CRITICAL THINKING

TOOLS FOR TAKING CHARGE OF YOUR LEARNING AND YOUR LIFE

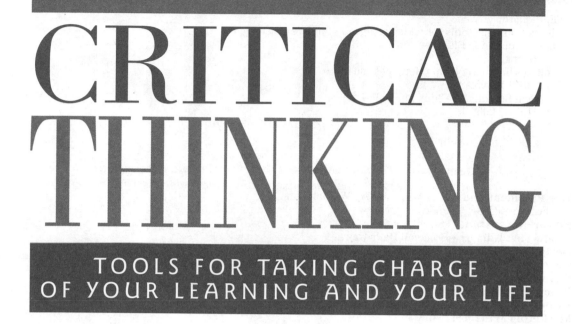

SECOND EDITION

Richard Paul
Linda Elder

PEARSON
Prentice
Hall

Upper Saddle River, New Jersey
Columbus, Ohio

Library of Congress Cataloging-in-Publication Data

Paul, Richard.
  Critical thinking : tools for taking charge of your learning and your life /
Richard Paul, Linda Elder. — 2nd ed.
      p. cm.
  Includes bibliographical references and index.
  ISBN 0-13-114962-8
  1. Critical thinking. I. Elder, Linda. II. Title.
  BF441.P385 2006

                                                      2005016122

Vice President and Publisher: Jeffery W. Johnston
Executive Editor: Sande Johnson
Editorial Assistant: Susan Kauffman
Production Editor: Holcomb Hathaway
Design Coordinator: Diane C. Lorenzo
Cover Designer: Jeff Vanik
Cover Photo: Corbis
Production Manager: Pamela D. Bennett
Director of Marketing: Ann Castel Davis
Marketing Manager: Amy Judd
Compositor: Carlisle Communications, Ltd.
Cover Printer: Phoenix Color Corp.
Printer/Binder: R. R. Donnelley & Sons Company

Pearson Prentice Hall™ is a trademark of Pearson Education, Inc.
Pearson® is a registered trademark of Pearson plc
Prentice Hall® is a registered trademark of Pearson Education, Inc.

Pearson Education Ltd.
Pearson Education Australia Pty. Limited
Pearson Education Singapore Pte. Ltd.
Pearson Education North Asia Ltd.

Pearson Education Canada, Ltd.
Pearson Educación de Mexico, S. A. de C.V.
Pearson Education-Japan
Pearson Education Malaysia Pte. Ltd.

16 15 14 13 12 11
ISBN 0-13-114962-8

CONTENTS

iii

Chapter 2

THE FIRST FOUR STAGES OF DEVELOPMENT: AT WHAT LEVEL OF THINKING WOULD YOU PLACE YOURSELF?   25

Chapter 3

SELF-UNDERSTANDING   41

Chapter 4

THE PARTS OF THINKING   53

Chapter 5

THE STANDARDS FOR THINKING   87

Chapter 6

ASK QUESTIONS THAT LEAD
TO GOOD THINKING   117

Chapter 7

MASTER THE THINKING, MASTER THE CONTENT   137

Chapter 8

DISCOVER HOW THE BEST THINKERS LEARN   147

Chapter 9

REDEFINE GRADES AS LEVELS OF THINKING AND LEARNING   175

Chapter 10

MAKE DECISIONS AND SOLVE PROBLEMS   185

Chapter 11

DEAL WITH YOUR IRRATIONAL MIND   211

Chapter 12

DETECT MEDIA BIAS AND PROPAGANDA IN NATIONAL AND WORLD NEWS   249

Chapter 13

RECOGNIZE FALLACIES: THE ART OF MENTAL TRICKERY AND MANIPULATION   291

Chapter 14

DEVELOP AS AN ETHICAL REASONER   337

Chapter 15

LEARN AND USE INFORMATION CRITICALLY AND ETHICALLY

Part One: Critique of Disciplines   359

Chapter 16

LEARN AND USE INFORMATION CRITICALLY AND ETHICALLY

Part Two: Method and a Model Case   379

Chapter 17

STRATEGIC THINKING: PART ONE   405

Chapter 18

STRATEGIC THINKING: PART TWO   421

Chapter 19

BECOMING AN ADVANCED THINKER: OUR CONCLUSION   439

Appendices

PREFACE

Whatever you are doing right now is determined by the way you are thinking. Whatever you feel—all your emotions—are determined by your thinking. Whatever you want—all your desires—are determined by your thinking. If your thinking is unrealistic, it will lead you to many disappointments. If your thinking is overly pessimistic, it will deny you due recognition of the many things in which you should properly rejoice.

Test this idea for yourself. Identify some examples of your strongest feelings or emotions. Then identify the thinking that is correlated with those examples. For example, if you *feel* excited about college, it is because you *think* that good things will happen to you in college. If you dread going to class, it is probably because you think it will be boring or too difficult.

In a similar way, if the quality of your life is not what you would wish it to be, it is most likely because it is tied to the way you think about your life. If you think about it positively, you will feel positively about it. If you think about it negatively, you will feel negative about it.

For example, suppose you came to college with the view that college was going to be a lot of fun, that you were going to form good friendships with fellow students who would respect and like you, and, what is more, that your love life would become interesting and exciting. And let's suppose that hasn't happened. If this were the thrust of your thinking, you now would feel disappointed and maybe even frustrated (depending on how negatively you have interpreted your experience).

For most people, thinking is often subconscious. For example, most people who think negatively would not say of themselves, "I have chosen to think about myself and my experience in a negative way. I prefer to be as unhappy as I can make myself."

The problem is that when you are not aware of your thinking, you have no chance of correcting it if it is poor. When thinking is subconscious, you are in no position to see any problems in it. And, if you don't see any problems in it, you won't be motivated to change it.

Since few people realize the powerful role that thinking plays in their lives, few gain significant command of it. Most people are in many ways victims of their thinking; that is, they are *hurt* rather than *helped* by it. Most people are their own worst enemy. Their thinking is a continual source of problems, preventing them from recognizing opportunities, keeping them from exerting energy where it will do the most good, poisoning relationships, and leading them down blind alleys.

Or consider your success as a student in college. The single most significant variable in determining that success is the quality of your thinking. If you think well when you study, you will study well. If you think well when you read, you will read well. If you think well when you write, you will write well. And if you study well, read well, and write well, you will do well in college. Certainly your instructors will play a role in your learning. Some of them will do a better job than others of helping you learn. But even the best teachers cannot get into your head and learn for you. Even the best teachers cannot think for you, read for you, or write for you. If you lack the intellectual skills necessary for thinking well through course content, you will not be successful in college.

Here is the key question we are putting to you in this book. If the quality of a person's thinking is the single most significant determinant of both happiness and success—as it is—why not discover the tools that the best thinkers use and take the time to learn to use them yourself? Perhaps you will not become proficient in all of them, but for every tool you learn, there will be a payoff.

This book will alert you to the tools the best thinkers use and will exemplify the activities and practice you can use to begin to emulate them. You will then have your destiny as a thinker in your own hands. The only thing that will determine whether you become a better and better thinker is your own willingness to practice. Here are some of the qualities of the best thinkers.

- **The best thinkers think about their thinking.** They do not take thinking for granted. They do not trust to fate to make them good in thinking. They *notice* their thinking. They *reflect* on their thinking. They act upon their thinking.

- **The best thinkers are highly purposeful.** They do not simply act. They know why they act. They know what they are about. They have clear goals and clear priorities. They continually check their activities for alignment with their goals.

- **The best thinkers have intellectual "tools" that they use to raise the quality of their thinking.** They know how to express their thinking clearly. They know how to check it for accuracy and precision. They know how to keep focused on a question and make sure that it is relevant to their goals and purposes. They know how to think beneath the surface and how to expand their thinking to include insights from multiple perspectives. They know how to think logically and significantly.

- **The best thinkers distinguish their thoughts from their feelings and desires.** They know that wanting something to be so does not make it so. They know that one can be unjustifiably angry, afraid, or insecure. They do not let unexamined emotions determine their decisions. They have "discovered" their minds, and they examine the way their minds operate as a result. They take deliberate charge of those operations. (See Chapter 1.)

- **The best thinkers routinely take thinking apart.** They "analyze" thinking. They do not trust the mind to analyze itself automatically. They realize that the art of analyzing thinking is an art one must consciously learn. They realize that it takes knowledge (of the parts of thinking) and practice (in exercising control over them). (See Chapter 2.)

- **The best thinkers routinely evaluate thinking—determining its strengths and weaknesses.** They do not trust the mind to evaluate itself automatically. They realize that the automatic ways that the mind evaluates itself are inherently flawed. They realize that the art of evaluating thinking is an art one must consciously learn. They realize that it takes knowledge (of the universal standards for thinking) and practice (in exercising control over them).

This book, as a whole, introduces you to the tools of mind that will help you reason well through the problems and issues you face, whether in the classroom, in your personal life, or in your professional life. If you take these ideas seriously, and practice using them, you can take command of the thinking that ultimately will command the quality of your life.

ACKNOWLEDGMENTS

We would like to thank the following reviewers, who read the manuscript in earlier forms and offered constructive suggestions: Brain J. Shelley, York Technical Institute; Jill Simons, Arkansas State University; and David Smith, Asheville-Buncombe Technical Community College.

DEDICATION

To all those who suffer cruelty and injustice due to the prejudiced, self-deceived, and unethical thinking that now dominates the world.

ACKNOWLEDGMENT

A special acknowledgment is due to Gerald Nosich—dedicated thinker, exemplary scholar, lifelong friend and colleague.

INTRODUCTION

The mind is its own place and in itself can make a hell of heaven or a heaven of hell.

John Milton, *Paradise Lost*

There are many ways to articulate the concept of critical thinking, just as there are many ways to articulate the meaning of any rich and substantive concept. But, as with any concept, there is an *essence* to critical thinking that cannot be ignored. In this introduction, we introduce the essence of critical thinking. We begin to unfold its complexities. We begin to show you its relevance to your life. Then, we will ask you to articulate your understanding of critical thinking, to demonstrate that you are beginning to make it your own.

A START-UP DEFINITION OF CRITICAL THINKING

Let us consider, then, a "start-up" definition of critical thinking.

> Critical thinking is the art of thinking about thinking while thinking in order to make thinking better. It involves three interwoven phases: it analyzes thinking,[1] it evaluates thinking,[2] it improves thinking.[3]

To think critically, you must be willing to examine your thinking and put it to some stern tests. You must be willing to take your thinking apart (to see it as something constructed out of parts). You must be willing to identify weaknesses in your thinking (while recognizing whatever strengths it may have). And, finally, you must be willing to creatively reconstruct your thinking to make it better (overcoming the natural tendency of the mind to be rigid, to want to validate one's current thoughts rather than improving them).

---

[1] By focusing on the parts of thinking in any situation—its purpose, question, information, inferences, assumptions, concepts, implications, and point of view.
[2] By figuring out its strengths and weaknesses: the extent to which it is clear, accurate, precise, relevant, deep, broad, logical, significant, and fair.
[3] By building on its strengths while reducing its weaknesses.

EXHIBIT I.1 *Critical thinkers use theories to explain how the mind works. Then they apply those theories to the way they live every day.*

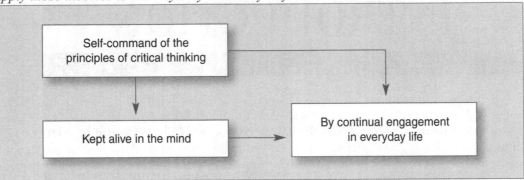

> The best thinkers pay close attention to thinking. They analyze it. They evaluate it. They improve it.

To think critically, you develop high standards for your thinking. You learn how to step back from it and make it meet those standards. This book will help you see how to act upon your thinking in this important and disciplined way, how to drag your thinking out into the light of day, take it apart, see it for what it is, and make it better.

HOW SKILLED ARE YOU AS A THINKER?

> The best thinkers use their ability to think well in every dimension of their lives.

There is nothing more practical than sound thinking. No matter what your circumstance or goals, no matter where you are or what problems you face, you are better off if you are in control of your thinking. As a student, shopper, employee, citizen, lover, friend, parent—in every realm and situation of your life—good thinking pays off. Poor thinking, in contrast, inevitably causes problems, wastes time and energy, and engenders frustration and pain.

Critical thinking is the disciplined art of ensuring that you use the best thinking you are capable of in any set of circumstances. The general goal of thinking is to figure out some situation, solve some problem, answer some question, or resolve some issue. We must all make sense of the world in which we live. How well or poorly we do this is crucial to our well-being.

Whatever sense we make of things, we have multiple choices to make. We need the best information to make the best choices. We need to figure out: What is really going on in this or that situation? Does so-and-so really care about me? Am I deceiving myself when I believe that . . . ? What are the likely consequences of failing to . . . ? If I want to do . . . , what is the best way to prepare? How can I be more successful in doing . . . ? Is this my biggest problem, or do I need to focus my attention on that? Successfully responding to questions such as these is the daily work of thinking.

Nothing you can do will guarantee that you will find the complete truth about anything, but there is a way to get better at it. Excellence of thought and skill in thinking are real possibilities. To maximize the quality of your thinking, however, you must learn how to become an effective critic of your thinking. And to become an effective critic of your thinking, you have to make *learning about thinking* a priority.

Consider for a minute all of what you have learned in your life: about sports, money, friendship, anger and fear, love and hate, your mother and father, nature, the city you live in, manners and taboos, human nature and human behavior. Learning is a natural and inevitable process. We learn in many directions. One direction in which learning is *not* natural is inward learning—self-knowledge, knowledge of the workings of our own mind, of how and why we think as we do.

Begin by answering these—rather unusual—questions: What have you learned about how you think? Did you ever *study* your thinking? What information do you have, for example, about the intellectual processes involved in how your mind thinks? More to the point, perhaps, what do you really know about how to analyze, evaluate, or reconstruct your thinking? Where does your thinking come from? How much of it is of high quality? How much of it is of poor quality? How much of your thinking is vague, muddled, inconsistent, inaccurate, illogical, or superficial? Are you, in any real sense, in control of your thinking? Do you know how to test it? Do you have any conscious standards for determining when you are thinking well and when you are thinking poorly? Have you ever discovered a significant problem in your thinking and then changed it by a conscious act of will? If someone asked you to teach him or her what you have learned about thinking thus far in your life, would you have any idea what that was or how you learned it?

> The best thinkers make the study of thinking second nature.

If you are like most people, the honest answers to these questions run along the lines of: "Well, I suppose I don't know much about my thinking or about thinking in general. I suppose in my life I have more or less taken my thinking for granted. I don't really know how it works. I have never studied it. I don't know how I test it, or even if I *do* test it. It just happens in my mind automatically."

Serious study of thinking, serious thinking about thinking, is rare in human life. It is not a subject in most schools. It is not a subject taught at home. But if you focus your attention for a moment on the role that thinking is playing in your life, you may come to recognize that everything you do or want or feel is influenced by your thinking. And if you become persuaded of that, you will be surprised that humans show so little interest in thinking. What is more, if you start to pay attention to thinking in a manner analogous to the way a botanist observes plants, you will be on your way to becoming a truly exceptional person. You will begin to notice what few others notice. You will be the rare person who is engaged in discovering what human thinking is about. You will be the rare person who knows how and why he or she is thinking, the rare person skilled in assessing and improving how he or she thinks.

Some things you will eventually discover are: All of us, somewhere along the way, have picked up bad habits of thinking. All of us, for example, make generalizations when we don't have the evidence to back them up, allow stereotypes to influence our thinking, form some false beliefs, tend to look at the world from one fixed point of view, ignore or attack points of view that conflict with our own, fabricate illusions and myths that we subconsciously confuse with what is true and real, and think deceptively about many aspects of our experience. As you discover these problems in your thinking, we hope you will begin to ask yourself some key questions: Is it possible for me to learn to avoid bad habits of thought? Is it possible for me to develop good habits of thought? Is it possible for me to think at a high, or at least *higher,* level?

These are problems and questions that few discover or ask. Nevertheless, every major insight you gain into good or bad thinking can enhance your life significantly. You can begin to make better decisions. You can gain power, important power that you presently lack. You can open up new doors for yourself, see new options, minimize significant mistakes, maximize potential understandings. If you're going to live your life as a thinker, why not get good at thinking about thinking?

I.1   *Think for Yourself*

BEGINNING TO THINK ABOUT YOUR THINKING

See if you can identify any discovery you made about your thinking before you started to read this book. If you can't think of any, write out your best explanation as to why not. If you do think of something, explain what you learned about your thinking.

GOOD THINKING REQUIRES HARD WORK

There is a catch—there almost always is. To make significant gains in the quality of your thinking, you will have to engage in a kind of work that most humans find unpleasant, if not painful: intellectual work. This is the price you have to pay if you want the gain. One doesn't become a skillful critic of thinking overnight any more than one becomes a skillful basketball player or dancer overnight. To become a student of thinking, you must be willing to put the work into thinking that skilled improvement requires. When thinking of what physical conditioning requires, we say, "No pain, no gain!" In this case, it would be more precise to say, "No intellectual pain, no *intellectual* gain!"

This means you must be willing to practice special "acts" of thinking that are, initially at least, uncomfortable, and sometimes challenging and difficult. You have to learn to do "moves" with your mind analogous to what accomplished athletes learn to do through practice and feedback with their body. Improvement in thinking, then, is similar to improvement in other domains of performance in which progress is a product of sound theory, commitment, hard work, and practice. Although this book will point the way to what you need to practice to become a skilled thinker, it cannot provide you with the internal motivation to do the required work. This must come from you. You must be willing, as it were, to be the monkey who comes down from the trees and starts to observe your fellow monkeys in action. You must be willing to examine mental films of your own monkeying around, as well.

Let's now develop further the analogy between physical and intellectual development. This analogy, we believe, goes a long way, and provides us with just the right prototype to keep before our minds. If you play tennis and you want to play better, there is nothing more advantageous than to look at some films of excellent players in action and then painstakingly compare how they, in comparison to you, address the ball. You study their performance. You note what you need to do more of, what you need to do less of, and you practice, practice, practice. You go through many cycles of practice/feedback/practice. Your practice heightens your awareness of the ins and outs of the art. You develop a vocabulary for talking about your performance. Perhaps you get a coach. And slowly, progressively, you improve. Similar points could be made for ballet, distance running, piano playing, chess playing, reading, writing, parenting, teaching, studying, and so on.

One major problem, however, is that all the activities of skill development with which we are typically familiar are visible. We could watch a film of the skill in action. But imagine a film of a person sitting in a chair *thinking*. It would look like the person was doing nothing. Yet, increasingly, workers are being paid precisely for the thinking they are able to do, not for their physical strength or physical activity. Therefore, though most of our thinking is invisible, it represents one of the most important things about us. Its quality, in all likelihood, will determine whether we will become rich or poor, powerful or weak. Yet we typically think without explicitly noticing how we are doing it. We take our thinking for granted.

For example, important concepts, such as love, friendship, integrity, freedom, democracy, and ethics, are often unconsciously twisted and distorted in common life and thought. Our subconscious interest is often in getting what we want, not in describing ourselves or the world truly and honestly.

In any case, most of our concepts are invisible to us, though implicit in our talk and behavior. So is much of our thinking. We would be amazed, and sometimes shocked, if we were to see all of our thinking displayed for us on a large screen.

To develop as a thinker, you must begin to think of your thinking as involving an implicit set of structures—concepts being one important set—whose use can be improved only when you begin to take the tools of thinking seriously. You develop as a thinker when you explicitly notice what your thinking is doing and when you become committed to recognizing both strengths and weaknesses in that thinking. You develop as a thinker as you build your own "large screen" on which to view your thinking.

Critical thinking, then, provides the tools of mind you need to think through anything and everything that requires thought—in college and in life. As your intellectual skills develop, you gain instruments that you can use deliberately and mindfully to better reason through the thinking tasks implicit in your short- and long-range goals. There are better and worse ways to pursue whatever you are after. Good thinking enables you to maximize the better ways and minimize the worse.

EXHIBIT I.2 *Critical thinking is the way we should approach everything we do.*

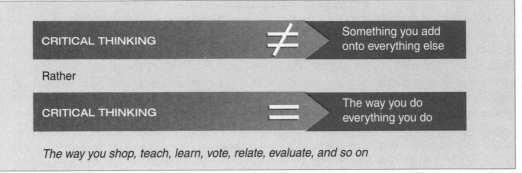

I.2 *Think for Yourself*

UNDERSTANDING THE IMPORTANCE OF CONCEPTS

See if you can think of a time in which you "misused" an important concept. Hint: Think of an idea that you commonly use in your thinking, such as friendship, trust, truthfulness, or respect. Have you ever implied you were someone's friend but acted against that person (such as gossiping behind that person's back)? Write out or orally explain your answer.

Only by applying the fundamentals to a wide range of human problems can one begin to appreciate their power and usefulness. Think of it this way. If we were coaching you in tennis, we would remind you again and again to keep your eye on the ball. Could you imagine saying to your coach, "Why do I have to keep my eye on the ball? I already did that once." The same logic applies to the principles of skilled thinking. If you want to be proficient, you have to redirect your eyes to the fundamentals, again and again and again.

EXHIBIT I.3 *Why is critical thinking so important? (A more elaborated "definition.")*

The Problem:

Everyone thinks. It is our nature to do so. But much of our thinking, left to itself, is biased, distorted, partial, uninformed, or downright prejudiced. Yet the quality of our life and that of what we produce, make, or build depends precisely on the quality of our thought. Shoddy thinking is costly, both in money and in quality of life. Excellence in thought, however, must be systematically cultivated.

DEFINING CRITICAL THINKING

Critical thinking is that mode of thinking—about any subject, content, or problem—in which the thinker improves the quality of his or her thinking by skillfully analyzing, assessing, and reconstructing it.

Critical thinking is self-directed, self-disciplined, self-monitored, and self-corrective thinking. It presupposes assent to rigorous standards of excellence and mindful command of their use. It entails effective communication and problem-solving abilities, as well as a commitment to overcome one's native egocentrism and sociocentrism.

To analyze thinking:

Identify its purpose, question, information, conclusion(s), assumptions, implications, main concept(s), and point of view.

To assess thinking:

Check it for clarity, accuracy, precision, relevance, depth, breadth, significance, logic, and fairness.

The Result

A well-cultivated critical thinker:

- raises vital questions and problems, formulating them clearly and precisely;
- gathers and assesses relevant information, using abstract ideas to interpret it effectively;
- comes to well-reasoned conclusions and solutions, testing them against relevant criteria and standards;
- thinks open mindedly within alternative systems of thought, recognizing and assessing, as need be, their assumptions, implications, and practical consequences; and
- communicates effectively with others in figuring out solutions to complex problems.

I.3   *Think for Yourself*

BEGINNING TO CONSIDER PROBLEMS IN THINKING

Exhibit I.3 shows that a big part of "the problem" critical thinking addresses is that "much of our thinking, left to itself, is biased, distorted, partial, uninformed, or downright prejudiced." Make a list of five significant problems in human life. Then see if you can identify the problems in *thinking* that lead to those problems. Be as specific as possible.

THE CONCEPT OF CRITICAL THINKING

The concept of critical thinking reflects an idea derived from roots in ancient Greek. The word *critical* derives etymologically from two Greek roots: *kriticos* (meaning "discerning judgment") and *kriterion* (meaning "standards"). Etymologically, then, the word implies the development of "discerning judgment based on standards." In *Webster's New World Dictionary,* the relevant entry for *critical* reads "characterized by careful analysis and judgment" and is followed by: "Critical, in its strictest sense, implies an attempt at objective judgment so as to determine both merits and faults." Considering these definitions together, then, critical thinking may be appropriately defined as

> thinking explicitly aimed at well-founded judgment, utilizing appropriate evaluative standards in an attempt to determine the true worth, merit, or value of something.

Critical thinking, then, has three dimensions: an analytic, an evaluative, and a creative component. As critical thinkers, we analyze thinking in order to evaluate it. We evaluate it in order to improve it.

In other words, critical thinking is the *systematic monitoring of thought with the end of improvement.* When we think critically, we realize that thinking must not be accepted at face value but must be analyzed and assessed for its *clarity, accuracy, relevance, depth, breadth,* and *logicalness.* We recognize that all reasoning occurs within *points of view* and frames of reference, that all reasoning proceeds from some *goals and objectives* and has an *informational base,* that all data when used in reasoning must be *interpreted,* that interpretation involves *concepts,* that concepts entail *assumptions,* and that all basic inferences in thought have *implications.* Because problems in thinking can occur in any of these dimensions, each dimension must be monitored.

When we think critically, we realize that in every domain of human thought, it is possible and important to question the parts of thinking and the standards for thought. Routine questioning in the critical mind looks something like this:

> Let's see, what is the most fundamental issue here? From what point of view should I approach this problem? Does it make sense for me to assume this? What may I reasonably infer from these data? What is implied in this graph? What is the fundamental concept here? Is this information consistent with that information? What makes this question complex? How could I check the accuracy of these data? If this is so, what else is implied? Is this a credible source of information?

And so forth. With intellectual language such as this in the foreground, one can come to recognize fundamental critical thinking "moves" that can be used in reasoning through any problem or issue, class or subject. To help you learn the language of critical thinking and to apply it on a regular basis to your learning and your life is a primary objective of this book. With the analytic and evaluative tools of critical thinking, you can learn how to raise the quality of your thinking.

EXHIBIT I.4 *Critical thinking applies to everything about which we think.*

Critical Thinking About:

Teaching and learning	Well-being	Speaking
Creativity	Listening	Politics
Emotions	Medicine	Religion
Intuition	Writing	Problem solving
Habits	Nursing	Reading

BECOME A CRITIC OF YOUR THINKING

One of the most important things you can do for yourself is to begin the process of becoming a critic of your thinking. You do this not to negate or "dump on" yourself but, instead, to improve yourself, to begin to practice the art of skilled thinking and lifelong learning. To do this, you must discover your thinking, see its structure, observe its implications, and recognize its basis and vantage point. You must come to recognize that, through commitment and daily practice, you can make foundational changes in your thinking. You need to learn about your bad habits of thought and about what you are striving for: good habits of thought. At whatever level you think, you need to recognize that you can learn to think better. Creative improvement is the end for which critical thinkers strive.

EXHIBIT I.5 *Critical thinking adds a second level of thinking to ordinary thinking. The second level analyzes, assesses, and improves our ordinary thinking.*

Second-order thinking is first-order thinking raised to the level of conscious realization (analyzed, assessed, and reconstructed).

First-order thinking is spontaneous and nonreflective. It contains insight, prejudice, truth and error, good and bad reasoning, indiscriminately combined.

I.4 *Think for Yourself*

BEGINNING TO THINK ABOUT YOUR THINKING

Consider your thinking in personal relationships, in dealing with friends, in relating to romantic partners, in sports, as a reader, as a writer, as a listener to lectures, as an employee, in planning your life, in dealing with your emotions, and in figuring out complex situations.

Complete these statements:

1. Right now, I believe my thinking across all domains of my life is of _____ quality. I base this judgment on _____.

2. In the following areas, I think very well:

    a. _____
    b. _____
    c. _____

3. In the following areas, my thinking is okay, not great, but not terrible either:

    a. _____
    b. _____
    c. _____

4. In the following areas, my thinking is probably poor:

    a. _____
    b. _____
    c. _____

ESTABLISH NEW HABITS OF THOUGHT

Most of us get through school by modifying our thinking the hard way—through trial and error. Most of us have little help in learning how to become a critic of our thinking. We develop few tools for working on our thinking. The result is that we use our native capacities to think in a largely unconscious fashion. We develop some good habits of thought and many poor habits of thought. The productive and unproductive habits of mind become intermixed and hard to disentangle. We learn without a clear sense of the ideal in thinking. We are not clear about our goals as thinkers. We treat each class like a new set of tasks to complete mechanically. We fail to learn important ideas that enable us to learn how to learn better and better.

To learn at a deeper level, you need to get powerful leverage on learning. You need a clearer perspective on what you should be striving to achieve, and you need powerful tools for upgrading your thinking and learning.

Critical thinking works. It is practical. It will enable you to be more successful, to save time and energy, and to experience more positive and fulfilling emotions. It is in your interest to become a better critic of your own thinking: as a student, scholar, parent, consumer, and citizen, and in other roles as well. If you are not progressively improving the quality of your life, you have not yet discovered the true power of critical thinking. We hope this book will serve as an impetus for this shift. Good thinking works—for everyone.

1.5   *Think for Yourself*

CHANGING YOUR HABITS

Have you ever changed a habit as a result of your conscious effort and planning? What do you have to do to change a habit? Is it easy? If not, why not? What do you think you would have to do to change habits of thought? Write out your answer or explain orally.

DEVELOP CONFIDENCE IN YOUR ABILITY TO REASON AND FIGURE THINGS OUT

No matter how well or poorly you have performed in school or in college, it is important to realize that the power of the human mind, *the power of your mind,* is virtually unlimited. But, if any of us are to reach our potential, we must take command of the workings of our minds. No matter where we are as thinkers, we can always improve.

As young children going through school, we usually get the impression that those students who are the quickest to answer questions, the quickest to turn in their papers, the quickest to finish tests are the "smartest" students. Those students who fall into this category often define themselves as "smart," and therefore as *better* than other students. They consequently often become intellectually arrogant. On the contrary, those students who struggle often see themselves as inferior, as incapable. And these students often give up on learning. They don't see that the race is to the tortoise, not the hare.

The fact is that standard measures of intelligence often impede learning. The point is that, whatever you have learned, or mislearned, about what it means to learn, you can now begin in earnest to develop your own mind, to take command of it. Critical thinking provides the tools for you to do just that. And it levels the playing field for all students. Some of the world's best thinkers—thinkers such as Einstein, Darwin, and Newton—are not the quickest thinkers. The best thinkers may be those who plod along, who ask questions, who pursue important ideas, who put things together in their minds, who figure things out for themselves, who create connections among important ideas. They are people who believe in the power of their own minds. They are people who appreciate the struggle inherent in substantive learning and thinking.

Consider how Darwin (1958) articulated his own struggles with learning:

> I have as much difficulty as ever in expressing myself clearly and concisely; and this difficulty has caused me a very great loss of time, but it has had the compensating advantage of forcing me to think long and intently about every sentence, and thus I have been led to see errors in reasoning and in my own observations or those of others. (p. 55)

In pursuing intellectual questions, Darwin (1958) relied upon perseverance and continual reflection, rather than memory and quick reflexes.

> I have no great quickness of apprehension or wit . . . My power to follow a long and purely abstract train of thought is very limited . . . My memory is extensive, yet hazy . . . So poor in one sense is my memory, that I have never been able to remember for more than a few days a single date or line of poetry . . . I have a fair share of invention, but not, I believe, in any higher degree . . . I think that I am superior to the common run of man in noticing things which easily escape attention, and in observing them carefully . . . I have had the patience to reflect or ponder for any number of years over any unexplained problem. (p. 55)

Einstein (Clark, 1984), for his part, performed so poorly in school that when his father asked his son's headmaster what profession his son should adopt, the answer was simply, "It doesn't matter; he'll never make a success of anything." He showed no signs of being a genius, and as an adult denied that his mind was extraordinary: "I have no particular talent. I am merely extremely inquisitive" (p. 27).

I.6   *Think for Yourself*

HOW DO YOU SEE YOURSELF AS A THINKER?

Think back to your previous school or college experience. Which pattern have you typically fallen into?

1. The quick student to whom teachers typically are drawn, because you can answer the factual questions they think are important.
2. The student who has difficulty remembering facts so that learning has been more difficult for you.
3. The student who does pretty well because, though you are not the quickest at remembering facts and answering factual questions, you still have a pretty good memory so you have done okay in school.
4. A different pattern entirely.

Complete these statements:

1. Given the categories outlined above, I would say that I am the following "type" of student: _____
2. I have/have not typically struggled in school/college because: _____
   _____
3. I generally see myself as capable/incapable as a student because: _____
   _____
4. To the extent that I see myself as incapable as a student, I can begin to change this view of myself by realizing: _____
   _____

The best thinkers are those who systematically and carefully reason their way through problems. They ask questions when they don't understand. They don't allow other people to define their level of intelligence. They don't allow intelligence tests or other standardized tests to define their level of intelligence. They realize that, no matter how difficult or easy it is for them to "remember" facts for tests, the real work of learning requires perseverance and commitment. The real work of learning requires skills of mind that you can develop, if and when you decide to. Learning these skills of mind is precisely what this book is all about.

Remember, the race is to the tortoise, not the hare. Be the tortoise.

EXHIBIT I.6 *Critical thinking: an elaborated definition.*

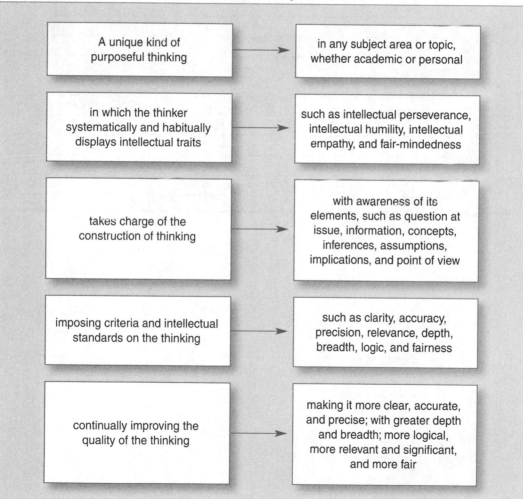

A unique kind of purposeful thinking	in any subject area or topic, whether academic or personal
in which the thinker systematically and habitually displays intellectual traits	such as intellectual perseverance, intellectual humility, intellectual empathy, and fair-mindedness
takes charge of the construction of thinking	with awareness of its elements, such as question at issue, information, concepts, inferences, assumptions, implications, and point of view
imposing criteria and intellectual standards on the thinking	such as clarity, accuracy, precision, relevance, depth, breadth, logic, and fairness
continually improving the quality of the thinking	making it more clear, accurate, and precise; with greater depth and breadth; more logical, more relevant and significant, and more fair

1.7   *Think for Yourself*

ARTICULATE YOUR UNDERSTANDING OF CRITICAL THINKING

R ead through this chapter again, highlighting the points made in the chapter that relate directly to the definition of critical thinking. Then complete these statements:

1. To me, critical thinking means: _____

_____

_____

_____

_____

2. In other words (this should be at least 4–5 sentences): _____

_____

_____

_____

_____

_____

_____

3. I can apply critical thinking to my life in the following ways: _____

_____

_____

_____

_____

BECOME A FAIR-MINDED THINKER

It is possible to develop as a thinker, and yet not to develop as a *fair-minded* thinker. It is possible to learn to use one's skills of mind in a narrow, self-serving way. Many highly skilled thinkers do just that. Think of politicians, for example, who manipulate people through smooth (fallacious) talk, who promise what they have no intention of delivering, who say whatever they need to say to maintain their positions of power and prestige. In a sense, these people are skilled thinkers because their thinking enables them *to get what they want*. But the best thinkers do not pursue selfish goals. They do not seek to manipulate others. They strive to be fair-minded, even when it means they have to give something up in the process. They recognize that the mind is not naturally fair-minded, but selfish. And they recognize that to be fair-minded, they also must develop specific traits of mind—traits such as intellectual humility, intellectual integrity, intellectual courage, intellectual autonomy, intellectual empathy, intellectual perseverance, and confidence in reason.

In this chapter we introduce what "fair-minded" means, and we discuss the traits of mind that accompany fair-mindedness. If you are to develop as a fair-minded thinker, you will have to "practice" being fair-minded. You will have to catch yourself in acts of selfishness and begin to correct your behavior. You will have to become committed to living a rational, compassionate, contributory life, to look outside yourself and see how your behavior affects other people. You will have to decide, again and again, that being fair-minded is crucial to your identity as a person.

WEAK VERSUS *STRONG* CRITICAL THINKING

Critical thinking can be used to serve two incompatible ends: self-centeredness or fair-mindedness. As we learn the basic intellectual skills that critical thinking entails, we can begin to use those skills in either a selfish or a fair-minded way. For example, when students are taught how to recognize mistakes in reasoning (commonly called fallacies), most students readily see those mistakes in the reasoning of others but not in their own reasoning. Using their understanding of fallacies, students develop some proficiency in making their opponents' thinking look bad, but they typically don't use their understanding of fallacies to analyze and assess their own reasoning.

Liberals see mistakes in the arguments of conservatives; conservatives see mistakes in the arguments of liberals. Believers see mistakes in the thinking of nonbelievers; nonbelievers see mistakes in the thinking of believers. Those who oppose abortion readily see mistakes in the arguments for abortion; those who favor abortion readily see mistakes in the arguments against abortion.

We call these thinkers *weak-sense* critical thinkers. We call the thinking "weak" because, though it is working well for the thinker in some respects, it is missing certain important higher-level skills and values of critical thinking. Most significantly, it fails to consider, in good faith, viewpoints that contradict its own viewpoint. It lacks fair-mindedness.

Another traditional name for the weak-sense thinker is found in the word *sophist*. Sophistry is the art of winning arguments regardless of whether there are problems in the thinking being used, regardless of whether relevant viewpoints are being ignored. The objective in sophistic thinking is to win. Period. Sophistic thinkers use lower-level skills of rhetoric, or argumentation, by which they make unreasonable thinking look reasonable and reasonable thinking look unreasonable. This form of thinking can be easily seen in unethical lawyers, prosecutors, and politicians who are more concerned with winning than with being fair. They use emotionalism and trickery in an intellectually skilled way. Consider the case of Delma Banks, a man convicted of murder in 1980. According to the *New York Times* (Feb. 25, 2004),

> The Supreme Court overturned a Texas inmate's death sentence on Tuesday on the ground that the prosecution deliberately withheld evidence that would have made jurors less likely to impose the death penalty had they been aware of it. . . . In her majority opinion, Justice Ruth Bader Ginsburg directly rebuked the Texas prosecutors for concealing facts they had a legal obligation to disclose and for permitting the state's witnesses to testify untruthfully. . . . Mr. Banks, who was convicted in 1980 of killing a 16-year-old co-worker at a Texarkana steak house to steal his car, came within 10 minutes of execution last March before the Supreme Court granted a stay and agreed to hear his appeal.

Or consider the case of Martin Tankleff, a man convicted of murdering his parents when he was 17 years old. According to the *New York Times* (April 4, 2004),

> K. James McCready, a veteran Suffolk County homicide detective, was off duty the morning of Sept. 7, 1988, when his beeper summoned him to a murder scene at a luxury waterfront home in Belle Terre. Inside was a gruesome sight. Arlen Tankleff had been stabbed and bludgeoned to death. Her brutally wounded husband, Seymour, was

unconscious and died weeks later in a hospital. Within hours of surveying the scene, Detective McCready declared the case solved. He singled out the couple's son, Martin, 17, as the prime suspect. In a long interrogation that day, the detective later boasted, he used deception to trick him into confessing. But Mr. Tankleff promptly disavowed the confession, refused to sign it, and the physical evidence did not implicate him. Yet he was convicted in 1990, based on the statement extracted by Detective McCready and his testimony as the star prosecution witness. . . . The Suffolk County system that prosecuted Mr. Tankleff [at that time] was under attack from many quarters as inept and even corrupt. . . . A State Investigation Commission report in 1989 found that the authorities had botched major cases . . . by coercing false confessions, brutalizing suspects, illegally tapping phones, lying on the witness stand, engaging in cover-ups and ignoring, losing or faking crucial evidence.

In both of these cases we see explicit examples of intellectual sophistry at work—in particular, skillfully hiding or distorting evidence in pursuit of an unjustifiable goal.

1.1   *Think for Yourself*

FINDING EVIDENCE OF INTELLECTUAL SOPHISTRY

In the next week, read articles in newspapers, news magazines, and similar sources for the purpose of identifying intellectual sophistry at work. Look for situations in which someone deliberately hides or distorts information in pursuing a goal. Note whether the person gets away with the sophistry.

Sophistic thinkers succeed only if they do not come up against what we call **strong-sense critical thinkers.** Strong-sense critical thinkers are not easily tricked by slick argumentation, by sophistry and intellectual trickery. The striking characteristic of strong-sense critical thinkers is their consistent pursuit of the fair and just. These thinkers strive always to be ethical—to behave in ways that do not exploit or otherwise harm others. They work to empathize with the viewpoints of others. They are willing to listen to arguments they do not necessarily hold. They change their views when faced with better reasoning. Rather than using their thinking to manipulate others and to hide from the truth (in a weak-sense way), they use thinking in an ethical, reasonable manner. Almost a century ago William Graham Sumner (1906) depicted strong-sense critical thinkers. He said they

cannot be stampeded . . . are slow to believe . . . can hold things as possible or probable in all degrees, without certainty and without pain . . . can wait for evidence and weigh evidence . . . can resist appeals to their dearest prejudices.

We believe that the world already has too many skilled selfish thinkers, too many sophists and intellectual con artists, too many unscrupulous lawyers and politicians who specialize in twisting information and evidence to support their selfish interests and the vested interests of those who pay them. We hope that you, the reader, will develop as a highly skilled, fair-minded thinker, one capable of exposing those who are masters at playing intellectual games at the expense of the well-being of innocent people. We hope as well that you develop the intellectual courage to argue publicly against what is unethical in human thinking. We write this book with the assumption that you will take seriously the fair-mindedness implied by strong-sense critical thinking.

To think critically in the strong sense requires that we develop fair-mindedness at the same time that we learn basic critical thinking skills, and thus begin to "practice" fair-mindedness in our thinking. If we do, we avoid using our skills to gain advantage over others. We treat all thinking by the same high standards. We expect good reasoning from those who support us as well as those who oppose us. We subject our own reasoning to the same criteria we apply to reasoning to which we are unsympathetic. We question our own purposes, evidence, conclusions, implications, and point of view with the same vigor that we question those of others.

Developing fair-minded thinkers try to see the actual strengths and weaknesses of any reasoning they assess. This is the kind of thinker we hope this book will help you become. From the beginning, then, we are going to explore the characteristics required for the strongest, most fair-minded thinking. As you read through the rest of the book, we hope you will notice how we are attempting to foster strong-sense critical thinking. Indeed, unless we indicate otherwise, from this point forward, every time we use the words "critical thinking," we will mean critical thinking in the strong sense.

In the remainder of this chapter, we will explore the various intellectual "virtues" that fair-minded thinking requires. Fair-mindedness entails much more than most people realize. Fair-mindedness requires a family of interrelated and interdependent states of mind.

One final point: In addition to fair-mindedness, strong-sense critical thinking implies higher-order thinking. As you develop your reasoning abilities and internalize the traits of mind in this chapter, you will develop a variety of skills and insights absent in the weak-sense critical thinker.

As we examine how the various traits of mind are conducive to fair-mindedness, we also will look at the manner in which the traits contribute to quality of thought (not simply a set of values added to a set of skills). In addition to the fairness that strong-sense critical thinking implies, it also implies depth of thinking and highly insightful thinking. Weak-sense critical thinkers develop a range of intellectual skills (for example, skills of argumentation) and may achieve some success in getting what they want, but they do not develop the traits highlighted in this chapter.

For example, some students are able to use their intelligence and thinking skills to get high grades without taking seriously the subjects they are studying. They become masters, if you will, of "beating the system." They develop test-taking and note-taking skills. They develop short-term memory skills. They learn to appeal to the prejudices of their teachers. They become academic sophists—skilled at getting by and getting what they want. They may even transfer these abilities to other domains of their lives. But they do not develop as fair-minded critical thinkers. (For example, see Chapters 12 and 13, on media bias and fallacies.)

EXHIBIT 1.1 *Critical thinkers strive to develop essential traits or characteristics of mind. These are interrelated intellectual habits that enable one to open, discipline, and improve mental functioning.*

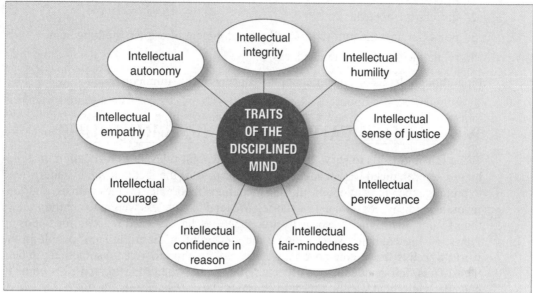

EXHIBIT 1.2 *These are the opposites of the intellectual virtues. Our natural disposition to develop them is an important reason why we need to develop countervailing traits.*

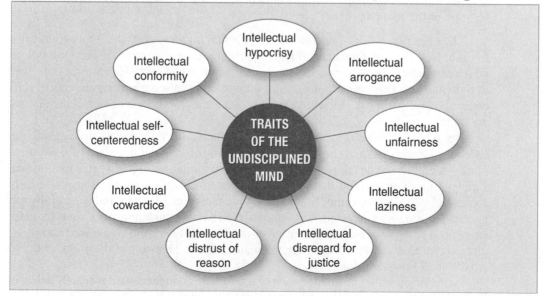

Let us now turn to the component traits of the strong-sense critical thinker. In each section we will:

1. introduce an intellectual trait or virtue,
2. discuss the opposite trait,
3. point out how the trait relates to the development of critical thinking, and
4. relate the trait to fair-mindedness.

First, though, let us be clearer about the concept of fair-mindedness.

WHAT DOES FAIR-MINDEDNESS REQUIRE?

To be fair-minded is to strive to treat every viewpoint relevant to a situation in an unbiased, unprejudiced way. It entails a consciousness of the fact that we, by nature, tend to prejudge the views of others, placing them into "favorable" (agrees with us) and "unfavorable" (disagrees with us) categories. We tend to give less weight to contrary views than to our own. This is especially true when we have selfish reasons for opposing views. If, for example, we can ignore the viewpoint of the millions of people in the world who live in extreme poverty, we can avoid having to give up something to help them. Thus, fair-mindedness is especially important when the situation calls on us to consider views that we don't want to consider.

> Fair-mindedness entails the predisposition to consider all relevant viewpoints equally, without reference to one's own feelings or selfish interests, or the feelings or selfish interests of one's friends, community, or nation. It implies adherence to intellectual standards (such as accuracy, sound logic, and breadth of vision), uninfluenced by one's own advantage or the advantage of one's group.

The opposite of fair-mindedness is *intellectual unfairness.* To be intellectually unfair is to lack a sense of responsibility to represent accurately and fairly viewpoints with which one disagrees. When we are intellectually unfair, we almost always see ourselves as right and just. Our unfair thoughts and actions almost always have an element of self-deception. We justify ourselves, rationalize our behavior, convince ourselves that we are "right."

Because each of us is naturally egocentric, each of us falls prey to unfair thinking. Indeed, egocentrism (and therefore unfair thinking) is the natural state of the human mind—a point to be developed when we deal with human irrationality (Chapter 6). We simply want to stress here that the traits discussed in this chapter can *never* be fully achieved by the human mind. No one is always fair-minded. The mind is naturally too egocentric, too self-interested. Any progress toward fair-mindedness is a constant inner struggle, a struggle to be faced each and every day. But the reward is a mind that is self-disciplined, that cannot easily be manipulated, that is able to see the truth, and that strives at all times to think fairly.

Achieving a truly fair-minded state of mind, then, is an ideal we never fully achieve. Fair-mindedness requires us to be, simultaneously, intellectually humble, intellectually courageous, intellectually empathetic, intellectually honest, intellectually perseverant, confident in reason (to be persuaded by good reasoning), and intellectually autonomous. Unless this family of traits functions in an integrated constellation, fair-mindedness is incomplete.

But these traits, singly and in combination, are not commonly valued. They are rarely discussed in everyday life, and are rarely taught. They are not discussed on television. They are not part of the school curriculum. They are not assessed in standardized testing. Yet, each of them is essential to fair-mindedness and inherent in strong-sense critical thinking. Let us see how and why this is so. We will begin with the fair-minded trait of intellectual humility.

Intellectual Humility: Strive to Discover the Extent of Your Ignorance

To explain intellectual humility in brief:

> To be intellectually humble is to develop knowledge of the extent of one's ignorance. Thus, intellectual humility includes an acute awareness that one's native egocentrism is likely to function self-deceptively (to tell the mind that it knows more than it does). It means being aware of one's biases and prejudices as well as the limitations of one's viewpoint. It involves being keenly aware of the extent of one's ignorance when thinking-through any issue, especially if the issue is emotionally charged. Intellectual humility depends on recognizing that one should not claim more than one actually knows. It does not imply spinelessness or submissiveness. It implies the lack of intellectual arrogance, pretentiousness, boastfulness, or conceit. It requires identifying and assessing the foundations of one's beliefs, looking especially for those that cannot be justified by good reasons.

The opposite of intellectual humility is *intellectual arrogance,* a natural tendency to think one knows more than one does know. Intellectual arrogance involves having little or no insight into self-deception or into the limitations of one's point of view. Intellectually arrogant people often fall prey to their own bias and prejudice, and frequently claim to know more than they actually know.

When we think of intellectual arrogance, we are not necessarily implying a person who is outwardly smug, haughty, insolent, or pompous. Outwardly the person may appear humble. For example, a person who uncritically follows a cult leader may be outwardly self-deprecating ("I am nothing. You are everything"), but intellectually he or she believes what does not make sense to believe and is at the same time fully confident in his/her beliefs.

Unfortunately, we are all capable of believing we know what we don't know. Our own false beliefs, misconceptions, prejudices, illusions, myths, propaganda, and ignorance seem to us as the plain, unvarnished truth. What is more, when challenged, we often resist admitting that our thinking is "defective." We then are intellectually arrogant, even though we might feel humble. Rather than recognizing the limits of our knowledge, we ignore and obscure those limits. From such arrogance, much suffering and waste result.

For example, when Columbus "discovered" North America, he believed that enslaving the Indians was compatible with God's will. He did not inwardly—as far as we know—recognize that only through intellectual arrogance could he believe he was privy to "God's will." Consider the following excerpt taken from Howard Zinn's *A People's History of the United States* (1995):

> The Indians, Columbus reported, "are so naïve and so free with their possessions that no one who has not witnessed them would believe it. When you ask for something they have, they never say no. To the contrary, they offer to share with anyone. . . ." He concluded his report by asking for a little help from their Majesties, and in return he would bring them from his next voyage "as much gold as they need . . . and as many slaves as they ask." He was full of religious talk: "Thus the eternal God, our Lord, gives victory to those who follow His way over apparent impossibilities." . . . Columbus later wrote, "Let us in the name of the Holy Trinity go on sending all the slaves that can be sold." (pp. 3–4)

Intellectual arrogance is incompatible with fair-mindedness because we cannot judge fairly when we are in a state of ignorance about that which we are judging. If we are ignorant about a religion (say, Buddhism), we cannot be fair in judging it. And if we have misconceptions, prejudices, or illusions about it, we will unfairly distort it. We will misrepresent it so as to discount it. Our false knowledge, misconceptions, prejudices, and illusions will keep us from being fair. We will be inclined to judge too quickly and be overly confident in our judgment. These tendencies are all too common in human thinking.

Why is intellectual humility essential to higher-level thinking? In addition to helping us become fair-minded thinkers, knowledge of our ignorance can improve our thinking in a variety of ways. It can enable us to recognize the prejudices, false beliefs, and habits of mind that lead to flawed learning. Consider, for example, our tendency to learn superficially. We learn a little and (by nature) think we know a lot. We get limited information and hastily generalize from it. We confuse memorized definitions with deep learning. We uncritically accept much that we hear and read—especially when what we hear or read agrees with our intensely held beliefs or the beliefs of groups to which we belong.

The discussion in the chapters that follow encourages intellectual humility and will help raise your awareness of intellectual arrogance. See if you, from this moment, can begin to develop in yourself a growing awareness of the limitations of your knowledge. Work on detecting your intellectual arrogance in action (which you should be able to see daily). When you do detect it, celebrate that awareness. Reward yourself for finding weaknesses in your thinking.

Consider *recognition* of weakness an important strength, not a weakness. As a starter, answer the following questions:

- Can you construct a list of your most significant prejudices? (Think of what you believe about your country, your religion, your friends, your family, simply because others—parents, friends, peer group, media—conveyed these to you.)
- Do you ever argue for or against views when you have little evidence upon which to base your judgment?

■ Do you ever assume that your group (your family, your religion, your nation, your friends) is correct (when it is in conflict with others) even though you don't have enough information to determine that it is correct?

1.2, 1.3 *Think for Yourself*

INTELLECTUAL HUMILITY

Name a person you think you know fairly well. Make two lists. In the first list include everything you know for sure about the person. In the second list include everything you know you don't know about him/her. For example: "I know for sure that my grandmother liked to cook, but I'm also sure that I never really understood what her fears and personal desires were. I knew many superficial things about her, but about her inner self I knew little." Be prepared to back up what you claim with an explanation of your thinking.

RECOGNIZING SUPERFICIAL LEARNING

Intellectual humility involves the ability to distinguish between learning that is deep and learning that is superficial. In this activity we ask you to test your ability to do this. Think of a course you completed in which you received a high or fairly high final grade. On a blank sheet of paper, write and elaborate on, without consulting any sources, answers to the following questions: What is (name of subject—for example, history, biology)? What is the main goal of studying this subject? What are people in this field trying to accomplish? What kinds of questions do they ask? What kinds of problems do they solve? What sorts of information or data do they gather? How do they go about gathering information in ways that are distinctive to this field? What is the most basic idea, concept, or theory in this field? How did studying this field change your view of the world?

If you find it difficult to answer these questions, consider the hypothesis that you might have received your high grade by cramming for tests or by some other means of superficial learning. Are you able to identify the difference between what you have learned superficially and what you have learned deeply?

Intellectual Courage: Develop the Courage to Challenge Popular Beliefs

A second trait of fair-mindedness is intellectual courage.

Having intellectual courage means facing and fairly addressing ideas, beliefs, or viewpoints even when this is painful. It means closely examining beliefs toward which one has strong negative emotions and to which one has not given a serious hearing. An important part of intellectual courage is recognizing that ideas that society considers dangerous or absurd are sometimes rationally justified (in whole or in part) or simply matters of subjective taste. Conclusions and beliefs inculcated in people by society are sometimes false or misleading.

To determine what makes sense to believe, one must not passively and uncritically accept what one has learned. Having intellectual courage is especially important because ideas considered dangerous or absurd may hold some truth and ideas strongly held by social groups to which we belong may hold some distortion or falsity. To be fair-minded thinkers in these circumstances, we must develop intellectual courage, recognizing that the penalties society places on us for nonconformity can be severe.

The opposite of intellectual courage, *intellectual cowardice,* is the fear of ideas that do not conform to one's own. If we lack intellectual courage, we are afraid to give serious consideration to ideas, beliefs, or viewpoints that we perceive as dangerous. We feel personally threatened by some ideas when they significantly conflict with our personal identity. We are unwilling to examine our beliefs—an indication that there may be some problem with the justifiability of those beliefs.

Each of the following ideas or its opposite is "sacred" in the minds of some people:

- being a conservative/being a liberal
- believing in God/disbelieving in God
- believing in capitalism/believing in socialism
- believing in abortion/disbelieving in abortion
- believing in capital punishment/disbelieving in capital punishment

No matter what side we are on, we often say of ourselves: "I am a(an) _____ [insert sacred belief here; for example, I am a Christian. I am a conservative. I am a socialist. I am an atheist]."

Once we define who we are through an emotional commitment to our beliefs, we are likely to experience inner fear when those beliefs are questioned. Giving into this fear is the first form of intellectual cowardice. Questioning our beliefs seems to mean questioning who we are as persons. The intensely personal fear that we feel keeps us from being fair (to opposing beliefs). When we "consider" opposing ideas, we subconsciously undermine them, presenting them in their weakest forms so we can reject them. We need intellectual courage to overcome self-created inner fear—the fear we ourselves have created by linking our identity to a specific set of beliefs.

Another important reason to acquire intellectual courage is to overcome the fear of rejection by others because they hold certain beliefs and are likely to reject us if we challenge those beliefs. This is where we invest others with the power to intimidate us.

Many people judge themselves according to the views of others and cannot approve of themselves unless they are approved of by others. Fear of rejection often lurks in the back of their minds. Few people challenge the ideologies or belief systems of the groups to which they belong. This is the second form of intellectual cowardice. Both forms make it impossible to consider either our own or others' ideas fairly.

The best thinkers do not connect their identities to their beliefs.

Instead of forming one's identity according to one's personal beliefs, it is far better to define oneself according to the *processes* by which one formulates beliefs. This is what it means to be a critical thinker. Consider the following resolution.

I will not *identify* with the content of any belief. I will identify only with the way I come to my beliefs. I am a critical thinker and, as such, am willing to examine my beliefs and abandon any that cannot be supported by evidence and rational considerations. I am ready to follow evidence and reason wherever they lead. My true identity is that of being a critical thinker, a lifelong learner, a person always looking to improve my thinking by becoming more reasonable in my beliefs.

When we refuse to connect our identity with our beliefs, we become more intellectually courageous and, by implication, more fair-minded. We are no longer afraid to consider beliefs that are contrary to our present beliefs. We are not afraid to be proven wrong. We freely admit to having made mistakes in the past. We are happy to correct any mistakes we are still making: "Tell me what you believe and why you believe it, and maybe I can learn from your thinking. I have cast off many early beliefs. I am ready to abandon any and all of my present beliefs that are not consistent with the way things are." Given this definition, how many people do you know who have intellectual courage?

> The best thinkers follow evidence and reason wherever they lead.

1.4, 1.5   *Think for Yourself*

INTELLECTUAL COURAGE I

Select one group to which you belong. Complete the following statements:

1. One main belief common to members of this group that might be questioned is . . . (here you want to identify at least one belief that may lead group members to behave irrationally)
2. This belief might be questioned because . . .
3. I would or would not be able to stand up to my group, pointing out the problems with this belief, because . . .

INTELLECTUAL COURAGE II

Try to think of a circumstance in which either you or someone you know defended a view that was unpopular in a group to which you belonged. Describe the circumstances, and especially how the group responded. If you can't think of an example, what is the significance of that realization?

Intellectual Empathy: Learn to Enter Opposing Views Empathically

Now let's consider another trait of mind necessary to fair-mindedness, intellectual empathy.

To have intellectual empathy is to put oneself imaginatively in the place of others on a routine basis, so as to genuinely understand them. It requires one to reconstruct the viewpoints and reasoning of others accurately and to reason from premises, assumptions, and ideas other than one's own. This trait requires the motivation to recall occasions when one was wrong in the past despite an intense conviction of being right, and the ability to imagine being similarly deceived in a case at hand.

The opposite of intellectual empathy is *intellectual self-centeredness,* thinking centered on self. When we think from a self-centered perspective, we are unable to understand the thoughts, feelings, and emotions of others. This, unfortunately, is the natural state of the human mind. From this perspective, most of our attention is focused on ourselves. Our pain, desires, and hopes are most pressing. The needs of others pale in significance to our own needs and desires. We are unable to consider issues, problems, and questions from a viewpoint that differs from our own and that, when considered, would force us to change our perspective.

How can we be fair to the thinking of others if we haven't genuinely tried to understand their thinking? Fair-minded judgment requires a good-faith effort to put oneself into the situation or perspective of another person (or other sentient creature). It requires an appreciation of the different contexts and situations within which varying perspectives emerge. Human thinking derives from the conditions of human life, from very different contexts and situations. If we do not learn how to take on others' perspectives and to accurately think as they think, we will not be able to fairly judge their ideas and beliefs. Trying to think within the viewpoint of others is not easy, though. It is one of the most difficult skills to acquire.

To develop your ability to empathize with others intellectually, practice using the following strategies:

1. During a disagreement with someone, switch roles. Tell the person, "I will speak from your viewpoint for 10 minutes if you will speak from mine. This way, perhaps we can better understand one another." Make sure you are accurately representing one another's viewpoint.

2. During a discussion, summarize what another person is saying, using this structure: "What I understand you to be saying is _____. Is this correct?"

3. When reading, say to yourself what you think the author is saying. This will enable you to bring ideas concretely into your mind so you then can think accurately within the author's viewpoint. Only then are you in a position to critique the author's viewpoint.

1.6, 1.7 *Think for Yourself*

INTELLECTUAL EMPATHY I

Try to reconstruct in your mind the last argument you had with someone (friend, parent, intimate other, supervisor). Reconstruct the argument from your perspective as well as that of the other person. Complete the statements below. As you do, take care that you do not distort the other person's viewpoint. Try to enter it in good faith, even if it means you have to admit you were wrong. (Remember that critical thinkers want to see the truth in the situation.) After you have completed this assignment, show it to the person you argued with to see if you have represented that person's view accurately.

1. My perspective was as follows (state and elaborate your view in detail):
2. The other person's view was as follows (state and elaborate the other person's view in detail):

INTELLECTUAL EMPATHY II

Think of an international political leader who is represented negatively in the news (for example, Castro in Cuba). Gather enough information about that person to be able to explain how he/she might defend himself/herself against the charges made in characterizing that person as "evil." Then ask yourself if you have ever seriously considered the possibility that any of the "enemies" of the United States might be more justified in opposing us than we are in opposing them. If you have never heard the defense of a national "enemy" from that person's point of view, how might that affect your ability to empathize with that person?

Intellectual Integrity: Hold Yourself to the Same Standards to Which You Hold Others

Let us now consider the trait of intellectual integrity.

Intellectual integrity means striving to be true to one's own disciplined thinking and holding oneself to the same standards that one expects others to meet. For example, it involves holding oneself to the same rigorous standards of evidence and proof to which one holds one's antagonists. It means practicing daily what one advocates for others. It requires honestly admitting discrepancies and inconsistencies in one's own thought and action, and identifying inconsistencies within one's thinking.

The opposite of intellectual integrity is *intellectual hypocrisy,* a state of mind unconcerned with true honesty. It is often marked by unconscious contradictions and inconsistencies. Because the mind is naturally egocentric, it is naturally hypocritical, yet at the same time skillfully able to rationalize whatever it thinks and however it leads us to act. Because of its innate need to project a positive image, the *appearance* of integrity is important to the egocentric mind. Therefore, we actively hide our hypocrisy from ourselves. And though we expect others to adhere to much more rigid standards than the standards we impose on ourselves, we see ourselves as fair. Though we profess certain beliefs, we often fail to behave in accordance with those beliefs.

Suppose I were to say to you that our relationship is really important to me, but you find out that I have lied to you about something important to you. My behavior lacks integrity. I have acted hypocritically. Yet, in my own egocentric, self-serving mind, I have rationalized my lying by telling myself things such as, "It's better that she not know. It will only upset her, and it won't help our relationship. The issue isn't that important anyway. It's really no big deal. She's better off not knowing." When I rationalize in this way, I can hide my hypocrisy from myself, which is vitally important. Though I have acted dishonestly, I can tell myself that everything I have done is the best thing to do in the situation. In short, I can appear *right* in my own mind.

To the extent that our beliefs and actions are consistent, we have intellectual integrity. We practice what we preach, so to speak. We don't say one thing and do another.

Clearly, we cannot be fair to others if we are justified in thinking and acting in contradictory ways. By its very nature, hypocrisy is a form of injustice. If we are not sensitive to contradictions and inconsistencies in our own thinking and behavior, we cannot reason well through ethical questions involving ourselves. We will distort other viewpoints in order to come out ahead.

Consider this political example: From time to time, the media disclose highly questionable practices by the CIA. These practices run anywhere from documentation of attempted assassinations of foreign political leaders (say, attempts to assassinate President Castro of Cuba) to the practice of teaching police or military representatives in other countries (say, in Central America or South America) how to torture prisoners to get them to disclose information about their associates. To appreciate how such disclosures reveal hypocrisy, we only have to imagine how we would respond if another nation were to attempt to assassinate our President or train American police or military in methods of torture. Once we imagine this, we recognize a basic inconsistency in our behavior and a lack of intellectual integrity on the part of those who plan, engage in, or approve of this kind of behavior.

All humans sometimes fail to act with intellectual integrity. When we do, we reveal a lack of fair-mindedness on our part, and a failure to think well enough to detect internal contradictions in our thought or life.

1.8 *Think for Yourself*

INTELLECTUAL INTEGRITY

Discuss a dimension of your life that you suspect holds some inconsistencies or contradictions (where you probably are not holding yourself to the same standard to which you hold someone else). Think of a situation in which your behavior contradicts what you say you believe. This might be in an intimate relationship, for example. Complete the following statements:

1. The context within which I fail to have intellectual integrity is . . .
2. In this context, I would (or do) expect others to behave as follows (though I am not willing to behave in the same way myself) . . .
3. The reason I fail to have intellectual integrity in this situation is that . . .
4. To change this situation, I need to . . .

Intellectual Perseverance: Refuse to Give Up Easily; Work Your Way Through Complexities and Frustration

Let us now consider intellectual perseverance.

Intellectual perseverance is the disposition to work one's way through intellectual complexities despite frustrations inherent in the task. Some problems are complicated and cannot be solved easily. One has intellectual perseverance when one does not give up in the face of complexity or frustration. The intellectually perseverant person understands that carefully and methodically reasoning-through complex issues and problems takes precedence over coming to conclusions quickly. Intellectual perseverance involves adhering to rational principles firmly despite the natural tendency to go with first impressions and simplistic answers. It also entails a realistic sense of the need to struggle with confusion and unsettled questions over an extended time to achieve understanding or insight.

The opposite of intellectual perseverance is *intellectual laziness,* demonstrated in the tendency to give up quickly when faced with an intellectually challenging task. The intellectually indolent, or lazy, person has a low tolerance for intellectual pain or frustration.

Intellectual perseverance is essential to almost all areas of higher-level thinking, because virtually all higher-level thinking involves some intellectual challenges. Without intellectual perseverance, those challenges cannot be overcome. Intellectual perseverance is required for high-quality reasoning in math, chemistry, physics, literature, art—and indeed any domain. Many students give up during early stages of learning a subject. Lacking intellectual perseverance, they cut themselves off from the many insights available to them only when they are willing to think-through a subject. They avoid intellectual frustration, no doubt, but they end up with the everyday frustrations of not being able to solve the complex problems they face.

Students often lack intellectual perseverance for at least two important reasons.

1. The mind is naturally averse to intellectual difficulties. It much prefers things to be easy, and it will take the simplest route to an answer when it can. This is the natural egocentric state of the mind.

2. Intellectual perseverance is rarely fostered in school. Instead, students are often encouraged to complete tasks quickly. Those who finish first are seen as the smartest and brightest. Slowly and carefully working through tasks is not usually valued. Consequently, students conclude that quickness is what matters most in *learning.* Those who are not able to finish tasks quickly come to view themselves as inadequate, stupid, inferior. Yet the most important questions we will reason-through in our lives most likely will be complex and, therefore, will require not speed but diligence and intellectual discipline. The thoroughness and attentiveness we bring to the process will determine whether, and to what extent, we can answer the questions.

Students who are intellectually quick are often the same students who give up when the intellectual task becomes difficult. They see themselves as capable of getting the "right" answer quickly and without intellectual pain. When the "right" answer does not come immediately and painlessly, they frequently blame the teacher for giving a "dumb assignment." Indeed, these students often fail to recognize that every question doesn't have a "right" answer; some instead have only better and worse answers. And there is no effective way to work-through these complex questions simply and easily.

How does a lack of intellectual perseverance impede fair-mindedness? Understanding the views of others requires intellectual work. It requires intellectual perseverance—insofar as those views differ from ours or are complex in nature. If we are unable or unwilling to work-through the views of others, to consider the information they use and how they interpret that information, to look closely at their beliefs, and analyze those beliefs for ourselves, to understand what they are trying to accomplish and how they see the world, we will not be able to think fairly within their viewpoint.

For example, suppose we are Christians wanting to be fair to the views of atheists. Unless we read and understand the reasoning of intelligent and insightful atheists, we cannot be fair to those views. Some intelligent and insightful atheists have written books to explain how and why they think as they do. Some of their reasoning is complicated or deals with complex issues. It follows that only those Christians who have the intellectual perseverance to read and understand atheists can be fair to atheist views. Of course, a parallel case could be made for atheists' understanding the views of intelligent and insightful Christians.

1.9   *Think for Yourself*

INTELLECTUAL PERSEVERANCE

Most people have much more physical perseverance than intellectual perseverance. On the one hand, most are ready to admit "No pain, no gain!" when talking about the body. On the other hand, most give up quickly when faced with a frustrating intellectual problem. Thinking of your own responses, especially in classes, how would you evaluate your own intellectual perseverance (on a scale of 0–10)? Explain to a classmate how you would support your score. On what do you base your conclusion?

Confidence in Reason: Respect Evidence and Reasoning, and Value Them as Tools for Discovering the Truth

Confidence in reason is another trait of fair-mindedness.

Confidence in reason is based on the belief that one's own higher interests and those of humankind at large are best served by giving the freest play to reason, by encouraging people to come to their own conclusions through the use of their own rational faculties. It is based on the belief that, with proper encouragement and cultivation, people can learn to think for themselves, form insightful viewpoints, draw reasonable conclusions, think clearly, accurately, relevantly, and logically, persuade each other by appeal to good reason and sound evidence, and become reasonable persons despite deep-seated obstacles in human nature and social life.

When one has confidence in reason, one is *moved* by reason in appropriate ways. The very idea of reasonability becomes one of the most important values, and a focal point in one's life. In short, to have confidence in reason is to use good reasoning as the fundamental criterion by which to judge whether to accept or reject any belief or position.

The opposite of confidence in reason is *intellectual distrust of reason.* Undisciplined thinkers feel threatened by good reasoning. By nature, people are not adept at analyzing their views. Yet, we tend to have complete confidence in our own views. The more we analyze our views, the more we see problems in our views and the less we want to hold on to views we have not analyzed. Without confidence in reason, people naturally will have confidence in the *truth of our own beliefs,* however flawed those beliefs might be. It is as if the mind engages unconsciously in something like the following inner dialogue:

> "I have formulated many beliefs throughout my life that I have not analyzed. If I were to *own* the beliefs I am often driven by, I would be appalled. Yet I cling to my beliefs because it would be too time-consuming and painful to analyze them closely. So I will just hang on to all of my beliefs, and everything will work out okay in the end."

In many ways, we live in an irrational world surrounded by curious forms of irrational beliefs and behaviors. For example, despite the success of science in providing plausible explanations based on careful study of evidence gathered through methodical and disciplined observations, many people still believe in unsubstantiated systems such as astrology. When faced with a problem, many follow their natural impulses. For example, they may follow leaders whose only claim to credibility is skill in manipulating a crowd and whipping up enthusiasm. Fewer people seem to recognize the power of sound thinking in helping us solve our problems and live a fulfilling life. Few, in short, have genuine confidence in reason. Instead, people tend to have uncritical or *blind* faith in one or more of the following, often resulting from irrational drives and emotions:

1. Faith in charismatic national leaders (think of leaders able to excite millions of people and manipulate them into supporting unjust wars or even to support genocide of an entire religious group [such as Hitler]).
2. Faith in charismatic cult leaders.
3. Faith in the father as the traditional head of the family (as defined by religious or social tradition).
4. Faith in institutional authorities (police, social workers, judges, priests, evangelical preachers, and so forth).
5. Faith in spiritual powers (such as a "holy spirit," as defined by various religious belief systems).

6. Faith in some social group, official or unofficial (faith in a gang, in the business community, in a church, in a political party, and so on).

7. Faith in a political ideology (such as right-wing fundamentalism, left-wing fundamentalism, communism, capitalism, Fascism).

8. Faith in intuition.

9. Faith in one's unanalyzed emotions.

10. Faith in one's gut impulses.

11. Faith in fate (some unnamed force that supposedly guides the destiny of all of us).

12. Faith in social or legal institutions (courts, schools, business community, government).

13. Faith in the folkways or mores of a social group or culture.

14. Faith in one's own unanalyzed experience (faith in the idea that one's interpretations about past experiences are the only *right* and *true* way to interpret those experiences).

15. Faith in people who have social status or position (the rich, the famous, the powerful).

Under certain conditions, confidence in reason may be compatible with some of the above. The key factor is the extent to which the form of faith is based on sound reasoning and evidence. The acid test, then, is: Are there good grounds for having that faith? For example, it makes sense to have faith in a friend if that friend has acted consistently as a friend over an extended time. But it does not make sense to have faith in a new acquaintance, even if one is emotionally attracted to that individual and that person professes his/her friendship.

As you think about your own thinking on the nature of different kinds of faith, and the extent to which you have appropriate confidence in reason and evidence, ask yourself to what extent you can be moved by well-reasoned appeals. Suppose you meet someone who shows so much of an interest in your boyfriend or girlfriend that you feel intensely jealous and negative toward that person. Would you shift your view if you knew that the person you are negative about is actually exceptionally kind, thoughtful, and generous? Could you shift your view even when you really would want your boyfriend or girlfriend to reject this person in favor of you? Would you be moved by reason if you thought your boyfriend or girlfriend would be *happier* with another person than with you? Have you ever given up a belief you held dear because, through your reading, experience, and reflection, you became persuaded that it was not reasonable to believe as you did? Are you ready and willing to admit that some of your most passionate beliefs (for example, your religious or political beliefs) may not be reasonable?

A direct relationship exists between confidence in reason and fair-mindedness. One cannot be fair-minded and yet be blind to the importance of *reason*. If I profess to be fair-minded, yet I am unwilling to consider good reasons with which I disagree, I demonstrate a mind that lacks confidence in reason and cannot be fair-minded. Fair-mindedness often requires one to consider reasoning not yet before considered, to consider that reasoning in good faith, and to change one's reasoning when faced with more *reasonable* reasoning, reasoning that is more logical, accurate, justifiable. All of this presupposes confidence in reason, confidence that when we place good reason at the heart of our thinking, we will do a better job of thinking.

1.10 *Think for Yourself*

CONFIDENCE IN REASON

Think of a recent situation in which you felt yourself being defensive and you now realize that you were not able to listen to an argument that you did not agree with, though the argument had merit. In this situation, you apparently could not be moved by good reasons. Briefly write what happened in the situation. Then write the reasonable arguments against your position that you were not willing to listen to. Why weren't you able to give credit to the other person's argument? In answering this question, see if you used any of the list of sources of faith that people usually rely on. In originally reasoning through the issue, were you relying on some form of blind faith?

Intellectual Autonomy: Value Independence of Thought

The final intellectual trait we will consider is intellectual autonomy.

> Intellectual autonomy means thinking for oneself while adhering to standards of rationality. It means thinking through issues using one's own thinking rather than uncritically accepting the viewpoints of others. Intellectually autonomous thinkers do not depend on others when deciding what to believe and what to reject. They are influenced by others' views only to the extent that those views are reasonable given the evidence.

In forming beliefs, critical thinkers do not passively accept the beliefs of others. Rather, they think-through situations and issues for themselves. They reject unjustified authorities while recognizing the contributions of reasonable authority. They carefully form principles of thought and action and do not mindlessly accept those presented to them. They are not limited by accepted ways of doing things. They evaluate the traditions and practices that others often accept unquestioningly. Independent thinkers strive to incorporate insightful ideas into their thinking, regardless of whether those ideas are considered acceptable or appropriate by the society within which they live. Independent thinkers are not willful, stubborn, or unresponsive to the reasonable suggestions of others. Independent thinkers are self-monitoring thinkers who are sensitive to mistakes they make and problems in their thinking. They freely choose the values by which they live.

Of course, intellectual autonomy must be understood not as a thing-in-itself. Instead, we must recognize it as a dimension of our minds working in conjunction with, and tempered by, the other intellectual virtues.

The opposite of intellectual autonomy is *intellectual conformity,* or intellectual dependence. Intellectual autonomy is difficult to develop because social institutions, as they now stand, depend heavily on passive acceptance of the status quo, whether intellectual, political, or economic. Thinking for oneself almost certainly leads to unpopular conclusions that are not sanctioned by the powers that be, while there are many rewards for those who simply conform in thought and action to social expectations.

Consequently, large masses of people are unknowing conformists in thought and deed, like mirrors reflecting the belief systems and values of those who surround them. They lack the intellectual skills and the incentive to think for themselves. They are intellectually conforming thinkers. And as long as people uncritically accept cultural values, as long as they conform to beliefs they have not analyzed for themselves, they cannot be intellectually free.

Even those who spend years getting a Ph.D. may be intellectually dependent, both academically and personally. They may uncritically accept faulty practices within their disciplines, uncritically defending these practices against legitimate critics. Despite all their years of school, they may yet be enslaved by social conventions and rules. They may have little or no insight into the human harm and suffering caused by these social rules.

One cannot be fair-minded and lack intellectual autonomy, because independent thinking is a prerequisite to thinking within multiple perspectives. When we intellectually conform, we are able to think only within "accepted" viewpoints. But to be fair-minded is to refuse to accept beliefs uncritically without thinking-through the merits (and demerits) of those beliefs for oneself. When we attempt to think within other viewpoints without the virtue of intellectual autonomy, we either are too easily swayed by those viewpoints (because we are unable to see through manipulation and propaganda) or we distort the viewpoints (because those viewpoints don't conform with the belief system we have uncritically formulated).

1.11, 1.12 *Think for Yourself*

INTELLECTUAL AUTONOMY I

Briefly review in your own mind some of the many influences to which you have been exposed in your life (influence of culture, family, religion, peer groups, teachers, media, personal relationships). Try to discriminate between those dimensions of your thought and behavior in which you have done the least thinking for yourself and those in which you have done the most thinking. What makes this activity difficult is that we often perceive ourselves as thinking for ourselves when we are actually conforming to others. What you should look for, therefore, are instances of your actively questioning beliefs, values, or practices to which others in your "group" were, or are, conforming.

By the way, don't assume that teenage rebellion against parents and school authorities (if you engaged in it) was necessarily evidence of independent thought. Teen rebellion is often simply the trading of one form of conformity (e.g., to parents) for another (conformity to peer group). Be prepared to explain how you arrived at your conclusions about your current extent of intellectual independence.

INTELLECTUAL AUTONOMY II

In analyzing some of the beliefs you have come to accept, complete the following statements:

1. One belief I have been taught by my culture about the way people should behave in groups is . . .

   I have been taught this by (whom?) . . .

   In analyzing this belief, I do/do not think it is rational because . . .

2. One belief I have been taught within or about religion is . . .

   I have been taught this by (whom?) . . .

   In analyzing this belief, I do/do not think it is rational because . . .

3. One belief I have been taught by my parents is . . .

   In analyzing this belief, I do/do not think it is rational because . . .

4. One belief I have learned from my peer group is . . .

   In analyzing this belief, I do/do not think it is rational because . . .

5. One belief I have been taught by teachers is . . .

   In analyzing this belief, I do/do not think it is rational because . . .

RECOGNIZE THE INTERDEPENDENCE OF INTELLECTUAL VIRTUES

The traits of mind essential for critical thinking are interdependent. Consider intellectual humility. To become aware of the limits of our knowledge, we need the intellectual courage to face our own prejudices and ignorance. To discover our own prejudices, in turn, we often must intellectually empathize with and reason within points of view with which we fundamentally disagree. To achieve this end, we typically must engage in intellectual perseverance, as learning to empathically enter a point of view against which we are biased takes time and significant effort. That effort will not seem justified unless we have the necessary confidence in reason to believe we will not be tainted or "taken in" by whatever is false or misleading in the opposing viewpoint.

Furthermore, merely believing we won't be harmed by considering "alien" viewpoints is not enough to motivate most of us to consider them seriously. We also must be motivated by an intellectual sense of justice. We must recognize an intellectual responsibility to be fair to views we oppose. We must feel obliged to hear them in their strongest form to ensure that we are not condemning them out of ignorance or bias on our part. At this point, we come full circle to where we began: the need for intellectual humility.

To begin at another point, consider intellectual integrity or good faith. Intellectual integrity is clearly a difficult trait to develop. We are often motivated—usually without admitting to or being aware of this motivation—to set up inconsistent standards in thinking. Our egocentric or sociocentric tendencies, for example, make us ready to believe positive information about those we like and negative information about those we dislike. Likewise, we are strongly inclined to believe what serves to justify our selfish interests or validate our strongest desires. Hence, all humans have some innate mental tendencies to operate with double standards, which is typical of intellectual bad faith. These modes of thinking often correlate quite well with getting ahead in the world, maximizing our power or advantage, and getting more of what we want.

Nevertheless, it is difficult to operate explicitly or overtly with a double standard. We therefore need to avoid looking at the evidence too closely. We need to avoid scrutinizing our own inferences and interpretations too carefully. At this point, a certain amount of intellectual arrogance is quite useful. I may assume, for example, that I know what you're going to say (before you say it), precisely what you are really after (before the evidence demonstrates it), and what actually is going on (before I have studied the situation carefully). My intellectual arrogance makes it easier for me to avoid noticing the unjustifiable discrepancy between the standards I apply to you and the standards I apply to myself. Not having to empathize with you makes it easier to avoid seeing my self-deception. I also can maintain my viewpoint more easily if I don't feel a need to be fair to your point of view. And a little background fear of what I might discover if I seriously consider the consistency of my own judgments can be quite useful as well. In this case, my lack of intellectual integrity is supported by my lack of intellectual humility, empathy, and fair-mindedness.

Going in the other direction, it will be difficult to use a double standard if I feel a responsibility to be fair to your point of view, to see that this responsibility requires me to view things from your perspective empathically, and to do so with some humility, recognizing that I could be wrong, and you, right. The more I dislike you personally, or feel wronged in the past by you or by others who share your way of thinking, the more pronounced in my character must be the trait of intellectual integrity and good faith to compel me to be fair.

1.13   *Think for Yourself*

A COMMITMENT TO SELF-TRANSFORMATION

To what extent would you like to become a person whose characteristics are defined by the intellectual traits explained in this chapter? How important is that goal to you? Discuss your commitment, or lack thereof, with a classmate. In this activity, honesty is the key.

EXHIBIT 1.3 *Natural versus critical thinking.*

- As humans we think; as critical thinkers we analyze our thinking.

- As humans we think egocentrically; as critical thinkers we expose the egocentric roots of our thinking to close scrutiny.

- As humans we are drawn to standards of thinking unworthy of belief; as critical thinkers we expose inappropriate standards and replace them with sound ones.

- As humans we live in systems of meanings that typically entrap us; as critical thinkers we learn how to raise our thinking to conscious examination, enabling us to free ourselves from many of the traps of undisciplined, instinctive thought.

- As humans we use logical systems whose root structures are not apparent to us; as critical thinkers we develop tools for explicating and assessing the logical systems in which we live.

- As humans we live with the illusion of intellectual and emotion freedom; as critical thinkers we take explicit intellectual and emotional command of who we are, what we are, and the ends to which our lives are tending.

- As human thinkers we are governed by our thoughts; as critical thinkers we learn how to govern the thoughts that govern us.

CONCLUSION

True excellence in thinking is not simply the product of isolated intellectual skills. Inevitable problems arise in the thinking of persons who, without knowing it, lack intellectual virtues. These people frequently display the traits of the undisciplined mind. To the extent that we are motivated unconsciously to believe what we want to believe, what is most comfortable to believe, what puts us in a good light, what serves our selfish interest, we are unable to function as rational persons. As you work through this book, we hope you find yourself thinking-through and beginning to internalize the essential traits. See how well you are able to resist the external influence of the conformist thinkers around you and the internal influence of the egocentric thinker within you.

THE FIRST FOUR STAGES OF DEVELOPMENT

AT WHAT LEVEL OF THINKING WOULD YOU PLACE YOURSELF?

M ost of us are not what we could be. We are less. We have great capacity, but most of it is dormant; most is undeveloped. Improvement in thinking is like improvement in basketball, ballet, or playing the saxophone. It is unlikely to take place in the absence of a conscious commitment to learn. As long as we take our thinking for granted, we don't do the work required for improvement.

Development in thinking is a gradual process requiring plateaus of learning and just plain hard work. It is not possible to become an excellent thinker by simply taking a beginning course in thinking. Changing one's habits of thought is a long-term process that occurs over years, not weeks or months. The essential traits of a critical thinker, which we examined briefly in Chapter 1, will develop only through long-term commitment.

EXHIBIT 2.1 *Most people have lived their entire lives as unreflective thinkers. To develop as thinkers requires commitment to daily practice.*

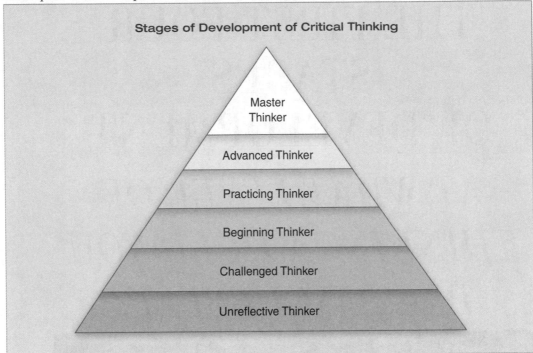

Stages of Development of Critical Thinking

Master Thinker

Advanced Thinker

Practicing Thinker

Beginning Thinker

Challenged Thinker

Unreflective Thinker

If we aspire to develop as thinkers, the stages all of us go through are:

Stage 1	The Unreflective Thinker (we are unaware of significant problems in our thinking)
Stage 2	The Challenged Thinker (we become aware of problems in our thinking)
Stage 3	The Beginning Thinker (we try to improve but without regular practice)
Stage 4	The Practicing Thinker (we recognize the necessity of regular practice)
Stage 5	The Advanced Thinker (we advance in accordance with our practice)
Stage 6	The Master Thinker (skilled and insightful thinking become second nature to us)

STAGE 1: THE UNREFLECTIVE THINKER

Are you an unreflective thinker? We all are born—and most of us die—as largely unreflective thinkers, fundamentally unaware of the role that thinking is playing in our lives. At this Unreflective Thinker stage we have no useful conception of what thinking entails. For example, as unreflective thinkers we don't notice that we are continually making assumptions, forming concepts, drawing inferences, and thinking within points of view. At this stage we don't know how to analyze and assess our thinking. We don't know how to determine whether our purposes are clearly formulated, our assumptions justified, our conclusions logically drawn. We are unaware of intellectual traits and so are not striving to embody them.

At this stage many problems in our lives are caused by poor thinking, but we are unaware of this. We don't question our beliefs. We don't question our decisions. We lack intellectual standards and have no idea what such standards might be. We lack the intellectual traits but are not aware that we lack them. We unconsciously deceive ourselves in many ways. We create and maintain pleasant illusions. Because our beliefs seem reasonable to us, we believe them with confidence. We walk about the world with confidence that things really are the way they appear to us. We judge some people to be "good" and some to be "bad." We approve of some actions. We disapprove of others. We make decisions, react to people, go our way in life, and do not seriously question our thinking or its implications.

Though we don't realize it, our egocentric tendencies at this stage play a dominant role in our thinking. We lack the skills and the motivation to notice how self-centered and prejudiced we are, how often we stereotype others, how frequently we dismiss ideas irrationally simply because we don't want to change our behavior or our comfortable way of looking at things.

2.1 *Think for Yourself*

REFLECTING ON YOUR KNOWLEDGE OF THINKING

Might you be at the Unreflective Thinker stage of development? Test yourself by writing your answers to the following:

1. Describe the role that thinking is playing in your life. (Be as clear and as detailed as you can.)
2. What was a recent assumption you made that you should not have made?
3. What is a concept you recently formed that you previously lacked?
4. List five inferences you made in the last hour.
5. Name and explain a point of view that you sometimes use to guide your thinking.
6. Briefly describe how you analyze and assess thinking.
7. Name some intellectual standards you use. Explain how you apply them.
8. Explain the role of egocentric thinking in your life.
9. Take one or two of the intellectual traits and explain what you are doing to try to embody them.

If you had trouble with your responses in the Think for Yourself exercise, you may well be at the Unreflective Thinker stage. If so, you do not need to apologize or feel badly about it. Most people are at this stage and don't know it. Traditional schooling and the way children are typically reared do not help people to become skilled thinkers. Often, parents and teachers themselves are unreflective thinkers. This is the product of a vicious circle. Unreflective persons raise unreflective persons. Once you explicitly recognize that you are at this stage, however, you are ready to move to the next stage. And when you move to the next stage, you may be close to breaking out of the vicious circle of unreflectiveness. To do so requires that we become honestly *reflective*—that we begin to notice some problems in our thinking, that we begin to recognize that our thinking is often egocentric and irrational, that changes in our own thinking are essential.

Honest reflectiveness leads to healthy motivation to change. It is functional and productive. You must not only see problems in your thinking but also have some sense of how those problems might be addressed. You must become reasonably articulate about what you have to do to improve. Motivation is crucial. Without a drive to change, nothing much of significance will happen.

STAGE 2: THE CHALLENGED THINKER

Are you ready to accept the challenge? We cannot solve a problem we do not own. We cannot deal with a condition we deny. Without knowledge of our ignorance, we cannot seek the knowledge we lack. Without knowledge of the skills we need to develop, we will not develop those skills.

As we begin to become aware that "normal" thinkers often think poorly, we move into the second stage of critical thinking development, the Challenged Thinker. We begin to notice that we often

- make questionable assumptions;
- use false, incomplete, or misleading information;
- make inferences that do not follow from the evidence we have;
- fail to recognize important implications in our thought;
- fail to recognize problems we have;
- form faulty concepts;
- reason within prejudiced points of view; and
- think egocentrically and irrationally.

We move to the Challenged Thinker stage when we become aware of the way our thinking is shaping our lives, including the recognition that problems in our thinking are causing problems in our lives. We are beginning to recognize that poor thinking can be life-threatening, that it can lead literally to death or permanent injury, that it can hurt others as well as ourselves. For example, we might reflect upon the thinking of

- the teenager who thinks that smoking is sexy;
- the woman who thinks that Pap smears are not important;
- the motorcyclist who reasons that helmets obstruct vision and, therefore, riding without one is safer;

- the person who thinks he can drive safely while drunk;
- the person who decides to marry a self-centered person with the thought that she will "change" after marriage.

We also recognize the difficulty involved in "improving" our thinking. If you are at this stage in your own thinking, you recognize that the problem of changing your habits of thought is an important challenge requiring extensive and difficult changes in your normal routines.

Some signs of emerging reflectiveness are that

- you find yourself striving to analyze and assess your thinking;
- you find yourself working with the structures of mind that create, or make possible, thinking (for example: concepts, assumptions, inferences, implications, points of view);
- you find yourself thinking about the qualities that make thinking sound—clarity, accuracy, precision, relevance, logicalness—even though you may have only an initial grasp of how to achieve these qualities;
- you find yourself becoming interested in the role of self-deception in thinking, even though your understanding is relatively "abstract" and you may not be able to offer many examples from your own life.

At this point in your development, there is a distinct danger of self-deception. Many resist accepting the true nature of the challenge—that their own thinking is a real and significant problem in their life. If you do as many do, you will revert to the Unreflective Thinker stage. Your experience of thinking about your thinking will fade. Your usual habits of thought will remain as they are. For example, you may find yourself rationalizing in the following way: "My thinking is not that bad. Actually I've been thinking well for quite a while. I question a lot of things. I'm not prejudiced. Besides that, I'm very critical. And I'm not nearly as self-deceived as lots of people I know."

If you reason in this way, you will not be alone. You will join the majority. This view—"if everyone were to think like me, this would be a fine world"—is the dominant view. Those who share this view range from the poorly schooled to the highly schooled. There is no evidence to suggest that schooling correlates with self-reflectiveness. Indeed, many college graduates are intellectually arrogant as a result of their schooling. Some unreflective thinkers did not go beyond elementary school, but others have done post-graduate work and now have advanced degrees. Unreflective people are found in all socioeconomic classes and include psychologists, sociologists, philosophers, mathematicians, doctors, senators, judges, governors, district attorneys, lawyers, and indeed people of all professions.

In short, absence of intellectual humility is common among all classes of people in all walks of life at all ages. It follows that active or passive resistance to the challenge of critical thinking is the common, not the rare, case. Whether in the form of a careless shrug or outright hostility, most people reject the challenge of critical thinking. That is why some soul-searching is important at this point in the process.

2.2, 2.3 *Think for Yourself*

DISCUSS THE CHALLENGED THINKER STAGE

Work in groups of three. The person whose first name is earliest in the alphabet will explain the second stage, that of the Challenged Thinker, to the other two, answering any questions they might have. Then the other two in the group will add any features that the first student missed and elaborate on the points they think are most important.

BEGIN TO IDENTIFY PROBLEMS IN YOUR THINKING

See if you can identify any problems in your thinking. The best way to do this is to analyze a behavior of yours that somehow is creating problems, either for you or others. Look at your personal relationships, your study habits, your interaction patterns. How do you behave when you are upset? How do you act when you don't get your way? Do you expect more of others than you expect of yourself? Consider these questions as starting points for challenging yourself as a thinker. If you cannot identify any problems in your thinking, think again.

STAGE 3: THE BEGINNING THINKER

Are you willing to begin? When a person actively decides to take up the challenge to grow and develop as a thinker, that person enters the stage we call the Beginning Thinker. In this stage of thinking, we begin to take thinking seriously. This stage prepares us for the next stages, with the ultimate goal of explicit command of thinking. It is a stage of dawning realizations. It is a stage of developing will power. It is not a stage of self-condemnation but, rather, of emerging consciousness. It is analogous to the stage in which people who are alcoholics recognize and fully accept the fact that they are alcoholics. Imagine an alcoholic saying, "I am an alcoholic, and only I can do something about it." Now imagine yourself saying, "I am a weak, undisciplined thinker, and only I can do something about it."

Once people recognize that they are "addicted" to poor thinking, they must begin to recognize the depth and nature of the problem. If we are at the Beginning Thinker stage, we should recognize that our thinking is sometimes egocentric. For example, we may notice how little we consider the needs of others and how much we focus on getting what we personally want. We may notice how little we enter the point of view of others and how much we assume the "correctness" of our own. We may even sometimes catch ourselves trying to dominate others to get what we want or, alternatively, acting out the role of submitting to others (for the gains that submissive behavior brings). We may begin to notice the extent to which we conform uncritically to the thinking of others.

As thinkers thinking about thinking, we are merely beginning to

- analyze the logic of situations and problems;
- express clear and precise questions;

- check information for accuracy and relevance;
- distinguish between raw information and someone's interpretation of it;
- recognize assumptions guiding inferences;
- identify prejudicial and biased beliefs, unjustifiable conclusions, misused words, and missed implications;
- notice when our viewpoint is biased by our selfish interests.

Thus, as Beginning Thinkers, we are becoming aware of how to deal with the structures at work in thinking (purposes, questions, information, interpretations, etc.). We are beginning to appreciate the value of thinking about our thinking in terms of its clarity, accuracy, relevance, precision, logicalness, justifiability, breadth, depth, and fairness. But we are still at a low level of proficiency in these activities. They feel awkward to us. We have to force ourselves to think in disciplined ways. We are like beginners in ballet. We feel foolish adopting the basic positions. We don't feel graceful. We stumble and make mistakes. No one would pay money to watch us perform. We ourselves don't like what we see in the mirror of our minds.

To reach this Beginning Thinker stage, our values must begin to shift. We must begin to explore the foundation of our thinking and discover how we have come to think and believe as we do. Let us consider this goal in a little more detail. Reflect now on some of the major influences that have shaped your thinking (and ours):

1. You were born into a culture (e.g., European, American, African, Asian).

2. You were born at some point in time (in some century in some year).

3. You were born in some place (in the country, in the city, in the North or South, East or West).

4. You were raised by parents with particular beliefs (about the family, about personal relationships, about marriage, about childhood, about obedience, about religion, about politics, about schooling).

5. You formed various associations (largely based on who was around you— associations with people with a viewpoint, values, and taboos).

If you were to change any one of these influences, your belief system would be different. Suppose you had been born in the Middle Ages as a serf in the fields in France. Can you see that if you were, virtually all of your beliefs would be altered? See if you can perform similar reflective experiments of your own. For example, imagine other changes in these influences and then imaginatively compare some of the beliefs you likely would have with the beliefs you actually do have. You will begin to appreciate how much you, and every other human, are a product of influences over which you, and they, had little or no control. Neither you nor they directed these influences. Their effects, clearly, were both good and bad.

For example, assume that many of these influences engendered false beliefs in us. It follows that our minds right now harbor false beliefs and we are acting on them. Yet, notice that the mind has no mechanism for screening out false beliefs. We all carry around in our minds prejudices from our culture, prejudices from where we were born and raised, prejudices from our parents, and prejudices from our friends and associates. Finding ways to locate those flawed beliefs and replace them with more reasonable beliefs is part of the agenda of critical thinking. Another way to look at the forces, rational and irrational, that have shaped our minds is in terms of "modes of influence."

2.4   *Think for Yourself*

PUTTING YOURSELF IN ANOTHER PLACE IN TIME

Imagine yourself in another place in time. Choose a different century, perhaps a different country, a different gender, a different socioeconomic group—in any case, an altogether different set of circumstances in which you might have lived. Complete the following:

1. The time within which I am imagining that I live is . . .
2. The details of the situation are (be specific) . . .
3. If I had lived in this place in time, I most likely would hold the following beliefs (about religion, my country, sexual conventions and taboos, gender issues, relationships, people of different races, etc. Again, be specific) . . .

For example, we think within a variety of domains: sociological, philosophical, ethical, intellectual, anthropological, ideological, political, economic, historical, biological, theological, and psychological. We ended up with our particular beliefs because we were influenced to do so in the following ways:

- *sociological:* our minds are influenced by the social groups to which we belong;
- *philosophical:* our minds are influenced by our personal philosophy;
- *ethical:* our minds are influenced by the extent to which we behave in accordance with our obligations and the way we define our obligations;
- *intellectual:* our minds are influenced by the ideas we hold, by the manner in which we reason and deal with abstractions and abstract systems;
- *anthropological:* our minds are influenced by cultural practices, mores, and taboos;
- *ideological and political:* our minds are influenced by the structure of power and its use by interest groups around us;
- *economic:* our minds are influenced by the economic conditions under which we live;
- *historical:* our minds are influenced by our history and by the way we tell our history;
- *biological:* our minds are influenced by our biology and neurology;
- *theological:* our minds are influenced by our religious beliefs and attitudes;
- *psychological:* our minds are influenced by our personality and personal psychology.

Reflections such as these should awaken in us a sense of how little we really know about our own minds. Within each of our minds is a largely unexplored world, an inner world that has been taking shape for the whole of our lives. This inner world is the most important fact about us, for it is where we live. It determines our joy and frustration. It limits what we can see and imagine. It highlights what we do see. It can drive us crazy. It can provide us with solace, peace, and tranquility. If we can appreciate these facts about us, we will find the motivation to take charge of our thinking, to be something more than clay in the hands of others, to become, in fact, the ruling force in our own lives.

2.5 *Think for Yourself*

DISCUSS THE BEGINNING THINKER STAGE

Work in groups of three. The person whose first name is last in the alphabet will explain the third stage, that of the Beginning Thinker, to the other two, answering any questions they might have. Then the other two in the group will add any features that the first student missed and elaborate on the points they think are most important.

Let's now consider two lurking traps that can derail the beginning thinker:

Trap # 1: the temptation of *dogmatic absolutism*—believing that truth is acquired not through reasoning and inquiry but, rather, through some predetermined, nonintellectual faith.

Trap # 2: the temptation of *subjective relativism*—believing that there are no intellectual standards by which to judge anything as true or false.

Both traps promise us easy answers. To advance as a beginning thinker and not fall into one or the other of these traps requires developing *confidence in reason* as a way of acquiring sound knowledge and insight. The two traps are mirror images of each other. If we become either a dogmatic absolutist or a subjective relativist, we will lose our motivation to develop as a critical thinker. As a dogmatic absolutist, we end up following wherever our "faith" leads us. As a subjective relativist, we will come to believe that everyone automatically acquires "their own truth" in some inexplicable subjective way. In both cases, there is no real place for the intellectual work and discipline of critical thinking. Both render critical thinking superfluous. Both free us from any intellectual responsibility.

If we avoid these traps, if we recognize how we have been shaped by forces beyond our control, if we discover that skills are available to help us begin to take charge of our minds, if we develop some initial confidence in reason, if we develop some intellectual humility and perseverance, we are ready to begin creating a genuine foundation on which we can rebuild our identity and character as thinkers and persons of integrity.

The key question is *how?* How exactly can we do this? We shall focus on this question for the rest of this chapter. In a sense, it is the most vital goal of the entire book.

2.6, 2.7 *Think for Yourself*

DISCUSS ABSOLUTISM AND SUBJECTIVE RELATIVISM

Work in groups of three. The person whose first name is second in the alphabet will explain the distinction between absolutism and subjective relativism to the other two, answering any questions they might have. Then the other two in the group will add any features that the first student missed and elaborate on the points they think are most important.

BEGINNING TO DEVELOP AS A THINKER

Make a list of some things you can do to begin your development as a disciplined thinker. Review Chapter 1 for ideas. Then answer this question: What do you think the benefits would be if you were to take this list seriously?

STAGE 4: THE PRACTICING THINKER

Good thinking can be practiced like basketball, tennis, or ballet. The only way to move from Beginning Thinker to Practicing Thinker is to commit yourself to daily practice in thinking well and begin to design your own plan for practice. When you do so, you become what we call a Practicing Thinker.

There are many ways to design practice regimens, some better, some worse for you. For example, you might glance through some of the other chapters of this book. Each provides suggestions for improving your thinking. You can use any of these suggestions as a starting point.

You might review the Think for Yourself activities. You might study the elements of thought, the standards for thought, and the traits of mind. You might analyze Chapter 10, on problem-solving, and Chapter 17, on strategic thinking. Think of it this way: Everything you read in this book represents a resource for you to use in devising a systematic plan for improving your thinking. As you move through the book, routinely ask yourself: What am I learning in this section or chapter that I can actively incorporate into daily practice?

If you are like most people, you can discover some practical starting points. The challenge will be in following through on any that you find. This is the challenge in most areas of skill development: People do not usually follow through. They do not establish habits of regular practice. They are discouraged by the strain and awkwardness of early attempts to perform well.

To develop as a thinker, you will have to work out a plan that will work for you, one that you can live with, one that will not burn you out or overwhelm you. Ultimately, success comes to those who are persistent and who figure out strategies for themselves.

Still, at this stage you probably don't know for sure what will work for you, only what seems like it *might*. You have to field-test your ideas. To be realistic, you should expect to experiment with a variety of plans before you find one that moves you forward as a thinker.

You should guard against discouragement. You can best avoid discouragement by recognizing from the outset that you are engaged in a process of trial and error. Prepare yourself for temporary failure. Success is to be understood as the willingness to work your way through a variety of relative failures. The logic is analogous to trying on clothes. Many that you try may not fit or look good on you, but you plod on anyway with the confidence that eventually you will find something that fits and looks good on you.

Consider another analogy: If you want to become skilled at tennis, you improve not by expecting yourself to begin as an expert player. You improve not by expecting to win every game you play or by mastering new strokes with little practice. Rather, you improve when you develop a plan that you can modify as you see what improves your game. Today you may decide to work on keeping your eye on the ball. Tomorrow you may coordinate watching the ball with following through as you swing. Every day you rethink your strategies for improvement. Development of the human mind is quite parallel to the development of the human body. Good theory, good practice, and good feedback are essential.

A "GAME PLAN" FOR IMPROVEMENT

As you begin to take your thinking seriously, you need to think about what you can do consistently every day to improve your thinking. Because excellence in thinking requires a variety of independent skills and traits that work together, you can choose to work on a range of critical thinking skills at any given point in time. The key is to focus on fundamentals and make sure you don't try to do too much. Choose your point of attack, but limit it. If you overdo it, you probably will give up entirely. But if you don't focus on fundamentals, you will never have them as a foundation in your thought.

Start slowly, and emphasize fundamentals. The race is won by the tortoise, not by the hare. Be a good and wise turtle. The solid, steady steps you take every day will determine where you ultimately end up.

A GAME PLAN FOR DEVISING A GAME PLAN

We have put together a few ideas to stimulate your thought about a game plan. There is nothing magical about our ideas. No one of them is essential. Nevertheless, each represents a plausible point of attack, one way to begin to do something plausible to improve thinking in a regular way. Though you probably can't do all of these at the same time, we recommend an approach in which you experiment with all of these. You can add any others you find in this book or come up with yourself. After you familiarize yourself with some of the options, we will explain how this game plan works.

1. Use "wasted" time. All humans waste some time. No one uses all of his or her time productively or even pleasurably. Sometimes we jump from one diversion to another without enjoying any of them. Sometimes we become irritated about matters beyond our control. Sometimes we fail to plan well, causing negative consequences that we easily could have avoided (for example, we spend time unnecessarily trapped in traffic—though we could have left a half hour earlier and avoided the rush). Sometimes we worry unproductively. Sometimes we spend time regretting what is past. Sometimes we just stare blankly into space.

The key is that the time is "spent," and if we had thought about it and considered our options, we would not have deliberately spent our time in that way. So our idea is this: Why not take advantage of the time you normally waste, by practicing good thinking during that time. For example, instead of sitting in front of the TV at the end of the day flicking from channel to channel in a vain search for a program worth watching, you could spend that time, or at least part of it, thinking back over your day and evaluating your strengths and weaknesses. You might ask yourself questions like these:

- When did I do my worst thinking today?
- When did I do my best thinking?
- What did I actually think about today?
- Did I figure out anything?
- Did I allow any negative thinking to frustrate me unnecessarily?
- If I had to repeat today, what would I do differently? Why?
- Did I do anything today to further my long-term goals?
- Did I act in accordance with my own expressed values?
- If I were to spend every day this way for 10 years, would I, at the end, have accomplished something worthy of that time?

Taking a little time with each question is important. It would be useful to review these questions periodically, perhaps weekly, to write your answers in a journal and in so doing to keep a record of how your thinking is developing.

2. Handle a problem a day. At the beginning of each day (perhaps driving to work or going to school), choose a problem to work on when you have free moments. Figure out the logic of the problem by identifying its elements. Systematically think-through the questions: What exactly is the problem? How can I put it into the form of a question? (See Chapter 10 for a template you might use.)

3. Internalize intellectual standards. Each week, study and actively bring into your thinking *one* of the universal intellectual standards presented in Chapter 5. Focus one week on clarity, the next on accuracy, and so on. For example, if you are focusing on *clarity* for the week, try to notice when you are being unclear in communicating with others. Notice when others are unclear in what they are saying. When you read, notice whether you are clear about what you are reading. When you write a paragraph for class, ask yourself whether you are clear about what you are trying to say and in conveying your thoughts in writing.

In doing this, you will practice four techniques of clarification: (1) stating what you are saying with some consideration given to your choice of words, (2) elaborating on your meaning in other words, (3) giving examples of what you mean from experiences you have had, and (4) using analogies, metaphors, pictures, or diagrams to illustrate what you mean. In clarifying thinking, you should state, elaborate, illustrate, and exemplify your points, and you will regularly ask others to do the same.

4. Keep an intellectual journal. Each week, write out a certain number of journal entries. Use the following format for each important event you write about:

- describe only situations that are emotionally significant to you (situations you care deeply about);

- describe only one situation at a time;

- describe (and keep this separate) how you behaved in the situation, being specific and exact (What did you say? What did you do? How did you react?);

- analyze, in the light of what you have written, what precisely was going on in the situation; dig beneath the surface;

- assess the implications of your analysis. (What did you learn about yourself? What would you do differently if you could relive the situation?)

5. Practice intellectual strategies. Choose a strategy from Chapter 17, on strategic thinking. While using that strategy, record your observations in a journal, including what you are learning about yourself and how you can use the strategy to improve your thinking.

6. Reshape your character. Each month, choose one intellectual trait to strive for, focusing on how you can develop that trait in yourself. For example, if concentrating on intellectual humility, begin to notice when you admit you are wrong. Notice when you refuse to admit you are wrong, even in the face of glaring evidence that you are truly wrong. Notice when you become defensive when another person tries to point out a deficiency in your work or your thinking. Notice when your arrogance keeps you from learning, when you say to yourself, for example, "I already know everything I need to know about this subject" or, "I know as much as he does. Who does he think he is, forcing his opinions onto me?"

7. Deal with your ego. Daily, begin to observe your egocentric thinking in action by contemplating questions like these: As I reflect upon my behavior today, did I ever become irritable over small things? Did I do or say anything irrational to get my way? Did I try to impose my will upon others? Did I ever fail to speak my mind when I felt strongly about something, and then later feel resentment?

Once you identify egocentric thinking in operation, you can work to replace it with more rational thought through systematic self-reflection. What would a rational person feel in this or that situation? What would a rational person do? How does that compare with what you did? (Hint: If you find that you continually conclude that a rational person would behave just as you behaved, you probably are engaging in self-deception.) (See Chapter 11 for more ways to identify egocentric thinking.)

8. Redefine the way you see things. We live in a world, both personal and social, in which every situation is defined; it is given a fundamental meaning. How a situation is defined determines how we feel about it and also how we act in it and what implications it has for us. Virtually every situation, however, can be defined in more than one way. This fact carries with it tremendous opportunities for all of us to make our life more of what we want it to be. In principle, it lies within your power to make your life much happier and more fulfilling than it is.

Many of the negative definitions that we apply to situations in our lives could in principle be transformed into positive definitions. As a result, we can gain when otherwise we would have lost. We can be happy when otherwise we would have been sad. We can be fulfilled when otherwise we would have been frustrated. In this game plan, we practice redefining the way we see things, turning negatives into positives, dead-ends into new beginnings, mistakes into opportunities to learn. To make this game plan practical, we should create some specific guidelines for ourselves. For example, we might make ourselves a list of five to ten recurring negative situations in which we feel frustrated, angry, unhappy, or worried. We then could identify the definition in each case that is at the root of the negative emotion. Next we would choose a plausible alternative definition for each, and then plan for our new responses as well as our new emotions.

Suppose you have a roommate who gets on your nerves by continually telling you about all the insignificant events in his or her life. Your present definition of the situation is, "What a bore! How am I going to last a whole semester listening to that brainless soap opera?" Your response might be: "Since I have to do a required research project for my introduction to psychology class, I will focus my project on the psychology of my roommate." Now, instead of sitting passively listening to the daily blow-by-blow description of your roommate's day, you actively question him or her to gather information you can use in your psychology paper. Because you are now directing the conversation, your roommate is not able to bore you with the details of his or her day, and you transform your interactions into a learning experience.

Another possibility is to redefine an "impossibly difficult class" into a "challenge to figure out new fundamental concepts and a new way of thinking." Let's look at this example: You redefine your initial approach to a member of the other sex not in terms of the definition— "His/her response will determine whether I am an attractive person"—but, instead, in terms of the definition, "Let me test to see if this person is initially drawn to me, given the way he or she perceives me."

With the first definition in mind, you feel personally put down if the person is not interested in you. With the second definition you explicitly recognize that people initially respond not to the way a stranger *is* but, rather, to the way the person subjectively *looks* to the other. You therefore do not perceive someone's failure to show interest in you as a defect in you.

9. Get in touch with your emotions. Whenever you feel some negative emotion, systematically ask yourself: "What, exactly, is the thinking that leads to this emotion? How might this thinking be flawed? What am I assuming? Should I be making these assumptions? What information is my thinking based on? Is that information reliable?" and so on. (See Chapters 3 and 17.)

10. Analyze group influences on your life. Closely analyze the behavior that is encouraged and discouraged in the groups to which you belong. For a given group, what are you required or expected to believe? What are you "forbidden" to do? If you conclude that your group does not require you to believe anything, or has no taboos, you can conclude that you have not deeply analyzed that group. To gain insight into the process of socialization and group membership, review an introductory text in sociology. (See Chapter 15.)

Integrating Strategies One by One

When designing strategies, the key point is that you are engaged in an experiment. You are testing strategies in your personal life. You are integrating them, and building on them, in light of your actual experience. All strategies have advantages and disadvantages. One plausible way to do this is to work with all of the strategies on the list below in any order of your choosing.

1. Use "wasted" time.
2. Handle a problem a day.
3. Internalize intellectual standards.
4. Keep an intellectual journal.
5. Practice intellectual strategies.
6. Reshape your character.
7. Deal with your ego.
8. Redefine the way you see things.
9. Get in touch with your emotions.
10. Analyze group influences on your life.

As you begin to design strategies to improve the quality of your life, suppose you find the strategy "Redefine the way you see things" to be intuitive to you. Therefore, it's a good strategy to begin with. As you focus intently on this idea and apply it in your life, you begin to notice social definitions within groups. You begin to recognize how your behavior is shaped and controlled by group definitions. You begin to see how you, and others, uncritically accept group definitions rather than creating your own definitions. Notice the definitions embedded in the following statements.

1. "I'm giving a *party.*"
2. "We're going to have a *meeting.*"
3. "Why don't you run for *election?*"
4. "The *funeral* is Tuesday."
5. "Jack is an *acquaintance,* not really a *friend.*"

When you internalize this idea, you begin to see how important and pervasive social definitions are. When you become more insightful about social definitions, you begin to redefine situations in ways that run contrary to commonly accepted social definitions. You then begin to see how redefining situations and relationships enables you to "get in touch with your emotions." You recognize that the way you define things generates the emotions you feel. When you *think* you are threatened (you define a situation as "threatening"), you feel *fear.* On the one hand, if you define a situation as a "failure," you may feel depressed. On the other hand, if you define that same situation as "a lesson or an opportunity to learn," you feel empowered to learn. When you recognize this control that you are capable of exercising, the two strategies begin to work together and reinforce each other.

You then might begin to integrate strategy #10 ("analyze group influences on your life") with the two strategies you have already internalized. One of the main ways in which groups control us is by controlling the definitions we are allowed to use. When a group defines some things as "cool" and some as "dumb," members of the group try to appear "cool" and not appear "dumb." When the boss of a business says, "That makes a lot of sense," his subordinates know they are not to say, "No, it is ridiculous." They know this because defining someone as the "boss" gives him or her special privileges to define situations and relationships. As a developing thinker, you begin to decide what groups you allow to influence your thinking and what group influences you reject.

You now have three interwoven strategies: You "redefine the way you see things," "get in touch with your emotions," and "analyze group influences on your life." The three strategies are integrated into one. At this point, you can experiment with any of the other strategies (listed below), looking for opportunities to integrate them into your thinking and your life.

- Use wasted time.
- Handle a problem a day.
- Internalize intellectual standards.
- Keep an intellectual journal.
- Practice intellectual strategies.
- Reshape your character.
- Deal with your ego.

2.8   *Think for Yourself*

BEGINNING TO DEVELOP A PLAN FOR YOURSELF

Focusing on strategies 1–10, which you have just read, write out a basic plan for beginning your development as a thinker. List the first three strategies you will incorporate into your thinking and how you plan to do this. Be specific and detailed. Then at the end of each day, revisit your list and see how you are progressing. Add to your list as you internalize previously learned ideas.

If you follow through on a plan, you are going beyond the Beginning Thinker stage. You are becoming a Practicing Thinker. We shall discuss this and the other two stages of development in Chapter 19.

CHAPTER 3

SELF-UNDERSTANDING

The preceding chapters emphasized that

- critical thinking requires the development of basic intellectual skills, abilities, and insights;
- becoming a skilled thinker is like becoming skilled in basketball, ballet, or saxophone playing;
- these skills can be used to serve two incompatible ends: self-centeredness or fair-mindedness;
- the skills of critical thinking can be learned in a "weak" sense (selfish thinking);
- we are focused on the development of critical thinking in a "strong" sense (i.e., serving fair-minded thinking);
- fair-mindedness requires that we develop a network of interrelated traits of mind;
- development as a critical thinker occurs in predictable stages;
- engaging in that development is challenging, requiring "planned practice" and happening over many years, not weeks or months.

Our goal in this chapter is to lay a foundation for better understanding the nature of the human mind. We will begin by taking a further look at human egocentrism and the obstacle it represents. We then will consider some basic distinctions we can use to achieve greater self-command. Our latent egocentrism, we shall see, asserts itself through each of the basic functions of the mind. We must understand those functions, as they work in relationship to each other. Only through practical insight into how our mind operates can we hope to understand, and transform, ourselves.

MONITOR THE EGOCENTRISM
IN YOUR THOUGHT AND LIFE

One of the fundamental challenges that most humans face in learning is that our life is dominated by a tendency to think and feel egocentrically. Our life is deeply situated in our own immediate desires, pains, thoughts, and feelings. We seek immediate gratification or long-term gratification based on an essentially selfish perspective. We are not typically or fundamentally concerned with whether our perceptions or meanings are accurate, though we may think we are. We are not significantly concerned with personal growth, self-insight, or ultimate integrity, though we think we are. We are not deeply motivated to discover our own weaknesses, prejudices, or self-deception. Rather, we seek to get what we want, avoid the disapproval of others, and justify ourselves in our own mind.

The tendency for humans to think in an egocentric fashion means that, typically, we have little or no real insight into the nature of our own thinking and emotions. For example, many of us unconsciously believe that it is possible to acquire knowledge without much thought, that it is possible to read without exerting intellectual energy, and that good writing is a talent one is born with—not a product of practice and hard work. As a result, we tend to evade responsibility for our own learning. We do not seek to learn new modes of thinking. Much of our thinking is stereotypical and simplistic, yet our egocentrism prevents us from recognizing this. We create the inner chains that enslave us.

These inner chains can have a negative effect on our relationships, success, growth, and happiness. It is not possible to get beyond the egocentrism that you and I inherit as human beings by ignoring our ego or pretending that we are decent people after all. We can restrain our egocentrism only by developing explicit habits that enable us to do so. We get beyond egocentric emotional responses not by denying that we ever respond in such a way but, rather, by owning these responses when they occur and restructuring the thinking that is feeding those emotions. For example, if you are gripped by the egocentric fear of appearing ridiculous or dumb when you want to ask a question in the classroom, you must explicitly target the egocentric thinking that is feeding that fear: "If I ask this question, the other students will think I am dumb or stupid." The thinking you could replace it with is something like: "Any question I might ask that would help me to learn would probably help other students as well. What's more, if any students think my question is stupid, that's their problem, their inability to understand the importance of asking questions as a means of learning. I will not let my learning be impeded because of other students' limited understanding of learning."

We will return to the problem of dealing with egocentrism later. Meanwhile, you should begin to think about what egocentrism is and begin to monitor your thinking for evidence of it.

3.1   *Think for Yourself*

BEGINNING TO UNDERSTAND EGOCENTRISM

Think of the most self-centered person you know. This may be someone who is fundamentally selfish or arrogant. Describe the person's behavior in detail. Based on the person's behavior, how would you describe his or her thinking? What types of feelings does he or she display? What is the person motivated to do? To what extent does the person use other people to get what he or she wants? To what extent does the person exhibit sincere concern for the thoughts and feelings of others?

MAKE A COMMITMENT TO FAIR-MINDEDNESS

Though no one defines himself or herself as an egocentric person, each of us should recognize that being egocentric is an important part of what we have to understand in dealing with the structure of our mind. One of the ways to begin to confront our own egocentrism is by exploring the extent to which we have allowed our identity to be egocentrically shaped. For example, as we previously emphasized, we are all born into a culture, a nation, and a family. Our parents inculcate into us particular beliefs (about the family, personal relationships, marriage, childhood, obedience, religion, politics, schooling, and so on). We form associations with people who have certain beliefs (which they have encouraged, or expected, us to accept). We are, in the first instance, a product of these influences. Only through self-understanding can we begin to be more than a product of influences.

If we uncritically believe what we were taught to believe, these beliefs are likely to become part of our egocentric identity. When they do, it affects the manner in which we believe. For example, we are all egocentric to the extent that an examination of our attitudes reveals that we unconsciously use egocentric standards to justify our beliefs:

1. **"It's true because *I* believe it."** People don't say this aloud, but we often find ourselves assuming that others are correct when they agree with us and incorrect when they do not. They way we respond to people indicates that we egocentrically assume we have a unique insight into the *truth.*

2. **"It's true because *we* believe it."** Our behavior indicates that we egocentrically assume that the groups to which we belong have a unique insight into the *truth.* In this way of thinking, our religion, our country, our friends are special—and better than other religions, countries, friends.

3. **"It's true because *I want* to believe it."** Our behavior indicates that we more readily believe what coincides with what we egocentrically want to believe, even to the point of absurdity.

4. **"It's true because *I have always believed it.*"** Our behavior indicates that we more readily believe what coincides with beliefs we have long held. We egocentrically assume the rightness of our early beliefs.

5. **"It's true because it is in *my selfish interest* to believe it."** Our behavior indicates that we more readily believe what coincides with beliefs that, when held, serve to advance our wealth, power, or position, even if they conflict with the ethical principles that we insist we hold.

If we consciously recognize these tendencies in ourselves and deliberately and systematically seek to overcome them by thinking fair-mindedly, our definition of ourselves can aid our development as thinkers. We then begin to divide our thoughts into two categories: (1) thoughts that serve to advance the agenda of our egocentric nature, and (2) thoughts that serve to develop our rational fair-mindedness. To effectively do this, we need to develop a special relationship to our mind. We must become a student of our mind's operations, especially of its pathology.

RECOGNIZE THE MIND'S THREE DISTINCTIVE FUNCTIONS

The mind has three basic functions: thinking, feeling, and wanting.

1. The function of *thinking* is to create meaning—making sense of the events of our lives, sorting events into named categories, finding patterns for us. It continually tells us: This is what is going on. This is what is happening. Notice this and that. It is the part of the mind that figures things out.

2. The function of *feeling* is to monitor or evaluate the meanings created by the thinking function—evaluating how positive and negative the events of our life are, given the meaning we are ascribing to them. It continually tells us: This is how you should feel about what is happening in your life. You're doing really well. Or, alternatively, watch out—you're getting into trouble!

3. The function of *wanting* allocates energy to action, in keeping with our definitions of what is desirable and possible. It continually tells us: This is what is worth getting. Go for it! Or, conversely, it tells us: This is not worth getting. Don't bother.

Looked at this way, our mind is continually communicating three kinds of things to us: (1) what is going on in our life; (2) feelings (positive or negative) about those

EXHIBIT 3.1 *The three basic functions of the mind are intricately interrelated.*

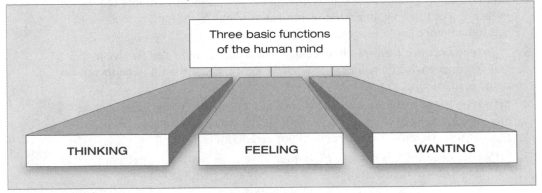

Three basic functions of the human mind

THINKING   FEELING   WANTING

events; and (3) things to pursue, where to put our energy (in the light of 1 and 2). What's more, there is an intimate, dynamic interrelation between thinking, feeling, and wanting. As we said, each is continually influencing the other two. When, for example, we *think* we are being threatened, we *feel* fear and we inevitably *want* to flee from or attack whatever we think is threatening us. When we *think* a subject we are required to study has no relationship to our lives and values, we *feel* bored by instruction about it and develop a negative motivation with respect to it.

UNDERSTAND THAT YOU HAVE A SPECIAL RELATIONSHIP TO YOUR MIND

It now should be clear that everyone lives in a special and intimate relationship to his or her mind—at least unconsciously. The trick is to make that unconscious relationship *conscious* and *deliberate*. All of our activity is a product of inward ideas of who and

EXHIBIT 3.2 *Thinking is the part of the mind that figures out what is going on. Feelings tell us whether things are going well or poorly for us. The wanting part of the mind propels us forward or away from action.*

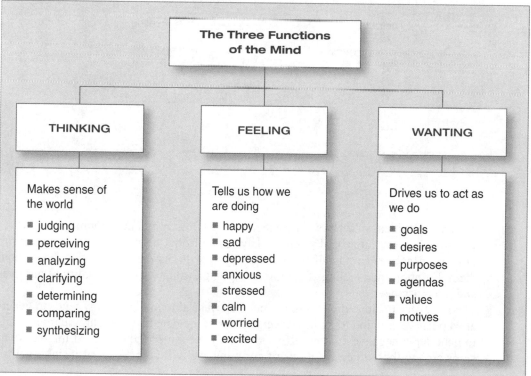

The Three Functions of the Mind

THINKING	FEELING	WANTING
Makes sense of the world	Tells us how we are doing	Drives us to act as we do
■ judging	■ happy	■ goals
■ perceiving	■ sad	■ desires
■ analyzing	■ depressed	■ purposes
■ clarifying	■ anxious	■ agendas
■ determining	■ stressed	■ values
■ comparing	■ calm	■ motives
■ synthesizing	■ worried	
	■ excited	

EXHIBIT 3.3 *Thinking, feeling, and wanting are interwoven. Where there is one, the other two are present as well. These three functions continually interact and influence one another in a dynamic process.*

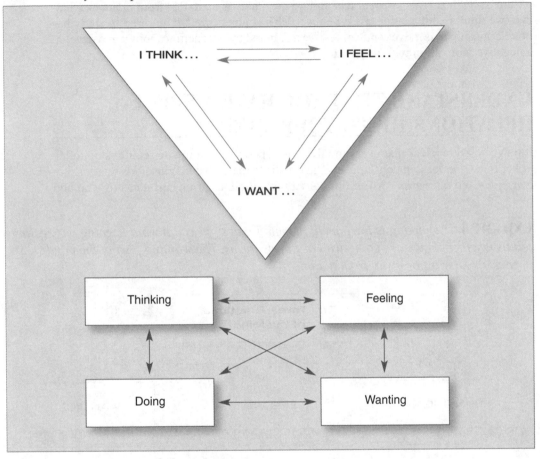

what we are, ideas of what we are experiencing (from moment to moment), of where we are going (our future), of where we have come from (our past). And, in addition, all of these ideas are in a state of continual interplay with our emotions and feelings about them. Emotions and feelings function as ongoing evaluators of the quality of our lives and circumstances.

For every positive thought the mind "believes," the mind naturally tends to generate a positive emotion to fit it. Conversely, for every negative thought, the mind tends to generate a negative emotion. If we explicitly recognize the continual interrelationships among these three functions of our mind, we will gain a central insight that we can begin to use to our advantage. Then we can begin to exercise command over our own mind's functions. Let's look into this idea more closely.

We experience joy, happiness, frustration, pain, confusion, desire, passion, and indifference because we give a meaning to every situation we experience, because we think about it in a particular fashion, because we connect it to feelings we experienced in what we perceived as similar or related circumstances. The meaning we create can be grounded in insight, objective reality, a fantasy, or even a dysfunctional interpretation of reality. For example, two people in the same situation might react entirely differently, with one person experiencing pain and frustration and the other experiencing curiosity and excitement.

Consider two students faced with the task of improving their writing ability. The first may experience difficulty, confusion, frustration, and ultimately give up. This person gives a negative meaning to the task of learning to improve her writing, defining it as a situation destined for failure. Because she *thinks* that learning to write should be easy, she feels frustrated when it is difficult. Another person in the same situation may experience improvement in writing as a challenge, exciting, even exhilarating, not because he possesses skills in writing that the other does not but, rather, because he brings a different mindset to the task. He *thinks* that learning to write should be difficult, that it should take lots of time, that it involves rewriting and rewriting and rewriting yet again if it is to be of high quality.

The actual task at hand is precisely the same. Nevertheless, the difficulty or ease with which a person handles the challenge, the decision to take up the challenge or avoid it altogether, ultimate success or failure, is determined fundamentally by the manner in which the situation is interpreted through one's *thinking*. Different *emotions* follow from these differences in thought and action.

Instruction that fails to address the affective side of our lives can turn us eventually into inveterate enemies of education unless we take active command of our thinking and our learning. For example, when we are force-fed math in a way that ignores our emotional response, we typically end up with a bad case of "math hatred" or "math phobia." For the rest of our life, we avoid anything mathematical. We view mathematics as unintelligible, as just a bunch of formulas, unrelated to anything important in our life, or we view ourselves as "too dumb" to understand it.

If, however, we take command of our thinking in our classes, we carefully analyze the content in our classes to determine what is most important for us to learn. We are self-motivated no matter how boring the class in itself may seem. We see ourselves as being capable of learning anything we put our minds to. When we feel frustrated during the learning process, we are intellectually persistent. When we feel confused, we realize that we need to ask questions so we can better understand what we are learning. We are not afraid to say, "I don't understand." We realize that the best thinkers are those who can differentiate that which they understand and that which they do not.

When we understand the interrelated roles of thoughts, feelings, and motivation, when we can see that for every feeling state we experience, a related thought process

EXHIBIT 3.4 *We change undesirable feelings and desires by changing the thinking that is leading to them.*

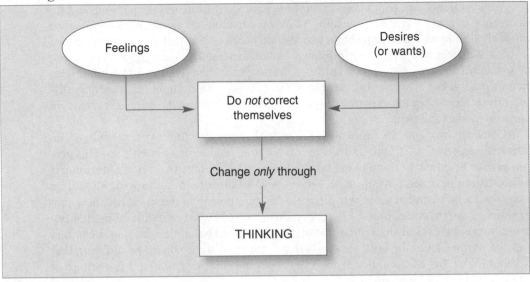

EXHIBIT 3.5 *By taking command of our thinking, we can take command of all three functions of the mind.*

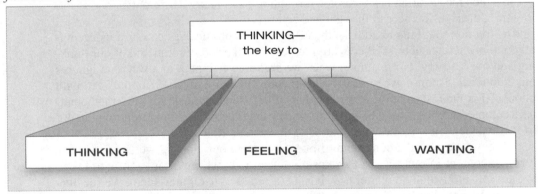

exists that motivates us to some action, we can begin to analyze thoughts underlying our emotions and desires. If I am bored in class, I can ask myself: *What is the thinking in my mind that is leading to this feeling of boredom?* If I am uninterested in what I am learning, I can ask myself: *What is the thinking that influences me not to want to learn this? What exactly is the value of learning this? Is this something I need to learn, that will be useful to me? If so, what do I need to do to learn it?*

EXHIBIT 3.6 *Your thinking controls every part of your life. But do you control your thinking?*

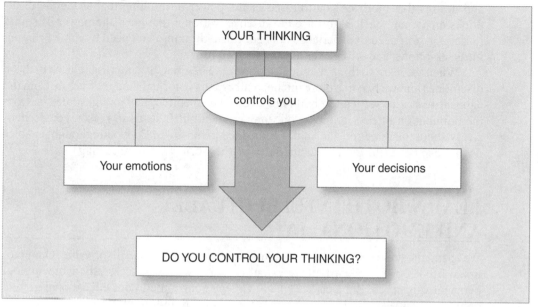

3.2 *Think for Yourself*

UNDERSTANDING THE RELATIONSHIP BETWEEN THE THREE FUNCTIONS OF THE MIND

Think of a situation you were in recently in which you experienced a negative emotion such as anger, frustration, depression, insecurity, or fear.

1. Write out in detail what was going on in the situation and how you felt in the situation.

2. Now try to figure out the thinking you were doing in the circumstance that led to the negative feeling. Write out the thinking in detail.

3. Then write how your thinking and feeling impacted your behavior. (Given the thinking and feeling, what were you motivated to do?)

CONNECT ACADEMIC SUBJECTS TO YOUR LIFE AND PROBLEMS

One challenge you face as a student is to learn to approach your classes with a fuller understanding of how your emotional life influences your learning, for good or ill. Your emotions can aid or hamper your learning. Your goals can facilitate or limit your insights.

If you typically don't learn at a deep level, you need to observe the thoughts, emotions, and desires that keep you from learning deeply. You must generate the thoughts and desires that motivate you to discover the powerful thinking that academic disciplines create and define. You need to discover rational thought—the power of sound reasoning. You need to experience nonegocentric thinking. You need to value bringing ideas, emotions, and will power together as you learn.

When we learn to think within disciplines, we begin to use important ideas in those disciplines and we become more intellectually free. Historical thought frees us from the egocentric stories we tend to build our lives upon. Sociological thought frees us from the domination of peer groups. Philosophical thought frees us to reason comprehensively about the direction and values embedded in our lives. Economic thought enables us to grasp powerful forces that are defining the world we are inhabiting.

LEARN BOTH INTELLECTUALLY AND EMOTIONALLY

We spend most of our time thinking about what we personally want or value. Our emotional life keeps us focused on the extent to which we are successfully achieving our personal values. The subjects we take in college contribute to our educational growth only insofar as we are able to relate what we are studying to our personal lives. If we are to personally value literature, for example—and hence be motivated to read it for more than the grade we will receive—we must discover the relevance of literary insights to our life. When we see connections between the issues and problems that the characters in stories face and the issues and problems that we face ourselves, literature comes alive to us. The characters we read about live in our minds. We identify with them. We puzzle with them, suffer with them, triumph with them.

When the logic of academic content makes intellectual sense in a dimension of our life, we value it. We are motivated to learn more, to figure out more, to "study" more. If we want to motivate ourselves—and it is no one else's responsibility but ours—we have to seek out connections between the academic content we study and our emotions and values.

Only you can build or create motivation in your life. If learning becomes sheer drudgery to you and you don't see value in it, you will put it off to the last minute and look for short-cuts (such as cramming) that typically substitute short-term memorization for long-term internalization. The thinking that then guides your study habits is: *"If I can get by through cramming, why should I work hard to internalize this (worthless) stuff?"* Your life, though still emotionally significant to you, becomes intellectually barren. As intellectual drudgery, your classes will inevitably be boring. On the one hand, you live within emotions that you don't intellectually analyze, and on the other hand, your intellectual life becomes an alienated set of rituals: you take notes (that mean little to you), cram for exams (that provide you with no insights), and crank out papers (that are mainly a patchwork of others' thoughts).

One key to integrating intellectual and emotional learning is found in the recognition that every academic discipline represents a powerful mode of thinking that can contribute to your development as a thinker. Until you discover this insight as a result of actually working your way into the thinking of one or more disciplines, you are unlikely to be strongly motivated by it. For example, until you experience the power of historical thinking, you will not value it. But if you do not value historical thinking in the first place, you will have little motivation to learn it.

This is the vicious circle that, in general, prevents the uneducated from becoming educated. When we are uneducated, we do not value education. But until we value education, we will not put the time, energy, and work into the deep learning that alone provides us with an education. It is your challenge to struggle with this dilemma. Will you be able to value the work of learning sufficiently to begin to discover the power of the disciplines to which college classes expose you? Or will you, like many students before you, simply become a "survivor"?

In some sense, all knowledge is personal, as no knowledge would exist without people to have that knowledge. In the long run, we acquire only the knowledge we value. We internalize only those modes of thinking that seem essential to what we want and what we think is important. It is up to each one of us to decide when, where, and how we learn.

The more emotionally powerful connections you can make between what you study and what you value in life, the easier you will find learning to be. Seek out the most basic concepts in the disciplines you study. Express those concepts in the most nontechnical manner you can. Relate those concepts to the most fundamental goals in the discipline. Relate those goals to your goals. The tools of this book can make possible the transition to higher-order thinking and learning. You, however, must summon the energy, the emotional reserves, to do the *intellectual* work required.

3.3 *Think for Yourself*

CONNECTING COURSE CONTENT TO WHAT YOU THINK IS IMPORTANT

Select one of your courses and try to write out the most fundamental, the most significant, concept in the course. Then make a list of ways in which you can use this idea in your life. Or make a list of important questions that thinkers within the field of study might ask. Write out your answer or explain orally.

THE PARTS
OF THINKING

I t should now be clear to you that

- critical thinking requires the development of basic intellectual skills, abilities, and insights;

- becoming a skilled thinker is like becoming skilled in basketball, ballet, or saxophone playing;

- these skills can be used to serve two incompatible ends: self-centeredness or fair-mindedness;

- the skills of critical thinking can be learned in a weak sense (skilled selfish thinking);

- we are focused, in this book, on the development of critical thinking in a strong sense (skilled fair-minded thinking);

- fair-mindedness requires us to develop a network of interrelated traits of mind;

- development as a critical thinker occurs in predictable stages;

- engaging in that development is challenging, requiring "planned practice" and emerging over many years, not weeks or months;

- human egocentrism represents a significant obstacle to fair-minded critical thinking;

- to conquer our egocentrism, we must understand, and exercise some control over, the three basic functions of the human mind: thinking, feeling, wanting.

This chapter focuses on how to take thinking apart—how to *analyze* it by examining its parts. Chapter 5 focuses on the *assessment* of thinking, on how to apply intellectual standards to the parts of thinking to ensure that the thinking you are examining is of high quality.

EXHIBIT 4.1 *Critical thinkers routinely apply the intellectual standards to the elements of reasoning in order to develop intellectual traits.*

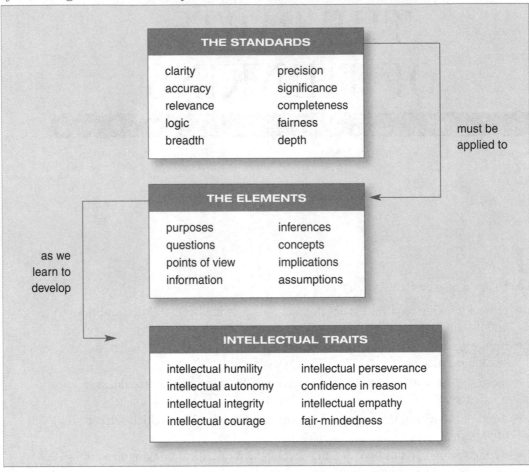

We begin with a brief discussion of *reasoning,* the mental process the mind uses to make sense of whatever we seek to understand.

REASONING IS EVERYWHERE IN HUMAN LIFE

The words *thinking* and *reasoning* are used in everyday life as virtual synonyms. *Reasoning,* however, has a more formal flavor. This is because it highlights the intellectual dimension of thinking.

Reasoning occurs whenever the mind draws conclusions on the basis of reasons. We draw conclusions whenever we make sense of things. The result is that whenever we think, we reason. Whenever we conceptualize the world, or any part of it, we reason. Usually, of course, we are not aware of the full scope of reasoning in our lives.

We begin to reason from the moment we wake up in the morning. We reason when we figure out what to eat for breakfast, what to wear, whether to stop at the store on the way to school, whether to go to lunch with this or that friend. We reason as we interpret the oncoming flow of traffic, when we react to the decisions of other drivers, when we speed up or slow down. One can draw conclusions, then, about everyday events or, really, about anything at all—about poems, microbes, people, numbers, historical events, social settings, psychological states, character traits, the past, the present, the future.

To reason well, we must scrutinize the process we are using. What are we trying to figure out? What information do we need? Do we have that information? How could we check it for accuracy? The less conscious we are of how we are thinking, the easier it is to make some mistake or error. To maximize your learning, try to approach your classes so you are going beyond noticing, to also analyzing and evaluating your reasoning.

4.1 *Think for Yourself*

BECOMING MORE AWARE OF THE ROLE OF REASONING IN YOUR LIFE

Make a list of all the things you did today. Then, for each act, figure out the thinking that led you to do, or guided you while doing, the act. (Remember that most of your thinking is *unconscious*.) For example, when you left your house this morning, you may have stopped at the store for food. This act makes no sense unless you somehow had come to the conclusion that you needed some food. Then, while at the store, you bought a certain number of items. This action resulted from the tacit conclusion you came to that you needed some items and not others.

Realize that every time you make a decision, that decision represents a view or conclusion you reasoned to. For each action you identify, answer these two questions: (1) What exactly did I do? and (2) What thinking is presupposed in my behavior? Write out your answer or explain orally.

REASONING HAS PARTS

The elements of thought also can be called the *parts of thinking* or the *fundamental structures of thought*. We will use these expressions interchangeably. The elements or parts of reasoning are those essential dimensions of reasoning that are present whenever and wherever reasoning occurs—independent of whether we are reasoning well or poorly. Working together, these elements shape reasoning and provide a general logic to the use of thought.

When we become adept at identifying the elements of our reasoning, we are in a much better position to recognize flaws in our thinking, by locating problems in this or that element. This ability is essential to critical thinking. The ability to identify the elements of reasoning, then, is an important ability in critical thinking.

Reasoning is a process whereby one draws conclusions on the basis of reasons. On the surface, reasoning seems somewhat simple, as if it has no component structures. Looked at more closely, however, it implies the ability to engage in a set of interrelated

EXHIBIT 4.2 *These parts or elements of reasoning are always present in human thinking.*

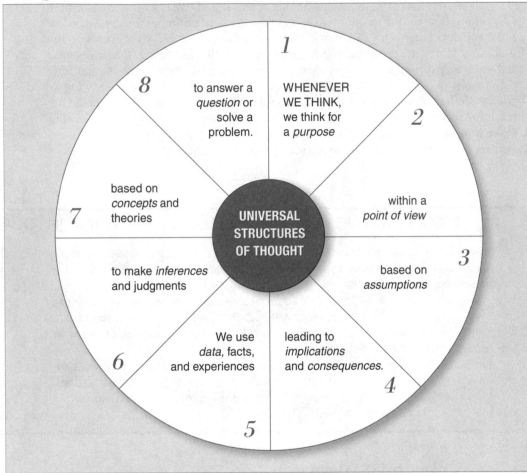

EXHIBIT 4.3 *Critical thinkers understand the importance of taking thinking apart in order to analyze it for flaws.*

intellectual processes. It is useful to practice making conscious what is subconscious in your thinking. Then you can better understand what's going on beneath the surface of your thought. In this chapter we introduce you to important ideas you can use for this task.

A First Look at the Elements of Thought

Let us begin by looking at the parts of thinking as they stand in an interrelated set. It is possible to name them in just one, somewhat complex, sentence:

> Whenever you reason,
>
> you do so in some circumstances,
>
> making some inferences (that have some implications and consequences)
>
> based on some reasons or information (and assumptions)
>
> using some concepts,
>
> in trying to settle some question (or solve some problem)
>
> for some purpose
>
> within a point of view.

If you like, you can put it in two sentences:

> Whenever you are *reasoning*,
>
> you are trying to accomplish some *purpose*,
>
> within a *point of view*,
>
> using *concepts or ideas*.
>
> You are focused on some *question, issue, or* problem,
>
> using *information*
>
> to come to *conclusions*,
>
> based on *assumptions*,
>
> all of which have *implications*.

Let us now examine, at least provisionally, each of these crucial concepts. We will be using them throughout this book, so it is essential that they become a comfortable part of your own critical thinking vocabulary. As you read these initial explanations, see if you can elaborate upon them in your own words, with an example drawn from your own experience.

By reasoning, we mean *to make sense of something by giving it some meaning in one's mind.* Virtually all thinking is part of our sense-making activities. We hear scratching at the door and think, "It's the dog." We see dark clouds in the sky and think, "It looks like rain." Some of this activity operates at a subconscious level. For example, all of the sights and sounds about me have meaning for me without my explicitly noticing that they do. Most of our reasoning is unspectacular. Our reasoning tends to become explicit to us only when someone challenges it and we have to defend it ("Why do you say that Jack is obnoxious? I thought he was quite pleasant.").

EXHIBIT 4.4 *If you understand the parts of thinking, you can ask the crucial questions implied by those parts.*

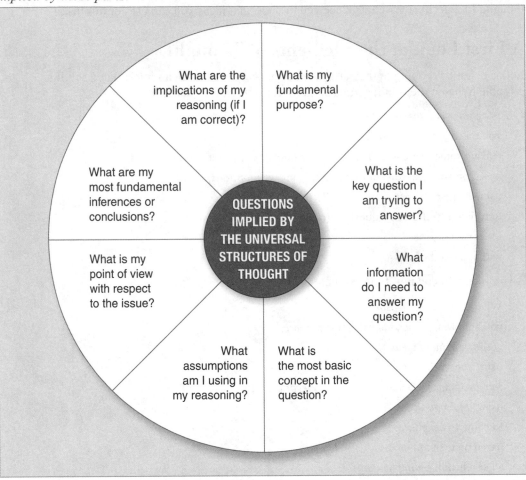

Throughout life, we begin with a goal or purpose and then figure out what to do to achieve our goal. Reasoning is what enables us to come to these decisions using ideas and meanings.

In saying that *reasoning has a purpose,* we mean that *when humans think about the world, we do not do so randomly but, rather, in line with our goals, desires, needs, and values.* Our thinking is an integral part of a patterned way of acting in the world, and we act, even in simple matters, with some set of ends in view. To understand someone's thinking—including our own—we must understand the functions it serves, what it is about, the direction it is moving, the ends that make sense of it. Most of what we are after in our thinking is not obvious to us, though. Raising human goals and desires to the level of conscious realization is an important part of critical thinking.

By *reasoning within a point of view,* we mean that *our thinking has some comprehensive focus or orientation.* Our thinking is directed *to* something *from* some angle. We can change either what we focus on or the angle of our focus. We often give names to the angle from which we are thinking about something. For example, we could look at something politically or scientifically, poetically or philosophically. We might look at something conservatively or liberally, religiously or secularly. We might look at something from a cultural or a financial perspective, or both. Once we understand how people are approaching a question or topic (what their comprehensive perspective is), we usually are much better able to understand the whole of their thinking.

By *using concepts in reasoning,* we mean the *general categories or ideas by which we interpret, classify, or group the information we use in our thinking.* For example, in this book the concepts of critical thinking and uncritical thinking are important. Everything written can be classified as an attempt to explain one or the other of these two important ideas. Each of these ideas is explained, in turn, by means of other ideas. Thus, the concept of thinking critically is explained by reference to yet other concepts such as "intellectual standards for thought." Out of each subject discipline (chemistry, geology, literature, math) arises its own set of concepts or technical vocabulary to facilitate its thinking. All sports require a vocabulary of concepts that enables those who are trying to understand or master the game to make sense of it. Try to explain baseball to someone without using these ideas: strike, ball, shortstop, inning, at bat, hit, run, safe, out, balk. To play the game, we must interpret everything we do in it by means of concepts such as these. The rules would not make sense without them. The game would be incomprehensible.

By *reasoning upon some question, issue, or problem,* we mean that *when we think about the world in line with our goals, desires, needs, and values, we often face questions we need to answer, problems we need to solve, issues we need to resolve.* Therefore, when we find ourselves confronting a difficulty, it makes sense to say, "What is the question we need to answer?" or, "What is the problem we need to solve?" or, "What is the issue we need to resolve?" To improve our ability to think well, we must learn how to put in a clear and distinct way the questions, problems, and issues we need to deal with. If we change the question, we change the criteria we have to meet to settle it. If we modify the problem, we need to modify how we are going to solve the problem. If we shift the issue, new considerations become relevant to its resolution.

By *using information in our reasoning,* we mean *using some set of facts, data, or experiences to support our conclusions.* Whenever someone is reasoning, it makes sense to ask, "Upon what facts or information are you basing your reasoning?" The factual basis for reasoning can be important. For example, in a newspaper ad, the following pieces of information were used in support of an argument against capital punishment:

- "Since the death penalty was reinstated by the Supreme Court in 1976, for every seven prisoners who were executed, one prisoner awaiting execution was found to be innocent and released."

- "At least 381 homicide convictions have been overturned since 1963 because prosecutors concealed evidence of innocence or presented evidence they knew to be false."

- "A study by the U.S. General Accounting Office found racial prejudice in death sentencing . . .: Killers of whites were proportionally more likely to be executed than were killers of blacks."
- "Since 1984, 34 mentally retarded people have been executed." (*New York Times,* November 22, 1999).

Can you see how information such as this—if true—gives strength to the reasoning? The opposing position, of course, would advance information of its own to try to challenge or counter this information. Important critical thinking axioms are: Check your facts! Check your data!

By *coming to conclusions,* we mean taking something (which we believe we know) and figuring out something else on the basis of it. When we do this, we *make inferences.* For example, if you walk by me without saying hello, I might come to the conclusion (make the inference) that you are angry with me. If the water kettle on the stove begins to whistle, I come to the conclusion (make the inference) that the water in it has started to boil. In everyday life, we are continually making inferences (coming to conclusions) about the people, things, places, and events of our lives.

By *reasoning based on assumptions,* we mean *whatever we take for granted as true* in order to figure out something else. Thus, if you infer that because a candidate is a Republican, he or she will support a balanced budget, you assume that all Republicans support a balanced budget. If you infer that foreign leaders presented in the news as "enemies" or "friends" of the United States are actually enemies or friends, you assume that the news is always accurate in its presentation of the character of foreign leaders. If you infer that someone who invites you to his or her apartment after a party "to continue this interesting conversation" is really interested in you romantically or sexually, you assume that the only reason for going to someone's apartment late at night after a party is to pursue a romantic or sexual relationship. All reasoning has some basis in the assumptions we make (but usually do not openly express).

By the *implications of reasoning,* we mean that which follows from our thinking. It means *that to which our thinking is leading us.* If you say to someone that you "love" him, you *imply* that you are concerned with his welfare. If you make a promise, you *imply* that you intend to keep it. If you call a country a "democracy," you imply that the political power is in the hands of the people at large (rather than being in the hands of a powerful minority). If you call yourself a "feminist," you imply that you are in favor of the political, social, and economic equality of the sexes. We often test the credibility of people by seeing if they are true to the implications of their own words. A sound principle of critical thinking (and of personal integrity, for that matter) is, "Say what you mean and mean what you say."

An Everyday Example: Jack and Jill

Now let's look at, and then analyze, a disagreement that might arise in everyday life—in this case, between lovers who come to different conclusions about a situation they both experienced. Suppose Jack and Jill, who are in a romantic relationship, go to a party, during which Jack spends most of the evening talking with Susan. On their way back, Jack, sensing that Jill is upset, asks, "What's wrong?"

After some hesitation, Jill says, "I didn't appreciate your spending the whole night flirting with Susan!"

Jack: Flirting . . . flirting, I was *not* flirting!

Jill: What would you call it?

Jack: Being friendly. I was being *friendly*.

Jill: When a guy spends the whole evening focused on one girl, sits very close to her, looks at her in a romantic way, and periodically touches her in supposedly casual ways, he is engaged in what can only be called *flirting*.

Jack: And when a girl spends her whole evening watching everything her boyfriend does, collecting evidence as if preparing for a trial, a boyfriend who has always been faithful to her, she is engaged in what can only be called *paranoia*.

Jill: Paranoid! How dare you call me that!

Jack: Well, how else can I describe your behavior? You're obviously distrustful and in-secure. You're accusing me without a good reason for doing so.

Jill: Don't act like this is the only time you have ever flirted. I have heard that you played the field before we got together.

Jack: And I have heard about your possessiveness and jealousy from your friends. I think you need to deal with your own problems before you attack me. If you ask me, I think you need counseling.

Jill: You're nothing but a typical male. You gauge your manhood on how many girls you can conquer. You're so focused on getting strokes for that male ego of yours that you can't see or admit what you're doing. If you aren't willing to change, I don't see how we can have a relationship!

Jack: I don't see how we can have a relationship either—not because I'm unfaithful but because *you're paranoid*. And unless I get an apology, I'm out of here!

Analysis of the Example

Let's analyze this exchange using the elements of thought.

- **Purpose.** Both Jack and Jill presumably seek a successful romantic relationship. That is their implied shared goal.

- **Problem.** They see a problem or issue standing in the way, a problem they conceptualize differently. To Jack, the problem is, "When is Jill going to deal with her paranoia?" To Jill, the problem is, "When is Jack going to take responsibility for his flirtatious behavior?"

- **Conclusions.** Jack's and Jill's inferences (conclusions) about the situation derive from the same behavior in the same circumstance, but they clearly see the behavior differently. To Jack, his behavior is to be understood as merely "friendly." To Jill, Jack's behavior can be understood only as "flirtation."

- **Facts.** The raw facts of the situation include everything Jack actually said and did at the party. Other relevant facts include Jack's behavior toward other women in his past. Additional facts include Jill's behavior toward former boyfriends and any other facts that bear on whether she is acting out of insecurity, or "paranoia."

- **Assumptions.** Jack is assuming that he is not self-deceived in his motivation with respect to Susan and other women. Jack also is assuming that he is competent to identify paranoia in another person's behavior. Further, he is assuming that a woman could not behave in the way that Jill did without being paranoid. Jill is assuming that Jack's behavior is not compatible with ordinary friendliness. Both of them assume that what they have heard about the other is accurate. Both assume themselves to be justified in their behavior in the situation.

- **Concepts.** Four key concepts are embedded in the reasoning: flirtation, friendliness, paranoia, and male ego.

- **Implications.** Both Jack and Jill imply by their reasoning that the other person is entirely to blame for any differences between them regarding Jack's behavior at the party. Both seem to imply that the relationship is hopeless.

- **Point of view.** Both Jack and Jill may be seeing the other through the bias of a gender-based point of view. Both see themselves as a victim of the other. Both see themselves as blameless.

Given what we know about the dispute, it is not possible to assess who is correct and to what extent. To decide whose interpretation of the situation is most plausible, we would need more facts. A variety of subtle but observable behaviors—if we could verify them in the behavior of Jack toward Susan—might lead us to conclude that Jill is correct and that Jack was behaving flirtatiously. Or, if we heard the conversation firsthand, we might decide that Jill's response is unjustified.

HOW THE PARTS OF THINKING FIT TOGETHER

The trick in learning the elements of thought is to express these ideas in a number of different ways until their nonlinear interrelationships begin to become intuitive to you. For example, you might think of the parts of reasoning as analogous to the essential parts of the human body. They are all present whether we are healthy or not. Like the parts of the body, the parts of thought function in an interdependent fashion. One way to express those interrelationships is that

- our purpose affects the manner in which we ask *questions;*
- the manner in which we ask *questions* affects the *information* we gather;
- the *information* we gather affects the way we *interpret* it;
- the way we *interpret* information affects the way we *conceptualize* it;
- the way we *conceptualize* information affects the *assumptions* we make;
- the *assumptions* we make affect the *implications* that follow from our thinking;
- the *implications* that follow from our thinking affect the way we see things—our *point of view.*

4.2   *Think for Yourself*

THINKING-THROUGH THE ELEMENTS OF YOUR REASONING

Select an important conclusion that you have reasoned to—for example, your decision to go to college. Identify the circumstances under which you made that decision, some of the inferences you made in the process (about the likely costs and advantages). State the likely implications of your decision, the consequences it has had, and will have, in your life, the information you took into account in deciding to go to college, the way you expressed the question to yourself, the way you looked at your life and your future (while reasoning through the question). See if you can grasp the inter-relationship of all of these elements in your thinking. Don't be surprised if you find this to be a difficult task.

In the remainder of this chapter, we will give a more detailed account of concepts, assumptions, inferences, implications, and point of view. We will direct special attention to the distinction between inferences and assumptions, as we find that students often have difficulty distinguishing these two initially. But once you become comfortable differentiating these two elements, the others tend to fall into place much more readily. Light is shed on all the elements throughout this book. There is even a chapter on one of them: the question. Periodically put down the book and see if you can elaborate on the elements of thought in your own words using your own examples. Success in these acts of active elaboration are what will make the concepts yours. You must *talk* ideas, *write* ideas, *think* ideas into your system.

THE RELATIONSHIP BETWEEN THE ELEMENTS

Because the elements do not exist in isolation but, rather, in relation to each other, we must not think of the distinctions between them as *absolute*. The distinctions are always *relative*. For example, if our *purpose* is to figure out how to spend less money, the *question* we have to figure out is, "What can I do to ensure that I spend less money?" The question is a virtual reformulation of the purpose. What's more, the point of view might be expressed as "viewing my spending habits to determine how to decrease my expenditures." This seems like a virtual reformulation of purpose and question. The point is that it is important to recognize an intimate overlap among all of the elements by virtue of their interrelationship.

At times, formulating some of the elements explicitly may seem to be redundant. Don't give way to this feeling. With practice, you will come to recognize the analytic power of making the distinctions explicit.

THE BEST THINKERS THINK TO SOME PURPOSE

A British scholar by the name of Susan Stebbing once wrote a book (1939) on the importance of purpose in thinking. In it, she said: "To think logically is to think relevantly to the purpose that initiated the thinking: all effective thinking is directed to an end." We agree. All thinking pursues a purpose. We do not think without having something we are trying to accomplish, without having some aim in view, something we want. When we think about the world, we do not do so randomly but, rather, in line with our goals, desires, needs, and values. Our thinking is an integral part of a patterned way of acting in the world, and we act, even in simple matters, with some set of ends in view. To understand someone's thinking—including our own—we must understand the functions it serves, what it is about, the direction it is moving, the ends that make sense of it.

Much of what we are after in our thinking is not obvious to us. Raising human goals and desires to the level of conscious realization is an important part of critical thinking. Though we always have a purpose in thinking, we are not always fully aware of that purpose. We may have some vague idea of it. Perhaps we have not clearly come to terms with our purpose. For example, you might be in college for the purpose of getting a degree, but you may not have analyzed precisely why you are seeking a degree. You may be going to college simply because all your friends are going. In this case, you have not thought seriously about your purpose. We are much more likely to achieve an end when we know exactly what we are trying to achieve.

One problem with human thinking is that we sometimes pursue contradictory ends. We might want to become educated and also want to avoid doing any intellectual work. We might want others to love us but not behave in loving ways toward them. We might want people to trust us but behave in ways that undermine trust. The purpose we might state explicitly may be simply what we would like to believe of ourselves. Our real purpose, however, might be one that we would be ashamed to admit. We might think we want to get into medical school to help and care for people when our actual purpose may be to make a lot of money, gain prestige and status, and be admired by others. We must be careful, therefore, not to assume that our purposes are consistent with one another or that our announced purposes are our actual purposes.

Further, the purposes that we pursue influence and are influenced by our point of view, by the way we see the world. Our purposes shape how we see things, and how we see things shapes what we seek. Each person formulates his or her purpose from a given point of view, determined by the context of his or her own experience. To understand our goals and objectives, then, we should consider the perspectives from which we see the world or some situation in it.

For example, a hairdresser, because of his perspective, might be more concerned than most janitors with personal appearance. Looking good and helping others to look good are more intimately connected with his view of himself and the world. An orthodontist would naturally think much more about teeth and their appearance than most other people would. Having straight teeth would naturally seem more significant to her than it might to, say, most professional football players. The orthodontist's purpose in fostering straight teeth arises out of her perspective or point of view.

4.3   *Think for Yourself*

IDENTIFYING YOUR PURPOSES: UNDERSTANDING YOUR THINKING

To begin to see the intimate interconnection of thinking to purpose, we suggest the following activity. First, make a list of five fundamental goals you have. Then comment on how your thinking is shaped by those goals. Fill in the blanks: "One of my purposes is _____. I can achieve this purpose best by _____."

Second, identify five things you think about a lot. Then comment on how those things are tied to your fundamental purposes. For example, if you spend a considerable amount of time thinking about people with whom you would like to explore a relationship, one of your purposes is probably to find a meaningful relationship. Or, if you spend a lot of time thinking about your future, one of your purposes is probably to figure out how you can prepare yourself to succeed.

THE BEST THINKERS TAKE COMMAND OF CONCEPTS

Concepts are like the air we breathe. They are everywhere. Although they are essential to our life, we rarely notice them. Yet, only when we have conceptualized a thing in some way can we think about it. Nature does not give us, or anyone else, instruction in how things are to be conceptualized. We must create that conceptualization, alone or with others. Once it is conceptualized, we integrate a thing into a network of ideas (as no concept stands alone).

We approach virtually everything in our experience as something that can be "decoded" or given meaning by the power of our mind to create a conceptualization and to make inferences on the basis of it—hence, to create further conceptualizations. We do this so routinely and automatically that we typically don't recognize ourselves as engaged in these processes. In our everyday life we don't first experience the world in "concept-less" form and then deliberately place what we experience into categories so as to make sense of things. Rather, it is as if things are given to us with their name inherent in them. So we see trees, clouds, grass, roads, people, children, sunsets, and on and on. We apply these concepts intuitively, as if the names belong to the things by nature, as if we had not created these concepts in our own minds.

If you want to develop as a critical thinker, you must come to terms with this human power of the mind—to create concepts through which we see and experience the world—for it is precisely this capacity of which you must take charge in taking command of your thinking. You must become the master of your own conceptualizations. You must develop the ability to mentally "remove" this or that concept from the things named by the concept, and try out alternative ideas. As general semanticists often say: "The word is not the thing! The word is not the thing!" If you are trapped in one set of concepts (ideas, words), you can think of things in only one way. Word and thing become one and the same in your mind.

To figure out the proper use of words, the proper way to conceptualize things, events, situations, emotions, abstract ideas, you first must achieve a true command of the uses of words. For example, if you are proficient in the use of the English language, you recognize a significant difference in the language between *needing* and *wanting,* between *having judgment* and *being judgmental,* between *having information* and *gaining knowledge,* between *being humble* and *being servile,* between *stubbornness* and *having the courage of your convictions.* Command of distinctions such as these, and many others, in the language has a significant influence upon the way you interpret your experiences. People who do not have this command confuse these important discriminations and distort the important realities they help us to distinguish.

4.4   *Think for Yourself*

TESTING YOUR UNDERSTANDING OF BASIC CONCEPTS

To the extent that you have a sound command of the English language, you should be able to state the essential differences between related but distinguishably different realities that are marked by words or expressions in our language. To the extent that you can, you are conceptualizing the ideas labeled with these words in keeping with educated use.

In this activity you will test your ability to do this. What follows is a set of related words, each pair illustrating an important distinction marked by the English language. For each set, working with a partner, discuss your understanding of each concept pair, emphasizing the essential and distinguishing difference. Then write down your understanding of the essential difference between each word pair.

After you have done this for each set of words, look up the words in the dictionary, and discuss how close your ideas of the essential difference of the word pair were to the actual distinctions the dictionary entries state or imply. (We recommend the *Webster's New World Dictionary.*)

1. clever/cunning	6. selfish/self-motivated
2. power/control	7. friend/acquaintance
3. love/romance	8. anger/rage
4. believe/know	9. jealousy/envy
5. socialize/educate	

In learning to speak our native language, we learn thousands of concepts. When used properly, these concepts enable us to make legitimate inferences about the objects of our experience. Unfortunately, nothing in the way we ordinarily learn to speak a language forces us to use concepts carefully or prevents us from making unjustifiable inferences in using them.

Often we misuse or confuse ideas because of our indoctrination into a social system, resulting in a distortion of our experience. As critical thinkers, we must continually distinguish the concepts and ideas implicit in our social conditioning from the concepts and ideas implicit in the natural language we speak. People from many different countries and cultures speak the same natural language. The peoples of Canada, Ireland, Scotland, England, Australia, Canada, and the United States all speak English. By and large, they implicitly share (to the extent to which they are proficient in the language) the same set of concepts (codified in the 23 volumes of the *Oxford English Dictionary*). Nevertheless, the people in these countries are not socially conditioned in the same way.

What's more, a person from China or Tibet could learn to speak the English language fluently without in any sense sharing in the same social conditioning. Because of this, natural languages (French, German, English, Swahili, and Hindi are examples) are repositories of concepts that, for the most part, are not to be equated with the concepts implicit in the social indoctrination of any social or cultural group speaking the language. This is a difficult insight to gain, but it is a powerful and essential one.

In the United States, for example, most people are socially conditioned to believe that our form of economic system (capitalism) is superior to any other (we call it "free enterprise"). We assume that no country can be truly democratic unless it has an economic system similar to ours. Furthermore, we assume that the major opposing systems, socialism or communism, are either wrong or enslaving or evil (an "Evil Empire"). We are encouraged to think of the world in these ways by movies, the news, schooling, political speeches, and many other social rituals. Raised in the United States, we internalize concepts, beliefs, and assumptions about ourselves and the world that are different from those we would have internalized had we grown up in China or Iran, for example.

Lexicographers would not confuse these socially implied meanings and psychological associations with the foundational meanings of the words in a decent dictionary of the English language. The term *communism* would not be defined as "an economic system that enslaves the people." The word *capitalism* would not have the definition, "an economic system essential to a democratic society."

Nevertheless, because we are socialized to believe that we, as a people, are *free, reasonable, just, and caring,* we assume that our behavior matches what these words imply. Words often substitute, in human life, for the realities named by them. Fundamental contradictions or inconsistencies in our life, then, go unquestioned. This is part of the self-deceptive tendencies to which the human mind is prone.

Critical thinkers learn how to strip off surface language and consider alternative ways to talk and think about things. For example, when thinking sociocentrically, we become trapped in the world view of our peer group and society with little or no conscious awareness of what it would be to rationally decide upon alternative ways to conceptualize situations, persons, and events. Most people are awed by social rituals and the trappings of social authority, status, and prestige and live their life, as it were, in surface structures. As a critical thinker, you will learn how to think sociologically, and thus how to recognize when your ideas are controlled by social rituals, social expectations, and taboos.

THE BEST THINKERS ASSESS INFORMATION

One cannot reason without using some set of facts, data, or experiences as a constituent part of one's thinking. Finding trustworthy sources of information and refining one's own experience critically are important goals of critical thinkers. We must be vigilant about the sources of information we use. We must be analytically critical of the use we make of our own experience. Experience may be the best teacher, but biased experience supports bias, distorted experience supports distortion, self-deluded experience supports self-delusion. We, therefore, must not think of our experience as sacred in any way but, instead, as one important dimension of thought that, like all other dimensions, must be critically analyzed and assessed.

The mind can take in information in three distinctive ways: (1) by memorizing factoids, or *inert information* (which is not understood well enough to be used by the mind), (2) by mislearning or partially learning information, or accepting illogical beliefs (which then leads to *activated ignorance*), and (3) by bringing significant ideas accurately into the mind (which then leads to *activated knowledge*).

Inert Information

By *inert information,* we mean *taking into the mind information that, though memorized, we do not understand*—despite the fact that we think we do. For example, many people have taken in, during their schooling, a lot of information about democracy that leads them to believe they understand the concept. Often, a good part of the information they have internalized consists of empty verbal rituals in their mind. Many children learn in school that "democracy is government of the people, by the people, for the people." This catchy phrase often sticks in their mind. It leads them to think they understand what it means, though most of them do not translate it into any practical criteria for assessing the extent to which democracy does or does not exist in any given country. To be explicit, most people could not intelligibly answer any of the following questions:

1. What is the difference between a government *of* the people and a government *for* the people?

2. What is the difference between a government *for* the people and a government *by* the people?

3. What is the difference between a government *by* the people and a government *of* the people?

4. What exactly is meant by "the people"?

Thus, students often do not sufficiently think about information they memorize in school to transform it into something truly meaningful in their mind. Much human information consists of, in the mind of the humans who "possess" it, merely empty words (inert or dead in the mind). Critical thinkers try to clear the mind of inert information by recognizing it as such and transforming it, through analysis, into something meaningful.

4.5   *Think for Yourself*

IN SEARCH OF INERT INFORMATION

Review information you were taught in school or at home. Look for what you may have repeated, often on command, to see if it qualifies for what we are calling *inert information*. Review, for example, the Pledge of Allegiance to the flag, slogans within subject fields, memorized bits and pieces of content, and sayings you have often heard but probably not made sense of. See how many candidates you can locate for inert information. Test each one with this criterion: If you cannot explain it or use it effectively, it is likely to be inert information in your mind. Be prepared to report what you found to your classmates. If, by any chance, you do not find this sort of information, don't assume that you are free of inert information.

Activated Ignorance

By *activated ignorance,* we mean *taking into the mind, and actively using, information that is false, though we mistakenly think it to be true.* The philosopher René Descartes came to confidently believe that animals have no actual feelings but are simply robotic machines. Based on this activated ignorance, he performed painful experiments on animals and interpreted their cries of pain as mere noises.

Some people believe, through activated ignorance, that they understand things, events, people, and situations that they do not. They act upon their false ideas, illusions, and misconceptions, often leading to needless waste, pain, and suffering. Sometimes activated ignorance is the basis for massive actions involving millions of people (think of the consequences of the Nazi idea that Germans were the master race and Jews an inferior race). Sometimes it is an individual misconception that is acted on by only one person in a limited number of settings. Wherever activated ignorance exists, it is dangerous.

It is essential, therefore, that we question our beliefs, especially when acting upon them has significant potential implications for the harm, injury, or suffering of others. It is reasonable to suppose that everyone has *some* beliefs that are really a form of activated ignorance. Eliminating as many such beliefs as we can is a responsibility we all have. Consider automobile drivers who are confident they can drive safely while they are intoxicated. Consider the belief that smoking does not have any significant negative effects on health.

It is not always easy to identify what is and is not activated ignorance. The concept of activated ignorance is important regardless of whether we determine whether information we come across is false or misleading. What we must keep in mind are clear-cut cases of activated ignorance so we have a clear idea of it, and personal vigilance with respect to the information we come across that is potentially false. Most people who have acted harmfully as a result of their activated ignorance have probably not realized that they were the agent of the suffering of others. Ignorance treated as the truth is no trivial matter.

4.6   *Think for Yourself*

IN SEARCH OF ACTIVATED IGNORANCE

Review what you were taught in school or at home in terms of what you formerly believed to be true but now have found to be false and harmful. When you were growing up, you probably picked up some activated ignorance from your peer group. Think of things you learned "the hard way." See how many candidates you can locate for activated ignorance. Test each one with this criterion: *At one time I thought this was true. Now I know it is false.*

Be prepared to report to your classmates what you found. If, by chance, you do not find any, don't assume that you are free of activated ignorance. Pursue why you are having trouble finding it.

Activated Knowledge

By *activated knowledge,* we mean *taking into the mind, and actively using, information that is true and also, when understood insightfully, leads us by implication to more and more knowledge.* Consider the study of history. Many students do no more than memorize isolated statements in the history textbook, to pass exams. Some of these statements—the ones they don't understand and could not explain—become part of the students' battery of inert information. Other statements—the ones they *misunderstand* and *wrongly explain*—become part of the students' battery of activated ignorance. Much of the information, of course, is simply forgotten shortly after the exam.

What is much more powerful, from a critical thinking perspective, is understanding the logic of historical thinking as a way of understanding the logic of history. When we understand these basic ideas, they become a form of activated knowledge. They enable us to build on historical knowledge by thinking-through previous historical knowledge.

We might begin, for example, by understanding the basic agenda of historical thinking: to construct a story or account of the past that enables us to better understand our present and make rational plans for the future. Once we have this basic knowledge of the logic of history, we are driven to recognize that we already engage in historical thinking in our daily life. We begin to see the connection between thinking within the subject and thinking in everyday-life situations. As a result of this provisional characterization of the logic of historical thinking, all humans clearly create our own story in the privacy of our mind. We use this story to make sense of our present, in the light of our conception of our past, and make plans for the future, given our understanding of our present and past. Most of us, however, do not think of ourselves as doing this.

If we reflect on our knowledge of the logic of history, and think-through some of its implications, we become aware that there is a logical similarity, for example, between historical thinking and ordinary, everyday "gossip." In gossip, we create a story about events in someone's recent past and pass on our story to others. If we reflect further on the logic of history, we recognize that every issue of a daily newspaper is produced by a kind of thinking analogous to historical thinking. In both cases, someone is constructing accounts of the past presented as making sense of some set of events in time.

Further reflection on the logic of history should lead us to ask ourselves questions such as, "In creating an account of some time period, approximately what percentage of what actually took place finds its way into any given historical account?" This should lead us to discover that, for any given historical period, even one as short as a day, countless events take place, with the implication that no historical account contains more than a tiny percentage of the total events within any given historical period. This should lead us to discover that historians must regularly make value judgments to decide what to include in, and what to exclude from, their accounts.

Upon further reflection, it should become apparent to us that the differing stories and accounts highlight different patterns in the events themselves—for example, accounts that highlight "high-level" decision-makers (great-person accounts), in contrast to accounts that highlight different social and economic classes (social and economic histories). It then should be apparent to us that the specific questions that any given historical thinker asks depend on the specific agenda or goal of that thinker.

It also should be apparent that:

- the historical questions asked are what determine which data or events are relevant;

- one and the same event can be illuminated by different conceptualizations (for example, different political, social, and economic theories about people and social change);

- different historians make different assumptions (each influencing the way they put their questions and the data that seem most important to them);

- when a given historian identifies with a given group of people and writes his or her history, it often highlights the positive characteristics of those people and the negative characteristics of those with whom they are or were in conflict.

It is by virtue of "discoveries" and insights such as these—which we must think-through for ourselves to truly grasp them as knowledge—that our view of history is transformed. They enable us to begin to "see through" historical texts. They lead us to value historical thinking, as its significance in everyday life becomes clear to us. They make more and more transparent to us our history, our use of history, and the effect of our use of history on the world and human welfare.

Activated knowledge, then, is knowledge born of dynamic seminal ideas that, when applied systematically to common experience, enable us to infer, by implication, further and further knowledge. Activated knowledge can be fostered in every legitimate human discipline. We begin with basic information about the most basic ideas and goals of a field. Grounded in basic concepts and first principles, we are able to experience the power of thought, knowledge, and experience working in unison. Developing a habit of studying to learn to seek the logic of things is one of the most powerful ways to begin to discover activated knowledge. It is one of the most important keys to making lifelong learning an essential ingredient in one's life.

4.7, 4.8, 4.9   *Think for Yourself*

IN SEARCH OF ACTIVATED KNOWLEDGE

Review what you were taught in school or at home. Seek what you learned so deeply and well that you were able to build further knowledge upon it. One possibility might be found in a sport that you took seriously, learning the basic moves of the game and the fundamental principles underlying those moves.

Don't be surprised if you conclude that you have not yet developed activated knowledge. This doesn't mean you don't know many things that are true. Rather, it means that you have not yet learned how to master basic principles to use as instruments in your thinking and learning. Be prepared to report to your classmates what you found.

IN SEARCH OF THE FACTS: KEY QUESTIONS TO ASK

One of the most important skills in critical thinking is that of evaluating information. This skill begins with the important recognition that information and fact, information and verification, are not the same thing. It requires also the important recognition that everything presented as fact or as true is not. It is important to recognize that the prestige or setting in which information is asserted, as well as the prestige of the person or group asserting it, is no guarantee of accuracy or reliability. Consider the following helpful maxim: *An educated person is one who has learned that information almost always turns out to be at best incomplete and very often false, misleading, fictitious, mendacious— just dead wrong.*

Careful professionals use a wide variety of safeguards in the disciplines in which they work. It is not possible to learn these safeguards separately from an actual study of the disciplines. It is possible, however, to develop a healthy skepticism about information in general, especially about information presented in support of a belief that serves the vested interests of a person or group. This skepticism is applied by regularly asking key questions about information presented to us:

- To what extent could I test the truth of this claim by direct experience?
- To what extent is this belief consistent with what I know to be true or in which I have justified confidence?
- How does the person who advances this claim support it?
- Is there a definite system or procedure for assessing claims of this sort?
- Does the acceptance of this information advance the vested interest of the person or group asserting it?
- Is the person asserting this information made uncomfortable by having it questioned?

These questions, both singly and as a group, represent no panacea. Everything depends on how we follow up on them. Used with good judgment, they help us to lower the number of mistakes we make in assessing information. They do not prevent us from making such mistakes. You should begin to practice asking the above questions when information is presented to you as true and important.

ASSESSING INFORMATION (PROVISIONALLY)

Assess the following claims by figuring out whether you think they are true or false. Explain your reasoning.

1. A friend of yours claims that astrology is accurate because he has used it to figure out why people he knew were behaving as they were. He also claims that you can use it to predict people's most likely behavior, including deciding who it would make sense to marry (or not to marry).

2. You hear someone say, "Science should use statements from the Bible to help assess scientific findings because anything that contradicts the Bible (the word of God) must be false."

3. You read about a person who is reported to have returned from the dead as the result of being resuscitated after a heart attack. The person says there is definitely a spirit world because he met a spirit while he was dead.

4. A friend of yours claims that the universe is run according to spiritual principles, citing the experience that once, when he was alone in the desert, the universe gave him a **mantra** (a chant).

5. You hear a woman say that no man can truly understand a woman because there is no way, as a man, that he can have the experience of a woman.

THE BEST THINKERS DISTINGUISH BETWEEN INFERENCES AND ASSUMPTIONS

As we have said, the elements of reasoning are interrelated. They are continually influencing and being influenced by one another. We now will focus at length on the crucial relationship between two of the elements: inference and assumption. Distinguishing inferences from assumptions is an important skill to learn in critical thinking. Many people confuse the two elements. Let us begin with a review of the basic meanings:

1. **Inference:** An inference is a step of the mind, an intellectual act by which one concludes that something is true in light of something else's being true, or seeming to be true. If you were to come at me with a knife in your hand, I probably would infer that you mean to do me harm. Inferences can be accurate or inaccurate, logical or illogical, justified or unjustified.

2. **Assumption:** An assumption is something we take for granted or presuppose. Usually it is something we learned previously and do not question. It is part of our system of beliefs. We assume our beliefs to be true and use them to interpret the world around us. If you believe that walking late at night in big cities is

dangerous and you are staying in Chicago, you will infer that it is dangerous to go for a walk late at night. You take for granted your belief that walking late at night in big cities is dangerous. If your belief is sound one, your assumption is sound. If your belief is not sound, your assumption is not sound. Beliefs, and hence assumptions, can be unjustified or justified depending upon whether we do or do not have good reasons for them. Consider this example: "I heard a scratch at the door. I got up to let the cat in." My inference was based on the assumption (my prior belief) that only the cat makes that noise, and that the cat makes the noise only when wanting to be let in.

We humans naturally and regularly use our beliefs as assumptions and make inferences based on those assumptions. We must do so to make sense of where we are, what we are about, and what is happening. Assumptions and inferences permeate our lives precisely because we cannot act without them. We make judgments, form interpretations, and come to conclusions based on the beliefs we have formed.

If you put humans in any situation, we start to give it some meaning or other. People automatically make inferences to gain a basis for understanding and action. So quickly and automatically do we make inferences that we do not, without training, notice them as such. We see dark clouds and infer rain. We hear the door slam and infer that someone has arrived. We see a frowning face and infer that the person is angry. If our friend is late, we infer that she is being inconsiderate. We meet a tall guy and infer that he is good at basketball, an Asian and infer that she gets good grades. We read a book and interpret what the various sentences and paragraphs—indeed what the whole book—is saying. We listen to what people say and make a series of inferences as to what they mean.

As we write, we make inferences as to what readers will make of what we are writing. We make inferences as to the clarity of what we are saying, what requires further explanation, what has to be exemplified or illustrated, and what does not. Many of our inferences are justified and reasonable, but some are not.

EXHIBIT 4.5 *Humans routinely draw conclusions in situations. Those conclusions are based on assumptions that usually operate at an unconscious level.*

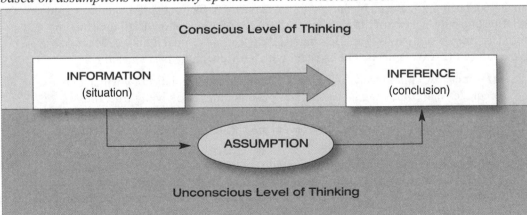

Important to critical thinking is the art of bringing what is subconscious in our thought to the level of conscious realization. This includes the skill of identifying and reconstructing the inferences we make so the various ways by which we shape our experiences through our inferences become more and more apparent to us. This skill enables us to separate our experiences into two categories. We learn to distinguish the *raw data* of our experience from our *interpretations of those data,* from the inferences we are making about them. Eventually we have to realize that the inferences we make are influenced heavily by our point of view and the assumptions we have made about people and situations. This puts us in the position of being able to broaden the scope of our outlook, to see situations from more than one point of view, and hence to become more open-minded.

Often, different people make different inferences because they bring different points of view to situations. They see the data differently. To put it another way, they have different assumptions about what they see. For example, if two people see a man lying in a gutter, one might infer, "There's a drunken bum." The other might infer, "There's a man in need of help." These inferences are based on different assumptions about the conditions under which people end up in gutters, and these assumptions are connected to the point of view about people that each has formed. The first person assumes, "Only drunks are to be found in gutters." The second person assumes, "People lying in the gutter are in need of help." The first person may have developed the point of view that people are fundamentally responsible for what happens to them and ought to be able to take care of themselves. The second may have developed the point of view that the problems people have are often caused by forces and events beyond their control. The reasoning of these two people, in terms of their inferences and assumptions, could be characterized in the following way:

Person One	**Person Two**
Situation: A man is lying in the gutter.	*Situation:* A man is lying in the gutter.
Inference: That man is a bum.	*Inference:* That man is in need of help.
Assumption: Only bums lie in gutters.	*Assumption:* Anyone lying in the gutter is in need of help.

As developing critical thinkers, we want to begin to notice the inferences we are making, the assumptions upon which we are basing those inferences, and the point of view about the world we are developing. To do this, we need lots of practice in noticing our inferences and then figuring out the assumptions that lead to them.

4.10   *Think for Yourself*

DISTINGUISHING BETWEEN INFORMATION, INFERENCES, AND ASSUMPTIONS

As thinkers, we have to be able to differentiate information, inferences, and assumptions. Whenever we are in a situation, we naturally make inferences. We come to conclusions about the situation or give it meaning through our interpretations. And these inferences result from the assumptions we made or are making.

For example:

- If it were 12:00 noon, what might you infer? (It's time for lunch.)
- If there are black clouds in the sky? (It's probably going to rain.)
- If Jack comes to school with a bump on his head? (He probably got hit.)
- If there are webs in the corners of the ceiling? (Spiders made them.)
- If Jill is in the eighth grade? (She is probably 13 or 14 years old.)
- If it were 12:00 noon and you inferred that it was time for lunch, what did you assume? (That whenever it is 12 noon, it is time for lunch.)
- If there are black clouds in the sky and you infer that it's probably going to rain, what did you assume? (That it usually rains when there are black clouds in the sky.)
- If Jack comes to school with a bump on his head and you infer that he must have been hit, what did you assume? (That the only time you develop a bump on the head is when you are hit.)

For this activity, use the table on p. 77. In it, we provide you with situations (information). We want you to figure out what someone might infer (rightly or wrongly) in the situation. Usually there is a range of possible inferences that different people might make, depending on their various beliefs.

Having stated what you think someone might infer, figure out the assumption that would lead someone to make that inference. As a suggestion, first figure out a likely inference (whether rational or irrational), then, and only then, try to figure out the assumption. The assumption will be a generalization that led the person to make the inference. We provide two examples to help you begin.

Our goal of becoming aware of the inferences we make and the assumptions that underlie our thinking enables us to begin to gain command over our thinking. Because all human thinking is inferential in nature, command of our thinking depends on command of the inferences embedded in it and, thus, of the assumptions that underlie it. Consider the way in which we plan and think our way through everyday events. We think of ourselves as preparing for breakfast, eating our breakfast, getting ready for class, arriving on time, sitting down in the appointed place, participating in class, making plans for lunch, paying bills, engaging in small talk, and so on.

Another way to put this is to say that we are continually interpreting our actions, giving them meanings, making inferences about what is going on in our lives. This is to say that we must choose among a variety of possible meanings. For example, am I "relaxing" or "wasting time"? Am I being "determined" or "stubborn"? Am I "joining" a conversation or "butting in"? Is someone "laughing *with* me" or "laughing *at* me"? Am I "helping a friend" or "being taken advantage of"? Every time we interpret our actions, every time we give them a meaning, we are making one or more inferences on the basis of one or more assumptions.

INFORMATION (SITUATION)	POSSIBLE INFERENCE THAT ONE MIGHT MAKE	ASSUMPTION LEADING TO THE INFERENCE
1. You see a woman in a wheelchair.	She must have a sad life.	All people in wheelchairs have a sad life.
2. A police officer trails your car closely for several blocks.	He is going to pull me over.	Whenever a police officer trails people, he or she is going to pull them over.
3. You see a child crying next to her mother in the grocery store.		
4. You meet a beautiful woman with blond hair.		
5. You notice a man in the library reading a book by Karl Marx.		
6. The teacher asks you to stay after class to tell you that your writing greatly needs improvement.		
7. While in a restaurant, your friend orders a steak cooked very rare.		
8. A friend tells you that she is pregnant and is going to have an abortion.		
9. Your roommate insists on listening to loud music while you are trying to study.		
10. The telephone rings in the middle of the night.		
11. Your significant other does not call you when he promised.		
12. Your significant other says she would rather spend time at the library than at parties.		

As humans, we continually make assumptions about ourselves, our jobs, our mates, our teachers, our parents, the world in general. We take some things for granted simply because we can't question everything. Sometimes we take the wrong things for granted. For example, I run off to the store (assuming that I have enough money with me) and arrive to find that I have left my money at home. I assume that I have enough gas in the car only to find that I have run out of gas. I assume that an item marked down in price is a good buy only to find that it was marked up before it was marked down. I assume that it will not (or that it will) rain. I assume that my car will start when I turn the key and press the gas pedal. I assume that I mean well in my dealings with others.

We make hundreds of assumptions without knowing it—without thinking about it. Most of these assumptions are sound and justifiable. Some, however, are not. The question then becomes: How can we begin to recognize the inferences we are making, the assumptions upon which we are basing those inferences, and the point of view—the perspective on the world that we are forming?

There are many ways to foster our awareness of our inferences and assumptions. For one thing, all disciplined subject-matter thinking requires that we learn to make correct assumptions about the content of what we are studying and that we become practiced in making justifiable inferences. As examples: In doing math, we make mathematical inferences based on our mathematical assumptions. In doing science, we make scientific inferences based on our scientific assumptions. In constructing historical accounts, we make historical inferences based on our historical assumptions. In each case, the assumptions we make depend on our understanding of fundamental concepts and principles.

As we become skilled in identifying our inferences and assumptions, we are in a good position to question the extent to which any one of our assumptions is justified. For example, are we justified in assuming that everyone eats lunch at 12:00 noon? Are we justified in assuming that it usually rains when there are black clouds in the sky? Are we justified in assuming that bumps on the head are caused only by blows? The point is that we all make many assumptions as we go about our daily life and we ought to be able to recognize and question them. As you develop these critical intuitions, you should increasingly notice your inferences and those of others. You should increasingly notice what you and others are taking for granted. You should increasingly notice how your point of view shapes your experiences.

4.11   *Think for Yourself*

GETTING MORE PRACTICE IN DIFFERENTIATING INFERENCES AND ASSUMPTIONS

Using the same format as we used in Think for Yourself 4.10, come up with 12 "episodes" of thinking for yourself, which include a situation, a possible inference in the situation, and the assumption leading to the inference. Use the table on p. 79.

INFORMATION (SITUATION)	POSSIBLE INFERENCE THAT ONE MIGHT MAKE	ASSUMPTION LEADING TO THE INFERENCE
1.		
2.		
3.		
4.		
5.		
6.		
7.		
8.		
9.		
10.		
11.		
12.		

THE BEST THINKERS THINK-THROUGH IMPLICATIONS

Among the most important skills of critical thinking is the ability to distinguish between what a statement or situation actually implies and what people may merely (and wrongly) infer from it. An inference, again, is a step of the mind that results in a conclusion. If the sun rises, we can infer that it is morning, for example. Critical thinkers try to monitor their thinking so they infer only that which is implied in a situation—no more, no less. If I feel ill and go to the doctor for a diagnosis, I want the doctor to infer exactly what my symptoms imply. For example, I do not want her to infer that I simply have a cold requiring no medication when I actually have a bacterial infection requiring antibiotics. My symptoms imply that I have a certain illness, which in turn implies a certain course of treatment. I want the doctor to accurately infer what my illness is, then accurately infer the proper treatment for it.

It is often the case that, in thinking, people fail to successfully think-through the implications of a situation. They fail to think-through the implications of a problem or decision. As a result, negative consequences often follow.

In any situation, three kinds of implications may be involved: possible ones, probable ones, and necessary ones. For example, every time you drive your car, one *possible* implication is that you could have an accident. If you drink heavily and drive very fast on a crowded roadway in the rain, one *probable* implication is that you *will* have an accident. If you are driving fast on a major highway and all the brake fluid drains out of your brake cylinders and another car immediately in front of you comes to a quick stop, one inescapable implication is that you *will* have an accident.

We reserve the word "consequences" for what actually happens in a given case. In short, a consequence is what *in fact* occurs in some situation. If we are good at identifying (making sound inferences about) possible, probable, and inevitable implications, we can take steps to maximize positive consequences and minimize negative ones. On the one hand, we do not want possible or probable negative implications to become real consequences. On the other hand, we do want to realize potential positive implications. We want to understand and take advantage of the real possibilities inherent in a situation.

We study the logic of things to become skilled in recognizing implications and acting accordingly. The art of doing this well is the art of making sound inferences about the implications of a situation by understanding exactly the logic of what is going on. As thinkers, then, we want to think-through all of the implications (possible, probable, and inevitable) of a potential decision before we make a decision and act on it.

In addition to implications that follow from concrete situations are implications that follow from the words we use. These follow from meanings inherent in natural languages. There are always implications of the words we use in communicating with people. If, for example, I tell my daughter that she cannot go to a friend's house because she failed to clean up her room, I am implying that she knew she had a responsibility to clean up her room if she wanted to go to a friend's house. My statement to my daughter and my view that she should have consequences for failing to clean her room are reasonable if:

1. I have previously communicated to her my desire for her to keep her room clean, and

2. I have adequately explained my reasoning and the consequences that will follow if she fails to comply with my request.

As thinkers, then, we want to be aware of what precisely we are implying when we say things. We also want to take into account the reasonability of what we are implying. If we do, we *say what we mean and mean what we say*—an important principle of integrity.

Just as the language we use in communicating has implications, the *way* we say things has implications. For example, the statement "Why didn't you clean the kitchen?" asked calmly has implications that are different from the same statement shouted aggressively. In the first instance, I perhaps am implying only that I think you should have cleaned the kitchen, and nothing more. In the second, I am implying that your failure to do so is a serious matter, warranting a severe reprimand.

Just as we may fail to notice the implications of a situation or of what we say, we also may fail to notice the implications of what others say to us. People often fail to infer precisely what others are, and are not, implying in their use of language. People often read things into what is being said, inferring more than what is being implied. If, for example, your teacher tells you that you need to work on your paper to improve it and he means to imply nothing more, you do not want to infer that he thinks you are not as smart as other students, that you are not capable of learning, or something else.

In sum, as developing thinkers, we want to realize the important role of implications in human life. When we are thinking-through a problem, issue, or question, we want to think-through all the significant implications of the decisions we might make. We want to infer only what is being implied in specific situations. When we use language, we want to be aware of what we are implying. When others are speaking to us, either verbally or in writing, we want to figure out what they are logically implying. In every case, we want to interpret precisely the logic of what is actually going on and infer only what is truly implied, no more, no less.

4.12 *Think for Yourself*

THINKING-THROUGH THE IMPLICATIONS OF YOUR POTENTIAL DECISIONS

As we have said, the ability to *think-through* the implications of a decision you are faced with or a problem you are trying to solve is an important critical-thinking skill. In this activity we want you to think of a problem for which you need to find a solution or a decision you need to make. Complete these statements:

1. The problem or decision I am facing is . . .
2. Some potential solutions to the problem, or decisions I might make, are . . .
3. For each of these solutions or decisions, some implications that would logically follow from my acting upon the solution or decision are . . .

THE BEST THINKERS THINK ACROSS POINTS OF VIEW

One of the most challenging elements to master is *point of view*. On the one hand, it is highly intuitive to most people that when we think, we think within a point of view. On the other hand, when we ask people, in the midst of reasoning-through something, to identify or explain their point of view, they are likely to begin expressing anything and everything they are thinking about. It becomes clear that most people do not have a clear sense of how to identify someone's point of view, including their own.

Let us begin by recognizing that our point of view has many potential sources: time, culture, religion, gender, discipline, profession, peer group, economic interest, emotional state, social role, or age group—to name just a few. For example, we can look at the world from

- a point in time (16th, 17th, 18th, 19th Century)
- a culture (Western, Eastern, South American, Japanese, Turkish, French)
- a religion (Buddhist, Christian, Muslim, Jewish)
- a gender (male, female, gay, straight)
- a profession (lawyer, teacher, . . .)
- a discipline (biological, chemical, geological, astronomical, historical, sociological, philosophical, anthropological, literary, artistic, musical, dance, poetic, medical, nursing, sport)
- a peer group
- an economic interest
- an emotional state
- an age group

Our dominant point of view as individuals reflects some combination of these dimensions. Unfortunately, most of us are little aware of the extent to which these factors shape our point of view. Typically, people do not say, "This is how I see it from the point of view of. . . . " Typically, people say something that implies, "This is the way things are." Our minds tend to absolutize our experience. We easily lose a sense of the partiality of how we look at things.

This is not an argument for *intellectual relativity* (the self-refuting view that everything is relative and therefore nothing can be proved). Looking at things from some point of view does not negate our ability to distinguish accurate from inaccurate statements. Doctors look at patients from the point of view of medical health, and that does not make their diagnoses "relative" or arbitrary.

As in the case of all the elements, we take charge of point of view by practicing bringing it out into the open. The more we recognize point of view at work in our thinking and in the thinking of others, the more points of view we learn to think within, the more effectively will we use point of view in our thinking.

4.13   *Think for Yourself*

PRACTICE IN MAKING EXPLICIT OUR POINT OF VIEW

What follows is a list of possible objects of our thinking. Choose from this list seven possible ones to think about. Then identify how you would look at each, from your point of view. For example, you might decide, "When I look at people, I see a struggle to find happiness" or, "When I look at the future, I see myself as a lawyer taking cases that protect the environment" or, "When I look at the health-care system, I see a system that does not provide adequately for the poor."

Once you write your sentence, see if you can characterize further how what you said explains your point of view.

life	the future of teaching	life in America
men	my economic future	income tax
women	education in the future	lifelong learning
human conflict	my future	the future
school	the problems we face as a nation	welfare
teaching	the problems we face as a species	welfare recipients
learning	mass transportation	drug use
mathematics	the environment	science
the past	people without health insurance	human values
peer groups	our health-care system	abortions
politics	modern lifestyle	the police
power	the modern American city	elections
art	religion	vegetarians
television	New Age ideas	liberals
computers	human sexuality	conservatives
the news	marriage	radicals

Complete the following, given the seven objects you have chosen to look at:

When I look at _____

I see (from my point of view) _____

When I look at _____

I see (from my point of view) _____

When I look at _____

I see (from my point of view) _____

When I look at _____

I see (from my point of view) _____

When I look at _____

I see (from my point of view) _____

When I look at _____

I see (from my point of view) _____

When I look at _____

I see (from my point of view) _____

THE POINT OF VIEW OF THE CRITICAL THINKER

The best thinkers share a common core of purposes with other critical thinkers, in keeping with the values of critical thinking. This has a variety of implications, one of the most important of which is that critical thinkers perceive explicit command of the thinking process as the key to command of behavior. Applied to the learning process, this entails that the best thinkers see reading, writing, speaking, and listening as modes of skilled thinking.

When these thinkers read, they see the text as a verbal representation of the thinking of the author. They strive to enter the writer's point of view. They strive to reconstruct the author's thinking in their own mind. When they write, they think explicitly about the point of view of their intended audience. They use their insight into the thinking of the likely audience to present their thinking in the most accessible way. Their speaking reflects a parallel emphasis. They use the dialogue to find out specifically the point of view and concerns of those with whom they are talking. They do not try to force their ideas on others. They recognize that people must think their own way to ideas and beliefs. They, therefore, share experiences and information more than final conclusions. They listen attentively to the thinking of others. They ask more questions than they make assertions.

They also recognize that every subject has a distinctive point of view. When studying a subject, they strive to enter that point of view and think within it. As a result, when studying math, they strive to develop a mathematical viewpoint. They strive to learn how to think like a mathematician. They seek fundamental principles, fundamental concepts, and fundamental processes and procedures. They seek to think within the logic of the subject. A parallel set of points can be made for every other subject.

The best thinkers have a distinctive point of view concerning themselves. They see themselves as competent learners. They have a "can do" vision of their own learning. They do not see opposing points of view as a threat to their own beliefs. They see all beliefs as subject to change in the face of new evidence or better reasoning. They see themselves as lifelong learners.

CONCLUSION

Just as the first step in learning basketball, tennis, soccer, or indeed any sport is to learn the most fundamental elements of the sport, the first step to learning critical thinking is to learn the most basic elements of thinking. These are the bread and butter of disciplined thinking, for if we cannot accurately analyze the parts of someone's thinking, we are in a poor position to assess it. Recognizing the elements of thought is therefore essential to the thinking of the best thinkers.

Analysis of the elements of thought is a *necessary*, but not a *sufficient*, condition of essential evaluation. To evaluate requires knowledge of the intellectual standards that highlight the qualities signaling strengths and weaknesses in thinking. For example, a strength in reasoning is to be *clear*, a weakness is to be *unclear*; a strength is to be *accurate*, a weakness is to be *inaccurate*. We shall focus on standards such as these in Chapter 5, explaining and illustrating how they apply to the elements of thought.

STANDARDS
FOR THINKING

One of the fundamentals of critical thinking is the ability to assess one's own reasoning. To be good at assessment requires that we consistently take apart our thinking and examine the parts with respect to standards of quality. We do this using criteria based on clarity, accuracy, precision, relevance, depth, breadth, logicalness, and significance. Critical thinkers recognize that, whenever they are reasoning, they reason to some purpose (element of reasoning). Implicit goals are built into their thought processes. But their reasoning is improved when they are clear (intellectual standard) about that purpose or goal. Similarly, to reason well, they need to know that, consciously or unconsciously, they are using information (element of reasoning) in thinking. But their reasoning improves if and when they make sure that the information they are using is accurate (intellectual standard).

Put another way, when we assess our reasoning, we want to know how well we are reasoning. We do not identify the elements of reasoning for the fun of it, or just to satisfy some authority. Rather, we assess our reasoning using intellectual standards because we realize the negative consequences of failing to do so. In assessing our reasoning, then, we recommend these intellectual standards as minimal:

- clarity
- relevance
- logic
- accuracy
- depth
- significance
- precision
- breadth
- fairness

These are not the *only* intellectual standards a person might use. They are simply among those that are most fundamental. In this respect, the elements of thought are more basic because the eight elements we have identified are *universal;* they are present in all reasoning of all subjects in all cultures for all time. On the one hand, one cannot reason with no information about no question from no point of view with no assumptions. On the other hand, there is a wide variety of intellectual standards from which to choose—such as credibility, predictability, feasibility, and completeness—that we don't use routinely in assessing reasoning.

As critical thinkers, then, we think about our thinking with these kinds of questions in mind: *Am I being clear? Accurate? Precise? Relevant? Am I thinking logically? Am I dealing with a matter of significance? Is my thinking justifiable in context?* Typically, we apply these standards to one or more elements.

5.1 *Think for Yourself*

IDENTIFYING INAPPROPRIATE STANDARDS

Can you identify a class you took in the past, either in high school or in college, in which you think your work was graded, at least in part, by one or more inappropriate standards? If so, what was the class? What was the standard? What was the result? Can you see the importance in education of basing all grades on appropriate intellectual standards? Write out or orally explain your answer.

TAKE A DEEPER LOOK AT UNIVERSAL INTELLECTUAL STANDARDS

Thinking critically requires command of fundamental intellectual standards. Critical thinkers routinely ask questions that apply intellectual standards to thinking. The ultimate goal is for these questions to become so spontaneous in thinking that they form a natural part of our inner voice, guiding us to better and better reasoning. In this section we focus on the standards and questions that apply across the various facets of your life.

Clarity

Questions that focus on clarity include:

- Could you elaborate on that point?
- Could you express that point in another way?
- Could you give me an illustration?
- Could you give me an example?
- Let me state in my own words what I think you just said. Tell me if I am clear about your meaning.

Clarity is a gateway standard. If a statement is unclear, we cannot determine whether it is accurate or relevant. In fact, we cannot tell anything about it because we do not yet know what it is saying. For example, the question "What can be done about the education system in America?" is unclear. To adequately address the question, we would need a clearer understanding of what the person asking the question is considering the "problem" to be. A clearer question might be, "What can educators do to ensure that students learn the skills and abilities that help them function successfully on the job and in their daily decision-making?" This question, because of its increased clarity, provides a better guide to thinking. It lays out in a more definitive way the intellectual task at hand.

5.2   *Think for Yourself*

CONVERTING UNCLEAR THOUGHTS TO CLEAR THOUGHTS

Can you convert an unclear thought to a thought that is clear? Suppose you are engaged in a discussion about welfare and one person says, "Let's face it—welfare is corrupt!" What does this mean? What could it mean?

It could mean some very different things. It could mean, "The very idea of giving people goods and services they have not personally earned is equivalent to stealing money from those who have earned it" (an ethical claim). Or it could mean, "The welfare laws have so many loopholes that people are receiving money and services that were not envisioned when the laws were initially formulated" (a legal claim). Or it could mean, "The people who receive welfare so often lie and cheat to falsify the documents they submit that they should be thrown in jail" (a claim about the ethical character of the recipients).

Now, for practice in making thoughts clear, take this statement: "She is a good person." This statement is unclear. Because we don't know the context within which this statement is being made, we aren't sure in what way she is "good." Formulate three possible meanings of this statement.

Now take the statement, "He is a jerk." Again, formulate three possible different meanings of this statement.

When you become skilled in differentiating what is clear and what is unclear, you will find that much of the time we are unclear both about what we are thinking and about what we are saying.

Accuracy

Questions focusing on making thinking more accurate include:

- Is that really true?
- How could we check to see if that is accurate?
- How could we find out if that is true?

A statement may be clear but not accurate, as in, "Most dogs weigh more than 300 pounds." To be accurate is to represent something in accordance with the way it actually is. People often present or describe things or events in a way that is not in accordance with the way things actually are. People frequently misrepresent or falsely describe things, especially when they have a vested interest in the description. Advertisers often do this to keep a buyer from seeing the weaknesses in a product. If an advertisement states, "Our water is 100% pure" when in fact the water contains small parts of chemicals such as chlorine and lead, it is inaccurate. If an advertisement states, "This bread contains 100% whole wheat" when the whole wheat has been bleached and enriched and the bread contains many additives, the advertisement is inaccurate.

Good thinkers listen carefully to statements and, when there is reason for skepticism, question whether what they hear is true and accurate. In the same way, they question the extent to which what they read is correct, when asserted as fact. Critical thinking, then, implies a healthy skepticism about public descriptions as to what is and is not fact.

At the same time, because we tend to think from a narrow, self-serving perspective, assessing ideas for accuracy can be difficult. We naturally tend to believe that our thoughts are automatically accurate just because they are ours, and therefore that the thoughts of those who disagree with us are inaccurate. We also fail to question statements that others make that conform to what we already believe, while we tend to question statements that conflict with our views. But as critical thinkers, we force ourselves to accurately assess our own views as well as those of others. We do this even if it means facing deficiencies in our thinking.

5.3, 5.4 *Think for Yourself*

RECOGNIZING INACCURATE STATEMENTS

Can you identify a statement that you heard recently that was clear but inaccurate? You will find an abundance of examples in everyday statements that people often make in praise or criticism. People in general have a tendency to make two kinds of inaccurate statements: *false positives* about the people they personally like (these would be untrue positive statements about people they like) and *false negatives* about the people they personally dislike (untrue negative things about people they don't like). Politically motivated statements tend to follow a similar pattern. See if you can think of an example of an inaccurate statement from your recent experience. Write out or orally explain your answer.

IN SEARCH OF THE FACTS

One of the most important critical thinking skills is the skill of assessing the accuracy of "factual" claims (someone's assertion that such-and-so is a fact). In an ad in the *New York Times* (Nov. 29, 1999, p. A15), a coalition of 60 nonprofit organizations accused the World Trade Organization (a coalition of 134 nation states) of operating in secret, undermining democratic institutions and the environment. In the process of doing this, the nonprofit coalition argued that the working class and the poor have not significantly benefited as a result of the last 20 years of rapid expansion of global trade. They alleged, among other things, the following facts:

1. "American CEOs are now paid, on average, 419 times more than line workers, and the ratio is increasing."
2. "Median hourly wages for workers are down by 10% in the last 10 years."
3. "The top 20% of the U.S. population owns 84.6% of the country's wealth."
4. "The wealth of the world's 475 billionaires now equals the annual incomes of more than 50% of the world population *combined*."

Using whatever sources you can find (including the website of the Turning Point Project, the nonprofit coalition, www.turnpoint.org, discuss the probable accuracy of the factual claims. For example, find the website (if there is one) of the World Trade Organization. The group might challenge some of the facts alleged or advance facts of its own that put the charges of the nonprofit coalition into a different perspective.

Precision

Questions focusing on making thinking more precise include:

- Could you give me more details?
- Could you be more specific?

A statement can be both clear and accurate but not precise, as in "Jack is overweight." (We don't know how overweight Jack is—1 pound or 500 pounds.) To be precise is to give the details needed for someone to understand exactly what is meant. Some situations don't call for detail. If you ask, "Is there any milk in the refrigerator?" and I answer, "Yes," both the question and the answer are probably precise enough for the circumstance (though specifying how much milk is there might be relevant). Or imagine that you are ill and go to the doctor. He wouldn't say, "Take 1.4876946 antibiotic pills twice per day." This level of specificity, or precision, would be beyond that which is useful in the situation.

In many situations, however, specifics are essential to good thinking. Let's say that your friend is having financial problems and asks you, "What should I do about my situation?" In this case, you want to probe her thinking for specifics. Without the full specifics, you could not help her. You might ask questions such as, "What precisely is the problem? What *exactly* are the variables that bear on the problem? What are some possible solutions to the problem—in detail?"

5.5   *Think for Yourself*

RECOGNIZING IMPRECISE STATEMENTS

Can you think of a recent situation in which you needed more details to figure out something, a circumstance in which, because you didn't have the details, you experienced some negative consequences? For example, have you ever been given directions to someone's house, directions that seemed precise enough at the time, but when you tried to find the person's house, you got lost because of lack of details in the directions?

First identify a situation in which the details and specifics were important (for example, in buying a computer, a car, or a stereo system). Then identify the negative consequences that resulted because you didn't get the details you needed to think well in the situation. Write out or orally explain your answer.

Relevance

Questions focusing on relevance include:

- How is this idea connected to the question?
- How does that bear on the issue?
- How does this idea relate to this other idea?
- How does your question relate to the issue we are dealing with?

A statement can be clear, accurate, and precise but not relevant to the question at issue. For example, students often think the amount of effort they put into a course should contribute to raising their grade in the course. Often, however, effort does not measure the quality of student learning and, therefore, is irrelevant to the grade. Something is relevant when it is directly connected with and bears upon the issue at hand. Something is relevant when it is pertinent or applicable to a problem we are trying to solve. Irrelevant thinking encourages us to consider what we should set aside. Thinking that is relevant stays on track. Thinking often is irrelevant because people lack discipline in thinking. They don't know how to analyze an issue for what truly bears on it. Therefore, they aren't able to effectively think their way through the problems and issues they face.

5.6   *Think for Yourself*

RECOGNIZING IRRELEVANT STATEMENTS

Can you identify a statement you heard recently that was clear, accurate, and sufficiently precise but irrelevant to the circumstance, problem, or issue? Though we all sometimes stray from a question or task, we need to be sensitive to when failure to stay on task may have a significant negative implication.

Identify, first, circumstances in which people tend to introduce irrelevant considerations into a discussion (for example, in meetings, in response to questions in class, in everyday dialogue when they have a hidden agenda—or simply want to get control of the conversation for some reason). Write out or orally explain your answer.

Depth

Questions focusing on depth of thought include:

- How does your answer address the complexities in the question?
- How are you taking into account the problems in the question?
- How are you dealing with the most significant factors in the problem?

We think deeply when we get beneath the surface of an issue or problem, identify the complexities inherent in it, and then deal with those complexities in an intellectually responsible way. Even when we think deeply, even when we deal well with the complexities in a question, we may find the question difficult to address. Still, our thinking will work better for us when we can recognize complicated questions and address each area of complexity in the question.

A statement can be clear, accurate, precise, and relevant, but superficial—lacking in depth. Let's say you are asked what should be done about the problem of drug use in America and you answer by saying, "Just say no." This slogan, which for several years was used to discourage children and teens from using drugs, is clear, accurate, precise, and relevant. Nevertheless, it lacks depth because it treats an extremely complex issue—the pervasive problem of drug use among people in our culture—superficially. It does not address the history of the problem, the politics of the problem, the economics of the problem, the psychology of addiction, and so on.

5.7   *Think for Yourself*

RECOGNIZING SUPERFICIAL APPROACHES

Identify a newspaper article containing a statement that is clear, accurate, precise, and relevant, but superficial with respect to a complex issue. For example, a number of laws take a Band-Aid approach to systemic problems such as drugs and crime.

1. State the problem at issue.
2. State how the article deals with the problem and why the approach taken is superficial.
3. Beginning to focus on the complexity of the issue, state how the problem might be dealt with.

Breadth

Questions focusing on making thinking broader include:

- Do we need to consider another point of view?
- Is there another way to look at this question?
- What would this look like from a conservative standpoint?
- What would this look like from the point of view of . . . ?

A line of reasoning may be clear, accurate, precise, relevant, and deep, but lack breadth. Examples are arguments from either the conservative or the liberal standpoint that get deeply into an issue but show insight into only one side of the question.

When we consider the issue at hand from every relevant viewpoint, we think in a broad way. When multiple points of view are pertinent to the issue, yet we fail to give due consideration to those perspectives, we think myopically, or narrow-mindedly. We do not try to enter alternative, or opposing, viewpoints.

Humans are frequently guilty of narrow-mindedness for many reasons: limited education, innate sociocentrism, natural selfishness, self-deception, and intellectual arrogance. Points of view that significantly disagree with our own often threaten us. It's much easier to ignore perspectives with which we disagree than to consider them, when we know at some level that to consider them would mean to be forced to reconsider our views.

Let's say, for example, that you and I live together and that I like to play loud music, which annoys you. The question at issue is: *Should I play loud music in a room when you are present?* Both your viewpoint and mine are relevant to the question at issue. When I recognize your viewpoint as relevant and then intellectually empathize with it—when I enter your way of thinking so as to actually understand it—I will be forced to see that imposing my loud music on you is unfair and inconsiderate. I will be able to imagine what it would be like to be forced to listen to loud music that I find annoying. But if I don't force myself to enter your viewpoint, I do not have to change my self-serving behavior. One of the primary mechanisms the mind uses to avoid giving up what it wants is unconsciously to refuse to enter viewpoints that differ from its own.

5.8   *Think for Yourself*

THINKING BROADLY ABOUT AN ISSUE

Take the question: Is abortion morally justified? Some argue that abortion is not morally justifiable, and others argue that it is. Try to state and elaborate on each of these points of view in detail. Articulate each point of view objectively, regardless of your personal views. Present each point of view in such a way that a person who actually takes that position would assess it as *accurate*. Each line of reasoning should be clear, accurate, precise, relevant, and deep. Do not take a position on it yourself.

Logic

Questions that focus on making thinking more logical include:

- Does all of this fit together logically?
- Does this really make sense?
- Does that follow from what you said?
- How does that follow from the evidence?
- Before, you implied this, and now you are saying that. I don't see how both can be true.

When we think, we bring together a variety of thoughts in some order. When the combined thoughts are mutually supporting and make sense in combination, the thinking is logical. When the combination is not mutually supporting, is contradictory in some sense, or does not make sense, the combination is not logical. Because humans often maintain conflicting beliefs without being aware that we are doing so, it is not unusual to find inconsistencies in human life and thought.

Let's say we know, by looking at standardized tests of students in schools and the actual work they are able to produce, that for the most part students are deficient in basic academic skills such as reading, writing, speaking, and the core disciplines such as math, science, and history. Despite this evidence, teachers often conclude that there is nothing they can do to change their instruction to improve student learning (and in fact that there is nothing fundamentally wrong with the way they teach). Given the evidence, this conclusion seems illogical. The conclusion doesn't seem to follow from the facts.

Let's take another example. Say that you know a person who has had a heart attack, and her doctors have told her she must be careful what she eats, to avoid problems in the future. Yet she concludes that what she eats really doesn't matter. Given the evidence, her conclusion is illogical. It doesn't make sense.

5.9 *Think for Yourself*

RECOGNIZING ILLOGICAL THINKING

Identify a newspaper article that contains an example of illogical thinking—thinking that doesn't make sense to you.

1. State the issue that the thinking revolves around.
2. State the thinking that you believe is illogical, and why you think it is illogical.
3. State some implications of the illogical thinking. What are some consequences likely to follow from the illogical thinking?

Significance

Questions that focus on making thinking more significant include:

- What is the most significant information we need to address this issue?
- How is that fact important in context?
- Which of these questions is the most significant?
- Which of these ideas or concepts is the most important?

When we reason-through issues, we want to concentrate on the most important information (relevant to the issue) in our reasoning and take into account the most important ideas or concepts. Too often we fail in our thinking because we do not recognize that, though many ideas may be relevant to an issue, it does not follow that all are equally important. In a similar way, we often fail to ask the most important questions and are trapped by thinking only in terms of superficial questions, questions of little weight.

In college, for example, few students focus on important questions such as, *What does it mean to be an educated person? What do I need to do to become educated?* Instead, students tend to ask questions such as, *What do I need to do to get an 'A' in this course? How many pages does this paper have to be? What do I have to do to satisfy this professor?*

5.10 *Think for Yourself*

FOCUSING ON SIGNIFICANCE IN THINKING

Think about your life, about the way you spend your time, in terms of the amount of time you spend on significant versus trivial things. As you do so, write the answers to these questions:

1. What is the most important goal or purpose you should focus on at this point in your life? Why is this purpose important? How much time do you spend focused on it?
2. What are the most trivial or superficial things you spend time focused on (things such as your appearance, impressing your friends, chatting about insignificant things at parties, and the like)?
3. What can you do to reduce the amount of time you spend on the trivial, and increase the amount of time you spend on the significant?

Fairness

Questions that focus on ensuring that thinking is fair include:

- Is my thinking justified given the evidence?
- Am I taking into account the weight of the evidence that others might advance in the situation?

- Are these assumptions justified?

- Is my purpose fair given the implications of my behavior?

- Is the manner in which I am addressing the problem fair—or is my vested interest keeping me from considering the problem from alternative viewpoints?

- Am I using concepts justifiably, or am I using them unfairly to manipulate someone (to selfishly get what I want)?

When we think-through problems, we want to make sure that our thinking is justified. To be justified is to think fairly in context. It is to think in accord with reason. If you are vigilant in using the other intellectual standards covered thus far in the chapter, you will (by implication) satisfy the standard of justifiability. We include fairness separately because of the powerful nature of self-deception in human thinking. For example, we often deceive ourselves into thinking that we are being fair and justified in our thinking when in fact we are refusing to consider significant relevant information that would cause us to change our view (and therefore not pursue our selfish interest). We often pursue unjustified purposes to get what we want even if we have to hurt others to get it. We often use concepts in an unjustified way to manipulate people. And we often make unjustified assumptions, unsupported by facts, that then lead to faulty inferences.

Let's focus on an example in which the problem is unjustified thinking as a result of ignoring relevant facts. Let's say, for instance, that Kristi and Abby live together. Kristi is cold-natured and Abby is warm-natured. During the winter, Abby likes to have the windows in the house open while Kristi likes to keep them closed. But Abby insists that it is "extremely uncomfortable" with the windows closed. The information she is using in her reasoning all centers on her own point of view—that she is hot, that she can't function well if she's hot, that if Kristi is cold, she can wear a sweater. But Abby is not justified in her thinking. She refuses to enter Kristi's point of view, to consider information supporting Kristi's perspective, because to do so would mean that *Abby would have to give up something.* She would have to adopt a more reasonable, or fair, point of view.

People who are manipulative often use concepts in ways that are not justified. Take John, for instance. Let's imagine that he is interested in borrowing Jay's portable stereo for a trip. John therefore begins to regularly hang out with Jay. When they are with others, John introduces Jay as his "friend." As a result, Jay comes to define John as his friend. So when John asks to borrow Jay's stereo, Jay readily agrees (because John is his friend). But when John fails to return the stereo and Jay asks for it back, John lies and says he lost it. The fact is that John never intended to return the stereo—and obviously never considered Jay a friend. John just used the term "friend" to get what he selfishly wanted. Therefore, his use of the concept of *friend* was for the purpose of manipulation and was not fair in context.

When we reason to conclusions, we want to check to make sure that the assumptions we are using to come to those conclusions are justifiable given the facts of the situation. For example, all of our prejudices and stereotypes function as assumptions in thinking. And no prejudices and stereotypes are justifiable given their very nature. For example, we often make broad, sweeping generalizations such as:

- Liberals are soft on crime.
- Elderly people aren't interested in sex.
- Young men are interested only in sex.
- Jocks are cool.
- Blondes are dumb.
- Cheerleaders are airheads.
- Intellectuals are nerds.
- Learning is boring.
- School doesn't have anything to do with life.

The problem with assumptions like these is that they cause us to make basic—and often serious—mistakes in thinking. Because they aren't justifiable, they cause us to prejudge situations and people and draw faulty inferences—or conclusions—about them. For example, if we believe that all intellectuals are nerds, whenever we meet an intellectual, we will infer that he or she is a nerd (and act unfairly toward the person).

In sum, justifiability, or fairness, is an important standard in thinking. It forces us to see how we are distorting our thinking to achieve our self-serving ends (or to see how others are distorting their thinking to achieve selfish ends).

5.11, 5.12   *Think for Yourself*

ANALYZING ASSUMPTIONS FOR JUSTIFIABILITY (FAIRNESS)

Look back at the assumptions you came up with for Think for Yourself 4.11. For each one, decide whether it is justifiable given the situation. For each assumption that is not justifiable, re-create an assumption that would be justified in context.

APPLYING INTELLECTUAL STANDARDS TO EVERYDAY LIFE DISCUSSIONS

Tape-record a discussion/debate between you and several other people (friends or family) on an important controversial issue (for example, "What is the best solution to the drug problem in this country?"). Then play back the recording two or three remarks at a time. Comment on which of the standards are being met and which are violated each "step" along the way. Notice how seldom people tend to use intellectual standards in their thinking. Notice how unclear everyday thinking often is. Notice how people may feel just as confident in their positions even after you point out violations of intellectual standards. What does that tell you about them?

EXHIBIT 5.1 *Powerful questions are implied by the intellectual standards. Critical thinkers routinely ask them.*

CLARITY	LOGIC
Could you elaborate? Could you illustrate what you mean? Could you give me an example?	Does all of this make sense together? Does your first paragraph fit in with your last one? Does what you say follow from the evidence?
ACCURACY	
How could we check on that? How could we find out if that is true? How could we verify or test that?	**SIGNIFICANCE** Is this the most important problem to consider? Is this the central idea to focus on? Which of these facts are most important?
PRECISION	
Could you be more specific? Could you give me more details? Could you be more exact?	**BREADTH** Do we need to look at this from another perspective? Do we need to consider another point of view? Do we need to look at this in other ways?
DEPTH	
What factors make this difficult? What are some of the complexities of this question? What are some of the difficulties we need to deal with?	**FAIRNESS** Is my thinking justifiable in context? Am I taking into account the thinking of others? Is my purpose fair given the situation? Am I using my concepts in keeping with educated usage, or am I distorting them to get what I want?
RELEVANCE	
How does that relate to the problem? How does that bear on the question? How does that help us with the issue?	

BRING TOGETHER THE ELEMENTS OF REASONING AND THE INTELLECTUAL STANDARDS

We have considered the elements of reasoning and the importance of being able to take them apart, to analyze them so we can begin to recognize flaws in our thinking. We also have introduced the intellectual standards as tools for assessment. Now let us look at how the intellectual standards are used to assess the elements of reason.

EXHIBIT 5.2 *Critical thinkers routinely apply the intellectual standards to the elements of reasoning.*

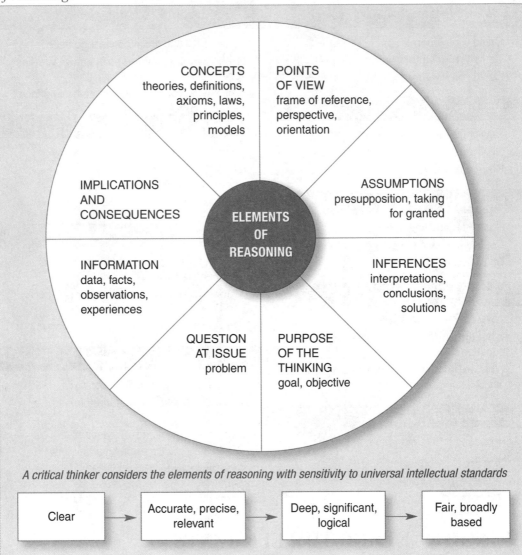

A critical thinker considers the elements of reasoning with sensitivity to universal intellectual standards

Clear	→	Accurate, precise, relevant	→	Deep, significant, logical	→	Fair, broadly based

Purpose, Goal, or End in View

Whenever we reason, we reason to some end, to achieve some objective, to satisfy some desire or fulfill some need. One source of problems in human reasoning is traceable to defects at the level of goal, purpose, or end. If the goal is unrealistic, for example, or contradictory to other goals we have, if it is confused or muddled, the reasoning we use to achieve it will suffer as a result.

As a developing critical thinker, you should get in the habit of explicitly stating the purposes you are trying to accomplish. You should strive to be clear about your purpose in every situation. If you fail to stick to your purpose, you are unlikely to achieve it. Let's say that your purpose in being in college is to obtain a degree so you can improve your chances of getting a good job and making a good income. If you keep that purpose clearly in mind and consistently work to achieve it, you are more likely to be successful. But it is easy to become so involved in the social life at college that you lose sight of your purpose and thus fail to achieve it.

As a student interested in developing your mind, you can begin to ask questions that improve your ability to focus on purpose in your classes. For example: *Am I clear as to my purpose—in an essay, a research project, an oral report, a discussion? Can I specify my purpose precisely? Is my purpose a significant one? Realistic? Achievable? Justifiable? Do I have contradictory purposes?*

5.13 *Think for Yourself*

BRINGING INTELLECTUAL STANDARDS TO BEAR UPON YOUR PURPOSE

Think of an important problem in your life. This can be a problem in a personal relationship, at your place of work, in college, or in another situation. Now state your purpose in the situation *clearly* and *precisely*. What exactly are you trying to accomplish? Is your purpose *fair*, or *justifiable*? Is it *realistic*? Explain to a classmate.

Question at Issue or Problem to Be Solved

Whenever you attempt to reason-through something, there is at least one question to answer—one question that emerges from the problem to be solved or issue to resolve. An area of concern in assessing reasoning, therefore, revolves around the very question at issue.

An important part of being able to think well is assessing your ability to formulate a problem in a clear and relevant way. It requires determining whether the question you are addressing is important, whether it is answerable, whether you understand the requirements for settling the question, for solving the problem.

As a student interested in developing your mind, you can begin to ask yourself questions that will improve your ability to focus on the important questions in your classes. You begin to ask: *What is the most fundamental question at issue* (in this lecture, in this chapter, in this discussion)? *What is the question, precisely? Is the question simple or complex? If it is complex, what makes it complex? Am I sticking to the question* (in this discussion, in this paper I am working on)? *Is there more than one important question to be considered here* (in this lecture, etc.)?

5.14 *Think for Yourself*

Point of View, or Frame of Reference

Whenever we reason, we must reason within some point of view or frame of reference. Any "defect" in that point of view or frame of reference is a possible source of problems in the reasoning.

A point of view may be too narrow, may be based on false or misleading information, may contain contradictions, and may be narrow or unfair. Critical thinkers strive to adopt a point of view that is fair to others, even to opposing points of view. They want their point of view to be broad, flexible, and justifiable, to be stated clearly and adhered to consistently. Good thinkers, then, consider alternative points of view when they reason through an issue.

As a person interested in developing your mind, you begin to ask yourself questions that will improve your ability to focus on point of view in your classes. These questions might be: *From what point of view am I looking at this issue? Am I so locked into my point of view that I am unable to see the issue from other points of view? Must I consider multiple points of view to reason well through the issue at hand? What is the point of view of this author? What is the frame of reference in this discipline? Are different world views implicit in these different perspectives?*

5.15 *Think for Yourself*

Information, Data, Experiences

Whenever we reason, there is some "stuff," some phenomena about which we are reasoning. Any "defect," then, in the experiences, data, evidence, or raw material upon which a person's reasoning is based is a possible source of problems.

Reasoners should be assessed on their ability to give evidence that is gathered and reported clearly, fairly, and accurately. Therefore, as a student, you should assess the information you use to come to conclusions, whether you are working on papers for class, reasoning-through issues within the subjects you take, or reasoning-through a problem in your personal life. You should assess whether the information you are using in reasoning is relevant to the issue at hand and adequate for achieving your purpose. You should assess whether you are taking the information into account consistently or distorting it to fit your own (often self-serving) point of view.

As a student interested in developing your mind, you begin to ask yourself questions that will improve your ability to focus on information in your classes. These questions might be: *What is the most important information I need to reason well through this issue? Are there alternative information sources I need to consider? How can I check to see if the information I am using is accurate? Am I sure that all of the information I am using is relevant to the issue at hand?*

5.16 *Think for Yourself*

BRINGING INTELLECTUAL STANDARDS TO BEAR UPON THE INFORMATION YOU ARE USING IN REASONING

Continue with the problem you have been working on. Now state the information you are using in your thinking. This could consist of data, facts, or experiences that, in conjunction with your assumptions, lead you to conclusions. It could come from your experience, word of mouth, research, the media, or other sources. State the information clearly. How could you determine whether the information is *accurate* and *relevant* to the question at issue?

Concepts, Theories, Ideas

All reasoning uses some ideas or concepts and not others. These concepts include the theories, principles, axioms, and rules implicit in our reasoning. Any defect in the concepts or ideas of this reasoning is a possible source of problems in our reasoning.

As an aspiring critical thinker, you begin to focus more deeply on the concepts you use. You begin to assess the extent to which you are clear about those concepts, whether they are relevant to the issue at hand, whether your principles are slanted inappropriately by your point of view. You begin to direct your attention to how you use concepts, what concepts are most important, how concepts are intertwined in networks.

As a student interested in developing your mind, you begin to ask questions that will improve your ability to focus on the importance of concepts in your classes. These questions may include: *What is the most fundamental concept I need to learn in this class to help me in my life? How does this concept connect with other key concepts in the course? What are the most important theories in this class? Am I clear about the important concepts in the class? What questions do I need to ask to get clear about the concepts the teacher is explaining?*

5.17 *Think for Yourself*

**BRINGING INTELLECTUAL STANDARDS TO BEAR
UPON THE CONCEPTS YOU USE**

Continue with the problem you have been working on. Now state the most important concepts you are using to guide your reasoning. For example, if you are concerned with how you can keep in physical shape while also dedicating enough time to classes, work, family, significant others, and so on, your key concepts might be physical fitness, quality learning, and good relationships. (You usually can find the key concepts you are using in your reasoning by looking at your question and purpose.) Elaborate on each of these concepts so you understand exactly how you are using them. State your concepts *clearly* and *precisely*.

Assumptions

All reasoning must begin somewhere. It must take some things for granted. Any defect in the assumptions or presuppositions with which reasoning begins is a possible source of problems in the reasoning.

Assessing skills of reasoning involves assessing our ability to recognize and articulate assumptions, again according to relevant standards. Our assumptions may be clear or unclear, justifiable or unjustifiable, consistent or contradictory.

As a student interested in developing your mind, you begin to ask questions that will improve your ability to utilize important assumptions in your classes. These questions could include: *What is taken for granted in this academic discipline* (or in this lecture, or this discussion, or this article, or this experiment)? *Are these assumptions justifiable, or should I question them? What does the author of this textbook assume in Chapter 2? Are these assumptions justified, or should they be questioned?*

5.18 *Think for Yourself*

BRINGING INTELLECTUAL STANDARDS TO BEAR UPON YOUR ASSUMPTIONS

Continue with the problem you have been working on. Now state the most important assumptions you are making in your reasoning. What are you taking for granted that might be questioned? Using the previous example of how to keep in physical shape while also dedicating enough time to learning and your key relationships, your main assumptions might be:

1. Intellectual work is/is not more important than relationships.
2. I know enough about fitness to do appropriate exercises.
3. I must spend some time working at a part-time job while in college (rather than getting a student loan).
4. I have enough time to do all of the above well.

State your assumptions *clearly* and *precisely*. Make sure they are *justifiable* in the context of the issue.

Implications and Consequences

Whenever we reason, implications follow from our reasoning. When we make decisions, consequences result from those decisions. As critical thinkers, we want to understand implications whenever and wherever they occur. We want to be able to trace logical consequences. We want to see what our actions are leading to. We want to anticipate possible problems before they arise.

No matter where we stop tracing implications, there always will be further implications. No matter what consequences we do see, there always will be other and further consequences. Any defect in our ability to follow the implications or consequences of our reasoning is a potential source of problems in our thinking. Our ability to reason well, then, is measured in part by our ability to understand and enunciate the implications and consequences of reasoning.

As a student interested in developing your mind, you begin to ask yourself questions that will improve your ability to focus on the important implications in your thinking as a student. These questions could include, for example: *What are the most significant implications of this biological theory, this phenomenon, this economic policy? What are the implications of this political practice? What are the implications of failing to act in this context? If we adopt this course of action, what are the likely consequences? What are the most significant implications of our tendency to solve this social problem in this way rather than that way? What were the implications* (social, political, economic, cultural) *of the United States' involvement in World War I?*

5.19 *Think for Yourself*

THINKING-THROUGH THE IMPLICATIONS OF YOUR REASONING

Continue with the problem you have been working on. Now state the most important implication of potential decisions you might make. Fill in these blanks: If I decide to do _____, then _____ is likely to follow. If I decide to act differently by doing _____, then _____ is likely to follow.

In this activity you are emphasizing the *logical* implications and potential consequences of each potential decision. Make sure you emphasize important implications of each decision. For further practice, what would be the most likely implications of (1) getting married, (2) not staying in college, (3) staying in your hometown for the whole of your life, (4) doing drugs for the fun of it?

Inferences

All reasoning proceeds by steps in which we reason as follows: "Because this is so, that also is so (or is probably so)" or, "Because this, therefore that." The mind perceives a situation or a set of facts and comes to a conclusion based on those facts. When taking this step of the mind, an inference results. Any defect in our ability to make logical inferences presents a possible problem in our reasoning. For example, if you see a person sitting on the street corner wearing tattered clothing, a worn bedroll beside him and a bottle wrapped in a brown paper bag in his hand, you might infer that he is a bum. This inference is based on the facts you perceive in the situation and what you assume about them. The inference, however, may or may not be logical in this situation.

Critical thinkers want to become adept at making sound inferences. First, you want to learn to identify when you or someone else has made an inference. *What are the key inferences made in this newspaper article? Upon what are the inferences based? Are they justified? What is the key inference* (or conclusion) *I made in this paper? Was it justified? What is the key inference in this theory, in this way of proceeding, in solving this problem in this way? Is this inference logical? Is this conclusion significant? Is this interpretation justified?* These are the kinds of questions you begin to ask.

As a student interested in developing your mind, you should ask questions that will improve your ability to spot important inferences wherever they occur. Given the facts of this case, is there more than one logical inference (conclusion, interpretation) one could come to? What are some other logical conclusions that should be considered? From this point on, develop an inference detector, the skill of recognizing the inferences you are making in order to analyze them.

5.20   *Think for Yourself*

BRINGING INTELLECTUAL STANDARDS TO BEAR UPON YOUR INFERENCES

Continue with the problem you have been working on. Now state the inferences, or conclusions, you might come to (about the information you have) in solving your problem. You may have stated these already in Think for Yourself 5.19.

Once you have thought-through the potential conclusions you might come to in reasoning-through the question at issue, state a possible final conclusion. Be clear and precise in stating each potential conclusion. Make sure your inferences make good sense, based on the information and concepts you are using.

BRIEF GUIDELINES FOR USING INTELLECTUAL STANDARDS

As we have emphasized, all reasoning involves eight elements, each of which includes a range of possible mistakes. Here we summarize some of the main "checkpoints" that the best thinkers use in reasoning. You should use these same checkpoints.

1. All reasoning has a *purpose.*
    - Take time to state your purpose *clearly.*
    - Choose *significant* and *realistic* purposes.
    - Distinguish your purpose from related purposes.
    - Make sure your purpose is *fair* in context (that it doesn't involve violating the rights of others).
    - Check periodically to be sure you are still focused on your purpose and haven't wandered from your target.

2. All reasoning is an attempt to figure out something, to settle some *question,* solve some problem.
   - Take time to state the question at issue *clearly* and *precisely.*
   - Express the question in several ways to *clarify* its meaning and scope.
   - Break the question into sub-questions (when you can).
   - Identify the type of question you are dealing with (historical, economic, biological, etc.) and whether the question has one right answer, is a matter of mere opinion, or requires reasoning from more than one point of view.
   - Think-through the complexities of the question (think-through the question *deeply*).

3. All reasoning is based on *assumptions.*
   - *Clearly* identify your assumptions and determine whether they are *justifiable.*
   - Consider how your assumptions are shaping your point of view.

4. All reasoning is done from some *point of view.*
   - *Clearly* identify your point of view.
   - Seek other *relevant* points of view and identify their strengths as well as weaknesses.
   - Strive to be *fair-minded* in evaluating all points of view.

5. All reasoning is based on data, *information,* and evidence.
   - Restrict your claims to those supported by the data you have.
   - Search for information that opposes your position as well as information that supports it.
   - Make sure that all information you use is *clear, accurate,* and *relevant* to the question at issue.
   - Make sure you have gathered *sufficient* information.
   - Make sure, especially, that you have considered all *significant* information relevant to the issue.

6. All reasoning is expressed through, and shaped by, *concepts* and ideas.
   - *Clearly* identify key concepts.
   - Consider alternative concepts or alternative definitions for concepts.
   - Make sure you are using concepts with care and *precision.*
   - Use concepts *justifiably* (not distorting their established meanings).

7. All reasoning contains *inferences* or interpretations by which we draw conclusions and give meaning to data.
   - Infer only what the evidence implies.
   - Check inferences for their *consistency* with each other.
   - Identify assumptions that lead you to your inferences.
   - Make sure your inferences *logically* follow from the information.

8. All reasoning leads somewhere or has *implications* and consequences.
   - Trace the *logical* implications and consequences that follow from your reasoning.
   - Search for negative as well as positive implications.
   - Consider all possible significant consequences.

5.21   *Think for Yourself*

CHECKPOINTS IN THINKING

For all of the eight categories outlined, transform each checkpoint into a question or a set of questions; figure out one or more questions that the checkpoint implies. When you have completed your list and you are actively using the questions you formulated, you will have powerful tools for thinking. Under the first category, *All reasoning has a purpose*, for example, the first checkpoint is: *Take time to state your purpose clearly*. Two questions implied by this checkpoint are: *What exactly is my purpose? Am I clear about my purpose?*

EXHIBIT 5.3

<table>
<tr><td colspan="3" align="center">**PURPOSE**</td></tr>
<tr><td colspan="3" align="center">*All reasoning has a purpose.*</td></tr>
<tr><td colspan="3">*Primary standards:* (1) clarity, (2) significance, (3) achievability, (4) consistency, (5) justifiability

Common problems: (1) unclear, (2) trivial, (3) unrealistic, (4) contradictory, (5) unfair

Principle: To reason well, you must clearly understand your purpose, and your purpose must be fair-minded.</td></tr>
</table>

Skilled Reasoners	Unskilled Reasoners	Critical Questions
take the time to state their purpose clearly.	are often unclear about their central purpose.	Have I made the purpose of my reasoning clear? What exactly am I trying to achieve? Have I stated the purpose in several ways to clarify it?
distinguish the purpose from related purposes.	oscillate between different, sometimes contradictory, purposes.	What different purposes do I have in mind? How do I see them as related? Am I going off in somewhat different directions? How can I reconcile these contradictory purposes?
periodically remind themselves of their purpose to determine whether they are straying from it.	lose track of their fundamental object or goal.	In writing this proposal, do I seem to be wandering from my purpose? How do my third and fourth paragraphs relate to my central goal?
adopt realistic purposes and goals.	adopt unrealistic purposes and set unrealistic goals.	Am I trying to accomplish too much in this project?
choose significant purposes and goals.	adopt trivial purposes and goals as if they were significant.	What is the significance of pursuing this particular purpose? Is there a more significant purpose I should be focused on?
choose goals and purposes that are consistent with other goals and purposes they have chosen.	inadvertently negate their own purposes and do not monitor their thinking for inconsistent goals.	Does one part of my proposal seem to undermine what I am trying to accomplish in another part?
regularly adjust their thinking to their purpose.	are unable to do the thinking necessary to achieve their purpose.	What thinking do I need to do to achieve my purpose?
choose purposes that are fair-minded, considering the desires and rights of others equally with their own desires and rights.	choose purposes that are self-serving at the expense of others' needs and desires.	Is my purpose self-serving or is it concerned only with my own desires? Does it take into account the rights and needs of other people?

EXHIBIT 5.4

QUESTION AT ISSUE OR CENTRAL PROBLEM

*All reasoning is an attempt to figure out something,
to settle some question, or to solve some problem.*

Primary standards: (1) clarity and precision, (2) significance, (3) answerability, (4) relevance

Common problems: (1) unclear and unprecise, (2) insignificant, (3) not answerable, (4) irrelevant

Principle: To settle a question, it must be answerable, and you must be clear about it and understand what is needed to answer it adequately.

Skilled Reasoners	Unskilled Reasoners	Critical Questions
are clear about the question they are trying to settle.	are often unclear about the question they are asking.	Am I clear about the main question at issue? Am I able to state it precisely?
can express a question in a variety of ways.	express questions vaguely and find questions difficult to reformulate for clarity.	Am I able to reformulate my question in several ways to recognize the complexities in the issue or problem?
can break a question into sub-questions.	are unable to separate the questions they are asking.	Have I broken down the main question into sub-questions? What are the sub-questions embedded in the main question?
routinely distinguish questions of different types.	confuse questions of different types and thus often respond inappropriately to the questions.	Am I confused about the type of question I am asking or being asked? For example: Am I confusing a legal question with an ethical one? Am I confusing a question of preference with a question requiring judgment?
distinguish significant from trivial questions.	confuse trivial questions with significant ones.	Am I focusing on trivial questions while other significant questions need to be addressed?
distinguish relevant questions from irrelevant ones.	confuse irrelevant questions with relevant ones.	Are the questions I'm raising in this discussion relevant to the main question at issue?
are sensitive to the assumptions built into the questions they ask.	often ask loaded questions.	Is the way I'm putting the question loaded? Am I taking for granted from the outset something I should be questioning?
distinguish questions they can answer from questions they can't answer.	try to answer questions they are not in a position to answer.	Am I in a position to answer this question? What information would I need to have before I could answer the question?

110

EXHIBIT 5.5

POINT OF VIEW		

All reasoning is done from some point of view.

Primary standards: (1) flexibility, (2) fairness, (3) clarity, (4) breadth, (5) relevance

Common problems: (1) restricted, (2) biased, (3) unclear, (4) narrow, (5) irrelevant

Principle: To reason well, you must identify those points of view relevant to the issue and enter these viewpoints empathetically and in good faith.

Skilled Reasoners	Unskilled Reasoners	Critical Questions
keep in mind that people have different points of view, especially on controversial issues.	do not credit alternative reasonable viewpoints.	Have I articulated the point of view from which I am approaching this issue? Have I considered opposing points of view regarding this issue?
consistently and accurately articulate other points of view and reason from within those points of view to understand them.	neither value nor practice reasoning within alternative viewpoints; cannot reason with empathy from other points of view.	Let me think aloud within this alternative viewpoint to see if I can accurately articulate it.
seek other viewpoints, especially when the issue is one they believe in passionately.	can sometimes give other points of view when the issue is not emotionally charged but cannot do so for issues they feel strongly about.	Am I presenting X's point of view in an unfair manner? Am I having difficulty appreciating X's viewpoint because I am emotional about this issue?
confine their monological reasoning to problems that are clearly monological.*	confuse multilogical with monological issues; insist that there is only one frame of reference within which a given multilogical question must be decided.	Is the question here monological or multilogical? How can I tell? Am I reasoning as if only one point of view is relevant to this issue when in reality other viewpoints are relevant?
recognize when they are most likely to be prejudiced for or against a viewpoint.	are unaware of their own prejudices.	Is this prejudiced or reasoned judgment? What is causing me to prejudge in this situation?
approach problems and issues with a richness of vision and an appropriately broad point of view.	reason from within inappropriately narrow or superficial points of view.	Is my approach to this question too narrow? Am I thinking broadly enough in order to adequately address the issue?

Monological problems are ones for which there are definite correct and incorrect answers and definite procedures for getting those answers. In *multilogical* problems, there are competing schools of thought to be considered. (See the Thinkers Guide to Asking Essential Questions.)

EXHIBIT 5.6

INFORMATION		

All reasoning is based on information: data, evidence, experience, research.

Primary standards: (1) clear, (2) relevant, (3) fairly gathered and reported, (4) accurate, (5) adequate, (6) consistently applied

Common problems: (1) unclear, (2) irrelevant, (3) biased, (4) inaccurate, (5) insufficient, (6) inconsistently applied

Principle: Reasoning can be only as sound as the information it is based on.

Skilled Reasoners	Unskilled Reasoners	Critical Questions
assert a claim only when they have sufficient evidence to support it.	assert claims without considering all relevant information.	Is my assertion supported by evidence? Do I have sufficient evidence to support my position?
can articulate and accurately evaluate the information behind their claims.	don't articulate the information they are using in their reasoning and so do not subject it to rational scrutiny.	Do I have evidence to support my claim that I haven't clearly articulated? Have I evaluated the information I am using for accuracy and relevance?
actively search for information *against* (not just *for*) their own position.	gather information only when it supports their own point of view.	Where is a good place to look for evidence on the opposite side? Have I looked there? Have I honestly considered information that doesn't support my position?
focus on relevant information and disregard what is irrelevant to the question at issue.	do not carefully distinguish between relevant information and irrelevant information.	Are my data relevant to the claim I'm making? Have I failed to consider relevant information?
draw conclusions only to the extent that they are supported by the data and sound reasoning.	make inferences that go beyond what the data support.	Does my claim go beyond the evidence I've cited?
state their evidence clearly and fairly.	distort the information or state it inaccurately.	Is my presentation of the pertinent information clear and coherent? Have I distorted information to support my position?

112

EXHIBIT 5.7

CONCEPTS AND IDEAS

All reasoning is expressed through, and shaped by, concepts and ideas.

Primary standards: (1) clarity, (2) relevance, (3) depth, (4) accuracy, (5) justifiability

Common problems: (1) unclear, (2) irrelevant, (3) superficial, (4) inaccurate, (5) justifiable

Principle: Reasoning can be only as clear, relevant, realistic, and deep as the concepts that shape it.

Skilled Reasoners	Unskilled Reasoners	Critical Questions
are aware of the key concepts and ideas they and others use.	are unaware of the key concepts and ideas they and others use.	What is the main idea I am using in my thinking? What are the main concepts others are using?
are able to explain the basic implications of the key words and phrases they use.	cannot accurately explain basic implications of their key words and phrases.	Am I clear about the implications of key concepts? For example: Does the word *cunning* have negative implications that the word *clever* does not?
are able to distinguish special, nonstandard uses of words from standard uses.	are not able to recognize when their use of a word or phrase departs from educated usage.	Where did I get my definition of this central concept? For example: Where did I get my definition of the concept of education, terrorism . . . ? Have I changed the meaning of a concept to fit my own purposes?
are careful to use words in keeping with educated usage.	often use words inappropriately or in ways not justified by the circumstances.	Am I using the concept of *love* appropriately? For example: Do I unknowingly act as if loving a person implies a right to treat him or her discourteously?
think deeply about the concepts they use.	fail to think deeply about the concepts they use.	Am I thinking deeply enough about this concept? For example: The concept of *health care,* as I describe it, does not take into account the patient's rights and privileges. Do I need to consider the idea of health care more deeply?

EXHIBIT 5.8

ASSUMPTIONS		

All reasoning is based on assumptions—beliefs we take for granted.

Primary standards: (1) clarity, (2) justifiability, (3) consistency

Common problems: (1) unclear, (2) unjustified, (3) contradictory

Principle: Reasoning can be only as sound as the assumptions it is based on.

Skilled Reasoners	Unskilled Reasoners	Critical Questions
are clear about the assumptions they are making.	are often unclear about the assumptions they make.	Are my assumptions clear to me? Do I clearly understand what my assumptions are based upon?
make assumptions that are reasonable and justifiable given the situation and the evidence.	often make unjustified or unreasonable assumptions.	Do I make assumptions about the future based on just one experience from the past? Can I fully justify what I am taking for granted? Are my assumptions justifiable given the evidence I am using to support them?
make assumptions that are consistent with each other.	often make assumptions that are contradictory.	Do the assumptions I made in the first part of my argument contradict the assumptions I am making now?
consistently seek to figure out their assumptions.	ignore their assumptions.	What assumptions am I making in this situation? Are they justifiable? Where did I get these assumptions?
recognize that assumptions lie at the unconscious level of thought and that those assumptions determine the inferences we make.	don't explicitly realize they make assumptions; don't understand the relationship between inferences and assumptions.	What assumptions in my thinking have I never explained? How might these assumptions lead to illogical inferences?

EXHIBIT 5.9

IMPLICATIONS AND CONSEQUENCES

*All reasoning leads somewhere. It has implications and,
when acted upon, has consequences.*

Primary standards: (1) significance, (2) logic, (3) clarity, (4) precision, (5) completeness

Common problems: (1) unimportant, (2) unrealistic, (3) unclear, (4) imprecise, (5) incomplete

Principle: To reason well through an issue, you must think-through the implications that follow from your reasoning. You must think-through the consequences likely to follow from the decisions you make.

Skilled Reasoners	Unskilled Reasoners	Critical Questions
trace out a number of significant implications and consequences of their reasoning.	trace out few or none of the implications and consequences of holding a position or making a decision.	Have I spelled out all the significant implications of the action I am advocating? If I were to take this course of action, what other consequences might follow that I haven't considered?
articulate the implications and possible consequences.	are unclear and imprecise in articulating possible consequences they articulate.	Have I clearly and precisely delineated the consequences likely to follow from my chosen action?
search for negative as well as positive potential consequences.	trace out only the consequences that come immediately to mind, either positive or negative, but usually not both.	I may have done a good job of spelling out some positive implications of the decision I am about to make, but what are some of the negative implications possible?
anticipate the likelihood of unexpected negative and positive implications.	are surprised when their decisions have unexpected consequences.	If I make this decision, what are some unexpected consequences? What are some variables out of my control that might lead to negative consequences?

EXHIBIT 5.10

INFERENCE AND INTERPRETATION

*All reasoning contains inferences from which we draw conclusions
and give meaning to data and situations.*

Primary standards: (1) clarity, (2) logic, (3) justifiability, (4) profundity, (5) reasonability, (6) consistency

Common problems: (1) unclear, (2) illogical, (3) unjustified, (4) superficial, (5) unreasonable, (6) contradictory

Principle: Reasoning can be only as sound as the inferences it makes (or the conclusions it comes to).

Skilled Reasoners	Unskilled Reasoners	Critical Questions
are clear about the inferences they are making and articulate their inferences clearly.	are often unclear about the inferences they are making, do not clearly articulate their inferences.	Am I clear about the inferences I am making? Have I clearly articulated my conclusions?
usually make inferences that follow from the evidence or reasons that are presented.	often make inferences that do not follow from the evidence or reasons presented.	Do my conclusions logically follow from the evidence and reasons presented?
often make inferences that are deep rather than superficial.	often make inferences that are superficial.	Are my conclusions superficial, given the problem?
often make inferences or come to conclusions that are reasonable.	often make inferences or come to conclusions that are unreasonable.	Are my conclusions reasonable?
make inferences or come to conclusions that are consistent with each other.	often make inferences or come to conclusions that are contradictory.	Do the conclusions I came to in the first part of my analysis seem to contradict the conclusions that I came to at the end?
understand the assumptions that lead to inferences.	do not seek to figure out the assumptions that lead to inferences.	Is my inference based on a faulty assumption? How would my inference be changed if I were to base it on a different, more justifiable assumption?

CHAPTER 6

ASK QUESTIONS THAT LEAD TO GOOD THINKING

From what we have emphasized thus far, it should be clear that to emulate the thinking of the best thinkers

- you must become interested in thinking
- you must become a critic of your own thinking
- you must be willing to establish new habits of thought
- you must develop a passion for thinking well
- you must study the interplay of thoughts, feelings, and desires
- you must become interested in the role of thinking in your life
- you must routinely analyze thinking into its elements
- you must routinely assess thinking for its strengths and weaknesses
- you must routinely assess your study (and learning) habits
- you must learn how to think within diverse systems of thought

In this chapter we shall explore the role of questions in thinking, to make explicit the questions the best thinkers ask.

THE IMPORTANCE OF QUESTIONS IN THINKING

It is not possible to become a good thinker and be a poor questioner. Thinking is not driven by answers but, rather, by questions. Had no questions been asked by those who laid the foundation for a field—for example, physics or biology—the field would not have been developed in the first place. Every intellectual field is born out of a cluster of questions to which answers are either needed or highly desirable. Furthermore, every field stays alive only to the extent that fresh questions are generated and taken seriously as the driving force in thinking.

> To learn a subject is to learn to ask the questions the best thinkers in the field routinely ask.

When a field of study is no longer pursuing answers to questions, it becomes extinct. To think-through or rethink anything, one must ask questions that stimulate thought.

On the one hand, questions define tasks, express problems, and delineate issues. Answers, on the other hand, often signal a full stop in thought. Only when an answer generates further questions does thought continue its life as such. This is why you are really thinking and learning only when you have questions. Moreover, the quality of the questions you ask determines the quality of your thinking. When you have no questions, you are not concerned with pursuing any answers.

For example, biologists and biochemists make progress when they ask questions such as: "What are we made of? How do our bodies work? What is life?" They make even more progress when they take their questioning to the subcellular and molecular level. They ask questions about isolated molecules and events on the molecular level: "What are proteins? What are enzymes? What are enzyme reactions? How do molecular events underlie macroscopic phenomena?" (Jevons, 1964). By focusing on these subcellular questions, they can move to important questions such as: "How do vitamins interact with chemistry in the body to produce healthier functioning? And how do cancer cells differ from normal cells? And what kinds of foods interact with the body's chemistry to lessen the likelihood of the development of cancerous cells?"

> A field is alive only to the extent that there are live questions in it.

The best teachers are usually those who understand the relationship between learning and asking questions. As Jevons (1964) says of his students, "Those who asked questions helped me most, but even those who merely looked puzzled helped a little, by stimulating me to find more effective ways of making myself understood."

QUESTIONING YOUR QUESTIONS

When you meet a person for the first time, what questions would you most like to answer about him or her? Another way to put this question is to ask, "What information do you seek about people when you first meet them?" What do these questions (and the information you seek) tell you about your values and concerns? What do they tell you, as well, about the nature of the relationships you tend to form?

Consider the following types of questions based on the elements of reasoning and intellectual standards.

- Questions of *purpose* force us to define our task.
- Questions of *information* force us to look at our sources of information as well as the quality of our information.
- Questions of *interpretation* force us to examine how we are organizing or giving meaning to information and to consider alternative ways of giving meaning.
- Questions of *assumption* force us to examine what we are taking for granted.
- Questions of *implication* force us to follow where our thinking is leading us.
- Questions of *point of view* force us to examine our point of view and to consider other *relevant* points of view.
- Questions of *relevance* force us to differentiate what does and what does not bear on a question.
- Questions of *accuracy* force us to evaluate and test for truth and correctness.
- Questions of *precision* force us to give details and be specific.
- Questions of *consistency* force us to examine our thinking for contradictions.
- Questions of *logic* force us to consider how we are putting the whole of our thought together, to make sure that it all adds up and makes sense within a reasonable system of some kind.

6.1   *Think for Yourself*

QUESTIONING THE DEPTH OF YOUR QUESTIONS

Write out your answers to these questions:

Are any of the questions you are focused on in your life *deep* questions?

To what extent are you questioning your *purposes* and goals?

Your *assumptions?* The *implications* of your thought and action?

Do you ever question your *point of view?*

Do you ever wonder whether your point of view is keeping you from seeing things from an opposing perspective? When?

Do you ever question the *consistency* of your thought and behavior?

Do you question the *logicalness* of your thinking?

What did answering the above questions, and your reflection on them, tell you about yourself and about your habits of questioning?

DEAD QUESTIONS REFLECT INERT MINDS

The best thinkers ask live questions that lead to knowledge and further questions that lead to knowledge and yet further questions.

Isaac Newton at age 19 drew up a list of questions under 45 headings. His goal was to constantly question the nature of matter, place, time, and motion.

Most students ask virtually none of these thought-stimulating types of questions. Most tend to stick to dead questions such as, "Is this going to be on the test?" This sort of question usually implies the desire not to think at all.

We must continually remind ourselves that thinking begins within some content only when questions are generated. No questions (asked) equals no understanding (achieved). Superficial questions equal superficial understanding; unclear questions equal unclear understanding. If you sit in class in silence, your mind probably will be silent as well. When this is the case, you either will ask no questions or your questions will tend to be superficial, ill-formed, and self-serving. You should strive for a state of mind in which, even when you are outwardly quiet, you are inwardly asking questions. You should formulate questions that will lead you to productive learning.

If you want to learn deeply and independently, you should always strive to study so that what you do stimulates your thinking with questions that lead to further questions.

6.2, 6.3 *Think for Yourself*

QUESTIONING AS YOU READ

Read a chapter in one of your textbooks for the primary purpose of generating questions. Only when you are asking questions as you read are you reading critically. After reading each section, or every few paragraphs, make a list of all the questions you have about what you are reading. Then see if you can answer these questions—either by looking in the textbook or by raising them in class.

QUESTIONING YOUR QUESTIONING ABILITY

At this point in your intellectual development, to what extent would you call yourself a skilled or deep questioner? That is, how would you rate the overall quality of the questions you are asking (those that you share with others and those you keep to yourself)? Do you know anyone who you would say is a deep questioner? If so, what makes you think this person questions deeply?

THREE CATEGORIES OF QUESTIONS

Before we go further in our discussion about how to question deeply, we want to introduce a useful way of categorizing questions. This way of classifying questions provides a sort of "jumpstart" in figuring out the kind of reasoning a question calls for.

The three categories of questions are:

1. Questions of fact. Questions with one right answer (factual questions fall into this category).

- What is the boiling point of lead?
- What is the size of this room?
- What is the differential of this equation?
- How does the hard drive on a computer operate?

EXHIBIT 6.1 *In approaching a question, it is useful to figure out what type it is. Is it a question with one definitive answer? Is it a question that calls for a subjective choice? Or does the question require you to consider competing answers?*

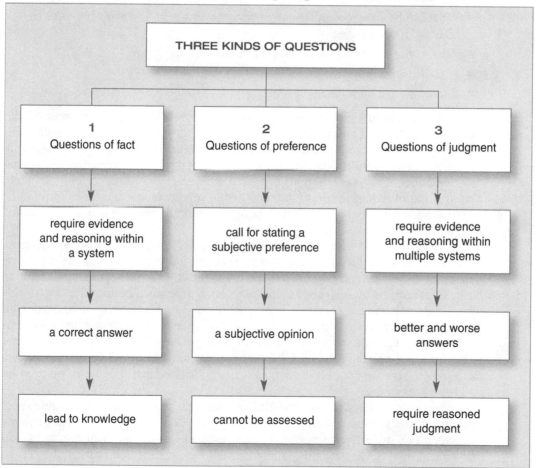

2. **Questions of preference.** Questions with as many answers as there are different human preferences (a category in which mere subjective opinion rules). These are questions that ask you to express a preference.

- Which would you prefer, a vacation in the mountains or one at the seashore?
- How do you like to wear your hair?
- Do you like to go to the opera?
- What is your favorite type of food?

3. **Questions of judgment.** Questions requiring reasoning, but with more than one defensible answer. These are questions that make sense to debate, questions with better-or-worse answers (well-reasoned or poorly reasoned answers). Here we are seeking the best possible answer given the range of possibilities.

- How can we best address the most basic and significant economic problems of the nation today?
- What can be done to significantly reduce the number of people who become addicted to illegal drugs?
- What is the best thing we can do to save the earth?
- Is abortion morally justifiable?
- Should capital punishment be abolished?

Only the second kind of question (a question of preference) calls for sheer subjective opinion. The third kind is a matter of reasoned judgment. We should rationally evaluate answers to the question using universal intellectual standards—as clarity, depth, consistency, and so forth. Some people think of all judgments as either fact or subjective preference. They ask questions that elicit either a factual response or an opinion. Yet, the kind of judgment most important to educated people—and the kind we most want to be good at—falls into the third, now almost totally ignored, category: reasoned judgment.

A judge in a court of law is expected to engage in reasoned judgment. The judge is expected to render a judgment and also to base that judgment on sound, relevant evidence and valid legal reasoning. A judge is under the ethical and legal obligation not to base her judgments on subjective preferences, on her personal opinions, as such.

Judgment based on sound reasoning goes beyond, and is never to be equated with, fact alone or mere opinion alone. Facts are typically used in reasoning, but good reasoning does more than state facts. Furthermore, a position that is well-reasoned is not to be described as simply "opinion." Of course, we sometimes call the judge's verdict an "opinion," but we not only expect but actually *demand* that it be based on relevant and sound reasoning.

When questions that require reasoned judgment are treated as matters of preference, counterfeit critical thinking occurs. In that case, some people come to uncritically assume that everyone's subjective opinion is of equal value. Their capacity to appreciate the importance of intellectual standards diminishes, and we can expect to hear questions such as these: What if I don't like these standards? Why shouldn't I use my own standards? Don't I have a right to my own opinion? What if I'm just an emotional person? What if I like to follow my intuition? What if I think spirituality is more important than reason? What if I don't believe in being "rational"? When people reject questions that call for reasoned judgment and deep thought, they fail to see the difference between offering legitimate reasons and evidence in support of a view and simply asserting the view as true.

Intellectually responsible people, by contrast, recognize questions of judgment for what they are: questions that require the consideration of alternative ways of reasoning. Put another way, intellectually responsible people recognize when a question calls for good reasoning, and they behave in accordance with that responsibility. This means that they realize when a question can be answered in more than one reasonable way. Moreover, they appreciate the responsibility they have to consider alternative ways of looking at the problem, of entering *in good faith* viewpoints that oppose their own before coming to final judgments.

To summarize, we all need to recognize that questions call on us to do one of three things:

1. to express a subjective preference,
2. to establish an objective fact (within a well-defined system), or
3. to come up with the best of competing answers (generated by competing systems).

We do not fully understand the task we are faced with until we know which of these three is called for in our thinking. Is the question calling for a subjective or personal choice? If so, let's make that choice in terms of our personal preferences. If not, is there a way to come up with one correct answer to this question (a definite system in which to find the answer)? Or, finally, are we dealing with a question that could reasonably be answered differently within different points of view? In other words, is it debatable? If the latter, what is the best answer to the question, all things considered?

6.4 *Think for Yourself*

DISTINGUISHING TYPES OF QUESTIONS I

Make a random list of clear and precise questions. Then decide which questions are a matter of fact (with a definite right or wrong answer), which questions are matters of subjective preference, and which questions require reasoning and judgment (within multiple perspectives). To make these determinations, you might think through each question in the following way:

1. Ask, "Are there any facts that a reasonable person would have to consider to answer this question?" (If there are some facts you need to consider, the question is not purely a matter of subjective preference.)
2. If any facts are relevant to the question, would all reasonable persons interpret the fact in the same way? If so, it is a question of fact. If not, the facts presumably can be rationally interpreted differently from different competing reasonable perspectives. It is therefore a question of judgment.

As you study a subject, distinguish among the three types of questions. Look for the questions that have definitive or correct answers. These will be matters settled by definition or fixed, established, and recognized procedures. Identify those questions that are ultimately a matter of personal choice. And, most important, identify those questions that can be legitimately, or at least arguably, approached from more than one point of view. These latter will arise most commonly when there are competing traditions or schools or theories within the discipline. For example, psychology incorporates many competing schools: Freudian, Jungian, Adlerian, rational–emotive, Gestalt, and so on. Many issues in psychology will be reasoned through differently depending on the reasoner's academic allegiance. These issues will call for considering argumentation from a variety of perspectives and will result in different reasoned judgments.

6.5   *Think for Yourself*

DISTINGUISHING TYPES OF QUESTIONS 2

Identify at least one subject you have studied in school that involves competing traditions or schools of thought. Then identify some questions that would be answered differently depending on the school of thought used to think-through the question. Which of the schools of thought do you best understand or most identify with? How might this school of thought be questioned from the perspective of another competing school of thought?

BECOME A SOCRATIC QUESTIONER

Now that you are beginning to understand how to categorize questions, let us discuss how we can approach questions in general so our questions will lead us to better thinking. As critical thinkers, we want to go beyond questions that are undisciplined, questions that go in multiple directions with neither rhyme nor reason. Therefore, we turn from merely questioning to what might be termed "Socratic questioning." What the word "Socratic" adds to ordinary questioning are systematicity, depth, and a keen interest in assessing the truth or plausibility of things.

One of the primary goals of critical thinking is to establish a disciplined, "executive" component of thinking in our thinking, a powerful inner voice of reason, to monitor, assess, and repair—in a more rational direction—our thinking, feelings, and action. Socratic questioning provides that inner voice. Here are some of the fundamentals of Socratic questioning, followed by examples of questions you might ask in Socratic dialogue to begin to deeply probe the thinking of another person.

- Seek to understand—when possible—the ultimate foundations for what is said or believed, and follow the implications of those foundations through further questions. (You might ask, for example, "On what do you base your beliefs? Could you explain your reasoning to me in more detail so I can more fully understand your position?")

- Recognize that any thought can exist fully only in a network of connected thoughts. Therefore, treat all assertions as connecting points to further thoughts. Pursue those connections. (You might ask, for example, "If what you say is true, wouldn't X or Y also be so?")

- Treat all thoughts as in need of development. (You might ask: "Could you elaborate on what you are saying so I can better understand you?")

- Recognize that all questions presuppose prior questions and all thinking presupposes prior thinking. When raising questions, be open to the questions they presuppose. (You might ask, for example, "To answer this complex question, what other questions do we need to answer?")

6.6 *Think for Yourself*

PRACTICING SOCRATIC QUESTIONING

When you become a Socratic questioner, a systematic questioner, you can question anyone about anything—effectively! Try out your questioning skills by questioning someone you know as systematically and as deeply as you can about something he or she deeply believes. Tape-record the discussion. Follow the suggestions given here. When finished, replay the tape and analyze your Socratic questioning abilities. Did you probe beneath the surface of the other person's thinking? Did you ask for elaboration when needed? Did you pursue connections? Overall, how you would rate yourself as a Socratic questioner?

EXHIBIT 6.2 *Socratic thinking is an integrated, disciplined approach to thinking.*

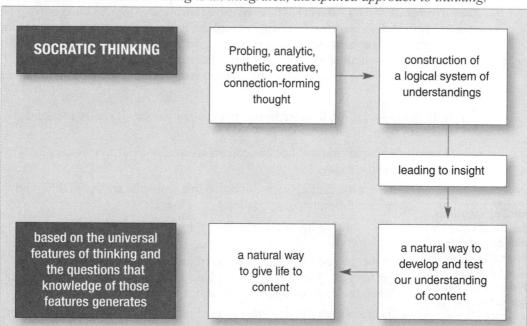

To take your thinking to the level of disciplined questioning, to think or question Socratically, you can go in several directions:

1. You can focus your questions on types of question (fact, preference, or judgment).
2. You can focus your questions on assessment, by targeting intellectual standards.
3. You can focus your questions on analysis, by targeting the elements of reasoning.
4. You can learn to "unpack" complex questions by developing questions one would have to answer prior to answering the lead question.
5. You can learn to determine the domains of questions inherent in a complex question.

In the following discussion we will elaborate on these forms of Socratic questioning. Of course, the questions you would ask in a given situation will be determined by the context within which you are thinking. When you become skilled at using these questions, you will begin to see the powerful role they can play in your thinking. And, with practice, they eventually will become intuitive to you. You will begin to naturally ask questions of clarification when you are unclear. You will begin to naturally ask questions focused on *information* when the data seem to be inaccurate or otherwise questionable. You will recognize intuitively when people are mistakenly answering questions of judgment with their subjective preference, and so on. Again, intuitive ability comes only after a lot of practice.

Focus Your Thinking on the Type of Question Being Asked

As discussed earlier in this chapter, when you approach questions systematically, you are able to recognize that all thought has three possible functions: to express a subjective preference, to establish an objective fact (within a well-defined system), or to come up with the best of competing answers (generated by competing systems). Assume that you do not fully understand thinking until you know which type of thinking the question is focused on.

Here are questions you can ask that focus on getting at the type of question you are dealing with:

- Is the question calling for a subjective or personal choice? If so, let's make that choice in terms of our personal preferences.
- If not, is this a question that has one correct answer, or a definite system in which to find the answer?
    - Or are we dealing with a question that would be answered differently within different points of view?
    - If the latter, what is the best answer to the question, all things considered?
    - Is this person treating a question of judgment as a question of preference by saying he doesn't have to give reasoning for his answer when the question implies that he does?
    - Is this person treating a question of judgment as a question for which there is one right answer?

In pursuing questions, Charles Darwin relied on perseverance and continual reflection: "I have never been able to remember for more than a few days a single date or line of poetry."

EXHIBIT 6.3 *Here are five ways to generate questions that lead to disciplined thinking.*

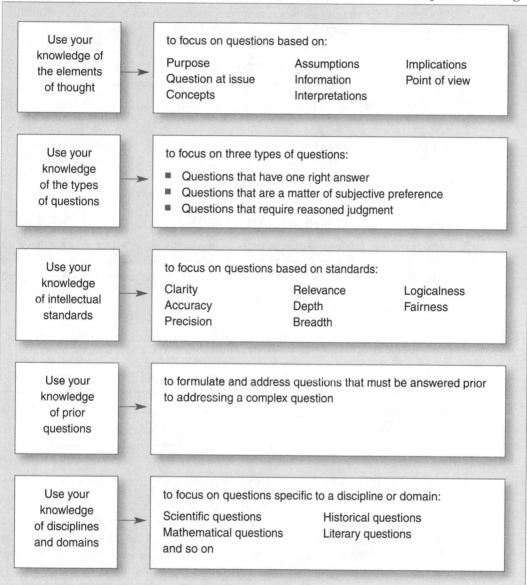

Use your knowledge of the elements of thought	→	to focus on questions based on: Purpose　　　Assumptions　　　Implications Question at issue　Information　　　Point of view Concepts　　　Interpretations
Use your knowledge of the types of questions	→	to focus on three types of questions: ■ Questions that have one right answer ■ Questions that are a matter of subjective preference ■ Questions that require reasoned judgment
Use your knowledge of intellectual standards	→	to focus on questions based on standards: Clarity　　　Relevance　　　Logicalness Accuracy　　　Depth　　　　　Fairness Precision　　　Breadth
Use your knowledge of prior questions	→	to formulate and address questions that must be answered prior to addressing a complex question
Use your knowledge of disciplines and domains	→	to focus on questions specific to a discipline or domain: Scientific questions　　　Historical questions Mathematical questions　Literary questions and so on

Focus Your Questions on Universal Intellectual Standards for Thought

When you approach questions systematically, you recognize when people are failing to use the universal intellectual standards in their thinking. You also recognize when you are failing to use these standards in your thinking. And you ask questions, specifically targeting the intellectual standards, that upgrade thinking.

From discussions in previous chapters, the guidelines are as follows.

1. Recognize that thinking is always more or less *clear.* Assume that you do not fully understand a thought except to the extent you can elaborate, illustrate, and exemplify it. Questions that focus on *clarity* in thinking are:

- Could you elaborate on what you are saying?
- Could you give me an example or illustration of your point?
- I hear you saying "X." Am I hearing you correctly, or have I misunderstood you?

2. Recognize that thinking is always more or less *precise.* Assume that you do not fully understand it except to the extent that you can specify it in detail. Questions that focus on *precision* in thinking are:

- Could you give me more details about that?
- Could you be more specific?
- Could you specify your allegations more fully?

3. Recognize that thinking is always more or less *accurate.* Assume that you have not fully assessed it except to the extent that you have checked to determine whether it represents things as they really are. Questions that focus on *accuracy* in thinking are:

- How could we check that to see if it is true?
- How could we verify these alleged facts?
- Can we trust the accuracy of these data given the questionable source from which they come?

4. Recognize that thinking is always capable of straying from the task, question, problem, or issue under consideration. Assume that you have not fully assessed thinking except to the extent that you have ensured that all considerations used in addressing it are genuinely *relevant* to it. Questions that focus on *relevance* in thinking are:

- I don't see how what you said bears on the question. Could you show me how it is relevant?
- Could you explain what you think the connection is between your question and the question we have focused on?

5. Recognize that thinking can either function at the surface of things or probe beneath that surface to deeper matters and issues. Assume that you have not fully assessed a line of thinking except to the extent that you have determined the *depth* required for the task at hand (and compared that with the depth that actually has been achieved). (To figure out whether a question is deep, we need to determine whether it involves complexities that must be considered.) Questions that focus on *depth* in thinking are:

- Is this question simple or complex? Is it easy or difficult to answer?
- What makes this a complex question?
- How are we dealing with the complexities inherent in the question?

6. Recognize that thinking can be more or less broad-minded (or narrow-minded) and that *breadth* of thinking requires the thinker to think insightfully within *more than one point of view or frame of reference.* Assume that you have not fully assessed a line of thinking except to the extent that you have determined how much *breadth* of thinking is required (and how much has actually been exercised). Questions that focus on *breadth* in thinking are:

- What points of view are relevant to this issue?

- What relevant points of view have I ignored thus far?

- Am I failing to consider this issue from an opposing viewpoint because I don't want to change my view?

- Have I entered the opposing views in good faith, or only enough to find flaws in them?

- I have looked at the question from an economic point of view. What is the moral point of view?

- I have considered a liberal position on the issue. What would conservatives say?

6.7 *Think for Yourself*

FOCUSING YOUR QUESTIONS ON INTELLECTUAL STANDARDS

For each of the categories of questions focusing on intellectual standards (see the previous section), try to come up with one situation in which your failure to use intellectual standards had negative consequences. This might be a situation in which you should have asked a question of clarification and didn't, or should have asked a question focusing on precision and didn't, and so on. State what happened as a result of each failure. For example, you might recall a time when you asked for directions to someone's house but got lost because you failed to ask questions focused on important details.

Focus Your Questions on the Elements of Thought

Another powerful way to discipline your questions is to focus on the elements or parts of thinking. As you formulate your questions, recall the following guidelines:

1. All thought reflects an agenda or *purpose.* Assume that you do not fully understand someone's thought (including your own) until you understand the agenda behind it. Questions that focus on purpose in thinking include:

- What are you trying to accomplish in saying this?

- What is your central aim in this line of thought?

- What is the purpose of this meeting?

- What is the purpose of this chapter?
- What is the purpose of our relationship?
- What is my purpose for being in college?

2. All thoughts presuppose an *information* base. Assume that you do not fully understand the thought until you understand the background information (facts, data, experiences) that supports or informs it. Questions that focus on information in thinking include:

- On what information are you basing that comment?
- What experience convinced you of this? Could your experience be distorted?
- How do we know this information is *accurate?*
- Have we left out any important information that we need to consider?

3. All thought requires making *inferences,* drawing conclusions, creating meaning. Assume that you do not fully understand a thought until you understand the inferences that have shaped it. Questions that focus on inferences in thinking include:

- How did you reach that conclusion?
- Could you explain your reasoning?
- Is there an alternative plausible conclusion?
- Given all the facts, what is the best possible conclusion?

4. All thought involves the application of *concepts*. Assume that you do not fully understand a thought until you understand the concepts that define and shape it. Questions that focus on concepts in thinking include:

- What is the main idea you are using in your reasoning?
- Could you explain that idea?
- Are we using our concepts justifiably?

5. All thought rests upon other thoughts, which are taken for granted or *assumed*. Assume that you do not fully understand a thought until you understand what it takes for granted. Questions that focus on assumptions in thinking include:

- What exactly are you taking for granted here?
- Why are you assuming that?
- Should I question the assumptions I am using about my roommate, my friends, my intimate other, my parents, my instructors, my country?

6. All thought is headed in a direction. It not only rests upon something (assumptions) but also is going somewhere (*implications* and consequences). Assume that you do not fully understand a thought unless you know the implications and consequences that follow from it. Questions that focus on implications in thinking include:

- What are you implying when you say that?
- What is likely to happen if we do this versus that?
- Are you implying that . . . ?

7. All thought takes place within a *point of view* or frame of reference. Assume that you do not fully understand a thought until you understand the point of view or frame of reference that places it on an intellectual map. Questions that focus on point of view in thinking include:

- From what point of view are you looking at this?
- Is there another point of view we should consider?
- Which of these possible viewpoints makes the most sense given the situation?

8. All thought is responsive to a *question*. Assume that you do not fully understand the thought until you understand the question that gives rise to it. Questions that focus on questions in thinking include:

- I am not sure exactly what question you are raising. Could you explain it?
- Is this question the best one to focus on at this point, or is there a more pressing question we need to address?
- The question in my mind is this: How do you see the question?
- How is your question related to the question we have been reasoning through?

6.8 *Think for Yourself*

FOCUSING YOUR QUESTIONS ON THE ELEMENTS OF REASONING

From each of the eight categories we just outlined, ask yourself at least one question about your view of marriage (or family). For example, you might begin with the question, "In my view, what is the basic purpose or goal of marriage?" (Answer each question after you ask it.)

Afterward, question a friend about his or her views, using the same questions (you should feel free to ask additional questions as they occur to you). Write out an analysis of your questioning process. Do you notice yourself beginning to think at a deeper level—given the questions you are now asking? Did you focus on all eight elements?

Focus Your Questions on Prior Questions

Whenever we are dealing with complex questions, another tool that is useful in disciplining our thinking is to construct prior questions—questions we need to answer before we can answer a more complex question. Hence, to answer the question, "What is multiculturalism?" we should be able to first settle the question, "What is culture?" And to settle that question, we should be able to settle the question, "What are the factors about a person that determine what culture he or she belongs to?" When you learn to formulate and pursue prior questions, you have another important "idea" that you can use to develop your ability to learn in any context.

To construct a list of prior questions, simply write down the main question upon which you are going to focus your discussion, and then formulate as many questions as you can think of that you would have to answer before you could answer the first. Then take this list and determine what question you would have to answer to answer these questions. Continue, following the same procedure for every new set of questions on your list.

As you proceed to construct your list, keep your attention focused on the first question on the list as well as on the last. If you do this well, you should end up with a list of questions that probe the logic of the first question. As an example of how to construct logically prior questions, consider this list of questions we would need to answer to address the larger question, "What is history?"

- What do historians write about?
- What is "the past"?
- Is it possible to include all of the past in a history book?
- How many of the events during a given time period are left out in a history of that time period?
- Is more left out than is included?
- How does a historian know what to emphasize?
- Do historians make value judgments in deciding what to include and what to leave out?
- Is it possible to simply list facts in a history book, or does all history writing involve interpretations as well as facts?
- Is it possible to decide what to include and exclude and how to interpret facts without adopting a historical point of view?
- How can we begin to judge a historical interpretation?
- How can we begin to judge a historical point of view?

6.9 *Think for Yourself*

CONSTRUCTING A LIST OF PRIOR QUESTIONS

Formulate a complex question to which you would like to find an answer. Then use the procedure of constructing prior questions until you have a list of at least 10 questions. Afterward, see if you have gained insight into how the first question has to be thought-through in light of the prior questions you formulated.

The best questions are those that keep us focused on achieving our most significant goals and purposes.

When you have practiced formulating prior questions to complex questions, you will begin to develop a Socratic questioning tool that you can use whenever you need to answer a complicated question. You will notice your mind coming up with questions that are inherent in other questions. You are unpacking questions to better answer them. You should also then begin to recognize when others are failing to consider the complexities in a question.

Focus Your Questions on Domains of Thinking

When you are addressing a complex question that covers more than one domain of thought, you can target your prior questions by figuring out the domains of thinking inherent in the question. Does the complex question, for example, include an economic dimension? Does it include a biological, sociological, cultural, political, ethical, psychological, religious, historical, or some other dimension? For each dimension of thinking inherent in the question, you can formulate questions that force you to consider complexities you otherwise may miss. Consider the following question, some of the domains imbedded in the question, and some of the questions imbedded in those domains.

Complex question: What can be done about the number of people who abuse illegal drugs?

EXHIBIT 6.4 *Complex questions have multiple domains.*

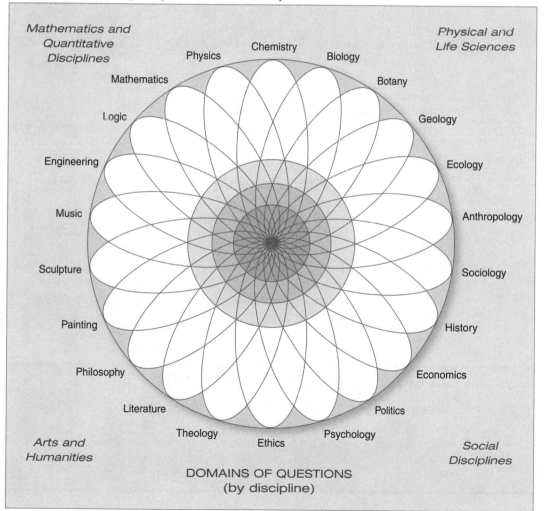

Domains inherent in the question, along with some questions we would have to address within each domain before we could answer our complex question, are:

1. Economic
   - What economic forces support drug use?
   - What can be done to minimize the influence of money involved in drug sales?

2. Political
   - What possible solutions to drug abuse are politically unacceptable?
   - Are there any realistic solutions that the power structure would accept?
   - To what extent does the political structure exacerbate the problem?

3. Social/Sociological
   - What social structures and practices support drug abuse?
   - How does gang membership contribute to drug abuse?
   - How does membership within any group contribute to the problem or, conversely, insulate group members from abusing drugs?

4. Psychological
   - How do factors such as stress, individual personality differences, and childhood traumas support drug abuse?
   - What role, if any, does human irrationality play in drug abuse?

5. Biological
   - How do genetics play a role in drug abuse?
   - What biological changes in the body resulting from drug abuse contribute to the problem?

6. Educational
   - What role are educational institutions now playing to support or diminish the problem?

7. Religious
   - What can religious institutions do to reduce the incidence of drug abuse?
   - What role are they now playing in regard to drug abuse?

8. Cultural
   - What cultural beliefs support the drug-abuse problem?
   - What can we learn from cultures that have a low incidence of drug abuse?

6.10   *Think for Yourself*

FORMULATING QUESTIONS WITHIN DOMAINS OF THINKING

Focus on the question: What can be done to significantly improve the health of the ecosystems on Earth? Using the model above, figure out the domains within the question that you would have to think within to address the complexities in the question. Then formulate as many questions as you can within each domain. (The question you are originally addressing determines the domains within which you need to think.)

When we can approach questions to target the domains inherent in them, we are able to ask questions such as:

- What domains of questions are inherent in this complex question?
- Is this person dealing with all the relevant domains within the question?
- Am I leaving out some important domains when reasoning through this issue?

CONCLUSION

Questions play an important role in the mind of the best thinkers. Three important types of questions are questions of fact, questions of preference, and questions of judgment. The best thinkers differentiate these forms of questions because the form of the question determines the kind of thinking the question calls for. The ability to ask questions is not enough in and of itself for the best thinkers. It is necessary to ask important questions relevant to the purposes we are pursuing (including questions that lead us to scrutinize our purposes). Socratic or systematic questioning is a means to disciplined thinking. One method of approaching Socratic questioning is to develop prior questions.

Because there is a sense in which "you think only as well as the questions you ask," you want to force yourself, as a developing thinker, to focus on the role that questions play in your thinking. To what extent are you asking significant questions? To what extent are you able to figure out whether a question is asking for a factual answer, preference, or reasoned judgment? To what extent are you asking questions that follow a disciplined path, leading to rationally defensible answers? To what extent are you able to take apart complex questions, to figure out questions you would have to answer prior to answering those questions? When you are practicing the fundamental questioning steps we have explored in this chapter, you will find yourself progressing as a questioner—and as a thinker.

MASTER THE THINKING, MASTER THE CONTENT

F rom what we have emphasized thus far, it now should be clear that

- critical thinking requires the development of basic intellectual skills, abilities, and insights;
- becoming a skilled thinker can be compared to becoming skilled in basketball, ballet, or saxophone playing;
- these skills can be used to serve two incompatible ends: self-centeredness or fair-mindedness;
- the skills of critical thinking can be learned in a weak sense (skilled but selfish thinking);
- we are focused in this book on the development of critical thinking in a strong sense (skilled, fair-minded thinking);
- fair-mindedness requires that we develop a network of interrelated traits of mind;
- development as a critical thinker occurs in predictable stages;
- engaging in that development is challenging, requiring planned practice and happening over many years, not weeks or months;
- human egocentrism represents a significant obstacle to fair-minded critical thinking;

- to conquer our egocentrism, we must understand, and exercise some control over, the three basic functions of the human mind: thinking, feeling, wanting;
- because humans spend most of our time thinking about what we personally want or value, we need to question our personal values.

GO BEYOND SUPERFICIAL MEMORIZATION TO DEEP LEARNING

As a student, it is important that you think seriously about what you want to accomplish in each of your classes, and in college in general. If you simply want to get by, to do no more than pass your courses, you know the logic of how to do so: You go to class. You find out the minimal requirements of the course. You fulfill those requirements with the least effort possible. You get the grade. You move on to the next semester. After four years and a certain number of course hours, you get a degree. Using this kind of thinking, you think of college merely as a vehicle to get a job. The problem with this "minimalist" strategy is that, in using it, you miss the opportunity to develop skills and insights that you can use for a lifetime. You graduate, but you do not become a lifelong learner.

If, however, you look at college as an opportunity to learn how to learn, to develop your mind, to seek out new ways to look at things, to expand your knowledge, to learn ideas that will help you figure out the problems of your life, you must seek to internalize a set of intellectual skills that will enable you to learn more deeply and more permanently in every one of your courses. With the proper vision of what you are after, you can begin to practice effective thinking in all your classes. And if you strive to develop certain habits of thought and characteristics of mind, such as intellectual humility, perseverance, and fair-mindedness, you can transform the way you operate in every challenging context and situation. You will acquire the tools of good thinking and learning. You then will go into each class with powerful questions on the tip of your tongue. You will ask these questions whenever possible. You will ask them while you are silently reading, while engaged in writing, while speaking, while listening.

You will recognize, then, that the content that defines college instruction can be learned only through thinking. You will recognize that when you think poorly while learning, you learn poorly, and that when you think well while learning, you learn well. So, if you are serious about acquiring powerful tools for learning, you must be committed to developing your ability to think well, to reason your way into any body of content, to organize content in your mind, to relate it to your experience, to assess it using appropriate standards.

If, however, you have become subconsciously habituated to rote memorization as your principal tool of learning, if your mode of preparing for an exam is to cram bits and pieces of content into your head, you may get by temporarily, but you will retain little of what you learned. The result, in the long run, will be poor performance, poor learning, and poor habits of thought. You will be of little value to an employer who wants to hire people who can systematically pursue important goals, recognize and analyze significant problems, communicate important meanings, and assess their own performance on the job.

7.1 *Think for Yourself*

THINKING DEEPLY ABOUT WHY YOU ARE IN COLLEGE

What are you trying to accomplish in college? Are you committed to developing your thinking in a deep way? Or are you going to college simply to get a job that requires a degree? Are you going to college just because your friends are going? Are you after the social life that college offers? Or are you not sure what your real motivation is? If you had to complete the following statements, what would you say? My fundamental purpose in going to college is . . . . I am committed to . . . . Write out your answer or explain orally.

THE RELATION OF CONTENT TO THINKING

A key insight into content—and into thinking—is that all content represents a distinctive mode of thinking. Math becomes easier as one learns to *think* mathematically. Biology becomes easier as one learns to *think* biologically. History becomes easier as one learns to *think* historically. Parenting becomes easier as one learns to *think* as a good parent. In Chapter 8 we elaborate on what it means to understand and think-through the logic of a course, or indeed of any domain of thinking.

EXHIBIT 7.1 *Thinking is the key to all content.*

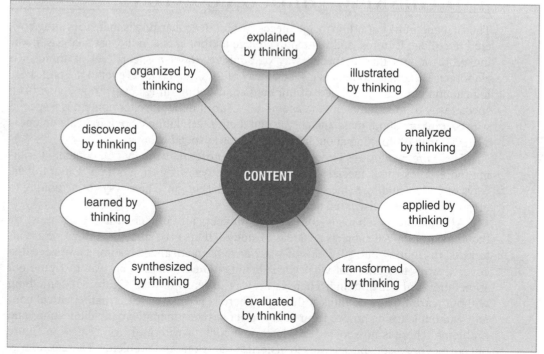

To become motivated to learn what you are studying, you have to understand the connection between content and thinking. If you do, what first appears as dull, dry stuff to memorize can come alive to you. Too many students—and, alas, too many teachers—fail to appreciate this intimate connection. As an opener, consider this: All subjects you study (that is, all content domains) were created by the thinking of humans. They are

generated by thinking, evaluated by thinking,

organized by thinking, restructured by thinking,

analyzed by thinking, maintained by thinking,

synthesized by thinking, transformed by thinking.

expressed by thinking.

They are

learned by thinking,

understood by thinking,

applied by thinking.

If you were to try to take the thinking out of content, you would have nothing, literally nothing, remaining. Learning a way to think is the key to learning any content whatsoever.

UNDERSTAND CONTENT THROUGH THINKING AND THINKING-THROUGH CONTENT

The first and most important insight necessary for deep learning is that everything covered in college lectures, and written in college textbooks, is, in the last analysis, nothing more or less than a special way of thinking about a special set of things. To elaborate: Historical content is a special way of thinking about events in the past. Biological content is a special way of thinking about living things. Algebraic content is a special way of thinking about the operations of arithmetic. Physics content is a special way of thinking about mass and energy and their interrelations. Sociological content is a special way of thinking about human behavior in social groups.

There are many ways to begin to grasp the profound truth that all content is nothing more or less than special ways of thinking, ways of figuring out particular things, ways of understanding some set of things through thought. Three ways of beginning to grasp this truth are discussed next.

All content in school is content in a subject; all content in a subject must be thought-through. All subjects are areas of study. All areas of study are things we are interested in figuring out. All fields of study have been advanced insofar as we have discovered ways to figure out whatever is being studied. There is no way to figure out something without thinking. There is no way to learn how to figure out something without learning how to think it through. There is no way to learn mathematical content without learning how to figure out correct answers to mathematical questions and problems. There is no way to learn historical content without learning how to figure out correct or reasonable answers to historical questions and problems. There is no way to learn biological content without learning how to figure out answers to biological questions and problems. Any subject or content area can therefore be understood as a mode of figuring out correct or reasonable answers to a certain body of questions. We study chemistry to figure out chemicals (to answer questions about chemicals). We study psychology to figure out human behavior (to answer questions about certain human problems). Subjects can be deeply understood only in this way.

7.2   *Think for Yourself*

UNDERSTANDING CONTENT AS SOMETHING TO BE THOUGHT-THROUGH

Select a subject that is the topic of a class you are now taking or have taken in the past. Make a list of the questions that professionals within the discipline pursue, questions they try to think-through to figure out important matters in the field. You may want to look through the first chapter of the textbook for the class, which should provide an overview of the purpose of the discipline, and key questions that thinkers within the discipline traditionally ask. You also might read through the relevant entry in an encyclopedia to identify these key questions. Write out your answer or explain orally.

All Content Is Organized by Concepts

There is no way to learn a body of content without learning the concepts that define and structure it. There is no way to learn a concept without learning how to use it in thinking something through. Hence, to learn the concept of democracy is to learn how to figure out whether some group is functioning democratically or not. To learn the concept of fair play is to learn how to figure out whether participants are being fair in the manner in which they are participating in a game. To learn the concept of a novel is to learn how to distinguish a novel from a play or a short story. To learn the concept of a family is to learn how to distinguish a family from a gang or a club. To learn any body of content, therefore, it is necessary to learn to think accurately and reasonably with the concepts that define the content.

7.3   *Think for Yourself*

IDENTIFYING THE MEANING OF KEY CONCEPTS

Choose a concept, the most basic concept, that is the focus of one of your classes. Write out in your own words your understanding of the concept. Write it out in such a way that you can readily see the significance of the concept in your life.

For example, if you are studying history, you first understand the role that historical thinking plays in our lives. Every human lives within a self-constructed inner history. That history is used every day to make decisions.

For example, if in your understanding of your past, you were always poor in writing or math, you probably would now seek to avoid writing or math classes.

Again, all of your plans for the future are a result of what seems possible and probable to you—given your understanding of your past. Understood in this way, there could be no more important study than that which enables us to improve our historical thinking. Can you see how that would be so? Can you see the study of history in a new light, given this way of understanding the basic concept (humans and historical thinkers)? Now try a key concept of your own choosing. Write out your answer or explain orally.

All Content Is Logically Interdependent

To understand one part of some content requires that we figure out its relation to other parts of that content. For example, we understand what a scientific experiment is only when we understand what a scientific theory is. We understand what a scientific theory is only when we understand what a scientific hypothesis is. We understand what a scientific hypothesis is only when we understand what a scientific prediction is. We understand what a scientific prediction is only when we understand what it is to scientifically test a view. We understand what it is to scientifically test a view only when we understand what a scientific experiment is, and so on. To learn any body of content, therefore, is to figure out (reason or think-through) the connections between the parts of that content. No *true* learning of the content is possible without this thinking process.

7.4   *Think for Yourself*

SEEING CONNECTIONS BETWEEN CONCEPTS WITHIN A SUBJECT

Select a subject you are taking currently (or have taken), and draw a diagram showing the links between the most basic concepts within the subject. Then state in your own words how each idea is linked to every other idea. Your thinking will be something like this: To understand "a," you must understand "b," and to understand "b," you must understand "c," and to understand "c," you must understand "d," and so on. Elaborate on each idea as you go so that you can see the connections between them.

Many teachers and students currently approach content not as a mode of thinking, not as a system for thought, or even as a system *of* thought but, rather, as a sequence of stuff to be routinely covered and committed to memory. When content is approached in this lower-order way, there is no basis for intellectual growth, no deep structures of knowledge are formed, and no basis for long-term grasp and control is developed.

By contrast, critical thinking approaches all content explicitly as thinking. It takes thinking apart. It weaves new thinking into old. It assesses thinking. It applies thinking.

It is thinking about thinking while thinking to make thinking better: more clear, more accurate, more relevant, more deep, more broad, and more effective.

THINK-THROUGH YOUR CLASSES USING YOUR KNOWLEDGE OF THINKING

If learning any content well involves understanding it as a mode of thinking, everything you can discover about thinking offers potential insight into how you should approach college classes. First, let us remind you of eight basic features of all thinking: Whenever we think, we think for a purpose within a point of view based on assumptions leading to implications and consequences. We use concepts and theories to interpret data, facts, and experiences to answer questions, solve problems, and resolve issues. Here are all the elements listed separately:

1. All thinking has a purpose or goal.
2. All thinking raises at least one question.
3. All thinking requires information.
4. All thinking requires concepts.
5. All thinking involves inferences.
6. All thinking involves assumptions.
7. All thinking involves implications.
8. All thinking involves a point of view.

Now let's think about how this knowledge might guide your thinking when thinking-through the process of learning college material. As examples:

1. If all thinking entails thinking for a *purpose,* you can always ask yourself, What is the purpose of this assignment? What was the purpose of this character in this story? What is the teacher's purpose in asking me this question? What is my purpose for being in class? What is my purpose for being in college? What are my long-term goals? If you keep central purposes in mind, you will accomplish them more fully.

2. If all thinking requires *information,* you can always ask yourself: What information do I need so I can to reason well through this problem? What information did the researchers use in coming to this conclusion? Upon what information does this historian base her conclusions? What information do I have about how to be successful in college? What information do I have about people who are successful in life? Do I have the information I need to accomplish my most important goals? If you make it a habit to consciously think about the information sources you are using, the quality of your thinking will improve.

3. If all sound thinking is focused on a *question,* you can always ask yourself: What is the key question at issue in this assignment? What is the key question that the researchers focused on? What is the key question at the heart of this story? What is the key problem that I face in becoming successful in college? In life? All good thinkers are good questioners. By learning powerful questions to ask, you will find that you learn more and more and that it becomes progressively easier.

These are just three of the structures of thought that serve as guides for improving thinking. A similar group of questions can be developed for each of the eight structures.

7.5 *Think for Yourself*

FOCUSING ON QUESTIONS IMPLIED BY THE STRUCTURES OF THOUGHT

Choose a subject in a class you are taking. Focus on a different subject than you have in previous Think for Yourself exercises. Complete the following sentences, and elaborate on your answer as much as possible.

1. The purpose of this subject is . . .
2. The main types of information that professionals in this field of study use are . . .
   (This might be research studies, in psychology for example; events from the past, in history for example; information about the universe, in astronomy for example.)
3. Some of the main questions that professionals within this discipline ask are . . .

A Caution

No one can do your thinking for you. No one can change you but you. The challenge of becoming the agent of your own growth and development is formidable. We are creatures of habit. We are masters of self-deception. We are highly skilled in self-justification, rationalization, and self-defense. We are not inclined to put burdens on ourselves that others are not requiring of us. Little in academic or social life encourages independent, critical thinking. Although college offers a wonderful opportunity to establish the habits of a lifelong learner, it would be naive to think that all college professors require critical thinking and teach for it.

You may take some history courses in which the professor covers so much historical content in lectures that historical thinking is obscured rather than encouraged. You may take some math courses in which mathematical thinking is sacrificed in favor of memorizing fixed procedures for solving standardized problems. You may take a psychology course in which the multilogical nature of psychological perspectives—that the many competing schools of psychology respond very differently to the same data or problem—is thrown into the background and the subject is presented as if it were a scientific discipline such as physics or chemistry. You may take a logic course so abstracted from the problems of everyday thinking that you conclude that logic is a waste of time rather than a necessary goal in thinking well.

In short, to some extent, if you are to truly benefit from the content you are studying, you may have to learn at a higher level than the mode of teaching in a class requires of you. To do this, you must develop for yourself the intellectual skills that will enable you to think-through the content in a disciplined way, in a way that leads to deep learning, in a way that results in your ability to take the ideas you learn in class, to give them meaning in your thinking and to use them in your life.

7.6 *Think for Yourself*

CRITIQUING THE QUALITY OF TEACHING

Select a class you are in now, or that you have taken in the past, which you think involved high-quality teaching. What precisely does/did the teacher do that led to deep, long-term learning? What can you do as a student to deepen your learning in every class you take? How can you learn as you learned in the best class you took by taking initiative in all your other classes? Or do you think the teacher determines how much you learn and you have little to do with it? Write out your answer or explain orally.

DISCOVER HOW THE BEST THINKERS LEARN

A man may hear a thousand lectures, and read a thousand volumes, and be at the end of the process very much where he was, as regards knowledge. Something more than merely admitting it in a negative way into the mind is necessary, if it is to remain there. It must not be passively received, but actually and actively entered into, embraced, mastered. The mind must go half-way to meet what comes to it from without.

John Henry Newman, *The Idea of a University* (1853)

The best thinkers are skilled learners. They take charge of their learning. They, in essence, design it—plan it out. You plan learning by becoming clear as to what your goals are, what questions you have to—or want to—answer, what information you need to get, what concepts you need to learn, what point of view or perspective you need to adopt. Skilled learners figure out the logic of what they are trying to understand. Skilled learners have strategies for studying well—and continue to develop strategies as they become more skilled at thinking. As you read through this chapter, you should begin to explicitly choose and practice a range of strategies that take you out of the mainstream of most students—who have in effect no powerful learning strategies.

We will begin with 18 ideas or strategies expressed simply. Most of these strategies will be explained and exemplified throughout the chapter. The strategies of close reading and substantive writing (two of the most important tools for learning) will be covered in a separate chapter.

EXHIBIT 8.1 *Critical thinkers have confidence in their ability to figure out the logic of anything they choose.*

The spirit of critical thinking

There is a logic to this, and I can figure it out!

THE LOGIC OF X

18 IDEAS FOR IMPROVING YOUR STUDIES

Idea # 1: Make sure you thoroughly understand the requirements of each class—how it will be taught and what will be expected of you. Ask questions about the grading policies and for advice on how best to prepare for class.

Idea # 2: Become an active learner. Begin to work ideas into your thinking by actively reading, writing, speaking, and listening.

Idea # 3: Think of each subject you study as a form of thinking. (If you are in a history class, your goal should be to think historically; in a chemistry class to think chemically; etc.)

Idea # 4: Become a questioner. Engage yourself in lectures and discussions by asking questions. If you don't ask questions, you probably won't discover what you do and do not know.

Idea # 5: Look for interconnections. The content in every class is a *system* of interconnected ideas, never a random list of things to memorize. Don't memorize like a parrot. Study like a detective, always relating new learning to previous learning.

Idea # 6: Think of your instructor as your coach. Think of yourself as a team member trying to practice the thinking exemplified by your instructor. For example, in an algebra class, think of yourself as going out for the algebra team and your teacher as demonstrating how to prepare for the games (thinking within the discipline).

Idea # 7: Understand the textbook as the thinking of the author. Your job is to think the thinking of the author. For example, role play the author frequently. Explain the main points of the text to another student, as if you were the author.

Idea # 8: Consider class time as a time in which you *practice* thinking (within the subject) using the fundamental concepts and principles of the course. Don't sit back passively, waiting for knowledge to fall into your head like rain into a rain barrel. It won't.

Idea # 9: Relate content whenever possible to issues and problems and practical situations in your life. If you can't connect it to your life, you don't understand it at a deep enough level to use it in your thinking.

Idea # 10: Figure out what study and learning skills you need to develop. Practice those skills whenever possible. Remember that recognizing and correcting your weaknesses is a strength.

Idea # 11: Frequently ask yourself: Can I explain this to someone well enough for them to accurately understand it? (If not, you haven't learned it.)

Idea # 12: Seek the key concept of the course during the first couple of class meetings. For example, in a biology course, try explaining what biology is in your own words. Then relate that definition to each segment of what you learn afterward. Fundamental ideas are the basis for all other ideas.

Idea # 13: Routinely ask questions to fill in the missing pieces in your learning. Ask yourself: "Can I elaborate on this? Can I give an example?" If you cannot give examples of what you are learning you are not connecting what you are learning to your life.

Idea # 14: Test yourself before each class by trying to summarize, orally or in writing, the main points of the previous class meeting. If you cannot summarize the main points, you haven't learned them.

Idea # 15: Learn to test your thinking using intellectual standards: "Am I being clear? accurate? precise? relevant? logical? Am I looking for what is most significant?"

Idea # 16: Use writing as a tool for learning by writing summaries in your own words of important points from the textbook or other reading material. Formulate your own test questions. Then write out answers to your questions.

Idea # 17: Frequently evaluate your listening. Are you actively listening for main points? Can you summarize what your instructor is saying in your own words? Can you elaborate what is meant by key terms?

Idea # 18: Frequently evaluate the depth of your reading. Are you reading the textbook actively? Are you asking questions as you read? Can you distinguish what you understand from what you don't understand?

8.1 *Think for Yourself*

WHERE DO YOU STAND?

To what extent have you "designed" any part of your learning (in high school or college)? Have you ever developed any strategies for learning? Can you name one? Did it work (if you can think of one)? If you can't think of any strategies you use to learn, why not? On a scale of 1 to 10, how skilled would you say you are as a learner?

THE LOGIC OF A TYPICAL COLLEGE CLASS

Because you are learning through the medium of college classes, it is helpful to understand the logic of college classes. To understand the logic of college classes, consider college in the light of its history and traditions.

College today is a product of college yesterday. Traditions alive in college instruction go back hundreds of years. For example, the most common way for professors to try to get students to learn a body of knowledge is to state that body of knowledge to them in a sequence of lectures, and then to ask students, largely on their own, to internalize that knowledge outside of class. In this design, quizzes and examinations are usually interspersed among the lectures as means of assessing the extent to which the students have learned what the lectures covered.

Often a quiz is not given for six weeks or more. When this traditional teaching approach is used, students often revert to two strategies, neither of which is conducive to deep learning:

1. Taking random, but disconnected, notes during the lecture (focusing on points that might be on the test);
2. Intensive cramming one or two nights before the quiz or test (striving to store a large amount of information in short-term memory).

Under these conditions, many students go from the passive to the desperate learner, from being largely inactive as a learner to being frantic as a learner. On the other hand, students who are naturally "good" at memorization generally get higher grades in lecture-based classes than students who struggle to memorize content. Consequently, these students erroneously connect high grades with skilled learning. In other words, because memorization leads to high grades, they conclude that when they memorize content, they are learning at a deep level. In this model, students formulate a concept of learning that is superficial and transitory.

8.2 *Think for Yourself*

ARE YOU A PASSIVE LEARNER?

To what extent would you say that you match the traditional college student learning pattern above (largely passive, periodically frantic)? To what extent do you think this pattern is effective for deep learning? Why have you fallen into this pattern (if you have)? Or why haven't you fallen into this pattern (if you have not)?

Becoming a Skilled Thinker

The ideal of college can be expressed in a number of ways. However, no matter how it is expressed, certain basic skills and dispositions must be included in the definition for it to accurately characterize the educated person. The educated person, for example, must be:

1. proficient in close reading and substantive writing;
2. able to acquire and effectively use significant information, reason well, communicate effectively, solve problems, and exercise sound personal and professional judgment;
3. proficient in formulating and assessing goals and purposes, questions and problems, information and data, conclusions and interpretations, concepts and theoretical constructs, assumptions and presuppositions, implications and consequences, points of view and perspectives;
4. able to think clearly, accurately, precisely, relevantly, deeply, broadly, and logically;
5. intellectually perseverant, intellectually responsible, intellectually disciplined, intellectually humble, intellectually empathic, and intellectually productive;
6. reasonable, ethical, and effective in reasoning through complex problems, both globally and in one's personal life;
7. a lifelong learner with the capacity to deal effectively with a world of accelerating change, intensifying complexity, and increasing interdependence.

It should be clear to you that these characteristics and skills will not emerge simply as the result of regularly taking notes in lecture and cramming for quizzes and exams. If you value the ends expressed in the above ideals, if you want to develop as an educated person, you will have to establish personal imperatives that set you apart from your fellow students. You will have to develop habits that few of your peers are developing. You must rise above peer-group expectation (and possibly peer group scorn), and learn for reasons of your own and at a deeper level.

You must recognize that to acquire knowledge, you must construct it in your mind. You must translate it from the thoughts of someone else into your thoughts. To think it into your mind, you must be able to state it, elaborate upon it, exemplify it, and illustrate it. You must become proficient in taking ownership of ideas. Ideas may come from lectures, from textbooks, or from other sources. But do not be deceived by your ability to restate ideas in the same words that the instructor or text originally expressed them. A parrot, a tape-recorder, a rote memorizer is not a knower. Until you can express an idea in your own words, and exemplify it from your own experience, it is not yours; you do not *know* it.

8.3   *Think for Yourself*

DO YOU OWN THE IDEAL?

Which of the goals stated above do you most identify with? Which the least? Why? Note that goals 3, 4, and 5 presuppose some knowledge of critical thinking. Take one of these goals—for example, learning to be more proficient in using "concepts and theoretical constructs." How could you begin to incorporate this goal more thoroughly into your strategies for learning?

The Design of a Typical College Class and the Typical College Student

Though all college students take college classes, few master the logic of any academic discipline they study. Few students understand how college classes get designed or what challenges they themselves face in the learning process. Here are some important background facts:

1. Every field of study is subject to continual and (in most cases) enormous expansion.
2. Textbooks, which are the basis for most college classes, are getting larger and larger, and lectures are, in turn, tending to cover more and more content.
3. Most students do not know how to organize content as a system of meanings, to bring content into their thinking as a connected, interrelated system.
4. Most students use periodic cramming to pass their exams.
5. Most students read, write, and listen at a superficial level.
6. Most students lack intellectual standards by which to assess their own thinking and learning.

8.4   *Think for Yourself*

RATING YOURSELF AGAIN

How would you rate yourself on items 3, 4, 5, and 6 above? Comment on each separately. Then comment on what you consider the implications of your answers to be. For example, for number 5, if you read at a superficial level, what is a consequence of your limited reading ability?

The facts presented above have a number of important implications:

1. Most college exams are constructed so that the majority of students can pass them—that is, the majority of students can memorize well enough to pass them. (If a significant number of students were to fail the exams, the instructor would get low evaluations from the students.)
2. Grade inflation is rampant.

3. Most students probably could not pass the final exams for courses six months after the courses end.

4. Most students do not learn to think in the broader context of the course (e.g., they take history courses but do not learn to think historically; they take science courses but do not learn to think scientifically).

An important implication of these facts is that college generates a great deal of self-deception: Instructors who certify students as understanding subjects they do not truly understand; students who forget most of what they temporarily cram into their heads; accrediting teams accrediting departments that show no real evidence that students are learning what they claim they are learning.

Skilled thinkers want to do more than survive in college. They want their college education to help them become effective lifelong learners and thinkers.

8.5   *Think for Yourself*

THE PROBLEM OF SELF-DECEPTION

To develop as a critical thinker, you must be willing to face the fact that humans engage in a great deal of self-deception. Self-deception in college is part of the broader problem of self-deception in human life. Do you see any ways in which you have deceived yourself in terms of your learning? In your personal relationships? Do you see any ways in which teachers you have had in the past deceived themselves? Do you see any ways in which your friends are deceiving themselves?

For each class you take, it is important for you to understand how that course is designed. This includes figuring out the logic of the course through an analysis of the course syllabus, the textbook, and how the instructor has introduced the course. Every course in which you enroll has some essential things to look for. First, what are the official requirements of the class? What is the assigned reading, writing, and planned testing or assessment? When will papers, if any, be due? When will quizzes and tests occur? These are some obvious things to look for.

However you study, you want to meet the formal requirements at a high level. But there is something more important than merely getting passing grades. It is learning to think within the disciplines you study, internalizing core concepts, and gaining the most basic insights underlying the disciplines. It is important to make the mode of thinking in the discipline a permanent part of your thinking. To aim at these high goals, you might routinely ask and pursue three interconnected key questions:

1. What is the central underlying concept of the course or subject?

2. What form(s) of thinking is (are) essential to this course or subject?

3. How can I begin to think within the logic of the subject?

Let us consider these in order.

FIGURE OUT THE UNDERLYING CONCEPT OF YOUR COURSES

If you look at the sequence of items a course covers as if they were random bits and pieces of information, the course will seem to lack any underlying unity. But virtually all courses have some inherent unity that, when understood, ties all the learning of the course together like a tapestry. This unity typically is found in foundational concepts that define the subject and its goals.

For example, if you understand that the important "facts" of history are the product of historical thinking, and recognize the basic patterns that underlie such thinking, you have a way of looking at everything covered in the textbook and lectures—namely, as products of historical thought. You then read the textbook and listen to the lectures in a special way, seeking to find components of historical thought. You recognize that, to understand any written history, you must understand

1. the historian's goals or purposes
2. the questions or problems that are the primary focus of the historian
3. the historian's specific selection of historical events that the historian considers relevant to his or her questions
4. the historian's interpretations of the events and the significance of those events
5. the theoretical concepts the historian is using to interpret the events
6. the underlying assumptions that help define the historian's perspective
7. the implications of studying the historical events from a given perspective
8. the historical point of view that shapes the historical reasoning throughout.

If, in addition, we recognize that everyone thinks historically every day of their lives, we study history differently. For example, each and every day of our lives, we use in our thinking a story that entails our personal history. That story, or the way we view our past, determines the decisions we make today and the plans we make for the future. Our own personal history, then, reflects our historical assumptions, concepts, and point of view. It leads us to ask certain questions with certain purposes in mind. It leads us to make particular inferences based on historical information that then leads to implications.

When you see history in this richly interconnected way, you look for the historical goals and questions that are defining the construction of any and all historical accounts. You notice what events are included and also look for what is left out of the historical account. You look at key historical conclusions historians come to, the key assumptions made, the underlying historical points of view. Yet, most history classes have little impact on the historical thinking of students. Therefore, most students lack the organizing idea behind the discipline of history. They lack insight into the logic of historical thinking. As a result, their own historical thinking remains unmodified by their "study" of history. They never internalize deep and important historical concepts that if internalized, would enable them to think critically about the past and to apply historical concepts in everyday life.

Consider another subject—economics. If we understand the concept of scarcity as the underlying concept in economics, we study economics in a special way. We realize that all other concepts that economists use are related to this central idea behind economics: that it is not possible for any one of us to have everything we want (the fact of scarcity) and, as a result, all of us have to give up some things to get other things. What people are willing to give up to get something else forms the basis for their economic decision-making. Power enters economics when some people control what is scarce and highly desired and can thereby "force" people who want what is scarce to make significant sacrifices in order to get such scarcities. This "power" is an important concept in economics.

Here is the skeleton for some other organizing ideas:

- *Mathematics* as the development of a language for quantification;
- *Algebra* as arithmetic with unknowns;
- *Sociology* as the study of how the life of humans is shaped by the groups in which they are members;
- *Physics* as the study of mass and energy and the interrelations between the two;
- *Philosophy* as the study of ultimate questions and their reasoned answers;
- *Biochemistry* as the study of the chemistry of life at the molecular level.

8.6   *Think for Yourself*

GETTING THE KEY IDEA

For practice, attempt to formulate the basic idea behind history, economics, or any other discipline. Explain that idea to a friend. Encourage him or her to ask you questions. See if you can explain the significance of understanding the underlying idea behind a subject as an important first step in understanding the subject—and that every concept within the subject must be integrated into this key organizing idea. (We recommend that you use textbooks and/or encyclopedias in formulating core concepts.)

FIGURE OUT THE FORM OF THINKING ESSENTIAL TO COURSES OR SUBJECTS

The organizing concept behind a course is often the organizing concept behind a subject or discipline. If you understand this core concept, you should be able to formulate the eight central structures that define any form of thought:

1. What are the *goals* or objectives of the course or discipline?
2. What *questions* or problems will be central?
3. What *concepts* will be fundamental?
4. What *information* will I use in reasoning well within the subject?
5. What *point of view* or frame of reference do I need to learn to reason within?
6. What *assumptions* define the course or discipline?
7. What kinds of *conclusions* will I need to learn how to reason to?
8. What are the pay-offs *(implications)* of reasoning well within this discipline?

If we are correct in what we said about all subjects being forms of thought, each of your classes offers an invitation to think within one or more of those forms. Your ability to reason well within any subject will directly depend upon your ability to understand the *thinking* that defines the subject, to think the kind of thinking that professionals in the discipline think.

Consider the following thinking on the part of a student taking a course in history:

> To do well in this course, I must begin to think historically. I must read the textbook not as a bunch of disconnected stuff to remember but, instead, as the thinking of the historian. I must begin to think like a historian myself. I must begin to be clear about historical purposes. (What are historians trying to accomplish?) I must begin to ask historical questions (and recognize the historical questions being asked in the lectures and textbook). I must begin to sift through historical information, drawing some historical conclusions. I must begin to question where historical information comes from.
>
> I must notice the historical interpretations that historians form to give meaning to historical information. I must question those interpretations (at least sufficiently to understand them). I must begin to question the implications of various historical interpretations and begin to see how historians reason to their conclusions. I must begin to look at the world as historians do, to develop a historical viewpoint. I will read each chapter in the textbook, looking explicitly for the elements of thought in that chapter. I will actively ask historical questions in class from a critical-thinking perspective. I will begin to pay attention to my own historical thinking in my everyday life. In short, I will try to make historical thinking a more explicit and prominent part of my thinking.

Students who approach history classes as historical thinking begin to understand the historical dimension of other subjects as well. For example, they begin to recognize that every subject itself has a history and that the present state of the subject is a product of its historical evolution. What's more, historically thinking students notice the overlap between history as a study of the relatively recent past of humans (in the last 30,000 years) and the much longer history of humans (canvassed in anthropology). They are able to place these last 30,000 years (which seem like such a long time when we first think about it) into the larger historical perspective of anthropology, which begins its study of the human past some 25,000,000 years ago when our ancestors were small, hairy, apelike creatures who used tools such as digging sticks and clubs, walked upright, carried their tools, and lived on plant food.

Further, they see this longer history as breaking down into stages: from hunting and gathering civilizations to agricultural civilizations to industrial civilizations to post-industrial civilizations. And that's not all. They then are able to take this historical perspective and put it into a still larger historical view by shifting from anthropological thinking to geographical thinking. They realize that human history is itself a small part of a much older history, that of mammals, and that the age of mammals was preceded by an age of reptiles, and that age by the age of coal plants, and that age by the age of fish, and that by the age of mollusks. They then can take the next step and grasp that geological history, even though reaching back thousands of millions of years, is comparatively short when compared to that of the solar system, and that of the solar system is comparatively short when compared to the galaxy, and that of the galaxy is comparatively short when compared to the history of the universe itself.

The capacity to think historically in larger and larger time spans continues to develop as the study of all subjects is transformed by a developing sense of the drama of time itself. Historical thinkers then are able to shift from history to pre-history, from pre-history to anthropological history, from anthropological history to geological history, and from geological history to astronomical history. In this ever expanding perspective, the history of human knowledge is pitifully short: a milli-second geologically, a milli-milli-second astronomically. Only a second ago, astronomically speaking, did a species emerge—*Homo sapiens*, which drives itself and creates the conditions to which it itself must adapt, in new and unpredictable ways. Only a milli-second ago did a species emerge that has the capacity, but not the propensity, to think critically.

8.7 *Think for Yourself*

DEVELOPING YOUR THINKING

Examine in detail the extract quoting a student thinking about history (see p. 156). Write out some thinking of your own about any subject you are studying. Construct parallel sentences if you wish, but try to begin to see how each of the parts fits and contributes to an organized way of understanding a body of content and learning within any system of thought.

Then read and explain to a classmate or a friend what you wrote. Encourage him or her to ask you questions whenever what you say is not clear. Only when you can accurately articulate the logic of a course in your own words and elaborate on that logic can you begin to use it in your thinking. Once you finish, you can begin to think about how your thinking within this discipline can help you gain insights into other disciplines as well.

THINK WITHIN THE LOGIC OF THE SUBJECT

Once you have some sense of what you are aiming at as a whole, when you can articulate the key organizing idea within a subject, begin to plan your learning in parts, in light of the order or sequence in which content is being presented in the class and in the textbook. Then go to class armed with questions generated by reading your class notes and the textbook. You also might read encyclopedia entries for help with the basic logic of a subject. Some possible start-up questions are:

What is the main *goal* of studying this subject?

What are people in this field trying to accomplish?

What kinds of *questions* do they ask? What kinds of problems do they try to solve?

What sorts of *information* or data do they gather?

How do they go about gathering information in ways that are distinctive to this field?

What is the most basic idea, *concept*, or theory in this field?

How should studying this field affect my *view* of the world?

How are the products of this field used in everyday life?

These questions can be contextualized for any given class day, chapter in the text-book, and dimension of study. For example, on any given day you might ask one or more of the following questions:

What is our main *goal* today?

What are we trying to accomplish?

What kinds of *questions* are we asking? What kinds of problems are we trying to solve?

What sort of *information* or data do we need?

How can we get that information?

What is the most basic idea, *concept*, or theory that we need to understand to solve the problem we are most immediately posing?

How should we look at this problem? What *point of view* should we adopt?

How does this problem relate to everyday life?

8.8 *Think for Yourself*

ASKING GOOD QUESTIONS

Using these questions as a stimulus for your thinking, write out, for any class you are taking, a series of questions that enable you to think your way into the subject of the course. Compare your questions with the questions of another student.

A CASE: THE LOGIC OF BIOCHEMISTRY

Let us now take one discipline and explicate its logic by analyzing some key passages from the kind of text you might find in a book on the subject. Consider the following quote:

> [In biochemistry] . . . attention is directed to the problems of finding out how molecular events underlie macroscopic phenomena, with special reference to the modes of action of vitamins, drugs, and genetic factors. One kind of job that biochemists undertake is, of course, to isolate compounds from living things and determine their structures. In this they share the preoccupation of other kinds of biologists with spatial form.
>
> Biochemistry includes a sort of submicroscopic anatomy that elucidates structure on the minute scale of molecules. The classical anatomists cut up bodies to describe the parts of which they are made insofar as they are visible to the naked eye. Microscopy revealed a whole new world of structure and organization smaller than this, and . . . cells became the focus of interest. With the advance of chemistry, it gradually became possible to tackle biological architecture even on the molecular scale.
>
> The grand strategy remains the same—a better understanding of living things in terms of their constituent parts. The tactics, however, . . . depend on the order of size of the parts being examined. For gross anatomy, the scalpel is appropriate; for cellular structure, the microscope; for parts as small as molecules, the relevant techniques are those we call chemical. . . . Seen in this light, biochemistry is the logical extrapolation of dissection. The idea is epitomized in the expression "molecular biology." . . .

Merely to determine structure, however, is far from the summit of the ambitions of biochemists. They are interested not only in what the constituents of living things are like, but also in what they do—in the way that chemical processes underlie the more obvious vital manifestations. The continuous change that is one of the most striking characteristics of life rests on unceasing chemical activity inside living organisms. Biochemistry thus continues another classical tradition of biology in linking form with function. Like anatomy divorced from physiology, static divorced from dynamic biochemistry . . . fails to . . . increase man's power over nature. Life, after all, is a matter of keeping events going, not only of maintaining structures; and biochemists seek to elucidate events as well as structures by isolation.

By and large, then, while the techniques of biochemistry are chemical, its problems are the basic ones of biology. Chemistry is its means, biology its end. It is the extreme extension of that approach to the phenomena of life that seek to explain them in terms of the sub-units of which living organisms are composed. Of this kind of biological analysis, it represents the ultimate state—ultimate because pushing the analysis a stage further, from the molecular level down to the atomic, leaves no characteristically biological kind of organization, the atoms being the same in the inorganic realm. . . . Biochemistry concentrates on the farthest removal from immediate biological reality; insofar as it concerns itself with molecules, it remains remote from intact organisms. Data on the molecular level have to be related to observations made on more highly organized, less disrupted systems. (Jevons, 1964)

Biochemical Goals

It is clear from this passage that the goals of biochemistry are to determine the biochemical foundations of life and, through those means, to develop a rational chemotherapy. It aims to be a fundamental kind of biology, to use chemistry and events on the molecular scale, typified by proteins and single enzyme reactions, and then "moves on to their collaboration and organization above the molecular level in subcellular particles."

Biochemical Questions

The chemical concepts address the phenomena of life: From isolated molecules and questions, biochemistry is concerned with the questions: What are we made of? How do our bodies work? What is life? More particularly: How do molecular events underlie macroscopic phenomena of life? What compounds underlie living things? What is their structure? And what do they do?

How do vitamins work in the body? How do drugs work? How do genetic factors influence both? What molecular parts of living organisms are the special concern of biochemistry? (What are proteins, carbohydrates, and fats? What do they do? What are nucleic acids? What do they do?) How do enzymes catalyze virtually every reaction in living organisms? What is the role of enzymes in biological thought? How can we understand the biochemical unity of living matter? What is the similarity of yeast and muscle? What do proteins do inside living organisms? How can we correlate observations made at different levels of organization? How can we design drugs and create a rational chemotherapy? How can we produce drugs that target undesirable events in living creatures?

Biochemical Information

From the questions above, we can begin to see the kinds of information that biochemists seek: information about proteins and enzymes as the kind of chemical units out of which life is constructed, about the process of catalysis as the means by which key chemical reactions essential to the construction of life take place, information about artificial lifelike reactions (such as the study of a single enzyme reaction in a test tube), information about the variety of enzymes in living cells, about the molecular structures within cells, about multi-enzyme systems and how they operate, and so on.

Biochemical Judgments

From the biochemical information above, biochemists clearly seek to make judgments about the important properties of enzymes, their protein nature, the agents that make things happen in living organisms, metabolism, the complex process of maintenance and growth of which life basically consists.

Biochemical Concepts

From the biochemical judgments above, we have to understand a number of essential concepts to understand the logic of biochemistry: the concept of levels of organization of life processes (at the molecular level, at the subcellular particle level, at the cellular level, at the organ level, and at the level of the total organism); the concept of life structures and life processes; the concept of the dynamics of life; the concept of proteins, enzymes, catalysis, metabolism as reducible to a consecutive series of enzyme-catalyzed reactions; the concept of the unity of life processes amid a diversity of life forms; and so on.

Biochemical Assumptions

From the biochemical concepts above, some key assumptions behind biochemical thinking are that life has biochemical foundations, that these foundations are found at the molecular level, that the techniques of chemistry are most fitting for the study of life at the molecular level, that it is possible to use chemical concepts to explain life, that it is possible to analyze and discover the structure and dynamics of isolated molecules and events on the molecular scale, that proteins and enzymes are key agents in fundamental life processes, that enzyme reactions are crucial to understanding life, that it is possible, ultimately, to develop a rational chemotherapy that can be used in medicine and everyday life planning, to kill unwanted life processes while strengthening or maintaining desirable ones.

Biochemical Implications

The present logic of biochemistry has specific and general implications. The specific implications have to do with the kind of questioning, the kind of information-gathering and information-interpreting processes that biochemists are using today. (For example, the state of the field implies the importance of focusing questions and analysis on the concepts above, of seeking key answers at the molecular level, involving proteins, enzymes, and catalyzed chemical reactions.) The general implications are that, if modern biochemical theory is on the right track, we will be increasingly able to enhance human and other forms of life and diminish disease and other undesirable states (by application of chemotherapy).

Biochemical Point of View

The biochemical viewpoint is directed at the molecular level of life and sees that level as providing for the most fundamental disclosures about the nature, function, and foundations of life. It sees the essential techniques to be chemical. It sees the essential problems to be biological. It sees life processes at the molecular level to be highly unified and consistent. It sees life processes at the whole-animal level to be highly diversified. It sees the processes at the molecular level to be the key, along with genetics, to the explanation of diversity at the macro-level.

Clearly, as soon as we understand the basic logic of biochemistry and situate ourselves somewhere in a course in biochemistry, the questions we bring to class will be contextualizations of this logic for the following generic types:

What is our main goal today?

What are we trying to accomplish?

What kinds of questions are we asking? What kinds of problems are we trying to solve?

What sort of information or data do we need?

How can we get that information?

What is the most basic idea, concept, or theory that we need to understand to solve the problem we are posing most immediately?

How should we look at this problem?

How does this problem relate to everyday life?

On one day the class may be focusing on a particular concept such as catalysis, on another day big molecules, on another day subcellular particles, on another coenzymes, on another energy transactions, on another DNA. Understanding the overall logic of biochemistry will enable you to make sense of where you are and why it is significant and how to relate it to what came before and what will come after.

MAKE THE DESIGN OF THE COURSE WORK FOR YOU

At the beginning of any course you take, ask yourself: How am I going to learn so as to make the design of the class work for me? What am I going to do to get actively involved? How am I going to develop essential insights, understandings, knowledge, and abilities? How am I going to learn to reason my way to the answers to questions in the field?

Early in the course, seek an explanation of the most fundamental concept of the course. As you proceed through the course, you should seek to integrate all features of the course into a comprehensive understanding, to see the course, and the subject, as a comprehensive whole.

EXHIBIT 8.2 *The logic of science.*

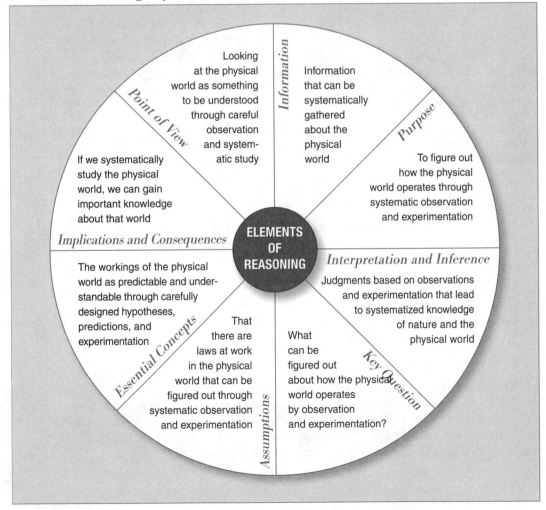

8.9 *Think for Yourself*

WRITING OUT THE LOGIC OF A COURSE

Using the example of Biochemistry, as well as the more abbreviated logic of American History on pages 164–165, write out the logic of a course you are now taking or have taken in the past. Use textbooks, encyclopedias, and other resources as references. You might refer to Exhibits 8.2–8.7, which give the basic logic of several subjects.

EXHIBIT 8.3 *The logic of history.*

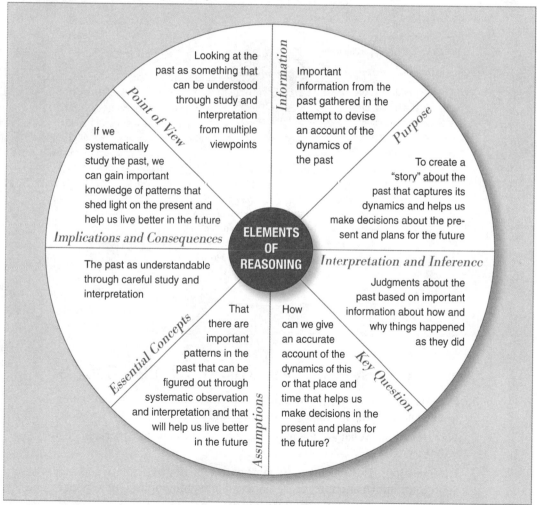

EXHIBIT 8.4 *The logic of business.*

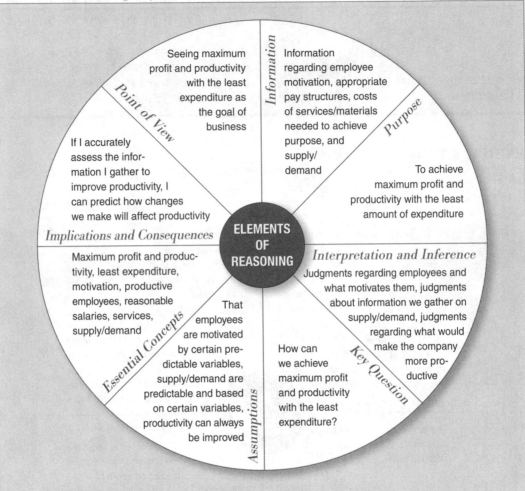

Sample Course American History, 1600–1800

1. **Purpose.** The purpose of the course is to think historically about the major trends and patterns in American History, 1600–1800.

2. **Key question.** What are the major patterns and trends in American History, 1600–1800?

3. **Information.** The students will work with a variety of primary and secondary sources of information: records, diaries, letters, biographies, newspapers, and historical accounts from textbooks and articles.

4. **Skills of interpretation.** The students will learn how to gather and interpret data from a variety of historical sources.

5. **Essential concepts.** The students will need to learn how to use basic historical, economic, political, and religious concepts, as well as those from social life and values.

6. **Assumptions.** The fundamental assumption behind this course is that it is possible for entry-level students to gain insight into the patterns and events in American life, 1600–1800, that shed light on contemporary problems.

7. **Implications.** Students who reason well about events in 17th- and 18th-century American life should be able to see connections with events in the 20th century.

8. **Point of view.** Students will learn how to reason as both a conservative and a liberal historian, integrating economic, political, and social analyses.

EXHIBIT 8.5 *The logic of abnormal psychology.*

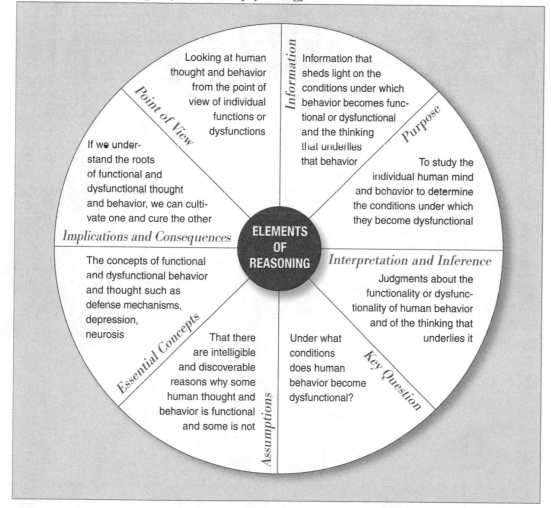

EXHIBIT 8.6 *The logic of philosophy.*

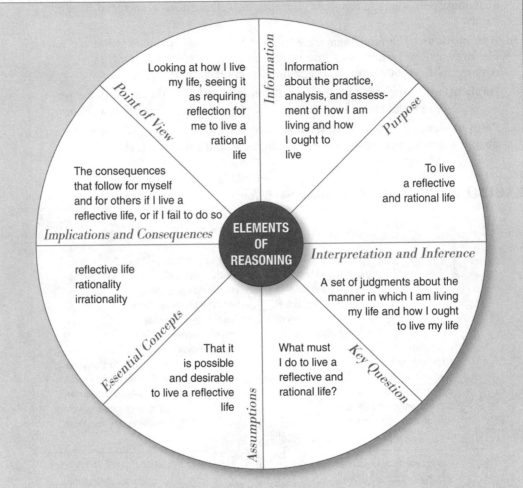

EXHIBIT 8.7 *The logic of sociology.*

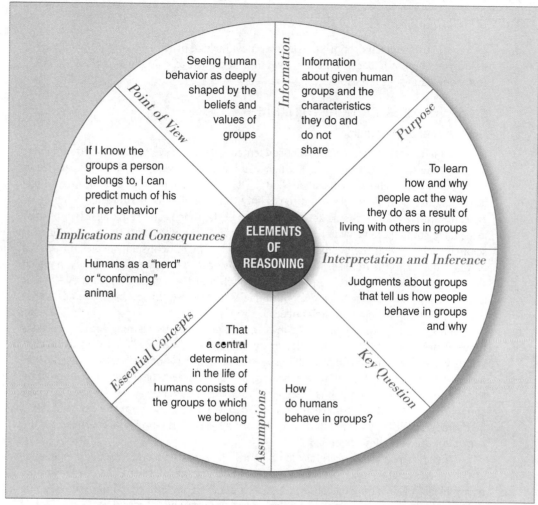

8.10   *Think for Yourself*

EVALUATING THE LOGIC OF A COURSE

xamine the course description below for a course in Critical Thinking. To what extent do you think it is based on the conception of critical thinking in this book? Support your conclusions with reasons.

CLASS SYLLABUS: CRITICAL THINKING

Key Concept of the Course

This course is entirely and exclusively concerned with the development of potential capacities that all of you have, even though you have not developed them—capacities in that part of your mind known as your "intellect." Most people don't develop their intellect. They use it ineffectively and often mainly to rationalize or justify their infantile or egocentric drives. Most people are not in charge of their ideas and thinking. Most of their ideas have come into their mind without their having thought about them. They unconsciously pick up what the people around them think. They unconsciously pick up what is on television or in the movies. They unconsciously absorb ideas from the family in which they were reared. They are the products, through and through, of forces they did not choose. They reflect those forces without understanding them. They are like puppets that don't know their strings are being pulled.

To become a critical thinker is to reverse that process—by learning to practice skills that enable one to start to take charge of the ideas that run one's life. It is to think consciously and deliberately and skillfully in ways that transform oneself. It is to begin to remake one's own mind. It is to run for the first time one's inner workings and to understand the "system" one is running. It is to develop a mind that is analogous to the body of a person who is physically fit. It is like an excellent dancer who can perform any dance that can be choreographed. It is like a puppet that discovers the strings, and figures out how to gain control of the way they are pulled.

Whenever you are doing a task in or for the class, ask yourself: Would an independent observer watching me closely conclude that I am engaged in taking charge of my mind, of my ideas, of my thinking, or would such a person conclude that I am merely going through the motions of formally doing an assignment, trying to get by with some rotely memorized formula or procedure?

General Plan

The class will focus on practice, not on lecture. It will emphasize your figuring out things using your own mind, not memorizing what is in a textbook. On a typical class day, you will be in small groups practicing "disciplined" thinking. You will be regularly responsible for assessing your own work using criteria and standards discussed in class. If at any time in the semester you feel unsure about your grade, you should request an assessment from the professor. For every class day, you will have a written assignment that involves disciplined thinking. Out of class, you will enter disciplined reflections in a journal, using a special format.

READING, WRITING, SPEAKING, LISTENING, AND THINKING

Let us turn now to reading, writing, speaking, and listening. Clearly, these activities are important to your success as a student. If you are a skilled *reader,* you are able to master a subject from a textbook alone, without benefit of lectures or class discussion. Many excellent readers have become educated through reading alone.

Or consider *writing.* The art of writing well forces us to make explicit the ideas we understand and how we understand those ideas in relation to each other. Often, we have the illusion that we understand an idea until we try to place our understanding into written words. Suddenly we see problems. We discover that we cannot state what we understand clearly, or we have trouble elaborating, or we find it difficult to give apt examples or illustrations. Writing to learn is a powerful tool in learning deeply and well. Those who cannot write out what they are learning are often poor learners.

Speaking is another powerful tool in learning. If we can explain to another person what we are learning, we typically take our learning to a deeper level. This is why we have the saying, "In teaching you will learn." Entering into an oral dialogue with other learners is a powerful tool in learning—if the speaking in that dialogue is skilled. Of course, poorly discussed ideas may lead to "activated ignorance," the illusion that we understand when we do not. In this case, speaking solidifies misunderstanding rather than furthering understanding. For this reason, you want to make sure that you acquire oral skills so you can express yourself well, ask appropriate questions, and assess your learning.

Listening well is probably the least understood of the four modalities of communication we are considering. Much student listening is unskilled—passive, associational, unquestioned, superficial. Poor listening leads to incomplete internalization and even to blatant misunderstanding.

Reading, writing, speaking, and listening are all modes of *thinking.* Your primary goals as a student should be to learn how to think like a good reader (while reading), like a good writer (while writing), like an effective speaker (while speaking), and like an insightful listener (while listening). Happily, these four different modes of thinking are interrelated, so that learning to take charge of one is significantly related to learning to take charge of the other three. This is true precisely because each is a form of thinking and all forms of thinking share generic characteristics—as we have emphasized throughout this book.

Irrespective of whether you are reading, writing, speaking, or listening, you want your thinking to be clear, precise, accurate, relevant, responsive to complexity, as broad as the issue requires, and focused on the appropriate point(s) of view. Good readers, writers, speakers, listeners, and thinkers recognize that they each have agendas, deal with questions and problems, utilize information, make inferences and draw conclusions, make assumptions, and reason within a point of view. And they consider the implications and consequences of their reasoning.

Consider writing as an example. All intellectual deficiencies in writing can be explained as deficiencies in the elements of thinking reflected. These deficiencies are, typically, in violations of the standards for thinking. Consider:

- When you write sentences that can be interpreted in many different ways and you do not make clear which meaning you intend, you demonstrate that you are writing, and presumably thinking, in a vague way.

- When you do not give concrete examples and illustrations to make your point clear, you demonstrate that you do not know how to clarify your thought, or for some reason have chosen not to.

- When you do not make clear—with appropriate transitional words and critical vocabulary—the logical relations between the sentences you write, you make evident that you are not thinking in terms of the logic of your thought, that you do not fully understand the structure of your own reasoning.

- When you do not analyze key concepts and lay bare their logic, you make evident that you are weak at conceptual analysis.

- When you do not make clear the question or issue you are dealing with or you drift, for no apparent reason, from one issue to another, you reveal that you lack the intellectual discipline and focus to appreciate what each issue you raise requires of you. You demonstrate that you lack a sense of relevance.

- When you make sweeping judgments about a philosophical position that you have not sufficiently analyzed empathetically, you demonstrate intellectual arrogance.

Take reading as another example. All intellectual deficiencies in reading can be explained as deficiencies in the elements of thinking reflected, typically, in violations of the standards for thinking. Consider:

- When you are unable to identify the *agenda* of a text, there is a problem in your reading (or in the text).

- When you are unable to identify the *key questions* of a text, there is a problem in your reading (or in the text).

- When you are unable to identify the *key information* in a text, there is a problem in your reading (or in the text).

- When you are unable to identify the *key concepts* in a text, there is a problem in your reading (or in the text).

- When you are unable to identify the *key assumptions* in a text, there is a problem in your reading (or in the text).

- When you are unable to identify the *key implications* in a text, there is a problem in your reading (or in the text).

- When you are unable to identify the *key point of view* in a text, there is a problem in your reading (or in the text).

Speaking and listening can be analyzed in a similar way. Let us now apply these principles to the reading of an article or essay.

FIGURE OUT THE LOGIC
OF AN ARTICLE OR ESSAY

One important skill for understanding an essay or article is the analysis of the parts of the author's reasoning. Once you have done this, you can evaluate the author's reasoning using intellectual standards.

8.11 *Think for Yourself*

ANALYZING THE LOGIC OF AN ARTICLE

Take an article that you have been assigned to read for class, completing the logic of it using the template below. When you become practiced in using this approach, you will have a powerful intellectual tool for understanding the reasoning of any author.

THE LOGIC OF "(NAME OF THE ARTICLE)"

1. The main *purpose* of this article is _____. *(Here you are trying to state as accurately as possible the author's purpose for writing the article. What was the author trying to accomplish?)*

2. The key *question* that the author is addressing is _____. *(Your goal is to figure out the key question that was in the author's mind when he or she wrote the article. What was the key question the article addressed?)*

3. The most important *information* in this article is _____. *(You want to identify the key information the author used, or presupposed, in the article to support his or her main arguments. Here you are looking for facts, experiences, data the author is using to support his or her conclusions.)*

4. The main *inferences/conclusions* in this article are _____. *(You want to identify the most important conclusions the author comes to and presents in the article.)*

5. The key *concept(s)* we need to understand in this article is (are) _____. By this concept the author means _____. *(To identify the concept, ask yourself: What are the most important ideas that you would have to understand to understand the author's line of reasoning? Then elaborate briefly on what the author means by these concepts.)*

6. The main *assumption(s)* underlying the author's thinking is (are) _____. *(Ask yourself: What is the author taking for granted that might be questioned? The assumptions are generalizations that the author does not think he or she has to defend in the context of writing the article, and they are usually unstated. This is where the author's thinking logically begins.)*

7. a. If we take this line of reasoning seriously, the *implications* are _____. *(What consequences are likely to follow if people take the author's line of reasoning seriously? Here you are to follow the logical implications of the author's position.*

You should include implications that the author states, if you believe them to be logical, but you should do your best thinking to determine what you think the implications are.)

    b. If we fail to take this line of reasoning seriously, the *implications* are _____. *(What consequences are likely to follow if people ignore or reject the author's reasoning?)*

8. The main *point(s) of view* presented in this article is (are) _____. *(The main question you are trying to answer here is: What is the author looking at, and how is he or she seeing it? For example, in this book we are looking at education and seeing it as involving the development of intellectual skills. We also are looking at learning as the responsibility of students.)*

FIGURE OUT THE LOGIC OF A TEXTBOOK

Just as you can understand an essay or article by analyzing the parts of the author's reasoning, so can you figure out the logic of a textbook by focusing on the parts of the author's reasoning within the textbook. To understand the parts of the textbook author's reasoning, use the template in Think for Yourself 8.12, below.

8.12 *Think for Yourself*

FIGURING OUT THE LOGIC OF A TEXTBOOK

Using the template below, figure out the logic of a textbook from a current class you are taking or any textbook you choose. Be as detailed as is necessary for someone new to the field of study you are focused on to understand the logic of the textbook.

1. The main *purpose* of this textbook is _____. *(Here you are trying to determine the author's purpose for writing the textbook. What was the author trying to accomplish?)*

2. The key *question(s)* that the author is addressing in the textbook is (are) _____. *(You are trying to figure out the key question(s) in the author's mind when he or she wrote the textbook. What is the key question the textbook answers? Here, you might identify the broadest question the textbook answers, along with the most important sub-questions it focuses on.)*

3. The most important kinds of *information* in this textbook are _____. *(You want to identify the types of information the author uses in the textbook to support his or her main arguments [e.g., research results, observations, examples, experience].)*

4. The main *inferences/conclusions* in this textbook are _____. *(You want to identify the most important conclusions the author comes to and presents in the textbook. Focus on this question: What are the most important conclusions the author presents, conclusions that, if you understand them, shed important light on key beliefs in the field?)*

5. The key *concept(s)* we need to understand in this textbook is (are) _____. By these concepts, the author means _____. *(To identify these concepts, ask yourself: What*

are the most important ideas that you would have to understand to understand the textbook? Then precisely elaborate on what the author means by these basic concepts. Begin with the most fundamental concept presented, such as science, biology, or psychology. These usually can be found in the first chapter. Then identify the other significant concepts that are deeply tied into the most fundamental concept.)

6. The main *assumption(s)* underlying the author's thinking is (are) _____. (*Ask yourself: What is the author taking for granted that might be questioned? Assumptions are sometimes generalizations that the author does not think he or she has to defend in the context of writing the textbook. The assumptions are sometimes stated in the first chapter as the key assumptions underlying the subject area.*)

7. a. If people take the textbook seriously, the *implications* are _____. (*What consequences are likely to follow if readers take the textbook seriously? Here you are to follow the logical implications of the information/ideas in the textbook. You should include implications that the author argues for, if you believe them to be well-founded, but you should do your best thinking to determine what you think the implications are.*)

   b. If people fail to take the textbook seriously, the *implications* are _____. (*What consequences are likely to follow if the author's thinking is ignored in a situation when it is relevant?*)

8. The main *point(s) of view* presented in this textbook is (are) _____. (*The main question you are trying to answer here is: What is the author looking at, and how is he or she seeing it? For example, the author might be looking at science and seeing it as "our main tool in helping us better understand the physical world and how it operates."*)

CRITERIA FOR EVALUATING AN AUTHOR'S REASONING

Now that you have worked through the logic of an article or a textbook, or both, you are ready to assess the author's reasoning by focusing on how well the author uses each of the elements of reasoning within the article or book. Choose the logic of either the article or the textbook. For the one you choose, go through each of the elements, or parts, of the author's reasoning and evaluate them using the intellectual standards outlined here:

1. Focusing on the author's *purpose:* Is the purpose well-stated? Is it clear and justifiable?

2. Focusing on the key *question* that the written piece answers: Is the question at issue well-stated (or clearly implied)? Is it clear and unbiased? Does the expression of the question do justice to the complexity of the matter at issue? Are the question and purpose directly relevant to each other?

3. Focusing on the most important *information* the author presents: Does the writer cite relevant evidence, experiences, and information essential to the issue? Is the information accurate and directly relevant to the question at issue? Does the writer address the complexities of the issue?

4. Focusing on the most fundamental *concepts* at the heart of the author's reasoning: Does the writer clarify key concepts when necessary? Are the concepts used justifiably?

5. Focusing on the author's *assumptions:* Does the writer show a sensitivity to what he or she is taking for granted or assuming (insofar as those assumptions might reasonably be questioned)? Or does the writer use questionable assumptions without addressing problems that might be inherent in those assumptions?

6. Focusing on the most important *inferences* or conclusions in the written piece: Do the inferences and conclusions the author makes follow clearly from the information relevant to the issue, or does the author jump to unjustifiable conclusions? Does the author consider alternative conclusions where the issue is complex? Does the author use a sound line of reasoning to come to logical conclusions, or can you identify flaws in the reasoning somewhere?

7. Focusing on the author's *point of view:* Does the author show a sensitivity to alternative relevant points of view or lines of reasoning? Does he or she consider and respond to objections framed from other relevant points of view?

8. Focusing on *implications:* Does the writer show a sensitivity to the implications and consequences of the position he or she is taking?

A TEST TO REPEAT IN EVERY CLASS AND SUBJECT

We have shown how every academic field has its own logic, or system of meanings. To learn the field is to learn to think within the system. This is true whether one is talking of poems or essays, paintings or choreographed dances, histories or anthropological reports, experiments or scientific theories, philosophies or psychologies, specific events or general theories. Whether we are designing a new screwdriver or working out a perspective on religion, we must create a system of meanings that makes sense to us. To learn the system underlying a discipline is to create it in our mind. This requires that our thinking be permanently re-shaped and modified. As you study a subject, periodically ask yourself:

Can I explain the underlying system of ideas that defines this subject? (This is like writing the encyclopedia entry for it.)

Can I explain its most basic ideas to someone who doesn't understand it (answering their questions about it)?

Could I write a glossary of its most basic vocabulary (minimizing technical terms in my explanations of meaning)?

Have I written out the basic logic of the subject? (Its key goal is . . . etc.)

Can I compare and contrast the logic of the subject I am learning with that of other subjects I have learned?

To what extent can I relate this subject to significant problems in the world?

To what extent has thinking in this field helped me become more intellectually humble, perseverant, autonomous . . . ?

REDEFINE GRADES AS LEVELS OF THINKING AND LEARNING

The best learners, like the best thinkers, continually assess their learning against standards of excellence. Being passionate about learning, they welcome standards they can use to strive for excellence. The best learners are not dependent on instructors to tell them how well they are doing. They have universal criteria that they apply across all dimensions of learning. To the extent that you need instructors to tell you how well you are doing, and have no independent sense yourself, you are not thinking critically. The best learners avoid being overly dependent on teachers and, rather, seek to develop an independent, disciplined, thinking mind.

Each step in learning, like the process of thinking critically, is tied to a self-reflective step of self-assessment. As a skilled learner, you do not simply have goals in learning; you know what your goals are. Your primary goal is to think within the logic of the subject, to think like a scientist, to think like a psychologist, to think like an artist, and so forth.

The best learners seek to enter the foundations of any subject they study and use that foundation to understand everything else within the subject. They seek to understand the most fundamental questions asked within the subject. They seek to identify the most basic kinds of information used by professionals within the field, the most basic concepts the field employs, the most fundamental assumptions that underlie it, the most basic point of view that defines it.

The best learners do not memorize random bits and pieces of information. Their learning is problem- or question-based. But they do not simply state a problem; they assess that formulation for its clarity. They do not simply gather information; they gather it and check it for its relevance and significance. They do not simply form an interpretation; they check their interpretation to see what it is based on and whether that basis is adequate.

DEVELOP STRATEGIES FOR SELF-ASSESSMENT

In Chapter 5, you were introduced to a host of universal intellectual standards that you can use to assess your thinking independent of what you are thinking about. Here we look at more holistic standards for assessing your learning within subjects. Virtually every day of study, for example, you should seek to assess the quality of your work as a learner. You should use intellectual standards regularly and explicitly. But you should go farther. You also should regularly examine your learning to determine the extent to which you are constructing in your mind the system that defines the subject or subjects you are studying.

In what follows you will find a set of performance criteria that you can use in any course to assess your studying overall, irrespective of the specific subject. You can use these criteria to give yourself grades, independently of your instructor. Of course, your instructor may officially adopt these criteria as grade profiles in the class.

USE PROFILES TO ASSESS YOUR PERFORMANCE

Performance profiles for five levels of quality in thinking and learning are: exemplary student, high-performing student, mixed-quality student, low-performing student, and (alas) incompetent student. Your thinking stands at one of these levels in every class you take and can be shown—if we have adequate documentation of your thinking on the tests and assignments in the class.

Most students have no sense that these levels of performance exist, even though these profiles are based on common-denominator academic values. You should get into the habit of reviewing your work with these criteria in mind. If you do so, you will grow as a learner and thinker. If you learn how to routinely perform at the high-performing or exemplary level, you will do well in every class you take.

As you read through these profiles, notice that you can take any statement in the criteria—for example, the statement that the exemplary student

> often raises important questions and issues, analyzes key questions and problems clearly and precisely, recognizes key questionable assumptions, clarifies key concepts effectively, uses language in keeping with educated usage, frequently identifies relevant competing points of view, and demonstrates a commitment to reasoning carefully from clearly stated premises in the subject, as well as marked sensitivity to important implications and consequences.

—and transform that statement into specific questions about your own performance:

To what extent do I:

raise important questions and issues in the class?

analyze key questions and problems clearly and precisely?

recognize key assumptions?

clarify key concepts?

use language in keeping with educated usage?

identify competing points of view?

reason carefully from clearly stated premises?

note important implications and consequences?

Exemplary Students (Grade of A)

Exemplary performance in thinking (within academic subjects) implies excellence in thinking within the domain of a subject (e.g., sound historical thinking, sound biological thinking, sound mathematical thinking). It also involves developing a range of knowledge acquired through exercising thinking skills and abilities. Exemplary work, on the whole, is clear, precise, and well-reasoned and also insightful and well-informed. Basic terms and distinctions are learned at a level that implies insight into basic concepts and principles.

The exemplary student has internalized the basic intellectual standards appropriate to the assessment of his or her own work in a subject and is highly skilled at self-evaluation. Exemplary students regularly

raise important questions and issues,

analyze key questions and problems (clearly and precisely),

recognize questionable assumptions,

clarify key concepts effectively,

use language in keeping with educated usage,

identify relevant competing points of view,

display sensitivity to important implications and consequences, and

demonstrate a commitment to reasoning carefully from clearly stated premises in the subject.

Exemplary students display excellent reasoning and problem-solving within a field and work consistently at a high level of intellectual excellence. They usually interrelate ideas within and among fields of study. They regularly apply what they are learning to issues and problems in their lives.

High-Performing Students (Grade of B)

High performance in thinking-through a subject implies sound thinking within the domain of a subject along with the development of a range of knowledge acquired through the exercise of thinking skills and abilities. High-level student thinking is, on the whole, clear, precise, and well-reasoned, but sometimes lacks depth of insight (especially into opposing points of view). Basic terms and distinctions are learned at a level that implies comprehension of basic concepts and principles.

High-level students internalize the basic intellectual standards appropriate to the assessment of their thinking in a subject and demonstrate competence in self-evaluation. High-level students

often raise questions and issues,

commonly analyze questions and problems clearly and precisely,

recognize most questionable assumptions,

clarify key concepts well,

typically use language in keeping with educated usage,

commonly identify relevant competing points of view,

display sensitivity to many important implications and consequences, and

frequently demonstrate the beginnings of a commitment to reasoning carefully from clearly stated premises in a subject.

High-performing students display sound reasoning and problem-solving within a field and work consistently at a commendable level of intellectual performance. They often interrelate ideas within and among fields of study. They often apply what they are learning to issues and problems in their lives.

Mixed-Quality Students (Grade of C)

Thinking of mixed quality implies inconsistent performance within the domain of a subject and course, along with limited development of knowledge acquired through the exercise of thinking skills and abilities. The mixed-quality student often tries to use memorization as a substitute for understanding. Thinking of mixed quality is—inconsistently—clear, precise, and well-reasoned. Moreover, except rarely, it does not display depth of insight. Basic terms and distinctions are learned at a level that implies the beginnings of, but incomplete comprehension of, basic concepts and principles.

Although thinkers of mixed quality have internalized a few of the basic intellectual standards appropriate to the assessment of their own work in a subject, they demonstrate inconsistency in self-evaluation. Mixed-quality students

sometimes raise questions and issues,

sometimes analyze questions and problems clearly and precisely,

recognize some questionable assumptions,

clarify some concepts competently,

sometimes use language in keeping with educated usage,

sometimes identify relevant competing points of view,

sometimes demonstrate a clear commitment to reasoning carefully from clearly stated premises in a subject, and

are inconsistently sensitive to important implications and consequences.

Mixed-quality students display inconsistent reasoning and problem-solving within a field and work, at best, at a competent level of intellectual performance. They sometimes interrelate ideas within and among fields of study. They sometimes apply what they are learning to issues and problems in their lives.

Low-Performing Students (Grade of D or F)

Low-performing students reason poorly within the domain of a subject and course. On the whole, they try to get through courses by means of rote recall, attempting regularly to acquire knowledge by memorization rather than through comprehension and understanding. Low-performing students do not develop critical thinking skills or insights requisite to understanding course content. They produce work that is typically unclear, imprecise, and poorly reasoned. Low-performing students achieve competence only at the lowest order of performance. They often use basic terms and distinctions incorrectly, reflecting superficial or mistaken comprehension of basic concepts and principles.

Low-performing students have not internalized the basic intellectual standards appropriate to the assessment of their own work in a subject. They also do poorly in self-evaluation.

Low-performing students

rarely raise questions and issues,

superficially analyze questions and problems,

do not recognize their assumptions,

clarify concepts only partially,

rarely use language in keeping with educated usage,

rarely identify relevant competing points of view,

show no understanding of the importance of a commitment to reasoning carefully from clearly stated premises in a subject, and

are insensitive to important implications and consequences.

Low-performing work displays poor reasoning and problem-solving within a field and works, at best, at a deficient level of intellectual performance. Low-performing students fail to interrelate ideas within and among fields of study. They rarely apply what they are learning to issues and problems in their lives, because they fail to see any relationship between course content and real-life situations.

9.1 *Think for Yourself*

HOW WOULD YOU RATE YOURSELF AS A THINKER?

Now that you have read through the student profiles for each competency level, rate yourself as a student. Write a brief paper, completing and elaborating on the following statements:

1. I see myself at the following skill level as a student (exemplary, high-performing, mixed-quality, or low-performing):

2. I support my position with the following evidence from my work in one or more classes (examples should include excerpts from papers, etc. that directly relate to the skills discussed in the profiles. For example, if you say that you are a mixed-quality student, you might give an equal number of examples of written work that are clear, as well as unclear.):

3. To improve as a student, I need to do the following (focus on the skills discussed at the exemplary or high-performing level to formulate a plan):

APPLY STUDENT PROFILES TO ASSESS YOUR PERFORMANCE WITHIN SPECIFIC DISCIPLINES

As a thinker developing your ability to apply knowledge to new situations, you can apply the skill levels you have been learning in this chapter to any subject you study. To provide an example, we apply these competency levels to the study of psychology.

Exemplary Thinking as a Student of Psychology (Grade of A)

Exemplary thinking as a student of psychology demonstrates real achievement in grasping what psychological thinking is, along with the clear development of a range of specific psychological thinking skills or abilities. The work at the end of the course is clear, precise, and well-reasoned. In exemplary work, the student uses psychological terms and distinctions effectively. The work demonstrates a mind that is taking charge of psychological ideas, assumptions, and inferences.

The exemplary student of psychology

analyzes psychological issues clearly and precisely,

formulates psychological information accurately,

distinguishes the relevant from the irrelevant,

recognizes key questionable psychological assumptions,

clarifies key psychological concepts and checks their use for justifiability,

uses psychological language in keeping with established professional usage, while at the same time questioning inappropriate conceptualizations of human behavior within the field of psychology,

thinks within competing psychological points of view, accurately representing each view,

shows a pronounced tendency to reason carefully from clearly stated premises, and

displays sensitivity to important psychological implications and consequences.

Exemplary work displays excellent psychological reasoning and problem-solving skills and is consistently at a high level of intellectual excellence. Students functioning at the exemplary level routinely interrelate ideas within psychology, and between psychology and related fields of study such as history, sociology, anthropology, and philosophy. When relevant, they regularly apply psychological principles and concepts to issues and problems in their lives.

High-Performing Thinking as a Student of Psychology (Grade of B)

Students of psychology who function at the high-performing level demonstrate achievement in grasping what psychological thinking is, as well as in a range of specific psychological thinking skills and abilities. At the end of the course, high-performing work is, on the whole, clear, precise, and well-reasoned, though with occasional lapses into weak reasoning. On the whole, the high-performing student of psychology uses psychological terms and distinctions effectively. The student's work demonstrates a mind that is beginning to take charge of psychological ideas, assumptions, and inferences.

The high-performing student of psychology

often raises important questions and issues,

commonly analyzes psychological questions and problems clearly and precisely,

recognizes most questionable psychological assumptions,

often clarifies key psychological concepts and checks their use for justifiability,

typically uses psychological language in keeping with established professional usage, while at the same time often questioning inappropriate conceptualizations of human behavior within the field of psychology,

commonly thinks within competing psychological points of view,

displays sensitivity to many important psychological implications and consequences, and

frequently demonstrates a commitment to reasoning carefully from clearly stated psychological premises.

High-performing students of psychology demonstrate sound psychological reasoning and problem-solving skills. They often interrelate ideas within psychology, and between psychology and related fields of study such as history, sociology, anthropology, and philosophy. When relevant, they often apply psychological principles and concepts to issues and problems in their lives.

Mixed-Quality Thinking as a Student of Psychology (Grade of C)

Students of psychology who function at the mixed-quality level illustrate some, but inconsistent, achievement in grasping what psychological thinking is, along with the development of modest psychological thinking skills and abilities. Mixed-quality work at the end of the course shows some emerging psychological thinking skills, but pronounced weaknesses as well. Though some assignments are done reasonably well, others are done poorly, or at best are mediocre. Lapses in reasoning are more than occasional. Though psychological terms and distinctions are sometimes used effectively, they are sometimes used ineffectively. Only on occasion does a thinker of mixed quality display a mind taking charge of psychological ideas, assumptions, and inferences. Only occasionally does mixed-quality thinking display intellectual discipline and clarity.

The thinker of mixed quality sometimes

analyzes psychological issues clearly and precisely,

formulates psychological information accurately,

distinguishes the relevant from the irrelevant,

recognizes key questionable assumptions,

clarifies key psychological concepts effectively, and can identify when psychological concepts are being used justifiably,

uses psychological language in keeping with established professional usage,

identifies relevant psychological competing points of view,

recognizes important psychological implications and consequences, and

reasons carefully from clearly stated psychological premises.

Sometimes the thinker of mixed quality (in psychology) seems to be simply going through the motions of the assignment, carrying out the form without getting into the spirit of it. On the whole, work of mixed quality shows only modest (and inconsistent) psychological reasoning and problem-solving skills and often displays weak reasoning and problem-solving skills. Students at the mixed-quality level sometimes interrelate ideas within psychology, and between psychology and related fields of study. When relevant, mixed-quality students sometimes apply psychological principles and concepts to issues and problems in their lives.

Low-Performing Thinking as a Student of Psychology (Grade of D or F)

Low-performing work shows little, if any, understanding of psychological thinking, and, at best, demonstrates low-level psychological thinking skills or abilities. Low-performing work at the end of the course shows only occasional (if any) psychological thinking skills combined with frequent uncritical psychological thinking. Most assignments are done poorly. There is little evidence that the student is reasoning through the assignment. Usually the student seems to be merely going through the motions of the assignment, carrying out the form without getting into the spirit of it. Low-performing work in psychology rarely shows any effort to take charge of psychological ideas, assumptions, and inferences. In general, low-performing thought lacks discipline and clarity.

In low-level work, the student generally

does not analyze psychological issues clearly and precisely,

does not formulate psychological information accurately,

does not distinguish the relevant from the irrelevant,

does not recognize key questionable assumptions,

does not clarify key psychological concepts effectively,

does not use psychological language in keeping with established professional usage,

does not identify relevant competing psychological points of view, and

does not reason carefully from clearly stated premises or recognize important implications and consequences.

Low-performing work rarely, if ever, demonstrates sound psychological reasoning and problem-solving skills and frequently displays poor reasoning and problem-solving skills. Students at this level almost never interrelate ideas within psychology, and between psychology and related fields of study. They rarely, if ever, apply psychological principles and concepts to issues and problems in their lives.

9.2 *Think for Yourself*

SELF-EVALUATION IN A SUBJECT YOU ARE STUDYING

Transform the example of thinking within the field of psychology that you have just read into a set of questions that you can use to assess the quality of your learning within a subject you are currently studying or have studied. For example, if you are taking a course in biology, you might formulate the following types of questions:

- Am I gaining command over a range of biological thinking skills and abilities that I use to acquire biological knowledge?

- Is my work (papers, exams) clear, precise, and well-reasoned?

- Am I gaining command of the key biological terms and distinctions?

- To what extent have I developed the ability to identify and solve fundamental biological problems?

Then answer each question, stating your answer, then elaborating upon it and giving an example of it.

CONCLUSION

To be a skilled learner, you must be a skilled thinker. To learn most effectively in the context of college, you must take charge of your learning. You must design it—plan it out. You plan learning by becoming clear as to what your goals are, what questions you have to—or want to—answer, what information you need to acquire, what concepts you need to learn, what you need to focus on, and how you need to understand it.

In this chapter we have laid out profiles that you can use throughout your college experience to assess how well you are functioning as a learner in each class you take, within each academic subject you study. With these profiles clearly in mind, you become the master of your own assessment in each class. You realize that your ability to think within a subject is determined by the *skills you develop* in thinking-through that subject, not by a grade the instructor gives you. Simply, you take command of your learning. You know how well you are doing in thinking through the content because you can assess your own development. You develop as an independent thinker.

MAKE DECISIONS AND SOLVE PROBLEMS

Everyday life is an endless sequence of decision-making and problem-solving. The quality of the decisions we make coupled with our competence in solving problems largely determine the quality of our lives. Most people work through decisions and problems in an intuitive way. They go with their first reactions and conclusions. They have no systematic way by which to deal with decisions and problems. Sometimes this haphazard approach works. But sometimes it doesn't. When we bring critical thinking tools into our decision-making and problem-solving processes, we are more likely to solve the problems we face and make rational decisions. In this chapter we provide an integrated approach to working-through decisions and problems. First we address decision-making, then problem-solving. As you work your way through the chapter, note the overlap between the two processes.

MAKING DECISIONS

To live is to act. To act is to decide. Every day you are faced with a myriad of decisions. Some of the decisions are small and inconsequential, and some are large and life-determining. When our pattern of decision-making is rational, we live a rational life. When our pattern of decision-making is irrational, we live an irrational life. Rational decisions maximize the quality of life without violating the rights or harming the well-being of others. Rational decisions maximize our chances for happiness, successful living, and fulfillment. When applied to decision-making, critical thinking enhances the rationality of our decisions by raising the pattern of decision-making to the level of conscious and deliberate choice.

No one *deliberately* chooses to live an irrational life. Many, however, *subconsciously* choose to live an irrational or unethical life. In doing so, they maximize their chances for unhappiness and frustration, or they do harm to others in seeking their own advantage.

Evaluating Patterns in Decision-Making

How can we determine the extent to which our decision-making is irrational? In the first place, our irrational decisions often are those we make without realizing we are making them. Let us begin, then, with an analysis of our subconscious decisions.

If you ask yourself how many decisions you made yesterday, you probably will be puzzled as to how to determine the number. In a sense, the absolute number is unimportant. What is important is to recognize the categories of decisions you made and find a way to begin to identify and evaluate patterns within those categories.

We all have basic human needs. We all make choices as to how to satisfy those needs. Further, we all have chosen values and make choices in relation to those values. We all assume that our basic values support our welfare and contribute to our well-being. No one says, even to himself or herself, "I choose to live in accordance with values that undermine my welfare and harm me."

And we all make choices that have implications for the well-being of others. When we make decisions that undermine or harm others' well-being, we make unethical decisions. When we make decisions or choose values that undermine or harm our well-being, we make irrational decisions.

Some common patterns of irrational or unethical decision-making are:

- deciding to behave in ways that undermine our welfare;
- deciding not to engage in activities that contribute to our long-term welfare;
- deciding to behave in ways that undermine another's welfare;
- deciding to associate with people who encourage us to act against our own welfare or the welfare of others.

These categories sound odd, for why would anyone make self-defeating or self-harming decisions? But there is a general answer to this query: These decisions are made for immediate gratification and short-term gain. This becomes more apparent when we look at more specific categories within these categories. For example, under "Deciding to behave in ways that undermine one's welfare" are:

- deciding to eat foods that are unhealthy (foods that shorten our lives or lead to disease or negative qualities of life);
- deciding to smoke, drink to excess, or use drugs that are harmful;
- deciding not to exercise or engage in adequate aerobic activities.

Clearly, we make these decisions with immediate pleasure and the short run uppermost in our minds. Indeed, our mind is "wired" for immediate and short-run gratification. Taking into account the long-term requires reflection. We must raise our behavior to the level, as Piaget put it, of *conscious realization*. Of course, we can be conscious of a problem without taking the steps to correct it. Putting our long-term insights into action requires self-discipline and will power.

When we identify a pattern of irrational decision-making in our life, we have discovered what sometimes is called a bad habit. When we replace a pattern of irrational decision-making with a rational pattern, we replace a bad habit with a good habit. The replacement is at the level of action. Because habits account for hundreds or thousands of decisions over an extended time, we can improve our decision-making significantly by identifying our bad habits and replacing them with good habits. For example, we can make hundreds of rational decisions over time by making the decision to eat healthy foods and not eat unhealthy foods. Once that decision is manifested in behavior over an extended time, it results in a productive habit.

"Big" Decisions

There are two kinds of big decisions to learn to watch for in one's life:

1. Those that have more or less *obvious* long-term consequences (basic career choices, choice of mate, choices of values, choice of philosophy, basic parental decisions)

2. Those whose long-term consequences must be "discovered" (such as the implications of our daily habits, including those implicit in our eating and exercise habits).

What is most dangerous in general are "unthought" decisions, the decisions that creep into our lives unnoticed and unevaluated. Clearly, it is not possible to raise all decisions to the level of conscious realization, for then we would have no habits whatsoever. Rather, we aim to evaluate *categories* or clusters of decisions (*big* in their collectivity) and the *individual big* decisions.

The Logic of Decision-Making

It is useful to consider the logic of decision-making. That logic is determined by the *goal* of decision-making and the *question* that follows from that goal.

- **The goal:** to decide between some set of alternatives, choosing the one most in keeping with our welfare and the welfare of others

- **The question:** put in terms of completing the following sentence: "At this point in my life, faced with the alternatives (A or B or C or D), which one is most likely to enhance my welfare and the welfare of others?"

The four keys to sound decision-making are

1. To recognize that you face an important decision,

2. To accurately identify the alternatives,

3. To logically evaluate the alternatives,

4. To have the self-discipline to act on the best alternative.

Each of these factors presents potential problems to the thinker.

10.1   *Think for Yourself*

UPGRADING YOUR THINKING ABOUT A FUTURE DECISION

Identify an important decision that you will have to make in the future or that you need to make now. (For example: Should I major in a subject that will lead to a job immediately upon graduation or in a subject that will broadly prepare me to live life well in the long run?) Prethink this decision by completing the following thoughts:

My main purpose in making this decision is . . .

I am looking at this decision from the point of view of . . .

The precise question I am trying to answer is . . .

The key idea I need to think-through to answer this question is . . .

The information I need to answer this question well is . . .

I think I am safe in assuming . . .

The likely implications of my decision are . . .

Write out or orally explain your answer.

Recognizing the Need for an Important Decision

Much of the worst decision-making is the result of the failure to recognize that a decision is at hand. The result, then, is that many decisions are made subconsciously—and, therefore, often egocentrically or sociocentrically. Many choices that people make about friends, associates, schoolwork, family, choice of amusement (including alcohol and drug use), and the satisfaction of personal needs are a result of "mindless" decisions ("It never occurred to me!" "I just didn't realize. . . !"). These are often the "after-the-fact" explanations when the negative implications of the decisions are realized.

Accurately Recognizing the Alternatives

Recognizing that a decision is at hand is not all there is to it. We also must recognize what our alternatives are. Here, many decisions go awry because of failure to accurately identify the alternatives. This failure comes in two forms:

1. Thinking that something is an alternative when it is not (thinking unrealistically)
2. Failing to recognize an alternative (thinking too narrowly).

Among the common decisions in the first category of failure are decisions such as these:

- "I know he's got major faults, but he loves me and I can help him change!"
- "I know there are lots of problems in our relationship, but we love each other and that's all that matters!"

- "I know I'm not doing well in school, but I'll make it in the NBA!" (or "become a rock star!")
- "I know I need to learn this, but I can learn it by cramming the night before the exam!"

The second category of failure (thinking too narrowly) is difficult to correct, as no one believes he or she is thinking too narrowly (when the person is). Actually, the more narrow the thinkers, the more confident the thinkers are that they are broad-minded. A good general rule is that if you can think of only one or two options, you probably are thinking too narrowly.

We have found the following twofold rule to be useful:

Rule One: There's always a way.

Rule Two: There's always another way.

In the light of what we have considered thus far, let's now look at the process of becoming a more skilled decision-maker.

Putting More Time Into Decision-Making

If we don't make time for reflective thought about our decisions, we cannot improve them. A real change of behavior requires some thought about our present behavior. The key here is to recognize that we lose a tremendous amount of time through bad decision-making. It is not unusual, for example, for a couple to spend 5 or 10 years in a bad marriage before recognizing it and leaving it. People often lose years through a poor career choice. Students often lose a great deal of time by their chosen—and inefficient—mode of studying. Putting more time into our decisions, and making better decisions as a result, is going to save us a tremendous amount of time that otherwise would result from the need to correct bad decisions.

Being Systematic

People need to think-through their major habits. They need to give time to the decisions they make around major needs and blocks of time: eating habits, exercise habits, free-time activities, social interactions, and so forth. People have to think critically about how the habits they develop in every part of life affect the overall quality of life. For example, if you spend many hours a day playing computer games, what are some implications of the decision to do so? What important things do you not have time to do?

Dealing With One Major Decision at a Time

Speed thinking usually does not help us think well through our decisions. The more things we try to do simultaneously, and the faster we try to do them, the more likely we will be to do each of the things poorly. Because we live in a fast-paced world, it is difficult to appreciate the importance of taking our time in reasoning-through the decisions we face. After making a bad decision, we sometimes say we didn't have enough time to think-through the problem. But the problem usually is that we had the time but didn't *take* the time. In general, the more deliberate our approach to decision-making is—the more time we spend thinking-through all the aspects of the problem—the better will be our decisions.

Developing Knowledge of Your Ignorance

We are ignorant about most of our decision-making. The more knowledge we gain of our ignorance (of decisions), the more thoughtful our decisions will become. Being able to recognize and face the things we don't know is instrumental in determining what we will have to figure out. We tend not to know what we need to know to make effective decisions, but the *primary* problem most of us face is that we think we already know everything relevant to making those decisions. We are intellectually arrogant.

Dimensions of Decision-Making

Using the elements of thought as our guide, we can identify at least nine dimensions of decision-making that represent potential problems for thought. These dimensions are similar to dimensions of problem-solving, explored later in the chapter. These dimensions do not define a procedure that can be followed mindlessly or mechanically. They presuppose good judgment and sound thinking in every dimension.

To be an effective and rational decision-maker:

1. Figure out, and regularly rearticulate, your most fundamental goals, *purposes,* and needs. Your decisions should help you remove obstacles and create opportunities to reach your goals, achieve your purposes, and satisfy your needs.

2. Whenever possible, take problems and decisions one by one. State the situation and formulate the alternatives as *clearly* and *precisely* as you can.

3. Study the circumstances surrounding the alternative possible decisions to make clear the kind of decision you are dealing with. Figure out what *implications* follow from the various possible alternatives before you. Differentiate decisions over which you have some control and decisions that seem forced on you. Concentrate your efforts on the most *important* decisions and those on which you can have the most impact.

4. Figure out the *information* you need, and actively seek that information.

5. Carefully analyze and interpret the information you collect, drawing what reasonable *inferences* you can.

6. Figure out your options for action. What can you do in the short term? In the long term? Recognize explicitly your limitations in money, time, and power.

7. Evaluate your options in the situation, taking into account their advantages and disadvantages.

8. Adopt a strategic approach to the decision, and follow-through on that strategy. This may involve direct action or a carefully thought-through wait-and-see strategy.

9. When you act, monitor the *implications* of your action as they begin to emerge. Be ready to revise your strategy at a moment's notice if the situation requires. Be prepared to shift your strategy or your analysis or statement of the kind of decision, or all three, as more information about the decision becomes available to you.

We will elaborate upon these dimensions in the problem-solving discussion to come later in the chapter.

10.2 *Think for Yourself*

CREATING PROBLEMS THROUGH POOR DECISION-MAKING

Consider the following strategies for dealing with, or making, decisions. Each represents poor decision-making. Can you see why? Discuss each strategy with another student or a friend. Do you see one or more of these examples as a good way to deal with decisions? If so, explain your contrary view.

1. Staying in an abusive relationship "for the sake of the children"
2. Taking drugs to gain an immediate escape from the pain of facing unpleasant realities in your life
3. Overeating to deal with depression
4. Establishing an escalating "get tough" policy on crime, leading to larger and larger prison cultures that create more and more hardened criminals
5. Smoking to win approval in a group
6. Establishing an escalating "get tough" policy on terrorists, leading to more and more resentment and hatred in the groups resorting to "terrorism," leading to even more violent responses
7. Getting angry and acting out by hitting things or people, throwing things, and shouting
8. Feeling self-pity when frustrated

The Early Decisions (2–11 Years of Age)

By reviewing some of the major decision-making that has shaped our lives, we can gain insight into the problems inherent in the process. For example, in our early life we are not in a position to exercise significant control over our decision-making. Our parents usually give us some opportunities to make decisions, certainly. But when we are very young, we have a limited capacity to take the long view. We are naturally dominated by the immediate, and our view of the world is highly egocentric. What's more, many parents exercise excessive control over their children's decision-making on the one hand, or insufficient control on the other.

When humans are very young, we need to be restrained from acting egocentrically and sociocentrically so these negative patterns can be modified as soon as possible and with as little damage to ourselves and others in the meantime. Even young children, however, need to exercise power in their lives and begin to learn to accept the consequences of their own decisions. Children cannot learn to be responsible for their behavior if they are given no opportunities to make their own decisions.

One of the problems with children's decisions is that they are often the result of the "party line" of the peer groups to which they belong. Youth culture—with its media, movies, music, and heroes—plays a large role in the decision-making of most children. Human insecurity drives children to seek recognition and acceptance from other children. Many of their decisions and their behavior reflect an attempt to be liked by and included in their peer group. The behavior patterns that result from these decisions often become the basis for short- and long-term problems.

One way or another, the decisions made by or for us have an impact on our personality and character. Decisions influence our beliefs and attitudes, our sense of ourselves, and our sense of the world in which we live.

10.3   *Think for Yourself*

EVALUATING GOOD DECISIONS

Review in your mind your earliest recollections about your life as a child. See if you can remember or reconstruct some of what proved to be significant decisions made either by you or for you. Ask yourself the following questions. If you cannot answer a question, simply move on to the next.

- To what extent did your parents give you opportunities to make decisions?
- When did you begin, or have you not begun, to take the long view in your decisions?
- To what extent were your early decisions highly egocentric?
- To what extent did your parents exercise excessive control over your decision-making?
- To what extent did your parents exercise insufficient control?
- To what extent did your parents restrain you from acting egocentrically and sociocentrically?
- To what extent would you say that you still are an egocentric or sociocentric decision-maker?
- To what extent did you exercise power in your life as a child and begin to learn to accept the consequences of your own decisions?
- To what extent do you think you have learned, by having to bear the consequences of your own decisions, to become responsible for your own behavior?

Adolescent Decisions (12–17 Years of Age)

The adolescent years are important in decision-making in our lives. As adolescents, we tend to seek more independence in decision-making, though sometimes without being willing to take more responsibility for those decisions. Indeed, some adolescents seem to take the view: "I have a right to make my own decisions, but you have the responsibility to help me escape the consequences of those decisions whenever those consequences are negative."

Like the very young, adolescents seem to have limited capacity to take the long view. Their immediate view of what is happening to them is often generalized as if it were a lifelong condition (egocentric immediacy). In their desire to achieve independence, adolescents often engage in power struggles with their parents and other authority figures.

Like the decisions of young children, the decisions of adolescents are often the result of the "party line" of the peer groups to which they belong. Adolescent youth culture—again, with its media, movies, music, and heroes—plays a key role in the decision-making of most adolescents. Human insecurity drives adolescents to seek recognition and acceptance from other adolescents. Like young children, many of their decisions and behaviors reflect an attempt to achieve this end. The behavior patterns that result from these decisions often become the basis for short- and long-term problems.

Love, sexuality, and a comprehensive view of the world become important to adolescents, though each of these is often understood superficially. The basis for adolescents' conceptions of these factors is often drawn from movies, music, and television programs that target the adolescent population. This is a formula tailor-made for poor decision-making and bad habits.

For example, media-created heroes often are presented as successful when they use violence to defeat those who are presented as evil. In this good guys/bad guys world, everything is black or white. The evil-doers use bullying and power to hurt and intimidate the weak and the good. The weak and the good are rescued only when someone who is good develops the courage to use violence against the evil-doer.

In media-created romantic relationships, love is typically automatic, irrational, and at first sight, and has no real relationship to the character of the person. Adolescent media have virtually no heroes who achieve their heroic status because of rational use of their mind or knowledge. If the decisions, behavior patterns, and habits developed in adolescence were to simply come and go with the early and adolescent years, one could simply wait them out. But this is not the case. All of us are shaped, often for a lifetime, by decisions and habits we form during these important years. As soon as possible, conscious intervention is needed.

10.4 *Think for Yourself*

EVALUATING ADOLESCENT DECISIONS

Review in your mind your recollections about your life as an adolescent. Which of your decisions proved to be most significant? Ask yourself the following questions. If you cannot answer a question, simply move on to the next.

- Can you identify some ways in which you were influenced by the media as an adolescent? Elaborate.

- To what extent did your decisions during adolescence reflect an attempt on your part to gain recognition and acceptance from other adolescents? What decisions can you specify?

- To what extent did any of these decisions become the basis for short- or long-term problems?
- To what extent were your decisions regarding romantic relationships based on influences from youth culture?
- Can you identify one bad habit you formed as a result of poor adolescent decision-making?
- To what extent is your conception of love or friendship a reflection of the manner in which love or friendship is treated in movies or music lyrics?

If you have difficulty answering any of the above questions (for example, because it seems to you that you were independent in your decision-making), does it seem plausible to you that someone lives in a culture and yet is not significantly influenced by it?

SOLVING PROBLEMS

We have emphasized that we all live a life driven by decisions, and that all of us can improve our decision-making by (1) reflecting, critically, on the nature and role of decisions in our lives and (2) systematically adopting strategies that enhance the reasonability of our decision-making in the light of that nature and role.

Most of the points we made about decision-making also can be made about problem-solving. Problems are embedded in the fabric of our lives almost to the same extent that decisions are. Every domain of decision-making is also a domain in which we have to solve problems. Every decision has an impact on our problems, either to minimize them or to contribute to them. Poor decisions create problems. Many problems can be avoided by sound decision-making early on.

We shall not attempt here to restate every point we made about decision-making with special reference to problem-solving. Rather, our goal is to help readers think-through problem-solving along lines that highlight its place in our lives, and to see how virtually all of the tools, values, and traits discussed in this book are relevant for effective problem-solving.

Becoming an Activist Problem-Solver

Some problems and difficult decisions, if left alone, solve or resolve themselves. An irritating roommate moves. A cold works its way through your system. Your parents send you the money you need. Your friend—who hurt your feelings—apologizes. You get a job offer you were not expecting.

Most problems, however, do not go away by themselves but must be dealt with actively, one way or another. If not dealt with, many problems get worse over time. It is therefore in your interest to become an *activist* problem-solver—to go after problems before they come after you—and to make difficult decisions in a rational manner. The ancient Hawaiians had a saying, "Either you eat life or life eats you!" And in Mother Goose we find the following observation:

> For every problem under the sun
>
> There is a solution or there is none
>
> If there be one, seek till you find it
>
> If there be none, then never mind it

Both of these sayings express the spirit of the activist problem-solver and decision-maker. Becoming an activist problem-solver requires more than an activist spirit. It takes understandings, insight, and skill. These are the factors we shall concentrate on. Happily, the understanding, insights, and skills we have already focused on in previous chapters are ones you can use. You take charge of your problems and decisions by creating the thinking that solves or resolves them.

You should begin by recognizing the kinds of problems you face. Problems can be divided into two types:

1. Problems that we ourselves have created by our own decisions and behavior.
2. Problems created by forces outside of us.

Let us then divide each of these into two groups:

1. Problems that we can solve, in whole or in part.
2. Problems beyond our control.

Clearly, we are apt to have the best chance of solving problems that we ourselves have created, for we often have the capacity to reverse decisions we made previously and modify behavior in which we previously engaged.

10.5 *Think for Yourself*

GAINING PERSPECTIVE ON YOUR PROBLEM-SOLVING

Make a list of 10 of the most important problems with which you have been confronted in the last 5 years of your life. Then comment briefly on each of the problems by answering the following questions:

1. To what extent did this problem arise as a result of a decision or behavior on your part? To what extent as a result of outside forces?
2. To what extent was this a problem that you had the power or capacity to solve? To what extent was it a problem beyond your control?

Evaluating Patterns in Your Problem-Solving

How can we determine the extent to which your problem-solving is irrational? Irrational problem-solving comes in at least two forms:

1. Pseudo-solutions (solutions that seem to solve the problem, but don't).
2. Solutions that solve the problem at the expense of the rights and needs of others.

Both forms of irrational problem-solving involve self-deception. Both require that we not notice the prime characteristic of the solution we have generated. Both are prevalent in human life. We all have basic needs, values, and desires. Frustration comes when we are not successfully getting what we need, value, or desire. Frequently we confuse true and false needs, rational and irrational values and desires. Consequently, we often seek to satisfy false needs and obtain irrational ends.

Dissolving Pseudo-Problems

Problems that exist because we are seeking to satisfy false needs or gain irrational ends have to be dissolved, not solved. We dissolve pseudo-problems by dissolving the "needs" or irrational ends that have generated the problems in the first place.

False Needs and Irrational Ends

To test an apparent need, ask yourself first the following question: "Do I *need* or just *want* this?" Most children and many adults use the word "need" as a synonym for "want." But when we are being precise, we recognize that it is possible to want many things one doesn't actually need. There is a world of difference between the statements, "I need food to live" and "I need a sports car to be happy." You may want to be wealthy, but you don't need to be. You might want to be in a romantic relationship with a certain person, but you don't need to be. You may want to have a high-status job, but you don't actually need it. We can all dissolve *some,* and sometimes *many,* of our problems by being careful in our use of the words "need" and "want."

10.6   *Think for Yourself*

DISTINGUISHING NEEDS FROM WANTS

Make a list of the various things that you, at one time or another, have talked about as a need when, at best, the thing so named was something you strongly or intensely wanted. You might begin with a romantic relationship. Consider also material desires—the various things you have thought were indispensable to you. Be prepared to explain how you would have acted and emotionally responded differently if you had been clearly aware of this important difference at the time.

Some irrational values and ends are manifested in our lives in ways other than being camouflaged by the word "need." For example, bureaucracies often create networks of regulations that create rather than solve problems. The true function of these regulations may be to make life easier for the bureaucrat at the same time that they make life inconvenient for the user of the bureaucracy. Politicians sometimes pass laws that sacrifice the public interest to the vested interest of their financial supporters.

An irrational value or end, then, is one that does more harm than good. Many fall into the category of practices that serve the interests or desires of a few at the expense of the many. In these cases, we must shift our energies and efforts away from satisfying the desires to dissolving the desires themselves, or the practice that has been generated to gain that satisfaction.

For example, some students rotely memorize the meanings of key ideas for a test because it is easier than taking the time to actually learn what the idea means. This is irrational, for subsequent work typically requires student understanding. Soon the students are lost and their work and self-esteem suffer accordingly. This irrational way to learn is common in math and science classes. It is a typical self-defeating behavior of students.

10.7 *Think for Yourself*

IDENTIFYING IRRATIONAL VALUES AND ENDS

See if you can identify some irrational values or ends that you have come to adopt subconsciously. Discuss briefly some of the problems that were generated, for you or others, as a result. Then discuss how you might begin to act to dissolve those problems by adopting more rational values and ends. We are *not* assuming that actually doing this will be easy!

"Big" Problems

The two kinds of big problems to learn to watch for in life are:

1. Problems for which our response will have obvious long-term consequences
2. Problems whose long-term consequences must be discovered

It is dangerous to respond to either of these types of big problems in a passive way.

Dimensions of Problem-Solving

Let us visit the dimensions of problem-solving, which are similar to the dimensions of decision-making. These dimensions do not define a procedure that can be followed mindlessly or mechanically. They presuppose good judgment and sound thinking.

1. Figure out and regularly rearticulate and reevaluate your goals, purposes, and needs. All of us live goal-directed lives. We form goals and purposes, and we seek to satisfy them. We form values and seek to acquire them. We have needs and seek to fulfill them. If we automatically were to achieve our goals and purposes and fulfill our needs, we would have no problems or challenging decisions to make. Problems, therefore, must be recognized as arising from two sources:

- Obstacles or opportunities to reaching our goals, achieving our purposes, and satisfying our needs
- Misconceptions in defining our goals, purposes, or needs.

Taking the second problem first, sometimes the misconception or mistake lies in our very definitions of what is worth seeking or achieving, or in what we think we need. Skilled critical thinkers regularly revisit their conceptions of what is worth pursuing. Very often human problems arise simply because people are pursuing what they ought not to pursue. For example, if you define your happiness in terms of controlling the lives and decisions of the key persons in your life, that goal is bound to create problems both for yourself and for those whom you seek to control. Humans often seek excess—excess of wealth (greed), excess of power (domination), excess of food (an unhealthy body). Humans often make unreasonable demands on others—demanding that everyone believe what we believe, value what we value, act as we act. Humans often set up inconsistent standards—expecting others to be satisfied with what we ourselves would not be satisfied with, or be judged by criteria that we would resent were that same criteria applied to us.

10.8 *Think for Yourself*

IDENTIFYING OBSTACLES TO REACHING YOUR GOALS

Identify a problem in your life that is caused by some obstacle to reaching a goal, achieving a purpose, or satisfying a need.

1. What precisely is the goal, purpose, or need?
2. What is the obstacle?
3. What are some possible ways to eliminate or reduce the power of the obstacle?

Identify a problem in your life that was caused by a misconception you formed in defining your goals, purposes, or needs. Sometimes the mistake lies in our very definitions of what is worth seeking or achieving, or in what we think we *need*.

2. Identify your problems explicitly, then analyze them. We cannot solve a problem that we don't recognize we have. The first step in becoming an activist problem-solver is to become an activist in stating problems. Many leave problems at the level of vague dissatisfaction—knowing that something is wrong but not clarifying exactly what that something is. Others express discontent but do not come to terms with the root cause. It is not in your interest to hide from problems or to wait for them to solve themselves. Whining and pining, bitching and complaining, or just sitting there vaguely discontented usually are not effective problem-solving stances, though sometimes a wait-and-see strategy *is* appropriate.

Once you have enumerated, articulated, and evaluated your goals, purposes, and needs, enumerate and articulate your problems explicitly. Wherever possible, attack your problems singly rather than in combination—unless they form a cluster that is deeply inseparable and requires an interrelated, holistic strategy.

State your problem as clearly and precisely as you can. Then study it to make clear the kind of problem you are dealing with. See it as a member of a group of problems having common features. Figure out what sorts of things you will have to do to solve it. As an activist problem-solver, you seek to state all your problems as clearly and precisely as you can. You take the time to formulate your problems explicitly in words but also to study your problems sufficiently to make clear to yourself the kind of problems you are dealing with.

Many of the problems we face are complex. And complex problems have multiple intricacies. Often problems can be approached from many different standpoints, from the point of view of different subjects. We therefore need to be skilled at determining the domains of thinking inherent in the problems we face and at doing our best thinking within each domain.

Take, for instance, the problem of drug abuse in the United States. The abuse of drugs has many dimensions. Suppose, then, the question we are pursuing is: What can be done to reduce the number of people who abuse drugs in this country? To effectively think-through this problem, we need to think within at least these domains of thinking:

- *cultural* (seeing the problem as caused, in part, by cultural norms)

- *sociological* (seeing the problem as caused, in part, by social group influences)

- *psychological* (seeing people as psychologically dependent on what makes them feel good—instant gratification—and seeing people as often unable to deal well with anxiety and other negative emotional states)

- *biological* (seeing many drug abusers as physically addicted to the drugs they use)

- *political* (seeing the barriers to solving the problem of drug abuse, given the power structure in this country).

When faced with complex questions, then, we do our best reasoning only when we have identified and thought-through all the important domains within those questions. As you think-through the problems you face, distinguish those problems over which you have some control from problems over which you have no control. Set aside the problems over which you have no control, concentrating your efforts on problems you potentially can solve. Worrying about problems you can't solve is pointless and diminishes the quality of your life.

10.9 *Think for Yourself*

IDENTIFYING PROBLEMS

Make a list of as many problems as you can think of that you face in your day-to-day life. Notice how many of them you would classify as personal rather than academic. For each problem, ask yourself why you have not yet solved it. Write out the reason in each case. Then read the reasons and ask yourself what that tells you about yourself and your approach to problems.

Consider: Most people leave most of their problems unformulated and deal with them in a piece-meal, as it-occurs-to-me-from-moment-to-moment way. Few people take the time to analyze their problems explicitly and to systematically evaluate their options.

3. Figure out the information you need, and actively seek that information. Virtually all problem-solving requires the acquisition of key relevant information. For any problem you are trying to solve, figure out the information you need and actively seek it.

The relevant information is determined by the nature of the question asked. If you ask a historical question, you need historical information. If you ask a biological question, you need biological information. If you ask a multidisciplinary question, you must seek information within all disciplines that bear on the question. If you ask a conceptual question, you must analyze at least one concept. If you ask an ethical question, you must identify at least one relevant ethical principle. If your question is sociological, you must gather sociological information. In short, as an activist problem-solver, you work to figure out the information you need to solve the problem.

10.10   *Think for Yourself*

UNDERSTANDING PROBLEMS BY TYPES

Review each of the problems you listed in Think for Yourself 10.5. Comment as well as you can on the kind of problem each problem is. Set aside for a moment the specific details of the problem and think of the general kind of problem that the problem you listed exemplifies (e.g., an economic problem, an ecological problem, a historical problem). Try to characterize what you would have to do to appropriately answer the question(s) the problem poses. For example, review the kinds of information you would need to settle the question. If you find this task too difficult, read on. Further explanation and examples will be provided later in the chapter.

4. Carefully analyze, interpret, and evaluate the information you collect, drawing what reasonable inferences you can. Having relevant information is a necessary condition to solving a problem, but it is never sufficient. To solve a problem, you must interpret the information you have, make sense of it, give it meaning. We live in a glut of information, much of it unreliable, slanted, distorted, or just plain false. Information must be analyzed and evaluated. As an activist problem-solver, you must be comfortable with a wide variety of information states, and you must check information sources for reliability and relevance.

10.11 *Think for Yourself*

WATCHING YOUR INFERENCES

Take one of the problems you have worked on recently (for example, Think for Yourself 10.5 or 10.6). List all the information you can think of that is relevant to the problem. Then make some inferences (draw some conclusions) based on the information. Ask yourself: Are these logical conclusions? Do they follow from the information? Or is there another way to interpret this information? Could I reasonably make inferences different from the ones I made?

For example, if someone you know walks right by you without saying hello, one possible inference you might draw is that this person is angry with you. But this is only one of a number of possible inferences. Another possibility is that the person was distracted by a personal problem. Another is that she just didn't notice you. The only logical inference you can make is that the person's behavior toward you was not in keeping with her ordinary response, and therefore some special explanation is in order.

In everyday life we often jump to conclusions—make inferences that go beyond what the evidence implies. As an activist critical thinker, you must seek to heighten your awareness of your interpretations of the information you get and infer only what the evidence implies. That is the spirit of critical thinking.

5. Figure out your options for action and evaluate them. Sometimes the information you collect will explicitly define your options for action. Sometimes, however, you will have to make further inferences—inferences from your inferences—to figure out your options for action. In one sense, these considerations are extensions of the information-interpreting process. In another sense, they go beyond it because they take us to the level of action.

For example, you might first figure out from observing a friend that he is behaving differently toward you than he did in the past. Your first inference may be something like: "Jack is behaving strangely toward me." Your second inference may be, "He is behaving more formally toward me than he ever has, as if he has lost confidence in me or has some grievance toward me."

Suppose you then ask him directly, "Jack, have I done something to upset you? You seem to be acting more distant toward me." Jack replies, "Oh, no, nothing is wrong. You didn't do anything. Everything is fine."

At this point, if Jack's behavior is of significant concern to you, you might begin to consider your options. You might, for example:

a. Observe Jack's behavior more closely to check on your first interpretation. Perhaps you were projecting into his behavior what was not there.

b. Reduce your closeness to him. You might avoid seeing him for a while.

c. Ask a mutual friend for his or her interpretation.

d. Re-question Jack.

e. Conclude that Jack is no longer your friend, and write him off.

As a critical thinker, you would carefully evaluate these options and not simply go with the first one that pops into your mind. Especially if you value Jack's friendship, you would want to make sure that you are not misinterpreting the situation. You would act, but be cautious in your action, sticking closely to the facts and being willing to re-interpret what is happening.

In any case, you will not solve real-world problems unless you are willing to act. The activist problem-solver is not simply a thinker but is also a doer. Yet, what we do is often significant. Different behavior has different implications. However we behave, consequences follow. As critical thinkers, we want to make sure that our actions are rational and wise, that they make good sense. As a result, we often review our options before we act, and we select an option with due consideration for its likely implications.

We routinely ask a variety of questions:

- Is this problem under my control?
- What are my options in the short term? In the long term?
- Am I looking at the situation so as to see multiple options for action, or am I limiting my options by being close-minded?
- What are my limitations in money, time, and power?

Many of your decisions have both advantages and disadvantages. Therefore, you must give due consideration to the implications of the options you have. An option may be tempting in the short run but have significant long-term negative implications. Many people have suffered grievous pain or damage or have caused grievous pain or damage to others as a result of their failure to give due consideration to the implications of their decisions.

As an activist problem-solver, you want to continually think of your decisions in terms of a long-term set of strategies. What do I want in the long run? What is worth achieving in the long run? What in the long run will make my life most meaningful? These are important questions for you to ask frequently. You should be alert to a self-deceptive dichotomy that often is present in human life: daily decision-making based on short-term gratification juxtaposed with episodic lip service to important long-term values on ceremonial occasions. In this common pattern, we live for values that we don't explicitly admit to, while we frequently espouse higher values that we ignore in our daily decision-making.

6. Adopt a strategic approach to the problem, and follow-through on that strategy. On some occasions, the best strategy to use in responding to a problem may be a carefully thought-through wait-and-see strategy. In most cases, however, a more direct strategy is called for. Once we have isolated the best option, we typically need to think-through how to act on that option. We need some strategy for action, or a set of multiple strategies.

7. When you act, monitor the implications of your action as they begin to emerge. Once we begin to act, our job as an activist problem-solver does not end. We must be ready at a moment's notice to revise our strategy, or strategies, if the situation requires it. We must be prepared to shift our strategy or our analysis or our statement of the problem, or all three, as more information about the problem becomes available to us. Life is often filled with surprises. What looks like the best option today may turn out to be a mistake tomorrow. What looks like our best course of action may shift as we see concretely where our first course of action is taking us.

As critical thinkers, we must be willing to backtrack, shift direction, turn ourselves inside out or outside in. We realize that the facts should be the final determinant in our thinking. We also realize that some facts do not emerge until we act. Thinking in this flexible manner can be challenging because the human mind naturally closes down, seeing its thinking as good enough even when it hasn't clearly thought-through the problem.

Avoiding the Pitfalls of Problem-Solving

Success in problem-solving is not merely a matter of walking through a set procedure or following someone's rules for problem-solving. Problem-solving can go wrong in too many ways. It is good to have general guideposts for problem-solving. It is also important to keep in mind the major ways by which thinking can go bad. Sensitivity to the elements and standards of reasoning is crucial. An examination of the dimensions of problem-solving that we have identified reveals that some of the elements of thought are prominent. Note the words in italics.

1. Figure out and regularly rearticulate your *goals, purposes,* and needs. Recognize problems as emergent obstacles to reaching your *goals,* achieving your *purposes,* and satisfying your needs.

2. Identify your problems explicitly, then analyze them. Wherever possible, take problems one by one. State the problem as clearly and precisely as you can. Study the problem to make clear the kind of problem you are dealing with. Figure out, for example, what sorts of things you are going to have to do to solve it. Distinguish problems over which you have some control from problems over which you have no control. Set aside the problems over which you have no control and concentrate your efforts on problems you can potentially solve.

3. Figure out the *information* you need, and actively seek that *information.*

4. Carefully analyze, interpret, and evaluate the *information* you collect, drawing whatever reasonable *inferences* you can.

5. Figure out your options for action and evaluate them. What can you do in the short term? In the long term? Distinguish what is under your control and what is not. Recognize explicitly your limitations in money, time, and power. Evaluate your options, taking into account their advantages and disadvantages in the situation.

6. Adopt a strategic approach to the problem and follow-through on that strategy. This may involve direct action or a carefully thought-through wait-and-see strategy.

7. When you act, monitor the *implications* of your action as they begin to emerge. Be ready at a moment's notice to revise your strategy if the situation requires it. Be prepared to shift your strategy or your analysis or your statement of the problem, or all three, as more *information* about the problem becomes available to you.

Missing elements in italics are *concept, assumption,* and *point of view.* These elements, too, are essential to effective problem-solving. The only reason they are not mentioned explicitly is that they would have to be mentioned for *each* of the dimensions. Let us look briefly at the first two dimensions of problem-solving and comment on how considerations regarding the concept, assumption, and point of view are relevant. We will leave it to the readers to reflect on the implications of these elements for each of the dimensions of problem-solving.

1. Figure out, and regularly rearticulate, your *goals, purposes,* and needs. Recognize problems as emergent obstacles to reaching your *goals,* achieving your *purposes,* and satisfying your needs.

Clearly we must pay close attention to how we *conceptualize* our goals, purposes, and needs, to recognize that different *conceptualizations* will have different implications. For example, if we conceptualize college as designed to provide us with a degree with which we can get a job upon graduation, our primary purpose in college will be to do only that which is needed in college to get the degree. By implication, then, we will place minor emphasis on learning. We will do little to pursue the development of our mind. Therefore our concept, or idea, of the purpose of college will serve as a barrier to our development.

We also should recognize that our goals and purposes will keenly reflect and define our *point of view,* and that changes in *point of view* typically will have significant implications. Again, if our purpose in college is merely to get a degree to get a good job, our *point of view* is to look at college as a vehicle for gainful employment, or a career. Again, by implication, this point of view may lead us through college with little or no concern with what or how we are learning. If, however, we alter our point of view to look at college as a means to expand our reasoning abilities and take control of the problems we will face in our lives, we will relate much differently to our coursework. We will be much more concerned with the development of our intellectual capacities.

Finally, whenever we frame goals and purposes or define our needs, we make significant *assumptions* about ourselves and about our world. If we change our *assumptions,* all of the other elements typically shift. In the case of the college example above, looking at college merely as a means to employment, some of our *assumptions* might be: The only good reason to go to college is to get a degree so as to get a good job; we should do only what we absolutely must do to obtain the degree; we should do only what is minimally required to pass each class so we can graduate; how much you learn in college is of secondary importance to obtaining the degree.

Conversely, if we *assume* that college represents an opportunity to develop skills and abilities we can use for a lifetime, our orientation will be very different from the "how-can-I-get-by?" approach.

2. Identify your problems explicitly, then analyze them. Wherever possible, take problems one by one. State the problem as clearly and precisely as you can.

Clearly we must pay close attention to how we *conceptualize* our problems, to recognize that different *conceptualizations* will have different implications. We also should recognize that how we *conceptualize* our problems will keenly reflect our *point of view,* and that change in *point of view* typically will have significant implications.

Finally, whenever we frame problems, we make significant *assumptions* about ourselves and about our world. If we change our *assumptions,* all of the other elements typically shift.

10.12   *Think for Yourself*

UNDERSTANDING THE SIGNIFICANCE OF THE ELEMENTS OF THOUGHT IN EFFECTIVE PROBLEM-SOLVING

Write out or orally discuss a brief commentary on each of the dimensions of problem-solving below, focusing, as in the examples above, on the significance of the elements of concept, assumption, and point of view.

1. Figure out the information you need, and actively seek that information.

2. Carefully analyze and interpret the information you collect, drawing whatever reasonable inferences you can.

3. Figure out your options for action and evaluate them. What can you do in the short term? In the long term? Distinguish what is under your control from what is beyond your control. Recognize explicitly your limitations in money, time, and power. Evaluate your options, taking into account their advantages and disadvantages in the situation.

4. Adopt a strategic approach to the problem, and follow through on that strategy. This may involve direct action or a carefully thought-through wait-and-see strategy.

5. When you act, monitor the implications of your action as they begin to emerge. Be ready at a moment's notice to revise your strategy if the situation requires it. Be prepared to shift your strategy or your analysis or your statement of the problem, or all three, as more information about the problem becomes available to you.

COMMENTS:

Analyzing Problems Using the Elements of Thought

It should be clear by now that the elements of thought play a central role in all thinking, including the thinking we use when attempting to solve our problems. In addition to thinking-through problems using the dimensions of problem-solving we have highlighted, we also could analyze the logic of the problem we are trying to solve using the elements of thought in an explicit and systematic way. Recall the elements of thought:

Whenever we reason, we reason with some *purpose* in mind, using *information*, based on *assumptions*, and leading to *implications*. Whenever we reason, we reason within a *point of view*, using *concepts*, to come to *inferences or conclusions* in an attempt to answer some *question*.

Because these parts of thinking are present whenever we reason-through an issue, we can analyze and assess them for quality. Put another way, whenever we are facing a problem in our lives, or something we are trying to figure out, we can look closely at each of the elements of our reasoning and upgrade how well we are using each of the elements. The better we are at identifying the parts, or elements, of thinking, the better we are at thinking.

Let us go back to a problem we worked on earlier: trying to figure out whether to work while you are in college. The situation is that your parents are paying your room and board, but only that. You would like to have extra money. You also realize that if you work, you will have less time for your schoolwork and your social life.

Let's look at how you might reason-through this issue using the elements of reasoning as an intellectual tool. For purposes of this example, we will analyze only five of the elements:

1. **Purpose.** Your purpose in reasoning-through this issue is to figure out whether it makes sense to get a job while in college, given the following facts:
   a. You want extra spending money.
   b. You need to have sufficient time for studying.
   c. You want to maintain an active social life.

2. **Question.** The key question you are trying to answer is: Does it make sense for me to get a job while I'm in college, or will having a job keep me from fulfilling my study needs and from maintaining the type of social life I would like to have?

3. **Information.** The information you use in your reasoning falls into at least three categories: (1) information about work possibilities, (2) information about college commitments and responsibilities, and (3) information about your desired social life:
   a. Information about the types of jobs you might qualify for and how many hours per week those jobs would require, as well as information about how stressful each job might be (which might cause you to do less well in your studies).
   b. Information about college such as (1) the approximate number of hours you need to spend each day and each week preparing for class. For example, if you have a class on Tuesday and Thursday and you have a paper due for each of these classes, you would need to have enough time prior to each class to write your papers; and (2) what type of class schedule you would have, and whether your schedule would allow you to work during the daytime or whether you would need to find a job at night.
   c. Information about your desired social life, such as when you would want to socialize and how often.
   d. How you would prioritize your (1) need and/or desire to succeed in college; (2) desire to have extra money; (3) desire to maintain a social life.

4. **Concepts.** The key concepts that you might use in reasoning are:
   a. Extra money—your idea of how much money you would want to make to have spending money while in college.
   b. Commitment to college—your idea of the commitment you should make to your education. When you think of how much time you should designate for class preparation, do you allocate the time necessary for deep learning or merely time for superficial learning? How exactly would you articulate your commitment?
   c. Social life—your idea of the kind of social life you want to have, including the amount of time you want to spend with your friends, whether you want to spend time during the days or in the evening, and so on.

5. **Assumptions.** The beliefs you might be taking for granted in reasoning-through this issue are that:
   a. You will attend all of your classes so you will not be able to work during class time.
   b. You need to have some social life.
   c. Learning deeply within the content of your courses is secondary to doing the amount of work that will result in an "A" for each course.
   d. Because all of your friends work, you should be able to work as well.

   Whatever assumptions you use in your thinking, they will play a key role in how well you think-though the problem.

10.13, 10.14 *Think for Yourself*

ANALYZING PROBLEMS USING THE ELEMENTS OF THOUGHT

Complete the final three elements for the problem above. Compare and discuss your analysis with that of another student.

CHOOSING A PROBLEM TO ANALYZE

Identify a significant problem in your life that you need to reason-through. Then, using the following template, analyze the problem and come up with a tentative solution.

- What is the problem? (*Study the problem to make clear the kind of problem you are dealing with. Figure out, for example, what sorts of things you are going to have to do to solve it. Distinguish problems over which you have some control from problems over which you have no control. Play special attention to controversial issues in which it is essential to consider multiple points of view.*)

- The key *question* that emerges from the problem is . . . (*State the question as clearly and precisely as you can. Details are important.*)

- My *purpose* in addressing the problem is . . . (*Know exactly what you are after. Make sure you are not operating with a hidden agenda and that your announced and real purposes are the same.*)

- Actively seek the *information* most relevant to the question. *(Include in that information your options for action, both short-term and long-term. Recognize your limitations in terms of money, time, and power.)*
- Some important *assumptions* I am using in my thinking are . . . *(Figure out what you are taking for granted. Watch out for self-serving or unjustified assumptions.)*
- If I solve this problem, some important implications are . . . If I fail to solve this problem, some important *implications* are . . . *(Evaluate your options, taking into account the advantages and disadvantages of possible decisions before acting. What consequences are likely to follow if you make this or that decision?)*
- The most important *concepts*, or ideas, I need to use in my thinking are . . . *(Figure out the significant ideas needed to understand and solve the problem. You may need to analyze these concepts. Use a good dictionary.)*
- The *point(s) of view* is/are as follows: *(Know the point of view from which your thinking begins. Be especially careful to determine whether multiple points of view are relevant.)*

After reasoning-through the parts of thinking above, the best *solution* (conclusion) to the problem is . . . *(If the problem involves multiple conflicting points of view, you will have to assess which solution is the best. If the problem is one-dimensional, it may have just one "correct" solution.)*

The Art of Problem-Solving

If you aspire to become a critical thinker, you must develop into an activist problem-solver. To develop as an activist problem-solver, you must recognize that critical thinking is an essential and defining orientation. Critical thinking sheds essential light on problem-solving, making clear that problem-solving cannot be reduced to a simplistic procedure. There are dimensions to problem-solving, dimensions we can use to guide our thinking, but these dimensions cannot be reduced to a strict method for finding correct answers. The more dimensions to a problem, the greater is its complexity. Consider the dimension of figuring out the information we need. As you remember:

> Virtually all problem-solving requires the acquisition of key relevant information. For any problem you are trying to solve, figure out the information you need and actively seek it.

But, as you also remember:

> The relevant information is determined by the nature of the question asked. If you ask a historical question, you need historical information. If you ask a biological question, you need biological information. If you ask a multidisciplinary question, you must seek information within all disciplines that bear on the question. If you ask a conceptual question, you must analyze at least one concept. If you ask an ethical question, you must identify

a relevant ethical principle. If your question is sociological, you must gather sociological information.

To achieve success as a problem-solver, therefore, you must begin to form a mental map of the variety of types of problems. But there are as many types of problems as there are types of questions we may seek to answer, and there is no easy way to develop such a map. We can divide questions into types in an unlimited number of ways. For example, in this book we have frequently drawn a distinction between types of question by discipline: chemical questions, mathematical questions, biological questions, and so on. We also have differentiated questions into types by "system" considerations: one-system questions, no-system questions, and multi-system questions. There are other helpful ways to divide questions into types.

The main point is that we can understand any question better when we can compare it to other questions similar to it in terms of what we would need to do to answer the question. Every question sets us a task to complete. It becomes a problem when we experience some difficulty in the task. Completing the task then becomes problematic. Every problem can be placed into a variety of types, depending on the main difficulties or complexities inherent in the problem.

There is no person or group to which we can turn for a definitive map of question types. Even if there were, we still would have to personally internalize the logic of those types to use them effectively in problem-solving. Therefore, each of us must begin to develop our own mental maps of question types based on two considerations:

1. our knowledge of established classifications (for example, the ones to which we have referred)
2. the kinds of questions that are especially important in our lives.

And we must approach all of the dimensions of problem-solving in a similar spirit.

Critical thinking theory provides a general guide to thinking, but it does not—cannot—take the work out of thinking. Critical thinking theory cannot think for us. Each of us must internalize the theory for ourselves and link it actively with our experience through practice. And we must apply it with good judgment and a sense of its own incompleteness. Effective problem-solving returns us to the basic principles of critical thinking, and it also reminds us where the responsibility for quality of thought finally remains: with us, the individual thinker. Effective problem-solving provides us with principles, but the application of those principles remains an art, not a science.

CONCLUSION

In this chapter we have focused on the importance of decision-making and problem-solving in human life. As you see, there is much overlap between the two processes. Decision-making is an inherent part of problem-solving, for whenever we think-through a problem we, in the end, must make a final decision. But, of course, many decisions we need to make are not necessarily related to a problem per se. Nevertheless, as you have seen in this chapter, the skills of mind that are useful in reasoning-through problems and coming to rational decisions are often the same.

Though no one fully masters decision-making and problem-solving, all of us can improve these processes by:

1. Reflecting critically on the nature and role of decisions in our lives.
2. Determining which problems in our lives are big problems, and focusing especially on those problems.
3. Systematically adopting strategies that enhance our ability to make reasonable decisions and solve problems effectively.

In constructing these strategies, it is in our interest to think and act so as to maximize our awareness of:

- knowledge of the major decisions of our childhood;
- knowledge of the major decisions of our adolescence;
- the patterns that underlie how we approach decisions and problems;
- the extent to which our decisions and approaches to problems are based on immediate gratification and short-term goals;
- our ultimate and most primary goals;
- the alternatives available to us;
- the self-discipline necessary to act on the "best" alternative when making decisions and solving problems;
- the need for adequate time to reflect while making decisions and solving problems;
- the need to be systematic;
- the dimensions of decision-making and problem-solving.

Becoming skilled at decision-making and problem-solving is intimately connected with becoming skilled at thinking. An excellent decision-maker and problem-solver has self-understanding, understands how to use the fundamentals of critical thinking, is well aware of the problem of egocentrism and sociocentrism in thought, and is intellectually humble, perseverant, and fair-minded.

DEAL WITH YOUR IRRATIONAL MIND

Humans often engage in irrational behavior. We fight. We start wars. We kill. We are self-destructive. We are petty and vindictive. We act out when we don't get our way. We abuse our mates. We neglect our children. We rationalize, project, and stereotype. We act inconsistently, ignore relevant evidence, jump to conclusions, and say and believe things that don't make good sense. We deceive ourselves in many ways. We are our own worst enemy.

Behind human irrationality are two overlapping and interrelated motivating impulses, which are the focus of this chapter:

- Human egocentrism, the natural human tendency "to view everything within the world in relationship to oneself, to be self-centered" (*Webster's New World Dictionary*); and

- Human sociocentrism, conceptualized most simply as *group egocentricity*. To define sociocentricity, we might take Webster's definition of egocentricity (above) and substitute *group* for *self*. Consider: *Sociocentric thinking is the natural human tendency to view everything within the world in relationship to one's group, to be group-centered.*

Human egocentricity is best understood as having two basic tendencies.

1. The tendency to see the world in *self-serving* terms, to constantly seek that which makes one feel good, that which one selfishly wants, at the expense of the rights and needs of others.

2. The desire to maintain its beliefs.

Egocentricity is a form of *rigidity of thought*. It views its irrational beliefs as rational.

The second motivating impulse, sociocentric thinking, is an extension of egocentric thinking. Humans are herd animals, largely influenced by and functioning within groups. And because most people are largely egocentric, or centered in themselves, they end up forming groups that are largely centered in themselves. As a result of egocentrism and sociocentrism, most people are self-serving, rigid, conform to group thinking, and assume the correctness of their own beliefs and that of their groups.

Sociocentric thought, then, is a direct extension of egocentric thought in that it fundamentally operates from the two primary tendencies of egocentric thought:

1. Seeking to get what it (or its group) wants without regard to the rights and needs of others; and

2. Rationalizing the beliefs and behavior of the group (irrespective of whether those beliefs and behaviors are irrational).

Sociocentric thought presupposes the egocentric tendencies of the human mind. The selfish mind finds its natural home in the *self-centered* group. And virtually all groups operate with *in-group* advantages denied to those in the *out-groups*. This is instanced in many forms of social conflict, punishment, and vengeance. It also is close to the root of most wars and war crimes. It enables some (advantaged) people to be comfortable in the face of the wretched suffering of masses of (disadvantaged) others. It enables some in a group (the elite) to manipulate others in the group (the non-elite).

Consider the similarity between street gangs and nations. Gangs collectively pursue irrational purposes and engage in violent behavior against other gangs—behavior that can seem to be justified only by one-sided, *group-serving* thought. In a similar way, countries frequently attack other countries using equally one-sided group-serving thought. The difference often is in sophistication, not in kind. The one is censured by society, the other validated.

In short, people are born into, and join, groups. They then identify with them egocentrically. They rarely dissent. They rarely think for themselves. They rarely notice their own conformity and irrationality. Humans seek what is in their selfish interests and see the world from the perspectives of the (sociocentric) groups to which they belong. Egocentric and sociocentric thought both represent enormous barriers to the development of rational thought. This is true, in part, because these two tendencies in the mind *appear to the mind as perfectly rational.* Unless we fully understand these overlapping tendencies and fight to combat them, we cannot fully develop as rational, autonomous, fair-minded thinkers. We shall elaborate further on these points in the last part of this chapter.

TAKE CHARGE OF YOUR EGOCENTRIC NATURE

Egocentric thinking stems from the condition that humans do not naturally consider the rights and needs of others, nor do we naturally appreciate the point of view of others or the limitations in our own point of view. As humans, we become explicitly aware of our egocentric thinking only if we are specially trained to do so. We do not naturally recognize our egocentric assumptions, the egocentric way we use information, the egocentric way we interpret data, the source of our egocentric concepts and ideas, the implications of our egocentric thought. We do not naturally recognize our self-serving perspective.

> The best thinkers realize they must confront their own egocentrism to improve.

Humans live with the unrealistic but confident sense that they have fundamentally figured out *the way things actually are,* and that they have done this objectively. They naturally *believe* in their immediate *perceptions*—however inaccurate they may be. Instead of using intellectual standards in thinking, humans often use self-centered psychological (rather than intellectual) standards to determine what to believe and what to reject. The most commonly used psychological standards in human thinking are:

"It's true because *I* believe it." *Innate egocentrism:* I assume that what I believe is true even though I have never questioned the basis for many of my beliefs.

"It's true because *we* believe it." *Innate sociocentrism:* I assume that the dominant beliefs within the groups to which I belong are true even though I have never questioned the basis for many of these beliefs.

"It's true because I *want* to believe it." *Innate wish fulfillment:* I believe in, for example, accounts of behavior that put me (or the groups to which I belong) in a positive light rather than a negative light even though I have not seriously considered the evidence for the more negative account. I believe what "feels good," what supports my other beliefs, what does not require me to change my thinking in any significant way, what does not require me to admit I have been wrong.

"It's true because I *have always believed it.*" *Innate self-validation:* I have a strong desire to maintain beliefs that I have long held, even though I have not seriously considered the extent to which those beliefs are justified, given the evidence.

"It's true because it is *in my selfish interest* to believe it." *Innate selfishness:* I hold fast to beliefs that justify my getting more power, money, or personal advantage even though these beliefs are not grounded in sound reasoning or evidence.

11.1 *Think for Yourself*

IDENTIFYING SOME OF YOUR IRRATIONAL BELIEFS

Using the above categories of irrational beliefs as a guide, identify at least one belief you hold in each of the categories.

It's true because *I* believe it.

It's true because *my group* believes it.

It's true because I *want* to believe it.

It's true because I *have always believed it.*

It's true because it is *in my selfish interest* to believe it.

On a scale of 1–10 (10 equating with "highly irrational" and 1 with "highly rational"), where would you place yourself? Why?

If humans are naturally prone to assess thinking in keeping with the above criteria, it is not surprising that they, as a species, have not developed a significant interest in establishing and teaching legitimate intellectual standards. There are too many domains of our thinking that humans, collectively, do not want to have questioned. They have too many prejudices that they do not want to be challenged. They are committed to having their selfish interests served. They typically are not concerned with protecting the rights of others. They typically are not willing to sacrifice our desires to meet someone else's basic needs. They do not want to discover that beliefs they have taken to be obvious and sacred might not be either obvious or sacred. They will ignore any number of basic principles if doing so enables them to maintain our power or to gain more power and advantage.

> Humans naturally see ourselves as right even in the face of clear evidence to the contrary.

Fortunately, humans are not always guided by egocentric thinking. Within each person are, metaphorically speaking, two potential minds: one emerges from innate egocentric, self-serving tendencies, and the other emerges from cultivated rational, higher-order capacities (if cultivated). We begin this chapter by focusing on the problem of egocentric tendencies in human life. We then contrast this defective mode of thinking with its opposite: rational or reasonable thinking. We explore what it means to use our minds to create rational beliefs, emotions, and values—in contrast to egocentric ones. We then focus on two distinct manifestations of egocentric thinking: dominating and submissive behavior.

Understand Egocentric Thinking

Egocentric thinking emerges from our innate human tendency to see the world from a narrow, self-serving perspective. We naturally think of the world in terms of how it can serve *us*. Our instinct is to continually operate within the world, to manipulate situations and people, in accordance with our selfish interests.

At the same time, we naturally assume that our thinking is rational. No matter how irrational our thinking is, no matter how destructive, when we are operating from an egocentric perspective, we see our thinking as reasonable. Our thinking seems to us to be right, true, good, justifiable. Our egocentric nature, therefore, creates perhaps the most formidable barrier to critical thinking.

> We naturally think of the world in terms of how *it* can serve *us*.

We inherit from our childhood the sense that we have basically figured out the truth about the world. We naturally *believe* in our sense of who and what we are and what we are engaged in. Therefore, if we behave or think irrationally, we are, in a sense, victims of the beliefs and thought processes we have developed throughout life (because egocentric thinking is commanding us).

As we age, our rational capacities develop to some extent. We come to think more reasonably in some areas of our lives. This can come from explicit instruction or experience. If we are in an environment that models reasonable behavior, we become more reasonable. Yet, it is hard to imagine making significant inroads into egocentric thinking unless we become explicitly aware of it and learn how to undermine or short-circuit

EXHIBIT 11.1 *These elements comprise the logic of egocentrism.*

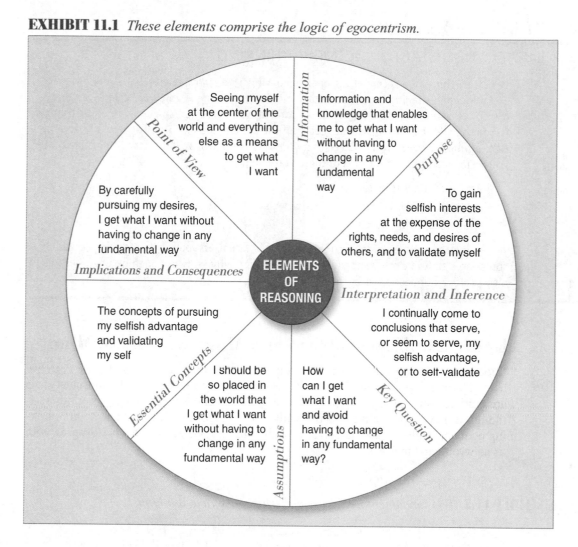

it in some way. The human mind can think irrationally in too many ways while masking itself within a facade of reasonability.

The mere appearance of rationality, of course, is not equivalent to its genuine presence. And, unfortunately, much apparently rational adult behavior is at root egocentric or sociocentric. This stems, in part, from the fact that people generally do not have a clear understanding of how the human mind functions. Most important, they fail to realize that thinking, if left to itself, is inherently flawed with prejudices, half-truths, biases, vagueness, arrogance, and the like.

11.2   *Think for Yourself*

BEGINNING TO UNDERSTAND EGOCENTRIC THINKING

Try to think of a recent disagreement in which you now realize you were not fair-mindedly listening to the views of someone else. Perhaps you were defensive during the conversation, or you were trying to dominate the other person. You were not trying to see the situation from the perspective of the person with whom you were interacting. At the time, however, you believed that you were being reasonable. Now you realize that you were close-minded. Complete these statements:

1. The situation was as follows . . .
2. My behavior/thinking in the situation was as follows . . .
3. I now realize that I was close-minded because . . .

If you cannot think of an example, think of a situation you were in recently in which someone else was close-minded. Also, ask yourself why you cannot think of any examples of close-mindedness on your part.

Understand Egocentrism as a Mind Within the Mind

Egocentric thinking functions subconsciously, like a mind within us that we deny we have. No one says, "I think I will think egocentrically for a while." Its ultimate goals are gratification and self-validation. It does not respect the rights and needs of others—though it may be protective of those with whom it ego-identifies. When we are thinking egocentrically, we see ourselves as right and just. We see those who disagree with us as wrong and unjustified.

EXHIBIT 11.2 *Two fundamental motives underlie egocentric thinking.*

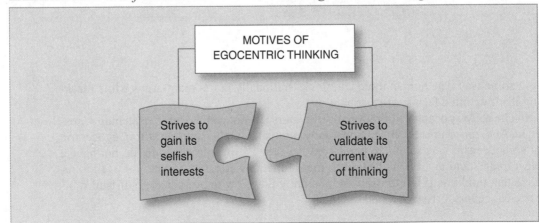

MOTIVES OF
EGOCENTRIC THINKING

Strives to gain its selfish interests

Strives to validate its current way of thinking

Our family, our children, our country, our religion, our beliefs, our feelings, our values—all are privileged in our egocentric mind. Our validation is crucial to us, and we seek it even if we have been unfair to others or irresponsibly harmed them in a flagrant way. We are interested only in facts we can twist to support us. We dislike or fear people who point out our inconsistencies. If we criticize ourselves, it is not the occasion for significantly changing our behavior but, rather, the means of avoiding such change. For example, if I think, "I know I have a short fuse, but I can't help it. I lose my temper just like my father did!" my criticism justifies my continuing to lose my temper.

> Egocentric thinking functions subconsciously, like a mind within us that we deny we have.

One of the ways we use egocentric thinking, then, is to validate our current belief system. When we feel internally validated, we live comfortably with ourselves even if what we are doing is actually unethical. For example, if I have been brought up to believe that people of a certain race are inferior, my egocentric thinking enables me to maintain all of the following beliefs: (1) I am not prejudiced (they simply are inferior), (2) I judge each person I meet on his or her own merits, (3) I am an open-minded person.

With these beliefs operating in my thinking, I do not see myself as jumping to conclusions about members of this race. I do not think of myself as wronging them in any way. I see myself as simply recognizing them for what they are. Though I ignore the evidence that demonstrates the falsity of what I believe, I do not see myself ignoring the evidence. I do not think of myself as a racist, for being a racist is bad and I am not bad.

Only when we explicitly develop our ability to analyze ourselves rationally can we begin to see these tendencies in ourselves. When we do, it is almost never at the precise moments when our egocentric mind is in control. Once egocentric thinking begins to take control, it spontaneously rationalizes and deceives itself into believing that its position is the *only* justifiable position. It sees itself as experiencing the truth, no matter how inaccurate is the picture of things it is painting. This skilled deceiving of self effectively blocks reasonable thoughts from correcting distorted thoughts. And the more highly self-deceived we are, the less likely we are to recognize our irrationality, the less likely we are to consider relevant information that our egocentricity is blocking from our view, and the less motivated we are to develop truly rational beliefs and views.

11.3 *Think for Yourself*

DISCOVERING PREJUDICES IN YOUR BELIEFS

As egocentric thinkers, we see ourselves as possessing the truth. At the same time, we form many beliefs without the evidence to justify them. We form many prejudices (judgments *before* the evidence). If this is true, we should be able to begin to unearth some of our prejudices, using our rational capacity. In an attempt to begin this process, complete the following statements:

1. One of the prejudices I have is . . . (Think of generalizations you tend to make even though you don't have the evidence to justify them. They can be about anything you please: a religion, atheists, men, women, homosexuals, heterosexuals, and so

on. Put your prejudice in this form: All X are Y, as in *all women are . . .* , or *all men are . . .*)

2. A more rational belief with which I should replace this faulty belief is . . .

3. If I use this new belief in my thinking, my behavior would change in the following ways . . .

Successful Egocentric Thinking

Though egocentric thinking is irrational by nature, it can be functional within a dysfunctional logic. For example, it often enables us to selfishly get what we want without having to worry about the rights of the people we deny in getting what we want. This type of thinking—though defective from the points of evidence, sound reasoning, objectivity, and fair play—is often "successful" from the point of view of self-gratification. Hence, though egocentric thinking is inherently flawed, it can be successful in achieving what it is motivated to achieve.

We see this in many persons of power and status in the world—successful politicians, lawyers, businesspeople, and others. They often are skilled in getting what they want and are able to rationalize unethical behavior with great sophistication. The rationalization can be as simple as, "This is a hard, cruel world. We have to be realistic. We have to realize we don't live in a perfect world. I wish we did. And, after all, we are doing things the way things have always been done." Conversely, rationalization can be as complex as that which is masked in a highly developed philosophy, ideology, or party platform.

> Though egocentric thinking is inherently flawed, it can sometimes successfully achieve what it wants.

Hence, though egocentric thinkers may use ethical terms in their rationalizations, they are not responsive to ethical considerations. They do not really respect ethical principles. They think of ethical principles only when those ethical principles seem to justify their getting what they want for other reasons.

Egocentric thinking, then, is inherently indifferent to ethical principles or genuine conscience. We cannot be focused exclusively, at one and the same time, on getting what we selfishly want and genuinely taking into account the rights and needs of others. The only time egocentric thinking takes others into account is when it is forced to do so to get what it wants. Hence, an egocentric politician may take into account the views of a public-interest group only when her reelection depends on the support of that group. She is not focused on the justice of the group's cause but, rather, on the realization that if she fails to publicly validate those views, that group will refuse to support her reelection. She cares only about what is in her selfish interest. As long as the concern is selfish, by definition, the rights and needs of others are not perceived as relevant.

Corporate executives who ensure that the expected earnings of the company are significantly overstated (to enable them to sell their stock at a high price) cause innocent people to lose money investing in a company that appears to be (but is not) on the upswing. Most CEOs who manipulate data in this way do not worry about the well-being of potential investors. Their justification must be, "Let the buyer beware!" By using this type of justification, they don't have to face the unethical nature of their behavior.

Highly skilled egocentric thought can be generated in every type of human situation, from situations involving the rights and needs of thousands of people to simple, everyday interactions between two people. Imagine that a couple, Max and Maxine, routinely go to the video store to rent movies. Inevitably Max wants to rent an action-filled movie while Maxine wants to rent a love story. Though Maxine is often willing to set aside her choices to go along with Max's desires, Max is never willing to go along with Maxine's choices. Max rationalizes his position to Maxine, telling her that his movie choices are better because they are filled with thrilling action, because love stories are always slow-moving and boring, because his movies are always award-winners, because "no one likes to watch movies that make you cry," because, because, because. . . . Many reasons are generated. Yet all of them camouflage the real reasons: that Max simply wants to get the types of movies he likes, that he shouldn't have to watch movies that he does not want to watch. In his mind, he should get to do it because he wants to. Period.

Max's egocentrism hides the truth even from himself. He is unable to grasp Maxine's viewpoint. He cannot see how his self-centered thinking adversely affects Maxine. Insofar as his thinking works to achieve his desires, and he is therefore unable to detect any flaws in his reasoning, he is egocentrically successful.

11.4 *Think for Yourself*

RECOGNIZING EGOCENTRIC THINKING IN ACTION

Think of a situation in which someone you know was trying to selfishly manipulate you into doing something incompatible with your interest. Complete the following statements:

1. The situation was as follows . . .
2. This person, X, was trying to manipulate me in the following way (by giving me these reasons for going along with him/her) . . .
3. At the time, these reasons (did/did not) seem rational because . . .
4. I now believe this person was trying to manipulate me because . . .
5. I think the real (irrational) reason he/she wanted me to go along with his/her reasoning is . . .

Unsuccessful Egocentric Thinking

When egocentric thought is unsuccessful, it creates problems for those influenced by the thinker and also for the thinker himself or herself. Let's return to Max and Maxine and the movies for a moment. Imagine that for many months Max and Maxine go through this video-store routine in which, through self-serving argumentation, Max is able to manipulate Maxine into going along with his video choices. But one day Maxine decides that she simply isn't going along with Max's selfish behavior in choosing which movie to rent. She begins to feel resentment toward Max. She begins to think that perhaps Max isn't truly concerned about her. The more she thinks about it, the more she begins to see that Max is selfish in the relationship in a number of ways. He is unwilling to go along with her movie choices and, further, tries to control where they go to lunch every day, when they eat lunch, when they visit with friends, and so on.

Maxine begins to feel manipulated and used by Max, and out of her resentment emerges a defensive attitude toward Max. She rebels. She no longer simply goes along with Max's unilateral decisions. She begins to tell him when she doesn't agree with his choices.

At this point, the table is turned for Max. His egocentric thinking is no longer working for him. He feels anger when he doesn't get his way. Because he lacks insight into his dysfunctional thinking, though, he doesn't realize that he is actually abusing Maxine and treating her unfairly. Because Maxine's resentment is now leading to acts of retaliation on her part, Max's life is less successful than it was. Maxine may end up deciding that she is not going to happily agree to Max's movie choices in the future. Her resentment may lead her to seek subtle ways to punish Max for his unfair treatment of her. If she does go along with his movie choices, she might sulk the entire time they are watching the movie. Both of them may become unhappy as a result of Maxine's rebellion, and they may interrelate in a perpetual state of war, as it were.

This is merely one pattern in a myriad of possible patterns of egocentric thinking leading to personal or social failure. Egocentric thinking and its social equivalent, sociocentric thinking (discussed later in the chapter), can lead to social prejudice, social conflict, warfare, genocide, and a variety of forms of dehumanization. Though on occasion some person or group might be "successful" as a result of the ability to wield superior power, quite often the consequences will be highly negative for themselves as well as their victims.

> When we are egocentrically unsuccessful, we create problems for ourselves and/or others.

Consider a gang that randomly chooses a person to harass who is wearing a sweatshirt of the same color as its group "color." The members begin with verbal assaults, which quickly lead to physical attacks, which in turn result in serious injury to the victim. Consequently, the gang members responsible for the attack are arrested on suspicion, then found guilty of a serious crime, which leads to their imprisonment.

Even if it does not cause direct harm to others, egocentric thinking may lead to chronic self-pity or depression. When problems emerge, it is easy to revert to this type of thinking:

> I don't know why I should always get the short end of the stick. Just when I think things are going well for me, I have to face another problem. Is there no end? Life seems to be nothing but one problem after another. My instructors expect too much of me. My parents won't give me the money I need to get by. My boss doesn't think I'm doing a good enough job. My wife is always complaining about something I do, and now I've got to figure out how to deal with this car. Life is just a pain in the neck. I don't know why things don't ever go my way.

EXHIBIT 11.3 *These are some of the many feelings that might accompany egocentric thinking. They often occur when egocentric thinking is "unsuccessful."*

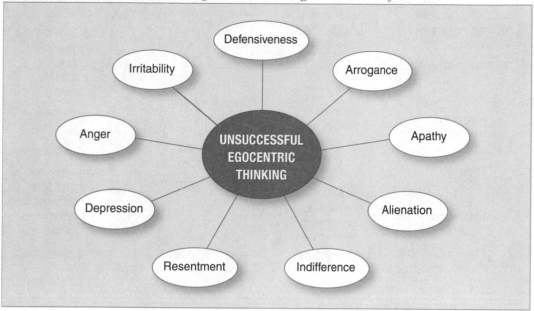

Egocentric, self-pitying persons fail to recognize the positives in life. They screen these out in favor of self-pity. They inflict unnecessary suffering on themselves. They say to themselves, "I have a right to feel all the self-pity I want, given the conditions of my life." In situations such as this, because the mind is unable to correct itself, it is its own victim. It chooses to focus on the negative and engage in self-punitive behavior.

11.5 *Think for Yourself*

UNEARTHING DYSFUNCTIONAL EGOCENTRIC THINKING

Try to think of a time when your desire to selfishly get what you wanted failed because of your egocentric behavior. Complete these statements:

1. The situation was as follows . . .
2. When I didn't get what I wanted, I thought . . . and behaved . . .
3. A more rational way to think would have been . . .
4. A more rational way to act would have been . . .

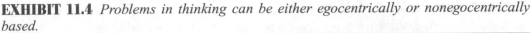

EXHIBIT 11.4 *Problems in thinking can be either egocentrically or nonegocentrically based.*

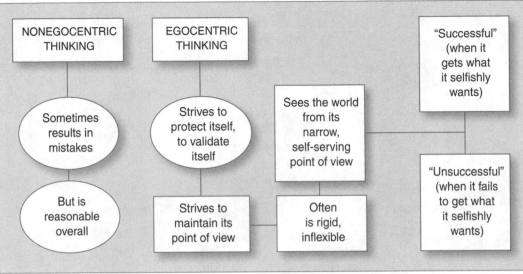

Rational Thinking

Although irrationality plays a significant role in human life, human beings are, in principle, capable of thinking and behaving rationally. Humans can learn to respect evidence even though it does not support our views. We can learn to enter empathically into the viewpoint of others. We can learn to attend to the implications of our own reasoning and behavior. We can become compassionate. We can make sacrifices for others. We can work with others to solve important problems. We can discover our tendency to think egocentrically and begin to correct for that tendency.

Hence, though egocentrism causes us to suffer from illusions of perspective, we can transcend these illusions by practicing the thinking that takes us into the perspective of others. Just as we can assimilate what we hear into our own perspective, so can we learn to role-play the perspectives of others. Just as egocentrism can keep us unaware of the thinking process that guides our behavior, critical thinking can help us to learn to explicitly recognize that thinking process. Just as we can take our own point of view to be absolute, we also can learn to recognize that our point of view is always incomplete and sometimes blatantly self-serving. Just as we can remain completely confident in our ideas even when they are illogical, we can learn to look for lapses of logic in our thinking and recognize those lapses as problematic.

> Though humans are naturally egocentric, they can learn to be rational.

We need not continually confuse the world with our own perspective of the world. We can learn to consider and understand others' points of view, to see situations from more than one point of view. We can learn to assess our thinking for soundness. We can strive to become conscious of our thinking, as we develop our "second nature."

EXHIBIT 11.5 *The logic of the nonegocentric mind.*

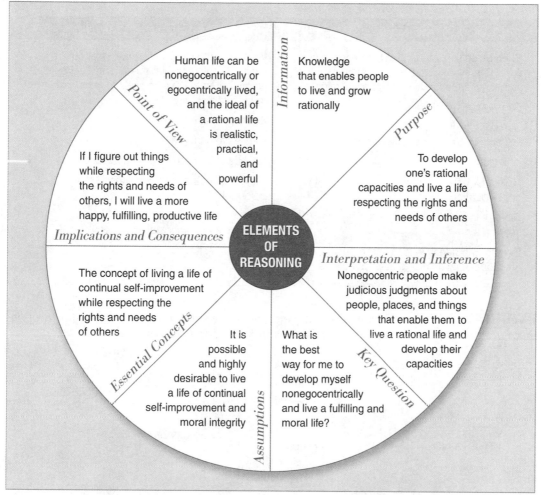

Each of us has at least the potential for developing a rational mind and using that development to resist or correct for egocentric thought patterns. This requires a certain level of command over the mind that few people have. It involves disciplined thinking. It means holding oneself accountable. It means developing an inner voice that guides thinking so as to improve it. It means thinking-through the implications of thinking before acting. It involves identifying and scrutinizing our purposes and agendas, explicitly checking for egocentric tendencies. It involves identifying irrational thinking and transforming it into reasonable thinking.

Let us imagine the case of Todd and Teresa, who are dating. Todd finds himself feeling jealous when Teresa talks with another man. Then Todd recognizes the feeling of jealousy as irrational. Now he can intervene to prevent his egocentric nature from

EXHIBIT 11.6 *This figure compares the tendencies of inherent egocentric thinking with those of cultivated nonegocentric thinking.*

THE EGOCENTRIC MIND	THE NONEGOCENTRIC MIND
Pursues selfish interests at the expense of the rights, needs, and desires of others while stunting development of the rational mind	Respects the needs and desires of others while pursuing its own needs and desires and is motivated to develop itself, to learn, and to grow intellectually
Seeks self-validation	
Can be inflexible (unless it can achieve its selfish interests through flexibility)	Is flexible, adaptable
	Strives to be fair-minded
Is selfish	Strives to interpret information accurately
Makes global, sweeping positive or negative generalizations	Strives to gather and consider all relevant information
Distorts information and ignores significant information	Reacts rationally to situations by taking charge of emotions and using emotional energy productively
Reacts with negative, counterproductive emotions when it fails to have its desires met	

EXHIBIT 11.7 *At any given moment, depending on the situation, the three functions of the mind are controlled by either egocentric or nonegocentric thinking.*

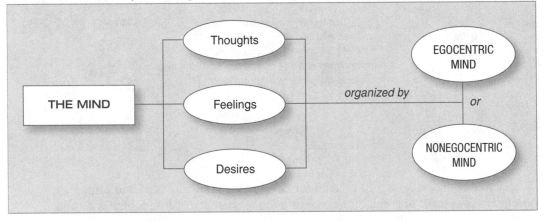

asserting itself. He can ask himself questions that enable him to begin to distance himself from his "ego": "Why shouldn't she talk to other men? Do I really have any good reason for distrusting her? If not, why is her behavior bothering me?"

Through this sort of self-scrutinizing, reasonable persons seek to understand what lies behind their motivations. They come to terms with their own egocentrism. They establish relationships characterized by reasonability and mutual respect. Rational thinking, then, is flexible, disciplined, and fair-minded in its approach. It is able to chart its own course while adhering to ethical demands. It guides itself deliberately away from irrational tendencies in itself.

Thus, just as unconscious, self-deceptive thinking is the vehicle for accomplishing irrational ends, conscious, self-perceptive thinking is the vehicle for achieving rational ends. An intrinsic dimension of rational thinking, therefore, is raising to the conscious level all instinctive irrational thought. We cannot improve by ignoring our bad habits, only by breaking them down. This requires that we admit we have bad habits. And it requires an active self-analytic stance.

Following this line of reasoning, a rational act is one that is able to withstand reasonable criticism when brought entirely into the open. All thought that we cannot own entirely up to should be suspect to us. Like a contract with many pages of fine print that the contract writer hopes the reader will not explicitly understand, the egocentric mind operates to hide the truth about what it is actually doing. It hides the truth both from itself and from others, all the while representing itself as reasonable and fair.

Rational thinking, by contrast, is justified by the giving of good reasons. It is not self-deceptive. It is not a cover for a hidden agenda. It is not trapped within one point of view when other points of view are relevant. It strives to gather all important relevant information and is committed to self-consistency and integrity. Reasonable people seek to see things as they are, to understand and experience the world richly and fully. Reasonable people are actively engaged in life. Reasonable people are willing to admit when they are wrong, and to learn from their mistakes. Indeed, they want to see themselves as wrong when they are wrong.

To develop your rational capacities, then, you have to understand that at any given moment, your thoughts, feelings, and desires can be controlled by either egocentric or rational thinking. For your rational mind to prevail over your egocentric tendencies, you will function in a way analogous to that of the orchestra leader. The leader controls the process of musical production, maintains discipline within the orchestra, assesses the quality of the sounds, listens for flaws in delivery, points out those flaws for correction, and, through routine scrutiny and continual practice, is finally able to elicit music of high quality.

For you to reach more of your rational potential, you must become a student of the interplay between rational and irrational thought and motivation in your life. You must come to see that, ultimately, your thinking is what is controlling who and what you are, determining the essential quality of your life.

11.6 *Think for Yourself*

TO WHAT EXTENT ARE YOU RATIONAL?

Now that you have read an introduction to rationality and irrationality (egocentrism), think about the extent to which you think you are either rational or irrational. Answer these questions:

1. If you were to divide yourself into two parts, one being egocentric and the other rational, to what extent would you say you are either? Would you say you are 100% rational, 50% rational and 50% egocentric, or how would you divide yourself?

2. What reasoning would you give to support your answer to number 1 above? Give examples from your life.

3. To the extent that you are egocentric, what problems does your egocentrism cause?

4. Does your egocentric thinking tend to cause more problems for yourself or for others? Explain.

Two Egocentric Functions

We have introduced you to the distinction between rationality and irrationality. Now we will discuss two distinctively different patterns of egocentric thinking. Both represent general strategies the egocentric mind uses to get what it wants; both represent ways of irrationally acquiring power.

First let's focus on the role that power plays in everyday life. All of us need to feel that we have some power. If we are powerless, we are unable to satisfy our needs. Without power, we are at the mercy of others. Virtually all that we do requires the exercise of some kind of power, whether small or large. Hence, the acquisition of power is essential for human life. But we can pursue power through either rational or irrational means, and we can use the power we get to serve rational or irrational ends.

Two irrational ways to gain and use power are given in two distinct forms of egocentric strategy:

1. The art of dominating others (a *direct* means to getting what one wants)

2. The art of submitting to others (an *indirect* means to getting what one wants).

> To get what we want egocentrically, we either try to dominate others or try to submit to them.

Insofar as we are thinking egocentrically, we seek to satisfy our egocentric desires either directly, by exercising overt power and control over others, or indirectly, by submitting to those who can act to serve our interest. To put it crudely, the ego either bullies or grovels. It either threatens those who are weaker or subordinates itself to those who are more powerful, or both.

Both of these methods for pursuing our interests are irrational, both fundamentally flawed, because both are grounded in unjustified thinking. Both result from the assumption that the needs and rights of egocentric persons are more important than those they exploit for their advantage. We will briefly explore these two patterns of irrational thinking, laying out the basic logic of each.

Before we discuss these patterns, one caveat is in order: As we have mentioned, many situations in life involve using power. Using power need not imply an inappropriate use, however. For example, in a business setting, hierarchical protocol requires managers to make decisions with which their employees may not agree. The responsibility inherent in the manager's position calls for that manager to use his or her power to make decisions. Indeed, managers who are unable to use the authority vested in their positions are usually ineffective. They are responsible for ensuring that certain tasks are completed. Therefore, they must use their power to see those tasks to completion. Of course, that does not justify their using power unjustifiably to serve selfish ends.

The use of power, then, is and must be part of human life. The fundamental point is that power can be used either rationally or irrationally, depending on the motivation and manner of the person wielding it. Thus, if power is used to serve rational ends, and pursues those ends in a reasonable manner, it is justified. In contrast, if power is used to control and manipulate others for irrational, self-serving ends, that is another matter entirely.

Let us now turn to the two predominant patterns of irrational thinking that all of us use to the extent that we are egocentric.

1. The dominating ego function: "I can get what I want by fighting my way to the top."
2. The submissive ego function: "I can get what I want by pleasing others."

The egocentric mind chooses one over the other either through habit or through an assessment of the situation. For example, it can either forcefully displace those at the top or please those on top and thereby gain its desires. Of course, we must remember that these choices and the thinking that accompanies them function subconsciously.

Egocentric Domination

Between the two functions of egocentric thinking, perhaps the one more easily understood is the dominating function—or the *dominating ego,* as we usually will refer to it for the purposes of this chapter. When we are operating within this mode of thinking, we are concerned, first and foremost, to get others to do precisely what we want by

EXHIBIT 11.8 *Whenever we think egocentrically to serve our interests, we attempt to either dominate or submit to others.*

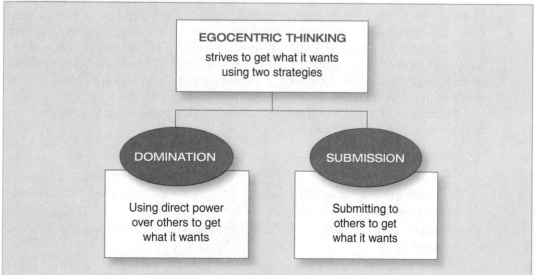

EGOCENTRIC THINKING
strives to get what it wants
using two strategies

DOMINATION

Using direct power
over others to get
what it wants

SUBMISSION

Submitting to
others to get
what it wants

means of exerting power over them. Thus, the dominating ego uses physical force, verbal intimidation, coercion, violence, aggression, "authority," and any other form of overt power to achieve its agenda. It is driven by the fundamental belief that to get what we want, we must control others in such a way that were they to resist us, we could force them to do what we want. At times, of course, domination may be quite subtle and indirect, with a quiet voice and what appears to be a mild manner.

For examples of the dominating ego at work, we need only to look to the many people who are verbally or physically abused by their spouses, or the many children similarly abused by their parents. The basic unspoken pattern is, "If others don't do what I want, I force them to do it." Or consider the man in a bar who gets into a fight to force another man away from his girlfriend. His purpose, on the surface, is to protect her. In reality, his purpose may be to ensure that she won't be tempted into a romantic relationship with someone else, or to embarrass the other man in front of his peers.

> The dominating ego uses force and control over others to get what it wants.

Domination over others typically generates feelings of power and self-importance. Through self-deception, it also commonly entails a high sense of self-righteousness. The dominator is typically arrogant. To the dominator, control over others seems to be right and proper. The dominator uses force and control "for the good" of the person being dominated. The key is that there is self-confirmation and self-gain in using power and forcing others to submit. Others must undergo undeserved inconvenience, pain, suffering, or deprivation as a result.

Given these mutually supporting mental structures, it is difficult for those who successfully dominate others to recognize any problems in their own behavior or reasoning. Why change when, in your mind, you are doing what ought to be done? Hence, as long as the dominating ego is "successful," it experiences positive emotions. To the extent that it is "unsuccessful"—unable to control, dominate, or manipulate others—it experiences negative emotions.

The negative emotions frequently generated from the frustrated failure to control include anger, rage, wrath, rancor, hostility, antagonism, depression, and sadness. Consider the abusive husband who, for many years, is successfully able to control his wife. When she decides to leave him, he may go into a fit of rage and kill her, and perhaps even himself. As long as he thinks he is in control of her, he feels satisfied. But when he no longer can dominate her, his irrational anger may well lead him to the extreme of physical violence.

Examples of the kinds of thinking that dominating persons use in justifying their irrational controlling behavior are:

"I know more than you do."

"Since I know more than you, I have an obligation to take charge."

"If I have to use force to make things right, I should do so because I understand better what needs to be done."

"If I have more power than you do, it is because I am superior to you in skill and understanding."

"I have a right to take the lead. I understand the situation best."

EXHIBIT 11.9 *The logic of the dominating ego encompasses these elements.*

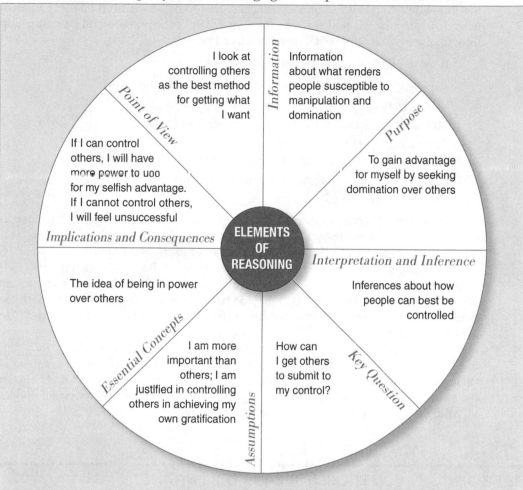

"You are behaving stupidly. I cannot let you hurt yourself."

"I am an expert. Therefore, there is nothing you can teach me that I need to know or that I don't already know."

Given these subconscious beliefs and thoughts, it follows that people who operate primarily from the dominating ego would be likely to have difficulties in interpersonal relationships, especially when they come up against another dominating ego or against a strong, rational person. Just as the unconscious tendency to dominate impedes healthy personal relationships, so it often impedes the learning process for students who previously have been able to avoid disciplined learning by using the strategy and tactics of a dominating ego.

Intellectual arrogance is a common byproduct of the tendency to dominate. All of the following thoughts—often unconscious—lead to or derive from intellectual arrogance on the part of students who have successfully avoided significant learning through the exercise of power over teachers and parents:

"Why should I have to learn this? It's useless to me."

"This is just theory and abstraction. I want practical knowledge."

"I know as much as I need to know about this subject."

"This isn't in my major. I will never have any use for it."

"I'm intelligent. If I don't understand what is being taught to me, there is obviously something wrong with the way the instructor is presenting it."

"I've always made good grades before. So if I don't make a good grade in this class, it's the teacher's fault."

Another benchmark of the dominating ego is its propensity to impose higher standards on others that it imposes on itself. For example, it may require something near perfection in others while ignoring blatant flaws in itself. For a simple, everyday example, we can turn to what often happens in traffic jams. People frequently drive as if their "rights" were sacred ("No one should ever cut me off") while they frequently cut off others ("I have to get into this lane—too bad if others have to wait."). In short, the dominating ego expects others to adhere to rules and regulations it has the "right" to thrust aside at will.

From an ethical point of view, those who seek control over others frequently violate the rights, and ignore the needs of, others. Selfishness and cruelty are common in these people. It is difficult to gain any ground by reasoning with people who are under the sway of their dominating ego, for they will use any number of intellectual dodges to avoid taking moral responsibility for their behavior.

11.7 *Think for Yourself*

TO WHAT EXTENT ARE YOU EGOCENTRICALLY DOMINATING?

Think about your typical patterns of interaction with friends, family members, fellow workers, and others. Complete the following statements:

1. I tend to be the most (egocentrically) dominating in the following types of situations . . .
2. Some examples of my dominating behavior are . . .
3. I usually am successful/unsuccessful in dominating others. My strategy is . . .
4. My controlling behavior creates problems because . . .

Next we lay out the logic of egocentric submissive thinking—thinking that seeks power and security through attachment to those who dominate and wield power. We are not assuming that everyone who has power has achieved it by dominating others. They may well have achieved power through rational means. With this caveat in mind, let us begin with a basic outline of the submissive ego.

Egocentric Submission

If the hallmark of the dominating ego is control over others, the hallmark of the submissive ego is *strategic subservience.* In this mode of thinking, people gain power not through the direct struggle for power but, instead, through subservience to those who have power. They submit to the will of others to get the powerful person to act in their selfish interest. In this way, people with submissive egos gain indirect power. To be successful, they learn the arts of flattery and personal manipulation. They must become skilled actors and actresses, appearing to be genuinely interested in the well-being and

EXHIBIT 11.10 *The logic of the submissive ego encompasses these elements.*

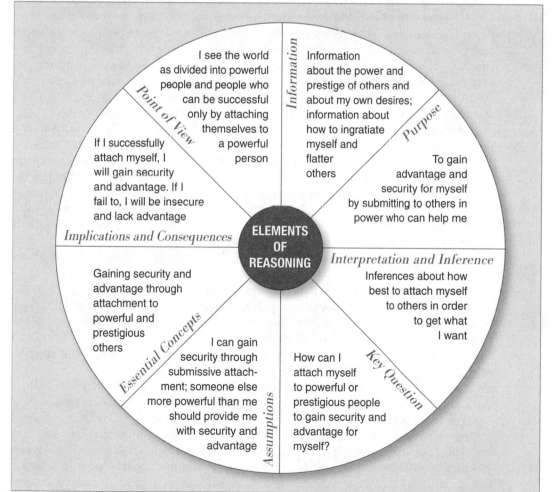

interests of the other while in reality pursuing their own interest through the other. At the same time, they must hide this mode of functioning from themselves, as they have to maintain some level of self-respect. If they had to consciously admit to themselves that they were submitting to others to have their own way, they would have trouble feeling justified.

There are countless examples of this mode of functioning in everyday life. The teenage female, for example, who pretends to enjoy fishing (while being inwardly bored by it) so her boyfriend will like her better is engaging in this type of thinking. She submits to his desires and his will only because she wants to gain specific ends (of having a prestigious boyfriend, gaining attention from him, feeling secure in the relationship, and so on). Though she readily agrees to go fishing with him, she probably will end up resenting having done so in the long run—especially once she secures his commitment to her. By virtue of the bad faith implicit in the strategies of the submissive ego, it is common for resentment eventually to develop in the person who functions consistently in this mindset.

> The submissive ego submits to those in power to get what it wants.

If the pattern of thinking of the submissive ego takes root in the young woman we just imagined, she eventually may marry a financially secure man so she can be taken care of, will not have to work, and can enjoy the luxuries of a life without personal sacrifice. Consciously, she may deceive herself into believing she loves the man. Yet, because she does not relate to him rationally, the relationship is likely to be dysfunctional.

A similar pattern often occurs in social groups. Within most groups there will be a structure of power, with some playing a dominant and others a submissive role.

Most people will play both roles, depending on the situation. Nazi Germany and the ideology of Fascism provide an excellent example of a system that simultaneously cultivated both dominating and submissive behavior. In this system, nearly everyone had to learn to function within both egocentric types, depending on the context. A hierarchy was established in which everyone was required to give absolute obedience to those above them and to have absolute authority over everyone below them. Only Hitler did not have to use the strategy of submission, as there was no one for him to submit to. Theoretically, no one in such a system has to rationally persuade anyone below him or her in the system. The expectation is clear: Anyone below submits; anyone above dominates.

In the ideology of most human cultures, a greater place is officially given to the use of reason in human life than it was in Fascist society. Much of the official ideology of any society, however, is more window dressing than reality. Suffice it to say that because all societies are stratified and all stratified societies have a hierarchical structure of power, all societies, to date, encourage the thinking of the dominating and submissive ego.

Part of that stratification is found in work-related contexts. In many work situations, men and women alike feel forced to operate in a submissive manner toward their supervisors, allowing themselves to be dominated and manipulated by their superiors so these employees can stay in favor, keep their jobs, or get promotions.

Thus, the submissive ego operates through artifice and skillful self-delusion to ensure its security, advantage, and gratification. To achieve its objectives, it engages in behavior that is compliant, servile, cowering, acquiescent—though all of these characteristics may be highly disguised. It continually capitulates, defers, caves in, succumbs, yields to the will of others to gain advantage and maintain its artificial self-esteem.

To avoid the feeling of caving in to superiors, one of the most effective image-saving devices is to adopt the point of view of the superior. In this case, the submission appears as simple agreement: "He didn't pressure me; I agree with him."

As long as the submissive ego achieves "success," it experiences positive emotions—satisfaction, happiness, fulfillment, pleasure, and the like. To the extent that it is not achieving its goals and fails to gain its ends through submission, however, it feels any of a number of negative emotions including bitterness, resentment, animosity, ill will, spitefulness, vindictiveness, enmity, antipathy, and loathing. What's more, depending on the situation, a sense of having failed may lead to insecurity, fear, helplessness, depression, and anxiety.

When unsuccessful, the submissive ego tends to punish itself inwardly, much more than the dominating ego, which, when experiencing pain, tends to respond by inflicting pain on others. Egocentric feelings mirror egocentric thought. Hence, when inflicting pain on itself, the submissive ego sees itself as justified in feeling bad. It experiences a form of sick pleasure in reminding itself that it has every reason to feel negative emotions.

Consider, for example, the woman who believes that her husband should deal with all the unpleasant decisions that have to be made. If he asks her to handle some of those decisions, she goes along with him but is resentful as a result. She may think thoughts such as: Why should I have to deal with these unpleasant decisions? They are his responsibility. I always have to do the things he doesn't want to do. He doesn't really care about me because if he did, he wouldn't ask me to do this.

She feels justified in thinking these negative thoughts, and in a way she enjoys the feelings of resentment that accompany the thoughts.

The submissive ego often has a "successful" relationship with a person who functions within the dominating-ego mindset. The paradigm case of this phenomenon can be found in marriages in which the male dominates and the female submits. She submits to his will. He may require that she do all the household chores. In return, either implicitly or explicitly, he agrees to take care of her (serve as the primary breadwinner). Although she may resent his domination at times, she understands and, at some level, accepts the bargain. Through rationalization she convinces herself that she probably couldn't do better with any other man, that this one provides the comforts she requires, that in essence she can put up with his domineering behavior because the payoffs are worth it.

Thus, the submissive ego can experience a form of dysfunctional "success" as long as it feels that it is having its desires met. Take the employee who behaves in a subservient manner to a verbally abusive manager to get promotions. As long as the manager takes care of the employee—by looking after his interests, by giving him the promotions he is striving toward—the employee has positive feelings. When the manager ceases doing this, however, and therefore no longer seems to be concerned with the employee's needs and desires, the employee may feel degraded and resentful of the manager and the subservient role he is forced to play. If given an opportunity, he may turn on his supervisor.

As the submissive ego relates to others, its feelings, behaviors, and thoughts are controlled by beliefs deriving from its own subconscious sense of inferiority. To justify its need to submit to the desires and will of another person, it must perceive itself as inferior to that person. Otherwise it would be unable to rationalize its subservience. It would be forced to recognize its dysfunctional thinking and behavior. Consider the following unconscious beliefs that drive the thinking of the submissive ego:

- "I must go along with this (decision, situation) even though I don't agree with it. Otherwise I won't be accepted."
- "For me to get what I want, I must submit to those who are more powerful than I am."
- "Since I'm not very smart, I must rely on others to think for me."
- "Since I'm not a powerful person, I must use manipulative strategies to get others to get what I want."

As is true with all manifestations of egocentric thinking, none of these beliefs exists in a fully conscious form. These beliefs require self-deception. Otherwise the mind would immediately recognize them as irrational, dysfunctional, absurd. Consequently, what the mind consciously tells itself is very different from the beliefs operating in egocentric functioning. Consider the first belief, "I must go along with this decision even though I don't agree with it. Otherwise I won't be accepted." The conscious thought parallel to this unconscious thought is something like: "I don't know enough about the situation to decide for myself. Even though I'm not sure this is the right decision, I'm sure the others are in a better position to decide than I am." This is the thought the mind believes it is acting upon, when in reality it is basing its reasoning on the other, unconscious belief. Thinking within this logic, the person is "dishonestly" going along with the decision, in a sense pretending to agree, but all the while doing so only to forward an agenda of acceptance.

In addition to serving as a major barrier to the pursuit of rational relationships, the submissive ego stunts the development of the rational mind, limiting its capacity for insight into self. The submissive ego is enabled to do this through any number of self-protecting beliefs:

- "I'm too stupid to learn this."
- "If I have a question, others might think I'm ignorant."
- "I'm not as smart as others."
- "No matter how hard I try, I can't do any better than I'm already doing."
- "I'll never be able to figure this out."
- "Since I know I'm too dumb to learn this, there's no point in really trying."

Thus, the submissive ego, like the dominating ego, creates significant barriers to development. It routinely turns to others for help when it is capable of performing without that help. The submissive ego experiences frustration, anxiety, and even depression when it fails, or when it anticipates failure, in learning situations. Whereas the dominating ego believes it already knows what it needs to know, the submissive ego often believes it is incapable of learning.

11.8, 11.9   *Think for Yourself*

TO WHAT EXTENT ARE YOU EGOCENTRICALLY SUBMISSIVE?

Think about your typical patterns of interaction with friends, family members, fellow workers, and others. Complete the following statements:

1. I tend to be the most (egocentrically) submissive in the following types of situations . . .
2. Some examples of my submissive egocentric behavior are . . .
3. I am usually successful/unsuccessful when I try to manipulate others through submissiveness. My strategy is . . .
4. My submissive behavior creates problems because . . .

TO WHAT EXTENT ARE YOU EGOCENTRICALLY DOMINATING VERSUS SUBMISSIVE?

Think about your typical patterns of interaction with friends, family members, fellow workers, and others. Do you tend to be more dominating or submissive in most situations in which you are egocentric? What about your friends, family members, co-workers? Do they tend to be dominating or submissive? Given your experience, what problems emerge from people behaving in dominating or in submissive ways?

Pathological Tendencies of the Human Mind

We now can put explicitly into words an array of interrelated natural dispositions of the human mind that follow as consequences of the pathology of the natural mind. To significantly develop our thinking, we must overtly identify these tendencies as they operate in our lives, and we must correct them through critical-thinking processes. As you read them, ask yourself whether you recognize these as processes that take place regularly in your own mind (if you conclude, "not me!" think again):

- **Egocentric memory:**   the natural tendency to "forget" evidence and information that do not support our thinking and to "remember" evidence and information that do

- **Egocentric myopia:**   the natural tendency to think in an absolutist way within an overly narrow point of view

- **Egocentric righteousness:**   the natural tendency to feel superior in the light of our confidence that we possess the *Truth* when we do not

- **Egocentric hypocrisy:**   the natural tendency to ignore flagrant inconsistencies— for example, between what we profess to believe and the actual beliefs our behavior implies, or between the standards to which we hold ourselves and those to which we expect others to adhere

- **Egocentric oversimplification:** the natural tendency to ignore real and important complexities in the world in favor of simplistic notions when consideration of those complexities would require us to modify our beliefs or values

- **Egocentric blindness:** the natural tendency not to notice facts and evidence that contradict our favored beliefs or values

- **Egocentric immediacy:** the natural tendency to overgeneralize immediate feelings and experiences, so that when one event in our life is highly favorable or unfavorable, all of life seems favorable or unfavorable to us

- **Egocentric absurdity:** the natural tendency to fail to notice thinking that has "absurd" consequences

Challenge the Pathological Tendencies of Your Mind

It is not enough to recognize abstractly that the human mind has a predictable pathology. As aspiring critical thinkers, we must take concrete steps to correct it. This requires us to develop the habit of identifying these tendencies in action. This is a long-term project that is never complete. To some extent, it is analogous to stripping off onion skins. After we remove one, we find another beneath it. To some extent, we have to strip off the outer layer to be able to recognize the one underneath. Each of the following admonitions, therefore, should not be taken as simple suggestions that any person could immediately, and effectively, put into action, but, rather, as strategic formulations of long-range goals. We all can perform these corrections, but only over time and only with considerable practice.

Correcting egocentric memory.   We can correct our natural tendency to "forget" evidence and information that do not support our thinking and to "remember" evidence and information that do, by overtly seeking evidence and information that do not support our thinking and directing explicit attention to them. If you try and cannot find such evidence, you should probably assume you have not conducted your search properly.

Correcting egocentric myopia.   We can correct our natural tendency to think in an absolutist way within an overly narrow point of view by routinely thinking within points of view that conflict with our own. For example, if we are liberal, we can take the time to read books by insightful conservatives. If we are conservative, we can take the time to read books by insightful liberals. If we are North Americans, we can study a contrasting South American point of view or a European or Far-Eastern or Middle-Eastern or African point of view. By the way, if you don't discover significant personal prejudices through this process, you should question whether you are acting in good faith in trying to identify your prejudices.

Correcting egocentric righteousness.   We can correct our natural tendency to feel superior in light of our confidence that we possess the *truth* by regularly reminding ourselves how little we actually know. In this case, we can explicitly state the unanswered questions that surround whatever knowledge we may have. By the way, if you don't discover that there is much more that you do not know than you do know, you should question the manner in which you pursued the questions to which you do not have answers.

Correcting egocentric hypocrisy.   We can correct our natural tendency to ignore flagrant inconsistencies between what we profess to believe and the actual beliefs our behavior implies, and inconsistencies between the standards to which we hold ourselves and those to which we expect others to adhere. We can do this by regularly comparing the criteria and standards by which we are judging others with those by which we are judging ourselves. If you don't find many flagrant inconsistencies in your own thinking and behavior, you should doubt whether you have dug deeply enough.

Correcting egocentric oversimplification.   We can correct our natural tendency to ignore real and important complexities in the world by regularly focusing on those complexities, formulating them explicitly in words, and targeting them. If you don't discover over time that you have oversimplified many important issues, you should question whether you have really confronted the complexities inherent in the issues.

Correcting egocentric blindness.   We can correct our natural tendency to ignore facts or evidence that contradicts our favored beliefs or values by explicitly seeking out those facts and evidence. If you don't find yourself experiencing significant discomfort as you pursue these facts, you should question whether you are taking them seriously. If you discover that your traditional beliefs were all correct from the beginning, you probably moved to a new and more sophisticated level of self-deception.

Correcting egocentric immediacy.   We can correct our natural tendency to overgeneralize immediate feelings and experiences by getting into the habit of putting positive and negative events into a much larger perspective. You can temper the negative events by reminding yourself of how much you have that many others lack. You can temper the positive events by reminding yourself of how much is yet to be done, of how many problems remain. You know you are keeping an even keel if you find that you have the energy to act effectively in either negative or positive circumstances. You know that you are falling victim to your emotions if and when you are immobilized by them.

Correcting egocentric absurdity.   We can correct our natural tendency to ignore thinking that has absurd consequences by making the consequences of our thinking explicit and assessing them for their realism. This requires that we frequently trace the implications of our beliefs and their consequences in our behavior. For example, we should frequently ask ourselves: "If I really believed this, how would I act? Do I really act that way?"

By the way, personal ethics is a fruitful area for disclosing egocentric absurdity. We frequently act in ways that are "absurd"—given what we insist we believe in. If, after what you consider to be a serious search, you find no egocentric absurdity in your life, think again. You probably are just developing your ability to deceive yourself.

The Challenge of Rationality

If the human mind has a natural tendency toward irrationality, in the form of dominating and submissive ego functions, it also has a capacity for rationality, in the form of capacity for self-knowledge. We all have a tendency toward hypocrisy and inconsistency, but we nevertheless can move toward greater and greater integrity and consistency. We can counteract our natural tendency toward intellectual arrogance by developing our capacity for intellectual humility. Put another way, we can learn to continually question what we "know" to ensure that we are not uncritically accepting beliefs that have no foundation in fact.

Moreover, we can counteract our tendency to be trapped in our own point of view by learning how to enter sympathetically into the points of view of others. We can counteract our tendency to jump to conclusions by learning how to test our conclusions for their validity and soundness. We can counteract our tendency to play roles of domination or submission by learning how to recognize when we are doing so. We can begin to see clearly why submission and domination are inherently problematic. We can learn to search out options for avoiding either of these modes of functioning. And we can practice the modes of self-analysis and critique that enable us to learn and grow in directions that render us less and less egocentric.

TAKE CHARGE OF YOUR SOCIOCENTRIC TENDENCIES

Just as all humans are egocentric by nature, we are sociocentric as well. *Sociocentric thinking,* as you may remember, is egocentric thinking raised to the level of the group. And it can be even more destructive than egocentric thinking, because it carries with it the sanction of a social group (which clearly wields more power than does the individual).* Egocentric and sociocentric thought are both implicitly or explicitly self-serving and dogmatic. Like egocentric thinking, sociocentric thinking is absurd at the level of conscious expression. In other words, if sociocentric thinking is made explicit in the mind of the thinker, its unreasonableness will be obvious. Thus our objective, as developing thinkers, is to make explicit in our own minds the sociocentic thinking that influences our behavior.

> Sociocentric thinking is egocentric thinking raised to the level of the group.

Note the following parallels for egocentric and sociocentric patterns of thought:

- **Egocentric standard.** "It's true because I believe it."

    Related sociocentric standard: "It's true because we believe it."

- **Egocentric standard.** "It's true because I want to believe it."

    Related sociocentric standard: "It's true because we want to believe it."

---

*Consider, for example, that close to 500,000,000 people died in the 20th century as a result of violent group conflicts (war, that is).

EXHIBIT 11.11 *The logic of sociology is composed of these elements.*

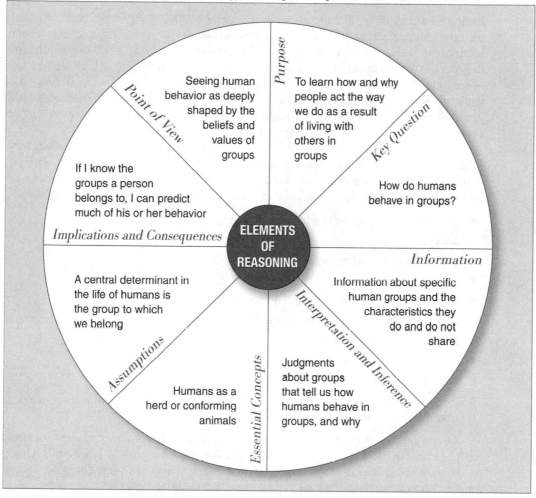

- **Egocentric standard.** "It's true because it's in my vested interest to believe it."
  Related sociocentric standard: "It's true because it's in our vested interest to believe it."

- **Egocentric standard.** "It's true because I have always believed it."
  Related sociocentric standard: "It's true because we have always believed it."

Just as individuals deceive themselves through egocentric thinking, groups deceive themselves through sociocentric thinking. Just as egocentric thinking functions to serve one's selfish interest, sociocentric thinking functions to serve the selfish interests of the group. Just as egocentric thinking operates to validate the uncritical thinking of the individual, sociocentric thinking operates to validate the uncritical thinking of the group.

The Nature of Sociocentrism

Living a human life entails membership in a variety of human groups. These typically include groups such as nation, culture, profession, religion, family, and peer group. Even before we are aware of ourselves as living beings, we find ourselves participating in groups. We find ourselves in groups in virtually every setting in which we function as persons. What's more, every group to which we belong has some social definition of itself and some usually unspoken "rules" that guide the behavior of all members. Each group to which we belong imposes some level of conformity on us as a condition of acceptance. This includes a set of beliefs, behaviors, and taboos.

All of us, to varying degrees, uncritically accept as right and correct whatever ways of acting and believing are fostered in the social groups to which we belong. This becomes clear to us if we reflect on what happens when, say, an adolescent joins an urban street gang. With that act, adolescents are expected to identify themselves with:

- a name that defines who and what they are;
- a way of talking;
- a set of friends and enemies;
- gang rituals in which they must participate;
- expected behaviors involving fellow gang members;
- expected behaviors when around the enemies of the gang;
- a hierarchy of power within the gang;
- a way of dressing and speaking;
- social requirements to which every gang member must conform;
- a set of taboos—forbidden acts that every gang member must studiously avoid under threat of severe punishment.

Group membership clearly offers some "advantages." But those advantages come with a price. Groups impose their rules (mores, folkways, taboos) on individuals. Group membership is in various ways "required" for ordinary acts of living. Suppose, for example, that you wanted to belong to no nation, to be a citizen not of a country but *of the world.* You would not be allowed that freedom. You would find that you were allowed no place to live, nor any way to travel from place to place. Every place in the world is claimed by some nation (as its "sovereign" possession), and every nation requires that all visitors to it come as a citizen of some other country (thus, with a "passport").

In addition, everywhere a nation imposes its "sovereignty," it requires the obedience of all persons to literally thousands (if not hundreds of thousands) of laws. Of course, no one can memorize thousands of laws, so it is virtually impossible to live in any society without breaking (unknowingly) many of its laws. One consequence of this is that the most powerful sub-groups in any complex society can usually find a way to "punish" weak members of the group.

For most people, blind conformity to group restrictions is automatic and unreflective. Most people effortlessly conform without recognizing their conformity. They internalize group norms and beliefs, take on the group identity, and act as they are expected to act—without the least sense that what they are doing might reasonably be questioned. Most people function in social groups as unreflective participants with a range of beliefs, attitudes, and behaviors analogous, in the structures to which they conform, to those of urban street gangs.

For most people, blind conformity to group restrictions is automatic and unreflective.

This conformity of thought, emotion, and action is not restricted to the masses, or the lowly, or the poor. It is characteristic of people in general, independent of their role in society, independent of status and prestige, independent of years of schooling. In all likelihood, it is as true of college professors and their presidents as students and custodians, as true of senators and chief executives as it is of construction and assembly-line workers. Conformity of thought and behavior is the rule in humans, and independence the rare exception.

11.10 *Think for Yourself*

THINKING ABOUT THE GROUPS YOU BELONG TO

Make a list of the groups you belong to. Then choose the group you think has influenced you the most in your beliefs, values, and behavior.
Complete the following statements:

1. The group that has influenced me the most is probably . . .
2. This group's main function or agenda is . . .
3. Comment on as many of the following variables as you can identify with, with respect to the group you have chosen to analyze. To what extent does your membership in this group involve
   - a name that defines who and what they are;
   - a way of talking;
   - a set of friends and enemies;
   - group rituals in which you must participate;
   - expected behaviors involving fellow members;
   - expected behaviors when around the "enemies" of the group;
   - a hierarchy of power within the group;
   - a way of dressing and speaking;
   - social requirements to which you must conform;
   - a set of taboos—forbidden acts, whose violation is punished.
4. One of the key "requirements" of this group is . . .
5. One of the key "taboos" (what I am forbidden to do) is . . .
6. A group that my group would look down upon is . . . . We think of this group as beneath us because . . .

The idea of sociocentric thinking is not new. Under one label or another, many books have been written on the subject. And it has been the focus of important sociological studies. Almost a hundred years ago, in his seminal book *Folkways,* originally published in 1902, William Graham Sumner wrote extensively about social expectations and taboos. One of the founders of the discipline of sociology, Sumner documented the manner in which *group think* penetrates virtually every dimension of human life. He introduced the concept of ethnocentrism in this way:

> Ethnocentrism is the technical name for this view of thinking in which one's own group is the center of everything, and all others are scaled and rated with reference to it. . . . Each group nourishes its own pride and vanity, boasts itself superior, exacts its own divines, and looks with contempt on outsiders. Each group thinks its own folkways the only right ones, and if it observes that other groups have other folkways, these excite its scorn. (p. 13)

Sumner describes folkways as the socially perceived "right" ways to satisfy all interests according to group norms and standards. He says that in every society:

> There is a right way to catch game, to win a wife, to make one's self appear . . . to treat comrades or strangers, to behave when a child is born. . . .
> The "right" way is the way which ancestors used and which has been handed down. The tradition is its own warrant. It is not held subject to verification by experience. . . . In the folkways, whatever is, is right. (p. 28)

In regard to expectations of group members, Sumner states:

> Every group of any kind whatsoever demands that each of its members shall help defend group interests. The group force is also employed to enforce the obligations of devotion to group interests. It follows that judgments are precluded and criticism silenced. . . . The patriotic bias is a recognized perversion of thought and judgment against which our education should guard us. (p. 15)

Even young children exhibit sociocentric thinking and behavior. Consider this passage from Piaget's study for UNESCO (Campbell, 1976), which is a dialogue between an interviewer and three children regarding the causes of war:

> **Michael M. (9 years, 6 months old):** Have you heard of such people as foreigners? *Yes, the French, the Americans, the Russians, the English* . . . Quite right. Are there differences between all these people? *Oh, yes, they don't speak the same language.* And what else? *I don't know.* What do you think of the French, for instance? *The French are very serious, they don't worry about anything, an' it's dirty there.* And what do you think of the Russians? *They're bad, they're always wanting to make war.* And what's your opinion of the English? *I don't know . . . they're nice* . . . Now look, how did you come to know all you've told me? *I don't know . . . I've heard it . . . that's what people say.*

> **Maurice D. (8 years, 3 months old):** If you didn't have any nationality and you were given a free choice of nationality, which would you choose? *Swiss nationality.* Why? *Because I was born in Switzerland.* Now look, do you think the French and Swiss are equally nice, or the one nicer or less nice than the other? *The Swiss are nicer.* Why? *The French are always nasty.* Who is more intelligent, the Swiss or the French, or do you think they're just the same? *The Swiss are more intelligent.* Why? *Because they learn French quickly.* If I asked a French boy to choose any nationality

he liked, what country do you think he'd choose? *He'd choose France.* Why? *Because he was born in France.* And what would he say about who's the nicer? Would he think the Swiss and French equally nice, or one better than the other? *He'd say the French are nicer.* Why? *Because he was born in France.* And who would he think more intelligent? *The French.* Why? *He'd say the French want to learn quicker than the Swiss.* Now you and the French boy don't really give the same answer. Who do you think answered best? *I did.* Why? Because Switzerland is always better.

Marina T. (7 years, 9 months old): If you were born without any nationality and you were given a free choice, what nationality would you choose? *Italian.* Why? *Because it's my country. I like it better than Argentina where my father works, because Argentina isn't my country.* Are Italians just the same, or more, or less intelligent than the Argentineans? What do you think? *The Italians are more intelligent.* Why? *I can see people I live with, they're Italians.* If I were to give a child from Argentina a free choice of nationality, what do you think he would choose? *He'd want to stay an Argentinean.* Why? *Because that's his country.* And if I were to ask him who is more intelligent, the Argentineans or the Italians, what do you think he would answer? *He'd say Argentineans.* Why? *Because there wasn't any war.* Now who was really right in the choice he made and what he said, the Argentinean child, you, or both? *I was right.* Why? *Because I chose Italy.*

Clearly these children are thinking sociocentrically. They have been indoctrinated into the belief systems, with accompanying ideologies, of their nation and culture. They cannot articulate why they think their country is better than others, but they have no doubt that it is. Seeing one's group as superior to other groups is both natural to the human mind and propagated by the cultures within which we live.

> Every group of any kind whatsoever demands that each of its members shall help defend group interests.
>
> William Graham Sumner

Social Stratification

Sociocentric systems are used in complex societies to justify differential treatment and injustices within a society, nation, or culture. This feature of complex social systems has been documented by sociologists who have specialized in the phenomenon of social stratification. As virtually all modern societies today are complex, the following characteristics of stratification presumably can be found in all of them. According to Plotnicov and Tuden (1970):

Each has social groups that

1. are ranked hierarchically,
2. maintain relatively permanent positions in the hierarchy,
3. have differential control of the sources of power, primarily economic and political,
4. are separated by cultural and invidious distinctions that also serve to maintain the social distances between the groups, and
5. are articulated by an overarching ideology which provides a rationale for the established hierarchical arrangements. (pp. 4–5)

Given this phenomenon, we should be able to identify, for any given group in our society, where approximately it stands in the hierarchy of power, what the sources of power and control are, how the distinctions that indicate status are formulated, how social distances are maintained between the groups, and the overarching ideology that provides the rationale for the way things are.

11.11   *Think for Yourself*

IDENTIFYING SOCIAL STRATIFICATION

Try to construct a hierarchy of the social groups within the culture with which you are most knowledgeable. First identify the groups with the most power and prestige. What characteristics do these groups have? Then identify the groups with less and less power until you reach the groups with the least amount of power. How do the groups with the most power keep their power? To what extent is it possible for groups with the least power to increase their power? To what extent do they seem to accept their limited power? To the extent that they accept their limited power, why do you think they do?

Sociocentric Thinking Is Unconscious and Potentially Dangerous

Sociocentric thinking, like egocentric thinking, appears in the mind of the person who thinks that way as reasonable and justified. Thus, although groups often distort the meaning of concepts to pursue their vested interests, they almost never see themselves as misusing language. Although groups almost always can find problems in the ideologies of other groups, they rarely are able to find flaws in their belief systems. Although groups usually can identify prejudices that other groups are using against them, they rarely are able to identify prejudices that they are using against other groups. In short, just as egocentric thinking is self-deceptive, so is sociocentric thinking.

Though the patterns of dysfunctional thinking are similar for egocentric and sociocentric thinking, there is at least one important distinction between the two. As we have already pointed out, egocentric thinking is potentially dangerous. Through self-deception, individuals can justify the most egregious actions, but individuals operating alone are usually more limited in the amount of harm they can do. Typically, groups engaging in sociocentric thinking can do greater harm to greater numbers of people.

> Although groups almost always can find problems in the ideologies of other groups, they rarely are able to find flaws in their own belief systems.

Consider, for example, the Spanish Inquisition, wherein the state, controlled by the Catholic Church, executed thousands of reputed heretics. Or consider the Germans, who tortured and murdered millions of Jews, or the "founders" of the Americas, who enslaved, murdered, or tortured large numbers of Native Americans and Africans.

In short, throughout history and to the present day, sociocentric thinking has led directly to the pain and suffering of millions of innocent persons. This has been possible because groups, in their sociocentric mindset, use their power in a largely unreflective, abusive way. Once they have internalized a self-serving ideology, they are able to act in ways that flagrantly contradict their announced morality without noticing any contradictions or inconsistencies in the process.

Sociocentric Uses of Language

Sociocentric thinking is fostered by the way groups use language. Groups justify unjust acts and ways of thinking through their use of concepts or ideas. For example, as William Sumner points out, sociocentrism can be exemplified by the very names groups choose for themselves and the way they differentiate themselves from what they consider lesser groups:

> When Caribs were asked whence they came, they answered, "We alone are people." The meaning of the name *Kiowa* is "real or principal people." The Lapps call themselves "men." Or "human beings." The Greenland Eskimo think that Europeans have been sent to Greenland to learn virtue and good manners from the Greenlanders. . . . The Seri of Lower California . . . observe an attitude of suspicion and hostility to all outsiders, and strictly forbid marriage with outsiders. (p. 14)

In the everyday life of sociocentric thinkers, we can find many self-serving uses of language that obscure unethical behavior. During the time when Europeans first inhabited the Americas, they forced Indians into slavery and tortured and murdered them in the name of progress and civilization. By thinking of the Indians as savages, they could justify their inhumane treatment. At the same time, by thinking of themselves as civilized, they could see themselves as bringing something precious to the savages—namely, civilization.

The words *progress, savagery, civilization,* and *the true religion* were used as vehicles to exploit the American Indians to gain material wealth and property. The thinking of the Europeans, focused on these ideas, obscures the basic humanity of the peoples exploited, as well as their rightful ownership of the land that they had occupied for thousands of years.

Sumner says that the language social groups use is often designed to ensure that they maintain a special, superior place:

> The Jews divided all mankind into themselves and the Gentiles. They were "chosen people." The Greeks called outsiders "barbarians." . . . The Arabs regarded themselves as the noblest nation and all others as more or less barbarous. . . . In 1896, the Chinese minister of education and his counselors edited a manual in which this statement occurs: "How grand and glorious is the Empire of China, the middle Kingdom!" . . . The grandest men in the world have come from the middle empire. . . . In all the literature of all the states equivalent statements occur. . . . In Russian books and newspapers the civilizing mission of Russia is talked about, just as, in the books and journals of France, Germany, and the United States, the civilizing mission of those countries is assumed and referred to as well understood. Each state now regards itself as the leader of civilization, the best, the freest and the wisest, and all others as their inferior. (p. 14)

Disclose Sociocentric Thinking
Through Conceptual Analysis

Concepts are one of the eight basic elements of human thinking. We cannot think without concepts. They form the classifications, and implicitly express the theories, through which we interpret what we see, taste, hear, smell, and touch. Our world is a conceptually constructed world. And sociocentric thinking, as argued above, is driven by the way groups use concepts.

If we thought using the concepts of medieval European serfs, we would experience the world as they did. If we thought using the concepts of an Ottoman Turk general, we would think and experience the world that he did. In a similar way, if we were to bring an electrician, an architect, a carpet salesperson, a lighting specialist, and a plumber into the same building and ask each to describe what he or she sees, we would end up with a range of descriptions that, in all likelihood, reveal the special "bias" of each observer.

Or again, if we were to lead a discussion of world problems between representatives of different nations, cultures, and religions, we would discover a range of perspectives on potential solutions to the problems and sometimes as to what a problem is in the first place.

It is hard to imagine a skilled critical thinker who is not also skilled in the analysis of concepts. Conceptual analysis is important in a variety of contexts:

1. The ability to identify and accurately analyze the range of distinctions available to educated speakers of a language (being able to distinguish between meanings of words, given educated usage).

2. The ability to identify the difference between ideological and nonideological uses of words and concepts (being able to figure out when people are giving special, unjustified meaning to words based on their ideology).

3. The ability to accurately analyze the network of technical meanings of words that define the basic concepts within a discipline or domain of thinking (being able to analyze the meanings of words within disciplines and technical fields).

Many problems in thinking are traceable to a lack of command of words and their implicit concepts. For example, people have problems in their romantic relationships when they are unclear about three distinctions: (1) between egocentric attachment and genuine love, (2) between friendship and love, and (3) between misuse of the word *love* (as exemplified by many Hollywood movies) and the true meaning of the word *love* shared by educated speakers of the English language.

Reveal Ideology at Work Through Conceptual Analysis

People often have trouble differentiating ideological and nonideological uses of words. They are then unable to use the following words in a nonloaded way: *capitalism, socialism, communism, democracy, oligarchy, plutocracy, patriotism, terrorism.* Let's look at this case in greater detail.

When the above words are used ideologically, they are applied inconsistently and one-sidedly. The root meaning of the word is often lost, or highly distorted, while the word is used to put a positive or negative gloss on events, obscuring what is really going on. Hence, in countries in which the reigning ideology extols capitalism, the ideologies of socialism and communism are demonized, democracy is equated with capitalism, and plutocracy is ignored. In countries in which the reigning ideology is communism, the ideology of capitalism is demonized, democracy is equated with communism, and oligarchy is ignored. The groups called "terrorist" by the one are called patriot by the other.

> In the everyday life of sociocentric thinkers, we can find many self-serving uses of language that obscure unethical behavior.

If we examine the core meanings of these words and use them in keeping with the core meanings they have in the English language, we can recognize contradictions, inconsistencies, and hypocrisy when any group misuses them to advance its agenda. Let us review the core meanings of these terms as defined by *Webster's New World Dictionary*:

- **capitalism:** an economic system in which all or most of the means of production and distribution, as land, factories, railroads, etc., are privately owned and operated for profit, originally under fully competitive conditions; it has generally been characterized by a tendency toward concentration of wealth.

- **socialism:** any of the various theories or systems of the ownership and operation of the means of production and distribution by society or the community rather than by private individuals, with all members of society or the community sharing in the work and the products.

- **communism:** any economic theory or system based on the ownership of all property by the community as a whole.

- **democracy:** a form of government in which the people hold the ruling power either directly or through elected representatives; rule by the ruled.

- **oligarchy:** a form of government in which the ruling power belongs to a few persons.

- **plutocracy:** (1) government by the wealthy, (2) a group of wealthy people who control or influence a government.

- **patriotism:** love, and loyal or zealous support of one's own country.

- **terrorism:** use of force or threats to demoralize, intimidate, and subjugate, especially such use as a political weapon or policy.

To this day, countries in which the reigning ideology is capitalism tend to use the words *socialism* and *communism* as if they meant "a system that discourages individual incentive and denies freedom to the mass of people." Countries in which the reigning ideology is socialism or communism, in their turn, tend to use the word *capitalism* to imply the exploitation of the masses by the wealthy few. Both see the use of force of the other as *terrorist* in intent. Both see the other as denying its own members fundamental human rights. Both tend to ignore their own inconsistencies and hypocrisy.

CONCLUSION

The thesis of this chapter is that we can successfully deal with our own egocentric and sociocentric tendencies only by facing, admitting, and undermining them. Without a clear understanding of our egocentric tendencies, we are trapped in a narrow and selfish perspective. Without a clear understanding of our sociocentric tendencies, we are trapped in groupthink.

Dealing with egocentrism and sociocentrism is no easy matter. Because both function subconsciously, it is difficult to identify them. And though no one will object to our being less selfish (personally), if we significantly and publicly dissent from group beliefs, we face an array of informal—if not formal—penalties.

What is important is that we begin to identify egocentrism and sociocentrism in our thinking and our lives. Every time we become aware of selfishness or narrow rigidity in our thinking, we create an opportunity to lessen those pathologies. Every group to which we belong is a possible place to identify sociocentrism at work in ourselves and others. When we begin to identify the many patterns of self-centeredness and social conformity in our lives, we can begin to break out of those patterns. We need not begin with the beliefs that are most challenging to ourselves or whose denial is most "explosive." Furthermore, we need not make all of what we find a matter of public statement. The key is that we do begin within the privacy of our mind, that we follow through with consistency, and that we give ourselves time to grow progressively into better thinkers and persons. By such inward acts we can become people who think for ourselves and adhere to conscious standards of rationality. By such acts we can develop intellectual integrity and emerge increasingly as fair and just persons.

HOW TO DETECT MEDIA BIAS AND PROPAGANDA IN NATIONAL AND WORLD NEWS

T he logic behind bias and propaganda in the news media is simple and it is the same the world over. Each society and culture has a unique world view, which colors what they see and how they see it. News media in the cultures of the world reflect the world view of the culture they write for. But the truth of what is happening in the world is much more complicated than what appears to be true in any culture. To be a critical reader of the news media in any society, one must come to terms with this truth and read accordingly. Critical thinking is a complex set of skills that reverses what is natural and instinctive in human thought.

As we pointed out previously, the uncritical mind is unconsciously driven to iden-tify truth in accordance with the following tacit maxims:

"It's true if I believe it."

"It's true if we believe it."

"It's true if we want to believe it."

"It's true if it serves our vested interest to believe it."

The critical mind consciously seeks the truth in accordance with the following instinct-correcting maxims:

"I believe it, but it may not be true."

"We believe it, but we may be wrong."

"We want to believe it, but we may be prejudiced by our desire."

"It serves our vested interest to believe it, but our vested interest has nothing to do with the truth."

Mainstream news coverage in a society operates with the following maxims:

This is how it appears to us from our point of view; therefore, this is the way it is.

These are the facts that support our way of looking at this; therefore, these are the most important facts.

These countries are friendly to us; therefore, these countries deserve praise.

These countries are unfriendly to us; therefore, these countries deserve criticism.

These are the stories most interesting or sensational to our readers; therefore, these are the most important stories in the news.

Critical readers of the news reverse each of these maxims. This chapter explains how to do this and thereby reduce the influence of bias and propaganda on the mind.

DEMOCRACY AND THE NEWS MEDIA

Nothing could be more irrational than to give the people power and to withhold from them information, without which power is abused. A people who mean to be their own governors must arm themselves with the power which knowledge gives. A popular government without popular information or the means of acquiring it is but a prologue to a farce or a tragedy, or perhaps both.

—James Madison

Democracy can be an effective form of government only to the extent that the public (that rules it in theory) is well-informed about national and international events and can think independently and critically about those events. If the vast majority of citizens do not recognize bias in their nation's news; if they cannot detect ideology, slant, and spin; if they cannot recognize propaganda when exposed to it, they cannot reasonably determine what media messages have to be supplemented, counter-balanced, or thrown out entirely.

On the one hand, worldwide news sources are increasingly sophisticated in media logic (the art of "persuading" and manipulating large masses of people). This enables them to create an aura of objectivity and "truthfulness" in the news stories they construct. On the other hand, only a small minority of citizens are skilled in recognizing bias and propaganda in the news disseminated in their country. Only a relatively few are able to detect one-sided portrayals of events or seek out alternative sources of information and opinion to compare to those of the mainstream news media. At present, the overwhelming majority of people in the world, untrained in critical thinking, are at the mercy of the news media in their own country. Their view of the world, which countries they identify as friends and which as enemies, is determined largely by those media (and the traditional beliefs and conventions of their society).

This slanted information is not a "plot" or a "conspiracy." It is simply a matter of educational background and economic reality. Journalists and news editors are themselves members of a culture (German, French, Mexican, Chinese, Korean, Japanese, Indonesian, Russian, Algerian, Nigerian, North American, etc.). They share a view of the world with their target audience. They share a nationalized sense of history and allegiance, often a religion, and a general belief system. An Arab editor sees the world differently than an Israeli editor. A Pakistani editor sees the world differently than an Indian editor. A Chinese editor sees the world differently than an American editor. The same is true of news reporters and other journalists.

What's more, news people work under severe time restrictions (in constructing their stories) and limitations of space (in laying out or presenting their stories). It is hardly surprising that profound differences are reflected in news coverage from nation to nation and from culture to culture.

In any case, only those who understand the conditions under which world media operate have a chance of controlling the influence of their national media upon them. Our goal in this chapter is to help our readers lay a foundation for transforming the influence of the media on their lives. It is in all of our interests to critically assess, rather than mindlessly accept, news media pronouncements. We hope we can aid readers to become more independent, insightful, and critical in responding to the content of news media messages and stories.

12.1   *Think for Yourself*

CONTRASTING WORLD VIEWS

Are you familiar with any world view that contrasts with the world view of your culture? If so, discuss with another student the similarities and differences between the beliefs of your culture and those of a different culture. If not, see if you can locate a characterization of one world view that contrasts with the world view of your home culture.

For example, if you see the world from the perspective of a North American "Christian" culture, accumulate some information about the perspective of a Middle Eastern "Muslim" culture. Find a news source on the Internet that provides coverage of world events from that alternative cultural perspective. Discuss the differences you find in the same events being covered in these contrasting ways. See if you can notice your prejudice in favor of your home culture.

MYTHS THAT OBSCURE THE LOGIC OF THE NEWS MEDIA

The media foster a set of myths regarding how they function. Believing these myths impedes the ability to view the news from a critical perspective. The myths include the following:

- that most news stories are produced through independent investigative journalism
- that news writers simply report facts in their stories and do not come to conclusions about them
- that fact and opinion are clearly separated in constructing the news
- that there is an objective reality (the actual "news") that is simply "reported" or described by the news media of the world (our news media writers reporting on this objectively; the media of foreign enemies systematically slanting and distorting it)
- that what is unusual (novel, odd, bizarre) is news; what is usual is not.

12.2   *Think for Yourself*

FINDING THE ROOT CAUSES OF MYTHS ABOUT THE MEDIA

D iscuss with another student what you think are the root causes of one or more of the above myths. Ask why people would believe these myths.

"OBJECTIVITY" IN THE NEWS MEDIA

The logic of constructing news stories is parallel to the logic of writing history. In both cases, for events covered there is *both* a massive background of facts *and* a highly restricted amount of space to devote to those facts. The result in both cases is the same: 99.99999% of the "facts" are never mentioned at all (see Exhibit 12.1).

If objectivity or fairness in the construction of news stories is thought of as equivalent to presenting all the facts and only the facts ("All the news that's fit to print"), objectivity or fairness is an illusion. No human knows more than a small percentage of the facts, and it is not possible to present all the facts (even if one did know them). It isn't even possible to present all the *important* facts, for many criteria compete for determining what is "important." We therefore must always ask: What has been left out of this article? What would I think if different facts had been highlighted here? What if this article had been written by those who hold a point of view opposite to the one embedded in the story as told?

Most people, having given up on getting a set of unadorned facts, align themselves with whichever spin outlet seems comfortable.

Wall Street Journal (May 7, 2004)

EXHIBIT 12.1 *What happens in the world on any given day.*

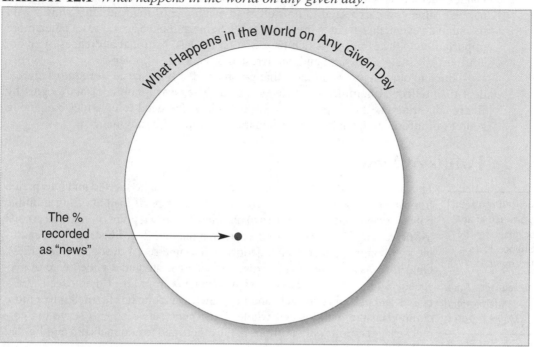

The % recorded as "news"

For example, people commonly consider facts to be important to the extent that the facts have significant implications for them personally: Is any given event going to affect what I want? How much is it going to cost me? How is it going to influence my income, my living conditions, my leisure, my convenience? How some given event is going to affect others, especially others far away and out of sight, is quite another matter. There is therefore a wide divergence among the news media of the world as to what is presented as "significant" in the world.

The media focus on what their readers personally care about. Thus, even if their readers are irrational in some belief (e.g., they harbor some irrational hate), the media nevertheless will treat that hatred as rational. Hence, when slavery was commonly accepted in the United States, the media presented slavery as "natural." When the country became divided on the issue, the media followed suit (each paper presenting as right what its readers believed to be right).

Consider how news media treat what is "shocking" or "exciting" or "disgusting" or "delightful" to a social group. For example, a woman sunbathing on a beach with bare breasts is commonplace on the French Riviera (and therefore is not condemned and her behavior is not treated as "news"), but the same woman would be arrested and punished for sunbathing in a similar way at a beach in Lebanon (and therefore would be condemned and her behavior treated as "news"). Or again, during the Olympic

Games each country's news media focus their attention on those events in which their nation's athletes are expected to do well. And when one of their athletes wins a gold medal in an event, this event is presented to the home audience as if it were much more important than the events in which they won no medals. National audiences often are "thrilled" by their "victories" and uninterested in victories of others.

Human "objectivity" is an ideal that no one perfectly achieves. It requires a great deal of intellectual humility (knowledge of our extensive ignorance) and begins by freely admitting one's own point of view, as well as the need to consider competing sources of information and opinion when making important judgments.

Points of View

> Newspapers tend to signal the importance of an article or image by the prominence of its placement.
>
> *New York Times International* (May 11, 2004)

The key point is this: Typically, any set of events can be viewed and interpreted from *multiple* points of view. Openness to a range of insights from multiple points of view and a willingness to question one's own point of view are crucial to "objectivity." This can be suggested in a diagram that illustrates how multiple viewpoints often stand in relation to the same set of events (Exhibit 12.2). Objectivity is achieved to the extent that one has studied a wide range of perspectives relevant to an issue, obtained insights from all of them, seen weaknesses and partiality in each, and integrated what one has learned into a more comprehensive, many-sided whole. Each perspective should serve to "correct" exaggerations or distortions in the others and to add facts not highlighted in the others.

EXHIBIT 12.2 *Six points of view focused on the same set of events.*

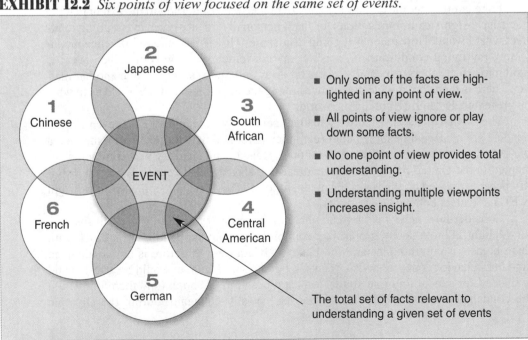

- Only some of the facts are highlighted in any point of view.
- All points of view ignore or play down some facts.
- No one point of view provides total understanding.
- Understanding multiple viewpoints increases insight.

The total set of facts relevant to understanding a given set of events

We gain in "objectivity" (in conceptualizing both history and the news) to the extent that we can put stories and narratives into a rich historical context and comment on them from multiple points of view. For example, to understand the war between Great Britain and its colonies in North America (1776–1783), one must look at the events from at least three points of view: that of the British government, that of the Colonial leaders, and that of the indigenous peoples.

To achieve objectivity, we need to:

1. identify the point of view from which a given news story or historical account is constructed
2. identify the audience it is written for
3. recognize what points of view it is negating or ignoring
4. distinguish the raw facts behind the story from the interpretation and spin being put on those facts.

When we do this, we are not as easily manipulated. We are able to exercise greater independence of judgment. We get a greater sense of what elements of the story or account are most credible and which are the least credible. Of course, it is hard to do any of these if we have not also discovered multiple sources for information and a way to determine when those sources are most credible.

12.3 *Think for Yourself*

IDENTIFYING THE INTERESTS OF READERS

Analyze the front section of a newspaper to identify the viewpoint of the paper's primary audience. See if you can figure out what the readers of that paper—the people willing to buy—think is important. How would you characterize the readers' primary point of view? How do they see the world? What do they want to read about? What would they rather not read about?

Forms of Objectivity

"Objectivity" may appear in three ways. Two are genuine. One is a façade, a counterfeit of objectivity. These forms of objectivity are discussed next.

The Objectivity of Intellectual Humility

The first form of objectivity is based on the possibility of developing intellectual humility, knowledge of our ignorance. Thus, a critical consumer of the news knows the difference between hearing a story and verifying the truth of that story. A critical consumer of the news knows that what is presented as fact in the news may not be fact. It may be propaganda, misinformation, distortion, or half-truth. Knowing this, critical consumers of the news "bracket" what they hear, read, and see in the news. Recognizing that they don't themselves know the facts, they "suspend" belief. They take in information in a tentative fashion. ("This may or may not be true.") For example, "objective" jurors will not come to a conclusion of guilt or innocence after hearing only one side of a case.

Unfortunately, intellectual humility is a rare quality in human life. The majority of people in the world have been exposed to a limited range of views and have been most influenced by the viewpoint that is dominant in their own culture. As a result, they take themselves to be in possession of the *Truth*. This confidence is actually proof of their lack of objectivity. They do not know what intellectual humility is, and they do not take steps to achieve it.

The Objectivity of Fair-Minded, Multidimensional Thinking

A second form of objectivity goes beyond the first. Fair-minded, multidimensional thinking is based on intellectual humility and also on having done substantial intellectual work in reasoning within multiple conflicting points of view in addressing questions, problems, and issues of significance. It is connected to positive insight into the complexity and many-sidedness of most important world issues and large-scale conflicts. Those who have achieved this state can insightfully role-play multiple perspectives on a multitude of issues. They can identify and weigh relative strengths and weaknesses within those perspectives. They are comfortable playing the role of dissenter, though they don't dissent for the sake of dissent. They reject party lines, sociocentric mindsets, and intellectual conformity. They are intellectually independent, are intellectually perseverant, and have intellectual integrity.

How many photos of naked Iraqis does one want to see?

Col Allan,
editor in chief,
New York Post,
(May 10, 2004)

Sophistic Objectivity

The third form of objectivity is "sophistic." This intellectual state results from studying a range of views with the overriding motivation to defend a predetermined choice. This mindset is common in intellectuals who make their income (and achieve their prestige) as apologists for powerful interests. The temptation to become an apologist for a well-established point of view or economic interest is enormous because money, position, and prestige are involved. Lawyers and politicians, as well as public relations experts, are typically ready to play such a role.

What is on the front page is more difficult to avoid than what is inside.

New York Times International
(May 11, 2004)

Most national news commentators routinely play such a role. They present positions consistent with a picture of the world shared by most of their readers or viewers. Their audience views them as objective only to the extent that what they present reflects mainstream views.

12.4   *Think for Yourself*

INTERNALIZE THE FORMS OF OBJECTIVITY

Explain to another student (in your own words) the three forms of objectivity described. Have your partner try to explain them to you. For each one, state your understanding, elaborate, and give an example from your own experience.

THE PERCEPTION OF BIAS IN THE MAINSTREAM

Quite naturally, but uncritically, people think of those who agree with them as objective and those who disagree with them as biased. Thus, if news commentators present mainstream views with a liberal spin, they are viewed as "objective" only by the liberals in the audience. If mainstream views are given a conservative spin, they are viewed as "objective" only by the conservatives in their audience. The media therefore present liberal or conservative slants on the news in accordance with their audience's views.

Propaganda and News Story Writing

Webster's New World Dictionary defines propaganda as "any systematic, widespread dissemination or promotion of particular ideas, doctrines, practices, etc. to further one's own cause or to damage an opposing one." Given this definition, there is no clear-cut dividing line between news story writing with a given cultural audience in mind, on the one hand, and constructing propaganda on the other hand. Both systematically play down or seek to minimize the worth of opposing perspectives or points of view. The logical similarity is striking. Even historical writing can take on the character of propaganda when it is written to "glorify" or "demonize" certain groups of people by suppressing or ignoring information that does not support its preconceptions and favored ideology.

> . . . because of the nudity and humiliation on display in the Iraq photographs, many newspapers have chosen to put articles about them on the front page, but the images inside.
>
> *New York Times International*
> (May 11, 2004)

Because the word "propaganda" carries with it a negative connotation (suggesting deception or distortion), few news writers would admit that the word applies to their stories. Yet, if one receives most of one's news from a single cultural or national source, the likely impact on the mind will be that of distortion and deception. Most people, as a result, are trapped in one world view (because they have received a steady diet of stories and accounts articulated from that perspective and have not seriously considered any alternatives).

This does not mean, of course, that a given world view is unvaried. Not everyone who shares a viewpoint agrees on every issue. Not every German agrees with every other German, Still, a significant difference exists between those who see the world from a German perspective and those who see it from, say, a Japanese or a Mexican perspective. What's more, although essentially every point of view carries some insight, it doesn't follow that each has *equal* insight.

It is usually much easier for people to recognize the truth of these tendencies when they are thinking about the news coverage in other nations or cultures—especially when those other nations and cultures differ greatly from their own. For example, Israelis easily recognize bias and propaganda in Arab coverage though they see little in their own coverage, and vice versa.

When President George W. Bush of the United States gave a speech identifying Iran, Iraq, and North Korea as an "axis of evil," his speech was received favorably by the majority of Americans. It was taken as a follow-up of the President's promise to "rid the world of evil." A wave of patriotic fervor was sweeping the nation. The national news media had engendered a communal sense of rage. For the overwhelming majority of Americans, the American government stands for high ideals (liberty, justice, democracy, free enterprise, human rights). The President defending the country against its enemies with the might of its armed forces is an image that inspires patriotic emotions.

The speech, however, was not received in the same way abroad. Bush was roundly condemned by the news media in Iran, Iraq, and North Korea and also was viewed as arrogant and out of touch with the complexities of reality by "allies" of the United States. Here are some of the ways the French and German media conceptualized the speech to their national audiences (*New York Times,* January 31, 2002, p. A12):

- "In France, the afternoon daily *Le Monde* ran a front-page cartoon of Mr. Bush in battle fatigues and a headline saying, 'Mr. Bush points out his latest enemies'."

- "A television editorialist on LCI, France's 24-hour news station, said the speech belonged to 'a sheriff convinced of his right to regulate the planet and impose punishment as he sees fit'."

- "In Germany, an editorial in the daily *Suddeutsche Zeitung* offered Chancellor Gerhard Schroder sympathy as he heads for Washington tonight. 'Poor Gerhard Schroder,' the editorial says. 'It can't be easy being the first grumpy European to appear at the throne of the freshly anointed American Caesar'."

Here is a sense of the news media coverage in Iran and North Korea, taken from the same source:

- "Bush intends to divert public opinion from the Middle East issue and to prepare the domestic grounds for continuing his support of Israel in its brutal oppression of the Palestinian nation." (Iran state radio report)

- "North Korea's official media scoffed at Mr. Bush for identifying the nation as among the world's most dangerous. It said his 'loudmouthed threat' was intended to justify an American military presence in South Korea."

In virtually every case, it is easier to persuade people that foreign press coverage is biased than to persuade those same people of their own national press bias. Every nation's press coverage of the "news" appears to the mass public of that culture as expressing self-evident truth—because the news is routinely presented within the world view of the mass public that consumes that news.

When trapped in a culture-bound view of the world, one thinks within a web of self-serving assumptions, thinking that it is others (our national or cultural enemies and opponents) who use propaganda and manipulation while we, being honest and just, always give the other side its due. Others use propaganda and manipulation. We freely express the truth. This mindset is not the product of a conspiracy or intrigue. It is the natural and predictable outcome of national news media attempting to make a profit by presenting events in the world to a home audience.

12.5   *Think for Yourself*

INTERNALIZE THE CONCEPT OF PROPAGANDA

E xplain to another student (in your own words) the concept of propaganda described above. Have your partner try to explain it to you. State your understanding, elaborate, and give an example. Do you have a different concept of propaganda? Explain.

Protecting the Home Audience from Guilt Feelings

The events for which news coverage is most taboo in mainstream media news are deeds that indict the home culture or society of ethical wrongdoing. Consider, for example, the extent of civilian suffering following the dropping of atom bombs on the cities of Hiroshima and Nagasaki by the United States military. Though some debate has taken place in the United States media on these acts, to our knowledge the U.S. mainstream media have presented little documentation of the enormous suffering caused by those events.

> We are certainly not going to let images with nudity or gore or violence go on the air.
>
> John Banner,
> executive producer of
> ABC's *World News Tonight*

One might compare, for example, documentation of the suffering of civilians in German extermination camps (which has been, and continues to be, extensive) with that of the Japanese populations of Hiroshima and Nagasaki when subjected to massive atomic radiation. Searching the 50 years since the event, we found only one article in one American newspaper, the Santa Rosa *Press Democrat* (in Northern California) documenting in detail the suffering of the civilian population. The article was a guest editorial by David R. Ford, who worked in 1965 for a CBS television affiliate in Honolulu and now lives in the Santa Rosa, California, area. Here are excerpts (without the horrific details) from his editorial:

> In 1965. . . I spent a vacation in Hiroshima, Japan. My purpose: To interview the sick and dying 20 years after the atomic bomb was exploded over that city on Aug. 6, 1944. . . . I began the visit in the women's ward.

What follows in the article are detailed images of suffering that American readers would find extremely painful to imagine their government as inflicting (200,000 civilians died in Hiroshima alone on that day). The American reporter said to a Japanese victim,

> "But we dropped millions of pamphlets warning citizens to evacuate the cities." He looked into my eyes. "No paper was ever dropped. No warning was ever given."

We cannot, of course, attest to the truth or falsity of the allegation of the U.S. failure to forewarn the civilian population. For our purposes, the significance is the almost complete absence of documentation of how the citizens of Hiroshima and Nagasaki suffered at the time and in the 50 years following the events. Given our analysis, the absence of documentation of these events by the American media is exactly what we would predict from a national mass news media. People do not pay for news that leads them to question the "goodness" of their own nation or makes them feel responsible for the large-scale suffering of others. They pay to see the events of the world in a way that validates their values and allegiances.

12.6 *Think for Yourself*

IDENTIFYING UNETHICAL GOVERNMENT ACTIONS

Identify a news story, either from the mainstream news or from an alternative news source, that focuses on one or more ethical wrongdoings sanctioned by your government or culture, actions that people within the country would like to avoid knowing or thinking about. Write a summary of the story and identify the reason(s) people would like to avoid thinking about the issue. How is the "wrongdoing" treated? Is it highlighted, or is it hidden?

FOSTERING SOCIOCENTRIC THINKING

The key insight is this: The major media and press in *all countries of the world* present events to the world in terms that presuppose or imply the "correctness" of the ideology (or ideologies) dominant in the country. Our hope is not in changing the news media. News reporters and editors operate within a system of economic imperatives and constraints that dominate their work. Their audience is captive to an enculturated conception of the world.

Rather, as aspiring critical consumers of the mass media, we must learn to recognize that mainstream news is inevitably based on a sociocentric view of the world. We must learn how to recognize national and cultural bias. There is no reason to suppose that the ideology dominant in our culture is more accurate or insightful than that of any other culture. Presuming that one's own culture is exceptionally truthful in presenting its picture of the world is evidence not of insight but instead of ethnocentrism. Sociocentrism is a fundamental characteristic of all countries and cultures. The news media function as unwitting agents of social conventions and taboos.

EXHIBIT 12.3 *A mutually reinforcing relationship fostering sociocentric thinking.*

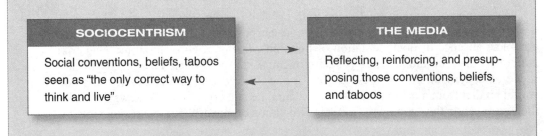

SOCIOCENTRISM	THE MEDIA
Social conventions, beliefs, taboos seen as "the only correct way to think and live"	Reflecting, reinforcing, and presupposing those conventions, beliefs, and taboos

Many examples of sociocentric thinking can be found in the mass media. The media are an inherent part of the culture within which they function. And, again, those in the media must "sell" their stories. Their papers, news broadcasts, and magazines must be economically successful to remain in business:

> Pressure to increase the profits of media companies has not been an isolated phenomenon. Throughout the American economy, there is unprecedented pressure to maximize profits, putting shareholder value ahead of all other considerations. The corporations that own the news media are subject to all the business trends and economic demands that have reshaped American business in the 1980s and 1990s, affecting nearly every part of society. (Downie and Kaiser, p. 25)

Because much of the thinking within any given culture is sociocentric in nature to begin with, the news media have little choice but to package what they produce within a sociocentric framework. The vehicles of large-scale social communication within a society inevitably serve that society and advance its self-image. Biased coverage is the rule, not the exception.

The mainstream news media around the world are thus biased toward their country's "allies" and prejudiced against their "enemies." They therefore present events occurring in the countries of their allies in as favorable a light as possible, highlighting their "positive" deeds while downplaying their negative ones. When generating news stories about their "enemies," the opposite treatment inevitably follows. Generating positive stories about the admirable characteristics of one's enemies is unacceptable. At the same time, negative stories about enemies are always popular, routinely generated and highlighted. The ability of a news consumer to identify these biased stories in action and mentally "rewrite" them with an opposing bias is a crucial critical thinking skill. With this skill, one sees slanted constructs everywhere in the news. And when one sees through the bias, its persuasive effect on the mind disappears.

12.7 *Think for Yourself*

IDENTIFYING SOCIOCENTRIC THINKING IN THE NEWS

Locate one news story exemplifying the fact that reporters, as a rule, uncritically accept the social conventions and taboos of their culture.

For example, on the front page of the typical American newspaper, it is common to see, from time to time, a picture of the President of the United States shaking hands with another leader, or arriving somewhere on an airplane, or walking on the front lawn of the White House with his dog, smiling and appearing happy—in other words, looking "Presidential." Somehow this makes people within the culture feel confident in their president. It is a form of "authority worship." The convention that this picture exemplifies is the cultural norm of idolizing persons in positions of power.

See if you can find a story wherein the reporter feeds into social conventions or taboos—for example, a story of a woman being taken to jail for appearing topless in public or a story of someone going to prison for growing and selling marijuana. These types of stories would be candidates because they represent cultural conventions.

SLANTING STORIES TO FAVOR PRIVILEGED VIEWS

Every journalist knows intuitively which terms to use when characterizing the favored and unfavored players on the world stage (as pictured within a cultural perspective). We *plan* . . . they *plot*. We are *clever* . . . they are *sneaky*. We form *strategies* . . . they *conspire*. We have *convictions* . . . they are *fanatics*. We are *proud* . . . they are *arrogant*. We *stand tall* . . . they *brag* and *bluster*. We build weapons to *defend* ourselves . . . they build weapons to *threaten* us. We *intervene* . . . they *invade*. We have *religious convictions* . . . they are *fanatics*. We are *freedom-fighters* . . . they are *terrorists*. We violate treaties when they are *obsolete* . . . they violate treaties because they are *irresponsible, untrustworthy, unethical*.

Journalists routinely select words that reinforce the prevailing views among the readership or audience for whom they are writing. Ironically, if newspersons writing for a mainstream audience were to adopt views that significantly diverged from those dominant in their society and presented the news in accordance with those views, they would be considered "biased" and "irresponsible." If you think in accordance with mainstream views, you are a "responsible" thinker; if not, you are "irresponsible."

The exception occurs, of course, if significant numbers of people in the culture hold conflicting views, as in the conflict between liberal and conservative perspectives (expressed differently in most cultures). In this case, both points of view are presented in both favorable and unfavorable terms (depending upon whether the source is dominated by conservatives or liberals). Nevertheless, if one's views do not fall into either the mainstream liberal or conservative purview, one is dismissed as a "radical." Radicals are irresponsible by definition (as they do not agree with one of the two traditional views).

The following newspaper excerpts exemplify how the news media across the world do not report the news objectively but instead cater to the views of their readers.

"Foreign Media Shows Different Iraq War Than U.S. Outlets"

Source: *Press Democrat,* March 26, 2003.

> Journalists from around the world are reporting the war in Iraq through a very different lens than U.S.-based media, one often colored by a mistrust of the Bush administration and U.S. intentions in general. "You see a lot more skepticism in other parts of the world," said Alice Chasan, editor of *World Press Review,* which compiles reports from media in other countries. The context of many foreign reports is "What is the United States really trying to do? Is the war necessary?" she said. "Whatever happens is being seen through the prism of President Bush being 'arrogant.'" By contrast, "among the U.S. press there tends to be bandwagon effect and a fog of patriotism that has at times appalled me," Chasan said. "It's something you don't see elsewhere." . . .
>
> "I think that most American journalists have been remarkably uncritical in covering the war," said Tom Buk–Swienty, U.S. bureau chief for the Danish *Weekendavisen.* "In an effort not to look unpatriotic and in order to please the majority of people in this country, some parts of the press have almost become a PR machine instead of being a watchdog that one would expect in a democracy," he said. Patriotic displays include a

U.S. flag adorning one corner of the front page of the *New York Post.* Meanwhile, broadcast reporters "embedded" with U.S. units in the region have begun to use the personal pronoun "we." U.S.-based outlets have agonized over matters of taste as they weigh their audiences' appetite for gruesome photos.

"The War Americans Don't See"

Source: *Press Democrat,* April 4, 2003, editorial by Rami G. Khouri, executive editor of the *Daily Star,* a Beirut newspaper.

> The Arab press—like Arab public opinion as a whole—predominantly opposes the British and American attack on Iraq, and does not hesitate to say so in its front page headlines, articles and photographs. Yet the press is neither monolithic nor uniformly anti-American. . . . Samples. . . from front pages this week in the Arabic language (and in Algeria's case, French-language) press demonstrate the United States and the Arab world do see a different war unfolding. But the front pages of leading newspapers in and around the Arab world include both American and Iraqi perspectives and feature dramatic photographs that show United States forces as both aggressors and humanitarians.
>
> One recent front page photo showed an Iraqi civilian pouring tea for an American soldier. More common, though, are images of dead and maimed Iraqi children, parents wailing over the coffins of relatives killed by American bombings, extensive damage of Iraqi civilian buildings and Iraqi civilians being humiliated by American and British troops. Sometimes, an image that would get an innocuous description in an American newspaper is given a more sinister interpretation in the Arab press.
>
> Coverage tends to mirror ideology. The quality regional press like *Asharq al Awsat* and *Al Hayat,* edited in London and printed throughout the Middle East, are the most balanced. More ideological papers with narrow readerships reflect the sentiments of their financial backers and tend to cater to the nationalistic, political and emotional views of their audiences. The tone of opinion columns and editorials is heavily anti-American. Only occasionally do Arab writers like Ghassan Tueni in Beirut's *AN Nahar* call for the end of Saddam Hussein and his regime (and that is coupled with a rejection of American occupation).

Commentary.   This editorial supports the thesis that the press in every country presents events in the world as confirming what their audience (and the backers of their newspaper) already believe. This thesis is borne out at a national level and a regional level as well. Hence, the *Press Democrat* (published in a liberal area of California) carries this editorial, which argues that the Arab press is not entirely biased against the U. S. Its title emphasizes the need for Americans to broaden their sources of information ("The War Americans Don't See"). In contrast, the *New York Times,* in reporting on the Arab press, strongly suggests that it is biased against the United States and Israel, while the U.S. press, we are tacitly led to believe, is objective, balanced, and fair. See the next excerpt.

"Arab Media Portray War as Killing Field"

Source: *New York Times,* April 4, 2003.

> It was a picture of Arab grief and rage. A teen-aged boy glared from the rubble of a bombed building as a veiled woman shrieked over the prostrate body of a relative. In fact, it was two pictures: one from the American-led war in Iraq and the other from the

Palestinian territories, blended into one image this week on the Web site of the popular Saudi daily newspaper *Al Watan*. The meaning would be clear to any Arab reader: What is happening in Iraq is part of one continuous brutal assault by America and its allies on defenseless Arabs, wherever they are.

"As the Iraq war moved into its third week, the media in the region have increasingly fused images and enemies from this and other conflicts into a single bloodstained tableau of Arab grievance. The Israeli flag is superimposed on the American flag. The Crusades and the 13th-century Mongul sack of Baghdad, recalled as barbarian attacks on Arab civilization, are used as synonyms for the American-led invasion of Iraq. Horrific vignettes of the helpless—armless children, crushed babies, stunned mothers—cascade into Arab living rooms from the front pages of newspapers and television screens. . . . The daily message to the public from much of the media is that American troops are callous killers, that only resistance to the United States can redeem Arab pride and the Iraqis are fighting a pan-Arab battle for self respect. . . . The rage against the United States is fed by this steady diet of close-up color photographs and television footage of dead and wounded Iraqis, invariably described as victims of American bombs.

In recent days, more and more Arabic newspapers have run headlines bluntly accusing soldiers of deliberately killing civilians. Even for those accustomed to seeing such images from Arab coverage of the Palestinian-Israeli conflict, the daily barrage of war coverage in newspapers and on hourly television reports has left many Arabs beside themselves with anger. "He is 'Shaytan,' that Bush," shouted Ali Mammouda, a newsstand operator in Cairo, using the Arabic word for Satan and pointing with shaking hands to a color photograph in one of his newspapers. The image, published in many Arabic papers, showed the bloody bodies of a stick-thin woman and a baby said to be victims of American shelling in central Iraq. They were lying in an open wooden coffin, the baby's green pacifier still in its mouth. "Your Bush says he is coming to make them free, but look at this lady," Mr. Hammouda exclaimed. "Is she free? What did she do? What did her baby do?"*

Commentary.   This article implies that there is no truth in the Arab media's coverage of civilian casualties in the Iraq war. The *New York Times* readership is basically conservative, overwhelmingly supporting both the Israeli government and the U.S.-led invasion of Iraq. The readership is therefore primed to reject any coverage of the war that negatively portrays U.S. forces, the U.S. government, or the Israeli government. Because the article heavily criticizes the Arab media's coverage of the Iraq war, the story is not "buried"; rather, it is given a prime place in the paper (front page).

12.8   *Think for Yourself*

IDENTIFYING BIAS AGAINST OTHER COUNTRIES

I dentify a news story that favors your country's viewpoint and therefore is biased against the viewpoint of another country. Use the format above to write a summary of the story (with quotes). Then comment on how the story is slanted to support your country's viewpoint.

---

*All excerpts from *The New York Times*, copyright © in the indicated year by The New York Times Co. Reprinted with permission.

How to Obtain Useful Information from Propaganda and Standard News Stories

Obtaining useful information, even from propaganda and one-sided news stories, is possible, but only if one learns to read, hear, or view the stories critically. This means that we must analyze the stories with a clear awareness of the point of view they embody, recognizing the attempt to influence our thinking and beliefs. We must analyze them as we analyze one side of a multi-sided argument. One-sided presentations are not the truth pure and simple, though they contain at least part of the truth, the part that supports the side in question. What's more, in standard news stories something of the opposing point of view is often mentioned (though, usually, in fine print, deemphasized in the last few paragraphs of the story, or couched in terms or quote marks, suggesting that the reader should dismiss it).

Critical readers recognize one-sidedness and seek out viewpoints that are dismissed or ignored. They also note which stories are highlighted (e.g., on the front page) and which are buried in the background (e.g., on page 24). Some key questions we should ask when analyzing and interpreting news stories are:

- What is the intended audience?
- What point of view is being privileged?
- What point(s) of view is (are) being dismissed or played down?
- How can I gain access to the point of view being negated (from those who most intelligently understand it)?
- Which stories are featured on the front page? Why?
- What information is "buried" in the article? Why?

12.9, 12.10 *Think for Yourself*

INTERNALIZING IDEAS

Based on your understanding of the logic of the media, discuss with another student why some stories are highlighted (put on the front page) and others are played down (placed in a small article in an obscure section of the paper).

ANALYZING NEWS STORY PLACEMENT

Read through the front section of a newspaper. Your local paper might do, but try to use a fairly large newspaper containing national and international news. Find examples of relatively unimportant but highlighted (on page 1, for instance) articles, and examples of important but buried stories.

Steps in Becoming a Critical Consumer of the "News"

1. Understand the basic agenda of "news story construction." Always keep in mind that the ultimate purpose of mainstream "news story fabrication" is to sell "stories" for a profit to specific audiences (each with certain beliefs, values, and prejudices). It is not to educate. It is not to be fair to all sides (all sides are rarely represented in the target audience). To sell news stories to an audience, one must construct those stories carefully in such a way as to engage intended readers and reinforce or validate their beliefs, values, prejudices, and world view. Journalists typically come from those who share the beliefs, values, prejudices, and world view of the intended audience. The "slanting" of the story then is achieved "naturally."

Constructing news stories for an audience requires that one determine:

a. what the audience would consider a "story" (what they would, and would not, be interested in),

b. what about a story would be considered most relevant and what about it would be considered least relevant to the audience (therefore, what to play up and what to downplay),

c. how to construct "leads" or "headlines" for a story (to create an initial definition for the reader),

d. how much space or time to give a particular story,

e. how to relate the story to other stories and to the audience's picture of themselves and their world, and

f. how to tell the story so it sounds "professional" (objective and unbiased to the readers, a mere accounting of bare facts).

2. Use one's knowledge of the logic of news story construction, first, to deconstruct stories in the news, and then to reconstruct them imaginatively with alternative biases and slants. One becomes a critical consumer of the news media, first, by understanding the agenda of the news media, the criteria the news media use in constructing the news (deciding what a "story" is, what stories to cover, how to cover them to get the highest ratings or sell the most newspapers or magazines). Skilled consumers of the news learn how to identify and assess national, social, and political emphases and agendas. They learn how to read between the lines and how to imaginatively recast *stories as-told* into alternative *stories-as-they-might-have-been-told* from other points of view.

3. Learn how to redefine issues, access alternative sources (both within and outside the mainstream), put events into a historical perspective, and notice and assess assumptions and implications. Systematic questioning and assessment are crucial to the critical processing of media messages.

4. Learn how to identify low-credibility stories by noticing vested interests or passion associated with content. Stories are least credible when the interests of the producer or receiver of a story are involved or when the passions of a mass audience are involved (mass fear, anger, hatred, patriotism, etc.). When a nation is at war, for example, stories about the war told by the nation's press (including all explanations of it) are suspect, as all nations produce mass propaganda during war to build support for it.

Another such a case would be stories about persons involved in taboo sexual acts (approved in other societies), because the reader's disgust would command telling the story in such a way as to justify that disgust as a reasonable response ("Nudists Arrested," "Sexual Predator Condemned"). Stories that arouse mass passions typically are highly one-sided in nature and thus should have low credibility to those who think critically.

12.11 *Think for Yourself*

IDENTIFYING AND ANALYZING BIASED NEWS STORIES

Locate a news story (in a newspaper) that appears biased or is told from a slanted view. Identify:

1. The bias(es) inherent in the story.
2. The viewpoints that are ignored or distorted.

Then state how the story would have to be constructed if it were to fairly represent all relevant viewpoints.

Media Awareness of Media Bias

To what extent are the news media aware of bias and propaganda in their own constructions? This question does not have a definitive answer. All journalists are aware that they are writing for an audience. It does not follow, however, that they have thought-through the implications of this. Certainly, some journalists are much more aware than others.

In the United States, Israel is a favored "ally," so mistreatment or abuse of the Palestinians by the Israelis is usually covered under the idea of "justified reprisal." Because Fidel Castro of Cuba is viewed within the United States as an enemy, mainstream news writers routinely present Castro and Cuba in a negative light, ignoring or explaining away any achievements of the Cuban government (such as universal medical coverage and a low infant mortality rate). If and when persons in the news media recognize patterns of news coverage such as these, they must be careful in writing about them—lest they themselves be labeled "irresponsible" and "biased."

Sensitivity to Advertisers

Every group within a culture is not equally important to the news media. National media are biased in favor of national culture, religion, dominant beliefs, and social values. But within any complex culture, some groups play a more powerful role than others within media logic. For example, much news media profit comes from advertisers. These advertisers are not pleased if they, or the interests they represent, are cast in a bad light by the media they finance. News media, therefore, avoid generating stories that negatively feature major advertisers.

Put another way, because news media outlets can select from among a large mass of potential stories and cannot, in any case, carry more than a small percentage of what is available, they naturally, all other things being equal, choose to avoid or play down stories that are irritating to their advertisers. There are, of course, exceptions to this pattern. A lot depends on the "splash" the story would make or whether it is already "out."

Sensitivity to Government

National news media are sensitive to the power of government. For one, national governments typically license and regulate news media by law. For another, much national news is given to news media through high governmental officials and agencies. For these reasons, news media personnel hesitate to criticize the national government in certain fundamental ways.

For example, if the national government names some other group or nation as an enemy, the national news media generally present the "enemy" as unfavorably as they can. If the government attacks another nation militarily, the national news media line up like cheerleaders at a sporting event. The news media are typically apologists for the policies and acts of the national government.

An exception occurs when elements in the national news media are linked to a political party not presently in power. Their protection then comes from the power and interests represented by the opposition party. Then they are beholden to the views and beliefs of their political supporters. In the United States, certain news outlets are sometimes more influenced by the Democrat or Republican parties, but both parties unite around the same basic world view and beliefs of the broader society. Both identify the same countries as friends or enemies; both are responsive to major economic forces and concentrations of wealth and power.

The basic logic is the same. The media are presenting the news within a point of view. The point of view represents interests affecting media profitability and is deeply entrenched in social ideology. The news media focus on profit, though that focus is obscured and kept in the background.

> 'The national television networks have trimmed their reporting staffs and closed foreign reporting bureaus to cut their owners' costs. They have tried to attract viewers by diluting their expensive newscasts with lifestyle, celebrity, and entertainment features, and by filling their low-budget, high-profit, prime-time "newsmagazines" with sensational sex, crime, and court stories. (Downie and Kaiser, 2002, p. 10)

12.12   *Think for Yourself*

IDENTIFYING NEWS STORIES THAT PANDER TO THE GOVERNMENT

Identify a news story in which one or both of the following is/are true:

1. An action of your government is shown in a positive light when it should be shown in an objective, or even negative, light given the circumstances.

2. Negative actions of your government are down-played when they should be highlighted (due to their implications).

Sensitivity to Powerful Interests

News media sources try to maximize their profit while minimizing costs. Investigative journalism is more expensive than prepackaged stories (news from press releases, news conferences, and speeches). Realizing that their position of power within the culture is threatened if they fail to maintain a favorable public image, powerful economic interests continually invest in marketing their image to the public. There is therefore a symbiotic relationship between powerful media sources (which need news stories) and powerful economic interests (which generate and disseminate news stories in their interest). This is true in virtually all nations.

Powerful industries such as manufacturing, communications, agriculture, weapons producers, airlines, the criminal justice industry (prisons, police, lawyers, social workers, prison contractors), construction, banking, auto, insurance, public relations and advertising, broadcasting, entertainment—all are involved in shaping the daily news in their interest. Governmental agencies and persons in positions of power in the executive, legislative, judicial, military, and intelligence communities are all involved in shaping the daily news in their interest. Religious groups, professional groups, unions, and other groups organize around vested interests and invest heavily in shaping the daily news in their interest.

> From the Great Depression in the 1930s through World War II and the beginning of the Cold War in the 1950s, reporters seemed to reflect establishment views more often than they exposed the failings and foibles of the powerful. They seldom challenged government news management or the press agentry of private business and the entertainment industry. (Downie and Kaiser, p. 19)

Because most people's fundamental source of information about the world comes through the mass media, favorable news media coverage is a significant variable in achieving a favorable public image.

12.13   *Think for Yourself*

IDENTIFYING STORIES THAT FAVOR BUSINESS INTERESTS

Identify a news story in which business interests are favored over the interests of the people (or the environment), and yet the media fail to highlight this fact in the story.

Sensitivity to Competitors

News media provide the news in light of the news that other media outlets focus on. When some of the major outlets treat a story as "big," the others typically pick it up so as not to be viewed as deficient in coverage. Major media move as one "herd," following the leaders slavishly. National and international coverage differ very little from one newspaper to another within any given country.

12.14   *Think for Yourself*

ANALYZING NEWSPAPERS FOR SIMILARITIES AND DIFFERENCES

For any given day, purchase three mainstream newspapers. Then analyze them to see how they differ and how they are similar (focusing on the front section). Consider these questions:

1. To what extent do the three papers cover the same national news?
2. To what extent do they cover the same international news?
3. To what extent do they cover the same stories in the same or a similar way (in terms of placement and slant of the stories)?
4. After completing your analysis, what do you conclude about how mainstream newspapers cover the news in your country?

The Bias Toward Novelty and Sensationalism

The "news" typically is constructed with a systematic bias in favor of reporting what is novel, bizarre, sensational, or odd. What happens every day—no matter how intrinsically important—is often sacrificed. But great social problems typically are embedded in day-to-day events that are repeated thousands of times. The individual events underlying these problems are often not dramatic or "odd" (but pathetically common).

On the one hand, if a large bank systematically overcharges millions of customers a small amount of money, it succeeds in stealing millions of dollars. But such a practice probably will not be considered news. If, on the other hand, a solitary bank robber makes off with $10,000, that will make the news. If millions of children are bullied in schools every day and suffer lifelong damage from that experience, that probably will not be considered news. But if a child has sex with another child at school, that will be considered news. If millions of children go to bed hungry every night all over the globe, that is not news. But if one school serves caviar during the school lunch, that is news. If women and children are sold every day in an international slave trade, that is not news. But if a solitary teacher has a sexual relationship with a student, that is news.

12.15   *Think for Yourself*

IDENTIFYING SENSATIONALISM IN THE NEWS

Identify a news story in which some behavior is sensationalized. You are looking for a story that is blown out of proportion in terms of importance (while other important stories are ignored).

Critical Consumers of the News

Manipulating critical consumers of the news is difficult because:

- They study alternative perspectives and world views, learning how to interpret events from multiple viewpoints.

- They seek understanding and insight through multiple sources of thought and information, not simply those of the mass media.

- They learn how to identify the viewpoints embedded in news stories.

- They mentally rewrite (reconstruct) news stories through awareness of how stories would be told from multiple perspectives.

- They analyze news constructs in the same way they analyze other representations of reality (as some blend of fact and interpretation).

- They assess news stories for their clarity, accuracy, relevance, depth, breadth, and significance.

- They notice contradictions and inconsistencies in the news (often in the same story).

- They notice the agenda and interests served by a story.

- They notice the facts covered and the facts ignored.

- They notice what is represented as fact (that is in dispute).

- They notice questionable assumptions implicit in stories.

- They notice what is implied (but not openly stated).

- They notice what implications are ignored and what implications are emphasized.

- They notice which points of view are systematically put into a favorable light and which in an unfavorable light.

- They mentally correct stories reflecting bias toward the unusual, the dramatic, and the sensational by putting them into perspective or discounting them.

- They question the social conventions and taboos being used to define issues and problems.

> The media world we inhabit is without exception a world of "spin"
>
> The *Wall Street Journal*
> (May 7, 2004)

12.16 *Think for Yourself*

REWRITE A NEWS STORY

Using a daily newspaper, choose a story you think you can rewrite from another viewpoint. Rewrite the story. Explain the changes you have made and why you have made them.

Questions for the News Media

Is It Possible for the News Media to Reform?

To provide their publics with nonbiased writing, journalists around the world would have to, first, enter empathically into world views to which they are not currently sympathetic. They would have to imagine writing for audiences that hold views antithetical to the ones they hold. They would have to develop insights into their own sociocentrism. They would have to do the things that we have suggested are done by critical consumers of the news.

The most significant problem is that, were they to do so, their articles would be perceived by their public as "biased" and "slanted," as propaganda. These reporters would be seen as irresponsible, as allowing their personal point of view to bias their journalistic writings. Imagine Israeli journalists writing articles that present the Palestinian point of view sympathetically. Imagine Pakistani journalists writing articles that present the Indian point of view sympathetically.

The most basic point is this: Journalists do not determine the nature and demands of their job. They do not determine what their readers want or think or hate or fear. The nature and demands of their job are determined by the broader nature of the society itself and the beliefs, values, and world views of its members. It is human nature to see the world, in the first instance, in egocentric and sociocentric terms. Most people are not interested in having their minds broadened. They want their current beliefs and values extolled and confirmed. Like football fans, they want the home team to win, and when it wins, to triumph gloriously. If it loses, they want to be told that the game wasn't important, or that the other side cheated, or that the officials were biased against them.

As long as the overwhelming mass of people in the broader society are drawn to news articles that reinforce, and do not question, their fundamental views or passions, the economic imperatives will remain the same. The logic is parallel to that of reforming a nation's eating habits. As long as the mass of people want high-fat, processed foods, the market will sell high-fat and processed foods to them. And as long as the mass of people want simplistic news articles that reinforce egocentric and sociocentric thinking, articles that present the world in sweeping terms of good and evil (with the reader's views and passions treated as good and those of the reader's conceived enemies as evil), the news media will generate such articles for them. The profit and ratings of news sources with their fingers on the pulse of their readers and viewers will continue to soar.

12.17 *Think for Yourself*

CAN THE MEDIA REFORM?

Explain in your own words the reasoning used in concluding that the news media will never reform. Discuss the implications of this reasoning. Do you agree?

Is the Emergence of a "Critical Society" Possible?

In a concluding chapter of his classic book, *Folkways*, published in 1906, William Graham Sumner raised the possibility of the development of "critical" societies, by which he meant societies that adopt critical thinking as an essential part of their way of life. Sumner recognized that critical thinking "is our only guarantee against delusion, deception, superstition, and misapprehension of ourselves and our earthly circumstances." He recognized education as "good just so far as it produces a well-developed critical faculty." He says:

> The critical habit of thought, if usual in a society, will pervade all its mores, because it is a way of taking up the problems of life. People educated in it cannot be stampeded. . . . [They] are slow to believe. They can hold things as possible or probable in all degrees, without certainty and without pain. They can wait for evidence and weigh evidence, uninfluenced by the emphasis or confidence with which assertions are made on one side or the other. They can resist appeals to their dearest prejudices and all kinds of cajolery. Education in the critical faculty is the only education of which it can be truly said that it makes good citizens.

No country or culture in the world routinely fosters education as Sumner conceived it. As things now stand, such education is the rare exception in any society. The detection of bias and propaganda in the news media is possible only for those who are willing to be diligent in pursuing news from multiple sources representing multiple alternative cultural and national standpoints. It is possible only for those who—in their reading and thinking and judging—are willing to swim against the tide.

12.18   *Think for Yourself*

IMAGINING A CRITICAL SOCIETY AND ITS IMPLICATIONS

What are some of the ways your life would probably have been different had you been raised in a critical society? What are some of the realities we face, given that people in the world are largely irrational?

FINDING ALTERNATIVE SOURCES OF INFORMATION

To find sources of information supporting the dominant views within a culture is not difficult. The problem for most of us is finding well-thought-through views that question the mainstream news. Thus, in the former Soviet Union, for example, it was hard to gain access to views that critiqued the Soviet line. It is always a minority of thinkers motivated to look beyond the dominant views who dig beneath the surface and bring forward what is unpleasant or painful to the majority. Critiques of a society within a society are typically hard to come by.

The main point is that every society in the world today has mainstream and dissenting views. And it is important to recognize that we are not saying that dissenting views are correct and mainstream views are incorrect. Insights can be gained from all major conflicting world views. What is most important is to locate both mainstream and dissenting views (expressed in their most articulate and insightful forms). The ideal, for any given important issue, is access to a full range of views, as expressed by their most skilled and insightful defenders.

In doing this, one faces two problems:

1. to locate a full range of views
2. to locate well-informed spokespersons for each major position in the spectrum.

Let us look at the United States. American mainstream views can be found in any of a large number of major American newspapers (the *New York Times,* the *Washington Post,* the *Baltimore Sun,* the *Boston Globe,* the *Chicago Tribune,* the *Cleveland Plain Dealer,* the *Los Angeles Times,* the *Minneapolis Star Tribune,* the *Philadelphia Inquirer,* the *Sacramento Bee,* the *San Francisco Chronicle,* and so on). Similar lists of mainstream newspapers could be produced for other countries in the world. Of course, there would be some overlap in viewpoints between mainstream newspapers from various nations and cultures, depending on the extent to which they share religious views, economic interests, and political traditions.

Locating dissenting views within nations and cultures is more difficult, depending on the extent to which dissenters are forced to go "underground." The best general source for the views of important dissenters is through the scholarly magazines and presses of the world. In some cases, a person can locate publications dealing with issues in greater depth than the mainstream news.

In the United States, for example, *The Nation* is one such publication. Founded in 1865, it has, from its beginnings, provided an outlet for intellectually dissenting points of view. Its contributors include: Nelson Algren, Hannah Arendt, W.H. Auden, James Baldwin, Willa Cather, Emily Dickinson, John Dos Passos, W.E.B. DuBois, Albert Einstein, Lawrence Ferlinghetti, Robert Frost, Carlos Fuentes, Emma Goldman, Langston Hughes, Henry James, Martin Luther King, Jr., D.H. Lawrence, Robert Lowell, Thomas Mann, H.L. Mencken, Arthur Miller, Pablo Neruda, Octavio Paz, Sylvia Plath, Ezra Pound, Bertrand Russell, Jean Paul Sartre, Upton Sinclair, Wallace Stevens, I.F. Stone, Gore Vidal, Kurt Vonnegut, Alice Walker, and William Butler Yeats. Clearly, this is a valuable source for non-mainstream points of view. In addition to providing a weekly magazine on controversial political and cultural issues, *The Nation* also has established a digital archive covering 6,500 issues. (see www.archive.thenation.com).

All sources of news and commentary should be read critically, carefully analyzed and assessed, and used as vehicles for intellectual independence, as sources for *part* of the truth, not as vehicles of *The Truth.* The ideal is freedom from any one point of view or perspective.

BECOMING AN INDEPENDENT THINKER

To detect bias and propaganda in the news media requires a commitment to thinking for oneself. The process of becoming an independent thinker is furthered significantly by reading the writings of famous dissenters, thinkers who in their day questioned the mainstream view. Each of the persons below critiqued the mainstream views of his or her day. Each thought outside the cultural box.

Tom Paine, *Common Sense,* 1776

William Lloyd Garrison, *The Journal of the Times and The Liberator,* 1831

Wendell Phillips, *Speeches, Lectures, and Letters,* 1863

Margaret Fuller, *Memoirs* (2 vols), 1852

Henry David Thoreau, *Essay on Civil Disobedience,* 1849

Emma Goldman, *My Disillusionment with Russia,* 1923

Henry George, *Social Problems,* 1883

Thorstein Veblen, *The Vested Interests and the Common Man,* 1919

John Peter Altgeld, *Our Penal Machinery and Its Victims,* 1884

Lincoln Steffens, *The Struggle for Self-Government,* 1906

William Graham Sumner, *Folkways,* 1906

Gustavus Myers, *History of the Great American Fortunes* (2 vols.) 1907

Jose Ortega y Gasset, *The Revolt of the Masses,* 1932

William J. Lederer, *A Nation of Sheep,* 1961

H.L. Mencken, *Prejudices* (6 vols.), 1977

Eric Hoffer, *The True Believer,* 1951

Matthew Josephson, *The Robber Barons,* 1962

Bertrand Russell, *Unpopular Essays,* 1952

C. Wright Mills, *The Power Elite,* 1959

Howard Zinn, *A People's History of the United States,* 1995

Ralph Nader, *The Ralph Nader Reader,* 2000

Edward S. Herman, Noam Chomsky, *Manufacturing Consent,* 2002

12.19, 12.20 *Think for Yourself*

FAMILIARITY WITH DISSENTING VIEWS

How many, if any, of these dissenting authors are you familiar with? Have you read a book by any of them? If not, why? Do you begin to see the extent to which you have been socially conditioned to think within a mainstream point of view?

READ VIEWS OF DISSENTING THINKERS

Get a book or article by any of the authors in our the above list and read some part of the book or article. You will have to read enough to get an idea of this author's views. Then write a short summary of her or his views. Why do you think we have placed this author's name on our list of independent thinkers?

Buried, Ignored, or Underreported Stories

Of the millions of events that take place in the world on any given day, only a tiny percentage of them (a couple of hundred) are made into "news" stories (for a given culture). The stories selected typically confirm the dominant cultural viewpoint of the society. Stories that disconfirm the dominant cultural viewpoint are ignored, underreported, or buried (given little coverage and attention). Stories that are buried in the reporting of one culture, however, may be front-page news in the reporting of another.

This phenomenon is intensified when there is conflict between cultures. In this case, when the same event is covered, it is conceptualized very differently. For example, in wartime, each side tells the story of the conflict to its home audience in self-serving terms. Hence, though both sides commit atrocities, the media on each side highlight only the atrocities of the enemy while suppressing, denying, or minimizing their own atrocities. Each side conceptualizes itself as representing the forces of good (decency, justice, and so on) and its enemies as representing the forces of evil. The predictability of this self-serving function of mass media is highlighted in research into the mutual "image of the enemy":

> Enemy-images mirror each other—that is, each side attributes the same virtues to itself and the same vices to the enemy. "We" are trustworthy, peace-loving, honorable, and humanitarian; "they" are treacherous, warlike, and cruel. In surveys of Americans conducted in 1942, the first five adjectives chosen to characterize both Germans and Japanese (enemies) included *warlike,* and *cruel,* none of which appeared among the first five describing the Russians (allies); in 1966 all three had disappeared from American characterizations of the Germans and Japanese (allies), but now the Russians (no longer allies, although more rivals than enemies) were warlike and treacherous. . . .
>
> The enemy-image acts like a distorting lens, which overemphasizes information that confirms it and filters out information that is incompatible with it. Thus the mass media play up incidents of an enemy's treachery or cruelty and ignore examples of humanitarian or honorable behavior. (Jerome Frank, *Chemtech,* August 1982, p. 467)

In the pages that follow, we provide examples of stories that were buried, ignored, or underreported in the U.S. mass media. The buried stories were given low priority and minimal coverage in the major media. The ignored stories were found in dissenting alternative, non–mass media publications. In each case of an ignored story, pay special attention to how the story would disconfirm the dominant U.S. image of itself and/or of its role in the world, were it to be highlighted in the mass media. If buried or ignored stories actually were emphasized in the mass media, they would damage the public image of the United States, as committed to freedom, justice, human rights, preservation of the earth's resources, international law, and democracy.

Keep in mind that the media in all countries project a favorable self-image of their own culture by selecting what is and is not covered, what is given a positive spin and what is given a negative spin. Our examples focus on what has been underreported or suppressed in the mass media in the United States, as we expect that the majority of our readers will be U.S. citizens. Our analysis could be paralleled in a similar study of the mass media's treatment of news *within any given country or culture.* Of course, the extent to which news is distorted within any country varies among countries and can be determined only through in-depth analysis, story by story.

1. Do respected countries in the world consider the U.S. a danger to world peace? **"Arrogance May Come Back to Haunt U.S.,"** editorial by Nicholas Kristof (Source: *New York Times,* Feb. 3, 2003.)

> The European edition of *Time* magazine has been conducting a poll on its web site: "Which country poses the greatest danger to world peace in 2003?" With 318,000 votes cast so far, the responses are: North Korea, 7 percent; Iraq, 8 percent; the United States, 84 percent.

Comment: We did not find this fact reported in the U.S. mass media, except as a passing comment in an editorial. The notion that the U.S. might be the country that poses the greatest danger to world peace is, of course, deeply incompatible with the U.S. self-image.

2. To what extent is the U.S. responsible for atrocities of its allies? **"The Death Convoy of Afghanistan,"** mass media news article (Source: *Newsweek,* Aug. 26, 2002. © 2002 Newsweek Inc. All rights reserved. Reprinted by permission.)

> In January, two investigators from the Boston-based Physicians for Human Rights had argued their way into Sheberghan prison [in Afghanistan]. What they saw shocked them. More than 3,000 Taliban prisoners—who had surrendered to the victorious Northern Alliance forces . . . were crammed, sick and starving, into a facility with room for only 800. The Northern Alliance commander of the prison acknowledged the charnel-house conditions, but pleaded that he had no money. . . .
>
> But stories of a deeper horror came from the prisoners themselves. However awful their conditions, they were the lucky ones. They were alive. Many hundreds of their comrades, they said, had been killed on the journey to Sheberghan from Konduz by being stuffed into sealed cargo containers and left to asphyxiate. . . .
>
> Pentagon spokesmen have obfuscated when faced with questions on the subject. Officials across the administration did not respond to repeated requests by *Newsweek* for a detailed accounting of U.S. activities in the Konduz, Mazar-e Sharif and Sheberghan areas at the time in question, and Defense Department spokespersons have made statements that are false. According to Aziz ur Rahman Razekh, director of the Afghan Organization of Human Rights, "I can say with confidence that more than a thousand people died in the containers."

Comment: This story is exceptional in that it was *not* "buried" in *Newsweek*. However, it was suppressed or buried in virtually all of the other major U.S. news magazines and media sources, and, to our knowledge, it has not been followed up in *Newsweek*.

3. Is the U.S. responsible for the deaths of more than half a million civilians in Iraq? **"The Betrayal of Basra,"** by Chuck Sudetic (Source: *Mother Jones,* Nov/Dec. 2001; *Mother Jones* is a dissenting, non–mass media source for news and commentary.)

> For ten years the United States has been the staunchest advocate of maintaining a tight blockade on Iraq's access to foreign goods and its oil revenues. These restrictions have failed to loosen Saddam's grip on power. They have failed to force him to give up what is left of Iraq's chemical, biological, and nuclear weapons programs. What the sanctions have done, however, is kill. . . .

According to an estimate by Amatzia Baram, an Iraq analyst at the University of Haifa in Israel, between 1991 and 1997 half a million Iraqis died of malnutrition, preventable disease, lack of medicine, and other factors attributable to the sanctions; most were elderly people or children. The United Nations Children's Fund puts the death toll during the same period at more than 1 million of Iraq's 23 million people.

According to this article, the Iraqi people

have come to see Saddam's worst enemy, the United States, as their enemy as well. . . . Washington abandoned [its] revolt against Saddam in 1991. Now [the] bitterness is tangible. And it will be ripe for exploitation by anti-American demagogues and terrorists for years after Saddam is gone.

The article quotes an Iraqi now living in the U.S.: "These people are not going to forget what has happened to them. In their eyes it is genocide. And people do not forget genocide."

4. Does the U.S. have a responsibility to live in accordance with the international treaties it signs? **"Bush Seeks Exemption for Pesticide"** (Source: *Press Democrat,* Feb. 9, 2003; mass media news source.)

According to this news source, in 1987, along with 182 other countries, the U.S. signed the Montreal Protocol, a treaty calling for the elimination of chemicals that harm the ozone layer. But according to the article, U.S. farmers say there are no good alternatives to the use of methyl bromide, "a clear, odorless gas that is injected into the soil every 18 months to kill worms, insects, rodents, and diseases. . . . The chemical was to be banned by 2005 in developed nations."

The article states that the Bush administration therefore directed the EPA to seek an exemption for 16 uses of the chemical. The article quotes David Doniger, policy director of the climate center of the Natural Resources Defense Council: "We knew there were going to be some hard cases that needed extra time. But we never anticipated that the agribusiness industry would abuse the process and the Bush administration would kowtow to the growers and chemical companies this bad. It is thumbing its nose at the international treaty."

According to this article, "bromide from methyl bromide is roughly 60 times more destructive to ozone on an atom-per-atom basis than the chlorine from CFCs" (chemicals once widely used in aerosols).

Comment: This article was buried toward the back of a local news section.

5. Does the U.S. army operate a school that trains military officers in torture and murder techniques? **"New Army Plan for Torturers' School"** (Source: *CounterPunch,* Feb. 1–15, 2000; *CounterPunch* is a dissenting, non–mass media source of news and commentary.)

According to *CounterPunch,* the School of the Americas, located in Fort Benning, Georgia, and run by the U.S. Army, is an institution "that has turned out 60,000 graduates, including many of the most vicious killers and torturers in the Latin American military. . . . Year after year the U.S. Army has seethed at the growing campaign aimed at the School of the Americas. . . . The annual protest rallies and civil disobedience out-side Fort Benning have swelled in numbers, with 15,000 demonstrating last fall and 900 committing civil disobedience."

The article goes on to say that because of these demonstrations, the Army recog-nizes the need to change its image. Thus the Secretary of the Army has drafted legisla-tion that would replace the School of the Americas with the United States Military Institute for Hemispheric Security Cooperation. According to the article, "same place, new name." The article contends that the function of the new school will mirror that of the old one, "which is, as it has always been, the preparation of fresh cadres of military officers able and willing to carry out the proper custodial functions required of them by the American Empire."

6. Is it humane for mentally ill inmates in U.S. prisons to be subjected to long-term solitary confinement? **"The SuperMax Solution,"** editorial by Regan Good (Source: *The Nation*, March 3, 2003; *The Nation* is a dissenting, non–mass media source for news and commentary.)

According to this editorial, mentally ill inmates are increasingly confined to long-term solitary cells—known as supermax confinement. "Confined to their cells, alone, twenty-three hours a day, inmates eat, sleep, defecate, urinate, read and write (if they are able), watch TV or listen to the radio (if they are allowed) in the same 8-by-12 cell, often for years on end. The monotony, sensory deprivation, and mandated idleness . . . is especially torturous for inmates who have a serious mental illness." The article states that inmates must "earn" their way out of such confinement by correcting their behav-ior. But as Jean Maclean Snyder, an attorney representing mentally ill prisoners at Tamms prison, points out, many mental ill inmates can't "behave" in solitary confine-ment, by definition. "There is nothing to be good at, there is no behavior allowed." This article points out that, at any given moment, "there are about 25,000 people in long-term solitary confinement in the United States."

Comment: On a related point, in 1998 the *New York Times* (Oct. 5) reported that Amnesty International was citing the United States for violating fundamental human rights within its own country, criticizing the U.S. criminal justice system for widespread cruelty and degrading practices. According to the *Times,* Pierre Sane, Secretary General of AI, said, "We felt it was ironic that the most powerful country in the world uses international human rights laws to criticize others but does not apply the same standards at home."

7. To what extent has America been involved in crimes against humanity? **"War Criminals, Real and Imagined,"** by Gregory Elich (Source: *CovertAction Quarterly,* Winter 2001; *CovertAction Quarterly* is a dissenting news source. The fol-lowing sections are summaries of information contained in this article, which cites 33 supporting references.)

Indonesia: In 1965, a CIA-backed military coup toppled President Sukarno of Indonesia and brought to power General Suharto. Following the coup, between 500,000 and 1 million civilians were killed by the Suharto government. These civilians were trade unionists, peasants, ethnic Chinese, and members of the Indonesian Communist

Party. During this time, the U.S. gave Suharto a list of thousands of communists within Indonesia it wanted killed and supplied him with covert military weapons. Once Suharto became acting president, the U.S. began to send economic aid to the country, and U.S. and Western European advisors helped chart economic policy. U.S. aid rose to $200 million by 1969, after Indonesia passed an investment law favorable to foreign companies. "In the years to come, New Order Indonesia would continue to imprison, torture, and execute several hundred thousand people."

Iran: In 1983, the CIA gave the Khomeini government a lengthy list of communists in the Tudeh Party, targeting these people as a threat, and hoping they would be arrested and executed. Eventually the entire party was eliminated by the Khomeini government, with deaths totaling 10,000 people. The Tudeh party leadership was tortured and forced to make false televised confessions. In 1989, again backed by the U.S. government, a special committee in Iran sentenced and executed 5,000 people from various political parties. Those executed were considered "leftists," and therefore a potential problem in a post-Khomeini government.

Cambodia: In 1975, the CIA-backed Khmer Rouge overthrew the government of Cambodia. Virtually the entire country was turned into a forced labor camp to implement a primitive agrarian economy. During the next four years, 2 million Cambodians died from starvation, disease, and executions. Several hundred thousand were tortured and murdered. When the Khmer Rouge invaded Vietnam, an uprising of Cambodian people and Vietnam troops drove the Khmer Rouge from power. The U.S. backed the Khmer Rouge in launching guerrilla war against the new Cambodian socialist government. Through U.S. efforts, Vietnamese troops that were in Cambodia in support of the fledgling socialist government were driven out. Prince Norodom Sihanouk and Son Sann were forced into power, with U.S. insistence that Khmer Rouge play a major role in the new government. But since the people of Cambodia revolted against this idea, and the possibility of an international tribunal was becoming imminent, the Khmer Rouge offered to turn over its leader, Pol Pot, to the U.S. government. The U.S. refused to take Pol Pot. Yet the U.S. managed to control the U.N. trials against the Khmer Rouge so that the role of the CIA in supporting the egregious actions of the Khmer Rouge were never uncovered.

8. Did the Bush administration threaten Mexico in order to get its U.N. vote for war on Iraq?   "Let Them Hate as Long as They Fear," editorial by Paul Krugman, a columnist for the *New York Times.* (Source: *Press Democrat,* March 10, 2003; first published in the *New York Times.*)

According to this editorial, the Bush administration has threatened Mexico in order to get its vote on the U.N. Security Council for an American war on Iraq. *New York Times* columnist Paul Krugman states, "Last week *The Economist* quoted an American diplomat, who warned that if Mexico didn't vote for a U.S. resolution, it could 'stir up feelings' against Mexicans in the United States. He compared the situation to that of Japanese Americans who were interred after 1941, and wondered whether Mexico 'wants to stir the fires of jingoism during the war. . . .' Then came President Bush's Monday interview with Copley News Service. He alluded to the possibility of reprisals if Mexico didn't vote America's way. . . . " According to Krugman's column, Bush said that if Mexico and other countries oppose the U.S., "There will be a certain sense of discipline." Krugman goes on to say, "These remarks went virtually unreported by the ever-protective U.S. media, but they created a political firestorm in Mexico. The White House has been frantically backpedaling, claiming that when Bush talked of 'discipline,' he wasn't making a threat. But in the context of the rest of the interview, it's clear that he was."

9. Is the U.S. government violating international law and the U.N. Declaration of Human Rights by setting up assassination teams to kill persons they suspect are enemies? **"Rumsfeld Weighs New Covert Acts by Military Units"** (Source: *New York Times,* Aug. 12, 2002.)

> Defense Secretary Donald H. Rumsfeld is considering ways to expand broadly the role of American Special Operations Forces in the global campaign against terrorism, including sending them worldwide to capture or kill Al Qaeda leaders far from the battlefields of Afghanistan, according to Pentagon and intelligence officials. . . . The discussion whether to give Special Operations Forces missions to capture or kill individual Al Qaeda leaders may at some point conflict with the executive order prohibiting assassinations.

Comment: The U.N. Declaration of Human Rights, to which the U.S. is a signatory, guarantees that anyone charged with a crime will have an opportunity to defend himself in a court of law. Those assassinated by American Special Forces, however, will be killed based on the presumption or suspicion of guilt. No neutral court of law will judge their evidence or provide an opportunity for the accused to defend themselves. It is clear that the U.S. would voice vehement objections if another country were to assassinate Americans under parallel conditions. This contradiction certainly would be pointed out if this news item were reported in a Muslim newspaper.

10. Is the United States "arrogant, self-indulgent, hypocritical, inattentive and unwilling or unable to engage in cross-cultural dialogue?" **"Panel Urges U.S. to Revamp Efforts to Promote Image Abroad"** (Source: *New York Times,* July 29, 2002.)

> In a report to be released this week, the Council on Foreign Relations asserts that many countries, in particular predominantly Islamic ones, see the United States as "arrogant, self-indulgent, hypocritical, inattentive and unwilling or unable to engage in cross-cultural dialogue. . .". The report acknowledges that American policies regarding Israel are a major impediment to improving the country's image in Muslim nations. But it chides the government for not doing more to . . . express concern about the "suffering and grievances of the Palestinian people." It also asserts that the Bush administration has weakened its standing abroad with "misunderstood and/or misguided" policies that angered allies, including rejecting treaties to reduce global warming, ban antipersonnel land mines and create an International Criminal Court.

Comment: Most mainstream media commentary on serious criticisms of the U.S. explains away the criticisms as based on jealousy and envy on the part of other countries. Most Americans (whose exposure to news is limited to mainstream mass media sources) believe that criticisms of U.S. policies are ill founded and without substance. Most versions of this report emphasized the need for the U.S. to do a better job presenting its image (as is indicated in the headline of this article), not in changing its policies.

11. Is the United States (in threatening to attack Iraq) taking the law into its own hands and introducing chaos in international affairs?   **"Nelson Mandela Condemns U.S. Threats to Attack Iraq"** (Source: Associated Press, Sept. 3, 2002.)

> Johannesburg, South Africa—Nelson Mandela said Monday that he is "appalled" by U.S. threats to attack Iraq and warned that Washington is "introducing chaos in international affairs. . . We are really appalled by any country, whether a superpower or a small country, that goes outside the U.N. and attacks independent countries. . . . No country should be allowed to take the law into [its] own hands. What they are saying is introducing chaos in international affairs, and we condemn that in the strongest terms."

Comment: This story was buried in most mainstream American media sources. Nelson Mandela is a Nobel Peace Prize winner and an internationally renowned leader, and it would be embarrassing to the U.S. government were his views to be given a major play in the U.S. mass media.

12. Did the United States try to block a U.N. anti-torture vote?   **"U.S. Fails to Block U.N. Anti-torture Vote"** (Source: Associated Press, July 25, 2002.)

> The United States failed to block a U.N. vote Wednesday on a plan to strengthen a treaty on torture, and was widely criticized by allies for trying to do so. The United States argued that the measure, known as a protocol, could pave the way for international and independent visits to U.S. prisons and to terror suspects being held by the U.S. military at Guantanamo Bay Naval Base in Cuba. . . . The objective of the protocol is "to establish a system of regular visits undertaken by independent and national bodies to places where people are deprived of their liberty, in order to prevent torture and other cruel, inhuman or degrading treatment or punishment. . . . People were tortured or ill-treated by authorities in 111 countries last year." according to an Amnesty International report.

Comment: This story was buried in most mainstream American media sources because it threatens the image of the U.S. as a country that stands for human rights and against practices such as the protocol condemns: "torture and other cruel, inhuman or degrading treatment and punishment."

13. Has the U.S. government tried to block the creation of an international war crimes tribunal and exempt America from its provisions?   **"War Crimes Tribunal Sworn In"** (Source: *Press Democrat,* March 12, 2003.)

> The World's first permanent war crimes tribunal was inaugurated Tuesday in the Netherlands, despite efforts by the Bush administration to hamper its creation and exempt America from its provisions. U.N. Secretary-General Kofi Annan presided as 18 international judges of the International Criminal Court took the oath of office at

a ceremony before international dignitaries representing some of the 89 countries that back the court's establishment. Notably absent was an official representative of the United States.

Comment: The explanation given by the U.S. State Department for its refusal to support a world court is, roughly, that any accusation of war crimes by a U.S. citizen brought before the court would be based on a "political" motivation. The unstated assumption seems to be that Americans are incapable of committing war crimes.

14. Did the U.S. try to defeat the World Health Organization sponsored treaty to ban cigarette ads worldwide?   "W.H.O. Treaty Would Ban Cigarette Ads Worldwide" (Source: *New York Times,* July 22, 2002.)

[Geneva] Negotiators have drawn up a draft of an international treaty that would phase in bans on cigarette advertising and sports sponsorships by tobacco companies as part of the World Health Organization's campaign to curb smoking worldwide. . . . The health agency says tobacco use is a serious threat to global health with more than 4 million people dying from smoking-related diseases each year. . . . Anti-smoking campaigners have charged that the Bush administration has worked to undermine some of the toughest proposals, particularly concerning the ban on cigarette advertising. The United States has opposed any across-the-board ban on grounds that it would violate American free speech guarantees. . . The draft would require all nations that sign and ratify the treaty to draw up legislation "for preventing and reducing tobacco consumption, nicotine addiction and exposure to tobacco smoke." Subsidies for tobacco farming and manufacturing would be phased out, and eventually eliminated. . . . The W.H.O has charged that the tobacco giants have been working behind the scenes to weaken the negotiating process.

15. Does the U.S. share blame for the slaughter of 800,000 people in Rwanda in 1994, in the light of its knowledge of the slaughter and its deliberate decision to avoid getting involved to stop it?   "Papers Show U.S. Officials Knew of Rwanda Genocide" (Source: *Houston Chronicle,* Aug. 22, 2001.)

A set of newly declassified government documents shows that several senior U.S. officials were aware of the dimensions of the genocide in Rwanda in the spring of 1994, even as some officials sought ways to avoid getting involved. The 16 documents released Tuesday by the National Security Archive, a private research group at George Washington University, provide new details of the deliberations within the Clinton administration from April through May of 1994 as the mass killings took place in Rwanda. By the end of June, an estimated 800,000 people had been killed by government-backed militias. . . . Former President Clinton, during a March 1998 visit to Rwanda, expressed deep remorse about his administration's inaction and said Western governments must share responsibility for what happened. . . . The documents also provide more details behind the U.S. government's decision to avoid calling the killings genocide. . . . The officials worried that if the term *genocide* were used, Washington would be obliged to act because it was a signatory to an anti-genocide convention of 1948.

16. Is the hard-line criminalization of drug addiction leading to unconscionable injustices in sentencing and an unmanageable and overly costly prison system? "Special Report on Fighting Addiction" (Source: *Newsweek,* Feb. 12, 2001. © 2001 Newsweek Inc. All rights reserved. Reprinted by permission.)

The aggregate consequences of addiction are staggering. Consider that the number of inmates in American prisons more than tripled over the last 20 years to nearly 2 million, with 60 to 70 percent testing positive for substance abuse on arrest. These inmates are the parents of 2.4 million children, all of whom are disproportionately likely to follow their parents to jail. According to the exponential math of a Brown University study, if the prison population were to continue growing at the current rate, by 2053 the United States would actually have more people in prison than out. . . .

George Pataki, once a major hard-liner, proposed cutting the minimum sentences for serious drug felons from 15 years to 8 and giving judges more discretion. In reviewing the clemency process, Pataki says he found "dramatically unfair sentences—people sentenced to 15 years when their involvement was minimal." But at the federal level, so-called mandatory minimum sentencing requirements are in no danger of being repealed any time soon. Spending priorities right now look pound foolish. The Center on Addiction and Substance Abuse released a study last week showing that states spend more than 13 percent of their total budgets just "shoveling up" the wreckage of addiction—as much as they appropriate for higher education and 100 times what they spend on prevention and treatment. Another study, by Rand Corp., shows that every dollar spent on treatment saves seven dollars in services. That's because even if addicts eventually relapse, they are clean during their time in treatment, saving millions in acute health-care costs and law enforcement.

17. Has the United States been a major supplier of biological agents to Iraq, agents used to make biological weapons? **"Iraq Links Germs For Weapons to U.S. and France"** (Source: *New York Times,* March 16, 2003.)

Iraq has identified a Virginia-based biological supply house and a French scientific institute as the sources of all the foreign germ samples that it used to create the biological weapons that are still believed to be in Iraq's arsenal, according to American officials and foreign diplomats who have reviewed Iraq's latest weapons declaration to the United Nations. . . . The document shows that the American and French supply houses shipped 17 types of biological agents to Iraq in the 1980's that were used in the weapons programs. Those included anthrax and the bacteria needed to make botulinum toxin, among the most deadly poisons known. . . . Gary Milhollin, director of the Wisconsin Project, an arms control research group, said that the biological supply houses should have realized that Iraq might use the germ samples to make weapons, especially since it was known then that Iraq used chemical weapons against Iranian troops in the Iran–Iraq war. "If you know that the buying country is involved in a chemical weapons program, you have an obligation to ask some questions rather than just send it out," Mr. Milhollin said.

18. Did the FBI and the Justice Department deliberately mislead judges in justifying the "need" for electronic surveillance? Did the FBI and the Justice Department misuse information it obtained during such surveillance? **"Secret Court Says FBI Aides Misled Judges in 75 Cases"** (Source: *New York Times,* August 23, 2002.)

The nation's secret intelligence court has identified more than 75 cases in which it says it was misled by the Federal Bureau of Investigation in documents in which the bureau attempted to justify its need for wire taps and other electronic surveillance, according to the first of the court's ruling to be released publicly. The opinion by the Foreign Intelligence Surveillance Court, which was issued in May but made public today by Congress, is stinging in its criticism of the FBI and the Justice Department, which the court suggested had tried to defy the will of Congress by allowing intelligence material to be shared freely with criminal investigators. . . . In essence, the court said that the FBI and the Justice Department were violating the law by allowing information gathered from intelligence eavesdropping to be used freely in bringing criminal charges, without court review, and that criminal investigators were improperly directing the use of counterintelligence wiretaps. . . .

Gregory T. Nojeim, associate director of the national office of the American Civil Liberties Union in Washington, said the opinion was "astounding" in demonstrating that the FBI and the Justice Department tried an "end run around the Fourth Amendment protections against reasonable searches."

19. Does the United States government sanction the use of torture?   "In Torture We Trust?," by Eyal Press (Source: *The Nation,* March 31, 2003. Reprinted with permission.)

The recent capture of Al Qaeda leader Khalid Shaikh Mohammed is the latest indication that the taboo on torture has been broken. In the days after Mohammed's arrest, an unnamed official told the *Wall Street Journal* that U.S. interrogators may authorize 'a little bit of smacky-face' while questioning captives in the war on terrorism. Others proposed that the United States ship Mohammed off to a country where laxer rules apply. "There's a reason why [Mohammed] isn't going to be near a place where he has Miranda rights or the equivalent" a senior federal law enforcer told the *Journal.* "You go to some other country that'll let us pistol-whip this guy.". . .

On December 26 of last year, the *Washington Post* published a front-page story detailing allegations of torture and inhumane treatment involving thousands of suspects apprehended since the September 11 terrorist attacks. Al Qaeda captives held at overseas CIA interrogations centers, which are completely off-limits to reporters, lawyers and outside agencies, are routinely "softened up"—that is beaten—by U.S. Army Special Forces before interrogation, as well as thrown against walls, hooded, deprived of sleep, bombarded with light and bound in painful positions with duct tape. . . .

The same article reported that approximately 100 suspects have been transferred to U.S. allies, including Saudi Arabia and Morocco, whose brutal torture methods have been amply documented. . . . "We don't kick the [expletive] out of them," one official told the *Post.* "We send them to other countries so they can kick the [expletive] out of them." . . . Death certificates released for two Al Qaeda suspects who died while in U.S. custody at the Bagram base in Afghanistan showed that both were killed by "blunt force injuries." Other detainees told of being hung from the ceiling in chains.

20. Did the U.S. government know that Iraq had destroyed its chemical weapons and lie rather than admit their knowledge?   "The Big Lie?," by Russ Baker* (Source: *The Nation,* April 7, 2003.)

In its March 3 issue, *Newsweek* disclosed that the Bush Administration had deliberately suppressed information exculpating Iraq—information from the same reliable source previously cited by the Administration as confirming that Iraq had developed weapons of mass destruction since the 1991 Gulf War. As damning as this disclosure was, *Newsweek* chose to underplay it. . . . Here's the background: In the summer of 1995 Saddam's then son-in-law, Lieut. Gen. Hussein Kamel, former minister of Iraq's military industry and the person in charge of its nuclear/chemical/biological programs,

---

*Used with permission of Russ Baker (www.russbaker.com), an award-winning investigative journalist and essayist.

defected and provided what was deemed scrupulously accurate, detailed accounts of those weapons. Kamel's information has been cited as central evidence and a key reason for attacking Iraq.

In his February 5 presentation to the U.N. Security Council, Secretary of State Colin Powell said: "It took years for Iraq to finally admit that it had produced four tons of the deadly nerve agent VX. . . . This admission only came out after inspectors collected documentation as a result of the defection of Hussein Kamel, Saddam Hussein's late son-in-law." But *Newsweek's* John Barry revealed that the Administration had excised a central component of Kamel's testimony—that he had personal knowledge that Iraq had "destroyed all its chemical and biological weapons stocks and the missiles to deliver them." . . . According to the story, U.N. inspectors had reasons to hush up this revelation, as they were trying to bluff Saddam into revealing more. But what is Powell's excuse for using only half of Kamel's claim? And why did *Newsweek* and the rest of the American media make so little of this major story? *Newsweek* chose to run a short, 500-word item in its "periscope" section rather than put the story on the cover or make it the focal point of a longer article showing that the Bush Administration is rushing to war for no reason at all. . . . Perhaps it's not surprising that other media failed to pick up on the Kamel story: The big papers and magazines hate to acknowledge they've been scooped by competitors. . . . The Hussein Kamel revelation is probably the biggest Iraq story to get punted, but it isn't the only significant example. . . . It's worth noting that British revelations that the National Security Agency spied on diplomats representing U.N. Security Council members during the Iraq deliberations got a small mention in the *Washington Post* and prompted no questions at Bush's press conference. . . . Cumulatively, Barry's item on Kamel, the revelation that Colin Powell was citing a graduate student's thesis as British "intelligence" and a new revelation that more British "evidence" of Iraqi nuclear arms development cited by the Administration was (according to weapons inspectors themselves) fabricated suggest that a monstrous Big Lie is in process—an effort to construct falsified evidence and to trick this country and the world.

Every citizen in the world needs access to news sources and commentary that question the self-image maintained by the home culture through its own mass media. No culture lives up to the image it projects of itself. How inconsistent the "self-serving" image is with "reality" is a matter for the critically well-informed public to judge. In the case of the United States, the stories above represent a small sampling of stories buried in the mass media coverage or largely unread in the dissenting non-mass media. Their portrayal of the U.S. is incompatible with the highly positive self-image in the preponderance of coverage in the mass media.

For most U.S. consumers of the news, the self-image of the United States as defender of human rights, individual freedom, democratic values, and social justice is unquestionably justified. What we need to remember, however, is that most consumers of the news media do not know how to bring forward "buried" information. They do not know how to read the news critically. Most have never seriously questioned their country's image. Therefore, they see no reason to seek out dissenting stories or to question highly nationalistic self-portraits. They cannot, therefore, exercise that higher patriotism that comes only through recognition of the vital need for constructive criticism—the patriotism that helps a country become more of what it has promised to be.

12.21 *Think for Yourself*

IDENTIFYING IGNORED AND IMPORTANT STORIES

Identify a buried, underreported, or ignored story in the mainstream media news. You can look for this story either in a mainstream or an alternative newspaper. Then write a summary of the story, with relevant quotes, as we have done for the preceding examples. Add your own commentary. The more skilled you are at finding such stories, the better you will be able to critically analyze the news.

Using the Internet

The Internet can be used to locate both mainstream and dissenting views from virtually any country in the world. Below are three sources we located for non-mainstream viewpoints. As always, we do not offer sources as *The Truth*, but rather as aids in obtaining alternatives to the content of mainstream media news.

1. Amnesty International. In some cases, particularly in countries where those with dissenting views are put in prison or killed, dissenting views must be sought from expatriates rather than from resident citizens. Amnesty International (www.amnesty.org) is a good source for discovering persons whose views are being forcibly suppressed. The organization publishes a quarterly news magazine focused on exposing the violations of human rights by nations all over the globe *(Amnesty Now).* (Visit www.aiusa.org)

2. Statewatch. Another example of the sort of important resource one can locate on the Internet is Statewatch. It serves as a watchdog organization and database whose goal is the monitoring of state and civil liberties in the European Union. To get a sense of its thoroughness, Statewatch has compiled 25,500 entries in its database since 1991, containing news features, sources, and reports. It publishes *Statewatch* six times a year, in addition to pamphlets and reports. (Visit www.statewatch.org)

3. Covert Action Quarterly. The goal of the publication *CovertAction Quarterly* (info@covertactionquarterly.org) is to document the involvement of intelligence agencies (such as the CIA, SDECE, MI-6, PIDE-DGS, SDC1, BOSS, MOSSAD, and American, French, British, Portuguese, Italian, South African, and Israeli intelligence services) in actions violating human rights and international and national laws. This publication documents acts that typically are "disowned" by the countries sponsoring them. The sources are freelance investigative journalists, scholars, and former agents.

Another strategy is to search the Internet under descriptors such as "Japanese perspectives," "Asian perspectives," "Chinese perspectives," "African perspectives," "Central American perspectives," "South American perspectives," "Islamic perspectives" and so on. This should help you locate a range of cultural and political standpoints.

Additional Alternative News Sources

Below are some non-mainstream scholarly sources of news, and background for the news. We assume that you will read these sources with the same criticality we are recommending for mainstream views. Once again, we do not offer these sources as *The Truth* but, instead, as helpful non-mainstream viewpoints providing alternatives to the content of mainstream media news.

Harpers, www.harpers.org

The Progressive, www.progressive.org

Counter Punch, www.counterpunch.org

Common Dreams, www.commondreams.org

Indy Media Center, www.indymedia.org

The Nation, www.thenation.com/

Mother Jones, www.motherjones.com/

Free Speech T.V., www.freespeech.org/

In These Times, www.inthesetimes.com/

Z Magazine, www.zmag.org/

AlterNet, www.alternet.org/

The Multinational Monitor, www.essential.org/monitor/

Dollars and Sense, www.dollarsandsense.org/

The Guardian, www.guardian.co.uk/

The Village Voice, www.villagevoice.com/

Project Censored, www.projectcensored.org/

12.22   *Think for Yourself*

CHECKING OUR ALTERNATIVE SOURCES OF THE NEWS

Visit any of the news sources in the above list. Identify two or three significant news stories that represent the stories in a way that differs from the mainstream view.

CONCLUSION

Learning to detect media bias and propaganda in the national and world news takes time to develop. Yet, this is an art essential to intellectual responsibility, integrity, and freedom. This chapter presents a starting place for the development of intellectual analysis and assessment applied to news stories. As we develop in this art, we experience a progressive shedding of layers of social indoctrination and ethnocentricity.

In the end, each of us must decide for ourselves what to believe and how to act. We can do this critically or uncritically, rationally or irrationally, egocentrically or fair-mindedly. We can either tacitly accept our social conditioning and its accompanying ideology, or we can make a deliberative, conscious choice to grow beyond that conditioning. The choice is ours. No one can legitimately make that choice for us. If we choose to go beyond our social conditioning and think for ourselves, we can become free persons and conscientious citizens.

FALLACIES: THE ART OF MENTAL TRICKERY AND MANIPULATION

To understand the human mind, understand self-deception.

—Unknown

The word "fallacy" derives from two Latin words, *fallax* ("deceptive") and *fallere* ("to deceive"). This is an important concept in human life because much human thinking deceives itself while deceiving others. The human mind has no natural guide to the truth, nor does it naturally love the truth. What the human mind loves is itself, what serves it, what flatters it, what gives it what it wants, and what strikes down and destroys whatever threatens it.

The study of fallacies can be pursued in at least two different ways. First, it can be approached traditionally, in which case one defines, explains, and exemplifies ways by which unsound arguments can be made to seem sound.

Second, it can be approached deeply, in which case one relates the construction of fallacies to the pursuit of human interests and irrational desires. Taking the first approach, on the one hand, students gain little by memorizing the names and definitions of fallacies. They soon forget them. Their minds are left largely untouched and therefore unmoved. Taking the second approach, on the other hand, makes possible the acquisition of lifelong insights into how the mind—every mind—uses unsound arguments and intellectual "tricks" to further its ends.

When we look closely at human decisions and human behavior, we can easily see that what counts in human life is not who is *right,* but who is *winning.* Those who possess power in the form of wealth, property, and weaponry are those who decide what truths will be trumpeted around the world and what truths will be ridiculed, silenced, or suppressed. The mass media of the world generate an unending glut of messages that continually sacrifice truth to "spin." When we reach beneath the surface of things, we find a world in which the word "communication" and the word "manipulation" collapse into virtual synonyms.

Students need seminal insights and intellectual tools that enable them to protect themselves from becoming intellectual victims in a world of swarming media piranhas or, just as bad, from joining the swarm as a junior piranha in training. The pursuit of insights and tools, grounded in intellectual integrity, should be the ultimate aim of the study of "fallacies." That has been our aim in this chapter.

TRUTH AND DECEPTION IN THE HUMAN MIND

The human mind is a marvelous set of structures and systems. It is a center of consciousness and action. It forms a unique identity. It creates a view of the world. Rich experience emerges from its interactions with the world. It thinks. It feels. It wants. It apprehends truths and suppresses errors. It achieves insights and fabricates prejudices. Useful truths and harmful misconceptions are its intermixed products. The mind can just as easily believe what is false as what is true.

The mind can see beauty in right conduct and justify what is flagrantly unethical. It can love and hate. It can be kind and cruel. It can advance knowledge or error. It can be intellectually humble or intellectually arrogant. It can be empathic or narrow-minded. It can be open or closed. It can achieve a permanent state of expanding knowledge or a deadening state of narrowing ignorance. It both transcends the creatures of lesser ability and insults their innocence and nobility by its self-deception and cruelty.

How can humans create within their own minds such an inconsistent amalgam of the rational and the irrational? The answer is self-deception. Indeed, the most accurate and useful definition of humans perhaps is that of "the self-deceiving animal." Deception, duplicity, sophistry, delusion, and hypocrisy are foundational products of human nature in its "natural," untutored state. Rather than reducing these tendencies, most schooling and social influences redirect them, rendering them more sophisticated, more artful, and more obscure.

To exacerbate this problem, not only are humans instinctively self-deceptive but they are naturally sociocentric as well. Every culture and society sees itself as special and justified in all of its basic beliefs and practices, in all its values and taboos. The arbitrary nature of its folkways is known to its anthropologists (if it has any) but not to its overwhelming majority.

13.1   *Think for Yourself*

INTERNALIZING THE IDEA OF TRUTH AND DECEPTION IN THE HUMAN MIND

Elaborate in your own words the "dual" capacity of the human mind ("Truth and Deception in the Human Mind"), explaining it to a partner. Have your partner ask you questions. Then both of you should re-read the section to determine how well you read and understood what was said.

THREE TYPES OF THINKERS

Uncritical Persons (intellectually unskilled thinkers)

The overwhelming preponderance of people have not freely decided what to believe but, rather, have been socially conditioned (indoctrinated) into their beliefs. They are unreflective thinkers. Their minds are products of social and personal forces they do not understand, control, or concern themselves with. Their personal beliefs often are based in prejudices. Their thinking consists largely of stereotypes, caricatures, over-simplifications, sweeping generalizations, illusions, delusions, rationalizations, false dilemmas, and begged questions. Their motivations often are traceable to irrational fears and attachments, personal vanity and envy, intellectual arrogance and simple-mindedness. These constructs have become a part of their identity.

These persons are focused on what immediately affects them. They see the world through ethnocentric and nationalistic eyes. They stereotype people from other cultures. When their beliefs are questioned—however unjustified those beliefs may be—they feel personally attacked. When they feel threatened, they typically revert to infantile thinking and emotional counter-attacks.

When *their* prejudices are questioned, they often feel offended and stereotype the questioner as "intolerant" and "prejudiced." They rely on sweeping generalizations to support their beliefs. They resent being "corrected," disagreed with, or criticized. They want to be reenforced, flattered, and made to feel important. They want to be presented with a simple-minded, black-and-white world. They have little or no understanding of nuances, fine distinctions, or subtle points.

They want to be told who is evil and who is good. They see themselves as "good" and their enemies as "evil." They want all problems to admit to a simple solution, and the solution to be one they are familiar with—for example, punishing those who are evil by use of force and violence. In their minds, visual images are much more powerful than abstract language. They are overly impressed by authority, power, and celebrity. They are eminently ready to be directed and controlled, as long as those doing the controlling flatter them and lead them to believe that their views are correct and insightful.

The mass media are structured to appeal to these people. Subtle and complex issues are reduced to simplistic formulas ("Get tough on crime! Three strikes and you're out! Adult crime, adult time! You are either for us or against us!"). Spin is everything; substance is irrelevant.

Skilled Manipulators (weak-sense critical thinkers)

A much smaller group is composed of people who are skilled in the art of manipulation and control. These people are focused shrewdly on pursuing their own interest without respect to how that pursuit affects others. Though they share many of the characteristics of uncritical thinkers, they have qualities that separate them from uncritical persons. They have greater command of the rhetoric of persuasion. They are more sophisticated, more verbal, and generally have higher status.

On average, they have more schooling and achieve more success than uncritical persons. They typically acquire more power and occupy positions of authority. They are accustomed to playing the dominant role in relationships. They know how to use the established structure of power to advance their interests. Because they are fundamentally concerned not with advancing rational values but, instead, with getting what they want, they are careful to present themselves as sharing the values of those they manipulate.

Skilled manipulators are rarely insightful dissenters, rebels, or critics of society. The reason is simple: They cannot effectively manipulate members of a mass audience if they appear to that mass to be invalidating their beliefs.

Manipulators do not use their intelligence for the public good. Rather, they use it to get what they want in alliance with those who share their vested interests. Manipulation, domination, demagoguery, and control are their tools.[1]

People who are skilled in manipulation want to influence the beliefs and behavior of others. And they have insight into what makes people vulnerable to manipulation. As a result, they strive to appear before others in a way that associates themselves with power, authority, and conventional morality. This impetus is evident, for example, when politicians appear before mass audiences with well-polished, but intellectually empty, speeches.

A number of alternative labels can be applied to the roles that "manipulators" play, including: spin master, con artist, sophist, propagandist, indoctrinator, demagogue, and, often, politician. Their goal is to control what others think and do so by controlling the way information is presented to them. They use "rational" means only when such means can be used to create the appearance of objectivity and reasonability. The key is that they try to keep some information and some points of view from being given a fair hearing.

It should be noted that 'manipulators' are often the victims of their own propaganda and devices. Caught up in their own propaganda and narrowness of vision, they sometimes fail as a result. Many businesses fail because of their inability to critique their own illusions. Nations often fail to act successfully because their leaders are caught up in their own unrealistic descriptions of the world (and of their enemies). Manipulators usually are not grand conspirators. Their one-sidedness is obvious only to those who can appreciate the difference between 'self-serving' and fair-minded thinking. Only those capable of self-critique and self-insight can accurately assess the extent to which they are involved in the social, psychological, and intellectual manipulation of others.

Fair-Minded Critical Persons (strong-sense critical thinkers)

Finally, an even smaller group consists of people who, though intellectually skilled, do not want to manipulate and control others. These are the people who combine critical thought, fair-mindedness, self-insight, and a genuine desire to serve the public good. They are sophisticated enough to recognize how self-serving people use their knowledge of human nature and command of rhetoric to pursue selfish ends. They are acutely aware of the phenomenon of mass society and of the machinery of mass persuasion and social control. Consequently, they are too insightful to be manipulated and too ethical to enjoy manipulating others.

---

[1]A demogogue is not a true critic of society but is, rather, a sophist, for he/she "tries to stir up the people by appeals to emotion, prejudice, etc. in order to win them over quickly and so gain power" (*Webster's New World Dictionary*.)

They have a vision of a better, more ethical world, which includes realistic knowledge of how far we are from that world. They are practical in their effort to encourage movement from "what is" to "what might be." They gain this insight by struggling with their own egocentric nature and coming to see (in deeper and deeper ways) their own involvement in irrational processes. No one becomes a fair-minded thinker first and a selfish person later. Selfish thinking is instinctive. It is an inborn state. We are focus initially on ourselves—our own pain, desires, concerns. In the first instance, we pay attention to the needs of others only to the extent that we are forced to do so. Only through a commitment to our own intellectual and ethical development can we develop the intellectual traits characteristic of fair-mindedness.

The key is that fair-minded people consistently strive to achieve the widest, most informed viewpoint. Fair-minded people want no point of view to be suppressed. They want public discussion to include equal coverage of dissenting as well as dominant points of view. They want people to learn how to detect when someone is trying to manipulate them into believing or doing what they would not believe or do if they were to have access to more information or further reasoning from dissenting points of view. They want everyone to see through the "dirty tricks" of manipulative persuasion. They want to publicly disclose situations in which people of wealth and power are manipulating people with little wealth and power. They want to help people recognize how the wealthy and powerful often prey on the credulity, gullibility, and vulnerability of the poor or poorly schooled.

> The word "fallacy" derives from two Latin words, *fallax* ("deceptive") and *fallere* ("to deceive")

13.2 *Think for Yourself*

INTERNALIZING THE IDEAS OF STRONG-SENSE AND WEAK-SENSE CRITICAL THINKING

In your own words elaborate on the distinction between uncritical people, weak-sense critical thinkers, and strong-sense critical thinkers, explaining the distinctions to a partner. Have your partner ask you questions. Then both of you should re-read the passages in which those distinctions are drawn to determine how well you read and understood what was said.

THE CONCEPT OF FALLACIES OF THOUGHT

The meanings of the word "fallacy," found in the *Oxford English Dictionary,* are:

> 1. Deception, guile, trickery, trick. 2. Deceptiveness, aptness to mislead, unreliability. 3. A deceptive or misleading argument, a sophism. In Logic esp. a flaw, material or formal, which vitiates a syllogism. Also, sophistical reasoning, sophistry. 4. A delusive notion, an error, esp. one founded on false reasoning. Also, the condition of being deceived, error. 5. Sophistical nature, unsoundness (of arguments); erroneousness, delusion.

To be a human thinker is often to be a "self-deceived" thinker and, hence, a "fallacious" thinker. But to think of ourselves as believing what is false (or as defending and justifying prejudices, stereotypes, and misconceptions) is a painful thought. The human mind has developed ways to protect itself from that pain.

Psychologists have labeled these ways "defense mechanisms." They deny or distort reality. Their use is not deliberate and conscious but, instead, unpremeditated and subconscious. They include repression, projection, denial, rationalization, and stereotyping.

Naming Fallacies

In commenting on tricks of persuasion, the philosopher Schopenhauer once remarked, "It would be a very good thing if every trick could receive some short and obviously appropriate name, so that when a man used this or that particular trick, he could at once be reproved for it." Unfortunately, one can make an unlimited number of maneuvers in camouflaging poor reasoning, making bad thinking look good, and obscuring what is really going on in a situation. Furthermore, most people are resistant to recognizing poor reasoning when it supports what they intensely believe. It is as if people subconsciously accept the premise that all is fair in the scramble for power, wealth, and status. Any argument, any consideration, any mental maneuver or construction that validates emotionally charged beliefs seems to the believer to be justified. The more intense the belief, the less likely that reason and evidence can dislodge it.

As we have said before, the human mind is often myopic, inflexible, and conformist, and at the same time it is highly skilled in self-deception and rationalization. People by nature are highly egocentric, highly sociocentric, and wantonly self-interested. Our goal is not truth but advantage. We have not acquired our beliefs through a rational process. We are highly resistant to rational critique. Blind faith, fear, prejudice, and self-interest are primary organizers of much human thinking. Self-delusion, in conjunction with lack of self-command, characterize much human thinking. Highly compromised integrity is the result. If you point out a mistake in thinking to most people, you may silence them momentarily. But most, like rubber bands that have momentarily been stretched and let go, will soon revert to whatever it was they believed in the first place.

This is the reason that cultivation of intellectual virtues is so crucial to human development. Without a long-term transformation of the mind, little can be done to produce deeply honest thought. When challenged, the human mind operates from its most primitive intellectual instincts. This can be verified in the history of politics, economics, religion, and war—indeed, in any history that deeply plumbs the human mind in action.

Consequently, it is important to learn to recognize the most common tricks of persuasion so we might better understand ourselves and others. When used on others, fallacies are intellectually indefensible tricks of persuasion and manipulation; when used on ourselves, they are instruments of self-deception. In this book we concentrate on the most common and flagrant intellectual tricks and snares. Sometimes these tricks are "counterfeits" of good thinking. For example, a false dilemma is the counterfeit of a true dilemma. We shall see this most obviously in dealing with errors of generalization and comparison.

13.3   *Think for Yourself*

Why, according to the text, would it be impossible to generate a name for every fallacy of which the mind is capable? Explain briefly.

Mistakes Versus Fallacies

"What about mistakes?" you might ask. Isn't it possible that some of the time we commit fallacies inadvertently, unintentionally, and innocently? The answer is, of course, *yes*. Sometimes people make mistakes without any intention of tricking anyone. The test to determine whether someone is merely making a mistake in thinking is relatively simple. After the mistake is pointed out to the person, and the person is explicitly faced with the problems in the thinking, observe to see whether he or she honestly changes. Once the pressure to change is removed, do people revert to the original fallacious way of thinking, or do they demonstrate that they have truly been persuaded (and modified their thinking accordingly)? If a person reverts, or invents a new rationalization for his or her behavior, we can conclude that the person was using the fallacy to gain an advantage and not making a simple mistake.

No Exhaustive List of Fallacies

It is not possible to create an exclusive and exhaustive list of fallacies. The intellectual tricks, traps, and snares that humans so commonly engage in (or fall prey to) can be described from many differing standpoints and in a variety of differing terms. In this book we deal only with those that are most common or most easily recognized. There is nothing sacred about our list or our analysis. Here is a list of common problems or fallacies in human thinking. See if you can add to this list. It is common for people (in their thinking) to:

- be unclear, muddled, or confused
- jump to conclusions
- fail to think-through implications
- lose track of one's goal
- be unrealistic
- focus on the trivial
- fail to notice contradictions
- use inaccurate information in one's thinking
- ask vague questions

- give vague answers
- ask loaded questions
- ask irrelevant questions
- confuse questions of different types
- answer questions one is not competent to answer
- come to conclusions based on inaccurate or irrelevant information
- use only the information that supports one's view

- make inferences not justified by one's experience
- distort data and represent it inaccurately
- fail to notice the inferences one makes
- come to unreasonable conclusions
- fail to notice one's assumptions
- make unjustified assumptions
- miss key ideas
- use irrelevant ideas
- form confused ideas
- form superficial concepts
- misuse words
- ignore relevant viewpoints
- fail to see issues from points of view other than one's own

- confuse issues of different types
- lack insight into one's prejudices
- think narrowly
- think imprecisely
- think illogically
- think one-sidedly
- think simplistically
- think hypocritically
- think superficially
- think ethnocentrically
- think egocentrically
- think irrationally
- be incompetent at problem-solving
- make poor decisions
- lack insight into one's own ignorance

Few of these flaws fall neatly under traditional fallacy labels. Nevertheless, it is useful to have some sense of what the common fallacies are and how to distinguish them from sound reasoning.

All fallacies result from an abuse of a way of thinking that is sometimes justified. Generalization, for example, is one of the most important acts of human thinking. Making comparisons by analogy and metaphor is another. As we begin to focus on fallacies, we will begin with a detailed emphasis on generalizations and comparisons (and the errors of thought that emerge from their misuse). We then will focus in detail on some of the most widely used fallacies.

We do not have the space to approach all fallacies in this same detailed way. In total, we point out 44 fallacies (which we introduce as "44 Foul Ways to Win an Argument"). We view these fallacies as unethical strategies for winning arguments and manipulating people. They are the "dirty tricks" of intellectual life. Those who use them with success are able to do so precisely because, at some level, they deceive themselves into believing that their reasoning is sound.

FAULTY GENERALIZATIONS

As humans, we live in a world of abstractions and generalizations. All words that name or characterize what we think about are products of the mental act of generalizing.[2] But as semanticists rightly remind us: "Cow 1 is not cow 2 is not cow 3." Each and every

---

[2]For example, when we call a person a "woman," we abstract from everything that is individual and personal about her and focus on what she has in common with everyone else of her gender. A parallel point can be made about

existing thing is unique. Bishop Butler put this point in a memorable way in remarking, "Everything is itself and not another."[3]

Despite the uniqueness of things, the words we use in categorizing what we experience gloss over uniqueness and concentrate on similarities or differences (in general). As such, we talk in general terms about tables, chairs, cows, crows, people, poems, and social movements. Even though we can say useful things about individual tables, chairs, cows, crows, people, poems, and social movements, we nevertheless are forced to generalize in countless ways. We talk in general terms about nearly everything that interests us: life and death, love and hate, success and failure, war and peace.

We should be careful, therefore, not to triumph in a discussion by saying "That's a generalization!" (and therefore "automatically" faulty). We must remember that generalizing is integral to the foundations of communication. It enables us to construct the concepts through which we conduct all our thinking.

13.4   *Think for Yourself*

IDENTIFYING GENERALIZATIONS

Make a list of 10 perfectly reasonable generalizations that you use in your thinking. As examples: *The earth will continue to rotate around the sun. When I go to work tomorrow, my desk will still be in my office. My car will start when I turn the key.* Note that these assumptions are so basic that we almost never state them. We unconsciously take them for granted.

For a given generalization to be a "fallacy," it must be based either on too few instances or on unrepresentative instances. For example, if we meet three amusing Italians while on a visit to Rome, we are not justified in making the generalization that all

---

nearly every word. The point is that we cannot live a human life except with the tools of (linguistic) abstraction. They enable us to do virtually all uniquely human activities. So, being indispensable, abstractions can't be all bad in and of themselves.

The function of generalizations is quite simple. Without generalizations we could not explain anything. Things would occur around us for no reason that we could fathom. We would stand around in a stupor, unable to relate anything to anything else, for a generalization is simply a way to take some set of things (that we don't understand) and compare them with something we do understand by means of some "abstract" words.

How does critical thinking help us with forming generalizations and abstractions? Again, the answer is quite simple. Critical thinking enables us to take command of the abstractions we create in our own minds, the generalizations we make about the world, and therefore, ultimately, the quality of our reasoning.

Why, then, do so many people mishandle abstractions and misuse generalizations? Once again, the answer is simple. Having very little understanding of abstractions, most people are uncomfortable with them. They don't understand reasoning. The whole notion of things intellectual is—if truth be told—pretty much of a puzzle to them. Without critical thinking skills, one doesn't know how to form reasonable and useful abstractions and generalizations. One does not know how to bring them alive in the mind or apply them with discipline in the world.

[3]Bishop Joseph Butler (1692–1752) was a theologia and author.

or most Italians are amusing (there is no reason to think that the three we met were representative of all or most Italians).

But determining whether a generalization is justified is not merely a matter of counting the number of instances. For example, if you touch a hot stove and burn your hand, one instance should be enough to convince you of the wisdom of the generalization, "Never touch a hot stove with your bare hand." On the basis of very few experiences, you would be justified in making the even wider generalization, "Never touch extremely hot objects with your naked flesh."

Well, then, how can we ensure that we are making justifiable generalizations? The answer is that we need to make sure we have sufficient evidence to justify our generalizations. The more diverse the group we are generalizing about, the harder it is to generalize in a justifiable way about it. Thus, it is easier to make generalizations about frogs (given the consistency in frog behavior) than it is about domesticated dogs (whose behavior varies more, from dog to dog and from dog species to dog species). In a like manner, it is easier to generalize about domesticated dogs than it is about humans (whose behavior varies along many parameters). Human behavior is highly diverse.

Consider yourself as an example:

You were born into a culture (European, American, African, Asian). You were born at some point in time (in some century, in some year). You were born in some place (in the country, in the city, in the North or South, East or West). You were reared by parents with certain beliefs (about the family, personal relationships, marriage, childhood, obedience, religion, politics, schooling, etc.). You came to the world with certain predispositions that influenced your development as you interacted with your environment. You formed various associations, based largely on who was around you, associations with people who had distinct viewpoints, and values, and who adhered to certain taboos. As a result of all of these influences, you are a complex and unique individual. Therefore, you should be cautious in forming generalizations about yourself, just as you should be cautious in forming generalizations regarding others.

This does not mean that we cannot make any important generalizations about humans. We share some features with all other humans. For instance, given what we know about the human mind, we can make the following generalizations:

1. It is essential for our intellectual growth that we come to know the scope and limits of our intellectual capacities.

2. Most people do not recognize their tendency to think egocentrically and ethnocentrically.

3. Most people resist understanding the implications of their social conditioning and the ethnocentrism inherent in it.

One important series of studies, the Milgram Experiments,[4] documents the human tendency to conform (uncritically) to the commands of authority figures, even when those authority figures have no power to punish or compel them to conform and even when the authority figures are asking them to do what they know to be "unethical."

---

[4]See studies by Stanley Milgram at www.stanleymilgram.com

Another series of studies of the "mutual images of the enemy" documents a striking intellectual disability of humans. It occurs when groups come in conflict with each other for the same goal. Each side to the conflict then attributes the same virtues to itself and the same vices to the enemy. *We* are "trustworthy, peace-loving, honorable, and humanitarian." *They* (our enemies) are "treacherous, warlike, and cruel."[5]

We can readily find examples of this phenomenon in the daily news, which is filled with positive characterizations of "our side" and caricatures of those who oppose us. Self-aggrandizing generalizations that feed the human ego are always welcome and easily believed. Negative generalizations of those who oppose us are also welcome, as easily believed, and for similar reasons. As social animals, we do not want to face our fear and distrust of members of groups we oppose. We avoid facing the reality that we are very much like the people we hate and fear. The pain, the suffering, the waste of resources that result from acting on the thinking we generate egocentrically and sociocentrically boggle the mind.

13.5 *Think for Yourself*

HOW DO GENERALIZATIONS WORK IN THE MIND?

Briefly discuss the role of generalization in the mind's attempt to understand the world. What criteria can we use to assess a generalization?

ANALYZING GENERALIZATIONS

If we are to aspire to reasonability, we must be willing to question our own generalizations as well as the generalizations of others. We must be willing to strip the labels off of the objects of our experience and ask ourselves (again and again), "What do we really know about this or that or that other?"

Traditionally, faulty generalizations have been labeled either "hasty" or "unrepresentative." We boil down these labels to two pieces of advice:

1. Begin to recognize when generalizations are being made.
2. Determine whether the generalization is supported by sufficient evidence to justify it. In other words, make sure you have taken the time to accumulate enough facts to support the generalization, and make sure the evidence you have is "representative" of the full range of relevant information.

Qualify your generalization whenever necessary (most, many, some, a few, rather than "all".

Remember that you are a human and speak a human language, and that the language you speak is shot-through with generalizations and abstractions. Try to develop

---

[5]See studies by Jerome K. Frank, et al., www.globalcommunity.org

the ability to strip off whatever language you are inclined to use in interpreting the facts inherent in your experience (i.e., confine yourself to the statement of specific facts without putting a "spin" on those facts). See whether you can be more accurate and precise and less biased in your descriptions by reducing your interpretive generalizations to a minimum.

Consider now the following examples of generalizations commonly made by people, some of which are reasonable, others not:

- **Example:** "Yesterday I met the most remarkable person—kind, considerate, sensitive, and thoughtful."

  Comment: Generalizations about the character of a person after spending less than one day with that person are rarely justifiable.

- **Example:** "Well, aren't you going to stand up for our country? I thought you were a patriot."

  Comment: The suppressed generalization here is: One should never criticize one's country, because such criticism is inconsistent with loyalty. By the way, people who unconsciously make this (political) generalization often make a similar one about love between humans: "If you really loved me, you wouldn't criticize me." Both generalizations ignore the proposition that reasonable critique is a necessary and healthy element of creating a better world. Many of our greatest critics have also been our greatest patriots. Tom Paine is a case in point.

- **Example:** "Why do you always have to be so critical? Can't you just be human for once?"

  Comment: Besides "so critical" being overly vague, we have the suppressed (and absurd) generalization that critique is "inhuman." Note also the suppressed generalization that you are "always" critical. That you are sometimes critical is probable; that you are often critical is possible, but that you are always critical is highly unlikely.

- **Example:** "No, I'm not a rational person. I have *feelings*!"

  Comment: These statements imply that *being reasonable and having feelings are incompatible.* Not so. A reasonable person can have feelings just as intense as those of an irrational person. The difference is that the emotional responses of a reasonable person make sense. They fit the circumstances. A reasonable person is more integrated, lives fewer contradictions, has greater insight. For a rational person, the consistency among thought, feeling, and desire lays a foundation for intensity and commitment. The generalization that being reasonable and having feelings are incompatible is based on a stereotype, not an insight.

- **Example:** "Let's face it. The answer is *love*. That's the only way to create a better world."

  Comment: If everyone were to love everyone else, no doubt we would have a better world. But how is all this love to be produced in a world shot-through with greed, violence, selfishness, and cruelty, all of which result from innate egocentricity and ethnocentricity? How could we change people's thinking so as to bring about this massive outpouring of love? The notion that "love is the answer" is not a helpful generalization. It has to be qualified in a multitude of ways.

- **Example:** "The money we are spending to save lives by preventing bioterrorism makes little sense when compared with what it would cost to save lives through other means. We spend hundreds of billions of dollars to save lives that might be at risk while we allow hundreds of people to die every day on the homefront. According to the Institute of Medicine, some 18,000 people die prematurely every year as a result of being uninsured. That's six 9/11s." This example was adapted from an article in the *San Francisco Chronicle,* April 27, 2003.

  Comment: If the facts asserted are correct, the reasoning in this example makes an important point. The generalization implicit here seems justifiable: Money spent to save lives should be spent where it will do the most good.

- **Example:** "Enough food is produced in the world to feed everyone. Why do I say so? Here's why: World production of grain alone is more than 1.5 billion tons, enough to supply the entire world population with two pounds of grain per day. This, with the current production of vegetables, fruits, nuts, and meat, is enough to supply each man, woman, and child with 3000 calories a day—equal to the consumption of an average American."

  Comment: If the facts asserted are correct, the reasoning makes an important point. The generalization, that enough food is produced in the world to feed everyone, is plausible.

- **Example:** "Hunger is the result of overpopulation. If people had fewer children, they wouldn't be hungry."

  Comment: In assessing this statement, let us consider some relevant facts. According to the Institute for Food and Development Policy (www.foodfirst.org), overpopulation is not the cause of hunger. It is usually the other way around: Hunger is one of the real causes of overpopulation. The more children a poor family has, the more likely some will survive to work in the fields or in the city to add to the family's small income and, later, to care for the parents in their old age. High birth rates are symptoms of the failures of a social system—inadequate family income, nutrition, education, health care, and old-age security. If the facts asserted in this report are correct, the generalization is not justified.

In examining generalizations, make sure you understand precisely what is being said. For example, if someone comments on the importance of loving one's country, one would do well to spend some time spelling out precisely what the expression does and does not imply. For example, what exactly is it that one is supposed to love—the land, the weather, the ideals, the mass media, Hollywood movies, the criminal justice system, the medical system, puritanical attitudes, the politicians, the laws that have been passed, the wealth, the military, the foreign policy? Once one is clear about what a generalization is saying (and not saying), it is important to determine the information and evidence that would be required to justify it. Moreover, as we have said before, it is important to minimize faulty generalizations by carefully using qualifiers such as "most," "some," "a few." Remember these rules:

- Don't say *all* when you mean *most.*
- Don't say *most* when you mean *some.*
- Don't say *some* when you mean *a few.*
- And don't say *a few* when you mean just *one.*

13.6   *Think for Yourself*

CONTRAST REASONABLE WITH UNREASONABLE ASSUMPTIONS

Following our examples above, construct one or two examples of either reasonable or unreasonable assumptions. Then write a critical commentary concerning each one.

Post Hoc Generalizations

Post hoc ergo propter hoc is a Latin phrase for a well-known mistake in generalizing. It literally means, "After that therefore caused by it," referring to the mistake of inferring that something that came before something else must necessarily have caused it. Here is an obvious example: "Yesterday I got a stomachache after doing algebra. I will avoid doing algebra in the future." And another: "Yesterday my son was in a car crash. Right before it happened, I had a feeling that something bad was going to happen. This proves that you can hurt the people you love by thinking negative thoughts about them."

Before any given event happens, other things happen, usually many, many things. That does not mean that all of these earlier events caused what came afterward. Monday comes before Tuesday but does not cause it. Summer comes before Fall but does not cause it. I put my shoes on before I eat my breakfast, but putting on my shoes does not cause me to eat my breakfast.

- **Example:** The last time we had a major strike of teachers, a student died in a fight. That just shows you the irresponsibility of teachers striking.

  Comment: Sorry, but no causal connection has been established. The mere fact that the strike occurred prior to the fight is no good reason to consider it a cause.

- **Example:** "Last time I had dinner at Jack's house, I had a bad stomachache the very next day. The food at Jack's house must have been bad."

  Comment: I'm afraid we must decline this post hoc generalization about the nature of the food at Jack's house. The stomachache in question has many other possible causes. You could check and see whether the other people who ate at Jack's house also got sick.

Analogies and Metaphors

We seek to understand new experiences and phenomena by likening them to what we already understand. When we explicitly recognize that the similarity is only *partial,* we should recognize that we are speaking analogically or metaphorically. The basic difference between an analogy and a metaphor is simple: When we put the work "like" in our description, we create an analogy *(He is like a rat.).* When we omit the word "like," we create a metaphor *(He is a rat.).*

Analogies and metaphors help us make sense of the world. We often explain something by comparing it (point by point) with something similar. Metaphors and analogies provide provisional models for understanding what we don't yet "literally" understand.

There are, in any case, three kinds of statements: literal statements, analogical statements, and metaphorical statements. Examples are:

There are many tree stumps in this forest. (literal)

A tree stump is like a chair in the forest. (analogical)

Every tree stump in this forest, and there are thousands, is a *tribute* to the power of the lumber industry and a *testament* to its indifference to ecology. (metaphorical)

Let us now move to some examples of analogies or metaphors. Both are used to make sense of things. Let us consider how useful or illuminating each attempt is. In some cases, we will need to clarify the statement and context before evaluating it.

- **Example:** "Life is like a beautiful and winding lane, on either side bright flowers, beautiful butterflies and tempting fruits, which we scarcely pause to admire and taste, so eager are we to hasten to an opening which we imagine will be more beautiful still."—G.A. Sala

  Comment: What do you think? Each of us must consult our own experience to decide how useful this analogy is.

- **Example:** "Life is the childhood of our immortality."—Goethe

  Comment: This analogy assumes the existence of God and the soul. If you grant that assumption, the analogy holds. If you don't, it doesn't.

- **Example:** "Common sense does not ask an impossible chessboard, but takes the one before it and plays the game."—Wendell Phillips

  Comment: The point behind this metaphor is that rather than trying to make the impossible happen, we should deal with the inescapable realities of our lives. Can anyone argue with that? Perhaps not, but there may be much argument about what is actually impossible and what is inescapable.

- **Example:** "The question is: Are you going to stand up for your country or not?"

  Comment: What does "stand up" mean? Why not "lie down" for your country or "jump up and down" for it? The speaker no doubt is asking us to act patriotically, but what does that mean? In one interpretation—"my country right or wrong"—you defend your country even when it is waging an unjust war. If you refuse to do so, you are labeled unpatriotic. In another interpretation, it is your duty to support your country in a war if it is justified and to oppose it if it is not.

■ **Example:** "War is the business of barbarians."—Napoleon

Comment: It is too bad that Napoleon did not mean what he said.

■ **Example:** "The blood, and only the blood, of the German people will determine our destiny."—Adolph Hitler

Comment: This is a typical statement by one of the world's most notorious sophists and demogogues—vague, threatening, and misleading. A probable paraphrase might be: "Germany will win in any conflict if Germans are willing to die to bring that about." Another possible interpretation might be: "Germany is the master race, and racial characteristics are what will determine who ultimately wins or loses."

■ **Example:** "The chief evil of war is more evil. War is the concentration of all human crimes. Here is its distinguishing, accursed brand. Under its standard gather violence, malignity, rage, fraud, perfidy, rapacity, and lust. If it only slew man, it would do little. It turns man into a beast of prey."—W.E. Channing[6]

Comment: Few people think of this metaphor when patriotic music is playing and the troops are marching off to wage war. Do you agree or disagree with the metaphor and/or the point behind our comment on it?

44 FOUL WAYS TO WIN AN ARGUMENT

If you want to become aware of how politicians, the news media, the advertising industry, public relations experts, government officials, and assorted friends and enemies use the arts of manipulation and con artistry against you, enter their point of view! Learn the art of intellectual dirty tricks so that, if necessary, you can out-think the tricksters.

First, remember that those who strive to manipulate you want something from you: your money, your vote, your support, your time, your soul—something! But they also need you to be unaware of what they are about. They have something (often a lot) to hide. Their goal is not the use of sound evidence and valid reasoning. They insult our intelligence by assuming that a manipulative trick will work on us, that we are not insightful enough to see what they are doing.

Your goal should be to recognize fallacies for what they are—the dirty tricks of those who want to gain an advantage. Fallacies, therefore, are stratagems for gaining influence, advantage, and power (over the "sheep" of society). You will withstand their impact more effectively when you know these fallacies inside and out. When you come to see how counterfeits of good reasoning pervade everyday life (and are the life blood of the mass media), you are better able to resist their influence. When you are inoculated

---

[6]William Ellery Channing (1780–1842) was a U.S. Unitarian clergyman and writer.

against fallacies, your response to them is transformed. You ask key questions. You probe behind the masks, the fronts, the fostered images, the impressive pomp and ceremony. You take charge of your own mind and emotions. You become (increasingly) your own person.

Let us now turn to some of the most prominent fallacies in thinking. As you read through these dirty tricks, imagine yourself instructing unscrupulous people in the art of manipulating the sheep of the world. Imagine yourself in the "business" of seeking influence over others. You want to get their vote, support, money, or what have you. Something is at stake that you care about. You face some opposition. You want to win the argument, gain the influence. And you don't care (at some level) what you have to do to achieve your goal?

What can you do? Use any one or more of the 44 foul ways to win an argument described next. If you don't mind being unscrupulous, you can manipulate and control the simple-minded. And these foul ways work even with otherwise highly sophisticated persons. You can observe the practices of politicians (and other propagandists) successfully using them every day. And don't worry about feeling guilty. Your instinctive skill in self-deception most likely will keep you from noticing that you are doing something unethical. Here is your battery of strategies for overcoming your conscience.

Dirty Trick # 1

Accuse your opponent of doing what he/she is accusing you of (or worse).[7] This trick is sometimes called "pointing to another wrong." When under attack and having trouble defending themselves, manipulators turn the tables. They accuse their opponent of doing what they are being accused of. "You say I don't love you! I think it is you who doesn't love me!"

Manipulators know this is a good way to put their opponents on the defensive. They may want to up the ante by accusing the opponent of doing something worse than what he/she is accusing them of: "How dare you accuse me of being messy? When was the last time you even took a shower?"

Dirty Trick # 2

Accuse him/her of sliding down a slippery slope (that leads to disaster). The manipulator uses the slippery slope trick when a person implies that if someone does one thing (A), it inevitably will lead to a domino effect of negative things that, in the end, will result in something terrible: "A" is not so bad, but A leads to B and B leads to C and C is horrible!

Imagine a mother lecturing her teenage daughter: "Okay, maybe there's nothing wrong with a kiss, but remember where kissing leads and where that leads and where that leads. Before you know it, you'll be the mother of an unwanted baby! Your young life will be ruined forever!" Manipulators who use the slippery-slope argument conveniently forget that many people walk carefully on slippery ground and don't fall down.

---

[7]Traditionally called "Tu Quoque"—literally, "you also."

Dirty Trick # 3

Appeal to authority.[8] Most people are in awe of those with power, celebrity, or status. In addition, people feel intense identification and loyalty to many sacred symbols (flags, religious images, sacred words, etc.). Though power, celebrity, and status rarely correlate in any way with knowledge and insight, people are mesmerized by them.

Demagogues that successfully manipulate people know that most people are readily tricked in this way, so they wrap themselves in the flag and associate themselves with power, celebrity, or status (in any way they can). This includes looking for scientists and other "knowledgeable" persons to support their views.

Cigarette companies once hired scientists who were (in effect) prepared to say that there was no *proof* that cigarettes caused lung cancer, though they knew (or should have known) that the proof was there. Cigarette companies also founded the American Tobacco Institute, a body of researchers supposedly seeking to discover the effects of smoking on health. In reality, the researchers were seeking to defend the interests of the tobacco industry under the guise of scientific authority. They deceived millions of people (and caused millions of deaths along the way). Naturally, they could do this only by deceiving themselves into thinking that they were simply being *scientifically careful*. And, of course, they made a lot of money in the process (which strongly influenced their ability to deceive themselves).

Dirty Trick # 4

Appeal to experience. Skilled manipulators, con artists, and politicians often imply that they have "experience" to back them up, even when their experiences are limited or nonexistent. They know it is much harder for someone to deny what they say if they speak with the voice of experience. Of course, they sometimes will come up against an opponent who has more experience than they do. In that case, they attack their opponent's experience—as not representative, as biased, as limited, as distorted, or as subjective.

Dirty Trick # 5

Appeal to fear. Deep down, most people have a lot of fears—fear of death, disease, loss of love, loss of attractiveness, loss of youth, loss of income, loss of security, rejection by others. Unprincipled manipulators know that people tend to react primitively when any of these fears are activated. Thus, they represent themselves as having the ability to protect people against these threats (even when they can't). You should distrust authorities who say that certain groups (or people) are inherently dangerous: "Remember, these people are threatening our freedom, our way of life, our homes, our property." Politicians often use this strategy quite effectively to make sure people line up behind governmental authority and do what the government—that is, what politicians—want.

---

[8]Traditionally called "Argumentum ad Verecundiam."

Dirty Trick # 6

Appeal to pity (or sympathy). Manipulators know how to portray themselves (and their situation) in such a way as to make people feel sorry for them or at least to gain their sympathy, especially when they don't want to take responsibility for something they have done.

Consider the student who, when confronted with the fact that she hasn't done her homework, whines and says something like, "You don't understand how hard my life is. I have so much to do. It's very difficult for me to get my homework done. I'm not lucky like some students. Since my parents can't afford to send me to college, I have to work thirty hours a week to pay my own way. When I come home from work, my roommate plays music until midnight so I can't study. What am I supposed to do? Give me a break!"

Appeal to pity also can be used to defend someone the manipulator identifies with, as in, "Before you criticize the President, recognize that he has the hardest job in the world. He must stay up late at night, worrying about our well-being, trying to find a way to act in the welfare of all of us. The fate (and weight) of the free world rests heavy on his shoulders. How about some consideration for the poor man!" Use of this ploy enables the manipulator to divert attention from the innocent people who are harmed by a presidential decision or policy.

Dirty Trick # 7

Appeal to popular passions.[9] Manipulators, and other masters of counterfeit, subterfuge, and ruse, are careful to present themselves as people who share the values and views of their audience, especially the "sacred" beliefs of the audience. Everyone has some prejudices, and most people feel hatred toward something or someone. Masters of spin stir up prejudices, hatred, and irrational fears. They imply that they agree with the audience. They act as if they share their views. They work to convince the audience that their opponent doesn't hold sacred the beliefs they hold sacred.

This strategy has many possible variations. One has been called the "Just Plain Folks Fallacy," in which the manipulator says or implies something like this:

> "It's good to be back in my home (city/state/country) and with people I can really trust. It's great to be with people who face things squarely, who use their common sense to get things done, people who don't believe in highfalutin' ways of thinking and action."

Dirty Trick # 8

Appeal to tradition or faith ("the tried and true"). Closely related to Dirty Trick # 7, this strategy emphasizes what seems to have passed the test of time. People are often enslaved by the social customs and norms of their culture, as well as traditional beliefs. What is traditional seems right: "This is the way we have always done things."

Manipulators imply that they hold firm to what their audience is familiar and comfortable with. They imply that their opponent will destroy these traditions and faith.

---

[9]Traditionally called "Argumentum ad Populum."

They don't worry about whether these traditions harm innocent people (like the cruel customs and laws against Blacks before the Civil Rights movement). They create the appearance of being independent in their views while the views they reach "independently" just happen to coincide with those of the crowd. They know that people are usually suspicious of those who go against present social norms and established traditions. They know enough to avoid openly opposing the social customs to which people are unconsciously (and slavishly) bound.

Dirty Trick # 9

Assume a posture of righteousness. People begin with the deep-seated belief that they (their nation, their religion, their motivation) is especially pure and ethical. We sometimes bungle things, but we are always pure of heart: "We hold the highest ideals of any country. Of course, we make mistakes and sometimes commit follies. But our intentions are good. Unlike others in the world, we are innocent of guile. We are good-hearted."

National and international news (designed for national consumption) is always written with this premise in the background. We may blunder, but we always intend to do the right thing. Manipulators take advantage of this questionable premise by speaking and writing with such assumptions in the background. This posture is related to the fallacy of begging the question and leads to question-begging epithets. (See "Beg the Question," Dirty Trick # 11.)

Dirty Trick # 10

Attack the person (and not the argument).[10] When the opponent makes reasonable arguments, manipulators ignore those arguments and instead find a way to personally attack the reasoner. Name-calling (even mud-slinging) often works (depending on how you do it). Spin artists know what a given audience will reject and insinuate that their opponent supports those *terrible* things. For example, the opponent might be labeled a communist or an atheist. Or it might be said of her that she supports terrorism, or is soft on crime.

This strategy is sometimes called "poisoning the well." It leads to the audience dismissing an opponent in a sweeping way—no matter what the opponent says in his defense. Of course, spin artists knows the importance of reading the audience correctly to make sure they don't go too far. They realize that the more subtle they can be, the more effective their manipulation will be.

13.7   *Think for Yourself*

INTERNALIZING THE FIRST 10 DIRTY TRICKS

Close your book and try to make a list of the first 10 dirty tricks we've covered. Try to write a paragraph about each of them. Then re-read the pages that cover them and

---

[10]Traditionally called "Argumentum ad Hominem."

evaluate what you have written. Have you accurately stated what the various fallacies are? Have you exemplified them well?

Dirty Trick # 11

Beg the question.[11] One easy way to "prove" a point is to assume it in the first place. Consider this example:

> "Well, what form of government do you want, a government by liberal do-gooders ready to spend your hard-earned dollars or a government led by business minds that understand how to live within a tight budget and generate jobs that put people to work?"

This statement includes the following assumptions that should not be taken for granted:

- That a liberal government would spend money unwisely
- That business people know how to live within a tight budget and generate jobs that put people to work.

One variation on this fallacy has been called "question-begging epithets"—using words or phrases that prejudge an issue by the way the issue is put. For example: "Shall we defend freedom and democracy or cave in to terrorism and tyranny?" By putting the question in this way, we avoid having to talk about uncomfortable questions such as: "But are we really advancing human freedom? Are we really spreading democracy (or just extending our power, our control, our dominance, our access to foreign markets)?" Pay close attention to the words people use when they are articulating the "facts" with respect to an issue. They often choose words that presuppose the correctness of their position on an issue.

Dirty Trick # 12

Call for perfection (demand impossible conditions). The opponent wants the manipulator to agree to X, and the manipulator realizes he can't argue against X without losing credit in the eyes of the audience. Fine—agree to X, but only under the following conditions: "Yes, we do want a democracy, but only when we can have a *true democracy,* and that means this and that, and that will have to be changed before we consider it."

By making a maneuver of this kind, the manipulator diverts those who hear it so they do not discover that the manipulator has no intention whatsoever of allowing X to take place. This is similar to Dirty Trick #32 ("Raise nothing but objections").

---

[11]Traditionally called "Petitio Principii."

Dirty Trick # 13

Create a false dilemma (the great either/or). A true dilemma occurs when we are forced to choose between two equally unsatisfactory alternatives. A false dilemma occurs when we are persuaded that we have only two, equally unsatisfactory choices, when we really have more than two possibilities available to us. Consider the following claim: "Either we are going to lose the war on terrorism or we will have to give up some of our traditional freedoms and rights."

People are often ready to accept a false dilemma because few feel comfortable with complexity and nuanced distinctions. We tend to like sweeping absolutes. We want clear and simple choices. So those who are skilled in manipulating people face others with false dilemmas (one alternative of which is the one the manipulator wants them to choose and the other alternative clearly unacceptable).

Manipulators present arguments in *black or white* form. For example: "You are either for us or against us. You support either democracy and freedom or terrorism and tyranny." They realize that only a small minority of people will respond to such a false dilemma with the observation: "But these are not our only choices. In between the extremes of A and Z are options B, C, D, E, F, G, H, I, J, K . . . ."

Dirty Trick # 14

Devise analogies (and metaphors) that support your view (even if they are misleading or "false"). An analogy or a metaphor is a comparison that is not literally true. Consider: "Don't you think it is about time for us to *slap down* those judges who are *soft* on crime!" Here, the two phrases in italics are used metaphorically. They are not intended literally. These metaphors are attractive to many people whose information about the criminal justice system comes principally from "cops and robbers" television shows and sensationalized stories in the mass media.

To win arguments, then, manipulators use comparisons that make them look good and their opponent look bad: "You're treating me like my father used to treat me! He was so unfair, and so are you." Or: "The way you're treating me is like kicking a horse when it's down. Can't you see I've had a hard day?!"

The analogies and metaphors that work depend in part on the prejudices and beliefs of the audience. This requires understanding the world view of the audience, as well as the root metaphors underlying it. For example, if manipulators are trying to influence someone with a religious world view, they are more likely to be successful using religious metaphors and analogies. The skilled manipulator knows that when talking to a fundamentalist Christian, it is a mistake to choose metaphors from the Koran.

Dirty Trick # 15

Question your opponent's conclusions. Manipulators want to lead the audience to accept their conclusions. They want the audience to reject the conclusions or interpretations of their opponents. If they remember the Latin phrase "non-sequitur" (which means, literally, "It does not follow"), they can accuse their opponents of being illogical and call into question the opponents' reasoning. As soon as an opponent asserts a conclusion, the manipulator might say:

"Wait a minute. *That doesn't follow!* Your conclusion doesn't follow from your premises. First you said "X," and now youre saying "Y." How did you get from X to Y? How can you justify such a leap? What you say isn't logical. You haven't proven Y, only X."

Through this strategy, manipulators/can obscure any legitimate points the opponent makes. At the same time, they themselves seem to be logical and dispassionate.

Dirty Trick # 16

Create misgivings: Where there's smoke, there's fire. The manipulator knows that once serious charges are made against a person, it may be difficult, if not impossible, for the accused to clear away the suspicion that there must have been *something* to the charge. Lingering suspicions may destroy the chance for people to maintain their honor in the public eye. Rumors take on a life of their own. This, therefore, is one of the foulest of the foulest of the 44 foul ways to win an argument.

During the McCarthy era, many families, friendships, and careers were destroyed because of the power of rumor and the "where there's smoke, there's fire" mentality. Senator Joseph McCarthy and his House Un-American Activities Committee dragged people before a public tribunal and implied that if they truly loved the country, they would cooperate with the committee by providing the names of persons with left-leaning views. If the request was refused, a vast television audience would draw the conclusion that the "uncooperative" citizens were communists and, therefore, "un-American."

Most of those who elected to challenge the Committee on Un-American Activities lost their jobs; their families were ostracized; and their children were mocked and bullied at school. Most were blackballed and could no longer find employment in their profession.

Of course, perverse charges often are made off the record, in private conversations. Once the rumor is launched, there is no need to do more. People like to spread stories: "Of course, I don't believe it, but did you know that there has been some talk of Jack beating his wife and children? Ugly, isn't it?"

When governmental officials use this trick, it usually is called spreading "disinformation" (false charges that the government knows will be believed). For example, planting stories about "atrocities" of one country (that never actually occurred) is effective for validating an aggressive attack by another country. Hitler used this strategy effectively. The U.S. government has often spread disinformation—for example, to justify sending Marines into Central or South American countries to depose one government and put a more "friendly" government into power.

That these stories will be discredited years later is of no consequence to the fabricators of such stories. Disinformation often works. The discrediting of information is usually too late to matter. Years later, people don't seem to care.

Because people tend to think in simplistic ways, manipulators and politicians often get them to reject someone simply by mentioning something about the person that seems inappropriate or that goes against social conventions. For example: "Kevin already has admittedly smoked marijuana. That tells us a lot about him!" Or, "Look at that teenage girl wearing that skimpy top. I guess we know what she's after."

Dirty Trick # 17

Create a strawman. Manipulators know the importance of making their opponents look bad. Whatever the views of the opponent, a skilled spinmaster can make the opponent appear to take another, far less believable, view. The trick of misrepresenting someone's views to gain an advantage is sometimes called creating a "strawman." A strawman is literally not real, though it may look like it is. A strawman argument, then, is a false or misleading representation of someone's reasoning.

Suppose someone wants to reform our criminal justice system (so fewer innocent people are wrongfully convicted and thrown into prison). Her opponent may well retort with the strawman argument: "So I guess what you want is to free all criminals and leave us even more threatened than we are now!"

Of course, no one said or wants that, so her opponent is arguing against a strawman. By misrepresenting a person's position and presenting it in a form that people will reject, he successfully uses the "strawman" strategy.

In addition to misrepresenting the opponent's argument, he also might claim that the opponent is misrepresenting *his* argument. In this case, the spinmaster then can claim that the opponent is the one who is attacking a "strawman."

In any case, the manipulator wants to ensure that the best representation of his reasoning is compared with the worse possible representation of his opponent's reasoning. Manipulators try to make their opponent look bad at the same time they make their own case look good.

Imagine that an environmentalist makes the following argument:

> "Each of us must do our part to reduce the amount of pollution we are creating on the planet. The automobile industry, for example, has to find alternative forms of fuel—cleaner forms of fuel. We need to move away from gasoline as our primary source of automobile fuel. Otherwise, our planet will continue to suffer needlessly."

A manipulator who is seeking to discredit the environmentalist might misrepresent him as follows:

> "What my opponent is really arguing for is more *big government*. He wants to take away your right to choose and give bureaucracy more and more power over your life. Don't let him get away with it."

Dirty Trick # 18

Deny or defend inconsistencies.   Manipulators know that a person looks bad when appearing to be inconsistent, saying one thing and doing another, or sometimes supporting X and sometimes attacking it. When caught in a contradiction, the manipulator has two choices. She can either deny that there is any contradiction at all ("I didn't really say that!") or she can admit the contradiction and defend it as a justifiable change ("The world is changing and we must change with it").

Human life and society are shot through with contradictions and inconsistencies. Those who have the most integrity are the ones who admit to contradictions and inconsistencies and work to minimize them. Manipulators work hard to cover them up.

Dirty Trick # 19

Demonize their side, sanitize yours. Most people are not sophisticated. To manipulate them, the manipulator systematically uses "good" words to characterize the manipulator's side while using "negative" words to characterize the opponent. Thus, the manipulator believes in democracy, freedom, stability, compromise, fairness, strength, peace, protection, security, civilization, human rights, sovereignty, reformation, being open, defending the innocent, honor, God's comfort, normalcy, pride, independence, a mission, facing hardship. . . .

The opponent believes in tyranny, suppression, conflict, terrorism, aggression, violence, subversion, barbarism, fanaticism, the spread of chaos, attacking the innocent, extremism, dictatorship, plots, cunning, cruelty, destruction,. . . .

A variation on this strategy consists in sanitizing one's own motives, by explaining one's reasons to be "righteous": "I'm not motivated by profit or greed. I don't want to enhance my power and influence. I don't want to control and dominate. Certainly not. I want to spread the cause of freedom, to share the good life, the blessings of democracy (bla, bla, bla)."

The manipulator obscures his real motives (which are often selfish and based on considerations of money and power) while playing up motives that sound good and make the manipulator appear high-minded. This strategy, sometimes called "finding the good reason," gives lip service to high-minded principles (asserting them loudly while ignoring them in practice).

Dirty Trick # 20

Evade questions, gracefully. Spin artists who face questions from an audience learn how to predict most of the hard questions they will face and how to evade them with skill and grace. One way to evade a hard question is to answer it with a joke that deflects the question. Another way is to give a truistic answer ("How long will the troops have to remain in country X?" Answer: "As long as it is necessary and not one day longer.") A third way is to give an answer so long and detailed that the length of the answer enables the manipulator to slide from one question (a hard one) to another question (an easy one).

Manipulators do not answer questions directly when direct answers would get them into trouble or force them to accept a responsibility they want to avoid facing. They learn to use vagueness, jokes, diversions, and truisms to their advantage.

13.8   *Think for Yourself*

INTERNALIZING THE SECOND 10 DIRTY TRICKS

Close your book and try to a list the second 10 "dirty tricks." Write a paragraph about each of them. Then re-read the applicable pages and evaluate what you have written. Have you accurately stated the various fallacies? Have you exemplified them well?

Dirty Trick # 21

Flatter your audience.   People are receptive to flattery: "It's good to be talking to an audience of people with good old-fashioned common sense and real insights into our social problems." "An intelligent person such as you will not be taken in by . . . ." Sometimes, however, manipulators have to be subtle or the audience will suspect them of being manipulators.

Most politicians are highly proficient in the art of flattery. Their objective is to win over their audiences. Politicians want to lower the defenses of their audiences, to minimize any tendency they might have to think critically about what is said.

Dirty Trick # 22

Hedge what you say. Manipulators often hide behind words, refusing to commit themselves or give direct answers. This allows them to retreat if necessary. If caught leaving out important information, they then can come up with some excuse for not being forthcoming in the first place. Or, if questioned closely, they can qualify their position so no one can prove them wrong. When pressed, they hedge. Effective manipulators must be effective weasels. They must weasel out of their mistakes, cover up their errors, and guard what they say whenever possible.

Dirty Trick # 23

Ignore the evidence.[12]   To avoid considering evidence that might cause them to change their position, manipulators often ignore evidence. Usually they ignore the evidence to avoid having to consider it in their own minds, because it threatens their belief system or vested interests. Imagine a close-minded Christian questioning whether it is possible for an atheist to live an ethical life (lacking the guidance of the Bible). If such a person were confronted with examples of atheists who have lived self-sacrificing, compassionate, lives, she would be uncomfortable in her view. She probably would find a way to put the subject out of her mind to avoid the implications of the evidence.

---

[12]Traditionally called Apiorism (invincible ignorance).

Dirty Trick # 24

Ignore the main point.[13] Manipulators know that if they can't win a point, they should divert their audience from that point and focus on another point—a point not relevant to the original issue. Those skilled in doing this know how to do it so their audience doesn't notice the shift.

Dirty Trick # 25

Attack evidence (that undermines your case). When manipulators cannot successfully dodge consideration of evidence that does not support their case, they often attack that evidence. You can see this in the U.S. government's refusal to accept that Iraq did not have a stockpile of weapons of mass destruction before the United States waged war against Iraq. The government had no hard evidence to support its position that Iraq had the weapons, so it tried to manufacture the evidence through flagrant stretches of the imagination. No evidence could convince the government that it was wrong, because it wasn't willing to consider that it might be wrong. These dodges also could be covered under the double-standard fallacy, Dirty Trick # 44.

Dirty Trick # 26

Insist loudly on a minor point. Manipulators know that, if it looks like they are losing the argument, a good way to distract most people is to insist loudly on some minor point. Because most people think superficially, few will notice that the point is minor, especially if they are emotionally attached to it.

   Thus, for example, people often miss big issues when the media focus loudly on small issues (as if they were big issues). The problem of malnutrition and starvation in the world is given little coverage in the media, except on special occasions (such as during a drought or after a hurricane). At the same time, a small country refusing to do what our government wants it to do is treated as an issue of great significance (as if our government had a right to impose its will on other governments).

Dirty Trick # 27

Use the hard-cruel-world argument (to justify doing what is usually considered unethical). We often say that noble ends do not justify foul means, but do we believe it? When engaging in unethical practices (such as assassinations, forced detentions, and torture) government spokespersons often use the "It's a hard, cruel world" argument in defense.

   When individuals or countries gain a lot of power, they soon come to believe that they should be able to do pretty much what they want to do. They do this by convincing themselves that their ends are always noble and just, that the only negative things they do in the world are forced on them by evil others who do not share their noble

---

[13]Traditionally called "Ignoratio Elenchi."

values. Manipulators, then, often win arguments by insisting that they are being forced to use the means they deeply wish they could avoid, but, alas, it's a hard, cruel world.

As examples: "We don't want war. We are forced into it." "We don't want unemployment, but free enterprise demands it." "If we give resources to people who haven't worked for them, they will become lazy and we will end up in a totalitarian communist state." "We don't want the CIA to engage in assassination, torture, disinformation, or dirty tricks of any kind, but, unfortunately, we are forced to use these tactics to defend freedom and democracy in the world."

Dirty Trick # 28

Make sweeping glittering generalizations. Manipulators, con artists, spinmasters, and politicians will use any generalizations that support their case and that their audience will accept, regardless of whether they have sufficient evidence to support those generalizations. They make positive generalizations that people will readily support—generalizations, for example, about "our" or "their" devotion to God, country, patriotism, family, and free enterprise. Their generalizations are chosen deliberately to coincide with the thinking of their audience. Of course, these manipulators keep their generalizations vague so they can weasel out of them if necessary.

Dirty Trick # 29

Make much of any inconsistencies in your opponent's position. There is inconsistency in the best of us. We all sometimes fail to practice what we preach. Everyone sometimes falls into a double-standard. Manipulators exploit any inconsistencies they can find in their opponents' arguments. They are quick to make the charge of hypocrisy, even when they are guilty of flagrant, deep, and multiple forms of hypocrisy themselves, hypocrisy that bothers them not at all.

Dirty Trick # 30

Make your opponent look ridiculous ("lost in the laugh"). Manipulators look for ways to make their opponents, or their positions, look ridiculous (and therefore funny). People like a good laugh, and they especially like laughing at views that seem threatening. A good joke is usually well-received, for it relieves audience members of the responsibility to think seriously about what is making them uncomfortable. Manipulators measure their audience to make sure that their jokes do not sound like sour grapes.

13.9   Think for Yourself

INTERNALIZING THE THIRD SET OF DIRTY TRICKS

Close your book and try to make a list of the third 10 "dirty tricks." Try to write a paragraph about each of them. Then re-read the pages that cover them and evaluate what you have written. Have you accurately stated what the various fallacies are? Have you exemplified them well?

Dirty Trick # 31

Oversimplify the issue.   Most people are uncomfortable making sense of deep or subtle arguments, and manipulators oversimplify the issue to their advantage: "I don't care what the statistics tell us about the so-called 'abuse' of prisoners. The real issue is whether we are going to be tough on crime. Save your sympathy for the victims of crime, not for the criminals." What is being ignored is that the abuse of prisoners is itself a crime. Unfortunately, people with a certain (over-simple) mindset don't care about criminal behavior that victimizes "criminals." After all (they think to themselves), the world divides into good guys and bad guys, and sometimes the good guys have to do bad things to bad guys. They think the bad guys deserve bad treatment. By oversimplifying the issue, they don't have to deal with what is wrong in our treatment of prisoners.

Dirty Trick # 32

Raise nothing but objections.   Suppose your opponent is giving good reasons to accept an argument but your mind is made up and nothing will change it (of course, you don't want to admit that your mind is closed). Skilled manipulators respond with objection after objection after objection. As their opponent answers one objection, they move on to another. The unspoken mindset of the manipulator is: "No matter what my opponent says (in giving me reasons), I'll keep thinking of objections (actually, nothing whatsoever will convince me of the validity of the opponent's view)."

Dirty Trick # 33

Rewrite history (have it your way).   The worst deeds and atrocities can disappear from historical accounts (or be made to appear minor) while fantasies and fabrications can be made to look like hard facts. This is what happens in what is sometimes called "patriotic history." The writing of a distorted form of history is justified by love of country and often defended by the charge of negativity: "You always want to focus on what is wrong with us! What about what is right about us?!"

Human memory is continually working to re-describe events of the past in such a way as to exonerate itself and condemn its detractors. Historical writing often follows suit, especially in the writing of textbooks for schools. So, in telling a story about the past, manipulators feel free to distort the past in whatever ways they believe they can get away with. As always, the skilled manipulator is ready with (self-justifying) excuses.

Dirty Trick # 34

Seek your vested interests.   Manipulators attack their opponents' motivation but insist that their own motives are pure. They cover their true motives (i.e. whatever is in their vested interest) by expressing high ideals (freedom, democracy, justice, the American way, which they in reality ignore).

When manipulators are seeking their advantage and their opponents call them on it, manipulators either deny the charge (usually indignantly) or counter-attack by saying that everyone has a right to protect their interests. If pressed further, they may use a "you-do-it-too" defense.

Dirty Trick # 35

Shift the ground.   When manipulators sense that they are losing the argument, they do not give in. They shift the ground to something else! Sometimes they do this by going back and forth between different meanings of the same word. So if a person says of another that she isn't educated because she isn't insightful and has very little knowledge, the manipulator may shift the ground and say something like: "Of course she's educated! Look how many years of school she completed. If that's not being educated, I don't know what is!"

Dirty Trick # 36

Shift the burden of proof.   The burden of proof refers to which party in a dispute has the responsibility to prove what he or she asserts. For example, in a criminal court the prosecutor has the responsibility to prove guilt beyond a reasonable doubt. The defense doesn't have to prove innocence. Manipulators don't want to take on the burden of proof for what they assert. They therefore develop skill in shifting the burden of proof to their opponents: "Wait a minute! Before I have to prove that the invasion of Iraq was justified, you have to prove that it wasn't."

Actually, any country that invades another has to have powerful evidence to justify that act. No country has the obligation to prove that it ought not to be invaded. By international law, the burden of proof is on the other side, the side that initiates violence.

Suppose a manipulator questions your patriotism. You ask him what evidence exists to show you are not. He tries to shift the burden of proof: "Wait a minute—what have you done to show your loyalty to the country? You have socialist views, don't you? Aren't you against free enterprise? Didn't you protest the Vietnam War?" All of these are fallacious attempts to shift the burden of proof.

Dirty Trick # 37

Spin, spin, spin.   In an editorial in the *Wall Street Journal* (May 7, 2004) on the prominence of the "spin game" in the media, Daniel Henniger says:

> The media world we inhabit is without exception a world of "spin." Most people, having given up on getting a set of unadorned facts, align themselves with whichever spin outlet seems comfortable.

"Most" people probably don't see through the media reliance on spin, as we are commonly victims of its power.

No skilled manipulator (spinmaster) underestimates the power of spin in manipulating consumers of the "news." Manipulators continually foster the spin that obscures viewpoints they oppose, while at the same time positively representing their own viewpoint (the one they want the audience to accept).

To juxtapose opposing spins and decide which facts are most significant and which interpretations are most plausible, critical consumers must become aware of the virtual omnipresence of spin and the selectivity of coverage in the media. Critical consumers expect the media to put a spin on *all articles of news* in keeping with the prejudices of the audience the media "serve." Critical consumers must consider alternative ways of looking at the issues in the news media, and alternative ways of thinking about what is being presented, what is most significant about it, and how it is best represented.

Dirty Trick # 38

Talk in vague generalities.   It's hard to prove people wrong when they can't be pinned down. Instead of focusing on particulars, manipulators talk in the most vague terms they can get away with. This dirty trick is especially popular with politicians: "Forget what the spineless liberals say. It's time to be tough—tough on criminals, tough on terrorists, tough on those who belittle our country."

Manipulators make sure they don't use specifics that might cause someone to question what they are doing. For example: Who exactly you are going to be tough on, and what exactly do you intend to do with these people when you "get tough" with them? Is torture okay? What about humiliation? What about unlimited detention without any charge registered against them? What about placing them in tiny cells without a toilet for days at a time? What about assassination?

When people use this strategy against you, ask them to give you specific examples of what they mean. Ask for definitions of key terms. Then insist that they show how their definitions are applied in the specific cases. Don't allow them to get away with vague generalities!

Dirty Trick # 39

Talk double-talk.   Let's face it—we often do what we accuse our opponents of doing. But we don't want to admit it because that would hurt our cause. Double-talk can be a powerful mode of attack or defense. In double-talk (sometimes called double-speak) we use a positive word or phrase when we do something and a negative word when our opponents do precisely the same thing.

For example, before World War II, the U.S. government called the department that wages war the "War Department." After the war, the name was changed to the "Defense Department." This change has come about because the government doesn't want to admit that it starts wars. Rather, it wants to manipulate people into thinking that it only *defends* the country against *aggressive* others. In short, politically, the word "defense" sells better than the word "war."

When a citizen of a government in which we are in secret conflict gives us information about that enemy, we label it a "brave" and "courageous" act. When someone in our country tells our secrets to that same enemy, we indict that person as a "traitor."[14] We are clever; they are cunning. We support freedom-fighters; they support terrorists. We set up holding centers; they set up concentration camps. We strategically withdraw;

---

[14]When innocent people on our side are killed (without even realizing they were in danger), they are called "heroes." When people on the side of our enemy deliberately sacrifice their lives to die for what they believe, we call them "cowards" or "fanatics." We wouldn't label anyone on our side a "fanatic." Interestingly, when the U.S. government trained Bin Ladin and other Muslim fundamentalists to use terror tactics in fighting the Russians in Afghanistan, we called these fundamentalists "freedom-fighters." Now these same people, because they are fighting us, have been transformed into "terrorists."

they retreat. We are religious; they are fanatic. We are determined; they are pig-headed. Literally thousands of words fall into "good-when-I-do-it, bad-when-you-do-it" doublets. Most people are not skilled in detecting double-speak.

Dirty Trick # 40

Tell big lies. Most people lie about small things but would be afraid to lie about big things. Manipulators are not afraid of telling big lies, and they know that if they insist on a lie long enough, many people will believe them—especially if they have the resources of mass media to air the lie. Skilled manipulators are focused on *what they can get people to believe,* not what is true or false. They know that the human mind does not naturally seek the truth; it seeks comfort, security, personal confirmation, and vested interest. People often don't want to know the truth, especially truths that are painful, truths that expose their contradictions and inconsistencies, truths that reveal what they don't want to know about themselves or their country.

Many manipulators are highly skilled in telling lies and thus in making those lies seem true. For example, in studying the history of the CIA, one can document any number of unethical deeds that have been covered up by lies (see any volume of *Covert Action Quarterly* for documentation of the misdeeds and dirty tricks of the CIA in every region of the world).[15] Virtually all of these unethical acts were officially denied at the time they were committed.

13.10   *Think for Yourself*

INTERNALIZING THE FOURTH SET OF DIRTY TRICKS

Close your book and try to make a list of the fourth 10 "dirty tricks." Write a paragraph about each of them. Then re-read the pages that cover them and evaluate what you have written. Have you accurately stated what the various fallacies are? Have you exemplified them well?

Dirty Trick # 41

Treat abstract words and symbols as if they were real things.[16]   Manipulators know that most people are not linguistically sophisticated. Most people don't reflect on the relationship between the way we use language and concrete particulars in the world. We do not deliberately strip off language from specific events and deeds and consider a range of interpretations for making sense of what is happening in the world. Most see their view of the world as accurately reflecting what is going on in the world, even when

---

[15] info@covertactionquarterly.org
[16] Traditionally called "reification."

that view is highly distorted. Abstractions are not abstractions, in their mind, but realities. Consider the following examples:

- Freedom supports us.
- Democracy calls.
- Justice insists that we . . .
- The flag marches on.
- Science says . . .

Note that in all of these examples an abstract idea is given a life of its own when it is coupled with an action verb. How, for example, can a flag march? It's not possible. But people are swayed by this colorful, though highly misleading, use of language.

Dirty Trick # 42

Throw in a red herring (or two).   In this strategy, manipulators divert attention from the issue by focusing on what is irrelevant (but emotionally loaded). Suppose that a manipulator can't refute the reasoning of her opponent. She doesn't bother trying. Instead, she throws in an emotionally charged issue that will distract the audience from the reasoning of her opponent.

Consider this example: The manipulator's opponent has said that the oceans of the world are rapidly dying because of human activity, specifically industry waste. Instead of arguing against the position taken by her opponent, the manipulator throws in a "red herring." She says:

> "What we really need to concern ourselves with is all of the government regulations facing industry today, and all of the jobs that will be lost if bureaucratic regulations continue to grow. We need a country where the people have jobs and their children have opportunities to grow and reach their potential!"

How is this retort relevant to the oceans dying? It's not. It's a red herring thrown in to avoid the issue altogether.

Dirty Trick # 43

Throw in some statistics.   People are impressed by numbers, especially precise numbers. So whenever they can, manipulators quote statistics in their favor, even if the source is questionable. Their audience is usually impressed: "By the way, did you know that 78% of the students who read this guide raise their gradepoint average by 1.33 grade levels within two semesters? It's even higher at your school!"

Dirty Trick # 44

Use double standards (whenever you can).   Manipulators often use double standards—one standard for us, another standard for them. We can't abide countries developing nuclear weapons (except for us and all our friends). We condemn aggression

44 DIRTY TRICKS TO WIN AN ARGUMENT

Accuse your opponent of doing what he or she is accusing you of (or worse)

Accuse him/her of sliding down a slippery slope (that leads to disaster)

Appeal to authority

Appeal to experience

Appeal to fear

Appeal to pity (or sympathy)

Appeal to popular passions

Appeal to tradition or faith ("the tried and true")

Assume a posture of righteousness

Attack the person (and not the argument)

Beg the question

Call for perfection (demand impossible conditions)

Create a false dilemma (the "great either/or")

Devise analogies (and metaphors) **that support your view** (even if they are misleading or "false")

Question your opponent's conclusions

Create misgivings: Where there's smoke, there's fire

Create a strawman

Deny or defend your inconsistencies

Demonize his/her side, sanitize yours

Evade questions, gracefully

Flatter your audience

Hedge what you say

Ignore the evidence

Ignore the main point

Attack evidence (that undermines your case)

Insist loudly on a minor point

Use the hard-cruel-world argument (to justify doing what is usually considered unethical)

Make (sweeping) glittering generalizations

Make much of any inconsistencies in your opponent's position

Make your opponent look ridiculous ("lost in the laugh")

Oversimplify the issue

Raise nothing but objections

Rewrite history (have it your way)

Seek your vested interests

Shift the ground

Shift the burden of proof

Spin, spin, spin

Talk in vague generalities

Talk double-talk

Tell big lies

Treat abstract words and symbols as if they were real things

Throw in a red herring (or two)

Throw in some statistics

Use double standards (whenever you can)

(except when we are the aggressors). We can't tolerate torture and human rights violations by our enemies (although, alas, sometimes we are forced to do these things ourselves).

13.11 *Think for Yourself*

INTERNALIZING THE LAST FOUR DIRTY TRICKS

Close your book and try to make a list of the last four "dirty tricks." Write a paragraph about each of them. Then re-read the pages that cover them and evaluate what you have written. Have you accurately stated what the various fallacies are? Have you exemplified them well?

FALLACY DETECTION: ANALYZING A SPEECH FROM THE PAST

Now test yourself on the fallacies you have just read. Read through the following excerpts from a historically important political speech, a speech whose persuasive power won a national election in 1897. See how many of the 44 dirty tricks to win an argument this writer used.

Imagine yourself a voter in the United States in 1898 listening to the following excerpts from a speech, "The March of the Flag," given by Albert J. Beveridge[17] (who soon would become a U.S. Senator). Referring to the 44 Dirty Tricks listed in the box, read through the excerpts and indicate which of the manipulative strategies are being used in this speech. Perhaps the best way to do this is to highlight or underline and identify the fallacies you notice as you read through these passages.

The Opening:

Fellow citizens: It is a noble land that God has given us; a land that can feed and clothe the world; a land whose coast lines would enclose half the countries of Europe; a land set like a sentinel between the two imperial oceans of the globe, a greater England with a nobler destiny. It is a mighty people that He has planted on this soil; a people sprung from the most masterful blood of history; a people perpetually revitalized by the virile, man-producing working folk of all the earth; a people imperial by virtue of their power, by right of their institutions, by authority of their heaven-directed purposes—the propagandists and not the misers of liberty.

It is a glorious history our God has bestowed on His chosen people; a history whose keynote was struck by the Liberty Bell; a history heroic with faith in our mission and our future; a history of statesmen who flung the boundaries of the republic out into unexplored lands and savage wildernesses; a history of soldiers who carried the flag across the blazing deserts and through the ranks of hostile mountains, even to the gates of sunset; a history of a multiplying people who overran a continent in half a century;

---

[17]Thomas Deed (1903).

a history of prophets who saw the consequences of evils inherited from the past, and of martyrs who died to save us from them; a history divinely logical, in the process of whose tremendous reasoning we find ourselves today.

Beveridge's Definition of the Issue:

Therefore, in this campaign, the question is larger than a party question. It is an American question. It is a world question. Shall the American people continue their resistless march toward the commercial supremacy of the world? Shall free institutions broaden their blessed reign as the children of liberty wax in strength, until the empire of our principles is established over the hearts of all mankind?

Have we no mission to perform, no duty to discharge to our fellow man? Has the Almighty Father endowed us with gifts beyond our deserts and marked us as the people of His peculiar favor, merely to rot in our own selfishness, as men and nations must who take cowardice for their companion and self for their deity—as China has, as India has, as Egypt has?

Shall we be as the man who had one talent and hid it, or as he who had ten talents and used them until they grew to riches? And shall we reap the reward that waits on our discharge of our high duty as the sovereign power of earth; shall we occupy new markets for what our farmers raise, new markets for what our factories make, new markets for what our merchants sell—aye, and, please God, new markets for what our ships shall carry?

. . . Shall our commerce be encouraged until, with Oceanica, the Orient, and the world, American trade shall be the imperial trade of the entire globe? . . .

. . . [We] must deal from this day on with nations greedy of every market we are to invade; nations with statesmen trained in craft, nations with ships and guns and money and men. . . .

The world still rubs its eyes from its awakening to the resistless power and sure destiny of this republic.

Beveridge Refers to the Spanish–American War as:

. . . the most holy ever waged by one nation against another—a war for civilization, a war for a permanent peace, a war which, under God, although we knew it not, swung open to the republic the portals of the commerce of the world.

His View of the History of U.S. Conquest:

God bless the soldiers of 1898, children of the heroes of 1861, descendants of the heroes of 1776! In the halls of history they will stand side by side with those elder sons of glory, and the opposition to the government at Washington shall not deny them.

No! They shall not be robbed of the honor due them, nor shall the republic be robbed of what they won for their country. For William McKinley is continuing the policy that Jefferson began, Monroe continued, Seward advanced, Grant promoted, Harrison championed, and the growth of the republic has demanded.

His View of Our Conquering Other Countries:

Hawaii is ours; Puerto Rico is to be ours; at the prayer of the people Cuba will finally be ours; in the islands of the East, even to the gates of Asia, coaling stations are to be ours; at the very least the flag of a liberal government is to float over the Philippines, and I pray God it may be the banner that Taylor unfurled in Texas and Fremont carried to the coast—the stars and stripes of glory.

Concerning the Objection that Subjugating Other Countries Conflicts With the Right of a People to Self-Determination:

The opposition tells us that we ought not to govern a people without their consent. I answer: the rule of liberty, that all just government derives its authority from the consent of the governed, applies only to those who are capable of self-government. I answer: We govern the Indians without their consent, we govern our territories without their consent, we govern our children without their consent. I answer: How do you assume that our government would be without their consent?

Beveridge Believes that People Would Welcome Our Domination:

Would not the people of the Philippines prefer the just, humane, civilizing government of this republic to the savage, bloody rule of pillage and extortion from which we have rescued them?

He Views Other Countries as Motivated by Power and Greed. He Sees Us as Guided by the Interests of the People We Conquer:

Shall we turn these people back to the reeking hands from which we have taken them? Shall we abandon them to their fate, with the wolves of conquest all about them—with Germany, Russia, France, even Japan, hungering for them? Shall we turn these people back to the reeking hands from which we have taken them? Shall we abandon them to their fate, with the wolves of conquest all about them?

Concerning the Objection That Countries Have a Right to Rule Themselves:

. . . [To give them self-rule] would be like giving a razor to a babe and telling it to shave itself. It would be like giving a typewriter to an Eskimo and telling him to publish one of the great dailies of the world.

Will you affirm by your vote that you are an infidel to American vigor and power and practical sense? Or, that we are of the ruling race of the world; that ours is the blood of government; ours the heart of dominion; our the brains and genius of administration.

Distance is no objection to our conquering foreign lands in keeping with our destiny, for technological development is conspiring with us: Steam joins us; electricity joins us, the very elements are in league with our destiny. Cuba not contiguous! Hawaii and the Philippines not contiguous! Our navy will make them contiguous. Dewey and Sampson and Schley have made them contiguous, and American speed, American guns, American heart and brain and nerve will keep them contiguous forever.

Think of the thousands of Americans who will pour into Hawaii and Puerto Rico when the republic's laws cover those islands with justice and safety! Think of the tens of thousands of Americans who will invade mine and field and forest in the Philippines when a liberal government, protected and controlled by this republic, if not the government of the republic itself, shall establish order and equity there!

Think the hundreds of thousands of Americans who will build a soap-and-water, commonschool civilization of energy and industry in Cuba, when a government of law replaces the double reign of anarchy and tyranny. Think the prosperous millions that empress of islands will support when, obedient to the law of political gravitation, her people ask for the highest honor liberty can bestow, the sacred Order of the Stars and Stripes, the citizenship of the Great Republic!

What does all this mean for every one of us? It means opportunity for all the glorious young manhood of the republic—the most virile, ambitious, impatient, militant manhood the world has ever seen. It means that the resources and the commerce of these immensely rich dominions will be increased as much as American energy is greater than Spanish sloth; for Americans henceforth will monopolize those resources and that commerce.

In Cuba alone there are 15,000,000 acres of forest unacquainted with the ax. There are exhaustless mines of iron. There are priceless deposits of manganese. . . .

There are millions of acres yet unexplored. . . .

The resources of Puerto Rico have only been trifled with. The riches of the Philippines have hardly been touched by the finger-tips of modern methods.

It means new employment and better wages for every laboring man in the Union. It means higher prices for every bushel of wheat and corn, for every pound of butter and meat, for every item that the farmers of this republic produce. It means active, vigorous, constructive investment of every dollar of moldy and miserly capital in the land.

It means all this tomorrow, and all this forever. . . . The commercial supremacy of the republic means that this nation is to be the sovereign factor in the peace of the world. For the conflicts of the future are to be conflicts of trade—struggles for markets—commercial wars for existence.

Ah! As our commerce spreads, the flag of liberty will circle the globe, and the highways of the ocean—carrying trade to all mankind—be guarded by the guns of the republic. And, as their thunders salute the flag, benighted people will know that the voice of liberty is speaking, at last, for them; that civilization is dawning, at last, for them—liberty and civilization, those children of Christ's gospel, who follow and never precede the preparing march of commerce.

The American people have the most tremendous tasks of history to perform. They have the mightiest commerce of the world to conduct. They cannot halt their imperial progress of wealth and power and glory and Christian civilization. . . . It is a time to cheer the beloved President of God's chosen people, till the whole world is vocal with American loyalty to the American government.

Fellow Americans, we are God's chosen people. Yonder at Bunker Hill and Yorktown His providence was above us. . . . We cannot fly from our world duties; it is ours to execute the purpose of a fate that has driven us to be greater than our small intentions. We cannot retreat from any soil where Providence has unfurled our banner; it is ours to save that soil for liberty and civilization. For liberty and civilization and God's promise fulfilled, the flag must henceforth be the symbol and the sign to all mankind—the flag!

FALLACY DETECTION: ANALYZING A CURRENT PRESIDENTIAL SPEECH

Following is President George W. Bush's opening statement at a news conference (April 14, 2004), concerning the state of the war in Iraq. Identify any fallacies you think are being used.

Thank you. Good evening. Before I take your questions, let me speak with the American people about the situation in Iraq. [These have] been tough weeks in that country. Coalition forces have encountered serious violence in some areas of Iraq. Our military commanders report that this violence is being instigated by three groups. Some remnants of Saddam Hussein's regime along with Islamic militants have attacked coalition forces in the city of Falluja. Terrorists from other countries have infiltrated Iraq to incite and organize attacks.

In the south of Iraq, coalition forces face riots and attacks that are being incited by a radical cleric named al-Sadr. He has assembled some of his supporters into an illegal militia and publicly supported the terrorists groups Hamas and Hezbollah.

Al-Sadr's methods of violence and intimidation are widely repudiated by other Iraqi Shia. He's been indicted by Iraqi authorities for the murder of a prominent Shia cleric. Although these instigations of violence come from different factions, they share common goals. They want to run us out of Iraq and destroy the democratic hopes of the Iraqi people.

The violence we have seen is a power grab by these extreme and ruthless elements. It's not a civil war. It's not a popular uprising. Most of Iraq is relatively stable. Most Iraqis, by far, reject violence and oppose dictatorship. In forums where Iraqis have met to discuss their political future and in all the proceedings of the Iraqi Governing Council, Iraqis have expressed clear commitments. They want strong protections for individual rights, they want their independence, and they want their freedom.

America's commitment to freedom in Iraq is consistent with our ideals and required by our interests. Iraq will either be a peaceful democratic country or it will again be a source of violence, a haven for terror, and a threat to America and to the world.

By helping to secure a free Iraq, Americans serving in that country are protecting their fellow citizens. Our nation is grateful to them all and to their families that face hardship and long separation. This weekend at a Fort Hood hospital, I presented a Purple Heart to some of our wounded, had the honor of thanking them on behalf of all Americans. Other men and women have paid an even greater cost. Our nation honors the memory of those who have been killed, and we pray that their families will find God's comfort in the midst of their grief. As I've said to those who have lost loved ones: We will finish the work of the fallen

America's armed forces are performing brilliantly, with all the skill and honor we expect of them. We're constantly reviewing their needs. Troop strength now and in the future is determined by the situation on the ground. If additional forces are needed, I will send them. If additional resources are needed, we will provide them.

The people of our country are united behind our men and women in uniform. And this government will do all that is necessary to assure the success of their historic mission. One central commitment of that mission is the transfer of a sovereignty back to the Iraqi people. We have set a deadline of June 30. It is important that we meet that deadline. As a proud and independent people, Iraqis do not support an indefinite occupation, and neither does America. We're not an imperial power, as nations such as Japan and Germany can attest. We're a liberating power, as nations in Europe and Asia can attest as well.

America's objective in Iraq is limited, and it is firm. We seek an independent, free, and secure Iraq. Were the coalition to step back from the June 30 pledge, many Iraqis would question our intentions and feel their hopes betrayed. And those in Iraq who trade in hatred and conspiracy theories would find a larger audience and gain a stronger hand. We will not step back from our pledge. On June 30, Iraqi sovereignty will be placed in Iraqi hands. Sovereignty involves more than a date and a ceremony. It requires Iraqis to assume responsibility for their own future.

Iraqi authorities are now confronting the security challenge of the last several weeks. In Falluja, coalition forces have suspended offensive operations, allowing members of the Iraqi Governing Council and local leaders to work on the restoration of central authority in that city. These leaders are communicating with the insurgents to ensure an orderly turnover of that city to Iraqi forces so that the resumption of military action does not become necessary. They are also insisting that those who killed and mutilated four American contract workers be handed over for trial and punishment.

In addition, members of the governing council are seeking to resolve the situation in the south. Al-Sadr must answer the charges against him and disband his illegal militia.

Our coalition is standing with responsible Iraqi leaders as they establish growing authority in their country. The transition to sovereignty requires that we demonstrate confidence in Iraqis. And we have that confidence. Many Iraqi leaders are showing great personal courage. And their example will bring out the same quality in others.

The transition to sovereignty also requires an atmosphere of security. And our coalition is working to provide that security. We will continue taking the greatest care to prevent harm to innocent civilians. Yet we will not permit the spread of chaos and violence. I have directed our military commanders to make every preparation to use decisive force if necessary to maintain order and to protect our troops.

The nation of Iraq is moving toward self-rule. And Iraqis and Americans will see evidence in the months to come. On June 30 when the flag of free Iraq is raised, Iraqi officials will assume responsibility for the ministries of government. On that day the transitional administrative law, including a bill of rights that is unprecedented in the Arab world, will take full effect. The United States and all the nations of our coalition will establish normal diplomatic relations with the Iraqi government. An American embassy will open, and an American ambassador will be posted.

According to the schedule already approved by the governing council, Iraq will hold elections for a national assembly no later than next January. That assembly will draft a new permanent constitution, which will be presented to the Iraqi people in a national referendum held in October of next year. Iraqis will then elect a permanent government by December, 15, 2005. An event that will mark the completion of Iraq's transition from dictatorship to freedom.

Other nations and international institutions are stepping up to their responsibilities in building a free and secure Iraq. We're working closely with the United Nations envoy Lakhdar Brahimi and with Iraqis to determine the exact form of the government that will receive sovereignty on June 30. The United Nations elections assistance team headed by Carina Pirelli is in Iraq developing plans for next January's election. NATO is providing support for the Polish-led multinational division in Iraq. And 17 of NATO's 26 members are contributing forces to maintain security. Secretary of State Powell and Secretary of [Defense] Rumsfeld and a number of NATO defense and foreign ministers are exploring a more formal role for NATO, such as turning the Polish-led division into a NATO operation and giving NATO specific responsibilities for border control.

Iraqis' neighbors also have responsibilities to make their region more stable. So I'm sending Deputy Secretary of State Armitage to the Middle East to discuss with these nations our common interest in a free and independent Iraq and how they can help achieve this goal.

As we made clear all along, our commitment to the success and security of Iraq will not end on June 30. On July 1 and beyond, our reconstruction assistance will continue and our military commitment will continue. Having helped Iraqis establish a new government, coalition military forces will help Iraqis to protect their government from external aggression and internal subversion.

The success of free government in Iraq is vital for many reasons. A free Iraq is vital because 25 million Iraqis have as much right to live in freedom as we do. A free

Iraq will stand as an example to reformers across the Middle East. A free Iraq will show that America is on the side of Muslims who wish to live in peace, as we've already shown in Kuwait and Kosovo, Bosnia and Afghanistan. A free Iraq will confirm to a watching world that America's word, once given, can be relied upon even in the toughest times.

Above all, the defeat of violence and terror in Iraq is vital to the defeat of violence and terror elsewhere, and vital, therefore, to the safety of the American people. Now is the time and Iraq is the place in which the enemies of the civilized world are testing the will of the civilized world. We must not waver. The violence we are seeing in Iraq is familiar. The terrorist who takes hostages or plants a roadside bomb near Baghdad is serving the same ideology of murder that kills innocent people on trains in Madrid and murders children on buses in Jerusalem and blows up a nightclub in Bali and cuts the throat of a young reporter for being a Jew.

We've seen the same ideology of murder in the killing of 241 marines in Beirut, the first attack on the World Trade Center, in the destruction of two embassies in Africa, in the attack on the U.S.S. Cole, and in the merciless horror inflicted upon thousands of innocent men and women and children on September 11, 2001. None of these acts is the work of a religion. All are the work of a fanatical political ideology. The servants of this ideology seek tyranny in the Middle East and beyond. They seek to oppress and persecute women. They seek the death of Jews and Christians and every Muslim who desires peace over theocratic terror. They seek to intimidate America into panic and retreat, and to set free nations against each other. And they seek weapons of mass destruction to blackmail and murder on a massive scale.

Over the last several decades, we've seen that any concession or retreat on our part will only embolden this enemy and invite more bloodshed. And the enemy has seen over the last 31 months that we will no longer live in denial or seek to appease them: For the first time, the civilized world has provided a concerted response to the ideology of terror, a series of powerful, effective blows.

The terrorists have lost the shelter of the Taliban and the training camps in Afghanistan. They've lost safe havens in Pakistan. They lost an ally in Baghdad, and Libya has turned its back on terror. They've lost many leaders in an unrelenting international manhunt. And perhaps most frightening to these men and their movement, the terrorists are seeing the advance of freedom and reform in the greater Middle East.

A desperate enemy is also a dangerous enemy, and our work may become more difficult before it is finished. No one can predict all the hazards that lie ahead or the costs they will bring. Yet, in this conflict there is no safe alternative to resolute action.

The consequences of failure in Iraq would be unthinkable. Every friend of America in Iraq would be betrayed to prison and murder as a new tyranny arose. Every enemy of America in the world would celebrate, proclaiming our weakness and decadence, and using that victory to recruit a new generation of killers.

We will succeed in Iraq. We're carrying out a decision that has already been made and will not change. Iraq will be a free, independent country. And America and the Middle East will be safer because of it. Our coalition has the means and the will to prevail. We serve the cause of liberty and that is always and everywhere a cause worth serving.

FALLACY DETECTION: ANALYZING A SPEECH FROM A PRESIDENTIAL CANDIDATE

Read the following excerpts from a text by third-party presidential candidate Ralph Nader in 2004, regarding the war in Iraq, foreign policy, and the "war on terrorism." Identify any fallacies you find within it.

The Bush Administration and the Democratic Party Are Putting the Interests of Their Corporate Paymasters Before the Interests of the People

Ralph Nader

Concerning the Invasion and Occupation of Iraq:

The quagmire of the Iraq war and occupation could have been averted and needs to be ended expeditiously, replacing U.S. forces with a U.N. peacekeeping force, prompt supervised elections and humanitarian assistance before we sink deeper into this occupation, with more U.S. casualties, huge financial costs, and diminished U.S. security around and from the Islamic world. The faulty and fabricated rationale for war has the U.S. in a quagmire. Already more than $155 billion has been spent, adding to huge Bush deficits, when critical needs are not being met at home. We should not be mired in the occupation of Iraq, risking further upheavals when our infrastructure, schools, and health care are deteriorating. Four years of free public college and university tuition for all students could be paid for by $155 billion.

Withdraw U.S. Troops:

Presence of military hinders progress in Iraq, drains U.S. economy. Every day our exposed military remains in war-torn Iraq we imperil U.S. security, drain our economy, ignore urgent domestic needs, and prevent Iraqi democratic self-frule. We need to announce a withdrawal of our troops, not increase them.

Calls by the major presidential candidates to indefinitely "stay the course" spur the spiral of violence. U.S. presence serves as a magnet for insurrection, kidnapping, terrorism, and anarchy. Announcing a definite withdrawal and ending the U.S. corporate takeover of the Iraqi economy and oil will separate mainstream Iraqis from the insurgents and give the vast majority of people there a stake in replacing occupation with independence.

Three Steps to an Announced Withdrawal:

1. Develop an appropriate peacekeeping force under United Nations auspices from neutral nations with such experience and from Islamic countries. This force should begin to promptly replace all U.S. troops and civilian contractors. General Wesley Clark described Bush foreign policy as cowboy unilateralism that goes against everything the U.S. is supposed to represent to the world. It is time for the U.S. to return to the family of nations. The U.S. will have to underwrite a portion of this less expensive short-term force.

2. Free and fair elections should be held as soon as possible under international supervision so democratic self-rule can be put in place in Iraq and allowing Iraq to provide for its own security. Iraq is a country long controlled by a brutal dictator, devastated by economic sanctions and torn apart by war. Some autonomy for Sunnis, Shiites and Kurds makes a new government more workable. Iraq will sort out these issues more easily without the presence of a U.S. occupying force and the projected 14 U.S. military bases that Iraqis see as installing a puppet government fronting for an indefinite military and oil industry occupation.

3. The U.S. and others should provide interim humanitarian aid to Iraq. Economic sanctions and war have resulted in tremendous damage to people, their children, and the Iraqi infrastructure. Until the 1991 Gulf War, Hussein was a U.S. anti-communist ally also used to keep Iran at bay. During the 1980s, under Reagan and Bush I, U.S. corporations were licensed to export materials to Iraq for chemical and biological weapons. U.S. oil and other corporations should not profit from the illegal invasion and occupation of Iraq. Control over Iraqi oil and other assets should be exercised by Iraqis.

Concerning the Effect of the "War on Terrorism" on Civil Liberties and Constitutional Rights:

Civil liberties and due process of law are eroding due to the "war on terrorism" and new technology that allows easy invasion of privacy. Americans of Arab descent and Muslim–Americans are feeling the brunt of these dragnet, arbitrary practices. [I support] the restoration of civil liberties, repeal of the Patriot Act, and an end to secret detentions, arrests without charges, no access to attorneys, and the use of secret "evidence," military tribunals for civilians, non-combatant status, and the shredding of "probable-cause" determinations. They represent a perilous diminishment of judicial authority in favor of concentrated power in the executive branch. Sloppy law enforcement, dragnet practices are wasteful and reduce the likelihood of apprehending violent criminals. [I seek] to expand civil liberties to include basic human rights in employment and truly equal rights regardless of gender, sexual orientation, race, or religion.

Concerning Foreign Policy:

Our foreign policy must redefine the elements of global security, peace, arms control, an end to nuclear weapons, and expand the many assets of our country to launch, with other nations, major initiatives against global infectious diseases (such as AIDS, malaria, tuberculosis and virulent flu epidemics) which have and are coming to our country in increasingly drug-resistant strains. Other low-cost, high-yield (compared to massive costs of redundant weapons) that extend the best of our country abroad include public health measures for drinking-water safety abroad; tobacco control; stemming soil erosion, deforestation and misuse of chemicals; international labor standards; stimulating democratic institutions; agrarian cooperatives; and demonstrating appropriate technologies dealing with agriculture, transportation, housing, and efficient, renewable energy.

WARNING

Most students who study fallacies begin to find them plentiful in the arguments of those with whom *they disagree*. Realizing that fallacies are being used with equal frequency by you, as well as your friends, test your integrity by diligently seeking fallacies in your own thinking. Remember Pogo's slogan: "We have met the enemy, and he is us!"

The U.N. Development Program and many NGOs working abroad provide essential experience and directions in this regard including ending the specter of hunger, malnutrition, and resultant diseases with known and proven remedies and practices. With these foreign policy orientation overhauls we will discover and facilitate the indigenous genius of the Third World, recalling Brazilian Paulo Freire (literacy), Egyptian Hasan Fathi (agrarian housing), and Bangladeshi Mohammed Yunis (microcredit).

AVOID TWO EXTREMES

The two extremes are:

1. Finding fallacies only in the thinking of others (none in yourself)
2. Finding an equal number of fallacies in everything you read

As you begin to identify fallacies in daily life, there are two dangers to avoid. The first is an unconscious bias toward identifying fallacies only in the thinking of others (those with whom you disagree) and none in yourself. In this case, you use fallacy labels as a way to attack anyone with whom you disagree, while you avoid a critical scrutiny of your own use of such fallacies. If your "opponent" uses an analogy, you immediately call it a false analogy. If your opponent makes a generalization, you immediately call it a hasty or unrepresentative generalization. Your mind is set against him, and therefore you find fallacies in all his thinking. Your mind is so prejudiced in favor of your own thinking that, as a result, you find no fallacies in it.

The second danger consists in coming to believe that everyone commits an equal number of fallacies, and, therefore, you have no reason to concern yourself with fallacies. "The situation is hopeless," you say to yourself.

In any case, fallacies are foul ways to try to win an argument (or to justify a belief) unfairly. Their use is widespread, especially among those who make it their business to manipulate people. All of us sometimes commit fallacies. But there is often a significant difference in quantity.

Compare the problem of using fallacies to the problem of air pollution. All air carries some pollutants, but all air is not highly polluted. It is impossible to think in so careful a way that one never uses a fallacy. But it is possible to minimize that usage.

To protect ourselves, we need to be able to recognize when people are trying to manipulate us with fallacious appeals. To maintain our integrity, we must try to avoid using fallacious appeals ourselves. We do this by learning to monitor our own thinking and the thinking of others, using the tools of critical thinking. We must recognize what is encompassed in our own point of view and the limitations of that point of view. We must enter sympathetically into the point of view of others. We must learn how to strip our thinking, and the thinking of others, down to essentials: essential concepts, essential facts, essential inferences, essential assumptions.

We must be willing to scrutinize our thinking with the same care and concern that we use in scrutinizing the thinking of our opponents and nay-sayers. Our thinking should be in a state of permanent evolution, systematically building on our strengths and removing our weaknesses—and thereby rooting out as many fallacies as we have come to use.

CONCLUSION

In a world of fair-minded critical thinkers, the list of those who reasoned best and the list of those with the most influence in the world would be one and the same. But we don't exist in an ideal world of intellectually disciplined, empathic thinkers. We live in fundamentally uncritical societies, societies in which skilled manipulators, masters of intellectual tricks and stratagems, are the ones who tend to achieve position, status, and advantage.

In the everyday world there is a continual struggle for power and control, and in that struggle, truth and insight have little chance of competing with big money driving big media. Big money routinely utilizes the resources of media logic, polished rhetoric, and mass propaganda techniques to gain its ends. Most people, being intellectually unsophisticated, respond to, and even unknowingly use, fallacious thinking.

As we hope you realize by now, most of what are traditionally called fallacies are actually highly effective strategies for shaping the opinions and beliefs of others. Fallacies are best understood as "counterfeits" of good reasoning, devices often successful in manipulating the intellectual "sheep" of the world. It is important to realize that those who manipulate others typically deceive themselves in the process. Otherwise they wouldn't be able to live with themselves. People want to view themselves as decent and fair-minded, not as manipulators of unsophisticated others. The result is that when people use bad reasoning to manipulate others, they must at the same time "deceive" themselves into believing that their thinking is justified.

In an ideal world, children would be taught to recognize fallacies at an early age. They would learn how common fallacies are in everyday discourse. They would practice identifying fallacies in every dimension of their lives. They would come to understand the frailties and weaknesses of the human mind. They would learn to recognize their own frailties and weaknesses—their own egocentrism and sociocentrism. They would become familiar with the differences between uncritical thinking, sophistic thinking, and fair-minded thinking.

And they would become adept at identifying and distinguishing their uncritical, sophistic, and fair-minded thinking. They would continually catch themselves about to slip, slipping, or having slipped into egocentric or sociocentric thought. They would have no trouble admitting mistakes. They would be eminently moveable by sound reasoning.

But we do not live in an ideal world. Fallacies are "foul ways" to win arguments, yet they are winning arguments and manipulating people every day. The mass media are filled with fallacies. They are the bread and butter of mass political discourse, public relations, and advertising. We all fall prey to them at times. And many live and breathe fallacies as if they were the vehicles of sacred truth.

Your goal should be to recognize fallacies for what they are—the dirty tricks of those who want to gain an advantage. They are stratagems for gaining influence, advantage, and power. You will withstand their impact more effectively when you know these fallacies inside and out. When you come to see how counterfeits of good reasoning pervade everyday life (and are the life blood of the mass media), you are better able to resist their influence.

When you are inoculated against fallacies, your response to them is transformed. You ask key questions. You probe behind the masks, the fronts, the fostered images, the impressive pomp and ceremony. You take charge of your own mind and emotions. You become (increasingly) your own person. And perhaps most important, as you pursue your own goals, you diligently work to avoid using fallacies yourself.

13.12   *Think for Yourself*

FINDING EVERYDAY FALLACIES

Search through a daily newspaper and look for examples of fallacies. Explain and document examples that seem to qualify.

DEVELOP AS AN ETHICAL REASONER

One of the most significant obstacles to fair-mindedness is the human tendency to reason in a self-serving or self-deluded manner. This tendency is increased by the extent to which people are confused about the nature of ethical concepts and principles. To understand ethical reasoning, the following foundations are essential:

1. Ethical principles are not a matter of subjective preference.

2. All reasonable people are obligated to respect clear-cut ethical concepts and principles.

3. To reason well through ethical issues, we must know how to apply ethical concepts and principles reasonably to those issues.

4. Ethical concepts and principles should be distinguished from the norms and taboos of society and peer group, religious teachings, political ideologies, and the law.

5. The most significant barriers to sound ethical reasoning are the egocentrism and sociocentrism of human beings.

First we will seek to clarify the problem posed by ethics in human life: what ethics is, its basis, what it is commonly confused with, its pitfalls, and how it is to be understood. Following that discussion, we emphasize three essential components in sound ethical reasoning: (1) the principles upon which ethics is grounded, (2) the counterfeits to avoid, and (3) the pathology of the human mind.

WHY PEOPLE ARE CONFUSED ABOUT ETHICS

The ultimate basis for ethics is clear: Human behavior has consequences for the welfare of others. We are capable of acting toward others in such a way as to increase or decrease the quality of their lives. We are capable of helping or harming others. What's more, we are capable of understanding—at least in many cases—when we are helping and when we are harming others. This is so because we have the raw (though usually undeveloped) capacity to put ourselves imaginatively in the place of others and recognize how we would feel if someone were to act toward us in the manner in which we are acting toward them.

Even young children have some idea of what it is to help or harm others. Children make inferences and judgments on the basis of that ethical awareness, and they develop an outlook on life that has ethical significance for good or ill. But children tend to have a much clearer awareness of the harm done to them than they have of the harm they do to others:

"That's not fair! He got more than me!"

"She won't let me have any of the toys!"

"He hit me and I didn't do anything to him. He's mean!"

"She promised me. Now she won't give me my doll back!"

"Cheater! Cheater!"

"It's my turn now. You had your turn. That's not fair."

Through example and encouragement, we can cultivate fair-mindedness in children. Children can learn to respect the rights of others and not simply focus on their own desires. The main problem is not so much the difficulty of deciding what is helpful and what is harmful but, instead, our natural propensity to be egocentric. Few humans think at a deep level about the consequences to others of their selfish pursuit of money, power, prestige, and possessions. The result is that, though most people, independent of their society, ethnicity, and religion, give at least lip service to a common core of general ethical principles—that it is ethically wrong to cheat, deceive, exploit, abuse, harm, or steal from others, that we have an ethical responsibility to respect the rights of others, including their freedom and well-being, to help those most in need of help, to seek the common good and not merely our own self-interest and egocentric pleasures, and to strive to make this world more just and humane—few act consistently upon these principles.

The United Nations' Declaration of Human Rights, which all countries have ratified, articulates universal ethical principles. And a core of ideas defines the domain of ethicality and ethics, for reasonable people, in a broad and global way. Many fail to act in accordance with ethical principles, though. At an abstract level, there is little disagreement. Most people would argue that it is not ethically justifiable to cheat, deceive, exploit, abuse, and harm others merely because one wants to or simply because one has the raw power to do so. At the level of action, though, mere verbal agreement on general principles does not produce a world that honors human rights. There are too many ways by which humans can rationalize their rapacious desires and feel self-justified in taking advantage of those who are weaker or less able to protect themselves. Too many forces in human life—social groups, religions, political ideologies—generate norms of right and wrong that ignore or distort ethical principles. What's more, humans are too skilled in the art of self-deception for mere verbal agreement on abstract ethical principles to translate into the reality of an ethically just world.

Further complicating the picture, the ethical thing to do is not always self-evident—even to those who are not significantly self-deceived. In complex situations, people of seeming good will often disagree as to the application of this or that ethical principle to this or that concrete case. One and the same act often receives ethical praise from some and condemnation from others.

We can put this dimension of the problem another way: However strongly motivated to do what is ethically right, people can do so only if they *know* what is ethically justified. And this they cannot know if they systematically confuse their sense of what is ethically right with their vested interests, personal desires, political ideology, or social mores, or if they lack the capacity to reason with skill and discipline in the ethical domain.

Because of complexities such as these, skilled ethical reasoning presupposes the art of self-critique and ethical self-examination. We must learn to check our thinking for egocentrism, sociocentrism, and self-deception. This, in turn, requires development of the intellectual dispositions described earlier in the book, including intellectual humility, intellectual integrity, and fair-mindedness.

Sound ethical reasoning often requires a thinker to recognize and get beyond the pitfalls of ethical judgment: ethical intolerance, self-deception, and uncritical conformity. Sound ethical reasoning often requires us to recognize when our reasoning is a reflection of our social indoctrination. Sound ethical reasoning often requires us to enter empathically into points of view other than our own, gather facts from alternative perspectives, question our assumptions, and consider alternative ways to put the question at issue.

Few adults, however, acquire the skills or insights to recognize the complexities inherent in many everyday ethical issues. Few people identify their own ethical contradictions or clearly distinguish their vested interests and egocentric desires from what is genuinely ethical. Few have thought about the counterfeits of ethical sentiment and judgment or have thought-through a coherent ethical perspective in light of the complexities and pitfalls of ethical reasoning. As a result, everyday ethical judgments are often an unconscious mixture of genuine and counterfeit ethics, of ethical insight on the one hand and prejudice and hypocrisy on the other—each in a web of beliefs that seem to the believer to be self-evidently true.

Inadvertently, we pass on to our children and students our own ethical blindness, ethical distortions, and closed-mindedness. As a result, many who trumpet most loudly for ethics to be taught in the schools merely want students to adopt their own beliefs and perspectives, however flawed those beliefs and perspectives might be. They take themselves to have *The Truth* in their pockets. They take their perspective to be exemplary of all ethical truths. What these same people fear most is someone else's ethical perspective taught as the truth: conservatives afraid of liberals being in charge, liberals fearful of conservatives, theists of nontheists, nontheists of theists, and so on.

All of these fears are justified. People—except in the most rare and exceptional cases—have a strong tendency to confuse what they *believe* with the truth. "It's true because I believe it" is, as we have already emphasized, a deep subconscious mindset in most of us. Our beliefs simply *feel* like "The Truth." They *appear to the mind* as the truth. In the "normal" human mind, it is always the others who do evil, are deceived, self-interested, closed-minded—never us. Thus, instead of cultivating genuine ethical principles in students, teachers often unknowingly indoctrinate them, systematically rewarding students for expressing the beliefs and perspectives the teachers themselves hold. To this extent, they *indoctrinate* rather than educate students.

14.1 *Think for Yourself*

DISTINGUISHING BETWEEN INDOCTRINATION AND EDUCATION

As a person interested in developing your thinking, you must clearly distinguish between indoctrination and education. These two concepts are often confused. Using a good dictionary as your reference, complete the following statements (you may want to look up these words in more than one dictionary for a comprehensive understanding of these terms).

1. According to the dictionary, the meaning of the word *indoctrination* that contrasts with the meaning of education is . . .
2. According to the dictionary, the most fundamental meaning of the word *education* that contrasts with the meaning of indoctrination is . . .
3. The main difference between education and indoctrination, therefore, is . . .

Once you feel reasonably clear about the essential differences between these terms, think about your previous schooling and figure out the extent to which you think you have been indoctrinated (in contrast to having been educated). Complete these statements:

1. As a student, I believe I have been mainly (educated or indoctrinated). My reasons for concluding this are . . .
2. For example . . .

THE FUNDAMENTALS OF ETHICAL REASONING

To become skilled in any domain of reasoning, we must understand the principles that define that domain. To be skilled in mathematical reasoning, we must understand fundamental mathematical principles. To be skilled in scientific reasoning, we must understand fundamental scientific principles (principles of physics, of chemistry, of astronomy, and so on). In like manner, to be skilled in ethical reasoning, we must understand fundamental ethical principles. Good-heartedness is not enough. We must be well-grounded in fundamental ethical concepts and principles. Principles are at the heart of ethical reasoning.

People thinking-through an ethical issue must be able to identify the ethical principles relevant to the specific ethical situation. We also must muster the intellectual skills required to apply those principles fairly to the relevant case or situation. Ethical principles alone, however, do not settle ethical questions. For example, ethical principles sometimes can be applied differently in cases that are ethically complex.

Consider, for instance, the question: Should the United States maintain relations with countries that violate human rights? The most important ethical concepts relevant to this question are justice and integrity, yet matters of practicality and effectiveness clearly must be considered as well. Justice and integrity would seem to require cutting off relations with any country that violates fundamental human rights. But is isolating and confronting these countries the most effective way to achieve these high ethical ends? What's more, history reminds us that nearly all countries violate human rights in one form or another—the United States not excluded. To what extent do we have the right to demand that others live up to standards that we ourselves often fail to meet? These are the kinds of challenging ethical issues often ignored by the naïve and the good-hearted on the one hand, and the self-deceived and cynical on the other.

Because ethical reasoning is often complex, we must learn strategies to deal with these complexities. The three intellectual tasks we believe to be the most important to ethical reasoning are:

1. Mastering the most basic ethical concepts and the principles inherent in ethical issues.

2. Learning to distinguish between ethics and other domains of thinking with which ethics is commonly confused.

3. Learning to identify when native human egocentrism and sociocentrism are impeding one's ethical judgments (probably the most challenging task of the three).

If any of these three foundations is missing in a person's ethical reasoning, that reasoning will likely be flawed. Let's consider these abilities in turn.

Ethical Concepts and Principles

For every ethical question, we must identify some ethical concept or set of concepts directly relevant to the question. We cannot reason well with regard to ethical issues if we do not clearly understand the force of ethical terms and distinctions. Some of the most basic ethical concepts include honesty, integrity, justice, equality, and respect. In many cases, application of the principles implied by these concepts is simple. In some cases it is difficult.

Consider some simple cases. Lying about, misrepresenting, or distorting the facts to gain a material advantage over others is clearly a violation of the basic principle inherent in the concept of honesty. Expecting others to live up to standards that we ourselves routinely violate is clearly a violation of the basic principle inherent in the concept of integrity. Treating others as if they were worth less than we take ourselves to be worth is a violation of the principles inherent in the concepts of integrity, justice, and equality.

Every day, human life is filled with clear-cut violations of basic ethical principles. No one would deny that it is ethically repugnant for a person to microwave cats for the fun of it. Nor is it ethically acceptable to kill people to get their money or to torture people because we think they are guilty and ought to confess.

Nevertheless, in addition to the clear-cut cases are also complicated cases, requiring us to enter into an ethical dialogue, considering counter-arguments from different points of view. Consider, for example, the question: Is euthanasia ever ethically justifiable?

Certainly there are any number of instances when euthanasia is not justified. To consider the question of whether it is ever justified, however, we must consider the various conditions under which euthanasia seems plausible. For example, what about cases involving people who are suffering unrelenting pain from terminal diseases? Within this group are some who plead with us to end their suffering by helping them end their lives (since, though in torment, they cannot end their lives without the assistance of another person).

Given the fact, then, that a person so circumstanced is experiencing intense terminal suffering, one significant ethical concept relevant to this question is the concept of cruelty. *Webster's New World Dictionary* defines *cruelty* as "causing, or of a kind to cause, pain, distress, etc. . . . ; *cruel* implies indifference to the suffering of others or a disposition to inflict it on others." Cruelty, in this case, means "of a kind to cause" unnecessary pain. It means allowing an innocent person to experience unnecessary pain and suffering when we have the power to alleviate it—without sacrificing something of equal value.

Once cruelty is identified as a relevant concept, one ethical injunction becomes clear: Strive to act so as to reduce or end the unnecessary pain and suffering of innocent persons and creatures. With this ethical principle in mind, we can seek to determine in what sense, in any given situation, refusing to assist a suffering person should be considered cruel and in what sense it shouldn't.

Another ethical concept that may be relevant to this issue is: Life is good in itself. The principle that emerges from this concept is: Life should be respected. Some would argue that, given this principle, life should not be terminated by humans under any circumstances.

As a reasoner, you should come to your own conclusions. At the same time, you must be prepared to state your reasoning in detail, explaining what ethical concepts and issues seem to you to be relevant, and why. You must be prepared to demonstrate that you have given serious consideration to alternative perspectives on the issue, that you are not ignoring other reasonable ways to think-through the question at issue. You must be ready to present what you take to be the most relevant and important facts in the case. You must be prepared to do what any good thinker would do in attempting to support reasoning on any issue in any domain of thought. The fact that an issue is ethical does not mean that you can abandon your commitment to disciplined, rational thought.

Or consider: Under what conditions, if any, is animal experimentation justifiable? Again, one relevant ethical concept is cruelty, for anyone informed about animal experimentation knows that sometimes animals are subjected to extreme pain, anxiety, and suffering in the name of scientific inquiry. People for the Ethical Treatment of Animals (PETA), a proactive animal rights organization, focuses on the negative implications of animal experimentation. PETA, at its Web site, makes claims such as the following:

■ Every year, millions of animals suffer and die in painful tests to determine the "safety" of cosmetics and household products. Substances ranging from eye shadow and soap to furniture polish and oven cleaner are tested on rabbits, rats, guinea pigs, dogs, and other animals, even though test results do not help prevent or treat human illness or injury. In these tests, a liquid, flake, granule, or powdered substance is dropped into the eyes of a group of albino rabbits. The animals often are immobilized in stocks from which only their heads protrude. They usually receive no anesthesia during the tests. Reactions to the substances include swollen eyes. The rabbits' eyelids are held open with clips. Many animals break their necks as they struggle to escape.

■ Chimpanzees are popular subjects for AIDS research, although their immune system does not succumb to the virus. Chimpanzees also are used in painful cancer, hepatitis, and psychological tests, as well as for research into artificial insemination and birth control methods, blood diseases, organ transplants, and experimental surgery. Their use in military experiments is suspected, but such information is kept secret and is hard to verify. Chimpanzees are highly active and socially oriented. When kept isolated in laboratories with no regular physical contact with either humans or chimps, they quickly become psychotic. Because adult chimpanzees are strong and often unmanageable, and because infected chimpanzees cannot be placed in zoos or existing sanctuaries, many chimpanzees are killed before the age of 10.

■ Sleep deprivation is recognized as a form of human torture. For decades, repressive governments have used it to extract classified information or false confessions from political prisoners. But some people do it legally. These people aren't called torturers. Because their subjects are animals, they're called "scientists."

The PETA Web site says:

For more than a quarter century, Allan Rechtschaffen, an experimenter at the University of Chicago, deprived animals of sleep. He started out keeping rats awake for up to 24 hours and then letting them recover. He moved on to total sleep deprivation—he kept rats awake until their bodies could no longer cope and they died of exhaustion. This took anywhere from 11 to 32 days. To prepare the gentle animals for this long, nightmarish journey to death, Rechtschaffen stuck electrodes in the rats' skulls, sewed wires to their hearts, and surgically buried thermometers in their stomachs so that he could track their temperatures and brain waves. To make blood-drawing easier (for him), he snaked catheters through their jugular veins, down their necks and into their hearts. . . .

Clinical studies have already shown that humans deprived of sleep suffer from lack of concentration and hallucinations, and that they recover quickly with even brief periods of sleep. So what did Rechtschaffen hope to discover? In his own words, "We established that rats died after 17 days of total sleep deprivation. Thus, at least, for the rat, sleep is absolutely essential."

Information such as this is relevant to the question of whether, to what extent, and under what conditions animal experimentation is ethically justified. Some argue that animal experimentation is justified whenever some potential good for humans might emerge from the experiment. Others argue that animal experimentation is unethical because there are alternative ways, such as computer simulations, to get the information being sought. At its Web site, PETA claims the following:

■ More than 205,000 new drugs are marketed worldwide every year, most after undergoing the most archaic and unreliable testing methods still in use: animal studies. Many physicians and researchers publicly speak out against these outdated studies.

They point out that unreliable animal tests allow dangerous drugs to be marketed to the public and also may prevent potentially useful drugs from being made available. Penicillin would not be in use today if it had been tested on guinea pigs—common laboratory subjects—because penicillin kills guinea pigs. Likewise, aspirin kills cats, while morphine, a depressant to humans, is a stimulant to cats, goats, and horses. Human reactions to drugs cannot be predicted by tests on animals because different species (and even individuals within the same species) react differently to drugs.

■ The Physician's Committee for Responsible Medicine reports that sophisticated non-animal research methods are more accurate, less expensive, and less time-consuming than traditional animal-based research methods.

Some argue that, in experiments in which animal suffering cannot be avoided, the suffering is ethically justified because in the long run the knowledge gained from this experimentation reduces the pain and suffering that humans would otherwise endure. These proponents of experimentation argue that minimizing human pain and suffering is a superior ethical end to that of minimizing animal pain and suffering.

When reasoning-through complex ethical questions, then, skilled ethical reasoners identify the ethical concepts and facts relevant to those questions and apply those concepts to the facts in a well-reasoned manner. In coming to conclusions, they consider as many plausible ways as they can of looking at the issue. As a result of such intellectual work, they develop the capacity to distinguish when ethical questions are clear-cut and when they are not. Even when ethical issues are not clear-cut, it may be important to exercise our best ethical judgment.

The Universal Nature of Ethical Principles

For every ethical issue, there are ethical concepts and principles to be identified and used in thinking-through the issue. Included in the principles implied by these concepts are the rights articulated in the Universal Declaration of Human Rights. This set of rights, established on December 10, 1948, by the General Assembly of the United Nations, holds that the

> recognition of inherent dignity and of the equal and inalienable rights of all members of the human family is the foundation of freedom, justice, and peace in the world. . . . Disregard and contempt for human rights have resulted in barbarous acts which have outraged the conscience of mankind, and the advent of a world in which human beings shall enjoy freedom of speech and belief and freedom from fear and want has been proclaimed as the highest aspiration of the common people.

The Universal Declaration of Humans Rights was conceived as "a common standard of achievement for all peoples and all nations." It is a good example of an explicit statement of important ethical principles. It is significant, we believe, that every nation on earth has signed the declaration.

Here are a few of the principles laid out in the 30 articles of the declaration:

- All humans are born free and equal in dignity and rights.
- Everyone has the right to life, liberty, and security of person.
- No one shall be held in slavery or servitude.
- No one shall be subjected to torture or to cruel, inhuman, or degrading treatment or punishment.
- Everyone has the right to a standard of living adequate for the health and well-being of himself/herself and of his/her family.
- Everyone has the right to education.
- Everyone has the right to freedom of peaceful assembly and association.
- Everyone is entitled to all the rights and freedoms set forth in this Declaration, without distinction of any kinds, such as race, color, sex, language, religion, political or other opinion, national or social origin, property, birth, or status.
- All are equal before the law and are entitled without any discrimination to equal protection of the law.

14.2 *Think for Yourself*

RECOGNIZING VIOLATIONS OF HUMAN RIGHTS BASED ON UNIVERSAL ETHICAL PRINCIPLES

One ability essential to sound ethical reasoning is the ability to identify ethical principles relevant to the ethical issue at hand. In this activity we will briefly describe an issue as presented in a *New York Times* article, "Iraq Is a Pediatrician's Hell: No Way to Stop the Dying" (see Appendix C for the complete article). We then will ask you to identify any violations of human rights suggested by the manner in which events are characterized.

This article focuses on the medical problems for sick children in Iraq "when the country's medical system is all but paralyzed as a result of economic sanctions imposed by the United Nations. . . ." The article states that hospitals cannot obtain the medical equipment and supplies they need to handle diseases from the complicated to the "easily curable ailments." This means that virtually all children with leukemia, for example, die in Iraq.

The article mentions a 3-year-old girl with leukemia, Isra Ahmed, who bleeds profusely from her nose, gums, and rectum. The hospital's chief resident, Dr. Jasim Mazin, says that the hospital lacks the equipment to perform the kind of operation she needs. He states, "We're helpless." He goes on to say, "Iraq used to be the best country in the Arab world in terms of science and medicine. Now we can't even read medical journals because they are covered by the embargo."

Dr. Mazin said the worst period came in April 1998 when 75 children were lost to chest infections and gastroenteritis. He believes that all of them could have been saved with antibiotics commonly available in neighboring countries.

Assume for this exercise that the factual claims in this article are accurate and complete the following statements:

1. If the United Nations sanctions are responsible for the conditions discussed in this article, the United Nations has violated the following human rights . . .
2. If you believe one or more violations of human rights exist in this situation, complete the following statements:
   a. The universal ethical principle violated was . . .
   b. For this ethical principle to be honored, the following action would have been called for in this situation . . .

Though the principles outlined in the Universal Declaration of Human Rights are universally accepted in theory, even democratic countries do not necessarily live in accordance with them. For example, the *New York Times* ("Amnesty Finds 'Widespread Pattern' of U.S. Rights Violations," Oct. 5, 1998, p. A11) reported that Amnesty International was citing the United States for violating fundamental human rights. The Amnesty International report stated that "police forces and criminal and legal systems have a persistent and widespread pattern of human rights violations."

In the report, Amnesty International protested a U.S. failure "to deliver the fundamental promise of rights for all." The report states, "Across the country thousands of people are subjected to sustained and deliberate brutality at the hands of police officers. Cruel, degrading, and sometimes life-threatening methods of constraint continue to be a feature of the U.S. criminal justice system."

Pierre Sane, Secretary General of Amnesty International for 6 years, said, "We felt it was ironic that the most powerful country in the world uses international human rights laws to criticize others but does not apply the same standards at home."

Every country agrees in theory to the importance of fundamental human rights. In practice, though, they often fail to uphold those rights.

14.3 *Think for Yourself*

IDENTIFYING VIOLATIONS OF HUMAN RIGHTS BASED ON UNIVERSAL ETHICAL PRINCIPLES

Identify a newspaper article that either directly or indirectly implies at least one governmental violation of human rights. Complete the following statements:

1. The main substance of this article is . . .
2. The reason this article suggests to me at least one governmental violation of human rights is . . .
3. The universal ethical principle(s) violated is/are . . .

Distinguishing Ethics from Other Domains of Thinking

In addition to understanding how to identify ethical concepts and principles relevant to ethical issues, skilled ethical reasoners must be able to distinguish between ethics and other domains of thinking such as social conventions, religion, and the law. Too often, ethics is confused with these other modes of thinking. Commonly, for example, social values and taboos are treated as if they define ethical principles.

Thus, religious ideologies, social "rules," and laws often are mistakenly taken to be inherently ethical in nature. If we are to accept this amalgamation of domains, by implication every practice within any religious system is necessarily ethical, every social rule is ethically obligatory, and every law is ethically justified. We could not judge, then, any religious practices—such as torturing unbelievers—as unethical.

In the same way, if ethics and social conventions were one and the same, every social practice within any culture would necessarily be ethical—including social conventions in Nazi Germany. We could not, then, ethically condemn any social traditions, norms, mores, and taboos—however ethically bankrupt we think them to be. What's more, if ethics and the law were inextricable, by implication every law within any legal system would be ethical by definition—including laws that blatantly violate human rights.

It is essential, then, to learn to routinely differentiate ethics and other modes of thinking that are commonly confused with ethics. This will enable us to criticize commonly accepted, yet unethical, social conventions, religious practices, political ideas, and laws. No one lacking in this ability can truly live a life of integrity.

Ethics and Religion

To exemplify some of the problems in confusing ethics with other disciplines, let us return for a moment to the question: Are there any conditions under which euthanasia is ethically justifiable? Rather than understanding this as an ethical question, some take it to be a religious question. Therefore, they think-through the question using religious principles. They see some religious principles—namely, the ones in which they happen to believe—as fundamental to ethics.

They argue, for example, that euthanasia is not ethically justifiable because "the Bible says it is wrong to commit suicide." Because they do not distinguish the theological from the ethical, they are likely to miss the relevance of the concept of cruelty. They are not likely to struggle with the problem. This may mean that they find it difficult to feel any force behind the argument for euthanasia in this case or to appreciate what it is to experience hopeless torment without end.

A commitment to some set of religious beliefs may prevent them from recognizing that ethical concepts take priority over religious beliefs when they conflict, as the former are universal and the latter are inherently controversial. Reasonable persons give priority allegiance to ethical concepts and principles, whether these concepts and principles are or are not explicitly acknowledged by a given religious group. Religious beliefs are, at best, supplementary to ethical principles but cannot overrule them.

Consider this example: If a religious group were to believe that the firstborn male of every family must be killed as a sacrifice and failed to exercise any countervailing ethical judgment, everyone in that group would think themselves to be ethically obligated to kill their firstborn male. Their religious beliefs would lead them to unethical behavior and lessen their capacity to appreciate the cruel nature of their behavior.

The genuinely ethical thing to do in a society that propagates the above religious belief would be to rebel and resist what others consider to be obligatory. In short, theological beliefs do not properly override ethical principles, for we must use ethical principles to judge religious practices. We have no other reasonable choice.

14.4 *Think for Yourself*

DISTINGUISHING BETWEEN ETHICS AND RELIGION

Focus on one commonly held religious belief system to identify possible confusion between theological beliefs and ethical principles. See if you can identify any practices within the religion that might be critiqued as unethical. See also if you can identify any practices that the religion considers unethical that one might argue are actually ethical. Select any religion about which you are sufficiently knowledgeable to find possible problems of the sort we are considering. As an example, remember the case of those religious believers who think that a woman who commits adultery should be stoned to death.

Ethics and Social Conventions

Let us return to the relationship of ethics and social conventions. For more than a hundred years in the United States, most people considered slavery to be justified and desirable. It was part of social custom. There can be no question that, all along, this practice was unethical. Moreover, throughout history, many groups of people, including people of various nationalities and skin colors, as well as females, children, and individuals with disabilities, have been victims of discrimination as the result of social convention treated as ethical obligation. Yet, all social practices that violate ethical principles deserve to be rejected by ethically sensitive, reasonable persons no matter how many people support those practices.

Unless we learn to soundly critique the social mores and taboos that have been imposed upon us from birth, we will accept those traditions as "right." All of us are deeply socially conditioned. Therefore, we do not naturally develop the ability to effectively critique social norms and taboos.

Schools and colleges often become apologists for conventional thought; faculty members often inadvertently foster the confusion between convention and ethics because they themselves have internalized the conventions of society. Education, properly so-called, should foster the intellectual skills that enable students to distinguish between cultural mores and ethical precepts, between social commandments and ethical truths. In each case, when conflicts with ethical principles are present, the ethical principles should rule.

14.5 *Think for Yourself*

DISTINGUISHING BETWEEN ETHICS AND SOCIAL CONVENTION

Prior to and during the civil rights movement in the United States, many whites believed that blacks were intellectually inferior to them. This belief gave rise to laws that denied basic human rights to blacks. It would be hard to find a clearer case of socially accepted conventions leading to socially defended unethical practices.

Identify one newspaper article that embodies the confusion between social conventions and ethical principles. What we are looking for is an article in which a commonly held social belief results in the denial of some person's or group's basic human right(s).

1. The substance of this article is . . .
2. The reason this article implies at least one violation of human rights is . . .
3. The universal ethical principle(s) violated was/were . . .

Ethics and the Law

As students who are interested in developing your ethical reasoning abilities, you should be able to differentiate not only ethics and social conventions but also ethics and the law. What is illegal may be ethically justified. What is ethically obligatory may be illegal. What is unethical may be legal.

Laws often emerge out of social conventions. Whatever is acceptable and expected in social groups becomes the foundation for many laws. But, because we cannot assume that social conventions are ethical, we cannot assume that human laws are ethical. What's more, laws ultimately are made by politicians whose primary motivation is often power, vested interest, or expediency. One should not be surprised, then, when politicians are not sensitive to ethical principles or confuse ethical principles with social values or taboos.

Ethics and Sexual Taboos

The problem here is that social taboos often are matters of strong emotions. People frequently are disgusted by someone's violating a taboo. Their disgust signals to them that the behavior is unethical. They forget that what is socially unacceptable may not violate any ethical principle but, instead, violate a social convention of one kind or other. Based on this common confusion, one obvious area to think-through is the area of human sexuality. Social groups often establish strong sanctions for unconventional behavior involving the human body.

Some social groups inflict strong punishments on women who do no more than appear in public without being completely veiled, an act that is socially considered indecent and sexually provocative. The question for us, then, is: When is human behavior that is considered illicitly sexual by some society a matter for ethical condemnation, and when is it properly considered a matter of social nonconformity?

Our overall goal—which we hope this chapter will inspire readers to pursue—is to become so proficient in ethical reasoning and so skilled in distinguishing matters of ethical principle from matters of social taboo, legal fact, and theological belief that you will rarely confuse these domains in your experience and, rather, render to each of them their due consideration and weight in specific cases as they might arise in your life.

14.6   *Think for Yourself*

ETHICS, SOCIAL TABOOS, AND CRIMINAL LAW

In this exercise you will read two news articles. Both articles depict cases in which a given social group has established a law with a significant punishment attendant on its violation, regarding behavior judged by that group to be highly unethical. Think-through how you would analyze and assess the act in question, using the distinctions discussed in this chapter.

As you read the articles, here are some questions to think about:

■ Would you conclude that the social group in question has treated the sexual behaviors in each case properly or improperly as matters worthy of ethical condemnation?

■ To what extent should these behaviors be considered serious crimes?

■ Ethically and rationally speaking, how in your judgment should the two cases be treated?

Read each article, and answer the questions above for each one. Explain your reasoning. In each case, you may have to make explicit some of your assumptions about important details of the case that may not be in the original article. Your judgment might vary depending on what details you suppose.

For example, you might come to a different judgment depending on whether violence or outright bodily harm is involved. As you work through the activities, take into account the probable reasoning that might be advanced against your position (for example, you might say, "Someone might object to my reasoning by saying: . . . To them, my reply would be: . . . ").

SAN FRANCISCO CHRONICLE   FEBRUARY 6, 1999, A 12

First Philippine Execution in 23 Years

Lethal injection for man who raped his stepdaughter, 10

CHRONICLE NEWS SERVICES

MANILA—For the first time in 23 years, the Philippines executed a prisoner yesterday, a house painter convicted of raping his 10-year-old stepdaughter.

Leo Echegaray, 38, was put to death by lethal injection after months of legal delays and an emotional nationwide debate over the death penalty. He was pronounced dead at 3:19 P.M., eight minutes after he was injected, Justice Secretary Serafin Cuevas told reporters after witnessing the execution.

Echegaray's wife, Zenaida Javier, was one of the witnesses to the execution. "His last words to me (were) that he loves me so much," she told a reporter a few hours later. "I knew he was going to die," she said. "But I still tried to fight for his life until the end." The two were married in December.

Prison authorities said Echegaray ate a final meal of shrimp, fish, boiled

(continued)

beef and rice. He went to the execution chamber wearing orange prison garb with a button pinned on that said: "Execute Justice not People."

His was the first execution among the 915 inmates sentenced to death since 1994, when the Philippines restored the death penalty amid an epidemic of crime. Eight prisoners could be executed this year.

President Joseph Estrada refused to stop Echegaray's execution despite pleas from the Vatican, the European Union and human rights groups.

He said the execution signifies "proof of the government's determination to maintain law and order."

Amnesty International, however, called Echegaray's death "a huge step in the wrong direction for human rights in the Philippines."

Security was tight around the national penitentiary in Muntinlupa, a Manila suburb. Nearby schools were closed and barbed wire barricades were erected at the prison gates to hold back more than 100 reporters and activists on both sides of the issue.

Church bells tolled at 3 P.M., the scheduled time of the execution. The Catholic Church has led the anti-death penalty campaign in Asia's only predominantly Catholic country.

At a jail in Quezon City, prisoners prayed together until the execution. When the news came that Echegaray was dead, they lit candles and pinned black ribbons on their chests as others sang an anti-death penalty song.

But many Filipinos praised the execution as a necessary step against crime.

"Starting today, criminals will think twice," said Rafael Carausehas, a motorcycle taxi driver among a group of death penalty supporters outside the penitentiary. "This is the signal Filipinos have been waiting for the government to send."

The Supreme Court delayed Echegaray's scheduled execution January 4 to allow Congress to review the death penalty statute. The Congress later voted not to revise the law, and the court ordered the execution to proceed.

THE NEW YORK TIMES
OCTOBER 21, 1999

Boy, 11, Held on Incest Charge, Protests Ensue

By the New York Times

DENVER, Oct. 20—The case of an 11-year-old Swiss-American boy charged with aggravated incest has led to an international dispute over the treatment of children in the American justice system.

The boy, identified only by his first name, Raoul, is accused of making inappropriate sexual contact with his 5-year-old sister when the children were in their yard. On Tuesday, after a hearing, a Jefferson County juvenile magistrate set an arraignment date of Nov. 8, and the boy was released into foster care. The boy's lawyer, Arnold Wegher, said the child would plead not guilty.

The boy had been living with his mother, stepfather, 13-year-old sister and two half-sisters, ages 5 and 3, in Evergreen, Colo., about 30 miles west of Denver. A neighbor, Laura Mehmert, testified at the hearing that in May she saw the boy touching the younger girl's genitals with his face and hands. After speaking with the boy's mother, the neighbor reported the incident to the authorities.

On Aug. 30, the boy was arrested and led in handcuffs from his home. Since then, he has been held without bail in a county juvenile center.

Manuel Sager, a spokesman for the Swiss Embassy in Washington, said the circumstances of the boy's arrest "seemed disproportionate to us to the charges." He said the boy was taken into the courtroom in handcuffs and "foot chains."

A spokeswoman for the Jefferson County District Attorney's office said the use of restraints was "standard procedure."

If the boy, who has dual American and Swiss citizenship, is found guilty, he could face up to two years in a juvenile center.

"It's just a travesty," said Hanspeter Spuhler, director of the Swiss-American Friendship Society, which is based in Denver, and a friend of the boy's family. "The reason why it's such a big deal to the Swiss and the Europeans is because this is part of growing up, playing doctor or something. If indeed he touched her inappropriately, then it will be talked over with the parents."

Mr. Spuhler said the boy's parents had fled to Switzerland with their other children out of fear that their three daughters would also be taken from them. He said the parents were seeking help from the Swiss Government to have their son returned.

Mr. Spuhler joined protesters in front of the Jefferson County courthouse on Tuesday during the hearing, where the case was being covered by more than two dozen European journalists.

ARTICLE 1 (*San Francisco Chronicle*, Feb. 6, 1999)

We read, "For the first time in 23 years, the Philippines executed a prisoner yesterday, a house painter convicted of raping his 10-year-old stepdaughter." Philippines president Joseph Estrada refused to stop the execution of Leo Echegaray, despite pleas from the Vatican, the European Union, and human rights groups. He went on to say that the execution signifies "proof of the government's determination to maintain law and order."

After reflecting on the questions we directed you to consider for both articles, come to a determination as to whether, in your best judgment, the punishment fits the crime. Then complete these statements:

1. I believe that the law leading to this execution is or is not an ethically justified law, because . . .

2. If you believe the law itself violated some human right or ethical principle, complete the following statements:
   a. The reason this case contains at least one violation of human rights is . . .
   b. The universal ethical principle(s) violated is/are . . .
   c. From a strictly ethical point of view, the following action would have been called for in this situation . . .

3. If you believe the law was ethically justified, complete the following statements:
   a. The reason this case does not contain any violations of human rights is . . .
   b. The relevant ethical principle(s) that justified this action is/are . . .

ARTICLE 2 (*New York Times*, Oct. 21, 1999)

After reflecting on the questions we directed you to consider for both articles, come to a determination as to whether, in your best judgment, ethics is being confused with religious ideology, social conventions, or the law in the main issue that is the focus of the article. For your consideration, we have provided a brief analysis of the two fundamentally different perspectives that might be said to be indirectly implied in the article as it is written.

A Traditional View of Children's Sexuality

Children are not naturally sexual beings. If they engage in sexual acts, they are behaving in a mentally unhealthy manner. What's more, if older children behave in a sexual way toward a younger child, the younger child will be permanently damaged and the older child should be punished as a criminal would be punished. If the parents of children who engage in sexual behavior fail to take harsh action against that behavior, they are contributing to unhealthy mental development of their children and, therefore, are not fit to rear those children.

An Opposing View

To engage in sexual behavior is a natural part of human life. It is normal and healthy for children to experience, explore, and appropriately express sexual desires. Very often, children invent games (such as "playing doctor") as a form of exploring their sexual feelings with other children. Parents who understand the biological make-up of humans and the natural desire of children to be curious about their sexual desires will not punish children for having, or appropriately acting upon, sexual thoughts and feelings. Rather, they should look upon exploratory forms of sexual behavior as part of most children's lives.

This latter view seems to be implied in the article by Hanspeter Spuhler, director of the Swiss–American Friendship Society, who states, "It's just a travesty. The reason why it's such a big deal to the Swiss and the Europeans is because this is part of growing up, playing doctor or something. If indeed he touched her inappropriately, then it will be talked over with the parents."

In this view, if problems seem to be present with the child's behavior respecting sexuality, the parents will be expected to help the child overcome the problem, as parents are generally expected to help children develop as responsible persons. The role of authorities, then, is to help the parents develop their abilities to deal with their children as effectively as possible rather than acting as punitive bodies.

Now, given these two differing perspectives, how would you answer the following questions?

1. From an ethical perspective, which of these points of view seems the more reasonable, given what you know from reading the article and from your own thinking?

2. To what extent do you think ethics is confused with social conventions in the minds of the legal authorities in this case?

3. To what extent do you think religious ideology might play a role in the thinking of either of the above perspectives?

4. To what extent do you think the law upholds what is ethical in this case or, conversely, reflects poor ethical reasoning?

5. How do you think this case should have been handled, given what is ethical for the children at issue and their parents? Do you agree with the way it was handled by the authorities, or would you have acted differently had you been in charge of the case? Explain your reasoning.

14.7, 14.8 *Think for Yourself*

CULTURAL PRACTICE AND ETHICS

On June 12, 1999, the *New York Times* (p. A4) reported that in Muslim West Beirut, Lebanon, women and men are expected to avoid sunbathing together except when they are engaged or married to one another. At one beach

only a handful of women could be seen, and most were fully clothed, and sheltered by tents or beach umbrellas. Those who swam simply strolled into the water, until their baggy dresses began to float along beside them. . . .

"I don't bring my fiancee here, because if someone said something like 'what a beautiful girl,' there'd have to be a fight," said Hassam Karaki, who sat with other men on an all-male beach.

Randa Harb, 27, wore a modest pair of shorts and a tank top as she sat under an umbrella with her bare-chested husband and young son. "If you wear a bathing suit, you're going to attract more attention," Mrs. Harb said. "So my husband won't let me, because he doesn't want people to look and talk. . . ."

Lebanon is not alone as home to a culture averse to women who show too much skin. In Iran, a strict Islamic republic, the insistence on female "modesty" means that women may not even enter hotel pools. In most Arab countries, except among elites, a standard woman's bathing costume is a dress.

Now answer the following questions:

1. To what extent does the cultural practice of denying women the right to wear swimsuits at beaches and swimming pools where men are present seem ethical or unethical to you?
2. On what ethical concepts and principles do you base your reasoning?

DETERMINING ETHICAL DIMENSIONS OF CULTURAL PRACTICES

On March 6, 1999, the *New York Times* (p. A15) reported:

In Maine, a refugee from Afghanistan was seen kissing the penis of his baby boy, a traditional expression of love by his father. To his neighbors and the police, it was child abuse, and his son was taken away. . . .

[Some sociologists and anthropologists] argue that American laws and welfare services have often left immigrants terrified of the intrusive power of government. The Afghan father in Maine who lost his son to the social services, backed by a lower court, did not prevail until the matter reached the state Supreme Court, which researched the family's cultural heritage—while making clear that this was an exceptional case.

The same article focuses on female circumcision, or genital mutilation, as some call it.

"I think we are torn," said Richard A. Shweder, an anthropologist and a leading advocate of the broadest tolerance for cultural differences. "It's a great dilemma right now that's coming up again about how we're going to deal with diversity in the United States and what it means to be an American."

Some, like Mr. Shweder, argue for fundamental changes in American laws, if necessary, to accommodate almost any practice accepted as valid in a radically different society if it can be demonstrated to have some social or cultural good.

The article states that Mr. Shweder and others defend controversial practices

including the common African ritual that opponents call female genital mutilation, which usually involves removing the clitoris at minimum. . . .

But going more than halfway to tolerate what look like disturbing cultural practices unsettles some historians, aid experts, economists, and others. . . .

Urban Jonsson, a Swede who directs the United Nations Children's Fund (UNICEF), said that there is "a global ethical minimum" regarding cultural practices. "There is a nonethnocentric global ethicality," and "scholars would be better occupied looking for it rather than denying it. . . . I'm upset by the anthropological interest in mystifying what we have already demystified. All cultures have their bad and good things."

Now answer the following questions:

1. Focusing separately on each case presented in this article, to what extent does each have an ethical component?

2. To what extent do you think that it is true that any culture has "bad" and "good" practices? Or do you think that all practices within a culture are to be honored?

3. To the extent that an ethical case exists for the opposing positions described by this article, what ethical concepts and principles would have to be taken into account when determining the most reasonably defensible position for each?

4. The cases inherent in this article focus on culturally accepted practices that other cultures consider unethical. To what extent do you think each case contains a violation of human rights? Explain your reasoning.

It is important that you develop your ability to determine for yourself whether any belief system, practice, rule, or law is inherently ethical. To be skilled at ethical reasoning means to develop a conscience that is not subservient to unethical laws, or to fluctuating social conventions, or to controversial, theological systems of belief. But consistently sound ethical reasoning, like consistently sound complex reasoning of every type, presupposes practice in thinking-through ethical issues. As you face ethical problems in your life, the challenge will be in applying appropriate ethical principles to those problems. The more often you do so, the better you will become at ethical reasoning.

Understanding Our Native Selfishness

In addition to the above, ethical reasoning requires command over our native tendency to see the world from a self-serving perspective. Chapter 11, on human irrational tendencies, focuses on the problem of human self-centeredness at length. Here we apply some of the major points of that chapter to problems in ethical reasoning.

Humans naturally develop a narrow-minded, self-centered point of view. We feel our own pain; we don't feel the pain of others. We think our own thoughts; we do not think the thoughts of others. And as we age, we do not naturally develop the ability to empathize with others, to consider points of view that conflict with our own. For this reason, we often are unable to reason from a genuinely ethical perspective. Empathy with the thinking of others, then, is not natural to humans. Nevertheless, it is possible to learn to critically think-through ethical issues. With the proper practice, we can acquire the skill of considering situations from opposing ethical perspectives.

As we have argued in previous chapters, the human tendency to judge the world from a narrow, self-serving perspective is powerful. Humans typically are masterful at self-deception and rationalization. We often maintain beliefs that fly in the face of the evidence before our eyes and engage in acts that blatantly violate ethical principles. What's more, we feel perfectly justified in doing so.

At the root of every unethical act lies some form and degree of self-delusion. And at the root of every self-delusion lies some flaw in thinking. For instance, Hitler confidently believed he was doing the right thing in carrying out egregious acts against the Jews. His actions were a product of the erroneous beliefs that Jews were inferior to the Aryan race, and that they were the cause of Germany's problems. In ridding Germany of the Jews, he believed himself to be doing what was in the best interest of his Germany. He therefore considered his actions to be completely justified. His unethical ethical reasoning resulted in untold human harm and suffering for millions of people.

To become skilled at ethical reasoning, we must understand that ethical reasoning means doing what is right even in the face of powerful selfish desires. To live an ethical life is to develop command over our native egocentric tendencies. It is not enough to espouse the importance of living an ethical life. It is not enough to be able to do the right thing when we ourselves have nothing to lose. We must be willing to fulfill our ethical obligations at the expense of our selfish desires. Thus, having insight into our irrational drives is essential to living an ethical life.

14.9   *Think for Yourself*

IDENTIFYING YOUR UNETHICAL BEHAVIOR

Each of us engages in unethical behavior, but few of us recognize that we do. To become highly skilled at ethical reasoning, we must become everyday observers of our own thoughts and actions. Over the next week, closely observe your behavior to catch yourself doing something unethical (such as being selfish or hurting someone unjustifiably).

Complete the following statements for five "unethical acts":

1. The situation in which I behaved unethically was as follows . . .
2. The unethical action I engaged in was . . .
3. The reason(s) why this act was unethical is/are . . .
4. The basic right(s) I violated is/are . . .
5. To avoid behaving unethically in future such situations, I should . . .

CONCLUSION

To develop as an ethical reasoner, then, we must deeply internalize the fundamental roots of ethics. This means learning to identify and express ethical concepts and principles accurately. It means learning how to apply these principles to relevant ethical situations and learning to differentiate ethics from other modes of thinking that are traditionally confused with ethics.

Finally, it means taking command, with intellectual humility, of one's native egocentrism. Without such an organized, well-integrated, critically based approach to ethics, some counterfeit of ethics, but not ethics itself, is the likely result. To date, all across the world, ethics has routinely been confused with other domains of thinking. The use of ethics and its misuse have been nearly one and the same.

LEARN AND USE INFORMATION CRITICALLY AND ETHICALLY

PART ONE: CRITIQUE OF DISCIPLINES

K nowledge is, among other things, a form of power. It gives advantages to those who have it and disadvantages to those who lack it. For example, knowledge can be used to minimize or maximize suffering. It can serve selfish human desires or meet basic human needs. It can be used to build weapons of mass destruction or create conditions that contribute to peace and understanding. It can be used to destroy or to preserve the environment and the life-forms that inhabit it. It can contribute to a less just or a more just world. It can advance irrational or rational ends.

THE IDEAL OF KNOWLEDGE ACQUISITION

To the extent that we are committed to the development of fair-mindedness, we are committed to knowledge being acquired and used to minimize human suffering, to meet basic human needs, to preserve rather than destroy the environment, to contribute to a more just world, and to serve rational rather than irrational ends. In providing justification for the funding of instruction, spokespersons for the disciplines argue that their disciplines serve fair-minded ends.

Ideally, disciplines seek knowledge not to benefit a selected few but, rather, to distribute benefits in the broadest and most just way. Even those who argue that the pursuit of knowledge must be free to support that argument with the view that the free search for knowledge will confer, in the long run, the greatest benefit to the largest number of people. But to what extent are disciplines serving these higher ends? To what extent are they fulfilling the promises made on their behalf when they seek funding for public instruction? How can we learn to think in the most powerful and rational way within the disciplines we study? These are the questions that lie behind the critique of disciplines.

This chapter presents a plausible argument for suspecting a significant gap between the promised benefits of the various disciplines and the actual effects of instruction. It makes no further claim. How large that gap is in any given field is a matter for systematic study. In Chapter 16, this general argument is followed up with a more detailed argument for the field of psychology and mental health. In both cases, we would expect numerous qualifications and corrections to emerge from further inquiry.

This chapter and the next are included in this book because, to become a critical consumer of information in any field of study, it is essential that you gain some sense of what you are and are not learning and become sensitive to the possible problem of malpractice. By malpractice we mean any avoidable use of knowledge or information that leads to needless waste, unnecessary suffering, gratuitous harm, or injustice. One cannot assume that any field of knowledge functions as it presents itself or that it does the good it claims to do.

For example, a report issued by the National Academy of Sciences on medical errors (*New York Times,* Front Page, November 30 and December 7, 2004), pointed out that medical mistakes cause up to 98,000 unnecessary deaths per year and also that health-care providers could reduce the number of errors by 50% in the next 5 years by simply collecting and analyzing data on unsafe practices, as the aviation industry does. If this article is accurate, present instruction in the health care professions is resulting in an unacceptable level of malpractice.

Learning to think "medically" should have preempted this large-scale problem from arising in the first instance. Learning to think within a discipline in a rational way requires that we understand both the strengths and weaknesses of the discipline and begin to use its foundational concepts and most basic principles responsibly to assess and improve our performance.

TRUE LOYALTY TO A DISCIPLINE

True loyalty to a discipline is born of recognition of the discipline's potential power for good in the world. It is not a commitment to practices in the discipline as it stands. It is not given by the intensity with which one defends the discipline. A person committed to the discipline of history, for instance, recognizes the importance and the power of historical thinking in the world. Such a person recognizes that

- we are creators of history;
- we are products of history;
- nonetheless, we are not successfully teaching historical thinking;
- history, as written and taught, often reflects personal and social prejudices.

When students are socialized into a discipline so as to become uncritical defenders of the present practices of the discipline, both the discipline and the potential good of the discipline suffer. To put this another way, a person retards the development of a discipline by defending it uncritically. This defensiveness engenders a false sense of loyalty. Conversely, when practitioners recognize weaknesses in a discipline, they are well on their way to contributing to its strengths. It is a strength—an important strength—to recognize one's weakness. Unfortunately, we have not yet reached the phase of development of human knowledge wherein each discipline, as taught, routinely raises to the level of conscious realization the important weaknesses in the discipline.

As you study various disciplines, therefore, ask yourself two questions:

1. Am I coming to recognize the power of the discipline as a form of thinking?
2. Am I coming to recognize the limitations of the discipline in the light of its present state of development?

In this chapter, we are concerned principally with how one begins to answer the second question.

THE GAP BETWEEN FACT AND IDEAL

Two phenomena—*human fallibility* and *vested interest*—account for why few, if any, disciplines are close to approximating the ideal of knowledge acquisition. These two phenomena are at the root of much of the misuse of knowledge in the world:

1. **Human fallibility.** All knowledge is acquired, analyzed, and put to use in the world by individuals who are subject to the pitfalls of human weakness, self-deception, and pathological states of mind (e.g., prejudice, egocentrism, sociocentrism).
2. **Vested interest.** Human knowledge exists in a world of power, status, and wealth, all of which significantly influence what information is acquired within any discipline, how it is interpreted, and how it is used.

It follows that we should be skeptical of any description of a human knowledge-constructing enterprise that characterizes itself as an approximation of an ideal. Rather, we should approach human disciplines as in some state of contradiction between an announced ideal and actual reality. In this way we can realistically take into account the weaknesses as well as the strengths of the discipline and thereby contribute to the higher state of development of the discipline.

In assessing a human discipline, we should conduct an inquiry with the hypothesis that, in addition to a powerful form of thinking that represents the strength of the discipline, there is also some gap between the ideal of the discipline and its actual practice, and that, to some extent and in some discoverable ways, the phenomena of human fallibility and vested interest are operating. Often, because of self-deception in the process of teaching and learning, the power of the discipline as a form of thinking is obscured rather than illuminated. In this case, students fail to learn how to think scientifically in science classes or artistically in art classes.

If we begin with this hypothesis, we are much more likely to identify the misuses of information and knowledge on the part of human disciplines. No discipline has isolated, or could isolate, itself from the irrational dimensions of the human mind in action in human affairs. As always, we deal with irrationality best by raising it to the level of conscious realization, not by sweeping it under the rug or denying it. All illusions about present practice become millstones around the neck of practitioners, impeding full development of the discipline. Students do not think effectively within a discipline when they develop an unrealistic conception of the discipline.

So we begin with two premises:

1. The form of thought within any and every discipline is learnable and has great potential for contributing to good in the world.

2. Nevertheless, the information and knowledge that disciplines generate are subject to distortion by human fallibility at every stage of collection, construction, and use.

Professional associations, academies, schools, universities—even ethics committees—we assume are potentially subject to the same irrational influences. Individual students often transform the content they are studying into inert information on the one hand, or "activated ignorance" on the other. Both modes of learning produce illusions of knowledge.

We should *notice*—actually, *expect*—that disciplines, at this time in history, are not yet primed to present their practices to us, in textbooks, encyclopedias, or class instruction, in a way that (1) helps us to see the power of the discipline as a mode of thinking, and (2) puts us on guard against self-deception or vested interest in the discipline's present practices. As an example, it is not in the vested interest of a department, institution, or discipline to document weaknesses in the professional preparation of its graduates. Therefore, little such documentation is developed. On the rare occasions when some documentation of this kind is developed, it frequently is marginalized or discredited at any of these levels.

How many professionals are prepared to say, "Many of the students we certify as knowledgeable and skilled in the discipline are likely to use poor judgment in their practice of the discipline"? To the contrary, a great deal of money is spent in advertising purported success at each of these levels. Furthermore, once students graduate and seek jobs, it is in their vested interest to claim for themselves knowledge, skills, and abilities that they often do not have.

Finally, once in a job and practicing, it certainly is not in the vested interest of practitioners to admit that they are lacking in basic knowledge, skills, and abilities. Those who certify and those who are certified have the same collective vested interests.

Accordingly, as students of critical thinking, it is helpful to make explicit a comparison between theory and practice. In every discipline, we should focus our learning on the mode of thinking that is at the heart of the strength of the discipline while being on the lookout for a gap between the real and the ideal. With the hypothesis that in all likelihood some gap exists, we are much more likely to discover one. With the recognition that any documentation of a gap is likely to be resisted, we are more likely not to be discouraged when it is discovered.

Our hypothesis of inconsistency between the ideal and real should not prevent us from noticing very different degrees and forms of inconsistency. Some disciplines are undoubtedly much closer to the ideal. Some disciplines are more vigilant about the pitfalls that attend their practice. We, in turn, should guard against our hypothesis becoming a self-fulfilling prophecy in our minds, for then it itself constitutes evidence of self-deception on our part. Though we should be alert to problems in a discipline, we should not see problems where none are present.

We believe that as you discover the true power of a discipline as a form of thinking and, at the same time, come to recognize the limitations of a field as it stands, you also will begin to value the discipline in a deeper and truer sense. For one thing, you will see much better how you might make a contribution to the field, how you might help to strengthen the field and help it to contribute more to human and environmental good.

As you study this chapter, therefore, you should read it in relationship to the chapters that deal with content as a mode of thinking. You should put the goal of this chapter into the context of the other chapters. You should keep in mind the central goal of critical thinking: to improve your thinking, and through that improvement, to improve your life. Your awareness of weaknesses and limitations should be tempered by your awareness of the potential power of disciplinary thinking for the good.

THE IDEAL COMPARED TO THE REAL

The first essential step is to recognize the discipline as a powerful mode of thinking and setting forth the ideal of the discipline. To set out the ideal, ask yourself if the discipline were striving to function in an optimal way in an optimal setting:

What would the discipline look like?

How would it function?

How would it be represented?

How would it be taught?

How would it be applied?

The most important goal here is that we set out the ideal as ideal and do not confuse it, in our mind, with the discipline as it actually functions.

The second step is that of setting out the discipline as it is functioning, as it is representing itself, as it is being taught and applied. Here we should strive to recognize how the discipline is influenced by its relationship to the everyday world of power, status, and wealth. We must identify any likely areas of self-deception on the part of practitioners of the discipline. We must recognize that practitioners have vary-ing degrees of command of the mode of thinking in the discipline. We must recog-nize that it is possible, for example, for individual scientists to violate the canons of sound scientific thinking and engage in what is sometimes called "pseudoscience."

This chapter introduces you to some initial elements of this critique. The examples are not advanced as flawless examples of critical thinking in action but, rather, as illustrations of how we might begin to put the above insights into action in our thinking. We will begin by looking at a variety of disciplines from this perspective, followed by some initial re-flections in each case. Chapter 16 presents a more extended critique of one field, provid-ing an example of what a deeper critique might begin to look like in the light of a set of questions that students should have in mind when initially introduced to a discipline.

We will begin with mathematics and then consider the so-called hard sciences of physics, chemistry, astronomy, geology, and biology as first cases. Then we will re-flect upon the human sciences, the so-called soft sciences, and finally, the fine arts and literature.

Each case is guided by two important insights:

1. All knowledge in use in the world is subject to the pitfalls of human fallibility on the part of the individuals using it.

2. Knowledge exists in a world driven by the pursuit of power, status, and wealth, each of which exacts its toll.

THE IDEAL OF MATHEMATICS: ABSTRACT QUANTIFICATION

If there is a subject free from human fallibility and vested interest, it is mathematics, for presumably the study of abstract quantification favors no group over any other and, therefore, seems least likely to encourage or engender self-deception in its prac-titioners. But even a cursory examination of the topic suggests a gap between ideal and reality.

Let us briefly review the promise of math instruction used to justify the large sums of money necessary to maintain math instruction at all levels of schooling. That prom-ise can be stated in something like the following terms:

> *The ideal:* We live today in a world in which mathematics proficiency is increasingly im-portant to success in life. Our world is complex and technological, and mathematics is crucial to understanding its complexity and operating within its technological dimen-sions. Our investment in mathematics is sensible because, through it, we are providing society with the mathematicians, engineers, and technical experts necessary to meet worldwide competition. What's more, mathematics proficiency is important to every-one. Many problems and issues of daily personal and public life have an important quantitative dimension. Large-scale math instruction provides the citizenry with the quantitative concepts, principles, and tools by means of which they are able to perform

successfully in both personal and public life. Through it, students learn to transfer logical thinking to other domains of knowledge and thought.

To what extent is the ideal realized? How far are we from it? What are some of the hidden consequences deriving from large-scale math instruction that the promise of the ideal does not take into account? What alternatives do we have to our present practice? To what extent are we getting what we are paying for? To what extent is our social investment in mathematics having the promised effect? To what extent are we realistic in our conception of the value and real consequences of large-scale math instruction at virtually every level of schooling?

In our view, there is a large gap between the promised social gain from math instruction and the actual result. The gap is twofold. The first problem is inherent in the negative consequences for students who are unable to perform at some minimal level at school—those who fail at school math. The second problem is the failure of citizens who are certified by schools as competent in math who do not use mathematics successfully in dealing with public and social issues. We are alleging, then, that the students who fail officially and those who pass officially constitute evidence of a major problem in math instruction.

The Pain and Suffering of Those Who Fail

Let us begin with the manner in which mathematics is taught and the high stakes associated with success or failure in math. Success in mathematics is given high status in the schools. Some level of mathematical proficiency is required to advance through elementary school, then middle school, high school, and college. Students who find themselves unable to perform at the essential level experience a great deal of mental distress and anguish.

Some proficiency in math is a college-entrance requirement. What's more, students who fail in math, except in rare circumstances, are not allowed to graduate from high school or college. Some level of proficiency in math is enforced as a precondition for graduation.

Loss of Self-Esteem and Opportunity to Receive Higher Education

We rarely talk about, or attempt to assess, the damage that comes from loss of self-esteem and loss of opportunity to advance in school on the part of the many students who perform poorly in mathematics. Isn't it possible that many of those who do not perform well in math might yet perform at high levels in other domains of learning? Aren't we wrongfully denying those who fail in math an opportunity to succeed in other areas, especially because many college courses involve virtually no math?

If we look at the everyday challenges in professional and personal life, how many require the levels of proficiency in mathematics that testing and certification require?

A case can easily be made for simple arithmetic, no doubt, but what about algebra and geometry? How often does the average person face a problem that requires the use of concepts and principles of algebra and geometry, beyond perhaps the most elementary ones?

It is not obvious that mathematical proficiencies beyond that of basic arithmetic should be required of all students. Might we be better off making math optional beyond elementary arithmetic and the simplest algebra? Might we not be better off merely providing incentives to motivated students to study and excel at math? What is the point of lifelong penalties for those who do poorly in math?

Low Level of Math Competency of Those Who Pass School Examinations

There is a second gap between the ideal and the real regarding mathematics instruction. Presumably, a society in which all citizens are taught to think mathematically will be able to use math successfully in dealing with public issues involving a quantitative dimension. For example, assessing the national budget involves comprehending large sums and their significance in a variety of budgetary issues.

Assessing the significance of damage to the environment from pollution, assessing the loss of natural resources, assessing public health issues, and many other public issues require people to make judgments involving large figures. But it seems reasonable to question how many citizens are actually able to make these judgments reasonably, even when simple math is involved. And consider the many people who cannot seem to manage a personal budget. Many who have passed the school exams in math are failing the real task of using math successfully in their lives.

15.1 *Think for Yourself*

MATH AND YOU

Think about your education and answer the following questions:

1. To what extent would you say that you have mastered fundamental concepts in math and, as a result, are able to use that knowledge effectively in coming to informed conclusions about public issues with a mathematical dimension? To what extent would you say that you have memorized definitions and procedures sufficient to pass tests but insufficient to understand the basic concepts underlying the math you were doing? Now, see if you can give examples of when you last used math in your daily life. What level of math was it?

2. To what extent would you say that the math requirements you have had to meet are appropriate measures to require of all students? Be prepared to justify your conclusions.

3. In your view, should students be prevented from being accepted by a college on the basis of low math scores alone?

4. How often have you faced a problem in your life that required the use of concepts and principles of algebra and geometry?

THE IDEAL OF SCIENCE: PHYSICS, CHEMISTRY, ASTRONOMY, GEOLOGY, BIOLOGY

Historically, the idea of science was based on the notion that it was important to ask questions about, and consequently think about, the world in a new way—a way that emphasized a carefully controlled empirical study of the world. The idea of science is based on the notion that, instead of thinking about what the world *must* be like, given our basic assumptions and preconceptions about it, we should discover, through empirical thinking and inquiry, what it is actually like.

We must assume that the fundamental ideas through which we think traditionally about the world may be incorrect or misleading. We must be willing to question our seemingly self-evident beliefs about the world and entertain the assumption that they might be false. The idea of empirical thinking and carefully controlled experimentation was taken to be the key to gaining sound knowledge of the world.

This ideal of science emerged as a critical response to previous human inquiry in which the reasoning of important thinkers seemed to be influenced inappropriately by beliefs of a highly egocentric and sociocentric nature. Among those great thinkers were Plato, Aristotle, Augustine, and Aquinas—whose qualities of reflection and reasoning were taken at one time to be self-evident guarantors of knowledge. Their views of the physical and natural world were rarely questioned. With the emergence of science, however, such wide-ranging thinkers were increasingly recognized to be biased by questionable assumptions at the root of their thought.

Most obviously, it seemed that prescientific thinkers often uncritically assumed metaphysical or religious concepts at the foundations of their thought about the world. What's more, the traditional questions asked seemed to focus only rarely on testable characteristics in the world.

In the "new" view, which emerged during the Renaissance (1400–1650), people became scientists when they committed themselves to modes of inquiry based on controlled experimentation. The fields of physical and natural sciences, then, separated themselves from the field of philosophy and became fields of their own. Many of the early scientists set up their own laboratories for this purpose. This commitment, it was assumed, would maximize discovery of the actual laws and principles that operate in the physical and natural worlds and minimize the influence of human preconceptions about the world. There can be no doubt that this notion of science represented a real advance in the pursuit of knowledge about the physical and natural worlds.

Physics, chemistry, astronomy, geology, and biology are among the best cases one can choose for disciplines in which human self-deception and vested interest have been minimized. It does not follow, however, that these factors are not present. So let us now turn briefly to an expression of the promise of instruction in the physical and natural sciences. That ideal is formulated in ways that parallel the justification and argument for social investment in instruction in mathematics.

> *The ideal:* We live today in a world in which scientific understanding and proficiency are increasingly important to success in life. Our world is complex, and technological and scientific thinking is crucial to understanding both its physical and natural complexity and its technological dimensions. Our investment in science instruction is well-spent because, through it, we are providing society with the scientific and technological experts it requires to be competitive. What's more, scientific understanding and proficiency are important to everyone. Many problems and issues, in daily personal life and also in public life, have an important scientific dimension. Large-scale science instruction provides the citizenry with the scientific concepts, principles, and tools by means of which they are able to perform successfully in both personal and public ways.

To what extent is this ideal being fulfilled by science instruction as it exists today? It can be argued that the reality is a long way from the ideal. Though virtually all citizens are given many years of instruction in science, is there not abundant evidence to suggest that most people do not think scientifically about everyday scientific problems and issues? For one, can most high school graduates distinguish why astronomy is a science and astrology is not? What accounts for many high school graduates believing in astrology? Isn't there ample evidence to demonstrate that

- many, if not most, people cannot explain the difference between theological and scientific questions?
- many people, despite years of science instruction, have not formulated a single scientific hypothesis or designed a single scientific experiment and would not be able to effectively distinguish well-designed from poorly designed scientific experiments?
- many people cannot explain the role of theory in science and, therefore, cannot explain why the theory of evolution in biology cannot be reasonably compared to the interpretation of one reading of the Bible that the world is no more than a few thousand years old?
- many people cannot explain how to distinguish a scientific question from any other kind of questions and, consequently, do not treat scientific questions differently from other kinds of questions?
- many people cannot accurately explain any basic concepts, laws, or principles of science and do not use those concepts, laws, or principles in accounting for the world they experience?
- many people do not read any scientific articles, books, or even magazines (such as *Scientific American* or *Discovery*) and would have trouble understanding them if they did?

These questions, and their most plausible answers, suggest a large gap between the promise of science instruction and the actual effect of that instruction on the lives of most people. What's more, these questions can be contextualized for each of the various physical and natural sciences. Everywhere the word *science* appears, one could substitute one of the sciences—physics, chemistry, astronomy, geology, biology. Consider the following reformulation for the field of biology:

- Though virtually all citizens are given instruction in biology, is there not abundant evidence to suggest that most people do not think biologically about everyday biological problems and issues?

- What accounts for the fact that many, if not most, people cannot explain the difference between a theological and a biological question?

- Isn't it true that most persons who are given instruction in biology have not formulated a single biological hypothesis or designed a single biological experiment and would not be able to effectively distinguish well-designed from poorly designed biological experiments?

- Isn't it true that most people cannot explain the role of theory in biology and cannot, therefore, explain why the theory of evolution in biology cannot be reasonably compared to the interpretation of one reading of the Bible that the world is no more than a few thousand years old?

- Isn't it true that most people cannot explain how to distinguish a biological question from any other kind of question and, consequently, do not treat biological questions differently than other kinds of questions?

- Isn't it true that most people cannot accurately explain any basic concepts, laws, or principles of biology and do not use biological concepts, laws, or principles in accounting for the biological features of the world they experience?

15.2 *Think for Yourself*

THE PHYSICAL AND NATURAL SCIENCES AND YOU

Answer the following questions regarding your education:

- Why is astronomy a science and astrology not? Do you believe in astrology? If you do, upon what do you base that belief? How do you reconcile that belief with the basic principles of science?

- Can you explain the difference between theological and scientific questions?

- Have you ever formulated a scientific hypothesis or designed a scientific experiment? If you answer "yes," explain what your hypothesis was and the design of your experiment.

- Explain the basic role of theory in science. Then explain why the theory of evolution in biology can, or cannot, be evaluated by citing passages in the Bible.

- Select any basic concept, law, or principle of science, state it, then explain it using examples from your experience.

THE IDEAL OF SCIENCE: HISTORY, SOCIOLOGY, ANTHROPOLOGY, ECONOMICS, PSYCHOLOGY

In light of the success of the physical and natural sciences, it was predictable that those interested in the study of human life and behavior would look to the paradigm of scientific methodology as a means by which questions about the nature of human behavior could be as definitively settled as those about gravity, chemical reactions, plants, and animal life. Many scholars in the disciplines focusing on humans expected a revolution within their disciplines as a result of a commitment to the application of controlled experiment. By this rigorous process, it was thought, hypotheses about human life could be confirmed or falsified. Foundational truths about human life and behavior could be discovered and built upon.

This conception of the study of human behavior has one major problem. Briefly, it might be expressed as follows: Human behavior is the result of the meaning-creating capacity of the human mind. Human behavior is much more a product of human thinking than human instinct. Furthermore, a variety of influences have an impact on how humans *think* (and therefore on how they *feel* and what they *want*). Humans are highly complex, multidimensional creatures, which makes the study of human behavior through the scientific method subject to many limiting qualifications at best.

For example, as humans we are born into a culture at some point in time in some place, reared by parents with particular beliefs. We form a variety of associations with other humans who are equally variously influenced. Our minds are influenced in all of the following dimensions but *not to the same extent or in the same way:*

- *sociologically:* Our mind is influenced by the social groups to which we belong;

- *philosophically:* Our mind is influenced by our personal philosophy;

- *ethically:* Our mind is influenced by our character;

- *intellectually:* Our mind is influenced by the ideas we hold, by the manner in which we reason and deal with abstractions and abstract systems;

- *anthropologically:* Our mind is influenced by cultural practices, mores, and taboos;

- *ideologically and politically:* Our mind is influenced by the structure of power and its use by interest groups around us;

- *economically:* Our mind is influenced by the economic conditions under which we live;

- *historically:* Our mind is influenced by our history and by the way we tell our history;

- *biologically:* Our mind is influenced by our biology and neurology;

- *theologically:* Our mind is influenced by our religious beliefs and attitudes;

- *psychologically:* Our mind is influenced by our personality and personal psychology.

What's more, these influences are not only subject to almost unlimited variation among themselves but humans are capable of discovering each of these influences, reflecting on them, and then acting to change them in an almost unlimited number of ways. Consider how much more difficult it would be to study the behavior of mice if each mouse were to vary its behavior from every other mouse depending on a unique combination of prior influences within each of the above categories.

Furthermore, consider what the study of behavior of mice would be like if the mice could discover that we were studying them and began to react to our study in the light of that knowledge. And how could we even proceed to study mice if they were to decide at the same time to study us studying them?

The very idea of studying human behavior scientifically faces enormous difficulties by virtue of the diverse nature of human behavior. It faces enormous difficulties by virtue of the diverse simultaneous influences upon humans as we think, feel, and act in the world, and our capacity to notice and modify virtually any aspect of the thoughts, feelings, and desires that drive our behavior. In light of these considerations, let us examine the sort of promissory claims made on behalf of the social sciences.

> The ideal of science is based on the premise that it is possible in principle to ask questions about any aspect of the world in a way that enables us to pursue its answer by means of carefully controlled empirical study rather than on the basis of abstract reasoning following from human preconception. There is no reason why, in principle, humans should not be studied empirically.
>
> In studying humans as well as in studying other animal species in the world, it is essential that carefully controlled experimentation correlated with falsifiable hypotheses are used as the guiding keys to gaining dependable knowledge of the human world. What's more, it is essential that humans be taught knowledge of themselves so we can make intelligent decisions about our own conditions of life.

Each discipline will make specific claims emerging from its potential (viewed ideally) approximately as follows:

History as an Ideal

If we as humans do not study the mistakes of the past, we are bound to repeat them. History enables us to grasp the nature of our own past, how we have come to be the way we are, the problems we have had to overcome, the forces that have acted, and are acting, upon us. Such study and such an understanding are essential to our well-being. In this way, we can appreciate our heritage, what we have lived and died for, the evolution of our culture as a people. Without it, we make our decisions in the dark.

Sociology as an Ideal

We humans are social animals. It is in our nature to live and function within groups. To be free creatures, we need to understand the social conditions under which we live and act. All human groups define themselves in predictable ways. These groups create social requirements and social taboos. They devise ways to identify the in-group and the out-group. They create a collective ideology that justifies the way power is divided and the manner by which wealth is distributed. If we understand ourselves as social beings, we can maximize the quality of our lives and the conditions under which we better ourselves. Insight into social reality is an important, if not crucial, need for freedom and social justice to emerge and thrive.

Anthropology as an Ideal

Professional historians trace human history back some 30,000 to 40,000 years. Anthropologists trace human history back one or two million years and link that history seamlessly with the history of other creatures on our planet. Instruction in anthropology provides the perspective and insight into human reality that no other discipline can provide. It gives us a much wider breadth of human reality than most other social disciplines. It helps remind us how variable human culture is and how hard it is to judge one culture from the perspective of another. Many of the world problems we are experiencing are traceable to an ethnocentrism that the study of anthropology serves to correct.

Economics as an Ideal

Much of human life is concerned with the striving of humans to meet our needs and fulfill our desires. The study of the conditions and systems in which and through which humans seek to satisfy our needs and fulfill our desires is economics. Most social institutions can be understood much more deeply if we understand them in relationship to economic forces.

Much of what happens in human life is a product of economic forces. Wars and depressions are the result of economic conditions. The extremes of starvation and plenty are both the result of economic conditions. Many, if not most, of the large decisions made by human groups are based on their perception of economic realities. Many of the cruelties and atrocities in the world are influenced highly by economic realities. Money, and all of those goods into which money can be transformed, are crucial determinants of human life. If we do not study and understand economic reality, we are likely to suffer as a result.

Psychology as an Ideal

The nature and operations of the human mind are a central determinant in human life. The scientific study of the mind, therefore, can enable us to maximize our control over our own mental health. We can identify the pathologies of the mind in a way parallel to the way we identify the pathologies of the body. We can study causes and consequences of human mental health and disease. We can train practitioners to use the knowledge that psychological research collects in counseling and therapy, thereby helping individuals who are in need of mental assistance.

With our knowledge, we can assist the courts in determining what prisoners are mentally safe to parole, which persons are of sound mind, and which parents are fit or unfit to rear children. We can advise lawmakers on which deviant social practices are mentally healthy and which are not. In general, psychology contributes to the mental health and optimal mental functioning of humans.

15.3 *Think for Yourself*

THE SOCIAL SCIENCES AND YOU

Choose one of the social disciplines that you have studied (history, sociology, anthropology, economics, or psychology). Read the above description of the promised aim of the discipline. Then assess the extent to which your learning approached that ideal. Explain what your reasoning is based on.

The Social Sciences as Taught and Practiced

Although the social disciplines have promised much, the promise clearly falls far short of the ideal. What's more, serious questions can be raised as to whether using the word "science" is even appropriate to characterize the status of the social disciplines. Typically, the social disciplines are highly "multilogical." Many divergent points of view and frames of reference compete within the social disciplines. Often, different practitioners in the social fields render contradictory judgments.

On the instructional level, we clearly are far from delivering the benefits that have been promised by those who argue for that instruction. To put it one way, few students learn, as a result of instruction in history, to think historically, or, as a result of instruction in the other social fields, to think sociologically, anthropologically, economically, or psychologically. Instruction is often designed so that students are certified as knowledgeable in the content of a course when they have done no more than successfully cram for a true/false or a multiple-choice exam.

It is not clear that the study of history, sociology, anthropology, economics, and psychology has led to a better world (that is, with less war, cruelty, human suffering, and injustice). Actually, our belief that we have been educated as a result of the instruction we have received may render us more self-deceived than we would be without that instruction.

The social sciences could, and should, make a significant contribution to a better world. Insights into historical, anthropological, and economic thinking are relevant to critical thinking. These disciplines, however, are rarely taught in such a way as to contribute to the development of critical thought. For example, although sociology as taught emphasizes that humans tend to behave in keeping with the mores and taboos of social groups, rarely are students given assignments in which they must make explicit and critically assess the mores and taboos of any of the groups to which they belong.

The result is that the students usually leave sociology classes with little insight into the nature of their own social indoctrination. They do not seem to gain in autonomy as a result of instruction. The mores and taboos of their social groups and of the broader society rule them as much at the end of their instruction, as far as we can see, as they did at the beginning. Students begin and end as consummate conformists in language, clothing, values, and behavior. They have not, on the whole, begun to think historically, anthropologically, sociologically, and economically.

THE IDEAL OF THE ARTS AND HUMANITIES: MUSIC, PAINTING, SCULPTURE, ARCHITECTURE, DANCE, LITERATURE, PHILOSOPHY

The disciplines that exist within the arts and humanities typically have a twofold dimension:

1. a dimension of appreciation and cultivation;
2. a dimension of performance.

The first dimension is much more questionable as an area of knowledge, and its contribution to the quality of life is a likely domain for debate. The second dimension is much more objective and demonstrable.

The Promise of the Fine Arts and Literature

The ideal of instruction in the fine arts and literature could be put briefly as follows:

> Two consequences follow from the study of the fine arts and literature with regard to appreciation and cultivation: esthetic appreciation and (high) culture. The fine arts and literature introduce the student to the study of what is beautiful in painting, sculpture, architecture, dance, music, drama, and literature. This study elevates the person's taste and provides insight into objects and experiences that are not available to those who have not come to appreciate fine art.
>
> Without this study, we will not see the beauty in fine painting, sculpture, dance, music, drama, and literature. Without it, many will prefer the superficial, the trivial, the vulgar, and the stereotyped to that which is truly unique and beautiful. Those who fail to achieve an appreciation of fine arts and literature are denied an important dimension of human experience and fulfillment.

The Reality of Instruction in the Fine Arts and Literature

The real results of instruction in literature and the fine arts seem distant from the above ideal. Consider the following:

- Though nearly all citizens are given years of instruction in some dimensions of at least some of the fine arts and literature (usually literature), is there not abundant evidence to suggest that most people do not think esthetically or artistically as a result? Attempts to elevate the taste of most people seem to be a failure. Most people, even after a college education, seem to prefer the products of the popular media to the products of the artistic community. What's more, it is hard to determine what percentage of those whose supposed preference for the products of the artistic community is in truth a pretense born of self-delusion, enabling them to feel superior to the common herd.

- What accounts for the reality that most of us cannot give an intelligible explanation for our judgments about what we consider beautiful in painting, sculpture, architecture, dance, music, drama, or literature?

- Isn't it true that most people have not thought about the role of beauty and art in our lives and are not interested in doing so?

- Isn't it true that most people cannot explain how to distinguish an artistic question or issue from any other kind of question and issue and tend to respond to such questions in superficial and uninterested ways?

- Isn't it true that most people cannot accurately explain any basic concepts or principles of any of the fine arts or literature and do not use those concepts or principles in accounting for the world we experience?

- Finally, isn't it true that few people change their reading habits as a result of instruction in literature and, consequently, are just as unlikely to read important literature at the end of instruction as they were at the beginning?

It seems likely that some exception must be granted to the judgments implied above in the domain of trained performance in the fine arts and literature. The most successful form of instruction in the fine arts and literature is in the area of skill development: basic painting, sculpting, dancing, singing, acting, and writing skills, as well as performing on a musical instrument. It is questionable, however, to what extent most of the performances made possible by this training rise to the level of esthetic or artistic excellence. In any case, only a small minority of persons, at best, develop a level of excellence in the performing arts.

The Promise of Philosophy

The discipline of philosophy makes an interesting case. On the one hand, it makes some of the most sweeping claims for itself and, on the other hand, seems to deliver so little. Let us look at the traditional case made for the value of instruction in philosophy.

> We as humans are capable of living two kinds of lives: an unreflective or a reflective life. When we live unreflectively, we live as a conformist, trapped in the world of our own unanalyzed desires and social conditioning. We do not live as free agents. We do not choose our basic and ultimate values. We do not understand the actual options implicit in a human life. We behave in ways that are contradictory to the values we say we believe. We do not understand the forces at work in our lives, nor do we understand what is valuable and wasteful in them. Often, as unreflective persons, our lives are shot-through with irrationality, prejudice, and self-delusion.
>
> Conversely, when we live reflectively, we become the agents of our own destiny. We begin to act as genuinely independent persons. We see a world beyond the world of our personal egocentrism and social ethnocentrism. We come to terms with our own basic and ultimate values. We make decisions based on the actual options available to us. We begin to understand the forces at work in our lives and act consciously

with respect to them. We discover the power of rationality and use that power to minimize our prejudices as well as our involvement in self-delusion. The study of philosophy lays the foundation for living a reflective life.

The Reality of Philosophy

Clearly, the promise of philosophy is rarely fulfilled. The most likely reason for this discrepancy is that living a reflective life is not the usual focus of the coursework offered in philosophy. Instead, the coursework focuses on highly abstract issues (What is being? What is reality? What is time? What is knowledge? What is beauty? What is freedom?) through the reading of arguments and counter-arguments of a highly abstract sort. The arguments themselves typically are the products of professional philosophers who make their way in the profession by addressing themselves successfully to others who are trained in the "moves" considered appropriate by philosophers in their traditions of abstract argumentation.

Except for rare occasions, philosophers write for a specialized audience (of philosophers) already familiar with a specialized terminology, a range of technical distinctions, and a way of talking, thinking, and arguing that is uncommon in everyday life. If it is reflective, it is reflective in a special, narrow, and technical sense, in the sense of specialists with an esoteric language of their own.

Philosophical issues are so posed by professional philosophers, typically, that no actual case, no possible evidence could in principle settle them. The findings of other disciplines often are ruled out of the discussion by definition: "You're turning the question into a sociological (psychological, historical, biological) one. Let's stick to the philosophical question!" The result is that the issues that philosophers argue about are not really subject to being settled by the discovery of any empirical evidence.

The various positions are ones that can be argued for and against without end. Positions in the field are not refuted. They are abandoned. As a result, few students understand the significance to philosophers of any of the positions taken. The predominant undergraduate student view is, "Who cares?" A small—typically exceedingly small—minority of students become philosophy majors who, after some years of graduate study, seem to understand how to think about a range of philosophical questions and philosophical positions (usually the ones treated as significant in their seminar classes) to the satisfaction of some group of professional philosophers.

The result is that few students develop the skills of argumentation that would qualify them as plausible contributors to the argumentation in which professional philosophers engage. Few students see any connection between the argumentation and the conditions of their own lives. Few students are more reflective about their own lives as a result of taking courses in philosophy. Actually, students often develop a positive dislike of the subject as a result of their classroom experience and carefully avoid taking additional courses in the subject or doing further reading in the field.

Finally, the most ironic fact about the field of philosophy is that it is far from clear that professional philosophers are any more reflective about the manner in which they are living their own lives than are members of any other profession. One of the reasons is that, rhetoric to the contrary, philosophers themselves have little or no training in, or professional incentive to engage in, self-reflection—as against the development and submission of abstract argumentation about abstract issues to professional journals that are read by a small number of professional philosophers.

Neither students nor professors in philosophy are expected to come to terms with the concepts, values, or principles implicit in their own life or behavior. Learning how to think reflectively about one's life seems to be an art rarely focused upon and, therefore, rarely mastered.

15.4 *Think for Yourself*

THE IDEAL AND THE REAL

At the beginning of this chapter we stated that a significant gap exists between the ideal and the real in academic and professional fields for two primary reasons: human fallibility and vested interest. Choose two of the subjects focused on in this chapter, and for each answer, complete the following:

1. Re-read the section in this chapter that focuses on the subject you have chosen. Write in your own words your understanding of the ideal as presented. State and elaborate on the main points. Then write your understanding of the real as presented by us. Again, state and elaborate the main points.
2. Assuming that we are correct in our view that a gap exists between the ideal and the real in this field of study, how do you think human fallibility and vested interest might play a role in creating this gap?
3. How might human fallibility and vested interest be reduced in this discipline?
4. If you do not believe there is a gap between the ideal and the real, how would you articulate the field as an ideal?

CONCLUSION

As critical thinkers, we must be careful not to assume that things are actually the way they are represented to be in human life. The human mind has a strong predisposition to fallibility and is highly susceptible to vested interest. Human nature and vested interest are to be found at work in all professional disciplines and in all domains of human life.

To understand a field of knowledge, we must understand it realistically. To contribute to it productively, we must view it as an imperfect construction. To use it effectively in our daily life, we must internalize the mode of thinking integral to the discipline, aware that when we or others think, we do so with fallible human minds operating in a world of power struggles and vested interest.

This is not an argument for cynicism but, rather, for healthy skepticism. This chapter presented one possible set of beginning points from the perspective of which we can begin to appreciate the limitations of human knowledge and of the conditions under which human knowledge is constructed and applied. The points covered are illustrative of a direction of thought rather than infallible pronouncements.

Some may respond to the statements of the ideal with the view that no such promises are being made. But what, then, justifies the large social investment in teaching the discipline as it is taught? Others may say that the discussion of the reality of the disciplines is too one-sided and should be corrected by adding the positive side of instruction in the disciplines in question. To them, the response is: Please add what has been left out.

In Chapter 16 the analysis is concentrated on one domain of instruction, and the critical assessment is taken to a level of much greater detail. Again, this is done for its suggestiveness and in the spirit of illustration. It is not intended to express the last—but only the *first*—word in what should become a dialogue in every discipline, a dialogue open to all comers.

To the extent that we are committed to the development of fair-mindedness, we are committed to knowledge being acquired and used to minimize human suffering, to meet basic human needs, to preserve rather than destroy the environment, to contribute to a more just world, and to serve rational rather than irrational ends.

We are historically far from accomplishing the ideal, and far less consideration is being given to narrowing this large gap than is deserved. We need to grant full credit to the powerful modes of thinking implicit in the best practices of disciplines, but we also must recognize that, for those modes of thinking to flourish, they must develop out of a realistic critique of present practice.

LEARN AND USE INFORMATION CRITICALLY AND ETHICALLY

PART TWO: METHOD AND A MODEL CASE

Men, whose life lies in the cultivation of one science, or the exercise of one method of thought, have no more right . . . to generalize upon the basis of their own pursuit but beyond its range, than the schoolboy. . . . You might think this ought to make such a person modest in his enunciations; not so: too often it happens that, in proportion to the narrowness of his knowledge, is not his distrust of it, but the deep hold it has upon him, his absolute conviction of his own conclusions, and his positiveness in maintaining them. He has the obstinacy of the bigot, whom he scorns, without the bigot's apology, that he has been taught, as he thinks, his doctrine from heaven. Thus he becomes, what is commonly called a man of one idea; which properly means a man of one science, and of the view, partly true, but subordinate, partly false, which is all that can proceed out of anything so partial.

John Henry Newman, *The Idea of a University,* 1852

As we emphasized in Chapter 15, true loyalty to a discipline is born of recognition of the discipline's potential power for good in the world. It is not a commitment to practices in the discipline as it stands. It is not given by the intensity with which one defends the discipline. When students are socialized into a discipline so as to become uncritical defenders of the present practices of the discipline, both the discipline and the potential good of the discipline suffer. One retards the development of a discipline by uncritically defending it. This defensiveness engenders a false sense of loyalty. But when practitioners recognize weaknesses in a discipline, they are well on their way to contributing to the strengths of it.

It is a strength, an important strength, to recognize one's weakness. Unfortunately, we have not yet reached the phase of development of human knowledge wherein each discipline, as taught, routinely raises to the level of conscious realization important weaknesses in professional practice.

REALISTIC UNDERSTANDING

In this chapter we will focus our analysis on one domain, that of psychology, and on the allied fields of mental health. We begin with the premise that the art of thinking psychologically is a powerful form of thought, important to human well-being and self-insight. We also begin with the hypothesis that the benefit from this powerful mode of thought is diminished by the manner in which it is sometimes taught and used by psychologists and by those trained by psychologists in the fields of mental health.

One of the themes of this book is that, because we are all daily consumers of information, we must internalize information in a critical manner. We need to examine all information with full awareness that, though virtually all the information we are presented with is presented to us as true—as something *known* and not just *believed*—it may well be false or mere half-truth. When we are the recipient of gossip, the gossiper doesn't say, "What I am about to tell you is merely gossip, so treat it as such." Advertisements, which are often misleading, do not come to us with warnings about the extravagance of their claims. Newspapers do not warn us that what they are presenting as the news is often the product of press releases by groups with a vested interest in how the news is presented.

Political leaders do not say, "Everything I am about to tell you in this speech is intended to get myself elected to a position of power and influence—not to reveal the full truth about what is really happening. I will therefore hide, to the best of my ability, everything that puts me or my party in a bad light." Schools typically do not tell us how we should go about distinguishing what, among the many claims of textbooks and teachers, is highly credible and what is highly questionable. Teachers typically do not warn us that they, like all human beings, have prejudices and misconceptions and, therefore, their views should not be accepted uncritically.

Professionals in a subject only infrequently remind us of the limitations of what is known in the field or of the many teachings of the field in the past that at the time were presented as the truth and now are recognized to be out-and-out false. They do not tell us how to correct their statements with the qualifications that come from examining the same phenomena from the standpoints of different fields and orientations.

Finally, our own mind does not have a built-in warning system to alert us to what we have already taken in uncritically from our parents, our peers, the media, and so on.

Our memory does not have an automatic warning signal when we have a flawed memory of events stored in our mind. In short, one of the important themes of this book is the need, on the part of all of us, to take up a critical stance, to take a critical look at anything that we or anyone else takes to be fact rather than fancy, truth rather than error.

In this chapter we reemphasize the theme that we are *ethically* responsible for the manner in which we take in and use information; that if we mislearn information, we are on our way to misusing it; and that an irresponsible use of knowledge often creates harm or suffering to innocent persons or creatures. To minimize our potential for mislearning, we must be careful not to assume that the disciplines we study are the way they are presented in textbooks, instruction, and descriptions of practice. Nor should we assume that our manner of internalizing a discipline is free from distortion as a result of the flawed nature of our own learning.

If we want to understand a field of knowledge, we must understand it realistically, that it is an imperfect construction. If we want to understand *our learning* of a field of knowledge, we must realistically understand the imperfections of our learning, that even at best we imperfectly learn what we learn.

When studying a subject, it is helpful to have a provisional sense of the limitations of the subject and of ourselves as learners. This includes a provisional sense of the likely difference between the ideal of learning and the probable or possible result. We must develop heightened sensitivity to the influence of self-deception and vested interest within the discipline as well as within ourselves.

As critical thinkers, therefore, we recognize our moral obligation to critically evaluate the information we internalize and use. We shall explore this responsibility in further detail and model how to begin to fulfill it, using the field of psychology, along with the allied fields of mental health, as the prime example.

We have chosen psychology: (1) because human good and harm seem especially germane to its practice, and (2) because there seems to be an especially large gap between the ideal promised by psychology and the realities of its actual practice. You should read the discussion with the awareness that it may mischaracterize the field in some ways. In addition, you should realize that a similar critique could and should be made with virtually every field.

This chapter includes four general recommendations beyond those suggested in Chapter 15. The fourth—which incorporates the emphasis of Chapter 15—will provide a lead into the critique of the mental health field. The chapter concludes with some implications that follow from the extended analysis.

In this chapter the emphasis is on discovering the limitations of knowledge within a field. We must not confuse the limitations of a field of knowledge with our own limitations as learners, though. Both are significant. Both must be discovered and dealt with.

BE A CRITIC, NOT A CYNIC

Becoming a critical consumer of information is not the same as being a cynic about knowledge in general. A cynic views all knowledge as baseless. Such an absolute negation of knowledge cannot be justified for it is, in effect, an arrogant claim to *know* the status of *all* knowledge—that there is nothing we can claim to know absolutely. The spirit of critical thinking, by contrast, is intellectually humble. It is based on evidence that each of us must assemble individually, and it requires heightened awareness of how frequently humans make mistakes.

If we stop to think, we recognize that, implicit in our experience, we all have a great deal of evidence of our own fallibility. We all can access that evidence if we overcome our egocentric defensiveness. Our experience tells us how often and how easily we are taken in—by the subtle manipulations of others as well as by our own prejudices and misconceptions. Neither our experience nor our thought, however, gives us an easy or sweeping way to determine the status of *all* knowledge. Instead, we must examine each claim to knowledge, one by one, evaluating each on its merits.

RECOGNIZE THE MENTAL NATURE OF KNOWLEDGE

We often talk about knowledge carelessly and imprecisely, as if it could exist by itself in a book or a library or on a computer. But to be precise, human knowledge does not float through space. It exists *as knowledge* only in the human mind. But the human mind is an imperfect learner. Using thinking and experience, we can acquire knowledge, but we also can end up with error, illusion, self-deception, prejudice, hate, and fear. Human minds are all eminently fallible. For this reason, we must learn to think critically when we are engaged in the learning process. We must get in the habit of evaluating what we come to think and believe.

No one can do this for us. Each of us must figure out the world for ourself. Although others can help us by setting good examples of rational thinking, sound observation, and disciplined learning, no one can give us knowledge. Further, though all minds are capable of possessing knowledge, all are also, without exception, possessed by prejudices, vested interests, fears, insecurities, and social ideology. Paradoxically, then, wherever knowledge exists, some degree of ignorance also exists in some relationship to it. Wherever the fruits of knowledge exist, the consequences of its misuse are lurking. Human knowledge is always stored in imperfect, flawed minds. You have such a mind. So do we. So did Einstein.

16.1 *Think for Yourself*

BEGINNING TO DISTINGUISH WHAT YOU KNOW FROM WHAT YOU *THINK* YOU KNOW

Make a list of 10 things you believe about people in general or about certain groups of people (e.g., Most people are fundamentally . . . , most _____ are fundamentally . . . , most students are in college for the purpose of . . .). Then, for each belief you list, try to identify what your belief is based on. As you do so, ask yourself whether there is any relevant evidence you are failing to consider that might force you to modify your belief. Complete these statements for each belief:

1. I believe that . . .
2. I base this belief on the following . . .
3. I now think this belief is possibly unjustified because, on reflection, I realize I failed to consider some relevant evidence in forming the belief. I failed to consider . . .
   or
4. After reflecting on whether there is some relevant evidence I did not consider in forming this belief, I am still confident in this belief because . . .

DEVELOP AWARENESS OF THE HARM FROM MISUSE OF INFORMATION

Few humans are skilled in distinguishing where our knowledge ends and our misconceptions and prejudices begin. Few are skilled in identifying how our personal prejudices or vested interests influence our professional or personal thoughts. Formal schooling—for example, accumulating enough units to graduate from college—does not guarantee the acquisition of important critical thinking skills. What's more, in the real world of competition, struggle, and strife, human knowledge is often misused by intelligent people who are unaware of their own limitations, their flawed decisions, and their irrational behavior.

Intelligent people with a lofty sense of their importance, pursuing their vested interests, are much more of a threat to the well-being of others than are unintelligent people stumbling along unskilled in the art of deception and manipulation. Put another way, highly skilled thinkers who have little or no command over their native ability to deceive themselves will inevitably misuse information to justify pursuing selfish goals and purposes. And because they are highly skilled as thinkers, they often will be able to manipulate people and systems to get what they want.

The ethical use of knowledge, then, begins with a recognition, however imperfect, of the limits of one's knowledge and of the various influences that are likely to undermine the proper use of that knowledge. As we have emphasized throughout this book, the human mind, when critically developed, functions with an awareness of its limitations, and targets its own irrational tendencies, rendering those tendencies less dangerous and destructive. Conversely, irrational tendencies, ignored by uncritical and selfishly critical people, often lead to the irresponsible and unethical use of knowledge.

For example, during the era of World War II, the Nazis had no difficulty hiring college graduates and other highly trained persons to put their knowledge to work for flagrantly unethical ends (such as designing gas chambers in which to kill large numbers of people or developing brilliant plans for crushing a nation before it recognized what had happened). Thousands of German university graduates and scholars used their knowledge to serve the Nazi war machine. Most did it with a sense of righteousness. Prejudice against Jews and other non-Germans coexisted, in German minds, with much knowledge, insight, and practical know-how.

This systematic, unconscious confusion of knowledge, prejudice, and ignorance is not unique to Nazi Germany. It is a universal human problem, present in all groups and all individuals. It is not a matter of whether we are subject to prejudices and self-deception but, rather, to what degree. Because humans tend to be overly impressed by how much we know rather than by how little, an excess of intellectual arrogance is common even among highly schooled persons. This arrogance is not usually arrogance of manner but, instead, arrogance of mind, the confident belief that we know much more than we do. This is especially dangerous where the knowledge gained is highly specialized.

When people know a great deal about comparatively little and spend most of our time thinking within that narrow specialty, we tend to lose perspective on the limitations of our knowledge. When we consider broader questions, we often wrongfully generalize from our specialized experience. And, because we are experts within our subject, we often fail to recognize deficiencies in our thinking. Sometimes this results from a lack of historical perspective. Sometimes it results from a lack of knowledge of other disciplines. Sometimes it results from a failure of insight into the flawed operations of our own mind. Sometimes it results from intellectual vanity. Usually it is a combination of all four.

16.2   *Think for Yourself*

IDENTIFYING QUESTIONABLE PROFESSIONAL THINKING

Newspapers sometimes carry stories that document professional misuse of information (for example, a district attorney who ignores evidence in favor of a person, leading to a wrongful conviction of that person) or contain questionable judgments by professionals. Scan a daily newspaper and see if you can find an article that documents, or plausibly involves, a professional misusing information. Often you will find that the view expresses some vested interest. Complete these statements:

1. The issue outlined in the article is . . .
2. The main information the professional seems to use in his or her thinking is . . .
3. Other information that the professional should consider, but apparently isn't, is information about . . .
4. This professional seems to be viewing the situation in a questionable manner because . . . (here you are trying to determine whether the professional seems to have been influenced by some vested interest to exclude relevant information or whether the professional was simply engaging in poor-quality thinking because of naiveté or a similar reason).

One result is that, as a student, you cannot depend on formal instruction, including textbooks, to call to your attention the limits of the knowledge taught. In many academic fields, students are inadvertently, though routinely, encouraged to believe that the state of the discipline they are studying is more advanced than it is. Textbooks rarely highlight the lack of knowledge in the field.

Furthermore, because of the prestige of science, many disciplines have a strong incentive to describe themselves as a science even when they lack the credentials for such a claim. This is especially true of disciplines that focus on some dimension of human nature—a subject that inevitably generates debate, and should generate debate, from an array of standpoints. Many of the central questions the human disciplines seek to answer are answered very differently by competing schools of thought within the discipline.

The field of psychology illustrates this well. In this field, many psychological traditions and perspectives—Freudian, Adlerian, Jungian, gestalt, behaviorist, humanist, and so on—compete against one another, each seeking to persuade psychologists to join its camp. Therefore, the professional field is, to some extent, a battleground between competing paradigms and conceptual frameworks. The guiding principles of one psychologist are sometimes highly questionable to another.

One and the same case may be analyzed and evaluated in very different ways. Yet, the field of psychology sees itself—and presents itself—as a science. Imagine what chemistry would be like if key questions (such as, "What is the chemical composition of this liquid?") were answered differently depending on the chemist's theoretical orientation! Imagine what physics would be like if different schools of physics were to define fundamental terms in the field in different ways and defend conflicting laws of physical nature!

And that's not all. The process of certifying a student as knowledgeable in a field involves more than formal instruction. All students also are socialized informally into a group (taught how to behave and think like others in their professional group). This socialization accompanies the academic processes (taking courses, being tested, getting a degree). During socialization, students internalize a conception of themselves and the field they are studying that can lead them to believe that they, or the field of knowledge itself, are more advanced than they actually are. This easily becomes a form of intellectual arrogance that influences their practice. People with degrees often graduate thinking that they know much more than they do and are competent to do much more than they are. The result often is various forms of misuse of knowledge, various forms of malpractice. Much waste, injury, and needless suffering result from misuse of knowledge.

Professionals and practitioners who are keenly aware of the limitations of knowledge in the field, and therefore sensitive to the many possibilities for malpractice, are typically a small minority in a field, and the professional core of "true believers" often ignores their voice. Yet, only those who know how to question the status of knowledge in a field and recognize its limitations can truly be called safe and responsible practitioners.

We need to transform the learning process so developing knowledge of our ignorance is an essential dimension of developing our knowledge. We need to notice, analyze, and assess the socialization process—the hidden curriculum—so we are minimally inculcated with the unspoken prejudices of our discipline.

What you need to ensure, then, is that, as you study, you become an ethically responsible consumer of information and so develop your capacity to routinely ask critical questions about the status of the information you are presented with, as well as the status of your own knowledge (and ignorance). You need to train yourself, as it were.

The following discussion first asks the kinds of questions you should routinely ask about the professional field you are studying. This is followed by a critical analysis of one field of study, mental health. In coming to terms with the status of knowledge in your major, you should plumb at least this depth of analysis.

QUESTION ACADEMIC AND "EXPERT" INFORMATION

Some critical questions to ask about a field of study are:

- To what extent are there competing schools of thought within this field?
- To what extent do experts in this field disagree about their answers to important questions?
- What other fields deal with this same subject, from a different standpoint perhaps? To what extent are there conflicting views about this subject in the light of these different standpoints?
- To what extent, if at all, is this field properly called a science?
- To what extent can questions asked in the field be answered definitively? To what extent are questions in this field matters of (arguable) judgment?
- To what extent is there public pressure on professionals in the field to compromise their professional practice in the light of public prejudice or vested interest?
- What does the history of the discipline tell you about the status of knowledge in the field? How old is the field? How common is controversy over fundamental terms, theories, and orientation?
- How wide is the likely gap between the promised ideal of instruction and the actual results?

Some critical questions to ask about a textbook are:

- If there are competing schools of thought within this field, what is the orientation of the textbook writers? Do they highlight these competing schools and detail the implications of that debate?
- Are other textbooks available that approach this field from a significantly different standpoint? If so, how should we understand the orientation or bias of this textbook?
- Would other experts in this field disagree with any of the answers to important questions given in this textbook? If so, how would they disagree?

- Are there textbooks in other fields that deal with this same subject, from a different standpoint perhaps? To what extent are there conflicting views about this subject in the light of these different standpoints?

- To what extent does this textbook represent this field as a science? Do some experts in the field disagree with this representation? In what sense is it not a science?

- To what extent do the questions asked in this textbook lead to definitive answers? Conversely, to what extent are questions in this textbook matters of (arguable) judgment? And does the textbook help you to distinguish between these very different types of questions?

16.3 *Think for Yourself*

THINKING CRITICALLY ABOUT TEXTBOOKS

Locate a textbook in any discipline outside of the hard sciences (such as a textbook in sociology, anthropology, social work, psychiatry, or history). Carefully read the introduction and the introductory chapter. Then read the table of contents and skim through the book. Read as much of the textbook as is necessary to accurately answer the "critical questions to ask about a textbook" as outlined above.

Some critical questions to ask yourself about your professor are:

- Does your professor welcome questions?

- Is your professor receptive to questions about the status of knowledge within the field?

- Does your professor seem to be knowledgeable about limitations of the field? About what is arguable in the field?

16.4 *Think for Yourself*

THINKING CRITICALLY ABOUT YOUR SCHOOLING

Think back over your schooling and the teachers you have had. Answer the following questions:

1. To what extent did your teachers welcome questions in class?

2. Do you remember any occasions in which students asked questions about the status of knowledge within the field? To what extent were your teachers receptive to such questions?

3. To what extent did your teachers seem to be knowledgeable about limitations of the field? About what is arguable in the field?

QUESTION THE STATUS OF KNOWLEDGE IN A FIELD

There is no simple way to get an accurate sense of the limitation of knowledge in a field. As we question what is presented as knowledge, we must do so in an intellectually humble and honest way. Here are some of the kinds of information we should seek out.

1. We should seek out critics of the field, especially those with established credentials in the field. (Most fields have internal critics whose criticisms are not given much general visibility in the field.)

2. We should trace the implications of whatever evidence there is of conflicting schools of thought within the field, or conflicting theories.

3. We should be on the watch for vested interest in research or practice (wherein the practitioners may be tempted to misrepresent what is known for reasons of personal or professional benefit).

4. We should try to put the information in a field into some historical perspective (for example, if a field of study is relatively young, we should expect that information within it may be on a shakier foundation than information in a field that is older).

5. We should be on the alert for those engaged in popularizing knowledge in a field (often, for example, they are tempted to exaggerate its status or significance).

6. We should seek out a provisional view of the likely gap between the promised ideal of instruction and the actual results.

16.5 *Think for Yourself*

SEEKING OUT CRITICS IN A FIELD

Take any field of knowledge and see if you can find at least one critic of a dominant position in the field. Then look at any textbook that explains that position. See if the critic is mentioned and, if so, how his or her views are canvassed. Complete these statements:

1. One of the dominant theories in the field of _____ is . . .
2. One reputable critic of this theory is . . .
3. In the textbook I considered, the criticism of the theory was/was not given adequate attention because . . .

A MODEL CASE: QUESTIONING PSYCHOLOGY AND THE MENTAL HEALTH PROFESSIONS

Here we are using psychology and the mental health professions as the exemplar because (1) psychology is typically, but inappropriately, presented as a science, and (2) serious negative consequences for people result from this misunderstanding.

What we shall say here is not definitive. Instead, it is illustrative. Some of the conclusions represent thinking with which others might well disagree. For the purposes here, though, the example need not be flawless. Rather, it works if it provides you with a provisional understanding of how a critical consumer of information might begin to lay a foundation for critical assimilation of information within a field of study and practice. We begin with short answers to the questions posed above. Most of these short answers could be inferred from a good encyclopedia entry on psychology and the mental health professions.

- **To what extent are there competing schools of thought within this field?** There are numerous competing schools of thought within the mental health professions.

- **To what extent do experts in this field disagree about the answers they give to important questions?** Experts in the field often disagree about the answers they give to mental health–related questions.

- **What other fields deal with this same subject, from a different standpoint perhaps? To what extent are there conflicting views about this subject in the light of these different standpoints?** The different fields of study deal with mental health–related questions in differing ways. For example, psychologists, psychiatrists, social workers, sociologists, anthropologists, historians, and philosophers all have claimed to have exclusive understanding of the most fundamental concepts for comprehending the human mind and its functioning.

- **To what extent, if at all, is this field properly called a science?** Many mental health professionals see themselves as operating scientifically. Psychologists and psychiatrists routinely use what they consider to be the scientific method in conducting experiments and refer to their fields of study as hard sciences. There are so many conflicting ways of viewing important problems within the field, however, that it seems misleading to compare the mental health field with fields—such as chemistry, biology, and physics—in which conceptions of the phenomena studied are determined in such a way that essentially everyone in the field concurs about foundational concepts and how they are to be assessed.

- **To what extent can questions asked in the field be answered definitively? To what extent are questions in this field matters of (arguable) judgment?** Many, if not most, of the key questions in the field are matters of judgment, not matters of fact. Yet, they are often treated as uncontestable.

- **To what extent is there public pressure on professionals in the field to compromise their professional practice in light of public prejudice or vested interest?** One of the fundamental challenges the mental health professional faces is that discoveries about the human mind may not be in accord with deeply held beliefs within a society or social group. At the same time, all research results must be applied in actual social settings. The potential for conflict between research results and public belief is great. Therefore, tensions inevitably arise between free inquiry and socially dominant beliefs. Sometimes the tension is resolved in the direction of free inquiry, but often free inquiry is tacitly suppressed in favor of popular belief. This suppression usually is covert rather than overt, tacit rather than public.

■ **What does the history of the discipline tell you about the status of knowledge in the field? How old is the field? How common is controversy over fundamental terms, theories, and orientation?** As recognizable professional fields, the mental health professions are quite recent, dating back little more than a hundred years, to the work of Wilhelm Wundt (1832–1920). Wundt claimed that it was possible to make psychology an empirical science, and he established the first laboratory. From that day to the present, there has been ongoing debate in psychology as to what psychology can reasonably study, how it should conduct its inquiry, and whether it can or cannot establish genuinely scientific findings. One fundamental question, still unanswered, is the extent to which mental life can even be observed. Some psychologists have claimed that only behavior can be observed (including much debate about what is and is not behavior). The controversy broadens when the fields of sociology, anthropology, biology, and psychiatry are included in the investigation of human behavior.

■ **How wide is the likely gap between the promised ideal of instruction and the actual results?** The answer follows.

Psychology as an Ideal

The nature and operations of the human mind are a central determinant in human life. The scientific study of the mind, therefore, can enable us to maximize our control over our own mental health. We can identify pathologies of the mind in a way parallel to the way we identify pathologies of the body. We can study causes and consequences of human mental health and disease. We can train practitioners to use the knowledge that psychological research collects in designing successful counseling and therapy, thereby helping individuals who are in need of mental assistance.

With our knowledge, we can assist the courts in determining what prisoners are mentally safe to parole, which persons are of sound mind, and which parents pose a danger to their children. We can advise lawmakers on which social practices are mentally healthy and which are not. In general, psychology contributes to the mental health and optimal mental functioning of humans.

Psychology as Taught and Practiced

Though much has been promised in the name of psychology, the promises clearly fall far short of the ideal. What's more, serious questions can be raised as to whether it is even appropriate to use the word "science" to characterize psychology. As a field, psychology is highly multilogical. Many divergent points of view and frames of reference compete within psychology. Very often it is possible to get contradictory judgments from different practitioners in psychology. At the same time, students graduate with a major in psychology thinking of the field as a science and themselves as making judgments that have the force of science behind them.

The above discussion is not intended to imply that scientific work cannot be done in the field of psychology. Many important scientific studies have been conducted. Before we proceed with further documentation of the weaknesses of the mental health professions, considered as bodies of knowledge, we shall explore one important example that demonstrates the potential for scientific work in the field, followed by a partial list of the many areas of scientific studies done in the general field of psychology.

THE MILGRAM EXPERIMENT

The Milgram experiment is an example of work that is genuinely scientific and also provides us potentially deep insight into our own mind and the manner in which we tend to deceive ourselves. This classic study, done by Stanley Milgram at Yale, focused on the manner in which humans are unaware of the influence that external authorities have over us. The study, documented in the book *Obedience to Authority* (1974), demonstrates one way by which psychology can contribute to our better understanding of human self-deception. Here is the kind of self-serving thinking that Milgram's experiment questioned.

Most people think of themselves as free agents. They believe they have formed their beliefs as a result of reasonable judgments based on sound experience and reflective thought. They believe that their behavior is guided by a freely chosen moral perspective and that generally they act in accordance with that perspective. Hence, they believe that, though there are evil persons in the world—or at least people who do evil things—they do not include themselves among them.

They believe, for example, that they would not have participated, like so many Germans, in the Nazi extermination of Jews. If a serious conflict were to arise between the demands of an authority and their own conscience, they are confident that they would follow their conscience. Milgram demonstrates that this confident belief is often mistaken. Milgram's own description of the experiment reads:

> A person comes to a psychological laboratory and is told to carry out a series of acts that come increasingly into conflict with conscience. The main question is how far the participant will comply with the experimenter's instructions before refusing to carry out the actions required of him. . . . Two people come to a psychology laboratory to take part in a study of memory and learning. One of them is designated as a "teacher" and the other a "learner." The experimenter explains that the study is concerned with the effects of punishment on learning. The learner is conducted into a room, seated in a chair, his arms strapped to prevent excessive movement, and an electrode attached to his wrist. He is told that he is to learn a list of word pairs; whenever he makes an error, he will receive electric shocks of increasing intensity.
>
> The real focus of the experiment is the teacher. After watching the learner being strapped into place, he is taken into the main experimental room and seated before an impressive shock generator. Its main feature is a horizontal line of thirty switches, ranging from 15 to 450 volts, in 15-volt increments. There are also verbal designations which range from Slight Shock to Danger—Severe Shock. The teacher is told that he is to administer the learning test to the man in the other room. When the learner responds correctly, the teacher moves to the next item; when the other man gives an incorrect answer, the teacher is to give him an electric shock. He is to start at the lowest shock level (15 volts) and to increase the level each time that man makes an error, going through 30 volts, 45 volts, and so on.
>
> The "teacher" is a genuinely naïve subject who has come to the laboratory to participate in an experiment. The learner, or victim, is an actor who actually receives no shock at all. The point of the experiment is to see how far a person will proceed in a

concrete and measurable situation in which he is ordered to inflict increasing pain on a protesting victim. At what point will the subject refuse to obey the experimenter?

Conflict arises when the man receiving the shock begins to indicate that he is experiencing discomfort. At 75 volts, the "learner" grunts. At 120 volts he complains verbally; at 150 he demands to be released from the experiment. His protests continue as the shocks escalate, growing increasingly vehement and emotional. At 285 volts his response can only be described as an agonized scream. . . .

Many subjects will obey the experimenter no matter how vehement the pleading of the person being shocked, no matter how painful the shocks seem to be, and no matter how much the victim pleads to be let out. This was seen time and again in our studies and has been observed in several universities where the experiment was repeated. It is the extreme willingness of adults to go to almost any lengths on the command of an authority that constitutes the chief finding of the study and the fact most urgently demanding explanation.

A commonly offered explanation is that those who shocked the victim at the most severe level were monsters, the sadistic fringe of society. But if one considers that almost two-thirds of the participants fall into the category of "obedient" subjects, and that they represented ordinary people drawn from working, managerial, and professional classes, the argument becomes very shaky.*

This experiment reveals how little most people understand the roots of their own behavior, and it also reveals how much human behavior today is typically determined by external authority. Whatever schooling Milgram's participants had, and some had a great deal, that schooling had little effect on their intellectual, emotional, or moral autonomy. Furthermore, Milgram's participants seemed to have been heavily influenced by their desire to do what the experimenter giving them orders told them to do. Milgram's adult participants maintained their rapport with the experimenter rather than refuse orders that apparently endangered the life of an innocent victim:

The subjects were so concerned about the show they were putting on for the experimenter that influences from other parts of the social field did not receive much weight. This powerful orientation to the experimenter would account for the relative insensitivity of the subject to the victim. . . .

The Milgram experiment demonstrates *not* that psychology is a science, for overall it is not. Rather, it demonstrates that some important scientific work can be done in the field and that perhaps, at some time in the future, a genuinely scientific discipline, or set of disciplines, can emerge out of the present field of conflicting paradigms.

16.6   *Think for Yourself*

LINKING NATIVE EGOCENTRISM TO THE MILGRAM STUDY

Using the theory you have learned about irrationality in this book, do you see any link between the logic of egocentric thinking and the obedience to authority displayed in the Milgram experiment? To what extent do you think the "teachers" in the study were

---

*Excerpts from pp. 3–5 of *Obedience to Authority: An Experimental View* by Stanley Milgram. Copyright © 1974 by Stanley Milgram. Reprinted by permission of HarperCollins Publishers.

operating in an egocentrically submissive manner in obeying the experimenter? If you think they were, what explanation could you give for why they did so? What assumptions do you think the "teachers" were using in their thinking? What implications were they ignoring? Do you think a fundamentally rational person would have obeyed the experimenters? Why or why not?

SCIENTIFIC STUDIES IN PSYCHOLOGY

The Milgram experiment is not the only scientific study in psychology. Many hundreds of studies have been conducted on a wide variety of phenomena. A random list might include scientific studies of aggression, sex drive, sleep patterns, drinking problems, altered states of consciousness, anger, depth perception, anxiety, various forms of attachment, brainwashing, cults, behavior modification, classical conditioning, operant conditioning, bystander apathy, concept formation, memory, learning, compensation, conflict, conformity, delusions, depression, learned helplessness, dieting, dreams, forms of drug abuse, sensation, perception, exhibitionism, effects of punishment, fear, frustration, grief, prejudice, hallucinations, illusions, impotence, insomnia, introversion, motor development, observer bias, panic, sleep walking, stress, transfer of learning, and test anxiety.

The problem, then, is not in finding empirical data of a specific sort. The problem is in adding up those data into generalizations and applying those generalizations accurately and insightfully in life situations. Psychologists often talk as if psychology became a science when psychologists began to do experiments and make observations and predictions. But this does not change the reality that there are still numerous competing schools of psychology and a range of alternative disciplines that also study the human mind and behavior. There is no known scientific way to resolve the disagreements between schools or make corrections of the excesses of one discipline by the insights of another.

In addition, it is not simply a matter of conflict among psychologists. It is a conflict between psychologists and other disciplines about the nature of the human mind and behavior. Sociology, anthropology, history, philosophy, literature, and other fields shed light on human life. Truth about the human mind and behavior is not one-dimensional; it is multidimensional. Each discipline dealing with human behavior tends to talk as if its discoveries could be accepted without being qualified and corrected by those of the other relevant human disciplines.

Among the variety of questions that should be asked that are unlikely to be answered scientifically are the following:

- To what extent is human self-deception a mental pathology?
- To what extent is irrationality evidence of mental pathology?
- Are there pathologies of mind that are not psychological in nature?
- What is the difference between deviance that is psychologically pathological and deviance that is mentally healthy?

- To what extent has psychology reinforced social injunctions and taboos in its identification of mental pathologies?

- To what extent does psychological therapy and counseling cause, rather than solve, human problems?

- To what extent does the misapplication of principles of psychology to human problems cause unnecessary human suffering and injustice?

A DARK SIDE OF THE MENTAL HEALTH PROFESSIONS

Let us now look at some further reasons to question the status of knowledge in the fields of mental health. We shall consider what some of the critics of the field have said, as well as some of the facts about the history of psychology in relation to social convention and ideology.

For many years, the dominant social belief about homosexuality was that it was ethically perverted, mentally pathological, and disgusting. Psychologists and psychiatrists often reinforced this conception. They classified homosexuality as a mental illness and treated it as such. They cooperated in its criminalization. This was true despite historical evidence indicating that many societies have considered homosexuality to be normal and healthy.

Much of the misunderstanding of homosexuality resulted from mental health professionals' mislabeling it as a mental disease in the 19th century. Only after social attitudes toward homosexuality began to be liberalized did psychologists and psychiatrists reconsider their "professional" views.

The manner in which this reconsideration took place is instructive. In 1974, the American Psychiatric Association removed homosexuality from its official list of mental disorders. This reclassification came about as a result of a poll taken of the association's general membership. The views of each association member were given equal weight even though most members had done no research on the subject. Imagine a science that determines what is true and what is false by taking polls of its members!

This vote was taken some 17 years after a 1957 landmark study at the University of California, Los Angeles, which concluded that no pathological differences exist between homosexuals and heterosexuals. Despite the evidence that homosexuality alone was not pathological, however, many psychiatrists were opposed to removing it from the official list of mental disorders.

Psychiatrist Lee Coleman (1984) describes the manner in which the official list changed:

> What particularly struck many observers was the obviously political rather than scientific basis for the change. Under growing pressure from the homosexual community, the trustees of the American Psychiatric Association (APA) declared, by a majority vote in December 1973, homosexuality to be no longer a mental disorder. So much controversy

resulted from this [that] a referendum was called to enable the entire APA membership to vote. Of the total votes cast, 5,854 called for elimination, 3,810 for retention, and 367 abstained. (p. 18)

The classification of a sexual practice as pathological is much more than a mere academic distinction. It has far-reaching implications for the well-being of millions of people. For example, as late as the 1940s, homosexual acts were classified as felonies in all the states, with punishment of up to life in prison. Homosexuals were fired, persecuted, scorned, and even physically attacked.

Awareness of the history of the mental health professions, therefore, should make us cautious in accepting without question the present dominant views in the field. Rather, we should expect that those views are transitory and will continue to change as political and social attitudes change. Until these attitudes change, the mental health professions will continue to serve the public by providing pseudoscientific determinations that give the public misplaced confidence in its present judgmental beliefs and practices. Mental health professionals, as a group, have not led the way to decriminalize social behavior that is not "normal." They have reflected public opinion more often than they have led it.

LEGITIMIZING DEEPLY HELD SOCIAL BELIEFS

As we have suggested, professionals within the mental health field apply the theories they have learned to human behavior when the outcome is of significant consequence to the persons involved. Unlike physical health and disease, about which the public welcomes discoveries and conclusions are based on sound evidence, what is mentally "abnormal" is largely synonymous in the public mind with what is disgusting and abhorrent. Furthermore, what is disgusting to the public seems to be in need of punishment.

The mental health profession is much more likely to validate cultural norms than to be critical of those norms, even, it seems, when this means turning their minds against the evidence. In their book *Making Monsters: False Memories, Psychotherapy, and Sexual Hysteria,* Ofshe and Watters (1996) point out the incompetent manner in which recovered-memory therapists, using a form of psychotherapy in widespread use, often "help" patients uncover memories from their childhood about events that did not take place. They state:

> The mistakes made in this therapy are not due to the lack of reliable information but are largely the result of reliable information being ignored. Although much research has been conducted regarding human memory, the coercive nature of the therapy setting, and the effect of techniques, this knowledge has been ignored by recovered-memory therapists. (p. 10)

Ofshe and Watters go on to say that social, political, and religious ideologies often inappropriately guide the way by which mental health professionals interpret data:

> It is clear that the issues of child abuse, sexual assault, and the victimization of women and children have in our time been invested with enormous social importance. . . . A close link between a type of treatment and popular political movement does not come without

costs. While academics and scientists have often been called upon to ratify the conclusions and beliefs of a given social, religious, or political movement, the resulting science has often been distorted by the predilection to find data that confirm the assumptions of the movement. The conclusions drawn by such science are often bitterly defended, not because of their scientific merit but because they further the cause at hand. (pp. 11–12)

Ofshe and Watters suggest that the same social forces that have pushed recovered-memory therapy into prominence among therapists have also shielded it from critical analysis. For example:

> For much of the past decade, to wonder aloud whether the frequency of childhood sexual abuse could actually be as high as one in every two women (as theorized) was to be labeled "in denial." Those who expressed concern for the rights of the accused were charged with "protecting the perpetrator." One misstep, and even well-intentioned researchers or journalists could find themselves accused of secretly trying to prolong centuries of ignorance of child abuse. (p. 12)

Humans historically have tended to avoid questioning the deep-seated traditions and conventions of society. Rather, they have subconsciously accepted as "right" the dominant views of their society, especially when those views were tied into deeply held beliefs. Mental health practitioners are subject to this same human predisposition, and often with tremendous cost to those who become victims of the mental health system.

This confusion of social ideology with objective fact is reflected in the failure of the mental health field to ensure that its fundamental evaluative concepts (such as "healthy" and "pathological") are established by truly independent research divorced from the influence of deeply held social beliefs. For example, behavior falling outside the normal distribution is often viewed by the mental health professions as "pathological."

Consider the very definition of "abnormal" as defined by J. P. Chaplin in the *Dictionary of Psychology* (1985). Note that even this definition is debatable among clinical practitioners. According to Chaplin, "abnormal" means

> diverging widely from the normal; descriptive of what is considered normative, healthy or psychological from an adjustmental point of view. . . . Some authorities have suggested that abnormality be defined in statistical terms—that individuals who fall outside certain limits along the normal probability curve be considered abnormal. . . . Others have suggested that normalcy and abnormalcy be defined in terms of cultural standards, thus allowing considerable latitude for cultural relativity. . . . In applying such a definition, considerable latitude must be allowed for clinical judgment. (pp. 3–4)

Clearly, defining healthy behavior in terms of how most people behave is problematic. Such a position would make mental health vary not only from culture to culture but even from social group to social group. It would make racist and chauvinistic practices healthy wherever they were, or are, socially dominant. Further, because wherever we find social groups, we find social prejudice, it follows that those who hold such prejudices are mentally healthier than those who do not. In short, there appears to be no good reason to think either that all "normal" behavior is "healthy" or that all "abnormal" behavior is "unhealthy."

16.7   *Think for Yourself*

THINKING-THROUGH "NORMAL" VERSUS "ABNORMAL"

Make a list of all the social conventions you can think of that are considered normal within certain social groups. Then, for each norm, state the opposing or "abnormal" behavior. For each convention you identify, complete these statements:

1. One social convention I can think of is . . .
2. The "abnormal" behavior violating this norm is . . .
3. Some important implications of considering this behavior "wrong" are . . .
4. The abnormal behavior should or should not be considered wrong because . . .

When you are finished, check your reasoning to see if you inadvertently based your conclusion on a social convention or taboo rather than on a moral principle that transcends social boundaries and conventions.

In his book *The Reign of Error* (1984), Lee Coleman, M.D., discusses the problems inherent in the power given to psychiatry by society, and the arrogance with which many psychiatrists (and psychologists) often conduct their work. Consider the following case described by Coleman:

> When the Chicago police started to arrest Robert Friedman for panhandling in front of a downtown bus station on August 2, 1975, he pleaded, "Don't take me in. I'm not broke. I didn't know this was a crime." He opened his briefcase and revealed to the officers $24,087 in small bills.
>
> "A few days later," according to a report by the Associated Press, "he was committed to a mental institution by a judge who said he was protecting Friedman from thugs who might be after his cash."
>
> Thugs didn't get Friedman's cash, but psychiatry did. He was forced to pay for his incarceration in a psychiatric hospital, and even had to pay the fees for the lawyer who convinced the judge to lock him up. Twelve thousand dollars later, Friedman was finally able to get help from DePaul University law professor Edward J. Bennet, who commented, "He was committed on the possibility that he would be mugged, beaten, robbed, and instead, he's locked up, filled with drugs, and his money is taken gradually instead of in one clean sweep."
>
> This is an example of what I call psychiatry's reign of error. I mean by this the exercise of the vast power that our society grants psychiatry and that psychiatry so readily accepts. The immense legal power given to psychiatry is based on faith, not reason. (p. 1)

16.8   *Think for Yourself*

ANALYZING THE PANHANDLER CASE

Consider the panhandler case above in terms of the way the man was treated in this situation. Based on what you have read about the case, to what extent do you think psychiatrists played a role in legally robbing the man? Give your reasoning for your answer.

Because those who are authorized to practice in the mental health professions tend to accept the dominant beliefs of the day, they commonly make mistakes in judgment. This is not surprising. After all, a great deal of money and power are at stake in the practice established by mental health professionals. Lawmakers, and those they answer to, are not about to authorize any professional group to undermine or act contrary to righteously held social beliefs.

As a society, then, it is only plausible to expect that psychiatrists, psychologists, and other mental health professionals will toe the line, to ensure that their practice does not upset social tranquility. For example, when mental health professionals render a judgment as to whether a parent is fit or unfit, whether a person is criminally dangerous, and the like, society does not expect its folk wisdom to be violated.

The result, it seems, is a dangerous "marriage." On the one hand, mental health professionals think of their judgments as purely scientific in nature, even though they conform their practice to deeply ideological belief systems. At the same time, this dimension of social conformity is obscured systematically. The textbooks and training of psychologists and psychiatrists represent as scientific the tools used to assess the mental health of individuals.

On the other hand, if truth be told, the determinations regarding a person's mental health or lack thereof seem to be principally a matter of interpretation or judgment. If these judgments are based on a process of sifting through, weighing, and making inferences from a variety of forms of information rooted in debatable concepts and assumptions, we should be critically skeptical of the findings.

Therefore, it is almost always possible to find "experts" in the mental health professions who will testify to opposite conclusions and interpretations of the same data. Mental health professionals, basing their assessment about the mental health of individuals on a variety of competing paradigms in the field, significantly diverge in their conclusions. What's more, those who practice the profession seem to tacitly recognize that the authorities (such as lawyers and judges) to which these professionals are answerable do not take a neutral position regarding what is healthy. Rather, these authorities fully expect mental health professionals to uphold the dominant ideology of the broader society as to what is healthy, harmful, or morally corrupting.

Consider two of the tools that mental health professionals use to determine one's personality and the state of one's mental health. Again we quote from Coleman (1984):

> One of the clearest examples of subjectivity masquerading as science in the field of psychological testing is the widespread use of computers to score the answers to a personality questionnaire such as the Minnesota Multiphasic Personality Inventory (MMPI). . . . The answers are graphed and appear to give objective measures of personality. But these graphs hide the fact that someone has previously decided what is a normal response and what is an abnormal response to each question. Since the designer's interpretation of possible responses rested on his personal views rather than empirical tests, the scoring of all later patients' responses must also be subjective.
>
> Such pseudoscience also prevails with the Rorschach test. A person is asked to interpret a standard series of cards, each of which contains an inkblot. The response to each card becomes the basis for the psychologist's evaluation of the patient's mental state.

Once again, the responses are compared with the alleged normal and abnormal response determined by the test's designer. . . .

Like psychiatry, psychology has no procedure to obtain objective findings. (pp. 4–5)

The problem we are concerned with, then, is what appears to be an inherent self-delusion that accompanies the very way by which mental health professionals conceptualize their work.

16.9 *Think for Yourself*

THINKING CRITICALLY ABOUT PSYCHOLOGICAL TESTS

Locate reference materials pertaining to either the Minnesota Multiphasic Personality Inventory or the Rorschach inkblot test. See if you can get actual copies of the test, as well as information about how the test is interpreted. Then write a brief report presenting your view of the extent to which the test actually measures mental health. Include a discussion of how much individual professionals' interpretations play a role in these "objective" measures.

QUESTIONING PSYCHOTHERAPY

Let us now turn our attention from a general critique of the knowledge base of the mental health professions to the practice, based on that supposed knowledge base, of psychotherapy. One way in which the mental health professions have been successful is by gaining public acceptance of psychotherapy for treatment of mental problems.

For example, when we are depressed, when we can't seem to find meaning in our lives, when we are experiencing pain stemming from an unhappy romantic or intimate relationship, we often are advised to see a therapist. When our children are acting out and we no longer can deal with them effectively, we often are advised to take the whole family to group therapy. The assumption is that if we feel mentally unwell, if we are experiencing mental pain, or if we just can't seem to cope, a reasonable way to seek aid is through psychotherapy. This assumption has been fostered by the mental health profession. Yet, given the critique above, we are driven to ask to what extent psychotherapy actually helps people. Further, can therapy actually harm people? Some critics think so.

In his book *Beware the Talking Cure: Psychotherapy May Be Hazardous to Your Mental Health,* Terence Campbell (1994) questions the effectiveness of psychotherapy and concludes that

it is neither remarkable nor original to say that psychotherapy is often ineffective. Its reputation for wasting time, money, and energy is infamous. Psychotherapy is hazardous not because of who does it but because of the futility of the techniques themselves. Legions of psychotherapists regularly rely on techniques that severely damage their clients. . . . These therapists *think* that their techniques effectively help distressed people, but they confuse reality with illusions. As a result, too many people find themselves more seriously disturbed after psychotherapy than they were before it—and at its worst, the consequences can be fatal. (p. 5)

Campbell goes on to argue:

> With the possible exception of some behavioral techniques, used for some specific fears, there is no evidence to verify the effectiveness of any specific psychotherapeutic technique. (p. 12)

In their book *Crazy Therapies: What Are They? Do They Work?*, Margaret Singer and Janja Lalich (1996) concur with Campbell's view that therapy can be harmful to patients. They state:

> Some consumers risk being harmed—psychologically and otherwise—by some of the therapies currently in vogue. Each year countless individuals . . . turn over their innermost thoughts and feelings to a trusted counselor, only to be exploited and abused by some of them. (p. xii)

In citing one example of negative consequences resulting from therapeutic techniques, they say:

> "Jennifer" was referred by her physician to Ms. "W," a hypnotherapist, for treatment of stress-related headaches. Using extensive trance sessions, Ms. W led Jennifer to believe that nearly four hundred human, animal, and other world-entities had invaded her body and were living and squabbling inside her. Prolonged treatment led to Jennifer's mental deterioration and multiple suicide attempts. (p. xiii)

Consider another example presented by Singer and Lalich. This excerpt exemplifies the absurd methods that therapists sometimes use to help people work out their problems:

> Mr. and Mrs. "Johnson" went to therapy for typical marital issues. Dr. "T" was a believer in aggressive methods of expressing feelings. Handing the couple some plastic bats, Dr. T instructed them to fight it out as hard as they could. When the couple responded rather limply, Dr. T sat on the sidelines yelling at them, insulting them, and urging them to be more forceful. The couple ended up bashing not only each other but a great deal of furniture in Dr. T's office, as well as taking a few swings at him. Afterwards, Mr. and Mrs. Johnson felt silly and never went back, but the following week they received a bill for $5,000 in damages to Dr. T and his office. (p. xiv)

Campbell (1994) comments on the deficient training that therapists often receive:

> Too often, absurdity prevails as standard procedure in the training of psychotherapists. For example, a practicing therapist recalled an occasion in his own training when he felt lost; a sullen, severely depressed client had thoroughly confused him. When he asked a supervisor how he could respond more effectively to this client, he was told: "You don't have to *do* anything—just be." The trainee considered this advice profound in its wisdom; others would consider it profoundly incompetent. (p. 18)

The upshot is that, despite the field of mental health seeing itself as largely scientific in nature, therapeutic practice may involve potentially harmful techniques. Singer and Lalich express concern that therapy patients are sometimes involved in experimental therapies misrepresented as established practice. They term these types of therapy "crazy therapies":

> We invariably see, with some of the crazy therapies, a form of experimentation in the types of treatments prescribed and the techniques used. Certain practitioners are in

effect toying with untested procedures. . . . These therapists are not getting "informed consent" from their clients because they are not advising their clients that there are alternative approaches and methods of treatment, they are not advising their clients of the risks and side effects, and they are not informing their clients that they are being asked to participate in unproven experimental procedures.

Aside from the unethical nature of such professional interactions, there is a degree of deception that is unacceptable. Some of it may be attributed to incompetence or lack of proper training. Some of it may be rooted in greed or ego gratification. And some of it may be based in evil intent. Whatever the source, there is no justification for the suffering and loss to the thousands who have been taken in by certain crazy therapies and their proponents.

LEARNING FROM SUSPECT CLAIMS OF PSYCHOLOGY AND THE MENTAL HEALTH PROFESSIONS

In suggesting a critique of the claims to knowledge of the mental health professions, we are not seeking to denigrate the importance of studying mental health, any more than the National Academy of Sciences was denigrating the importance of studying physical health when it issued a report claiming that "medical errors kill 44,000 to 98,000 people a year" (*New York Times,* Front Page, Nov. 30, 1999).

We are not denying the power and value of psychological thinking. We are not seeking to discourage the teaching of courses in these fields. We are not advising students to avoid majoring in them. Finally, we are not saying that the field of psychology is doing *no* "scientific" work. Rather, we are saying that there are significant reasons for questioning the authority of the field of psychology if and when it is represented, on the whole, as a science. You, the learner, must ultimately decide what credibility you grant to the claims of any given field, including claims in the mental health professions. What we have done is to suggest that, beneath the rhetoric of a field of study, even an established one, may lie significant problems.

For example, the National Academy of Sciences report on medical errors indicated that the number of medical errors yearly "exceeds the number of people who die annually from highway accidents (about 43,450), breast cancer (42,300), or AIDS (16,500). The chairman of the panel that conducted the study, William C. Richardson, said, 'These stunningly high rates of medical errors—resulting in deaths, permanent disability, and unnecessary suffering—are simply unacceptable in a medical system that promises first to 'do no harm.' " The present practice of the mental health professions calls for similar analysis and report.

Although these are important findings, they should not surprise us, as critical thinkers aware of the pervasive presence of human fallibility and vested interest. Furthermore, there is little question but that the misuse of knowledge is more likely in some fields than in others. The fields of study that concentrate on human nature and human behavior seem most open to critique, whereas mathematics and the physical sciences seem most resistant to it.

Nevertheless, critique is required with respect to all fields of study and with respect to all information in that field. We should be ever cautious regarding the status of information we have taken in if we have not explored its potential for falsity or distortion. We should be especially skeptical of information that seems to validate passionately held beliefs or that directly supports the claims of monied interests.

If we know little or nothing about the history of a field, we should be wary of the knowledge claims of the field. Human disciplines require human scrutiny, especially as those disciplines are put into practice in the real world of affairs. If we are critical thinkers, we approach all disciplines as necessarily involving both strengths and weaknesses. We must continually remind ourselves that human knowledge can only be embodied in human minds and that all human minds are subject to self-deception, self-interest, and error. We must seek critics in all fields to make sure that we recognize the weaknesses and the strengths of any given field we study. We also must critically monitor the use we make of the information we acquire.

Finally, we must learn to internalize information *conditionally*. A conditional belief is one that we qualify with conditions. To illustrate, there is a difference between the statement, "X is true" and the statement, "If A and B are true, then X is true." Here are some other examples of conditional statements:

- If the experiment was conducted as it claims to have been, then its results are important.
- If the textbook description of Freud's view of the unconscious is accurate, then Freud also must have believed that . . .
- If we make the following assumptions, then it follows that she is probably guilty.
- If we consider his statements to be credible, then so-and-so is implicated in the act.

If we notice the conditions under which information comes to us, we can store it in our mind in conditional form.

To conclude our analysis, every field of study requires insightful critics and also students who study it critically and use its information responsibly. The potential for misuse of information (activated ignorance) is enormous. It should be sobering to recognize that self-deception exists at the individual level as well as at the group level, and that professional groups, like all other human groups, are subject to collective deception.

Recognizing that people are being harmed every day by the misuse of information by well-meaning persons and authorities, we should minimize contributing to this harm. Recognizing that most of what we learn comes to us in a conditioned form, we should use or communicate what we learn with the conditions attached, as it were. Although we are far from this practice now, only through it, and the development of our critical faculties, can we begin to minimize the misuse of information.

THINKING PSYCHOLOGICALLY: A POSTSCRIPT

For the art of psychological thinking to flourish, it must be understood as requiring an interface with all of the other forms of thought that influence the human mind and underlie human behavior patterns. These forms of thought include:

Sociological thinking. Our mind is influenced by the social groups to which we belong;

Philosophical thinking. Our mind is influenced by our personal philosophy;

Ethical thinking. Our mind is influenced by our character;

Anthropological thinking. Our mind is influenced by cultural practices, mores, and taboos;

Ideological and political thinking. Our mind is influenced by the structure of power and its use by interest groups around us;

Economic thinking. Our mind is influenced by the economic conditions under which we live;

Historical thinking. Our mind is influenced by our history and by the way we tell our history;

Biological thinking. Our mind is influenced by our biology and neurology.

This makes psychological thinking much more complicated and challenging. We, as humans, need to think deeply about the nature of our own mind and the manner in which it operates. But the manner in which the human mind operates is not simply a psychological question. It is a sociological, philosophical, ethical, anthropological, ideological, political, economic, historical, and biological question. Each of these represents an important dimension of human thought and behavior. What's more, we cannot side-step these complicated interfaces by restricting psychological thinking to what is normal (as against abnormal) or healthy (as against pathological). Each of these key concepts must be understood in relationship to each of the above modes of thinking. For example, what is ideologically normal (think of Fascism) in a society or culture may contribute to what is ethically pathological.

Is it psychologically healthy for a culture to encourage individuals to blindly conform to the social values, mores, and taboos of the social groups to which they belong? Is it psychologically healthy to be undisturbed by the amount of human suffering and injustice in the world? When is adjustment to a social, political, or economic reality a form of mental pathology? Politicians, military decision-makers, and corporate executives often seem to adjust comfortably to situations in which there is massive human suffering and injustice. Is this to be considered psychologically healthy? Many important questions about psychological thinking and human psychology emerge as soon as we place both of these into an interface with other forms of thinking about the human mind and its operations.

CHAPTER 17

STRATEGIC THINKING
PART ONE

Strategic thinking has two phases:

1. The understanding of an important principle of mental functioning.
2. Using that understanding strategically to produce a mental change in ourselves.

In this chapter and the next, we move back and forth between important understandings and strategies based on them. Strategic thinking is the regularization of this practice. From understanding to strategy, and from strategy to self-improvement, is the pattern we are looking for.

UNDERSTANDING AND USING STRATEGIC THINKING

If we understand that the mind has three functions—thinking, feeling, and desire (want)—and that these functions are interdependent, by implication we realize that any change in one of these functions is going to produce a parallel shift in the other two. It follows, then, that if we change our thinking, there should be some shift at the level of feeling and desire. So if I *think* you are insulting me, I will *feel* some resentment and develop some *desire* to respond to that insult.

By the same token, if we *feel* some emotion (say, sadness), there should be some *thinking* (say, thinking we have lost something of significance) that accounts for that feeling. It follows, then, that if I experience an irrational negative emotion or an irrational *desire,* I should, in principle, be able to figure out the irrational thinking that is creating that feeling and desire.

Once we discover the irrational thinking, we should be able to modify that thinking by more reasonable thinking. Finding the thinking to be irrational, we should be able to construct a more reasonable substitute. We then work to replace irrational thinking with rational thinking. As the new, reasonable thinking takes root, we should experience some shift in our emotions and desires. More reasonable emotions and desires should emerge from more reasonable thinking.

Now to a specific case: Suppose you recently ended a romantic relationship and are dating someone else now. In the meantime, you learn that your ex is dating your roommate. You suddenly *feel* a powerful surge of jealousy and the desire to lash out at your roommate. Your irrational *thinking* is something like this:

> I should get to control whom my roommate and my ex date. It is unfair that they are now dating when I don't want them to. Even though I have given up the relationship, I still should be able to control her. She is still really mine! My roommate has no right to do something so upsetting to me. He should know how I feel, and my feelings should come first. So what if he's attracted to my ex-girlfriend? He can just find someone else. If he's my friend, I should come first.

This thinking—if we have accurately reconstructed it—is largely subconscious. Virtually no one would consciously own such thinking. Through active work, however, you can bring it to the surface of your thinking. You can do this by first recognizing that underlying every irrational *feeling* is an irrational *thought* process. In this case, you should first figure out exactly what feeling you are experiencing. Then you should trace the feeling to the thinking that is leading to it. Hence, as in the case above, you should be able to spell out the probable unconscious thoughts that are fueling your irrational jealousy of, and anger toward, your roommate.

You usually will find that the thoughts are highly egocentric and infantile. These covert thoughts are what cause you to feel negative emotions. If you can determine the irrational thinking that is driving your emotions and behavior, you have a better chance of changing the emotions and behavior by working on the unreasonable thinking that is causing them.

In short, through active scrutiny and analytic reconstruction, you can begin to see how unreasonable and self-centered your thinking is in such cases. Then, using self-determined, strategic thinking, you can replace irrational thinking with thinking that makes sense, thinking such as:

> Wait a minute—what's wrong with my ex dating? I'm seeing new people myself. And what's wrong with my roommate dating my ex? She has no obligation to consult me before she dates a person. If I really care for my ex, I should wish her well. And if she is attracted to my roommate, shouldn't I wish them both well? If the situation were reversed, wouldn't I want my ex to respond in this way?

Whenever you feel your irrational jealousy emerging, you deliberately think-through the above reasoning. You do it again and again until you find productive, rational feelings and desires emerging. Some of the most powerful thoughts, feelings, and desires, though, are unconscious and primitive. Therefore, we should not expect ourselves to be able to completely displace all irrationality. Yet, by making our irrational thoughts explicit, we can better attack them with reason and good sense. We can be better people with healthier emotions and desires if we learn how to undermine, and thereby diminish, our irrational emotions and desires.

Now let's look at how we proceeded from understanding to strategy and from strategy to improvement in the example above:

The understanding. The human mind has three interrelated functions: thinking, feeling, and desiring, or wanting. These functions are interrelated and interdependent.

The strategy. Whenever you find yourself having what may be irrational emotions or desires, figure out the thinking that probably is generating those emotions and desires. Then develop rational thinking with which to replace the irrational thinking you are using in the situation. Finally, whenever you feel the irrational negative emotions, rehearse the rational thinking, using this format:

1. Explicitly state what the feelings and desires are.
2. Figure out the irrational thinking leading to it.
3. Figure out how to transform the irrational thinking into rational thinking—thinking that makes sense in context.
4. Whenever you feel the negative emotion, repeat to yourself the rational thoughts you decided you needed to replace the irrational thoughts, until you feel the rational emotions that accompany reasonable thinking.

In Chapters 17 and 18 we briefly review some key concepts, principles, and theories discussed thus far in the book, followed by examples of strategic thinking based on the examples. The aim is *illustration,* not comprehensiveness.

We hope you will develop ideas of your own for improvement. There are no formulas for a simple and painless life. Like you, we are working on the problem of targeting and removing our defective thinking. Like you, we are working to become more rational and fair-minded. We must recognize the challenge that this development represents.

As with all forms of personal development, development of thinking means transforming deeply ingrained habits. It can happen only when we take responsibility for our own growth as rational persons. Learning to think strategically must become a lifelong habit. It must replace the habit most of us have of thinking impulsively, of allowing our thinking to gravitate toward its own, typically unconscious, egocentric agenda.

Are you willing to make self-reflection a lifelong habit? Are you willing to become a strategic thinker? Are you willing to unearth the irrational thoughts, feelings, and desires that lurk in the dark corners of your mind? Are you willing to develop a compassionate mind? If so, you should find these two chapters on strategic thinking useful.

COMPONENTS OF STRATEGIC THINKING

Before proceeding to examples of strategic thinking, you will have to add two components to your intellectual repertoire as you seek to implement the strategies outlined in this chapter:

1. **An identifying component.** You must be able to figure out when your thinking is irrational or flawed.

2. **An intellectual action component.** You must actively engage and challenge the acts of your own mind.

In the *intellectual action component,* you must figure out four things:

1. What is actually going on in the situation as it stands.

2. Your options for action.

3. A justifiable rationale for choosing one of the options.

4. Ways of reasoning with yourself when you are being unreasonable, or ways of reducing the power of your irrational state of mind.

17.1 *Think for Yourself*

AN INTRODUCTION TO STRATEGIC THINKING

Identify an area of your life in which you use thinking that is possibly irrational. If you are having trouble, think of a situation in which you felt a powerful negative emotion and had difficulty dealing with it. Write out the answers to these questions:

1. What is actually going on in the situation as it stands? Elaborate on the details.

2. What are your options for action?

3. Which option seems best? How do you know? Can you view the situation in any other competing ways?

4. Construct the reasoning you need to rehearse when you are again in this situation or a similar situation.

If you have trouble completing this assignment, read the example on the next page.

THE BEGINNINGS OF STRATEGIC THINKING

Let us now consider some basic concepts, principles, and theories of critical thinking, providing examples of strategic thought as implied by those principles. In each case we will start with a key idea. We then will explore strategies for improving thinking based on that idea. We will begin with a more formal approach to the example given at the beginning of this chapter.

Key Idea #1: Thoughts, Feelings, and Desires Are Interdependent

As noted, the mind is composed of three functions: thinking, feeling, and desiring or wanting. Wherever one of these functions is present, the other two are present as well. These three functions are continually influencing and being influenced by one another. Our thinking influences our feelings and desires. Our feelings influence our thinking and desires. Our desires influence our thinking and feeling.

We cannot immediately change our desires or feelings. We have direct access only to thinking. It makes no sense for someone to order you to feel what you do not feel or to desire what you do not desire. We do not change feelings by substituting other feelings, or desires by substituting other desires. But someone can suggest that we consider a new way to think. We can role-play new thoughts but not new emotions or desires. It is possible to reason within a point of view with which we do not agree. By rethinking our thinking, we may change our thinking. And when our thinking changes, our feelings and desires will shift in accordance with our thinking.

Strategic Idea

With a basic understanding of the interrelation among thoughts, feelings, and desires, we should be able to routinely notice and evaluate our feelings. If, for example, I experience a degree of anger that I sense may be unreasonable, I should be able to determine whether the anger is or is not rational. I should be able to evaluate the rationality of my anger by evaluating the thinking that gave rise to it.

Has someone truly wronged me, or am I misreading the situation?

Was this wrong intentional or unintentional?

Are there ways to view the situation other than the way I am viewing it?

Am I giving a fair hearing to these other ways?

By pursuing these questions, I can come closer to a rational view of the situation.

Even if my way of viewing the situation is justified and I do have good reason to feel some anger, it does not follow that I have acted reasonably, given the full facts of the situation. I may have good reason to feel angry, but not to act irrationally as a result of that anger.

This strategy might be roughly outlined as follows:

1. Identify a *feeling* you have experienced that you suspect might be irrational (a feeling such as irritability, resentment, arrogance, or depression).

2. What thinking would account for the feeling? There may be more than one possibility here. If so, figure out which possibility is most likely.

3. Determine the extent to which the thinking is reasonable. Pay close attention to the reasons you give to justify the thinking. Is it possible that these are not your

actual reasons? Can you think of any other motives you might have? Consider alternative interpretations of the situation.

4. If you conclude that the feeling is irrational, express precisely why you think so.

5. Construct thinking that would represent a rational response in the situation.

Actively attack the irrational thinking with the thinking that is rational. Actively rehearse the thinking that represents a rational response.

For example, suppose I read an article about a fatal disease and come to the conclusion, from reading the symptoms, that I probably have the disease. I then become depressed. Late at night I think about how I will soon be dead, and I feel more and more depressed as a result. Clearly, the irrational feeling is the depression I am feeling. It is irrational because, until a doctor examines me and confirms a diagnosis, I have no good reason for believing that I actually have the disease in question. My irrational thinking is something like this:

> I have all the symptoms described in the article. So I must have this awful disease. I am going to die soon. My life is now meaningless. Why is this happening to me? Why me?

In the same situation, rational thinking would be something like this:

> Yes, it is possible that I have this disease, given that I seem to have the symptoms of it, but very often the same symptoms are compatible with many different bodily states. This being the case, it is not likely that I have this rare disease, and, in any case, it will do me no good to jump to conclusions. Still, as a matter of prudence and for peace of mind, I should go to the doctor as soon as possible to get a professional diagnosis. Until I get this diagnosis, I should focus my thinking on other, more useful things to think about than an unsubstantiated possibility.

Whenever I find myself feeling depressed about what the article said, I rerun the rational thinking through my mind and give myself a good talking-to as well:

> Hey, don't go off the deep end. Remember, you'll see the doctor on Monday. Don't put yourself through unnecessary pain. There are probably a lot of possibilities to account for your symptoms. Come back down to earth. Remember the Mother Goose rhyme, "For every problem under the sun, there is a solution or there is none. If there be one, seek 'til you find it. If there be none, never mind it." Don't wallow in misery when it doesn't do any good and only diminishes the quality of your life today.
>
> And now, how about scheduling some tennis for this afternoon, and a good movie for tonight?

17.2   *Think for Yourself*

FOCUSING ON THE RELATIONSHIP BETWEEN THOUGHTS, FEELINGS, AND DESIRES: PART I

Focusing on a negative feeling you sometimes or often experience, go through the five-point strategy outlined above, writing out your answers in detail.

A similar approach can be taken to changing irrational behavior grounded in irrational desires or motivations:

1. Identify the questionable behavior (behavior that is getting you in trouble, causing problems for you, or causing problems for someone else).

2. Identify the precise thinking leading to that behavior. What is the thinking that is generating the motivation to act in this manner?

3. Analyze the extent to which the thinking is justified, without leaving out any significant relevant information.

4. If the thinking is irrational, develop thinking that would be reasonable in this situation.

5. Actively attack the unreasonable thinking with reasonable thinking.

We might use many examples here to illustrate our point. But let's choose one that deals with a large segment of irrational human behavior. Here we are thinking of the many times when people abandon a commitment to change a bad habit because they are unwilling to work through the pain or discomfort that accompanies changing habits. Here's how the irrational behavior arises:

1. We notice that we have developed a bad habit that we would like to end. We realize, quite reasonably, that we shall have to make a change in our behavior. This could involve giving up any of the following habits: smoking, drinking too much alcohol, eating foods that are not good for us, not exercising enough, spending too much time watching television, spending too much money, not studying until just before an examination, or some other habit.

2. We make a resolution to change our bad habit.

3. For a short time, we do change our behavior, but during that time we experience pain or discomfort. These negative emotions discourage us. So we give up.

The irrational feelings are not the sensations of pain or discomfort. These emotions are to be expected. The irrational feeling is the discouragement that emerges from the discomfort and causes us to give up our resolution to change. This feeling is a result of irrational thinking (probably subconscious), which can be put into words roughly as:

I should be able to change my behavior without experiencing any pain or discomfort, even if I have had this habit for years. This pain is too much. I can't stand it. Furthermore, I really don't see how my changed behavior is helping much. I don't see much progress given all of my sacrifice. Forget it. It's not worth it.

This thinking makes no sense. Why should we expect to experience no pain or discomfort when we change a habit? Indeed, the reverse is true. Discomfort or pain of some kind is an essential byproduct of going through a process of withdrawal from almost any habit. The appropriate rational thinking is something like this:

Whenever I am trying to change a habit, I must expect to feel discomfort, and even pain. Habits are hard for anyone to break. But the only way I can expect to replace the habit with rational behavior is to endure the necessary suffering that comes with change. If I'm not willing to endure the discomfort that goes hand-in-hand with breaking a bad habit, I'm not really committed to change. Rather than expecting no pain, I must welcome it as a sign of real change. Instead of thinking, "Why should I have to endure this?" I rehearse the thinking, "Enduring this is the price I must pay for success." I must apply the motto: No pain, no gain.

17.3   *Think for Yourself*

FOCUSING ON THE RELATIONSHIP BETWEEN THOUGHTS, FEELINGS, AND DESIRES: PART 2

Focusing on some questionable behavior you sometimes engage in, go through the five-point strategy outlined above and write out your answers in detail. As soon as you have a chance, experiment with making some change in your behavior that you have been wanting to make. See if you can succeed with the new thinking at your disposal. Don't forget the essential ingredient of predicting, and accepting, discomfort or pain as a likely hurdle in the process of change.

Key Idea #2: There Is a Logic to This, and You Can Figure It Out

As a critical thinker, you approach every dimension of learning as requiring the construction of a system of meanings in your mind that makes sense and enables you to make logical inferences about the subject of your focus. The expression, "The logic of . . . " designates such a system. As a critical thinker, you recognize that there is a logic to academic subjects (a logic to chemistry, physics, mathematics, sociology). There is also a logic to questions, problems, and issues (a logic to economic questions, social problems, controversial issues, personal problems).

There is a logic to situations. There is a logic to personal behavior. There are explicit and implicit logics, admitted and hidden logics. There is a logic to warfare and a logic to peace, a logic to offense and a logic to defense. There are political logics, social logics, institutional logics, cultural logics.

There is a logic to the way the human mind works, a logic to power, a logic to domination, to mass persuasion, to propaganda, to manipulation. There is a logic to social conventions and a logic to ethical concepts and principles. There is theo-logic, bio-logic, and psycho-logic. There is even patho-logic (the logic of disease and malfunctioning). Each can be figured out by the disciplined, critical mind.

Using the elements of thought to figure out the basic logic of something is a practice to which we hope you are becoming accustomed. It is a powerful strategy for achieving perspective and gaining leverage or command. The following discussion is confined largely to the logic of personal life.

In every human situation or context, multiple systems of meaning are usually present. As a critical thinker, you engage in a process of figuring out why your parents, friends, teachers, and employers relate to you in the way they do. This is true because everyone makes sense of the situations of their own life in some way. To do this, they must make use, at least implicitly, of the eight elements of thought. If you can identify the elements of others' thinking, you can better understand where they are coming from.

You can assume all of the following:

Everyone you interact with has *purposes* or objectives they are trying to achieve.

Everyone has *problems* that relate to those purposes.

They are basing their reasoning on some *information*.

They come to *conclusions* based on that information, conclusions that may or may not be logical in the circumstance.

They take certain things for granted, or make certain *assumptions*.

They use certain key ideas or *concepts* in their thinking.

They think within a *point of view*, within a frame of reference that may keep them from seeing things objectively.

There are *consequences* that result from their thinking.

By assuming that there is always a logic to what happens in the world and also in the mind of those who operate in the world, you are empowered in your pursuit of understanding. You therefore are led to question superficial explanations and seek deeper ones. You are led to question:

the goals and *purposes* of those you interact with,

the way they define their *questions* and problems,

the *assumptions* they are making,

the *information* they are using to support their arguments,

the *conclusions* (inferences) they come to,

the *concepts* that guide their thinking,

the *implications* inherent in their thinking, and

the *point of view* from which they are looking at situations.

Just as you question the logic of the thinking of those around you, you also question the logic of your own thinking.

Strategic Idea

When you realize that there is a logic to everything, you can think-through the logic of the situations in which you find yourself. You can apply this principle in a number of directions, depending on your precise goals and objectives. Consider the questioning "inner voice" of the activist thinker focused on understanding the logic of his or her own thinking or the logic of others' thinking:

1. Questioning goals, purposes, and objectives. What is the central purpose of this person? This group? Myself? I realize that problems in thinking are often the result of a mistake at the level of basic purpose. I realize that I must develop skill in shifting my goals and purposes. I realize that I must be clear about my purposes, about others' purposes, about alternative purposes. I realize that I can always question my purposes, as well as the purposes of others.

2. Questioning the way in which questions are framed, problems are posed, issues are expressed. What issues have to be addressed in this situation? What is the key question I should raise? I realize that if the problem is misconceptualized, it will not be solved. If I have misconceived the question, I will not find the answer. Furthermore, I understand the value of sticking to the question at hand, of not wandering to other issues before effectively dealing with the question at issue. I want to be aware of situations in which others are failing to stick to the question at issue.

3. Questioning information and sources of information. What information do I need to gather to figure out what is going on? Where can I get it? How can I test it? What information are others using? Is it accurate? Is it relevant to the issue at hand? I realize that if I lack the information I need to effectively deal with this issue, my reasoning will be impaired. I also understand the problems inherent in using incorrect information in reasoning.

4. Questioning interpretations or conclusions. What interpretations, judgments, or conclusions are crucial to this situation? What conclusions am I coming to? What conclusions are others coming to? I understand that there is often more than one way to interpret situations. I value the ability to consider multiple ways to do so, weighing the pros and cons of each, before coming to a decision. I also want to be able to assess the quality of the conclusions that others are coming to.

5. Questioning the assumptions being made. What is being taken for granted? Is this a reasonable assumption? What would be reasonable to assume in this situation? I recognize that, because assumptions usually are unconscious in thinking, it is often difficult to determine what is being taking for granted. I want to be able to identify and correct my faulty assumptions. I also want to be able to accurately assess the assumptions others are using.

6. Questioning the concepts being used. What main ideas or concepts are being used? What implications follow from these ideas? What main ideas, or concepts, are crucial to making sense of this situation? I understand that whenever we think, we use concepts, and the way we use them both determines and is determined by the way we think in situations. Therefore, I must continually raise my awareness of the way concepts are being used, both by myself and by others.

7. Questioning the point(s) of view being considered. What point(s) of view have to be considered? Have I failed to take into account some point(s) of view that are relevant to understanding and thinking-through the issue? I realize that good reasoning often involves considering more than one way of looking at things. I therefore understand the value in being able to consider issues from multiple viewpoints. I recognize when others are unable or unwilling to see things from alternative viewpoints.

8. Questioning implications. Given the reasoning I am doing, what are the likely implications, positive and negative? What are the implications if I reason to this conclusion versus that conclusion? I understand that, whenever I reason, implications follow from my reasoning. Thus, I need to think-through the potential consequences of decisions I am considering. I also question the implications of others' thinking.

Just as we can seek to understand our own logic, we can seek to understand the logic of others. Perhaps an example will be helpful here. Imagine a person whose every-day life is based on the following thinking:

> The simple pleasures are the key to happiness: sleeping, gardening, walking, enjoying nature, telling jokes, listening to music, reading books. Don't seek more power or money than is necessary to get by. Don't seek to change the world in significant ways, because no matter what you do, nothing much will change. The people at the top will always be corrupt, and they will always have the power to hurt you. The large masses of people are lazy and irresponsible and always will be. Don't get involved in the affairs of others. Avoid gossip.

> Do not worry about what other people have. Don't worry about injustice; those who do unjust acts will naturally suffer negative consequences. Take things as they come. Don't take yourself too seriously. Be ready to laugh at yourself. Avoid conflict. When you do a job, do it well. Value your friends and support them. They will help you when you need them.

It would be of no use to attempt to persuade this person to become active in any social, political, or ethical cause. If you understand the basic logic of her thinking, you recognize that her response will always be the same: "You can't fight city hall. Don't worry about it. Those people will get their just desserts. Stay out of the battle. You can't do any good. And you probably will do yourself some harm."

The logic of this thinking has many implications, some positive, some negative. On the positive side, this thinking leads this person to enjoy life far beyond that enjoyed by most people, as she is continually seeing ordinary events—which most people treat as unimportant and insignificant—as objects of pleasure and delight. The simple act of looking out the window at a bird on a tree limb engenders inner warmth. On the negative side, she assumes no ethical responsibility for any action that is not directly within her immediate control. The logic of her thinking makes her indifferent to the fate of others who are not immediately connected to her. Though she is a reader, she reads only fiction, and that only for distraction and amusement.

Now let's put our commentary into the logic of this thinking in such a way as to pin down the elements of the logic inherent in it:

1. The main goal or *purpose* of this person is to enjoy life and to avoid involvement in any painful struggle. The first part of this purpose is fully justifiable because people have a right to enjoy life. The second part is questionable, and there is more than one way to evaluate it. Here is one reasonable way: On the one hand, insofar as this person would expect others to be concerned when injustice was done to her, she is obligated to help others who experience injustice. On the other hand, if she would not expect others to be at all concerned about any injustice she might experience, she is justified in not concerning herself with injustice being done to others.

2. The main issue or *question* for this person is something like this: How can I arrange the affairs of my life in such a way as to maximally enjoy the simple things of life and avoid involvement in any problems beyond those of my immediate family? In evaluating this question, the same reasoning would apply as that expressed in evaluating the purpose (in number 1 above).

3. The main *information* this person used in pursuing her goals was information about immediate matters of daily life. Again, use of this information is partially justified. It is justified in that this particular information enables the thinker to achieve her purpose. But the thinker fails to use information in her thinking that would enable her to contribute to making the world more just (information about the large number of people who are acting every day to improve conditions in the world, information about the large numbers of people who could be helped through some basic acts of kindness, and so on).

4. The main *assumptions* this person uses in thinking are: Simple pleasures are always available to everyone and are more important than socially praised possessions; in the world of power, nothing ever really changes; and only immediate family members have any ethical claims on us. Again, the first assumption is justifiable for the reason stated in *purpose* (number 1 above). The second assumption is simply not true. Even though power structures are difficult to change, they certainly can be changed through dedication and hard work. Many examples can be cited to support this point. With respect to the third assumption, she most likely would expect others, outside of her immediate family, to help her if some injustice were being done to her. Therefore, a likely unconscious assumption in her thinking is: "If some injustice is being done to me, I expect others to help me out. After all, I have a right to justice."

5. Some of the main *concepts* or principles this person uses in thinking are: The best way to live is to enjoy life's simple pleasures; no matter what you do, you can't change city hall; and people who behave in unethical ways will suffer the law of natural consequences. The first concept or principle, concerned with "simple pleasures," is being used justifiably because it helps her enjoy the small pleasures in life, to appreciate all of the many simple everyday joys. The second principle, "you can't change city hall," is not logical because every day, through diligence and perseverance, people help bring about improvement within institutions. The third principle, involving "natural consequences," is also illogical because many people are behaving unethically each and every day and suffering not at all while they are causing suffering to innocent others. By using this idea in thinking, she irrationally justifies her unwillingness to help make the world a more humane place.

6. The main *conclusion* (inference) this person comes to is: I can best enjoy life by keeping to myself and to my immediate family, by surrounding myself with the things I like, by taking time every day to appreciate the small joys that life brings. Given the information she uses in her thinking, her conclusions logically follow. Because she does not take into account information that would imply an ethical obligation to help reduce injustice, she concludes that she has no ethical obligations outside her immediate family.

7. The *points of view* of this person are: seeing every day as uncomplicated and filled with simple delights; and seeing her ethical obligations as applying only to her immediate family. This person is concerned only with her own point of view and those of her family members, but not of others.

8. The main *implications* of this person's thinking are that she will appreciate the many small pleasures in life but do nothing to contribute to the well-being of society. This person is concerned only with the implications that come with enjoying life. She is unconcerned about her doing nothing to help make the world a more just and humane place within which to live.

17.4   *Think for Yourself*

FOCUSING ON THE LOGIC OF SOMEONE'S THINKING

Think of someone you know well—a parent, a brother or sister, an employer, a friend. Try to figure out the logic of this person's thinking by focusing on the eight elements of his or her thought. Humans in many circumstances and contexts act with a hidden agenda. As a consequence, human behavior is often other than it seems to be. After figuring out the logic of this person's thinking, try to assess the thinking that he or she does within each element.

Complete this template:

1. The main purpose of this person is . . .
   I think this person is or is not justified in pursuing this purpose because . . .
2. The main issue for this person, and its related question, is . . .
   I think this question is/is not worth pursuing because . . .
3. The main information this person uses in pursuing his or her goals is . . .
   This information should/should not be used in this person's thinking because . . .
4. The main assumptions this person uses in thinking are . . .
   These assumptions are/are not justifiable because . . .
5. The main concepts this person uses in thinking are . . .
   These concepts are/are not being used justifiably because . . .
6. The main conclusions this person comes to are . . .
   These conclusions are/are not logical because . . .
7. The point of view of this person is . . .
   This person is/is not fully considering the relevant viewpoints of others because . . .
8. The main implications of this person's thinking are . . .
   This person is/is not concerned about these implications because . . .

Key Idea #3: For Thinking To Be of High Quality, We Must Routinely Assess It

Consistently high-quality thinking routinely assesses itself for flaws and then improves itself by replacing low-quality thinking with higher-quality thinking. As rational people, strongly motivated to improve our thinking, we not only think, but we think about our thinking from a critical vantage point. We routinely apply universal intellectual standards to our thought. That is, we continually strive to think in a clear, precise, accurate, relevant, logical, broad, deep, significant, and defensible way. We learn how to check our thinking regularly using these criteria.

Strategic Idea

As disciplined thinkers, we routinely apply intellectual standards to our thinking so as to assess and improve its quality. Consider the voice of a thinker focused on applying intellectual standards:

- **Focusing on clarity in thinking.** Am I clear about my thinking? Can I state it precisely? Can I elaborate on it in detail? Can I give an example from my experience? Can I illustrate it with an analogy or a metaphor? What about the thinking being expressed to me? Should I ask for the main point? Do I need an elaboration? Do I need an example? An illustration?

- **Focusing on precision in thinking.** Am I providing enough details for the other person to fully comprehend my meaning? Do I need more detail and specifics on the thinking of so-and-so?

- **Focusing on accuracy in thinking.** Am I certain that the information I'm using is accurate? If not, how can I check to see whether it is? How can I check on the accuracy of the information in this book?

- **Focusing on relevance in thinking.** How does my point bear on the issue at hand? Or does it? How does my statement relate to what he just said? How is his question related to the question we are discussing?

- **Focusing on logicalness in thinking.** Given the information I have gathered, what is the most logical conclusion I can come to in this situation? Or what is one of several logical conclusions? I'm not sure whether what he is saying is logical. What is another feasible conclusion? What is another conclusion that makes more sense? What are the logical consequences that might follow from this decision?

- **Focusing on breadth in thinking.** I wonder whether I need to consider another viewpoint, or other relevant viewpoints, before coming to a conclusion. In thinking-through the issue at hand, what points of view am I obligated to consider if I'm reasoning in a disciplined manner?

- **Focusing on depth in thinking.** What complexities are inherent in this issue? Am I inadvertently dealing with a complex issue in a superficial way? How can I dig beneath the surface of the situation and deal with what is most problematic in it?

■ **Focusing on justification in thinking.** Is his purpose justified? Is my purpose justified, given the circumstances, or is it somehow unfair or self-contradictory or self-defeating, given the facts? How is he using these terms? Is he using them in keeping with established usage? Is he stretching the meaning of the key words beyond the limit of their meaningfulness?

17.5 *Think for Yourself*

FOCUSING ON INTELLECTUAL STANDARDS IN QUESTIONING

Tape-record a conversation between you and a roommate, a parent, or someone else, in which you ask questions pertaining to intellectual standards. Select a complex question of interest to both of you, a question such as, "Is euthanasia ethically justifiable?" Or, "Should capital punishment be legal?" Or, "Are teachers fostering the development of intellectual skills that enable students to use their mind effectively?"

Begin with the broad question. Then practice asking the questions outlined in the strategy above, as appropriate. (This discussion should feel somewhat awkward to you, as you are still in the initial stages of learning the art of asking good questions.)

After you finish, play back the tape and analyze how well you asked questions of clarification, precision, relevance, and the rest. Use the questions we provided in this strategy as guidelines for your analysis.

STRATEGIC THINKING

PART TWO

As we learned in Chapter 17, strategic thinking is based on a two-part process that involves

1. Understanding a key idea.
2. Developing a strategy for action based on that idea.

This chapter is devoted to egocentrism—the most significant barrier to development of critical thinking. Chapter 17 covered the first three key ideas, so we begin with key idea #4.

Key Idea #4: Our Native Egocentrism Is a Default Mechanism

To understand the human mind, we must recognize its essential duality. On the one hand, the human mind has an instinctive tendency toward irrationality. On the other hand, the mind has a native capacity for rationality. To effectively take command of our mind, we must develop the ability to (1) monitor the mind's tendency toward egocentric or irrational thinking, and (2) attack it with corrective rational thought.

Our irrational mind is not concerned with the rights or needs of others. It has no ethical dimension. Properly developed, our rational mind is both intellectual and ethical. It has intellectual command of itself and ethical sensitivity as well. Intellectual skill and fair-mindedness are joined into one integrated mode of thinking. When our rational mind is underdeveloped or not engaged, however, our native egocentrism functions as a default mechanism. If we don't control it, it controls us!

Strategic Idea

It is possible for us to use our knowledge of egocentric thought to combat it. The more we know about human egocentrism, the more we can recognize it in ourselves, and thus the more we can attack or overrule it. One of the ways to achieve this end is to develop the habit of analyzing the logic of our own thinking. In the example that follows, we model the inner voice of the critical thinker using this strategy and these questions:

1. We can analyze our goals and purposes. What am I really after in this situation? Are my goals reasonable? Am I acting in good faith? Do I have any hidden agenda?

2. We can question the way we define problems and issues. Is this a reasonable way to put the question at issue? Am I biasing or loading the question by the way I am putting it? Am I framing the question in a self-serving way? Am I asking a question simply to pursue my selfish interests?

3. We can assess the information base of our thinking. What information am I basing my thinking on? Is that a legitimate source of information? Is there another source of information I need to consider? Am I considering all the relevant information— or only the relevant information that supports my view? Am I distorting the weight of the information in a self-serving way, blowing some of the information out of proportion while diminishing the value of other relevant information? Am I egocentrically refusing to check on the accuracy of some information because, if I find out it is not accurate, I will be forced to change my view?

4. We can rethink our conclusion or interpretation. Am I coming to an illogical conclusion because it is in my interest to do so? Am I refusing to look at this situation more logically because I simply don't want to, because if I do, I will have to behave differently?

5. We can analyze the ideas or concepts we are using in our thinking. How am I using the ideas most basic to my thinking? Am I using words in keeping with educated usage, or am I slanting or misusing some words to serve my vested interest?

6. We can identify and check our assumptions. What am I assuming or taking for granted? Are those assumptions reasonable? Are they in any way self-serving or one-sided? Am I making egocentric assumptions in my thinking (such as, "Everyone always dumps on me" or, "Life should be without problems" or, "There's nothing I can do; I'm trapped")? Are my expectations of others reasonable, or am I assuming a double standard?

7. We can analyze our point of view. Am I refusing to consider another relevant point of view so I can maintain my own self-serving view? Am I fully taking into account the viewpoint of others, or am I just going through the motions of "hearing" without actually listening to what others are saying? Put another way, am I honestly trying to understand the situation from another perspective, or am I merely trying to win an argument, to score points?

8. We can follow through on the implications of our thinking. Am I genuinely thinking-through the implications, or possible consequences, of my thoughts and behavior, or would I rather not consider them? Am I avoiding thinking-through implications because I don't want to know what they are (because then I will be forced to change my thinking, to think more rationally about the situation)?

Now let's walk through an example that suggests how a person might use reasonable thinking to detect irrational thought. What follows is a snapshot of the thinking of a hypothetical person as he examines a recent situation in his life. The numbered items 1 through 8 correspond to the list above.

The situation is as follows:

> I was in the video store on Friday night with my girlfriend, and we were choosing a movie to watch that evening. She wanted to watch a love movie, and I wanted to watch an action movie. I gave her all the reasons I could think of why the movie I wanted to watch was better. But now I realize that I was simply trying to manipulate her into going along with me. As I was giving her all of these good reasons for going along with my movie, all the while I was subconsciously thinking, "I should get to watch what I want to. I don't like love movies, so I shouldn't have to watch them. In addition, since I'm paying for the movie, I should get to choose it."

1. In this situation, my *purpose* was to convince my girlfriend that my reasoning for choosing the movie I wanted was better than her reasoning. I realize my purpose was egocentric because, now that I think of it, my reasoning wasn't any better than hers. My true purpose was to get what I wanted, even if I had to manipulate my girlfriend to get it.

2. The key *question* I was posing was: "What do I need to say to convince (or really manipulate) her into going along with my choice of movies?" I now realize this question was egocentric because it is unethical to act in bad faith toward anyone, especially toward someone I love. My question was completely selfish and shows that I really didn't care at all what my girlfriend wanted.

3. The main *information* I used in my reasoning was that I was paying for the movie, as well as information about how best to manipulate my girlfriend. This would mainly be what I have learned about her through my experience. For example, she usually goes along with me if I push hard enough, because she likes to please me. Also, I have learned that if I tell her that she always ends up liking the movies I choose, that usually convinces her to go along with me. Now that I think about it, I don't know if she really likes those movies or just says she does to please me. I know that I used this information in an egocentric way because I wasn't trying to look at information that would support our choosing *her* movie, just information to support my position. I wasn't noticing how I was leaving out relevant information that would support her position.

4. The main *conclusions* I came to were that we should choose the movie I wanted to watch, and that she probably would like it, too. I realize these conclusions were irrational because they were based completely on selfish thinking and enabled me to feel good about choosing the movie I wanted.

5. The key *concepts* I was using in my thinking were manipulation, because my main purpose was to manipulate her into going along with me, and the principle, "Whoever is paying for the movie should get to choose what we will watch." I realize I wasn't justified in using these concepts in my thinking, because they were completely self-serving and caused me to act in an unethical way.

6. The main *assumptions* I was using in my thinking were: "If I can effectively manipulate my girlfriend, I can get what I want. If my girlfriend acts like she likes the movies I choose, she does like them. Whoever pays for the movie should get to choose it." I realize these assumptions were egocentrically formulated because they are not based in sound reasoning. And they were enabling me to justify my unethical behavior.

7. The *point of view* from which I was reasoning was in seeing my girlfriend as someone to be easily manipulated, and seeing myself as justified in choosing the movie because I was paying for it. I realize these points of view were egocentric because I cannot be justified in acting in bad faith toward someone I love.

8. The *implications* that followed from my thinking were that I was able to manipulate her, but she probably resented having to go along with my choice of movie. Also, she was not able to enjoy the movie she wanted because I insisted on having my way. I realize these implications would not have occurred if I had been thinking and behaving rationally. If I had been rational, I would have thought and behaved in a way that demonstrated that I respected the desires of my girlfriend. She would have enjoyed the time we spent together more by watching what she wanted, and knowing that I was willing to do something for her rather than always expecting her to sacrifice for me.

18.1   *Think for Yourself*

FOCUSING ON THE LOGIC OF YOUR EGOCENTRIC THINKING

Identify a situation you were recently in where, in looking back on the situation, you realize you probably were irrational. Go through each of the elements of your reasoning as described in the strategy above, analyzing the justifiability of your thinking and behavior. Try to be as honest as you possibly can, remembering that our egocentrism is ready to deceive us. Complete the following statements:

The situation was as follows . . .

1. In this situation my purpose was . . .
   I realize my purpose was egocentric because . . .
2. The key question I was posing was . . .
   I realize this question was egocentric because . . .
3. The main information I used in my reasoning was . . .
   I know that I used this information in an egocentric way because . . .
4. The main conclusions I came to were . . .
   I realize these conclusions were irrational because . . .
5. The key concepts I was using in my thinking were . . .

I realize I wasn't justified in using these concepts in this way, and that I was irrationally distorting them, because . . .

6. The main assumptions I was using in my thinking were . . .

   I realize these assumptions were egocentrically formulated because . . .

7. The point of view from which I was reasoning was . . .

   I realize this point of view was egocentric because . . .

8. The implications that followed from my thinking were . . .

   I realize these implications would not have occurred if I had been thinking and be-having rationally. If I had been rational, I would have thought and behaved in the following way . . .

Key Idea #5: We Must Become Sensitive to the Egocentrism of Those Around Us

Because human beings are, by nature, egocentric and few are aware of how to exercise control over our egocentric thinking, it is important that we develop the ability to rec-ognize egocentrism in the thinking of those around us. We must recognize, though, that even highly egocentric people sometimes act rationally, so we must be careful not to stereotype. Nevertheless, it is reasonable to expect that everyone will behave irra-tionally sometimes, so we must learn to evaluate behavior in an open-minded, yet real-istic, way. When we understand the logic of egocentrism, when we become adept at identifying its self-serving patterns, we can begin to master it.

We draw a distinction between attacking our own irrationality and attacking that of others. Often with others, we must bite our lip, as it were, and distance ourselves from people who are fundamentally irrational. Or, at least, we must learn to deal with their egocentrism indirectly. Few people will thank us for pointing out egocentrism in their thinking. The more egocentric people are, the more resistant they are to owning it. The more power egocentric people have, the more dangerous they are. As rational persons, then, we learn to better deal with the irrationality of others rather than be controlled or manipulated by it.

When thinking irrationally, people find it difficult to think within the perspective of another. We unconsciously refuse to consider information that contradicts our ego-centered views. We unconsciously pursue purposes and goals that are not justifiable. We use assumptions in our thinking that are based in our own prejudices and biases. Unknowingly, we are engaging systematically in self-deception to avoid recognizing our egocentrism in operation.

Another problem relevant to dealing with the egocentric reactions of others is our own egocentric tendency. When we interact with others who are relating to us egocen-trically, our own irrational nature is easily stimulated into action or, to put it more in-formally, our buttons are easily pushed. When others relate to us in an ego-centered way, violating our rights and/or ignoring our legitimate needs, our own native egocen-trism likely will assert itself. Ego will meet ego in a struggle for power. When this happens, everyone loses. We therefore must anticipate our own egocentric reactions and come up with the appropriate rational thinking to deal with it.

Strategic Idea

Once we are aware that humans are naturally egocentric, and that most people are unaware of their native egocentrism, we can conclude that, in any given situation, we well may be interacting with the egocentric rather than the rational dimensions of those persons' minds. We therefore can question whether they are presenting rational ideas and pursuing rational purposes, or whether they are operating with irrational motives of which they themselves are unaware. We will not take for granted that others are relating to us in good faith. Rather, we will observe their behavior carefully to determine what their behavior actually implies.

Moreover, because we know that our irrational nature is easily activated by irrationality in others, we can carefully observe and assess our own thinking to ensure that we do not become irrational in dealing with others who are egocentric. We will be on the lookout for our own ego-centered thinking, and when we recognize it, we will take steps to "wrestle it down" and refuse to be drawn into irrational games—whether initiated by others or by our own egocentric tendencies. When we realize we are dealing with an irrational person, we will not let that person's irrationality summon our irrational nature. We will refuse to be controlled by the unreasonable behavior of others.

Strategically, the best thing to do is to avoid contact with highly egocentric people whenever possible. When we find ourselves deeply involved with that sort of people, we should seek a way to disengage ourselves when possible. When disengagement is not possible, we should minimize contact or act in such a way as to minimize stimulating their ego.

We can minimize the stimulation to a person's ego by recognizing the conditions under which most highly egocentric reactions take place—namely, when people feel threatened, humiliated, or shamed, or when their vested interest or self-image is significantly involved. By getting into the habit of reconstructing in our own minds the point of view of others, and therefore of frequently thinking within the perspective of others, it is possible to anticipate many of the egocentric reactions of those around us. We then can choose a course of action that sidesteps many of the land mines of human egocentrism.

18.2, 18.3   *Think for Yourself*

DEALING WITH THE EGOCENTRISM OF OTHERS

Think of a recent situation in which you believed someone you were interacting with became irrational in his or her response to you. Complete these statements:

1. The situation was . . .
2. What I did/said was . . .
3. The reaction of this person was . . .

4. I believe this person's thinking was . . .

5. I think this reaction/thinking was egocentric because . . .

6. The best response I could have made to this egocentric behavior would have been . . .

7. I might have been able to avoid stimulating an egocentric response in the first place by . . .

RECOGNIZING WHEN ANOTHER PERSON'S EGOCENTRISM BRINGS OUT YOUR EGOCENTRISM

Think of a recent situation in which you felt yourself becoming irrational in reaction to someone else's irrationality. Complete these statements:

1. The situation was . . .

2. I reacted in the situation by . . .

3. In thinking through the situation, I realize that a more rational way to respond to the other person would have been . . .

Key Idea #6: The Mind Tends to Generalize Beyond the Original Experience

One of the important truths that Jean Piaget, the noted child psychologist, discovered about children is that they overgeneralize their immediate feelings. If something good happens to them, the whole world looks good to them. If something bad happens to them, the whole world looks bad to them. He called this phenomenon egocentric immediacy.

What Piaget did not emphasize, however, is that the same reaction patterns are found in much adult thinking. It is fair to say that everyone has some difficulty putting the ups and downs of daily life into a long-range perspective. Given the strength of our immediate (emotional) reactions, it is not easy to keep things in proper perspective.

Once we begin to interpret situations or events in our life as negative, we also tend to generalize that negativity and even, on occasion, to allow it to cast a gloom over our whole life. A broad-based pessimism or a foolish optimism can come to permeate our thinking when negative or positive events happen to us. We move rapidly from thinking of one or two events in our lives as negative (or positive) to thinking of everything in our lives as negative (or positive). Egocentric negative thinking easily leads to indulgent self-pity. And egocentric positive thinking easily leads to an unrealistic state of complacent comfort.

Even a whole nation can be stampeded into an unrealistic state of complacent comfort by the reporting of one positive event. Hence, in England in 1938, after Neville Chamberlain returned to England from Munich, holding an agreement with Hitler in his hand, he declared, "Peace for our time!" Most of the people in England rejoiced triumphantly over the success of having obtained Hitler's agreement, without factoring into their thinking Hitler's consistent record of broken promises. The entire nation was transformed into a state of national euphoria brought on by egocentric immediacy.

Rational voices like that of Winston Churchill, expressing skepticism that Hitler would be satisfied with this concession, were thrust aside as alarmist and without foundation. But Churchill had looked at the events at hand using a long-term, realistic perspective.

Consider an everyday problem for many people who tend to see the world in largely negative terms. They wake up in the morning and have to deal with a few unexpected minor problems. As the day progresses, and as they deal with more "problems," everything in their lives appears negative. The snowball of bad things happening gets bigger and bigger as the day passes. By the end of the day, they are unable to see any positive things in their lives. Their thinking (usually tacit of course) is something like this:

> Everything looks bad. Life isn't fair. Nothing good ever happens to me. I always have to deal with problems. Why does everything bad happen to me?

Controlled by these thoughts, they lack the ability to counteract unbridled negativity with rational thoughts. They can't see the many good things in their lives. Their egocentric mind is shielding them from the full range of facts that would change their way of thinking so they could see things in a more realistic and, in this case, a more positive light.

Strategic Idea

If we intervene with rational thoughts at the point at which egocentric negativity begins, before it completely pervades the mind's functioning, we have a better chance of reducing or overthrowing it. The first step requires that we become intimately familiar with the phenomenon of egocentric immediacy. Then we should begin to identify instances of it in our own life as well as the lives of those around us.

The second step requires that we develop a rich and comprehensive list of the facts of our lives. It is important that we develop this list not when we are in the throes of an egocentric "fit" but, instead, when we are viewing the world from a rational perspective.

We also want to develop a long-range perspective to call upon when necessary to give the proper weight to individual events, whether positive or negative. We must establish in our mind what our most important values are. We must frame in our mind a long-range historical perspective. We must bring those values and this perspective strongly before our mind when lesser values and the distortions of egocentric immediacy begin to dominate our thoughts and feelings. When we have a well-established "big picture" in our mind, what are in effect small events will remain small, not blown out of proportion.

When we perceive that our thinking is tending toward egocentric immediacy, we can actively undermine it through comprehensive rational thinking. This involves reasoning with ourselves, pointing out flaws in our thinking, identifying and presenting relevant information we are ignoring, pointing out information we are distorting, checking our assumptions, and tracking the implications of our thinking.

In short, by developing a deep and comprehensive "big picture" in our mind, by keeping this comprehensive view as much as possible in the foreground of our thinking in daily life, we can minimize our own tendency toward egocentric immediacy. We can become skilled in recognizing what is truly small and large in our life. We can chart our course more effectively, navigating through passing storms and deceptively quiet seas alike.

18.4 *Think for Yourself*

"BIG PICTURE" THINKING

Think of a situation you were recently in where you felt an intense negative emotion that generated a chain reaction of further negative states in your mind, leading to a generalized feeling of depression. At that moment, your life looked bleak and unforgiving. Figure out the "big picture" thinking that was missing from your mind as you fell prey to egocentric immediacy.

Complete these statements:

1. The objective situation was as follows:
2. I responded irrationally to the situation by . . .
3. I felt these negative emotions:
4. The "big picture" thinking that I needed but didn't develop is something like the following:
5. The information I was failing to consider in my thinking was . . .
6. I can best avoid this situation in the future by . . .
7. I now realize . . .

Key Idea #7: Egocentric Thinking Appears to the Mind as Rational

One of the primary reasons human beings have difficulty recognizing egocentric thinking is that it appears to the mind as perfectly reasonable. No person says to himself or herself, "I shall think irrationally for a while." When we are most under the sway of irrational states (for example, in a state of irrational rage), we typically feel indignant and unfairly put-upon. Egocentric thinking blinds us in a variety of ways. We deceive ourselves.

When we are irrational, we feel rational. Our perceptions seem totally justified. And not recognizing any flaws in our thinking, we see no reason to question those thoughts. We see no reason to behave differently. The result is that there is little or no chance of overriding the dysfunctional behavior that is dominating us. This is especially true when our egocentric thinking is working to get us what we want.

Strategic Idea

Once we recognize that egocentric thinking appears in the human mind as rational thinking, once we can exemplify this truth with specific examples from our own life, we are potentially in a position to do something. We can learn to anticipate egocentric self-deception. For one thing, we can educate ourselves about the signs of it. We look for signs of shutting down—not really listening to those who disagree with us, stereotyping those who disagree with us, ignoring relevant evidence, reacting in an emotional manner, and rationalizing our irrational behavior (thinking of justifications for our behavior that have little to do with our actual motivation). Consider the following examples:

Situation 1: You are driving to school. You fail to notice that the off-ramp you must get off on is near. You recognize it at the last moment. You cut off someone to get to the off-ramp. He blows his horn at you and shouts. You shout back. You then are cut off by yet another car in a few minutes, and you blow your horn and shout at him.

During such events, you feel an inner sense of "rightness." After all, you had to get to school on time. You didn't mean to cut off anyone. The other guy clearly had no right to cut you off. We often use this kind of simplistic thinking when we deceive ourselves. We ignore evidence against our view. We highlight evidence for our view. We experience negative emotions accordingly. And we easily feel an acute sense of righteousness about how we think, feel, and act.

Situation 2: You come back to your room after performing badly on a test. Your roommate is playing music loudly and singing in the kitchen. You say, "Could we please have some peace and quiet around here for once!" Your roommate says, "What's bugging you?" You slam the door to your room and stay there for an hour, feeling depressed and angry. You come out and your roommate is talking with a friend. They ignore you. You say, "Well, you two are really friendly, aren't you!" You walk out, slamming the door.

Sometimes in cases like this, we recover from our egocentric immediacy after we cool off. But during the actual events that set us off, we feel righteous in our anger and justified in our depression. We have no trouble thinking of reasons to feed our righteousness or intensify our anger. We can dig up grievances from the past. We can go over them in our mind, blowing them up as much as we care to. We do this with no sense of our own self-deception.

In principle, we are capable of learning to catch ourselves in the process of engaging in deception or distortion. We can develop the habit of doing the following:

1. Looking at all events from the point of view of those we disagree with, as well as from our own. If we are in a conversation, we can check ourselves by repeating to the person our understanding of what he or she is saying, and why.

2. Becoming suspicious of our account of things whenever we seem completely correct to ourselves while those we disagree with seem completely wrong.

3. Suspending judgment of people and events when we are in the throes of intense emotions. Reserving judgment for moments when we can quietly question ourselves and review facts with relative objectivity.

18.5 *Think for Yourself*

RECOGNIZING AND REPLACING IRRATIONAL THINKING

Think of a situation you were in recently when you thought at the time that you were perfectly rational—which you now realize consisted of self-deception. Complete these statements:

1. The situation was as follows:
2. I behaved in the situation by . . .
3. At the time, I thought I was rational because . . .
4. Now I think I may have been irrational because . . .
5. I rationalized my behavior by telling myself . . .
6. The real reason I behaved the way I did is . . .

Key Idea #8: The Egocentric Mind Is Automatic in Nature

Egocentric thinking, unlike rational thought, operates in a highly automatic, unconscious, impulsive manner. Based in primitive, often "childish," thought patterns, it reacts to situations in programmed and mechanistic ways. We must recognize, therefore, that it often will spring into action before we have a chance to sidestep or prevent it. It fights. It flees. It denies. It represses. It rationalizes. It distorts. It negates. It scapegoats. And it does all of these in the blink of an eye with no conscious awareness of its deceptive tricks.

Strategic Idea

Because we know that the irrational mind operates in predictable, preprogrammed, automated ways, we become interested observers of the egocentric mechanisms of our own mind. We begin to observe the mechanistic moves our mind makes. Rather than allowing thoughts to operate strictly at the unconscious level, we can actively strive to raise them to conscious realization, as Piaget put it. We can work to bring them into full consciousness. This typically will be after the fact—especially in the beginning of our development as critical thinkers. After a time, when we become keenly aware of how our personal ego functions, we can often forestall egocentric reactions by the prior activity of rational thought.

For instance, as presented in key idea #7, we can begin to recognize when our mind rationalizes in predictable ways. We also can become familiar with the kinds of rationalization our mind tends to use. For example, "I don't have time to do this!" is a favorite rationalization. We could limit its use by remembering the insight, "People invariably have time for the things that are most important to us." We then are forced to face the truth about what we are doing: "I don't want to make room in my priorities for this," or,

"Since I continually say this is important to me, I'm only deceiving myself by saying, 'but I don't have time for it.'"

After time, and with practice, we can begin to notice when we are denying some important truth about ourselves. We can begin to see when we are refusing to face some reality rather than dealing with it openly and directly. We can begin to recognize when we are automatically thinking in a dishonest way, in attempting to avoid working on a solution to a problem.

In principle, then, we can study the tricks and stratagems of our mind to determine its automated patterns. Furthermore, and most important, we can learn to intervene to disengage irrational thought processes—if necessary, after they have begun to operate. In short, we can refuse to be controlled by primitive desires and modes of thinking. We can actively work to replace automatic egocentric thinking with reflective rational thinking.

18.6   *Think for Yourself*

FOCUSING ON DENIAL AS A MECHANISM OF IRRATIONALITY

Although the egocentric dimension of the mind uses many defense mechanisms to maintain its self-centered view, we will single out just one for this activity: denial. Think of a relationship you are in now in which you have a selfish interest in seeing things a certain way though the facts probably don't support your view. Let's say you want to believe that your boyfriend or girlfriend really loves you, even though his or her actual behavior toward you indicates that he or she likely is using you (perhaps as a vehicle of his or her self-gratification).

As another example, let's say that you want to believe you are treating your significant other respectfully, though the facts show that you often treat him or her with little respect and consideration. Admitting the truth would be painful to you. Complete these statements:

1. The situation is . . .
2. What I have denied accepting in this situation is . . .
3. I have avoided the truth by telling myself the following untruth:
4. I realize I have denied looking at the truth in the situation because . . .
5. Some implications that have followed from my denial about this situation are . . .

Key Idea #9: We Often Pursue Power Through Dominating or Submissive Behavior

When thinking irrationally or egocentrically, the human mind often seeks to achieve its goals by either dominating or submissive behavior. Put another way, when under the sway of egocentrism, we try to get our way either by dominating others or by gaining their support through outward submission to them. Although bullying (dominating) and groveling (submitting) are often subtle in nature, they nonetheless are common in human life.

Power is not bad in itself. We all need some power to rationally fulfill our needs. But in human life it is common for power to be sought as an end in itself, or used for unethical purposes. One of the typical ways for egocentric people and sociocentric groups to gain power is by dominating weaker people or groups. Another way is by playing a subservient role toward a more powerful other to get what they want. Much of human history could be told in terms of the use of these two egocentric functions of individuals and groups. Much individual behavior can be understood by seeing the presence of these two patterns in the behavior of individuals.

Though everyone tends to use one of these behavior patterns more than the other, everyone uses both of them to some extent. Some children, for example, play a role of subservience toward their parents while abusively bullying other children. Of course, when a bigger and tougher bully comes along, the weaker bully often becomes subservient to the stronger one.

When we are egocentrically dominating or submitting, we do not readily recognize that we are doing so. For example, people presumably attend rock concerts to enjoy the music. But members of the audience often act in a highly submissive (adoring, idolizing) way toward the musicians. Many people literally throw themselves at the feet of celebrities or take their own definition of significance from distantly attaching themselves to a celebrity, if only in their imagination. In like manner, sports fans often idolize and idealize their heroes, who appear bigger than life to them. If their team or their hero is successful, they vicariously feel successful and more powerful. "We really whipped them!" translates as, "I'm important and successful just as my hero is."

Rational people may admire other people but do not idolize or idealize them. Rational people may form alliances, but not ones in which they are dominated by others. They expect no one to submit to them blindly. They blindly submit to no one. Although none of us fully embodies this rational ideal, critical thinkers continually work toward it in all their relationships.

By the way, traditional male and female sex-role conditioning entails the man dominating the woman and the woman playing a submissive role toward her man. Women were to gain power by attaching themselves to powerful men. Men displayed power in achieving domination over women. These traditional roles are far from dead in present male/female relationships. In many ways the media, for example, still portray men and women in traditional gender roles. Because of these and other societal influences, men tend to be more dominating than submissive. Conversely, women *tend* to be more submissive, especially in intimate relationships.

Strategic Idea

If we realize the prominent role that egocentric domination and submission play in human life, we can begin to observe our own behavior to determine when we are irrationally dominating or submitting to others. When we understand that the mind naturally uses numerous methods for hiding its egocentrism, we recognize that to identify dominating and submissive patterns we must scrutinize our own mental functioning carefully. With practice, we can begin to identify our own patterns of domination and submission. At the same time, we can observe others' behavior, looking for similar patterns.

We can look closely at the behavior of our supervisors, our friends, our significant others, our parents, noticing when they tend to irrationally dominate and/or submit to the will of others.

In short, the more we study patterns of domination and submission in human life, the more we are able to detect them in our own life and behavior. And only when we become adept at detecting them can we take steps toward changing them.

18.7   *Think for Yourself*

RECOGNIZING SUBMISSIVE AND DOMINATING BEHAVIOR IN OURSELVES

During the next week, closely observe your behavior patterns to determine whether you tend to behave in a dominating or a submissive manner when you are egocentrically pursuing your desires. Take notes on your behavior during the week. At the end of the week, complete the following statements:

1. I observed myself behaving in a dominating way in the following situations:
2. Some implications of this behavior are . . .
3. In future similar situations, I will modify my behavior in the following ways:
4. I observed myself behaving in a submissive way in the following situations:
5. The implications of this behavior were . . .
6. In future similar situations, I will modify my behavior in the following ways:

Key Idea #10: Humans Are Naturally Sociocentric Animals

In addition to humans' being naturally egocentric, we are easily drawn into sociocentric thinking and behavior. Groups offer us security to the extent that we internalize and unthinkingly conform to their rules, imperatives, and taboos. When growing up, we learn to conform to many groups. Peer groups especially tend to dominate our life. Our unconscious acceptance of the values of the group leads to the unconscious standard: "It's true if we believe it." There seems to be no belief so absurd but that some group of humans irrationally accepts it as rational.

Not only do we accept the belief systems of the groups to which we belong but, most important, we act on those belief systems. For example, many groups are anti-intellectual in nature. Groups may expect any number of dysfunctional behaviors. For example, some youth groups expect members to abuse outsiders verbally and physically (as proof of power or courage).

In addition to face-to-face groups we are in, we are influenced indirectly by large-scale social forces that reflect our membership in society at large. In capitalist societies, for example, the dominant thinking is that people should strive to make as much money as possible, though this form of thinking, it might be argued, encourages people to accept a large gap between the "haves" and "have-nots" as right and normal.

Or consider this: Within mass societies, the nature of and solution to most public issues and problems are presented in sensationalized soundbites by the television and news media. As a result, people often come to think about complex problems in terms of simplistic, media-fostered solutions. Many people are led to believe that expressions such as "Get tough with criminals!" and "Three strikes and you're out!" represent plausible ways to deal with complex social problems.

What's more, the portrayal of life in Hollywood movies exerts a significant influence on how we conceptualize ourselves, our problems, and our lives. Sociocentric influences are at work at every level of social life in both subtle and blatant ways. There are many sociocentric forces in society.

Strategic Idea

Humans are naturally sociocentric. We must take possession of the idea that, because we are all members of social groups, our behavior reflects the imperatives and taboos of the groups to which we belong. We all, to a greater or lesser extent, conform uncritically to the rules and expectations of the groups of which we are members. When we recognize this, we can begin to analyze and assess that to which we conform. We can actively analyze the rules and taboos of the groups we are aligned with. We can rationally think-through the groups' expectations to determine the extent to which they are reasonable.

When we identify irrational expectations, we can refuse to adhere to those requirements. We can shift our group memberships from those that are flagrantly irrational to those that are more rational. Indeed, we can actively create new groups, groups that emphasize the importance of integrity and fair-mindedness, groups that encourage their members to develop independence of thought and work together in that pursuit.

Or we can minimize the groups we belong to—except the social groups we cannot escape. With respect to the large-scale sociocentric influences to which we are subjected by the mass media, we can develop an ongoing critical sensitivity that minimizes our falling prey to group think. In short, by understanding our personal relationship to sociocentric thinking, we can begin to take charge of the influence that groups have over us. We can significantly reduce that influence.

18.8   *Think for Yourself*

RECOGNIZING PROBLEMS IN SOCIOCENTRIC THINKING

Identify a group to which you belong. It can be a small group of friends, a club, a religious group, or a large, non–face-to-face cultural group of which you are a part. Complete the following statements:

1. The group I am focused on is . . .
2. The taboos or behaviors not allowed within the group are . . .
3. The injunctions or requirements are . . .

4. In analyzing my behavior in this group, I realize . . . about myself.

5. After analyzing this group's taboos and injunctions, I think it is/is not in my interest to be involved in this group, for these reasons:

Key Idea #11: Developing Rationality Requires Work

Significant development of one's rational capacities takes many years. The "gotta have it now" attitude prevalent in our culture creates a significant barrier to the development of higher-order human capacity. If we want to reap the benefits of a developed mind, there are no easy shortcuts. If we want to become better at reasoning-through the complex issues we inevitably will face, we must be committed to that end. Just as baseball players must practice the moves of baseball again and again to be highly skilled at the game, so must committed thinkers.

Strategic Idea

Because we understand that daily practice is crucial to the development of our rational capacity, we can develop the habit of asking ourselves what we are doing today to further our intellectual growth. We realize that we must make it a habit to identify our selfish interests—and correct for their influence over our thinking. When we discover that our selfish nature is often driving the decisions we are making, we can intervene through good-faith empathy with alternative points of view.

We can develop the habit of assessing the extent to which we use the intellectual standards of clarity, accuracy, logicalness, significance, breadth, depth, and justifiability to assess and improve our thinking. For example, to develop the habit of checking our thoughts for clarity, we can regularly elaborate, and give examples and illustrations when we are presenting our views to others. We also can regularly ask others to elaborate upon, illustrate, and exemplify their ideas when they are expressing their ideas to us. We can aim to develop similar habits with respect to using the other standards, and periodically assess ourselves to determine whether and to what extent those habits are developing. We can, and should, practice developing an inner voice that leads to routine questioning of ourselves and others.

18.9   *Think for Yourself*

GETTING IN THE HABIT OF DAILY CRITICAL THINKING

During the next 7 days, document something you do every day that develops your ability to think well. Complete the following statements for each day:

1. Today I engaged in the following thinking/behavior that demonstrates my commitment to becoming a critical thinker:

2. Before I started learning about critical thinking, I would have behaved in the following way in similar situations, rather than in the way described in number 1:

3. My new way of thinking/behaving is better because . . .

CONCLUSION

To develop a disciplined mind—a mind that takes responsibility for the quality of its inner workings and continually seeks to upgrade its abilities—presupposes two overlapping, yet distinct principles. First, we must develop a deep understanding of how our mind functions. Concepts, principles, and theories serving this end are the focus of this book. It is not enough to read about these concepts, principles, and theories, though. We must internalize them to the point at which we can use them routinely to develop unique strategies for targeting and improving the quality of our thinking. When we haven't internalized them well enough to effectively improve our thinking, they are of little or no use to us.

Authentic strategic thinking is thinking that takes a principle or an idea from the theoretical plane and, following out its implications on the practical plane, develops a course of action designed to improve what we think, feel, or do. As you think-through your behavior, and the patterns of thought that now rule your life, the important question is: How are you going to take important ideas and work them into your thinking so your behavior will change for the better? How will you move from abstract understanding to applying understanding to improve your life? Only when you are doing strategic thinking regularly—the strategic thinking outlined in this chapter—can you begin to significantly improve as a thinker.

BECOMING AN ADVANCED THINKER

OUR CONCLUSION

I n any domain of skills, well-designed practice should result in improvement, and consistent improvement in advancement. The chapters in this book provide ample exercises and tools for beginning to practice the art of skilled thinking. If we make a personal commitment to develop as thinkers, we all should be able to practice in such a way as to advance. As our practice becomes more and more intuitive, we should move in the direction of mastering the tools.

For example, we would expect advanced thinkers to develop the habit of analyzing their thinking. We would expect that, with advanced practice, significant insight into problems at deeper levels of thought would emerge. We would expect advanced thinkers to acquire significant command over our innate egocentric and sociocentric nature. We would expect significant evidence of emerging fair-mindedness and intellectual humility and perseverance.

PRACTICING SKILLED THINKING

We would withhold the term *advanced thinker*—the fifth stage of development—from those who do not systematically monitor the role in their thinking of concepts, assumptions, inferences, implications, points of view—in other words, from anyone who cannot take apart their thinking. We also would withhold this descriptor from those who do not develop the habit of evaluating their thinking for clarity, accuracy, precision, relevance, logicalness, and significance.

Some other important characteristics of advanced thinkers as we are conceptualizing them are

- an understanding of the powerful role that thinking plays in the quality of their life;
- an understanding of the intimate relationships among thoughts, feelings, and desires;
- regular monitoring of their thoughts, feelings, and desires;
- effective use of a range of strategies for improving their thinking;
- the habit of regularly critiquing their plans for improvement;
- the intellectual insight and perseverance to develop new, fundamental habits of thought;
- a deep commitment to intellectual integrity;
- sensitivity to inconsistency and contradictions in their life;
- the intellectual empathy necessary to put themselves in the place of others;
- the intellectual courage to face and fairly address ideas, beliefs, or viewpoints toward which they have strong negative emotions.

STAGE 5: REACHING THE ADVANCED STAGE OF DEVELOPMENT

There is a broad continuum in both the practicing and the advanced stages. No magic divide unambiguously separates these stages. Nevertheless, we know, roughly speaking, that we are reaching the stage we call the *advanced thinker* when we find that our regimen for rational living is paying off in significant ways. Here is a list of patterns that we take to be characteristic of those who have moved to an advanced stage in their command of thought. We don't assume that anyone will be equally developed in all of these patterns:

- We now are routinely identifying problems in our thinking and are working successfully to deal with those problems rationally.
- We have successfully identified the significant domains in our lives in which we need to improve (e.g., as student, employee, parent, husband, wife, consumer) and are making significant progress in all or most of these domains.
- We find aspiring to reasonability is no longer a strain.
- We continue to find evidence of egocentricity in our thoughts, emotions, and behavior, but at the same time we are finding that we can often, if not usually, overcome those thoughts and emotions and shift our behavior accordingly.
- We no longer find it difficult to admit when we are wrong.

- We are attracted to people who give us constructive criticism.

- We now are enjoying the process of observing our mind in action.

- We enjoy entering into the points of view of others.

- We take satisfaction from learning from the thinking of those with whom we have significant differences.

- We now see assumptions in our thinking whenever we think.

- We are no longer concerned with the image we maintain, are largely indifferent to what others think of us, are comfortable standing up in opposition to popular beliefs in the groups to which we belong.

- We find satisfying and fulfilling the process of assessing our behavior, motivations, and feelings to determine the extent to which they result from faulty thinking.

- We continue to find many ways to correct our thinking and shift our feelings.

- Because we have used our thinking as the leverage point for changing our feelings, desires, and action on many occasions, we now find ourselves doing so more intuitively, and often without significant effort.

- We have come to understand, through routine analysis of our behavior and thoughts, the problems that egocentricity and sociocentricity create in human lives.

- We now realize that our development is directly dependent on the extent to which we are successfully decreasing the role of egocentric thinking in our daily life. We now understand our use of domination and submissiveness.

- We now realize that egocentric thinking is not a reasonable mode of thinking—however natural it might be.

- We now are skilled in detecting egocentric thinking in ourselves and also in identifying it in others.

- We now routinely figure out the logic of the thinking of other people and frequently recognize when others are acting egocentrically.

- We recognize when others are attempting to manipulate us inappropriately into submission, or when they are trying to force us to back down through domination.

- We routinely write down our thoughts so we can better analyze them.

- We articulate our thoughts to other rational people as a check to ensure that we are not interpreting the situation illogically, to ensure against our unconsciously thinking in a self-centered manner.

- We recognize that we must give active voice to what is going on in our mind because of our natural tendency toward deception.

- We often use inner dialogue to check our thinking and improve it. Consider the following examples of the kind of inner dialogue that advanced thinkers engage in.

EXAMPLES OF INNER DIALOGUE

- I'm not clear about what this person is trying to communicate to me. I need to ask questions of clarification. I should ask her to elaborate on her point. I think I also need an example of what she's talking about.

- I'm not sure whether what he is saying is relevant to the issue at hand, whether his information is relevant to the question we are trying to solve, whether his question is relevant to the focus of this meeting.

- It seems that there is something illogical about the way I have interpreted this situation. Perhaps I've jumped to some conclusions before gathering all the relevant information. Perhaps I've come to this conclusion based on inaccurate information. Perhaps my interpretation is based strictly on my self-interest. It could be that my native egocentrism is keeping me from rethinking my conclusion because then I will be forced to consider another person's feelings and desires and I won't get what I want in the situation.

- I'm beginning to realize that I don't want to hear what this other person is saying because then I will have to rethink my position. Whenever I feel this type of defensiveness, I know that I'm being egocentric, that my mind is not allowing me to enter her point of view, because if I think within her view, I will have to alter my self-indulgent position. My mind will recognize its absurdity in pursuing its own desires at the expense of her needs and desires. I must force myself to rationally consider this opposing position, to operate in good faith rather than try to hide from something my egocentric mind doesn't want to see.

- I see what my mind is doing. Instead of trying to resolve a conflict, I'm trying to force this other person to accept my views. I want to make him do exactly what I say, even if that means I must hurt him to do so. I detect my dominating ego at work, and I know that whenever I'm thinking within this logic, I'm being irrational and I'm likely to hurt someone. I must recognize my dominating ego as a hurtful mode of thinking and reject it in any form.

- I wonder why I'm allowing this person to intimidate me. I feel like I must submit to her will in order to function. Whenever I'm being submissive, I need to ask myself what I'm trying to achieve in the situation. What is it that I want from this other person? Why do I let her treat me like this? Why do I think I must be submissive instead of being rational in this circumstance? Perhaps I'm not willing to admit that I'm simply manipulating her to get what I want. If were to tell her the truth, would I still be able to get what I want, or would I detect absurdity in my desires?

Reaching an advanced stage in thinking may take years. Many variables affect evolution in this direction. The most important variables are motivation, commitment, and regular practice.

STAGE 6: BECOMING A MASTER THINKER

There is a wide continuum in the advanced and master stages, and no magical divide unambiguously separates these stages. Nevertheless, roughly speaking, we know that we are reaching the stage we call *mastery* when we intuitively are doing what took deliberate effort at the practicing and advanced stages. Skilled performers make difficult moves look easy. What others find difficult feels easy and natural. Highly skilled performance becomes second nature to us. Excellence of performance is characteristic rather than unusual. When we have these attributes, we are moving into what properly can be called a mastery level.

The idea of "mastery" in thinking can be further explained by the following patterns:

- Master thinkers have systematically taken charge of their thinking. They are continually monitoring, revising, and rethinking strategies for continual improvement of their thinking.

- Master thinkers have deeply internalized the basic skills of thought, so critical thinking is, for them, both conscious and highly intuitive. They regularly raise their thinking to, as Piaget would put it, the level of "conscious realization."

- Through extensive experience and practice in engaging in self-assessment, master thinkers are actively analyzing their thinking in all the significant domains of their lives and also continually developing new insights into problems at deeper levels of thought.

- Master thinkers are deeply committed to fair-minded thinking and have a high level of—although imperfect—control over their egocentric nature.

- Master thinkers are actively and successfully engaged in systematically monitoring the role in their thinking of concepts, assumptions, inferences, implications, and points of view and also are improving that practice.

- Master thinkers have a high level of knowledge of thinking and a high level of practical insight into it as well.

- Master thinkers intuitively assess their thinking for clarity, accuracy, precision, relevance, logicalness, and, indeed, all of the intellectual standards.

- Master thinkers have deeply internalized critical thinking into their habits.

- Master thinkers deeply understand the role that egocentric thinking and sociocentric thinking play in the lives of human beings, as well as the complex relationships among thoughts, emotions, drives, and behavior.

- Master thinkers regularly, effectively, and insightfully critique their own use of thinking in their lives, and thereby improve it.

- Master thinkers consistently monitor their own thoughts.

- Master thinkers effectively, insightfully, and regularly articulate the strengths and weaknesses inherent in their thinking.

- Master thinkers are keenly aware of their fallibility as thinkers.

- Master thinkers have intellectual humility, intellectual integrity, intellectual perseverance, intellectual courage, intellectual empathy, intellectual autonomy, intellectual responsibility, and fair-mindedness.
- Egocentric and sociocentric thought is uncommon in master thinkers.

Most of us will not become master thinkers, any more than most high school basketball players will develop the skills or abilities of a professional basketball player or student writers will develop the writing skills of a published novelist. Nevertheless, it is important that we learn what it would be to become a master thinker so we can hold it out as an ideal to strive for. It is important that we see this as a real possibility, perhaps more realistically for a society to come, in which critical thinking is a highly honored social value.

The sixth stage of development—the master thinker stage—is best described in the third person, as it is not clear that any humans living in this age of irrationality qualify as master thinkers. It may be that the extent of deep social conditioning that all of us experience renders it unlikely that any of us are master thinkers. Nevertheless, the concept is useful, for it sets out what we are striving for and is, in principle, a stage that some humans can reach.

The emergence of master thinkers requires the emergence of a critical society—a society that so values critical thinking that it systematically rewards those who develop it, a society in which parenting, schooling, social groups, and the mass media cultivate and honor it. When people must develop their rationality in the face of large-scale irrationality in virtually every domain of life, as they must today, it is much less plausible that anyone will achieve the highest possible stage of development as a thinker.

QUALITIES OF MIND OF A MASTER THINKER

The most significant qualities of mind of a master thinker are as follows. Master thinkers are:

> conscious of the workings of their mind,
>
> highly integrated
>
> rationally powerful
>
> logical
>
> far-sighted
>
> deep
>
> self-correcting
>
> emancipated, or free.
>
> Each of these qualities is outlined below.

Master thinkers are conscious of the workings of their mind. They:

- are aware of their own patterns of thought and action
- are deliberate in the intellectual moves they make
- give explicit assent to their inner logic

Master thinkers have a highly integrated mind. They:

- transfer knowledge between different categories of experience
- apply insight into foundational concepts and principles to organize large bodies of information

Master thinkers have a powerful mind. They:

- are able to generalize knowledge
- are in command of the logic of language
- function well with the logic of concepts and questions
- are able to reason multilogically
- use the mind so as to "multiply" comprehension and insight

Master thinkers have a logical mind. They:

- routinely analyze the logic of things
- are committed to comprehensive principles of reason and evidence
- have a keen sense of the need for deep consistency

Master thinkers are far-sighted. They:

- take the long view
- plan their own development
- focus on ultimate values

Master thinkers think deeply. They:

- have insight into their own foundational beliefs and values
- grasp the roots of their own thought and emotion
- make sure their beliefs are rationally grounded
- consider the deep motives that guide thought, feeling, and action

Master thinkers have a self-correcting mind. They:

- apply intellectual criteria to their own thoughts, feelings, and behavior
- recognize and critique their own egocentrism and sociocentrism
- are sensitive to their own contradictions

Master thinkers have a free mind. They:

- are energized by rational passions
- are able to make fundamental changes in their own life patterns, habits, and behavior
- are models of reasonability and fair-mindedness

THE INNER LOGIC OF THE MASTER THINKER

Because master thinkers achieve a high level of success in bringing their thoughts, emotions, and actions in line with their espoused ideals, it follows that they function with a high level of fulfillment and sense of well-being. Having formed their identity by a commitment to reasonability, they are able to shift their beliefs without trauma or self-doubt. Seeing through the strategies used by those who would intimidate them by status and external authority, they are able to quietly dissent where others shy away in fear. Being keenly aware of the brevity of human life, they are able to prize and savor ordinary pleasures of daily life. Being committed to growth and deep honesty, they are able to form intimate relationships without mutual self-deception, hidden agendas, or bad-faith discontent.

Being aware of their place in a much larger world, master thinkers act with a realistic sense of what one person can and cannot achieve. They can plan without being possessed by their plans, believe without being trapped in those beliefs, and act without being blind to mistakes implicit in those acts.

THE IDEAL THINKER

Whether there are, or ever will be, master thinkers, there cannot be "ideal" thinkers, for it is not possible for the human mind to function in an "ideal" way. All actual human development is qualified by human fallibility. However much we develop our potential for rationality, our native egocentricity and conditioned sociocentricity will sometimes become activated. However much we develop our integrity, some contradictions and inconsistencies will escape our notice. However much we develop our insights, there will be other insights that we will not develop. However many points of view we internalize, there will be others that we have no time to enter, master, or profit from. However rich our experience, there will be experiences we shall never have the benefit of.

Our mind, however well-developed, always will be the mind of finite, fallible, potentially egocentric, potentially sociocentric, potentially prejudiced, potentially irrational creatures. As such, master thinkers are keenly aware of these limitations in themselves and, therefore, of how far they are from becoming "ideal" thinkers. Therefore, they never cease to appreciate the need to grow and learn, never cease to discover dimensions of their mind in need of critique and rethinking, and never cease to develop those critiques and enact that rethinking.

19.1 *Think for Yourself*

ASSESSING YOUR DEVELOPMENT AS A THINKER

Write a paper in which you assess your own stage of development as a thinker. Compare the stage at which you began this book with the stage you believe yourself to be in presently. What are the major barriers to your further development?

In what ways will your egocentrism create barriers to your development?

What strategies have you used in the past that have been most effective in dealing with these barriers?

What do you intend to do to try to overcome the barriers to your development as a thinker?

Support your assessment with specific examples from your life. Show your reasoning. Make your analysis useful to you.

APPENDICES

CRITICAL QUESTIONS ABOUT CRITICAL THINKING

W e have strongly emphasized recognition of the limitations of a field as an integral part of its study. Therefore, it is appropriate that we answer the same questions about critical thinking that we advocate for the questioning of any other field.

To what extent do competing schools of thought exist within this field?

In the first place, critical thinking is not a professional field in the usual sense. No degrees are granted in critical thinking. There are no departments of critical thinking. The few journals that include articles in critical thinking tend to have a pronounced subject-specific bias in their conception of critical thinking.

What is critical thinking, then, if not a recognized field of study? It is an intellectual interest with historical roots across multiple disciplines and subjects. It represents an interest, transcending any given subject, in the concepts, tools, and values that would enable motivated persons to take steps to correct for the deep-seated tendencies of the human mind to confuse ignorance with knowledge, prejudice with insight, and falsity with the truth. Part of the history of critical thinking is the documentation of irrational tendencies or flawed thinking of the human mind; part of it suggests concepts, tools, and values for combatting those tendencies and correcting for these flaws.

The concept of critical thinking reflects an idea derived from roots in ancient Greek. The word *critical* derives etymologically from two Greek roots: *kriticos* (meaning *discerning judgment*) and *kriterion* (meaning *standards*). Etymologically, then, the word implies the development of "discerning judgment based on standards." In *Webster's New*

World Dictionary, the relevant entry reads "characterized by careful analysis and judgment" and is followed by: "Critical, in its strictest sense, implies an attempt at objective judgment so as to determine both merits and faults." Applied to thinking, then, we might provisionally define critical thinking as thinking that explicitly aims at well-founded judgment and hence utilizes appropriate evaluative standards in an attempt to determine the true worth, merit, or value of something.

The tradition of research into critical thinking reflects the common perception that human thinking, left to itself, often gravitates toward prejudice, overgeneralization, common fallacies, self-deception, rigidity, and narrowness. The critical thinking tradition seeks ways of understanding the mind and then training the intellect to minimize these "errors," "blunders," and "distortions" of thought. It assumes that the capacity of humans for good reasoning can be nurtured and developed by an educational process aimed directly toward that end. The history of critical thinking documents the development of this insight in a variety of subject-matter domains and in a variety of social situations.

Each major dimension of critical thinking has been carved out in intellectual debate and dispute through 2,400 years of intellectual history. That history allows us to distinguish two contradictory intellectual tendencies: (1) a tendency on the part of the large majority to uncritically accept whatever is presently believed as more or less eternal truth, and (2) a conflicting tendency on the part of a small minority—those who think critically—to systematically question what has been commonly accepted (and seek, as a result, to establish sounder, more reflective criteria and standards for judging what it does and does not make sense to accept as true).

The operational (minimalist) assumptions behind the treatment of critical thinking we are providing are that

- critical thinking enables thinkers who are proficient in it to better produce and assess intellectual work, as well as to act more reasonably and effectively in the world of affairs and personal life;
- the possibility of assessing intellectual work and action in the world requires intellectual standards essential to sound reasoning and personal and professional judgment;
- self-assessment is an integral dimension of such reasoning and judgment;
- as one learns to think critically, one is better able to master content in diverse disciplines;
- critical thinking is essential to and made manifest in all academic disciplines, including sound reasoning and expert performance in diverse fields such as biology, chemistry, mathematics, sociology, history, anthropology, literature, and philosophy, as well as in all of the arts and professions;
- as one becomes proficient in critical thinking, one becomes more proficient in using and assessing goals and purposes, questions and problems, information and data, conclusions and interpretations, concepts and theoretical constructs, assumptions and presuppositions, implications and consequences, and points of view and frames of reference;
- mastery of language contributes to critical thinking;

- as one becomes more proficient in critical thinking, one improves one's capacity to think more clearly, more accurately, more precisely, more relevantly, more deeply, more broadly, and more logically;

- as one becomes more proficient in critical thinking, one becomes more intellectually perseverant, more intellectually responsible, more intellectually disciplined, more intellectually humble, more intellectually empathic, and more intellectually productive;

- as one becomes more proficient in critical thinking, one becomes a better reader, writer, speaker, and listener;

- proficiency in critical thinking is integral to, and reflective of, a commitment to lifelong learning.

One way to assess the reasonability of these assumptions is to randomly choose a few of them, negate them, and see if their negations have any plausibility. What you will find, we suggest, is that negating the minimalist assumptions we made leads to views that are inconsistent with virtually any reasonable construct of critical thinking and its traditional agenda, given its history and semantics.

Suppose someone denied our first four assumptions. They would, therefore, have to assert that

- critical thinking *does not* enable thinkers who are proficient in it to better produce and assess intellectual work or to act more reasonably and effectively in the world of affairs and personal life;

- the possibility of assessing intellectual work and action in the world *does not* require intellectual standards essential to sound reasoning and personal and professional judgment;

- self-assessment *is not* an integral dimension of such reasoning and judgment; and

- as one learns to think critically, one is *no better able* to master content in diverse disciplines.

Of what possible use would this alternative notion of critical thinking be? It would be one in which students would learn something that *does not entail better intellectual work, does not make them more reasonable or effective, has no intellectual standards, involves no self-assessment, and does not improve their ability to learn the content of the disciplines.*

A close examination of our minimalist assumptions reveals that they are in keeping with the semantics of the words *critical thinking,* with the history of the concept, with what is tested in established critical-thinking tests, and with the variety of ways by which critical thinking is typically defined.

DEFINITIONS

No one definition of critical thinking will do. Given the complexity of critical thinking—its rootedness in 2,400 years of intellectual history, as well as the wide range of its application—it is unwise to put too much weight on any one definition. Any brief formulation of critical thinking is bound to have important limitations. Some theoreticians provide a range of useful definitions, each with its limitations.

In *Educating Reason: Rationality, Critical Thinking, and Education,* Harvey Siegel (1988) defines critical thinking as "thinking [that is] appropriately moved by reasons." This definition highlights the contrast between the mind's tendency to be shaped by phenomena other than reasons: desires, fears, social rewards and punishments, and so on. Robert Ennis (1985) defines critical thinking as "rational reflective thinking concerned with what to do or believe." This definition usefully calls attention to the wide role that critical thinking plays in everyday life, for since all behavior depends on what we believe, all human action depends upon what we in some sense decide to do. Matthew Lipman (1988) defines critical thinking as "skillful, responsible thinking that is conducive to judgment because it relies on criteria, is self-correcting and is sensitive to context." This definition highlights the need for intellectual standards and self-assessment.

Scriven and Paul (Paul, 1995) define critical thinking (for the National Council for Excellence in Critical Thinking) as follows:

> Critical thinking is the intellectually disciplined process of actively and skillfully conceptualizing, applying, analyzing, synthesizing, and/or evaluating information gathered from, or generated by, observation, experience, reflection, reasoning, or communication, as a guide to belief and action. . . . Critical thinking can be seen as having two components: (1) a set of information and belief generating and processing skills, and (2) the habit, based on intellectual commitment, of using those skills to guide behavior. It is thus to be contrasted with: (1) the mere acquisition and retention of information alone, because it involves a particular way in which information is sought and treated; (2) the mere possession of a set of skills, because it involves the continual use of them; and (3) the mere use of those skills ("as an exercise") without acceptance of their results.

To look at the question of definition from another point of view, we now will review basic explanations of critical thinking expressed in interviews of a number of scholars in research conducted by John Esterle and Dan Cluman (1993) of the Whitman Institute of San Francisco. One of the questions asked of all interviewees was, "What is your conception of critical thinking?" A review of these answers demonstrates, as above, that despite diversity of expression, there is a core of common meaning among those interviewed. One possible limitation of the interviews is that most of those interviewed are philosophers.

CAROLE WADE. "In our introductory psychology book, Carol Tavris and I have a definition we thought quite a bit about. We define critical thinking as 'the ability and willingness to assess claims and make objective judgments on the basis of well-supported reasons.' We wanted to get in the willingness as well as the ability because a person can master critical thinking skills without being the least bit disposed to use them. Also, we didn't want critical thinking to be confined to problem solving. Unless you construe problem solving extremely broadly, critical thinking goes beyond that, to include forming judgments, evaluating claims, defending a position. We said 'well-supported reasons' rather than 'evidence' because, although our own discipline emphasizes empirical evidence, we wanted to recognize that you don't reach all conclusions or assess all claims on the basis of such evidence. Sometimes there is no empirical evidence and critical thinking is purely a process of reasoned judgment."

MICHAEL SCRIVEN. ". . . it's the skill to identify the less obvious alternatives to positions, claims, arguments, generalizations, and definitions, and to evaluate the alternatives with reasonable objectivity. Both are equally important. You may be commenting on what's there, but often that's only the tip of the iceberg. If you haven't seen the hidden presuppositions or the built-in point of view, then you're not thinking critically, however smart you are in analyzing the stuff that's actually presented. And the other way around: You may be good at seeing the presuppositions, the prejudices and so on, but very poor at actually analyzing them. So both those skills are key."

Browne and Keeley were interviewed together.

STUART M. KEELEY. "Rather than using a formal definition, we emphasize primarily the questions critical thinkers *think* should be questions and *want* to be questions. In other words, there is a set of questions that constitutes a rubric of what it means to be a critical thinker."

M. NEIL BROWNE. "And it's *a* set of questions, not *the* set of questions. I would add that a *sine qua non* of critical thinking is a focus on assessment, or evaluation, of the link between a claim and the basis for the claim. If there's not some orientation designed to move toward improved judgment—not right judgment but improved judgment—then I would be reluctant to label such a thing critical thinking. Our questions were not generated out of any theoretical framework but from our teaching practice. We were led to questioning as a format to express our standards because, unlike declarative stipulations of standards, there's greater openness to questioning, there's greater curiosity implied by questioning, and there's a requirement of action on the part of the person receiving the question.

"We're personally not as interested in a process that improves reflection as we are in a process that improves living, that improves practice, and that thus improves judgment. I don't think I'd want to put a lot of energy into something that just enables me to reflect more profoundly. Not that there's not merit in that, but I prefer something that people can use to address problems in their lives."

RICHARD PAUL. "I think the best way to get to the nub of it is to see that everyone thinks and that their thinking is deeply involved in every dimension of their daily life. If there's one thing that you can't escape, it's your own thinking. It's everywhere you are, and it's always shaping and influencing everything you do—including your emotions and decisions. Every nook and cranny that's in you is thought-ful, i.e., full of thought. The key question is: Are you in charge of your thinking, or is your thinking in charge of you? You discover critical thinking when you realize how deeply the quality of your life is dependent on the quality of your thinking, and that it's possible to take charge of your thinking—to make it what you want it to be rather than what it has been made to be by your environment, your parents, your society, the media, and so on. That's the basic idea behind critical thinking. It's intrinsically connected with a self-determining way of living. It's a commitment to continually upgrade the quality of your thinking so as to upgrade the quality of your life."

CAROL TAVRIS. "We developed what we called eight guidelines to critical thinking. We don't care about the number—there could be fourteen, there could be six. Several people have said, 'You know, really you've got four and a half here and several of them should be combined.' I don't care! They work. They're handy. And they identify different steps in critical thinking, different dispositions, and different skills: How to ask questions. Why are things this way? The fact that everybody says it's so doesn't mean it's so. You need to examine evidence, look for other interpretations of phenomena, and tolerate uncertainty; some things we're never going to know. By the second edition of our book, we realized that many people were confusing 'critical thinking' with exclusively negative thinking—debunking, tearing down. So we now speak of 'critical *and* creative thinking,' to show that the other face of critical thinking is the ability and willingness to envision new possibilities and solutions.

"Since this book came out, we've developed our ideas in a handbook called *Critical and Creative Thinking: The Case of Love and War,* which introduces these guidelines and shows how they might be applied to subjects that many people think irrationally about—love, attraction, and intimacy, and prejudice, hostility, and war.

"Carole Wade and I have become interested in the psychological impediments to clear thinking, and the way in which the mind is designed to serve itself, to protect self-esteem, to protect its own way of seeing the world, to keep things orderly so that everything fits into the existing framework."

JOHN CHAFFEE. "To understand the nature of critical thinking, we first have to define the concept of *thinking.* From my perspective, thinking is a very practical, holistic, integrated mental activity we engage in to make sense of the world. We use thinking in many different contexts: to solve problems, move toward goals, analyze complex issues, communicate with other people, and make informed decisions. So the thinking process is a global, purpose-seeking, meaning-seeking activity that is the essence of being human.

"Critical thinking builds on this fundamental process. The heart of thinking critically is developing a reflective orientation toward our minds. It involves exploring our thinking and the thinking of other people so that we can understand how our minds work, how we conceptualize the world and construct knowledge. Becoming a critical thinker goes beyond developing intellectual abilities. It also involves developing basic attitudes and dispositions. In a way, it's a whole philosophy of life, a process of personal transformation. A critical thinker views the world in a qualitatively different way from someone who is not a critical thinker. In this sense, there are intrinsic qualities that characterize a critical thinker: thinking actively, carefully exploring issues with penetrating questions, developing independent viewpoints based on analysis and reasoning, exploring issues from different perspectives, engaging in dialogue with other people, and exchanging views with them. Thinking critically is a community activity as well as a reflective process. By listening to and sharing ideas with others, our own thinking is expanded, clarified, and enriched.

"The other distinction that's important is that while people *think* all the time, that doesn't mean they are *thinking critically.* A critical thinker is not only *capable* of reflecting, exploring, and analyzing but *chooses* to think in these advanced, sophisticated ways. For example, seeing something from a variety of perspectives involves the intellectual capability to empathize or identify with somebody else, but it also involves the desire to do it.

Becoming a critical thinker is a melding of our intellect with our emotions, attitudes, and dispositions."

MARLYS MAYFIELD. "Ideally, I would say a critical thinker shows awakeness and alertness, particularly to incongruities, and a willingness to challenge incongruities. And all this takes courage and initiative. A critical thinker also appreciates clarity and precision, really relishes these qualities, and values the truth—whatever that might be—over being right. By my definition, those are the traits necessary to be a critical thinker."

Each of these explorations of critical thinking, as many others, cuts in fundamentally the same direction. All deal, whether broadly or narrowly, with the problem of upgrading the quality of human thinking by the cultivation of special skills, abilities, and insights that enable thinkers to take mindful command of their thinking and related behavior. What is most obvious from a serious examination of these multiple characterizations of critical thinking is how much they share a common set of concerns and objectives—quite in line with the history of the concept.

The most basic theme underlying all traditional approaches to critical thinking runs something like this. Though it is certainly of the nature of the human mind to think—spontaneously, continuously, and pervasively—it is not of the nature of the human mind to think critically about the standards, principles, and motivations guiding its spontaneous thought. The human mind has no built-in drive to question its innate tendency to believe what it wants to believe, what makes it comfortable, what is simple rather than complex, and what is commonly believed and socially rewarded. The human mind is ordinarily at peace with itself as it internalizes and creates biases, prejudices, falsehoods, half-truths, and distortions. The human mind—in a natural state of uncriticality—spontaneously experiences itself as in tune with reality, as directly observing and faithfully recording it. It takes a special intervening process to produce the kind of self-criticality that enables the mind to effectively and constructively question its own creations.

Learning to think critically is therefore, as we conceive it, an extraordinary process that cultivates capacities merely potential in human thought, counteracting the irrational tendencies spontaneously activated from within and reinforced by normal socialization. It is not normal and inevitable or even common for a mind to discipline itself intellectually and direct itself toward intellectually defensible rather than egocentric beliefs, practices, and values. This generic problem is reflected in the history of critical thought.

A BRIEF HISTORY OF THE IDEA OF CRITICAL THINKING

The intellectual roots of critical thinking are as ancient as its etymology, traceable ultimately to the teaching practice and vision of Socrates, 2,400 years ago, who discovered by a method of probing questioning that most people cannot rationally justify their confident claims to knowledge. Confused meanings, inadequate evidence, and self-contradictory beliefs often lurk beneath smooth but largely empty rhetoric.

Socrates found that one cannot depend upon those in authority to have sound knowledge and insight. He demonstrated that people may have power and high position, yet be deeply confused and irrational. He established the importance of asking deep questions that probe profoundly into thinking before we accept ideas as worthy of belief. He established the importance of seeking evidence, closely examining reasoning and assumptions, analyzing basic concepts, and tracing out implications not only of what is said but of what is done as well. This method of questioning, now known as Socratic questioning, is the best known critical thinking teaching strategy. In his mode of questioning, Socrates highlighted the need in thinking for clarity and logical consistency.

Socrates set the agenda for the tradition of critical thinking: to reflectively question common beliefs and explanations, carefully distinguishing those beliefs that are reasonable and logical from those that—however appealing they may be to our native egocentrism, however much they serve our vested interests, however comfortable or comforting they may be—lack adequate evidence or rational foundation.

Socrates' practice was followed by the critical thinking of Plato, Aristotle, and the Greek skeptics, all of whom emphasized that things are often very different from what they appear to be and that only the trained mind is prepared to see through the way things look to us on the surface (delusive appearances) to the way they really are beneath the surface (the deeper realities of life).

In the Middle Ages, the tradition of systematic critical thinking was embodied in the writings and teachings of thinkers such as Thomas Aquinas, who—to ensure that his thinking met the test of critical thought—systematically answered the most fundamental potential criticisms of his ideas as a necessary stage in developing his thinking. Aquinas, and other medieval thinkers, heightened our awareness not only of the potential power of reasoning but also of the need for reasoning to be systematically cultivated and cross-examined. Disputation and debate became an established tradition in the medieval university as a mode of both teaching and learning. As Felix Markham (1967) remarks in his book *Oxford:*

> The rise of the medieval universities is associated with a shift of interest from grammar and rhetoric to logic. It was valued not merely as an intellectual training, but as a method of reasoning which must lead to valid and demonstrable conclusions about the nature of reality. (p. 29)

Precision and discipline of thought were sound preparation for the "new learning" that was to come.

In the Renaissance (15th and 16th centuries), a flood of scholars in Europe began to think critically about religion, art, society, human nature, law, and freedom. They proceeded with the assumption that most of the domains of human life were in need of searching analysis and critique. Among these scholars were Colet, Erasmus, and More in England. They followed up on the insight of the ancient Greek thinkers.

Francis Bacon (England) explicitly analyzed the way the human mind, in its normal state, is entrapped by ignorance, prejudice, self-deception, and vested interest. He recognized explicitly that the mind cannot safely be left to its natural tendencies. In his book *The Advancement of Learning,* he argued for the importance of studying the world empirically. He laid the foundation for modern science with his emphasis on the information-gathering processes. He also called attention to the fact that most people, if left to their own devices, develop bad habits of thought (which he called "idols") that lead them to believe what is unworthy of belief. He called attention to "Idols of the Tribe" (the ways our mind naturally tends to trick itself), "Idols of the Marketplace" (the ways we misuse words), "Idols of the Theater" (our tendency to become trapped in conventional systems of thought), and "Idols of the Cave" (the ways our thinking is distorted according to individual experiences). His books could be considered some of the earliest texts in critical thinking, for his agenda was very much the traditional agenda of critical thinking.

Some 50 years later in France, Descartes wrote what might be called the second text in critical thinking, *Rules for the Direction of the Mind.* In it, Descartes argued for the need for a special systematic disciplining of the mind to guide it in thinking. He articulated and defended the need in thinking for clarity and precision. He developed a method of critical thought based on the principle of systematic doubt. He emphasized the need to base thinking on well-thought-through foundational assumptions. Every part of thinking, he argued, should be questioned, doubted, and tested.

In the same time period, Sir Thomas More developed a model of a new social order, *Utopia,* in which every domain of the present world was subject to critique. His implicit thesis was that established social systems are in need of radical analysis and critique. The critical thinking of these Renaissance and post-Renaissance scholars opened the way for the emergence of science and for the development of democracy, human rights, and freedom for thought.

In the Italian Renaissance, Machiavelli (*The Prince*) critically assessed the politics of the day and laid the foundation for modern critical political thought. He refused to assume that government functioned as those in power said it did. Rather, he critically analyzed how it did function and laid the foundation for political thinking that exposes both, on the one hand, the real agendas of politicians and, on the other hand, the many contradictions and inconsistencies of the hard, cruel world of the politics of his day.

Hobbes and Locke (in 16th- and 17th-century England) displayed the same confidence in the critical mind of the thinker that we find in Machiavelli. Neither accepted the traditional picture of things dominant in the thinking of their day. Neither accepted as necessarily rational that which was considered normal in their culture. Both looked to the critical mind to open up new vistas of learning. Hobbes adopted a naturalistic view of the world in which everything was to be explained by evidence and reasoning. Locke defended a common sense analysis of everyday life and thought. He laid the theoretical foundation for critical thinking about basic human rights and the responsibilities of all governments to submit to the reasoned criticism of thoughtful citizens.

It was in this spirit of intellectual freedom and critical thought that people such as Robert Boyle (in the 17th century) and Sir Isaac Newton (in the 17th and 18th centuries) did their work. In his *Sceptical Chymist,* Boyle severely criticized the chemical theory that had preceded him. Newton, in turn, developed a far-reaching framework of thought that roundly criticized the traditionally accepted world view. He extended the critical thought of minds such as Copernicus, Galileo, and Kepler. After Boyle and Newton, it was recognized by those who reflected seriously on the natural world that egocentric views of the world must be abandoned in favor of views based entirely on carefully gathered evidence and sound reasoning.

The thinkers of the French enlightenment—Bayle, Montesquieu, Voltaire, and Diderot—made another significant contribution to critical thinking. They all began with the premise that the human mind, when disciplined by reason, is better able to figure out the nature of the social and political world. What is more, for these thinkers, reason must turn inward upon itself to determine weaknesses and strengths of thought. They valued disciplined intellectual exchange, in which all views had to be submitted to serious analysis and critique. They believed that all authority must submit in one way or another to the scrutiny of reasonable critical questioning.

Eighteenth-century thinkers extended our conception of critical thought even further, developing our sense of the power of critical thought and of its tools. Applied to the problem of economics, it produced Adam Smith's *Wealth of Nations*. In the same year, applied to the traditional concept of loyalty to the king, it produced the Declaration of Independence. Applied to reason itself, it produced Kant's *Critique of Pure Reason*.

In the 19th century, critical thought was extended even further into the domain of human social life by Comte and Spencer. Applied to the problems of capitalism, it produced the searching social and economic critique of Karl Marx. Applied to the history of human culture and the basis of biological life, it led to Darwin's *Descent of Man*. Applied to the unconscious mind, it is reflected in the works of Sigmund Freud. Applied to cultures, it led to establishment of the field of anthropological studies. Applied to language, it led to the field of linguistics and to many deep probings of the functions of symbols and language in human life.

In the 20th century, our understanding of the power and nature of critical thinking emerged in increasingly more explicit formulations. In 1906, William Graham Sumner published a groundbreaking study of the foundations of sociology and anthropology, *Folkways,* in which he documented the tendency of the human mind to think sociocentrically and the parallel tendency for schools to serve the uncritical function of social indoctrination:

> Schools make persons all on one pattern, orthodoxy. School education, unless it is regulated by the best knowledge and good sense, will produce men and women who are all of one pattern, as if turned in a lathe. . . . An orthodoxy is produced in regard to all the great doctrines of life. It consists of the most worn and commonplace opinions which are common in the masses. The popular opinions always contain broad fallacies, half-truths, and glib generalizations. (p. 630)

At the same time, Sumner recognized the deep need for critical thinking in life and in education:

> Criticism is the examination and test of propositions of any kind which are offered for acceptance, in order to find out whether they correspond to reality or not. The critical faculty is a product of education and training. It is a mental habit and power. It is a prime condition of human welfare that men and women should be trained in it. It is our only guarantee against delusion, deception, superstition, and misapprehension of ourselves and our earthly circumstances. Education is good just so far as it produces well-developed critical faculty. . . . A teacher of any subject who insists on accuracy

and a rational control of all processes and methods, and who holds everything open to unlimited verification and revision, is cultivating that method as a habit in the pupils. Men educated in it cannot be stampeded. . . . They are slow to believe. They can hold things as possible or probable in all degrees, without certainty and without pain. They can wait for evidence and weigh evidence. . . . They can resist appeals to their dearest prejudices. . . . Education in the critical faculty is the only education of which it can be truly said that it makes good citizens. (pp. 632, 633)

John Dewey agreed. From his work, we have increased our sense of the pragmatic basis of human thought (its instrumental nature), and especially *its grounding in actual human purposes, goals, and objectives.* From the work of Ludwig Wittgenstein we have increased our awareness not only of the importance of *concepts* in human thought but also of *the need to analyze concepts* and assess their power and limitations. From the work of Piaget, we have increased our awareness of the *egocentric and sociocentric tendencies of human thought* and of the special need to develop critical thought that is able to *reason within multiple standpoints,* and to be raised to the level of "conscious realization."

From the work of scholars such as C. Wright Mills, we have increased awareness of the manner in which democratic institutions are undermined and social exploitation takes place in mass societies. From the contribution of depth-psychology and other researchers, we have learned how easily the human mind is self-deceived, how easily it unconsciously constructs illusions and delusions, how easily it rationalizes and stereotypes, projects and scapegoats.

From the work of Irving Goffman, we have an increased awareness of how "social definitions" can dominate the mental life of individuals in a society. From the work of many sociologists we have increased awareness of how the "normal" socialization process serves to perpetuate the existing society—its ideology, roles, norms, and values—however inconsistent these might be with a society's announced picture of itself. From the work of economists such as Robert Heilbroner, we have increased awareness of how unbridled economic forces influenced by vested interest groups may act to undermine or negate ethical values and human rights.

From the massive contribution of all the physical and natural sciences, we have learned *the power of information* and the *importance of gathering information with great care and precision,* and with sensitivity to its potential inaccuracy, distortion, or misuse.

To conclude, the potential tools and resources of the critical thinker have been vastly increased by virtue of the history of critical thought. Hundreds of thinkers have contributed to its potential development. Each major discipline has made potential contributions to critical thought. Because critical thinking is not a true discipline, however, there has been no systematic integration of these insights into one unified framework. Indeed, most typically, disciplines are taught in such a way that the potential contribution to critical thought of the discipline is unexpressed or obscured. Successful, large-scale integration would require many scholars working across disciplinary boundaries. Let us consider now some of the foundation stones of that integration.

COMMON DENOMINATORS OF CRITICAL THINKING

Critical thinking, by its very nature, requires the *systematic monitoring of thought*. Thinking, to be critical, must not be accepted at face value but must be analyzed and assessed for its *clarity, accuracy, relevance, depth, breadth, and logicalness*. Critical thinking requires the recognition that all reasoning occurs within *points of view* and frames of reference, that all reasoning proceeds from some *goals and objectives* and has an *informational base,* that all data when used in reasoning must be *interpreted,* that interpretation involves *concepts,* that concepts entail *assumptions,* and that all basic inferences in thought have *implications*. Each of these dimensions of thinking has to be monitored. Problems of thinking can occur in any of them.

The basic questions of Socrates now can be framed and used much more powerfully and focally. In every domain of human thought, and within every use of reasoning within any domain, it is now possible to question:

- ends and objectives;
- the status and wording of questions;
- the sources of information and fact;
- the method and quality of information collection;
- the mode of judgment and reasoning used;
- the concepts that make that reasoning possible;
- the assumptions that underlie concepts in use;
- the implications that follow from their use;
- the point of view or frame of reference within which reasoning takes place.

Questioning directed at these fundamentals of thought and reasoning are *baseline* in critical thinking. It is beyond question that intellectual errors or mistakes can occur in any of these dimensions, and that critical thinkers need to be fluent in talking about these structures and standards.

Independent of the subject, critical thinkers need to be in command of the intellectual dimensions of thought: Let's see, what is the most fundamental issue here? From what point of view should I approach this problem? Does it make sense for me to assume this? From these data may I infer this? What is implied in this graph? What is the fundamental concept here? Is this consistent with that? What makes this question complex? How could I check the accuracy of these data? If this is so, what else is implied? Is this a credible source of information? And so forth.

With intellectual language such as this in the foreground, one can come to recognize that at least minimal critical thinking moves within any subject field. What is more, one can take the basic tools of critical thought learned in one domain of study and extend them (with appropriate adjustments) to all the other domains and subjects of study. For example, having questioned the wording of a problem in math, I am more likely to question the wording of a problem in the other subjects I study.

For example, because critical thinkers can learn generalizable critical thinking moves, they need not study history simply as a body of facts to memorize; they now can study history as historical reasoning. Classes can be designed so students learn to think historically and develop skills and abilities essential to historical thought. Math can be learned by focusing on mathematical reasoning. Students can learn to think geographically, economically, biologically, chemically, in courses within these disciplines. In principle, then, all students can learn how to bring the basic tools of disciplined reasoning into every subject they study. Yet we are far from this ideal state of affairs.

To what extent do experts in this field disagree about the answers they give to important questions?

The answer to this question is complicated because of the lack of an official field and "official" experts. Textbooks on critical thinking have been written principally by philosophers, psychologists, rhetoricians, and scholars from the fields of literature and the language arts. Part of their differences mirror the differences in the concepts and tools most reflective of their respective backgrounds. If critical thinking is to be an integrated concept of value, it must not reflect the concepts and tools of any one discipline.

To what extent, if at all, is this field properly called a science?

Critical thinking is not a science. It is an art.

To what extent can questions asked in critical thinking be answered definitively? To what extent are questions asked by critical thinkers matters of arguable judgment?

The questions that critical thinkers ask are sometimes open to definitive settlement; sometimes they are matters of reasoned judgment.

To what extent is there public pressure on professionals in the field to compromise their professional practice in the light of public prejudice or vested interest?

In answering this question, we should comment upon two kinds of thinkers: (1) those who write books on critical thinking, and (2) those who engage in critical thinking in their daily life. Because critical thinking is a term that carries with it prestige, and because many want to think of themselves as critical thinkers (without having to undergo the discipline it takes to become a critical thinker), those who write books or develop positions that oversimplify the challenge of critical thinking often do well in the commercial and academic marketplace. In this sense, there is public pressure to market superficial or one-sided books and claim expertise with little justification for doing so.

Those who engage in critical thinking in their daily life can do so either (1) in a fair-minded way, a way that serves their interests as well as the interests of relevant others (as strong-sense critical thinkers) or (2) as weak-sense critical thinkers, using their intellectual skills to pursue their selfish interests while disregarding how their behavior impacts others.

What does the history of the discipline tell us about the status of knowledge in the field? How old is the field? How common is controversy regarding fundamental terms, theories, and orientation?

Because there is no established discipline or field, it is difficult to discuss controversy within it. Looking at the history of the concept and examining multiple definitions, one finds a great deal of convergence. But as yet there is no established forum for the discussion between multiple disciplines to take place.

SOME CRITICAL QUESTIONS TO ASK ABOUT A TEXTBOOK

If this field has competing schools of thought, what is the orientation of the textbook writers? Do they highlight these competing schools and detail the implications of that debate?

Because there is no field of study properly so called, there cannot be competing schools of thought. There are different orientations in those who have incorporated the idea of critical thinking into their writings—most of the differences reflecting differing agendas and home disciplines. Philosophers tend to approach critical thinking as formal or informal logic. Political thinkers tend to emphasize the political dimension of critical thought, psychologists the psychological dimension, sociologists the social dimension, economists the economic dimension, historians the historical dimension, linguists the linguistic dimension.

The difficulty with many of these approaches is that they fail to recognize the insights of other orientations. For the most part, they seem to be unaware of other orientations. They have no sense of common purpose or shared concerns and questions.

Are other textbooks available that approach this field from a significantly different standpoint? If there are, how should we understand the orientation or bias of this textbook?

The most salient characteristic of this orientation to critical thinking is that it is comprehensive (recognizing the need to incorporate insights from all disciplines) and minimalist (recognizing explicitly that we are beginning with necessary concepts, tools, and values, not with complete concepts, tools, and values). Many other approaches are more discipline-specific rather than comprehensive and emphasize a subset of the essential concepts, tools, and values.

Would other experts in this field disagree with any of the answers to important questions given in this textbook? If so, how would they disagree?

Because there is no field of study as such but, rather, individuals from different disciplines writing about critical thinking from the perspective of their disciplines, there would be probable disagreement about the adequacy of any given discipline to define the nature and limits of critical thinking. For example, some philosophers apparently argue that critical thinking is an intellectual possession of philosophy.

Since 1970, there are two identifiable waves of interest in critical thinking. The first was initiated by college and university faculty who were concerned that students were not, under standard instruction, learning to think critically. Critical thinking courses were established primarily in philosophy departments. Content in these courses usually consisted of some combination of formal and informal logic. Learning how to identify fallacies in argumentation was a main, and sometimes the exclusive, focus. The main intellectual standard emphasized was *formal validity.*

Students were taught to divide thinking into two types: (1) that which contained an argument, and (2) that which did not. All arguments were to be analyzed into premises and conclusions. The key question was then, "Do the conclusions *follow* from the premises?" The assumption was that all arguments can be divided into those whose conclusions follow and those whose conclusions do not follow (only the first type is considered *valid*).

A further refinement consisted of teaching students to distinguish *deductive* from *inductive* arguments. But there was never a satisfactory explanation of how inductive conclusions followed from the premises on which they were based. Because the focus in these courses was predominantly on argumentation, and particularly on identifying fallacies, students' ability to transfer what they had learned to other courses and to their everyday life was distinctly limited. The original purpose of developing courses in critical thinking that could help students reason better, generally speaking, was not achieved in the first wave.

Instructors and other academicians in other disciplines began to question the value of the first-wave courses. To some, the courses did not deal enough with one or more of a number of issues, insights, or concerns. Some thought traditional critical thinking courses did not deal adequately with the creative side of thinking or the political nature of thought or with feminist or sociological insights. Some thought it was too Western in its orientation or failed to take into account the role of emotion in thought. Some approached it from the perspective of science or engineering or the social disciplines or nursing or literary studies or rhetoric. There was pressure to widen the scope of critical thinking instruction to include what seemed to be left out, but there was no general agreement about what exactly was left out.

One can say, then, that the second wave, beginning roughly in 1985, was an unorganized attempt to broaden and enrich the treatment of critical thinking and to attend more to the problem of bringing it across the curriculum and into everyday life. The heterogeneity of recommendations coupled with the variety of disciplines brought into the discussion, however, tended to make the discussion itself more confusing and seemed to sacrifice some of the rigor and exactitude that, however narrow, seemed to be emphasized in formal and informal logic courses.

What is needed now is a third wave, a response to the problems inherent in both the first and second waves. The third wave should join rigor, breadth, comprehensiveness, and practicality. This textbook should be viewed as advancing a deliberate third-wave view. Rather than simply looking at the premises and conclusions of thinking, it recommends that we routinely examine purpose, question, information, inference, assumption, concept, implications, and point of view. Rather than looking principally at logicalness, it recommends that we in addition routinely examine thinking for its clarity, precision, relevance, depth, breadth, and significance.

Further, this book emphasizes the traits of mind essential to critical thinking and explicitly provides ways to understand how it can be taught across the disciplines. The fundamental objective is to bring both rigor and comprehensiveness to the educational process, to stress the need for students to learn what it means to be intellectually disciplined through consistent application of the standards to their thinking, and to teach students how to apply the skills of critical thinking in every dimension of their life—in everyday decision-making, in learning, in parenting, in the workplace.

To what extent does this textbook represent this field as a science? If it does, do some experts in the field disagree with this representation? In what sense is it not a science?

Critical thinking, as a potential third-wave phenomenon, is not a science but, rather, an art very much in the process of development and very much at the beginning of its having significant impact on education or social life.

To what extent do the questions asked in this textbook lead to definitive answers? Conversely, to what extent are questions in this textbook matters of arguable judgment? Does the textbook help you to distinguish between these very different types of questions?

We emphasize the importance of distinguishing questions with definite answers from those that are a matter of reasoned judgment and those that are a matter of subjective preference. Many of the questions regarding the identification of elements and assessment using basic standards have definite answers. Some are a matter of reasoned judgment. Most of the questions treated in this book are delineated into these categories, though the reader should cross-check our treatment of any given question using his or her independent thinking.

SAMPLE ANALYSIS OF THE LOGIC OF . . .

EXHIBIT B.1   *The logic of love.*

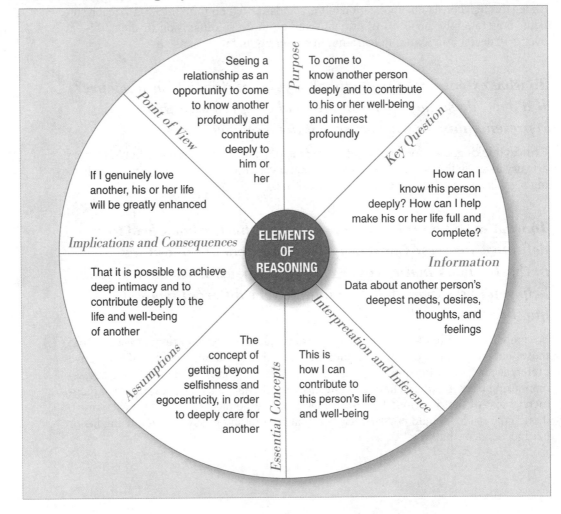

EXHIBIT B.2 *The logic of fear.*

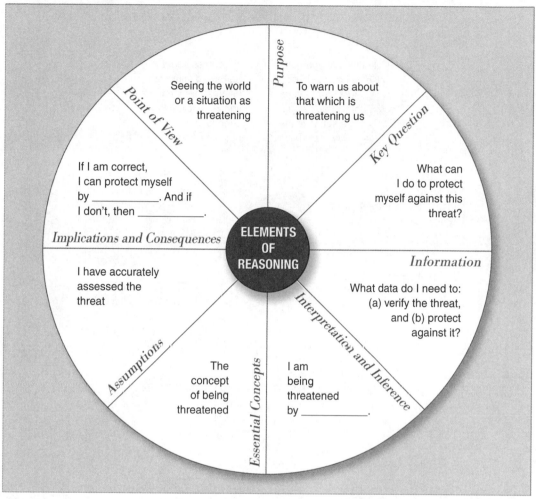

EXHIBIT B.3   *The logic of anger.*

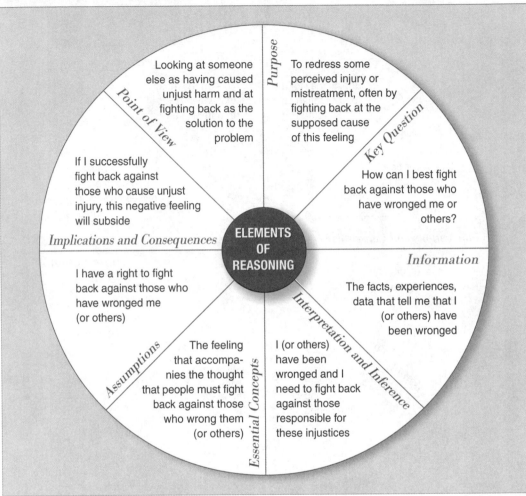

EXHIBIT B.4 *The logic of Christianity.*

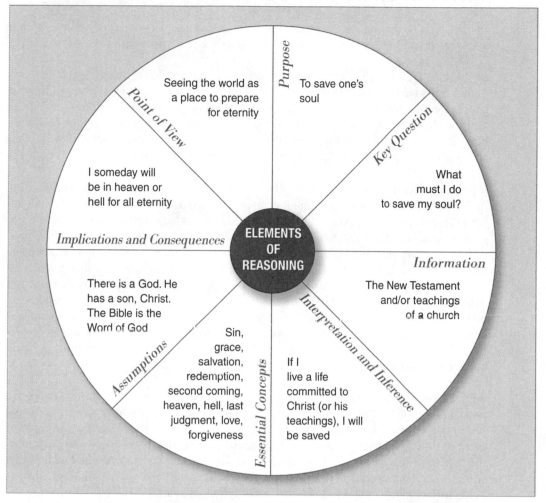

THE LOGIC OF ECONOMICS

PURPOSE: To develop theories that explain the distribution of goods and services within a society, as well as theories that define how goods and services should be distributed.

KEY QUESTIONS: How are goods and services produced, distributed, and consumed within any given society? How should they be? What is the best way to determine what people should get and how they should be allowed to get it? For example, to what extent should people be encouraged to pursue wealth and power principally for their own benefit? To what extent should society try to provide equal access to education, wealth, and power? What are the strengths and weaknesses of competing economic theories?

INFORMATION: Economists from differing schools of thought disagree on the information they use in reasoning through economic problems. Those who favor capitalism, for example, focus on information about supply of products versus demand, consumer preferences, consumer spending, business investments, and government support of business. In solving economic problems, they emphasize information about how to keep aggregate demand high. Those who favor socialism focus on information that reveals the impact of the distribution of wealth on the well-being of everyone, especially the poor and disadvantaged. Their ideal is to distribute wealth so that resources are made available as equally as possible, taking into account the crucial problem of how to motivate people to contribute to the well-being of others as well as themselves. The information that economists use is ultimately determined by the way they conceptualize ideal economic systems and the questions implied by the economic theories that guide their thinking.

KEY CONCEPTS: Economics is the study of how goods, services, and resources are and should be distributed and used within human societies. Leading economic concepts have evolved, especially through the last 200 years. Some of them are: the principle of competition, law of supply and demand, utilitarianism, capitalism, socialism, communism, Marxism, exploitation, class conflict between economic strata (especially between workers and employers), private property, free markets, self-interest, psychological variables influencing economic behavior, assumption of scarcity, law of diminishing returns, principles of marginal utility and productivity, aggregate demand, labor theory of value, Malthusian population doctrine, and Keynesian economics.

ASSUMPTIONS: By economists' studying the ways and means for distributing goods and services, economic systems can become more stable and more fair to the people who vie for resources within those systems. Beyond this shared assumption, economists' assumptions differ according to their philosophies, values, and theories. Those who favor capitalism assume that humans are fundamentally selfish and that only a system that utilizes the driving force of human selfishness will be realistic. Socialists, in contrast, assume that education can be used to shift the emphasis in human activity from self-aggrandizement to altruism.

INFERENCES: Economists make inferences about how best to stabilize and enhance the distribution, production, and use of goods and services. They make these inferences in accordance with their economic philosophies, considering trends and patterns of individual business and government spending, economic health, and distribution of wealth.

IMPLICATIONS: The implications that economic theories generate vary from theory to theory. Which of the theoretical implications become actual consequences is a matter of continual debate. The debate focuses on what actual consequences seem to be accounted for by this or that economic theory and what consequences (good or bad) result from variables other than those postulated by a given theory. For example, did the Great Depression of the 1930s result from a deep flaw in capitalist theory, or did it result from a failure to practice the theory thoroughly enough?

POINT OF VIEW: Economists look at the distribution of goods and services within a society, along with the distribution of power that distribution entails, as a crucial object of systematic study.

THE LOGIC OF SCIENCE

GOALS SCIENTISTS PURSUE: Scientists seek to figure out how the physical world operates through systematic observation, experimentation, and analysis. By analyzing the physical world, they seek to formulate principles, laws, and theories useful in explaining natural phenomena and in guiding further scientific study.

QUESTIONS SCIENTISTS ASK: How does the physical world operate? What are the best methods for figuring things out about the physical world? What are the barriers to figuring things out about the physical world? How can we overcome those barriers?

INFORMATION SCIENTISTS USE: Scientists use virtually any type of information that can be gathered systematically through observation and measurement, though most specialize in analyzing specific kinds of information. To name just some of the information scientists use, they observe and examine plants, animals, planets, stars, rocks, rock formations, minerals, bodies of water, fossils, chemicals, phenomena in the earth's atmosphere, and cells. They also observe interactions between phenomena.

JUDGMENTS SCIENTISTS MAKE: Scientists make judgments about the physical world based on observations and experimentation. These judgments lead to systematized knowledge, theories, and principles helpful in explaining and understanding the world.

CONCEPTS THAT GUIDE SCIENTISTS' THINKING: The most fundamental concepts that guide the thinking of scientists are (1) physical world (of nature and all matter); (2) hypothesis (an unproved theory, proposition, or supposition tentatively accepted to explain certain facts or to provide a basis for further investigation); (3) experimentation (a systematic and operationalized process designed to figure out something about the physical world); and (4) systematic observation (the act or practice of noting or recording facts or events in the physical world). Other fundamental concepts in science include: theory, law, scientific method, pure sciences, and applied sciences.

KEY ASSUMPTIONS SCIENTISTS MAKE: (1) There are laws at work in the physical world that can be figured out through systematic observation and experimentation; (2) much about the physical world is still unknown; (3) through science, the quality of life on earth can be enhanced.

IMPLICATIONS OF SCIENCE: Many important implications and consequences have resulted from scientific thinking, some of which have vastly improved the quality of life on earth, others of which have resulted in decreased quality of life (the destruction of the earth's forests, oceans, natural habitats, etc.). One important positive implication of scientific thinking is that it enables us to replace mythological thinking with theories and principles based in scientific fact.

THE SCIENTIFIC POINT OF VIEW: Scientists look at the physical world and see phenomena best understood through careful observation and systematic study. They see scientific study as vital to understanding the physical world and replacing myth with scientific knowledge.

THE LOGIC OF ECOLOGY

GOALS OF ECOLOGISTS: Ecologists seek to understand plants and animals as they exist in nature, with emphasis on their interrelationships, interdependence, and interactions with the environment. They work to understand all the influences that combine to produce and modify a given animal or plant, and thus to account for its existence and peculiarities within its habitat.

QUESTIONS THAT ECOLOGISTS ASK: How do plants and animals interact? How do animals interact with each other? How do plants and animals depend on one another? How do the varying ecosystems function within themselves? How do they interact with other ecosystems? How are plants and animals affected by environmental influences? How do animals and plants grow, develop, die, and replace themselves? How do plants and animals create balances between each other? What happens when plants and animals become unbalanced?

INFORMATION THAT ECOLOGISTS USE: The primary information used by ecologists is gained through observing plants and animals themselves, their interactions, and how they live within their environments. Ecologists note how animals and plants are born, how they reproduce, how they die, how they evolve, and how they are affected by environmental changes. They also use information from other disciplines including chemistry, meteorology, and geology.

JUDGMENTS THAT ECOLOGISTS MAKE: Ecologists make judgments about how ecosystems naturally function, about how animals and plants within them function, and about why they function as they do. They make judgments about how ecosystems become out of balance and what can be done to bring them back into balance. They make judgments about how natural communities should be grouped and classified.

CONCEPTS THAT GUIDE ECOLOGISTS' THINKING: One of the most fundamental concepts in ecology is *ecosystem,* defined as a group of living things that are dependent on one another and living in a particular habitat. Ecologists study how differing ecosystems function. Another key concept in ecology is *ecological succession,* the natural pattern of change occurring within every ecosystem when natural processes are undisturbed. This pattern includes the birth, development, death, and then replacement of natural communities. Ecologists have grouped communities into larger units called *biomes,* regions throughout the world classified according to physical features, including temperature, rainfall, and type of vegetation. Another fundamental concept in ecology is *balance of nature,* the natural process of birth, reproduction, eating, and being eaten, which keeps animal/plant communities fairly stable. Other key concepts include imbalances, energy, nutrients, population growth, diversity, habitat, competition, predation, parasitism, adaptation, co-evolution, succession and climax communities, and conservation.

KEY ASSUMPTIONS THAT ECOLOGISTS MAKE: Patterns exist within animal/plant communities; these communities should be studied and classified; animals and plants often depend on one another and modify one another; balances must be maintained within ecosystems.

IMPLICATIONS OF ECOLOGY: The study of ecology leads to numerous implications for life on Earth. By studying the balance of nature, for example, we can see when nature is out of balance, as in the current population explosion. We can see how pesticides, designed to kill pests on farm crops, also lead to the harm of mammals and birds, either directly or indirectly through food webs. We can also learn how over-farming causes erosion and depletion of soil nutrients.

POINT OF VIEW OF ECOLOGISTS: Ecologists look at plants and animals and see them functioning in relationship with one another within their habitats, and needing to be in balance for the earth to be healthy and sustainable.

THE LOGIC OF ASTRONOMY

GOALS OF ASTRONOMERS: Astronomers study the universe in order to better understand what it is comprised of and how celestial bodies and energy function within it. Astronomers seek to understand the origins, evolution, composition, motions, relative positions, size, and movements of celestial bodies, including planets and their satellites, comets and meteors, stars and interstellar matter, galaxies and clusters of galaxies, black holes and magnetic fields, and so forth.

QUESTIONS ASTRONOMERS ASK: How did matter and energy in the universe ever come to be? How is the universe structured? What energy forces exist in the universe and how do they function? Will the universe continue to expand forever? How are celestial bodies born? How do they function? How do they evolve? How do they die? Do planets similar to Earth exist in the universe? What questions remain to be asked about the universe?

INFORMATION ASTRONOMERS USE: Astronomers gather information about celestial bodies and energy through direct observation and indirect measurements. Developing methods for gathering information about the universe is a key ongoing focus of astronomers' work. For example, they use telescopes, as well as images taken from balloons and satellites. They gather information about the radiation of bodies in the universe through the electromagnetic spectrum, including radio waves, ultraviolet and infrared radiation, X-rays, and gamma rays. Telescopes placed on orbiting satellites gather information about radiation blocked by the atmosphere. Astronomers rely on computers with image processing software that notes the power and shape of light. They also use the interferometer, a series of telescopes that collectively have tremendous power.

JUDGMENTS ASTRONOMERS MAKE: Astronomers make judgments about the universe and how it functions. Using the instruments they design and continually seek to refine, they make judgments about suns, stars, satellites, moons, nebulae and galaxies, black holes, magnetic fields, gas clouds, comets, and so forth. They make judgments about the distances, brightness, and composition of celestial bodies and their temperature, radiation, size, and color. From a practical perspective, astronomers make judgments that include making astronomical tables for air and sea navigation, and determining the correct time.

CONCEPTS THAT GUIDE ASTRONOMERS' THINKING: The universe is the most fundamental concept in astronomy. The universe is the total of all bodies and energy in the cosmos that function as a harmonious and orderly system. Other important concepts in astronomy include: gravity, electromagnetism, nuclear forces (strong and weak), and quantum theory.

KEY ASSUMPTIONS ASTRONOMERS MAKE: (1) There are laws governing the universe, though we don't yet know them all; (2) the universe is largely unexplored and at present unexplained; (3) we need to develop better instruments of observation and measurement to understand the universe; (4) judgments in astronomy are limited by the observational instruments and research methods currently available.

IMPLICATIONS OF ASTRONOMY: One important implication of astronomy is that, as we improve our understanding of the universe, based on scientific observations and conclusions, we improve our understanding of life as an organic process, and we therefore rely less on myth to explain the universe. Furthermore, advances in astronomy help us see the earth as a minuscule body within a vast, expanding universe, rather than the earth (and therefore humans) as the center of the universe.

THE POINT OF VIEW OF ASTRONOMERS: Astronomers look at the universe and see a vast system of systems and a hugely unexplored space waiting to be discovered and understood.

IRAQ IS A PEDIATRICIAN'S HELL

NO WAY TO STOP THE DYING

BY STEPHEN KINZER

Baghdad, Iraq, Dec. 27—The greatest misfortune that has been visited on three-year-old Isra Ahmed was not contracting leukemia. It was contracting leukemia in Iraq at a time when the country's medical system is all but paralyzed as a result of economic sanctions imposed by the United Nations eight years ago.

Since Isra's illness was diagnosed earlier this year, she has spent most of her time in the Saddam Central Teaching Hospital for Pediatrics in Baghdad. She bleeds profusely from her nose, gums and rectum. Her mother has bought her earrings and a colorful clip to bind her thinning hair into a pony tail, but whatever diversion she has is likely to be only temporary.

In developed countries, the cure rate for leukemia approaches 70 percent. In Iraq it is near zero.

"It's still not too late to save this girl's life if we can give her a bone-marrow transplant," said Dr. Jasim Mazin, the hospital's chief resident. "But we don't have the equipment to perform that kind of operation. We're helpless."

In his five years at Saddam Central, virtually all of his leukemia patients have died. Their deaths, coupled with those who die of gastrointestinal diseases, diarrhea, dehydration and other easily curable ailments, have clearly taken a toll on him. He often works 20 hours a day, and although he is just 28, he looks nearly twice that age.

"Iraq used to be the best country in the Arab world in terms of science and medicine," Dr. Mazin said as he made his rounds on a recent morning. "Now we can't even read medical journals, because they are covered by the embargo."

"I can't believe I use disposable syringes on one patient after another, or perform operations with worn-out instruments in operating theaters that are not even disinfected," he said. "It's very difficult to work very hard on a patient, try to care for him, and then lose him because you can't get some silly thing that you could pick up in a drug store in any other country.

"And this is the best-supplied children's hospital in Iraq. If you go out into the provinces, you see that things are much worse."

The coordinator of United Nations relief programs here, Hans von Sponeck, toured hospitals outside Baghdad last month and reported that much of the equipment he saw "was fit only for a museum."

He said some of it is actually endangering the health of patients and staff, and cited X-ray machines that leak radiation and malfunctioning incinerators that leave residues of toxic medical waste.

Although the effect of sanctions is evident in every aspect of Iraqi life, there are few places where it is more poignantly visible than at hospitals like Saddam Central. According to United Nations figures, Government spending on medicine and medical equipment has fallen by more than 90 percent since the sanctions were imposed after Iraq invaded Kuwait in 1990 and the country began spiraling into economic collapse. Not a single new hospital has been built in that time, although the country's population has grown from 15 million to 22 million.

Iraqi doctors say conditions have improved since 1996, when the United Nations began allowing the Government to sell limited amounts of oil and use some of the income it earns to buy food and medicine. About $450 million worth of drugs and medical supplies have entered the country since then, though the United Nations says distribution is inadequate owing to "transport and logistic difficulties."

The Clinton Administration defends sanctions as an indispensable part of the Western campaign to bring down President Saddam Hussein, whom Western powers have accused of threatening the Middle East by building weapons of mass destruction. The Administration has, however, signaled its willingness to consider an expansion of the oil-for-food program that could allow Iraq to improve the abysmal conditions into which its health care system has fallen.

Any improvement would probably come too late for most of the children now lying listlessly in their hospital beds here.

"Inside the hospitals is where you have to go if you want to see why so much antagonism and resentment is building up here," said Kathy Kelly, who runs a Chicago-based group called Voices in the Wilderness that is campaigning against the sanctions and who is making her ninth visit to Iraq since 1990. "I've seen doctors go from superheroes to almost clinically depressed."

At Saddam Central, Dr. Mazin said he maintains his equilibrium by concentrating his mind on the children he has been able to save. He said his worst period came last April, when he lost about 75 children during a two-week epidemic of chest infections and gastroenteritis. Every one of them, he believes, could have been saved with antibiotics that are commonly available in neighboring countries.

Some patients at Saddam Central need more than medicine. Among them is 16-month-old Affaf Hussein, whose facial irregularities suggest congenital deformity. He suffers from recurrent pneumonia, and his mother spends several hours each day holding a respirator over his face so he can inhale moist oxygen.

"This child is very sick," Dr. Mazin said. "I believe he has some kind of genetic disorder, but we don't have the tools to diagnose what it is. We can't do anything for him."

One of the few bright spots at Saddam Central is a beaming 10-year-old named Marua Tariq, who comes in for a check-up every month wearing her favorite brightly-patterned sweater. She has leukemia, but was released from the hospital six months ago after her case stabilized, and has shown no symptoms since then. If she can stay healthy for another four and a half years, she will be considered cured, the first such case since the sanctions began.

"I'm feeling good and I'm studying hard at school," Marua said with a broad smile. "When I grow up, I want to be a doctor who treats children."

GLOSSARY

A GUIDE TO CRITICAL THINKING TERMS AND CONCEPTS

ACCURATE Free from errors, mistakes, or distortion. By comparison, *correct* connotes little more than absence of error; *accurate* implies a positive exercise to obtain conformity with fact or truth; *exact* stresses perfect conformity to fact, truth, or some standard; *precise* suggests minute accuracy of detail. Accuracy is an important goal in critical thinking, though this is almost always a matter of degree. It is also important to recognize that making mistakes is an essential part of learning, and that it is far better that students make their own mistakes than that they parrot the thinking of the text or the teacher. It also should be recognized that some distortion usually results whenever we think within a point of view or frame of reference. Students should think with this awareness in mind, with some sense of the limitations of their own, the text's, the teacher's, and the subject's perspective. *See also* perfection of thought.

AMBIGUOUS Having two or more possible meanings. Sensitivity to ambiguity and vagueness in writing and speech is essential to good thinking. A continual effort to be clear and precise in language usage is fundamental to education. Ambiguity is a problem more of sentences than of individual words. Furthermore, not every sentence that can be construed in more than one way is problematic and deserving of analysis. Many sentences are clearly intended one way; any other construal is obviously absurd and not meant. For example, "Make me a sandwich" is not seriously intended to request metamorphic change. It is a poor example for teaching genuine insight into critical thinking.

For an example of a problematic ambiguity, consider the statement, "Welfare is corrupt." Among the possible meanings of this sentence are the following: (1) Those who administer welfare programs take bribes to administer welfare policy unfairly; (2) welfare policies are written in such a way that much of the money goes to people who don't deserve it rather than to those who do; (3) a government that gives money to people who haven't earned it corrupts both the giver and the recipient. The first makes moral claims about administrators. The second makes legal claims about policy. The third questions the very principle of welfare. If two people are arguing about whether welfare is corrupt but interpret the claim differently, they can make little or no progress because they aren't arguing about the same point. Evidence and considerations relevant to one interpretation may be irrelevant to others. Therefore, before taking a position on an issue or arguing a point, it is essential to be clear about the issue at hand. *See also* clarify.

ANALYZE To break up a whole into its parts; to examine in detail so as to determine the nature of; to look more deeply into an issue or a situation. All learning presupposes some analysis of what we are learning, if only by categorizing or labeling things in one way rather than another. Students routinely should be asked to analyze their own ideas, claims, experiences, interpretations, judgments, and theories, and those they hear and read. *See also* elements of thought.

ARGUE (1) To engage in a quarrel; bicker; (2) to persuade by giving reasons. As developing critical thinkers, we strive to move from the first sense of the word to the second—we try to focus on giving reasons to support our views without becoming egocentrically involved in the discussion. This is a fundamental problem in human life. To argue in the critical-thinking sense is to use logic and reason and to bring forth facts

479

to support or refute a point. It is done in a spirit of cooperation and good will.

ARGUMENT   A reason or reasons offered for or against something; the offering of such reasons; a discussion in which there is disagreement, suggesting using logic and bringing forth facts to support or refute a point.

ASSUME   Take for granted or presuppose. Critical thinkers make their assumptions explicit, assess them, and correct them. Assumptions can vary from the mundane to the problematic: I heard a scratch at the door. I got up to let the cat in. I assumed that only the cat makes that noise, and that he makes it only when he wants to be let in. Someone speaks gruffly to me. I feel guilty and hurt. I assume that she's angry at me, that she's angry at me only when I do something bad, and that if she's angry at me, she dislikes me. People often equate making assumptions with making *false* assumptions. When people say, "Don't assume," this is what they mean. But we cannot avoid making assumptions, and some are justifiable. (For instance, we have assumed that people who buy this book can read English.) Rather than saying "Don't assume," we are saying, "Be aware of and careful about the assumptions you make, and be ready to examine and critique them." *See also* assumption, elements of thought.

ASSUMPTION   A statement accepted or supposed as true without proof or demonstration; an unstated premise or belief. All human thought and experience are based on assumptions. Our thought must begin with something we take to be true in a given context. We typically are unaware of what we assume and, therefore, rarely question our assumptions. Most of our assumptions are unconscious. They operate in our thinking without our knowing it. Much of what is wrong with human thought can be found in the uncritical or unexamined assumptions that underlie it. All of our prejudices, biases, and preconceived generalizations are based on assumptions.

We often experience the world in such a way as to assume that we are observing things just as they are, as though we were seeing the world without the filter of a point of view. People we disagree with we recognize as having a point of view. One of the key dispositions of critical thinking is the ongoing sense that, as humans, we think within a perspective, that we almost never experience things totally and absolutistically. There is a

connection, therefore, between thinking so as to be aware of our assumptions and being intellectually humble.

By "reasoning based on assumptions," we mean "whatever we take for granted as true" to figure out something else. Thus, if you infer that because a candidate is a Republican, he or she will support a balanced budget, you assume that all Republicans support a balanced budget. If you infer that foreign leaders presented in the news as "enemies" or "friends" are truly enemies or friends, you assume that the news is always accurate in its presentation of the character of foreign leaders.

If you infer that someone who invites you to his or her apartment after a party "to continue this interesting conversation" is really interested in you romantically or sexually, you assume that the only reason for going to someone's apartment late at night after a party is to pursue a romantic or sexual relationship. All reasoning has some basis in the assumptions we make (but usually do not express openly).

AUTHORITY   (1) The power or supposed right to give commands, enforce obedience, take action, or make final decisions; (2) a person with much knowledge and expertise in a field, and hence reliable. Critical thinkers recognize that ultimate authority rests with reason and evidence, as it is only on the assumption that purported experts have the backing of reason and evidence that they rightfully gain authority. Much instruction discourages critical thinking by encouraging students to believe that whatever the text or teacher says is true. As a result, students do not learn how to assess authority. *See also* knowledge.

BIAS   (1) A mental leaning or inclination; (2) partiality, prejudice. We must clearly distinguish two different senses of the word "bias." One is neutral, the other negative. In the neutral sense, because of one's point of view, one notices some things rather than others, emphasizes some points rather than others, and thinks in one direction rather than others. This is not in itself a criticism because thinking within a point of view is unavoidable. In the negative sense, we are implying blindness or irrational resistance to weaknesses within one's own point of view or to the strength or insight within a point of view one opposes. Fair-minded critical thinkers try to be aware of their bias (in the first sense) and try hard to avoid bias (in the second sense). Many people confuse these two senses. Many confuse bias with emotion or with evaluation, perceiving any expression of emotion or any use of evaluative words to be biased (the second sense). Evaluative words that can be justified by reason and evidence are not biased in the negative sense. *See also* criteria, evaluate, judgment, opinion.

CLARIFY   To make easier to understand, to free from confusion or ambiguity, to remove obscurities. *Clarity* is a fundamental perfection of thought, and *clarification* is a fundamental aim in critical thinking. It is important that students see why it is important to write and speak clearly, why it is important to say what they mean and mean what they say. Concrete, specific examples provide the key to clarification. *See also* accurate, ambiguous, logic of language, vague.

CONCEPT   An idea or thought. especially a generalized idea of a thing or of a class of things. Humans think within concepts or ideas. We cannot achieve command over our thoughts unless we learn how to achieve command over our concepts or ideas. Thus, we must learn how to identify the concepts or ideas we are using, contrast them with alternative concepts or ideas, and clarify what we include and exclude by means of those concepts.

In this book, the concepts of critical thinking and uncritical thinking are important ideas. Everything written can be classified as an attempt to explain one or the other of these two ideas. Each of these ideas is explained, in turn, by means of other ideas. Thus, the concept of *thinking critically* is explained by reference to yet other concepts such as *intellectual standards for thought.* Each discipline develops its own set of concepts or technical vocabulary to facilitate its thinking. All sports develop a vocabulary of concepts that enables those who are trying to understand or master the game to make sense of it. One cannot understand ethics without a clear concept of justice, kindness, cruelty, rights, and obligations.

People are often unclear about the concepts they are using. For example, most people say they believe strongly in democracy, but few can clarify with examples what the word "democracy" does and does not imply. Most people confuse the meaning of words with cultural associations, with the result that *democracy,* to many, means whatever *our* government does, and that any country that practices democracy in a different way is undemocratic. We must distinguish the concepts implicit in the English language from the psychological associations surrounding those concepts in a given social group or culture. The failure to develop this ability is a major cause of uncritical thought and selfish critical thought. *See also* logic of language.

CONCLUDE/CONCLUSION   To decide by reasoning, to infer, to deduce; the last step in a reasoning process; a judgment, decision, or belief formed after investigation or reasoning. All beliefs, decisions, and actions are based on human thought, but seldom as the result of conscious reasoning or deliberation. All that we believe is, one way or another, based on conclusions that we have come to during our lifetime. By "coming to conclusions" we mean taking something we believe we know and figuring out something else on the basis of it. When we do this, we make inferences. For example, if you walk by me without saying hello, I might come to the conclusion (make the inference) that you are angry with me. If the water kettle on the stove begins to whistle, I come to the conclusion (make the inference) that the water in the kettle has started to boil.

In everyday life, we continually are making inferences (coming to conclusions) about the people, things, places, and events in our lives. Yet, we rarely monitor our thought processes, and we don't critically assess the conclusions we come to, to determine whether we have sufficient grounds or reasons for accepting them. We seldom recognize when we have come to a conclusion—confusing our conclusions with evidence—and so cannot assess the reasoning that took us from evidence to conclusion. Recognizing that human life is inferential, that we continually come to conclusions about ourselves and the things and persons around us, is essential to think critically and reflectively.

CONSISTENCY   Thinking, acting, or speaking that is in agreement with what has been thought, done, or expressed already; intellectual or moral integrity. Human life and thought are filled with inconsistency, hypocrisy, and contradiction. We often say one thing and do another, judge ourselves and our friends by one standard and our antagonists by another, lean over backward to justify what we want or negate what does not serve our interests. Similarly, we often confuse desires with needs, treating our desires as equivalent to needs, putting what we want above the basic needs of others. Logical and moral consistency is a fundamental value of fair-minded critical thinking. Social conditioning and native egocentrism often obscure social contradictions, inconsistency, and hypocrisy. *See also* human nature, intellectual integrity, personal contradiction, social contradiction.

CONTRADICT/CONTRADICTION   To assert the opposite of; to be contrary to, go against; a statement in opposition to another; a condition in which things tend to be contrary to each other; inconsistency; discrepancy; a person or thing containing or composed of contradictory elements. *See also* personal contradiction, social contradiction.

CRITERION (CRITERIA, PL)   A standard, rule, or test by which something can be judged or measured. Human life, thought, and action are based on human values. Criteria are the standards by which we determine whether those values are achieved in any situation. Critical thinking depends upon making explicit the standards or criteria for rational or justifiable thinking and behavior. *See also* evaluate.

CRITICAL LISTENING   A mode of monitoring how we are listening to maximize our accurate understanding of what another person is saying. By understanding the logic of human communication—that everything spoken expresses point of view, uses some ideas and not others, has implications, and so on—critical thinkers can listen so as to enter sympathetically and analytically into the perspective of others. *See also* critical reading, critical writing, elements of thought, intellectual empathy.

CRITICAL PERSON   One who has mastered a range of intellectual skills and abilities. If that person generally uses those skills to advance his or her own selfish interests, that person is a critical thinker only in a weak or qualified sense. If that person generally uses those skills fair-mindedly, entering empathically into the points of view of others, he or she is a critical thinker in the strongest or fullest sense. *See also* critical thinking.

CRITICAL READING   An active, intellectually engaged process in which the reader participates in an inner dialogue with the writer. Most people read uncritically and so miss some part of what is expressed and distort other parts. Critical readers realize the way in which reading, by its very nature, means entering into a point of view other than our own, the point of view of the writer. Critical readers actively look for assumptions, key concepts and ideas, reasons and justifications,

supporting examples, parallel experiences, implications and consequences, and any other structural features of the written text, to interpret and assess it accurately and fairly. Critical readers do not evaluate written pieces until they accurately understand the author's viewpoint. *See also* elements of thought.

CRITICAL SOCIETY   A culture that rewards adherence to the values of critical thinking and hence does not use indoctrination and inculcation as basic modes of learning. Instead, it rewards reflective questioning, intellectual independence, and reasoned dissent. Socrates is not the only thinker to imagine a society in which independent critical thought becomes embodied in the concrete, day-to-day life of individuals. William Graham Sumner, North America's distinguished anthropologist, explicitly formulated the ideal:

The critical habit of thought, if usual in a society, will pervade all its mores, because it is a way of taking up the problems of life. Men educated in it cannot be stampeded by stump orators and are never deceived by dithyrambic oratory. They are slow to believe. They can hold things as possible or probable in all degrees, without certainty and without pain. They can wait for evidence and weigh evidence, uninfluenced by the emphasis or confidence with which assertions are made on one side or the other. They can resist appeals to their dearest prejudices and all kinds of cajolery. Education in the critical faculty is the only education of which it can be truly said that it makes good citizens. (Folkways, 1906)

Nevertheless, until critical habits of thought pervade our society, schools as social institutions will tend to transmit the prevailing world view more or less uncritically, to transmit it as reality, not as a picture of reality. Education for critical thinking, then, requires that the school or classroom become a microcosm of a critical society. *See also* dialogical instruction, didactic instruction, intellectual virtues, knowledge.

CRITICAL THINKING   (1) Disciplined, self-directed thinking that exemplifies the perfections of thinking appropriate to a specific mode or domain of thinking; (2) thinking that displays mastery of intellectual skills and abilities; (3) the art of thinking about one's thinking while thinking, to make one's thinking better: more clear, more accurate, or more defensible; (4) thinking that is fully aware of, and continually guards against, the natural human tendency to self-deceive and rationalize to selfishly get what it wants. Critical thinking can be differentiated by two forms: (1) "selfish" or "sophistic," on the one hand, and (2) "fair-minded," on the other. In thinking critically, we use our command of the elements of thinking and the universal intellectual standards to adjust our thinking successfully to the logical demands of a type or mode of thinking. *See also* critical listening, critical person, critical reading, critical society, critical writing, domains of thought, elements of thought, intellectual virtues, perfection of thought.

CRITICAL WRITING   Expressing ourselves in written language by arranging our ideas in some relationship to each other. When accuracy and truth are at issue, we must understand what our thesis is, how we can support it, how we can elaborate on it to make it intelligible to others, what objections to it can be raised from other points of view, what the limitations are to our point of view, and so forth. Disciplined writing requires disciplined thinking; disciplined thinking is enhanced by disciplined writing. *See also* critical listening, critical reading, logic of language.

CRITIQUE   An objective judging, analysis, or evaluation of something. The purpose of critique is the same as the purpose of critical thinking—to appreciate strengths as well as weaknesses, virtues as well as failings. Critical thinkers critique in order to redesign, remodel, and make better.

CULTURAL ASSOCIATION   A personal and cultural idea about relationships and linkages absorbed or formed uncritically. If a person who treated me cruelly as a child had a certain tone of voice, I may find myself disliking other persons with the same tone of voice. Media advertising juxtaposes and joins logically unrelated things to influence our buying habits. When we grow up in a certain country or within a certain group within it, we form mental links that, if they remain unexamined, unduly influence our thinking. *See also* concept, critical society.

CULTURAL ASSUMPTION   An unassessed, often implicit, belief adopted by virtue of upbringing in a society. We unconsciously take on our society's point of view, values, beliefs, and practices. At the root of each of these are many kinds of assumptions. Not knowing that we perceive, conceive, think, and experience within assumptions we have taken in, we take ourselves to be perceiving things as they are, not

things as they appear to be from a cultural vantage point. A crucial dimension of critical thinking is to become aware of our cultural assumptions so we might critically examine them. This dimension is almost totally absent from schooling. Although lip service to this ideal is common enough, realistic emphasis is essentially absent. *See also* ethnocentricity, prejudice, social contradiction.

DATA   Facts, figures, or information from which conclusions can be inferred, or upon which interpretations or theories can be based. Critical thinkers must make certain to distinguish hard data from the inferences or conclusions drawn from them.

DIALECTICAL THINKING   Thinking within more than one perspective (dialogical thinking), conducted to test the strengths and weaknesses of opposing points of view. (Court trials and debates are, in a sense, dialectical.) When thinking dialectically, reasoners pit two or more opposing points of view in competition with each other, developing each by providing support, raising objections, countering those objections, raising further objections, and so on. Dialectical thinking or discussion can be conducted so as to win by defeating the positions one disagrees with— using critical insight to support one's own view and point out flaws in other views (associated with critical thinking in the restricted or weak sense), or fair-mindedly, by conceding points that don't stand up to critique, trying to integrate or incorporate strong points found in other views, and using critical insight to develop a fuller and more accurate view (associated with critical thinking in the fuller or strong sense). *See also* multilogical problems, strong-sense critical thinkers, weak-sense critical thinkers.

DIALOGICAL THINKING   Thinking that involves a dialogue or extended exchange between different points of view or frames of reference. Students often learn effectively in dialogical situations, in circumstances in which they continually express their views to others and try to fit others' views into their own. *See also* Socratic questioning, monological thinking, multilogical thinking, dialectical thinking.

DIDACTIC INSTRUCTION   Teaching by telling. In didactic instruction, the teacher directly tells the student what to believe and think about a subject. The student's task is to remember what the teacher said and reproduce it on demand. In its most common form, this mode of teaching assumes falsely that one can give a person knowledge directly without that person having to think his or her way to it. It falsely assumes that knowledge can be separated from understanding and justification. It confuses the ability to state a principle with understanding it, the ability to supply a definition with knowing a word, and the act of saying that something is important with recognizing its importance. *See also* critical society, knowledge.

DOMAINS OF THOUGHT   Different modes of thinking determined by their fundamental purposes and agendas. Critical thinkers learn to discipline their thinking to take into account the nature of the issue or domain. We see this most clearly when we consider the difference between issues and thinking within different academic disciplines or subject areas. Hence, mathematical thinking is quite different from, say, historical thinking. Mathematics and history, we can say then, represent different domains of thought. *See also* logic of questions.

DOMINATING EGO   The irrational tendency of the mind to seek what it wants through the irrational use of direct control or power over people. Dominating strategies are an inherent part of one mode of egocentric thinking. This form of thinking seeks to gain advantage by irrationally wielding power over another. It is contrasted with *submissive* egocentric thinking, in which one irrationally seeks to gain some end by submitting to a person with power. Domination may be overt or covert. On the one hand, dominating egocentrism can involve harsh, dictatorial, tyrannical, or bullying behavior (e.g., a physically abusive spouse). On the other hand, it might involve subtle messages and behavior that imply the use of control or force if "necessary" (e.g., a supervisor reminding a subordinate, by quiet innuendo, that his or her employment is contingent upon unquestioning loyalty to the organization).

Human irrational behavior is always some combination of dominating and submissive acts. No one's irrational acts are exclusively one or the other. In the ideal of a Fascist society, for example, everyone except the dictator is submissive to everyone above him and dominating to everyone below him. Opposite is *submissive ego*.

EGOCENTRICITY   A tendency to view everything in relationship to oneself, to confuse immediate perception (how things seem) with reality; the tendency to be self-centered, or to consider only oneself and one's own interests; selfishness. One's desires, values, and beliefs (seeming to be self-evidently correct or superior to those of others) are often used uncritically as the norm of all judgment and experience. Egocentricity is one of the fundamental impediments to critical thinking. As one learns to think critically in a strong sense, one learns to become more rational and less egocentric. *See also* ethnocentricity, human nature, personal contradiction, sociocentricity, strong-sense critical thinkers.

ELEMENTS OF THOUGHT   A universal set of components of thinking, each of which can be monitored for quality. These are: purpose, question, point of view, assumptions, inferences, implications, concepts, and information. When we understand the elements of thought, we have a powerful set of tools for analyzing thinking. We can ask questions such as: Are we clear about our purpose or goal? About the problem or question at issue? About our point of view or frame of reference? About our assumptions? About the claims we are making? About the reasons or evidence upon which we are basing our claims? About our inferences and line of reasoning? About the implications and consequences that follow from our reasoning? Critical thinkers develop skills of identifying and assessing these elements in their thinking and in the thinking of others.

EMOTION   A feeling aroused to the point of awareness, often a strong feeling or state of excitement. Our emotions are integrally related to our thoughts and desires. These three mental structures—thoughts, feelings, and desires—are continually influencing one another in reciprocal ways. We experience negative feelings, for example, when we *think* things are not going well for us. Moreover, at any given moment, our thoughts, feelings, and desires are under the influence of either our rational faculties or our native irrational tendencies. When our *thinking* is irrational, or egocentric, irrational feeling states emerge. When this happens, we are excited by (what is at base) infantile anger, fear, and jealousy, and our objectivity and fair-mindedness decrease.

Critical thinkers strive to recognize when dysfunctional thinking is leading to inappropriate or unproductive feeling states. They use their rational passions (for example, the passion to be fair) to reason themselves into feelings appropriate to the situation as it really is, rather than egocentrically reacting to distorted views of reality. Thus, emotions and feelings are not in themselves irrational; they are irrational only when they arise from egocentric thoughts. Strong-sense critical thinkers are committed to living a life in which rational emotions predominate and egocentric feelings are reduced to a minimum. *See also* rational emotions/passions, intellectual virtues, strong-sense critical thinkers.

EMPIRICAL   Relying or based on experiment, observation, or experience rather than on theory or meaning. It is important to continually differentiate considerations based on experiment, observation, or experience from those based on the meaning of a word or concept or implications of a theory. Uncritical thinkers often distort facts or experience to preserve a preconceived meaning or theory. For example, uncritical conservatives may distort the facts that support a liberal perspective to prevent empirical evidence from counting against a theory of the world that he or she holds rigidly; uncritical liberals return the favor by a parallel distortion of facts that support a conservative perspective. Indeed, within all perspectives and belief systems many will distort the facts rather than admit to a weakness in their favorite theory or belief. *See also* data, fact, evidence.

EMPIRICAL IMPLICATION   That which follows from a situation or fact, not resulting from the logic of language but, rather, from experience or scientific law. The redness of the coil on the stove empirically implies a high level of heat.

ETHICAL REASONING   Thinking-through ethical problems and issues. Despite popular beliefs to the contrary, ethical reasoning is to be analyzed and assessed in the same way as any other domain of reasoning. Ethical reasoning involves the same elements and is to be assessed by the same standards of clarity, accuracy, precision, relevance, depth, breadth, logic, and significance. Ethical thinking, when reasonable, is ultimately driven by ethical concepts (for example, *fairness*) and principles (for example, "Like cases must be treated in a like manner"), as well as sound principles of critical thought. Understanding ethical principles is as important to sound ethical reasoning as understanding principles of math and biology is to mathematical and biological reasoning.

Ethical principles are guides for human conduct and imply what contributes to good or harm and what

one is either obligated to do or obligated not to do. They enable us to determine the ethical value of a behavior even when that behavior is not, strictly speaking, an obligation. Ethical questions, like questions in any domain of thought, can be either questions with a clear-cut answer or questions with competing reasonable answers, matters about which we must strive to exercise our best judgment. They are *not* matters of personal preference. It makes no sense to say, "Oh, you prefer to be fair. Well, I prefer to be unfair!"

ETHNOCENTRICITY   A tendency to view one's own race or culture as privileged, based on the deep-seated belief that one's own group is superior to all others. Ethnocentrism is a form of egocentrism extended from the self to the group. Much uncritical or selfish critical thinking is either egocentric or ethnocentric in nature. (*Ethnocentrism* and *sociocentrism* are used synonymously, for the most part, though sociocentricity is broader, relating to any social group, including, for example, sociocentricity regarding one's profession.)

The "cure" for ethnocentrism or sociocentrism is empathic thought (thinking within the perspective of opposing groups and cultures). Empathic thought is rarely cultivated. Instead, many give lip service to tolerance while privileging the beliefs, norms, and practices of their own culture.

Critical thinkers are aware of the sociocentric nature of human groups everywhere and resist the pressure of group-think that emerges from in-group thinking. They realize that universal ethical standards supersede group expectations and demands when questions of an ethical nature are at issue. They do not assume that the groups to which they belong are inherently superior to other groups. Instead, they attempt to critique every group accurately, seeking to determine its strengths and weaknesses. Their loyalty to a country is critically based on the principles and ideals of the country and is not based on uncritical loyalty to person, party, or national traditions.

EVALUATE   To judge or determine the worth or quality of something. Evaluation has a logic and should be carefully distinguished from mere subjective preference. The elements of its logic may be put in the form of questions to ask whenever an evaluation is to be carried out: (1) Do we clearly understand what we are evaluating? (2) Are we clear about our purpose? Is our purpose legitimate? (3) Given our purpose, what are the relevant criteria or standards for evaluation? (4) Do we have sufficient information about that which we are evaluating? Is that information relevant to the purpose? (5) Have we applied our criteria accurately and fairly to the facts as we know them? Uncritical thinkers often treat evaluation as mere preference or treat their evaluative judgments as direct observations not admitting of error.

EVIDENCE   The data on which a judgment or conclusion might be based or by which proof or probability might be established. Critical thinkers distinguish the evidence or raw data upon which they base their interpretations or conclusions from the inferences and assumptions that connect data to conclusions. Uncritical thinkers treat their conclusions as something given to them in experience, as something they directly observe in the world. As a result, they find it difficult to see why anyone might disagree with their conclusions. After all, the truth of their views, they believe, is there for everyone to see! These people find it difficult or even impossible to describe the evidence or experience without confusing that description with their interpretation.

EXPLICIT   Stated openly and directly; distinctly expressed; definite. The term *explicit* is applied to that which is so clearly stated or distinctly set forth that there is no doubt as to its meaning. What is explicit is exact and precise, suggesting that which is made unmistakably clear. Critical thinkers strive to make explicit what is implicit in their thinking when that practice enables them to assess the thinking. They realize that problems in thinking often occur when thinking is unclear, vague, or ambiguous.

FACT   What actually happened, what is true; verifiable by empirical means; distinguished from interpretation, inference, judgment, or conclusion; the raw data. There is a range of distinct senses of the word *factual.* For example, sometimes it means simply "true" as opposed to "claimed to be true," or "empirical" as opposed to "conceptual" or "evaluative." Sometimes it means "that which can be verified or disproved by observation or empirical study." People often confuse these two senses, even to the point of accepting as true a statement that merely seems factual—for example, the scientific-sounding claim, "29.23 percent of Americans suffer from depression." Purported facts should be assessed for their accuracy, completeness, and relevance to the issue. Sources of purported facts should be assessed for their qualifications, track record, and impartiality. *See also* intellectual humility, knowledge.

FAIR   Treating both or all sides alike without reference to one's own feelings or interests; implies adhering to a standard of rightness or lawfulness without reference to one's own inclinations. *Impartial* and *unbiased* both imply freedom from prejudice for or against any side; *dispassionate* implies the absence of passion or strong emotion—hence, disinterested judgment; *objective* implies viewing persons or things without reference to oneself or one's interests.

FAIR-MINDEDNESS   A cultivated disposition of mind that enables the thinker to treat all perspectives relevant to an issue in an objective manner. It implies being conscious of the need to treat all viewpoints alike without reference to one's own feelings or selfish interests, or the feelings or selfish interests of one's friends, community, or nation. It implies adherence to intellectual standards without reference to one's own advantage or the advantage of one's group.

FAITH   (1) Blind belief that does not require proof or evidence; (2) complete confidence, trust, or reliance. A critical thinker does not accept faith in the first sense, "blind" faith, for every belief is reached on the basis of some thinking, which therefore may be assessed. Critical thinkers have faith or confidence in reason, but this confidence is not "blind." They recognize that reason and reasonability have proved their worth in the acquisition of knowledge. Ask yourself what it would be not to have faith in evidence, not to have faith in accuracy, or relevance.

FAITH IN REASON   Confidence that in the long run one's own higher interests and those of humankind at large will best be served by giving the freest play to reason—by encouraging people to come to their own conclusions through a process of developing their own rational faculties; confidence that, with proper encouragement and cultivation, people can learn to think for themselves, form rational viewpoints, draw reasonable conclusions, think coherently and logically, persuade each other by reason, and become reasonable, despite the deep-seated obstacles in the native character of the human mind and in society.

Confidence in reason is developed through experiences in which one reasons one's way to insight, solves problems through reason, uses reason to persuade, and is persuaded by reason. Confidence in reason is undermined when one is expected to perform tasks without understanding why, to repeat statements without having verified or justified them, to accept beliefs on the sole basis of authority or social pressure.

FALLACY/FALLACIOUS   An error in reasoning, a flaw or defect in argument; an argument that doesn't conform to rules of good reasoning (especially an argument that appears to be sound); containing or based on a fallacy; deceptive in appearance or meaning; misleading; delusive.

HIGHER-ORDER LEARNING   Learning by thinking-through the logic of disciplines, by thinking-through the foundations, justification, implications, and value of facts, principles, skills, concepts, issues; learning so as to deeply understand. One can learn in keeping with the rational capacities of the human mind or in keeping with its irrational propensities, cultivating the capacity of the human mind to discipline and direct its thought through commitment to intellectual standards; or one can learn through mere association.

Education for critical thought produces higher-order learning by helping students actively think their way to conclusions; discuss their thinking with other students and the teacher; entertain a variety of points of view; analyze concepts, theories, and explanations in their own terms; actively question the meaning and implications of what they learn; compare what they learn to what they have experienced; take seriously what they read and write; solve nonroutine problems; examine assumptions; and gather and assess evidence. When students are engaged in thinking within a subject—when they are learning to think historically, to think mathematically—they are developing higher-order thinking skills. *See also* critical society, dialogical thinking, domains of thought, knowledge, lower-order learning, principle.

HUMAN NATURE   The qualities common to all people. People have both a primary and a secondary nature. Our primary nature is spontaneous, egocentric, and strongly prone to the formation of irrational belief. It is the basis for our instinctual thought. People need no training to believe what we want to believe: what serves our immediate interests, what preserves our sense of personal comfort and righteousness, what minimizes our sense of inconsistency, and what presupposes our own correctness. People need no special training to believe what those around us

believe: what our parents and friends believe, what is taught to us by religious and school authorities, what is repeated often by the media, and what is commonly believed in the nation in which we grow up.

People need no training to think that those who disagree with us are wrong and probably prejudiced. People need no training to assume that our own most fundamental beliefs are self-evidently true or easily justified by evidence. People naturally and spontaneously identify with our own beliefs. We experience most disagreements as personal attacks. The resulting defensiveness interferes with our capacity to empathize with or enter into other points of view.

But we need extensive and systematic practice to develop our secondary nature, our implicit capacity to function as rational people. We need extensive and systematic practice to recognize the tendencies we have to form irrational beliefs. We need extensive practice to develop a dislike for inconsistency, a love of clarity, a passion to seek reasons and evidence and to be fair to points of view other than our own. We need extensive practice to recognize that we indeed have a point of view, that we live inferentially, that we do not have a direct pipeline to reality, that it is entirely possible to have an overwhelming inner sense of the correctness of our views and still be wrong. *See also* intellectual virtues.

IDEA (CONCEPT)   Anything existing in the mind as an object of knowledge or thought; *concept* refers to a generalized idea of a class of objects, based on knowledge of specific instances of the class. Critical thinkers are aware of the ideas (or concepts) they are using in their thinking. They recognize that all disciplines are driven by key concepts. They recognize that all thinking presupposes concepts in use. They seek to identify irrational ideas. They seek to use words (expressive of ideas) in keeping with educated usage. *See also* clarify, concept, logic, logic of language.

IMPLICATION   A claim or truth that follows from other claims or truths. By the "implications of reasoning," we mean that which follows from our thinking. It means *that to which our thinking is leading us.* If you say to someone that you "love" him or her, you *imply* that you are concerned with the person's welfare. If you make a promise, you *imply* that you intend to keep it. If you call a country a democracy, you imply that the political power is in the hands of the people at large (instead of a powerful minority). If you call yourself a feminist, you imply that you are in favor of political, social, and economic equality of the sexes. We often test the credibility of a person by seeing if he or she is true to the implications of his or her own words. A sound principle of critical thinking (and of personal integrity as well, for that matter) is, "Say what you mean and mean what you say."

One of the most important skills of critical thinking is the ability to distinguish between what a statement or situation actually implies and what people may carelessly infer from it. Critical thinkers try to monitor their inferences to keep them in line with what is actually implied by what they know. When speaking, critical thinkers try to use words that imply only what they can legitimately justify. They recognize that there are established word usages that generate established implications. *See also* clarify, critical listening, critical reading, elements of thought, logic of language, precision.

INFERENCE   A step of the mind, an intellectual act by which one concludes that something is so, in light of something else's being so or seeming to be so. If you come at me with a knife in your hand, I probably would infer that you mean to cause me harm. Inferences can be accurate or inaccurate, logical or illogical, justified or unjustified. Inferences are based upon assumptions. *See also* implication.

INFORMATION   Statements, statistics, data, facts, diagrams gathered in any way, as by reading, observation, or hearsay. Information itself does not imply validity or accuracy. By "using information in our reasoning," we mean using some set of facts, data, or experiences to support our conclusions. Whenever someone is reasoning, it makes sense to ask, "What facts or information are you basing your reasoning on?" The informational basis for reasoning is always important and often crucial. For example, in deciding whether to support capital punishment, we need factual information to support our side of the argument. Statements representing information that one might present to support the position that capital punishment is unjustified might be:

- "Since the death penalty was reinstated by the Supreme Court in 1976, for every seven prisoners who were executed, one prisoner awaiting execution was found to be innocent and released."
- "At least 381 homicide convictions have been overturned since 1963 because prosecutors

concealed evidence of innocence or presented evidence they knew to be false."
- "A study by the U.S. General Accounting Office found racial prejudice in death sentencing. . . . Killers of whites were proportionally more likely to be executed than were killers of blacks."
- "Since 1984, 34 mentally retarded people have been executed."[*]

A separate question is whether the information presented is accurate. Also, we should recognize that the other side has information to back it as well.

INSIGHT   The ability to see and understand clearly and deeply the inner nature of things. Instruction for critical thinking fosters insight rather than mere performance. It cultivates the achievement of deeper knowledge and understanding through insight. Thinking one's way into and through a subject leads to insights as one synthesizes what one is learning, relating one subject to other subjects and all subjects to personal experience. Rarely is insight formulated as a goal in present curricula and texts. *See also* dialogical instruction, didactic instruction, higher-order learning, intellectual humility, lower-order learning.

INTELLECTUAL AUTONOMY   Having rational control of one's beliefs, values, and inferences. The ideal of critical thinking is to learn to think for oneself, to gain command over one's thought processes. Intellectual autonomy does not entail willfulness, stubbornness, or rebellion. It entails a commitment to analyzing and evaluating beliefs on the basis of reason and evidence, to questioning when it is rational to question, to believing when it is rational to believe, and to conforming when it is rational to conform. *See also* know, knowledge.

INTELLECTUAL CIVILITY   A commitment to take others seriously as thinkers, to treat them as intellectual equals, to grant respect and full attention to their views—a commitment to persuade rather than browbeat. It is distinguished from intellectual rudeness—verbally attacking others, dismissing them, stereotyping their views. Intellectual civility is not a matter of mere courtesy but, instead, arises from a sense that communication itself requires honoring others' views and their capacity to reason.

INTELLECTUAL COURAGE   Willingness to face and fairly assess ideas, beliefs, or viewpoints to which we have not given a serious hearing, regardless of our

---

[*]*Moratorium Now, New York Times,* Nov. 22, 1999.

strong negative reactions to them; arises from the recognition that ideas considered dangerous or absurd are sometimes rationally justified, in whole or in part, and that conclusions or beliefs that those around us espouse or inculcate in us are sometimes false or misleading. To determine for ourselves which is which, we must not passively and uncritically accept what we have learned. Intellectual courage comes into play here because we will inevitably come to see truth in some ideas considered dangerous and absurd and distortion or falsity in some ideas strongly held in our social group. To be true to our own thinking in these circumstances takes courage. Examining cherished beliefs is difficult, and the penalties for nonconformity are often severe.

INTELLECTUAL CURIOSITY   A strong desire to deeply understand, to figure out things, to propose and assess useful and plausible hypotheses and explanations, to learn, to find out. People do not learn well, do not gain knowledge, unless they want knowledge—deep, accurate, complete understanding. When people lack passion for figuring out things—have intellectual apathy—they tend to settle for an incomplete, incoherent, sketchy sense of things incompatible with a critically developed, richer, fuller conception. This trait can flourish only when it is allowed and encouraged, when people are able to pose and pursue questions of interest to them, and when their intellectual curiosity pays off in increasing understanding.

INTELLECTUAL DISCIPLINE   The trait of thinking in accordance with intellectual standards, intellectual rigor, carefulness, order, conscious control. Undisciplined thinkers do not recognize when they come to unwarranted conclusions, confuse ideas, fail to consider pertinent evidence, and so on. Thus, intellectual discipline is at the very heart of becoming a critical person. It takes discipline of mind to stay focused on the intellectual task at hand, to locate and carefully assess needed evidence, to systematically analyze and address questions and problems, to hold one's thinking to intellectual standards such as clarity, precision, completeness, and consistency. Intellectual discipline is achieved slowly, bit by bit, and only through deep commitment.

INTELLECTUAL EMPATHY   Understanding the need to put oneself imaginatively in the place of others to genuinely understand them. We must recognize our egocentric tendency to identify truth with our immediate perceptions or longstanding beliefs. Intellectual empathy correlates with the ability to reconstruct accurately the viewpoints and reasoning of others and to reason from premises, assumptions, and ideas other than our own. This trait also requires that we remember occasions when we were wrong, despite an intense conviction that we were right, and consider that we might be similarly deceived in a case at hand.

INTELLECTUAL HUMILITY   Awareness of the limits of one's knowledge, including sensitivity to circumstances in which one's native egocentrism is likely to function self-deceptively; sensitivity to bias and prejudice in, and limitations of, one's viewpoint. Intellectual humility is based on the recognition that no one should claim more than he or she actually knows. It does not imply spinelessness or submissiveness. It implies the lack of intellectual pretentiousness, boastfulness, or conceit, combined with insight into the strengths or weaknesses of the logical foundations of one's beliefs.

INTELLECTUAL INTEGRITY   Recognition of the need to be true to one's own thinking, to be consistent in the intellectual standards one applies, to hold oneself to the same rigorous standards of evidence and proof to which one holds one's antagonists, to practice what one advocates for others, and to honestly admit discrepancies and inconsistencies in one's own thought and action. This trait develops best in a supportive atmosphere in which people feel secure and free enough to honestly acknowledge their inconsistencies and can develop and share realistic ways of ameliorating them. It requires honest acknowledgment of the difficulties in achieving greater consistency.

INTELLECTUAL PERSEVERANCE   Willingness and consciousness of the need to pursue intellectual insights and truths despite difficulties, obstacles, and frustrations; firm adherence to rational principles despite irrational opposition from others; a sense of the need to struggle with confusion and unsettled questions over an extended time to achieve deeper understanding or insight.

INTELLECTUAL RESPONSIBILITY   A sense of obligation to fulfill one's duties in intellectual matters. Intellectually responsible people feel strongly obliged to achieve a high level of precision and accuracy in their reasoning and are deeply committed to gathering complete, relevant, adequate evidence. This sense of obligation arises when people recognize the need for meeting the intellectual standards required by rational, fair-minded thought.

INTELLECTUAL SENSE OF JUSTICE   Willingness and consciousness of the need to entertain all viewpoints sympathetically and to assess them with the same intellectual standards, without reference to one's own feelings or vested interests, or the feelings or vested interests of one's friends, community, or nation; implies adherence to intellectual standards without reference to one's own advantage or the advantage of one's group.

INTELLECTUAL STANDARDS   Concepts and principles by which reasoning should be judged to determine its quality or value. Because their contextualized application generates the specific criteria by which reasoning is assessed, intellectual standards are fundamental to critical thinking. Critical thinkers are able to take apart their thinking (focusing on the elements of reasoning) and assess the parts of thinking based on intellectual standards. The most important intellectual standards for thinking are clarity, accuracy, relevance, precision, breadth, depth, logicalness, significance, consistency, fairness, completeness, plausibility, probability, and reliability.

INTELLECTUAL VIRTUES   The traits of mind and intellectual character traits necessary for right action and thinking; the traits essential for fair-mindedness. They distinguish the narrow-minded, self-serving critical thinker from the open-minded, truth-seeking critical thinker. Intellectual traits are interdependent, each developing simultaneously in conjunction with the others. They cannot be imposed from without; they must be developed from within. The intellectual virtues include intellectual sense of justice, intellectual perseverance, intellectual integrity, intellectual humility, intellectual empathy, intellectual courage, intellectual confidence in reason, and intellectual autonomy.

INTERPRET   To give one's own conception of, to place in the context of one's own experience, perspective, point of view, or philosophy. Interpretations should be distinguished from the facts, the evidence, the situation. (I may interpret someone's silence as an expression of hostility toward me. This interpretation may or may not be correct. I may have projected my patterns of motivation and behavior onto that person, or I may have accurately noticed this pattern in the other.) The best interpretations take the most evidence into account. Critical thinkers recognize their interpretations, distinguish them from evidence, consider alternative interpretations, and reconsider their interpretations in the light of new evidence. All learning involves personal interpretation, because we must integrate into our own thinking and action whatever we learn. What we learn we must give a meaning to. It must be meaningful to us, and hence involves interpretive acts on our part. In attempting to directly implant knowledge in students' minds, *didactic instruction* typically ignores the role of personal interpretation in learning.

INTUITION   The direct knowing or learning of something without the conscious use of reasoning. We sometimes seem to know or learn things without recognizing how we came to that knowledge. When this occurs, we experience an inner sense that what we believe is true. The problem is that sometimes we are correct (and have genuinely experienced an intuition) and sometimes we are incorrect (having fallen victim to one of our prejudices). Critical thinkers do not blindly accept what they think or believe but cannot prove as true. They realize how easily they confuse intuitions and prejudices. Critical thinkers may follow their inner sense that something is so, but only with a healthy sense of intellectual humility.

A second sense of intuition that is important for critical thinking is suggested in the following sentence: To develop your critical thinking abilities, it is important to develop your critical thinking intuitions. We can learn concepts at various levels. If we learn nothing more than an abstract definition for a word and do not learn how to apply it effectively in a wide variety of situations, we end up with no intuitive basis for applying it. We lack the insight into how, when, and why it applies. We develop critical thinking intuitions when we gain the practical insights necessary for a ready and swift application of concepts to cases in a wide array of circumstances. We want critical thinking to be intuitive to us, ready and available for immediate translation into everyday thought and experience.

IRRATIONAL/IRRATIONALITY   (1) Lacking the power to reason; (2) contrary to reason or logic; (3) senseless, absurd. Uncritical thinkers have failed to develop the ability or power to reason well. Their beliefs and practices, then, are often contrary to what is reasonable, sensible, and logical and sometimes are blatantly absurd. The terms can be applied to persons, acts, emotions, policies, laws, social practices, belief systems, even whole societies—to virtually any human construct. *See also* logic, rationality, reason.

IRRATIONAL LEARNING Learning that is not based on rational assent. Not all learning is automatically or even commonly rational. Much that we learn in everyday life is quite distinctively irrational. It is quite possible—and indeed the bulk of human learning is unfortunately of this character—to come to believe any number of things without knowing how or why. We believe for irrational reasons—because those around us believe, because we are rewarded for believing, because we are afraid to disbelieve, because our vested interest is served by belief, because we are more comfortable with belief, or because we have ego-identified ourselves, our image, or our personal being with belief. In all of these cases, our beliefs are without rational grounding, without good reason and evidence, without the foundation a rational person demands. Conversely, we become rational to the extent that our beliefs and actions are grounded in good reasons and evidence; to the extent that we recognize and critique our own irrationality; to the extent that we are not moved by bad reasons and a multiplicity of irrational motives, fears, and desires; to the extent that we have cultivated a passion for clarity, accuracy, and fair-mindedness. These global skills, passions, and dispositions, integrated into behavior and thought, characterize the rational, the educated, and the critical person. *See also* didactic instruction, higher-order learning, knowledge, lower-order learning.

JUDGMENT (1) The act of deciding; (2) understanding and good sense. A person has good judgment when he or she typically reaches decisions on the basis of understanding and good sense. Whenever we form a belief or opinion, make a decision, or act, we do so on the basis of implicit or explicit judgments. All thought presupposes making judgments concerning what is so and what is not so, what is true and what is not. To cultivate people's ability to think critically is to foster their judgment, to help them develop the habit of judging on the basis of reason, evidence, logic, and good sense. Good judgment is developed not by merely learning about principles of good judgment but also by frequent practice in judging and assessing judgments.

JUSTIFY/JUSTIFICATION To show a belief, opinion, action, or policy to be in accord with reason and evidence; ethical acceptability. Education should foster reasonability in students. This requires that teachers and students develop the disposition to ask for and give justifications for beliefs, opinions, actions, and policies. Asking for a justification should not be viewed as an insult or attack but, rather, as a normal act of a rational person.

KNOW To have a clear perception or understanding of, to be sure of, to have a firm mental grasp of. *See also* knowledge.

KNOWLEDGE A clear and justifiable grasp of what is so or of how to do something. Knowledge is based on understanding or skill, which in turn is based on thought, study, and experience. "Thoughtless knowledge" is a contradiction. "Blind knowledge" is a contradiction. "Unjustifiable knowledge" is a contradiction. Knowledge applies to any body of facts gathered by study or observation, and to the ideas inferred from these facts, and connotes an understanding of what is known. By contrast, *information* applies to data gathered in any way, as by reading, observation, or hearsay, and does not necessarily connote validity. Critical thinkers distinguish knowledge from opinion and belief. Knowledge implies justifiable belief or skilled action. Hence, when students blindly memorize and are tested for recall, they are not being tested for knowledge.

In present-day schooling, knowledge is continually confused with mere recall. This confusion is a deep-seated impediment to the integration of critical thinking into schooling. Genuine knowledge is inseparable from thinking minds. We often wrongly talk of knowledge as if it could be divorced from thinking, as though it could be gathered by one person and given to another in the form of a collection of sentences to remember. When we talk in this way, we forget that knowledge, by its very nature, depends on thought. Knowledge is produced by thought, analyzed by thought, comprehended by thought, organized, evaluated, maintained, and transformed by thought.

Knowledge can be acquired only through thought. Knowledge exists, properly speaking, only in minds that have comprehended and justified it through thought. Knowledge is not to be confused with belief or with symbolic representation of belief. Humans easily and frequently believe things that are false or believe things to be true without knowing them to be so. A book contains knowledge only in a derivative sense, only because minds can read it thoughtfully and through that process gain knowledge.

LOGIC (1) Correct reasoning or the study of correct reasoning and its foundations; (2) the relationships between propositions (supports, assumes, implies, contradicts, counts against, is relevant to); (3) the system of principles, concepts, and assumptions that underlies any discipline, activity, or practice; (4) the set of rational considerations that bear upon the truth or justification of any belief or set of beliefs; (5) the set of rational considerations that bear upon the settlement of any question or set of questions.

The word *logic* covers a range of related concerns, all bearing upon the question of rational justification and explanation. All human thought and behavior are based to some extent on logic rather than instinct. Humans try to figure out things using ideas, meanings, and thought. This intellectual behavior inevitably involves logic or considerations of a logical sort—some sense of what is relevant and irrelevant, of what supports and what counts against a belief, of what we should and should not assume, of what we should and should not claim, of what we do and do not know, of what is and is not implied, of what does and does not contradict, of what we should or should not do or believe.

Concepts have a logic in that we can investigate the conditions under which they do and do not apply, of what is relevant or irrelevant to them, of what they do or do not imply. Questions have a logic in that we can investigate the conditions under which they can be settled. Disciplines have a logic in that they have purposes and a set of logical structures that bear upon these purposes: assumptions, concepts, issues, data, theories, claims, implications, consequences.

The concept of logic is a seminal notion in critical thinking. It takes considerable time, however, before most people become comfortable with its many uses. This stems in part from our failure to monitor our own thinking in keeping with the standards of reason and logic.

This is not to deny that logic is involved in all human thinking. Rather, it is to say that the logic we use is often implicit, unexpressed, and sometimes contradictory. *See also* higher-order thinking, knowledge, logic of a discipline, logic of language, logic of questions, lower-order learning.

LOGIC OF A DISCIPLINE   The notion that every technical term has logical relationships with other technical terms, that some terms are logically more basic than others, and that every discipline relies on concepts, assumptions, and theories, makes claims, gives reasons and evidence, avoids contradictions and inconsistencies, and has implications and consequences. Though all students study disciplines,

most are ignorant of the logic of the disciplines they study. This severely limits their ability to grasp the discipline as a whole, to think independently within it, to compare and contrast it with other disciplines, and to apply it outside the context of academic assignments.

Typically, students do not look for seminal terms as they study an area. They do not strive to translate technical terms into analogies and ordinary words they understand, or distinguish technical from ordinary uses of terms. They do not look for the basic assumptions of the disciplines they study. On the whole, they do not know what assumptions are or why it is important to examine them. What they have in their heads exists like so many BBs in a bag. Whether one thought supports or follows from another, whether one thought elaborates on another, exemplifies, presupposes, or contradicts another, are matters that students have not learned to think about. They have not learned to use thought to understand thought—another way of saying that they have not learned how to use thought to gain knowledge.

Instruction for critical thinking cultivates students' ability to make explicit the logic of what they study. This emphasis gives depth and breadth to study and learning. It lies at the heart of the differences between lower-order and higher-order learning. *See also* knowledge.

LOGIC OF LANGUAGE   For a language to exist and be learnable by people from a variety of cultures, it is necessary that words have definite uses and defined concepts that transcend any culture. The English language, for example, is learned by many peoples of the world who are unfamiliar with English or North American cultures. Critical thinkers must learn to use their native language with precision, in keeping with educated usage.

Many students do not understand the significant relationship between precision in language use and precision in thought. Consider, for example, how most students relate to their native language. Questioned about the meanings of words, they often say that people have their own meanings for all the words they use. If this were true, we could not understand each other. Students often speak and write in vague sentences because they do not have rational criteria for choosing words; they simply write whatever words pop into their heads. They do not realize that every language has a highly refined logic that one must learn in order to express oneself precisely. They do not realize that even words that are similar in meaning typically have different implications.

Consider, for example, the words *explain, expound, explicate, elucidate, interpret,* and *construe. Explain* implies the process of making clear and intelligible something that is not understood or known. *Expound* implies a systematic and thorough explanation, often by an expert. *Explicate* implies a scholarly analysis developed in detail. *Elucidate* implies shedding light by clear and specific illustration or explanation. *Interpret* implies bringing out meanings that are not immediately apparent. *Construe* implies a specific interpretation of something whose meaning is ambiguous. *See also* clarify, concept.

LOGIC OF QUESTIONS   The range of rational considerations that bear upon settlement of a given question or group of questions. Critical thinkers are adept at analyzing questions to determine what, precisely, a question asks and how to go about rationally settling it. Critical thinkers recognize that different kinds of questions often call for different modes of thinking, different kinds of considerations, and different procedures and techniques. Uncritical thinkers often confuse distinct questions and use considerations irrelevant to an issue while ignoring relevant considerations.

LOWER-ORDER LEARNING   Learning by rote memorization, association, and drill. Schools use a variety of forms of lower-order learning that we can identify by understanding the relative lack of logic informing them. Because lower-order learning is learning by sheer association or rote, students come to think of history class, for example, as a place where they hear names, dates, places, events, and outcomes; where they try to remember these and state them on tests. Math comes to be thought of as numbers, symbols, and formulas—mysterious things they mechanically manipulate as the teacher told them to do to get the right answer. Literature is often thought of as uninteresting stories to remember, along with what the teacher said is important about them.

Consequently, these students leave with a jumble of undigested fragments, scraps left over after they have forgotten most of what they stored in their short-term memory for tests. They do not grasp the logic of what they learn. Rarely do they relate what they learn to their own experience or critique each by means of the other. Rarely do they try to test what they learn in everyday life. Rarely do they ask, "Why is this so? How does this relate to what I already know? How does this relate to what I'm learning in other classes?"

In a nutshell, few students think of what they are learning as worthy of being arranged logically in their mind or have the slightest idea of how to do so. *See also* didactic instruction, monological problems, multilogical problems, multilogical thinking.

MONOLOGICAL PROBLEMS   One-dimensional problems that can be solved by reasoning exclusively within one point of view or frame of reference. Consider the following problems: (1) 10 full crates of walnuts weigh 410 pounds, whereas an empty crate weighs 10 pounds. How much do the walnuts alone weigh? and (2) In how many days of the week does the third letter of the day's name immediately follow the first letter of the day's name in the alphabet? We call these *problems,* and the means by which they are solved are *monological,* settled within one frame of reference with a definite set of logical moves. When the proper set of moves is performed, the problem is settled. The answer or solution proposed can be shown by standards implicit in the frame of reference to be the right answer or solution.

Most important human problems are multilogical rather than monological. They are nonatomic problems inextricably joined to other problems, having some conceptual messiness, often with important values lurking in the background. When the problems have an empirical dimension, that dimension tends to have a controversial scope. In multilogical problems, it is often arguable how some facts should be considered and interpreted and how their significance should be determined. When they have a conceptual dimension, the concepts usually can be pinned down in different ways.

While life presents us with predominantly multilogical problems, schooling today overemphasizes monological problems. Worse, present instructional practices frequently treat multilogical problems as if they were monological. The posing of multilogical problems and their consideration from multiple points of view play an important role in cultivating critical thinking and higher-order learning.

MONOLOGICAL THINKING   One-dimensional thought conducted exclusively within one point of view or frame of reference—figuring out how much this $67.49 pair of shoes with a 25% discount will cost me; learning what signing this contract obliges me to do; finding out what year John F. Kennedy was elected President. A person can think monologically whether the question is or is not genuinely monological. (For example, if one considers the question, "Who caused the Civil War?" only from a Northerner's perspective, one is thinking monologically about a multilogical question.)

Strong-sense critical thinkers avoid monological thinking when the question is multilogical. Moreover, higher-order learning requires multilogical thought even when the problem is monological (for example, learning a concept in chemistry), as students must explore and assess their original beliefs to develop insight into new ideas.

MULTILOGICAL PROBLEMS   Multidimensional problems that can be analyzed and approached from more than one (often from conflicting) points of view or frames of reference. For example, many ecological problems have a variety of dimensions—historical, social, economic, biological, chemical, moral, political. A person who is comfortable thinking-through multilogical problems is comfortable thinking within multiple perspectives, engaging in dialogical and dialectical thinking, practicing intellectual empathy, thinking across disciplines and domains. *See also* dialogical instruction, intellectual empathy, logic of a discipline, logic of questions, monological problems.

MULTILOGICAL THINKING   Thought that sympathetically enters, considers, and reasons within multiple points of view. *See also* dialectical thinking, dialogical instruction, multilogical problems.

NATIONAL BIAS   Prejudice in favor of one's country, its beliefs, traditions, practices, image, and world view; a form of sociocentrism or ethnocentrism. It is natural, if not inevitable, for people to be favorably disposed toward the beliefs, traditions, practices, and world view within which they grew up. This favorable inclination commonly becomes a form of prejudice—a more or less rigid, irrational ego-identification that significantly distorts one's view of one's own nation and the world at large. It is manifested in a tendency to mindlessly take the side of one's own government, to uncritically accept governmental accounts of the nature of disputes with other nations, to uncritically exaggerate the virtues of one's own nation while playing down the virtues of enemy nations.

National bias is reflected in the press and media coverage of every nation of the world. Events are included or excluded according to what seems significant within the dominant world view of the nation, and are shaped into stories to validate that view. Though constructed to fit into a certain view of the world, the news stories are presented as neutral, objective accounts, and are uncritically accepted as such because people tend to uncritically assume that their own view of things is the way things really are.

To become responsible, critically thinking citizens and fair-minded people, students must practice identifying national bias in the news and in their texts, and to broaden their perspective beyond that of uncritical nationalism. *See also* bias, critical society, dialogical instruction, ethnocentricity, intellectual empathy, knowledge, prejudice, sociocentricity.

OPINION   A belief that typically is open to dispute. Sheer unreasoned subjective opinion or preference should be distinguished from reasoned judgment—beliefs formed on the basis of careful reasoning. *See also* evaluation, judgment, justify, know, knowledge, reasoned judgment.

PERFECTION OF THOUGHT   A natural excellence or fitness to thinking, viewed in an attempt to understand or make sense of the world. This excellence is manifest in its clarity, precision, specificity, accuracy, relevance, consistency, logicalness, depth, completeness, significance, fairness, and adequacy. These perfections are general achievements of thought. Their absence represents legitimate concerns irrespective of the discipline or domain of thought. To develop one's mind and discipline, one's thinking with respect to these standards requires regular practice and long-term cultivation. Achieving these standards is a relative matter and varies to some extent among domains of thought. Being precise while doing mathematics is not the same as being precise while writing a poem, describing an experience, or explaining a historical event.

What's more, skilled propaganda, skilled political debate, skilled defense of a group's interests, skilled deception of one's enemy may require the violation or selective application of any of the above standards. Perfecting one's thought as an instrument for success in a world based on power and advantage differs from perfecting one's thought for the apprehension and defense of fair-minded, balanced truthfulness.

To develop one's critical thinking skills merely to the level of adequacy for social success is to sacrifice the higher perfections of thought for pragmatic gain and generally involves more than a little self-deception.

PERSONAL CONTRADICTION An inconsistency in one's life wherein people say one thing and do another, or use a double-standard, judging themselves and their friends by an easier standard than they use for people they don't like; typically a form of hypocrisy accompanied by self-deception. Most personal contradictions remain unconscious. People too often ignore the difficulty of becoming intellectually and morally consistent, preferring instead to merely admonish others. Personal contradictions are more likely to be discovered, analyzed, and reduced in an atmosphere in which they can be openly admitted and realistically considered without excessive penalty. *See also* egocentricity, intellectual integrity.

POINT OF VIEW Perspective. Human thought is relational and selective. It is impossible to understand simultaneously any person, event, or phenomenon from every vantage point. Our purposes often control how we see things. Critical thinking requires that we take this into account when analyzing and assessing thinking. This is not to say that human thought is incapable of truth and objectivity, but only that human truth, objectivity, and insight are limited and partial, not total and absolute. By reasoning within a point of view, then, we mean that our thinking inevitably has some comprehensive focus or orientation. Our thinking is focused *on* something *from* some angle.

We can change either what we are focusing on or the angle of our focus. We often give names to the angle from which we are thinking about something. For example, we could look at something politically or scientifically, poetically or philosophically. We might look at something conservatively or liberally, religiously or secularly. We might look at something from a cultural or a financial perspective, or both. Once we understand how someone is approaching a question or topic (his or her comprehensive perspective) we usually are much better able to understand the logic of that person's thinking as an organized whole.

PRECISION The quality of being accurate, definite, and exact. The standards and modes of precision vary according to subject and context. *See also* logic of language, elements of thought.

PREJUDICE A judgment, belief, opinion, or point of view—favorable or unfavorable—formed before the facts are known, resistant to evidence and reason, or in disregard of facts that contradict it. Self-announced prejudice is rare. Prejudice almost always exists in obscured, rationalized, socially validated, functional forms. It enables people to sleep peacefully at night even while flagrantly abusing the rights of others. It enables people to get more of what they want, or to get it more easily. It often is sanctioned with a superabundance of pomp and self-righteousness. Unless we recognize these powerful tendencies toward selfish thought in our social institutions, even in what seem to be lofty actions and moralistic rhetoric, we will not face squarely the problem of prejudice in human thought and action.

Uncritical and selfishly critical thought are often prejudiced. Most instruction in schools today, because students do not think their way to what they accept as true, tends to give students prejudices rather than knowledge. For example, partly as a result of schooling, people often accept as authorities those who sprinkle their statements liberally with numbers and intellectual-sounding language, however irrational or unjust their positions. This prejudice toward pseudo-authority impedes rational assessment. *See also* insight, knowledge.

PREMISE A proposition upon which an argument is based or from which a conclusion is drawn; a starting point of reasoning. For example, in commenting on someone's reasoning, one might say, "You seem to be reasoning from the premise that everyone is selfish in everything they do. Do you hold this belief?"

PRINCIPLE A fundamental truth, law, doctrine, value, or commitment upon which others are based. Rules—which are more specific than principles, and often are superficial and arbitrary—are based on principles. Rules are more algorithmic; they needn't be understood to be followed. Principles must be understood to be applied or followed appropriately. One important type of principle consists of ethical principles, which are guides for human conduct. Critical thinking is dependent on principles, not rules and procedures. Critical thinking is principled, not procedural, thinking. Principles must be practiced and applied to be internalized. *See also* higher-order learning, judgment, lower-order learning.

PROBLEM A question, matter, situation, or person that is perplexing or difficult to figure out, handle, or resolve. Problems, like questions, can be divided into many types, each with a certain logic. *See also* logic of questions, monological problems, multilogical problems.

PROBLEM-SOLVING The process of reaching solutions. Whenever a problem cannot be solved formulaically or robotically, critical thinking is required—first, to determine the nature and dimensions of the problem, and then, in the light of the first, to determine the considerations, points of view, concepts, theories, data, and reasoning relevant to its solution. Extensive practice in independent problem-solving is essential to developing critical thought. Problem-solving rarely is best approached procedurally or as a series of rigidly followed steps. For example, problem-solving schemas typically begin, "State the problem." Rarely can problems be stated precisely and fairly prior to analysis, gathering of evidence, and dialogical or dialectical thought wherein several provisional descriptions of the problem are proposed, assessed, and revised.

PROOF Evidence or reasoning so strong or certain as to demonstrate the truth or acceptability of a conclusion beyond a reasonable doubt. How strong evidence or reasoning has to be to demonstrate what it purports to prove varies from context to context, depending on the significance of the conclusion or the seriousness of implications following from it. *See also* domains of thought.

PURPOSE Object, aim, goal, end in view; something one intends to get or do. In saying that reasoning has a purpose, we mean that when humans think about the world, we do not do so randomly but, rather, in line with our goals, desires, needs, and values. Our thinking is an integral part of a patterned way of acting in the world, and we act, even in simple matters, with some set of ends in view. To understand someone's thinking—including our own—we must understand the functions it serves, what it is about, the direction it is moving, the ends that make sense of it. Most of what we are after in our thinking is not obvious to us. Raising human goals and desires to the level of conscious realization is an important part of critical thinking.

QUESTION A problem or matter open to discussion or inquiry, something that is asked, as in seeking to learn or to gain knowledge. By reasoning upon some *question, issue,* or *problem,* we mean that when we think about the world in line with our goals, desires, needs, and values, we often come up against questions we need to answer, problems we need to solve, issues we need to resolve. Therefore, when we find ourselves facing a difficulty, it makes sense to say, "What is the question we need to answer?" or, "What is the problem we need to solve?" or, "What is the issue we need to resolve?" To improve our ability to think well, it is important to learn how to put the questions, problems, and issues we need to deal with in a clear and distinct way. If you change the question, you change the criteria you have to meet to settle it. If you modify the problem, you need to modify how you are going to solve the problem. If you shift the issue, new considerations become relevant to its resolution.

RATIONAL/RATIONALITY That which conforms to principles of good reasoning, is sensible, shows good judgment, is consistent, logical, complete, and relevant. When we refer to something or someone as rational, we have in mind the quality of being based on or informed by sound reasoning or justified evidence. *Rationality,* like *virtue* or *goodness,* is a summary term. It is manifested in an unlimited number of ways and depends on a host of principles. It has some ambiguity, depending on whether one considers only the consistency and effectiveness by which one pursues one's ends, or whether it includes the assessment of ends themselves.

There is also ambiguity in whether one considers selfish ends to be rational, even when they conflict with what is just. Does a rational person have to be just or only skilled in pursuing his or her interests? Is it rational to be rational in an irrational world? *See also* intellectual virtues, irrational/irrationality, logic, perfection of thought, strong-sense critical thinkers, weak-sense critical thinkers.

RATIONAL EMOTIONS/PASSIONS The affective side of reason and critical thought. R. S. Peters (1973) explained the significance of "rational passions" as follows:

There is, for instance, the hatred of contradictions and inconsistencies, together with the love of clarity and hatred of confusion without which words could not be held to relatively constant meanings and testable rules and generalizations stated. A reasonable man cannot, without some special explanation, slap his sides with delight or express indifference if he is told that what he says is confused, incoherent, and perhaps riddled with contradictions.

> *Reason is the antithesis of arbitrariness. In its operation it is supported by the appropriate passions which are mainly negative in character—the hatred of irrelevance, special pleading, and arbitrary fiat. The more developed emotion of indignation is aroused when some excess of arbitrariness is perpetuated in a situation where people's interests and claims are at stake. The positive side of this is the passion for fairness and impartial consideration of claims. . . .*

> *A man who is prepared to reason must feel strongly that he must follow the arguments and decide things in terms of where they lead. He must have a sense of the giveness of the impersonality of such considerations. Insofar as thoughts about persons enter his head, they should be tinged with the respect which is due to another who, like himself, may have a point of view which is worth considering, who may have a glimmering of the truth which has so far eluded himself. A person who proceeds in this way, who is influenced by such passions, is what we call a reasonable man.*

RATIONALIZE   To devise socially plausible explanations or excuses for one's actions, desires, and beliefs, when these are not one's actual motives. To rationalize is to give reasons that sound good but are not honest and accurate. Rationalization is often used in situations in which one is pursuing one's vested interests while trying to maintain the appearance of high moral purpose. Politicians, for instance, are continually rationalizing their actions, implying that they are acting from high motives when they usually are acting as they are because they have received large donations from vested interest groups that profit from the action taken. Those who held slaves often rationalized that slavery was justified because the slaves were like children and had to be taken care of.

Rationalization is a defense mechanism that the egocentric mind uses to enable people to get what they want without having to face the reality that their motives are selfish or their behavior unconscionable. Rationalizations enable us to keep our actual motives beneath the level of consciousness. We then can sleep peacefully at night while we behave unethically by day.

RATIONAL SELF   Human character and nature to the extent that we seek to base our beliefs and actions on good reasoning and evidence. Who we are, what our true character is or our predominant qualities are, are typically different from who we think we are. Human egocentrism and accompanying self-deception often stand in the way of our gaining more insight into ourselves. We can develop a rational self, become a person who gains significant insight into what our true character is, only by reducing our egocentrism and self-deception. Critical thinking is essential to this process.

RATIONAL SOCIETY   *See* critical society.

REASONED JUDGMENT   Any belief or conclusion reached on the basis of careful thought and reflection, distinguished from mere or unreasoned opinion on the one hand and from sheer fact on the other. Few people have a clear sense of which of their beliefs are based on reasoned judgment and which on mere opinion. Moral or ethical questions, for example, are questions that usually require reasoned judgment. One way of conceiving subject-matter education is as developing students' ability to engage in reasoned judgment in accordance with the standards of each subject.

REASONING   The mental processes of those who reason; especially the drawing of conclusions or inferences from observations, facts, or hypotheses; the evidence or arguments used in this procedure. By reasoning, we mean making sense of something by giving it some meaning in your mind. Almost all thinking is part of our sense-making activities. We hear scratching at the door and think, "It's the dog." We see dark clouds in the sky and think, "It looks like rain." Some of this activity operates at a subconscious level (for example, all of the sights and sounds about me have meaning for me without my explicitly noticing that they do).

Most of our reasoning is quite unspectacular. Our reasoning tends to become explicit to us only when it is challenged by someone and we have to defend it. ("Why do you say that Jack is obnoxious? I thought he was quite pleasant.") Critical thinkers try to develop the capacity to transform thought into reasoning at will or, rather, the ability to make their inferences explicit, along with the assumptions or premises upon which those inferences are based. Reasoning is a form of explicit inferring, usually involving several steps.

RECIPROCITY   Entering empathically into the point of view or line of reasoning of others; learning to think as others do and that means sympathetically assessing that thinking. (Reciprocity requires creative imagination as well as intellectual skill and a commitment to fair-mindedness.)

RELEVANT Bearing upon or relating to the matter at hand. *Relevant* implies a close logical relationship with, and importance to, the matter under consideration. By comparison, *germane* implies such a close natural connection as to be highly appropriate or fit; *pertinent* implies an immediate and direct bearing on the matter at hand (e.g., a pertinent suggestion); *applicable* refers to that which can be brought to bear upon a particular matter or problem. People often have problems with sticking to an issue and distinguishing information that bears upon a problem from information that does not.

Merely reminding people to limit themselves to relevant considerations fails to solve this problem. Sensitivity to (ability to judge) relevance can be developed only with continual practice—practice distinguishing relevant from irrelevant data, evaluating or judging relevance, arguing for and against the relevance of facts.

SELF-DECEPTION Deceiving oneself about one's true motivations, character, or identity. The human species might well be called the self-deceiving animal! Self-deception is a fundamental problem in human life and the cause of much human suffering. Overcoming self-deception through self-critical thinking is a fundamental goal of strong-sense critical thinking. *See also* egocentricity, intellectual virtues, personal contradiction, rational self, social contradiction.

SELFISH INTEREST What is perceived to be useful to oneself without regard for the rights and needs of others. To be selfish is to seek what one desires without due consideration for others. Being interested in one's own welfare is one thing; trampling on the rights of others while one pursues desires unrelated to human needs is another. As fundamentally egocentric creatures, humans naturally are given to pursue our selfish interests, using rationalization and other forms of self-deception to disguise our true motives and the true character of what we are doing. To develop as fair-minded critical thinkers is to work actively to diminish the power of one's native selfishness without sacrificing any legitimate concerns for one's welfare and long-term good. *See also* egocentricity, fair-mindedness, rationalization, self-deception, vested interest.

SOCIAL CONTRADICTION An inconsistency between what a society preaches and what it practices. Every society has some degree of inconsistency between its image of itself and its actual character. Social contradiction typically correlates with human self-deception on the social or cultural level. Critical thinking is essential for the recognition of inconsistencies, and recognition is essential for reform and eventual integrity.

SOCIOCENTRICITY The assumption that one's own social group is inherently and self-evidently superior to all others. When a group or society sees itself as superior, and so considers its views as correct or as the only reasonable or justifiable views, and all its actions as justified, it has a tendency to presuppose this superiority in all of its thinking and, thus, to think closed-mindedly. Dissent and doubt are considered disloyal and are rejected. Few people recognize the sociocentric nature of much of their thought. *See also* ethnocentricity.

SOCRATIC QUESTIONING A mode of questioning that deeply probes the meaning, justification, or logical strength of a claim, position, or line of reasoning. Socratic questioning can be carried out in a variety of ways and adapted to many levels of ability and understanding. *See also* dialogical instruction, elements of thought, knowledge.

SPECIFY/SPECIFIC To mention, describe, or define in detail; limiting or limited; specifying or specified; precise; definite. Much human thinking, speech, and writing tend to be vague, abstract, and ambiguous rather than specific, concrete, and clear. Learning how to state one's views specifically is essential to learning how to think clearly, precisely, and accurately. *See also* perfection of thought.

STRONG-SENSE CRITICAL THINKERS Those who are characterized predominantly by the following traits: (1) an ability to question deeply one's own framework of thought; (2) an ability to reconstruct sympathetically and imaginatively the strongest versions of points of view and frameworks of thought opposed to one's own; and (3) an ability to reason dialectically (multilogically) in such a way as to determine when one's own point of view is at its weakest and when an opposing point of view is at its strongest.

Strong-sense critical thinkers are not routinely blinded by their own viewpoints. They know they have points of view and therefore recognize the framework of assumptions and ideas upon which their own thinking is based. They recognize the necessity of putting their own assumptions and ideas to the test of the strongest objections that can be leveled against them.

Teaching for critical thinking in the strong sense is teaching so that students explicate, understand, and critique their own deepest prejudices, biases, and misconceptions, thereby discovering and contesting their own egocentric and sociocentric tendencies. Only if we contest our inevitable egocentric and sociocentric habits of thought can we hope to think in a genuinely rational fashion. Only dialogical thinking about basic issues that genuinely matter to the individual provides the kind of practice and skill essential to strong-sense critical thinking.

To achieve genuine fair-mindedness, people need to develop critical-thinking skills in dialogical settings. If critical thinking is taught simply as atomic skills separate from the empathic practice of entering into points of view that students are fearful of or hostile toward, students will simply find additional means of rationalizing prejudices and preconceptions, or convincing people that their point of view is the correct one. They will be transformed from vulgar to sophisticated (but not to strong-sense) critical thinkers. Opposite is *weak-sense critical thinkers. See also* fair-mindedness.

SUBMISSIVE EGO The irrational tendency of the mind to psychologically join and serve people it deems as more powerful, to get what it wants. Humans naturally are concerned with their interests and are motivated to satisfy their desires. In a world of psychological power and influence, one can succeed in two basic ways: (1) to psychologically conquer or intimidate (subtly or openly) those who stand in one's way, or, alternatively, (2) to psychologically join and serve more powerful others, who then: (a) give one a sense of personal importance, (b) protect one, and (c) share with one some of the benefits of their success. The irrational person uses both techniques, though not to the same extent.

Those who seem to be more successful in submitting to more powerful others have what has been called a submissive ego. By contrast, those who seem to be more successful in using overt force and control have what might be called a dominating ego. This behavior can be seen publicly in the relationship of rock stars and sport stars to their admiring followers. Most social groups have an internal "pecking order," with some people playing roles of leader and most playing roles of followers. A fair-minded rational person seeks

neither to dominate nor to blindly serve someone else who dominates. Opposite is *dominating ego.*

TEACH To impart knowledge or skills. Teaching usually connotes some individual attention to the learner. By comparison, *instruct* implies systematized teaching, usually in a specific subject; *educate* stresses the development of latent faculties and powers by formal, systematic teaching, especially in institutions of higher learning; *train* implies the development of a certain faculty or skill or instruction toward a specific occupation, as by methodical discipline or exercise. *See also* knowledge.

THEORY A systematic statement of principles involved in a subject; a formulation of apparent relationships or underlying principles of certain observed phenomena that have been verified to some extent. Often without realizing it, we form theories that help us make sense of the people, events, and problems in our lives. Critical thinkers put their theories to the test of experience and give due consideration to the theories of others. Critical thinkers do not take theories to be facts.

THINK To exercise the mental faculties so as to form ideas and arrive at conclusions. By comparison, *reason* implies a logical sequence of thought, starting with what is known or assumed and advancing to a definite conclusion through the inferences drawn; *reflect* implies a turning back of one's thoughts on a subject and connotes deep or quiet continued thought; *speculate* implies reasoning on the basis of incomplete or uncertain evidence and therefore stresses the conjectural character of the opinions formed; *deliberate* implies careful and thorough consideration of a matter to arrive at a conclusion. Though everyone thinks, few people think critically. We don't need instruction to think; we think spontaneously. We need instruction to learn how to discipline and direct our thinking on the basis of sound intellectual standards. *See also* elements of thought, perfection of thought.

TRUTH Conformity to knowledge, fact, actuality, or logic; a statement proven to be or accepted as true, not false or erroneous. Most people uncritically assume their views to be correct and true; they assume themselves to possess the truth. Critical thinking is essential to avoid this, if for no other reason.

UNCRITICAL PERSON One who has not developed intellectual skills; is naive, conforming, easily manipulated, dogmatic, easily confused, unclear, closed-minded, narrow-minded, careless in word choice, inconsistent, unable to distinguish evidence from interpretation. Uncriticalness is a fundamental problem in human life, for when we are uncritical, we nevertheless think of ourselves as critical. The first step in becoming a critical thinker consists of recognizing that we are uncritical.

VAGUE   Not clearly, precisely, or definitely expressed or stated; not sharp, certain, or precise in thought, feeling, or expression. Vagueness of thought and expression is a major obstacle to the development of critical thinking. We cannot begin to test our beliefs until we recognize clearly what they are. We cannot disagree with what someone says until we are clear about what he or she means. Students need much practice in transforming vague thoughts into clear ones. *See also* ambiguous, clarify, concept, logic, logic of language, logic of questions.

VERBAL IMPLICATION   That which follows, according to the logic of the language. If I say, for example, that someone used flattery on me, I imply that the compliments were insincere and given only to make me feel positive toward that person, to manipulate me against my reason or interest for some end. *See also* elements of thought, empirical implication, implication, inference.

VESTED INTEREST   (1) Involvement in promoting personal advantage, usually at the expense of others; (2) people functioning as a group to pursue collective selfish goals and exerting influences that enable them to profit at the expense of others. For example, many groups that lobby Congress do so to gain money,

power, and advantage for themselves by provisions in law that specially favor them. The term *vested interest* classically contrasts with the term *public interest*. A group that lobbies Congress in the public interest is not seeking to gain special advantage for a comparative few but, rather, protection for all or the large majority. Preserving the quality of the air is a *public interest*. Building cheaper cars by including fewer safety features is a *vested interest* (it makes more money for car manufacturers). *See also* selfish interest.

WEAK-SENSE CRITICAL THINKERS   (1) Those who do not hold themselves or those with whom they ego-identify to the same intellectual standards to which they hold opponents; (2) those who have not learned how to reason empathically within points of view or frames of reference with which they disagree; (3) those who tend to think monologically (within one narrow perspective); (4) those who do not genuinely accept, though they may verbally espouse, the values of critical thinking; (5) those who use the intellectual skills of critical thinking selectively and self-deceptively to foster and serve their selfish interests at the expense of truth; (6) those who use critical-thinking skills to identify flaws in the reasoning of others and sophisticated arguments to refute others' arguments before giving those arguments due consideration; (7) those who are able to justify their irrational thinking with highly skilled rationalizations. Opposite is *strong-sense critical thinkers. See also* irrational/irrationality, monological thinking, rationalization.

REFERENCES

Campbell, S. (Ed.) (1976). *Piaget Sampler: An Introduction to Jean Piaget Through His Own Words.* New York: John Wiley & Sons.

Campbell, T. (1994). *Beware the Talking Cure: Psychotherapy May Be Hazardous to Your Mental Health.* Boca Raton, FL: Social Issues Resources Series.

Chaplin, J. P. (1985). *Dictionary of Psychology.* New York: Dell.

Clark, R. (1984). A. Einstein: The Life and Times. New York: Avon Books.

Coleman, L. (1984). *Reign of Error.* Boston: Beacon Press.

Darwin, F. (Ed.) (1958). *The Autobiography of Charles Darwin.* New York: Dover Publications.

Downie, L. and Kaiser, R. (2002). *The News About the News.* New York: Knopf.

Ennis, R. (1985). *Goals for Critical Thinking/Reasoning Curriculum* (Illinois Critical Thinking Project). Champaign, IL: University of Illinois.

Esterle, J. & Cluman, D. (Eds.) (1993). *Conversations with Critical Thinkers.* San Francisco: Whitman Institute.

Frank, J. (1982, Oct.). *Chemtech,* p. 467.

Fromm, Erich. (1956). *The Art of Loving.* New York: Harper & Row, pp. 1–2, 23–24, 47.

Guralnik, D. B. (Ed.) (1986). *Webster's New World Dictionary.* New York: Prentice Hall.

Jevons, F. R. (1964). *The Biochemical Approach to Life.* New York: Basic Books.

Lipman, M. (1988, March). Critical thinking and the use of criteria. *Inquiry: Newsletter of the Institute for Critical Thinking.* Upper Montclair, NJ: Montclair State College.

Markham, F. (1967). *Oxford.* Holland: Reynal & Co.

Milgram, S. (1974). *Obedience to Authority.* New York: Harper & Row.

Newman, J. H. (1912). *The Idea of a University.* New York: Longman's Green & Co. (The lectures that formed this book were originally given in 1852.)

New York Times (1998, Oct. 5). Amnesty finds "widespread pattern" of U.S. rights violations.

New York Times (1998, Dec. 28). Iraq is a pediatrician's hell: No way to stop the dying.

New York Times (1999, March 6). Testing the limits of tolerance as cultures mix: Does freedom mean accepting rituals that repel the West?

New York Times (1999, June 12). Beautiful beaches and bronzed men, but no bathing belles.

New York Times (1999, June 20). Arab honor's price: a woman's blood.

New York Times (1999, July 1). U.S. releases files on abuses in Pinochet era.

New York Times (1999, Oct. 21). Boy, 11, held on incest charge, and protests ensue.

New York Times (1999, Nov. 22). Moratorium now.

New York Times (1999, Nov. 27). Spanish judge is hoping to see secret files in U.S.

New York Times (1999, Nov. 29). Advertisement by the Turning Point Project entitled "Invisible government."

New York Times (1999, Nov. 30). Group asking U.S. for vigilance in patient safety: Wants a federal agency: Academy of Sciences asserts that rate of medical errors is "stunningly high."

New York Times (2004, Feb. 25). Prosecutorial misconduct leads justices to overturn death sentence in Texas.

New York Times (2004, April 4). Convicted of killing his parents, but calling a detective the real bad guy.

Ofshe, R. & Watters, E. (1996). *Making Monsters: False Memories, Psychotherapy, and Sexual Hysteria.* Berkeley, CA: University of California Press.

Paul, R. (1995). *What Every Student Needs to Survive in a Rapidly Changing World.* Dillon Beach, CA: Foundation for Critical Thinking.

PETA. (1999). 501 Front St., Norfolk, VA 23510, www.peta.com.

Peters, R. S. (1973). *Reason and Compassion.* London: Routledge & Kegan Paul.

Plotnicov, L. & Tuden, A. (Eds.) (1970). *Essays in Comparative Social Stratification.* Pittsburgh: University of Pittsburgh Press.

San Francisco Chronicle (1999, Feb. 6). First Philippine execution in 23 years: lethal injection for man who raped his stepdaughter, 10.

San Francisco Chronicle (1999, June 11). Treatment is new salvo fired by reformers in war on drugs: Courts, voters beginning to favor therapy, not prisons, to fight crack. (Article taken from the *New York Times.*)

San Francisco Chronicle (1999, Oct. 2). U.S. order to kill civilians in Korea illegal, experts say. Prosecution seen as impossible now. (Article taken from the Associated Press.)

Siegel, H. (1988). *Educating Reason: Rationality, Critical Thinking, and Education.* New York: Routledge Chapman Hall.

Singer, M. & Lalich, J. (1996). *Crazy Therapies: What Are They? Do They Work?* San Francisco: Jossey-Bass.

Stebbing, S. (1952). *Thinking to Some Purpose.* London: Penguin Books.

Sumner, W. G. (1940). *Folkways: A Study of the Sociological Importance of Usages, Manners, Customs, Mores, and Morals.* New York: Ginn and Co.

Zinn, H. (1995). *A People's History of the United States.* New York: Harper Collins.

INDEX